A VISION OF REALITY

A STUDY OF LIBERALISM
IN TWENTIETH-CENTURY VERSE

By the same Author

★

TITLE DEEDS AND OTHER POEMS
(Longmans)

A VISION OF REALITY

A STUDY OF LIBERALISM
IN TWENTIETH-CENTURY VERSE

By

Frederick Grubb

1965
CHATTO AND WINDUS
LONDON

Published by
Chatto and Windus Ltd
42 William IV Street
London W.C.2

★

Clarke, Irwin & Co. Ltd
Toronto

Printed in Great Britain by
Butler & Tanner Ltd, Frome and London

For my Parents

The rhetorician would deceive his neighbours,
The sentimentalist himself; while art
Is but a vision of reality.

W. B. YEATS

Art is not a solitary delight. It is a means of stirring the greatest number of men by giving them a privileged vision of our common sufferings and joys. It thus compels the artist to avoid isolation; it subjects him to the humblest and most universal truth . . .

If our societies are going to plunge into either totalitarian or bourgeois nihilism, those who do not wish to conform will be cut off and have to accept the fact. But in their places and within their abilities, they must do what is required so that life for all, with all, may again become possible.

ALBERT CAMUS

CONTENTS

ACKNOWLEDGMENTS

My thanks are due to the authors, or to the literary executors of authors, and to the publishers, of the following books from which quotation is made. Works quoted briefly are acknowledged in the footnotes.

Collected Poems of W. B. Yeats, Macmillan, 1950; T. S. Eliot, *Collected Poems 1909–1962*, Faber, 1963; *Collected Poems of Wilfred Owen*, ed. C. Day Lewis, Chatto & Windus, 1963; *Collected Poems of Isaac Rosenberg*, ed. Gordon Bottomley and Denys Harding, Chatto & Windus, 1949; Herbert Read, *Collected Poems*, Faber, 1946, *Moon's Farm*, Faber, 1955; Edwin Muir, *Collected Poems 1921–1958*, Faber, 1960; *Collected Poems of Kathleen Raine*, Hamish Hamilton, 1956; Robert Graves, *Collected Poems 1959*, Cassell, 1959; *Collected Poems of Norman Cameron*, intr. Robert Graves, Hogarth Press, 1957; William Empson, *Collected Poems*, Chatto & Windus, 1955; W. H. Auden, *Poems* (second edition 1933), *Look, Stranger!*, 1936, *Journey to a War*, 1939, *Another Time*, 1940, all Faber: for purposes of clarity, poems not christened in the volumes are provided with the names given in *Collected Shorter Poems*, Faber, 1950; *John Cornford: A Memoir*, ed. Pat Sloan, Cape, 1938; *Julian Bell: Essays, Poems, and Letters*, ed. Quentin Bell, Hogarth Press, 1938; Dylan Thomas, *Collected Poems 1934–1952*, Dent, 1952; Peter Porter, *Once Bitten, Twice Bitten*, Scorpion Press, 1961; Thom Gunn, *Fighting Terms*, Faber, 1962 (first edition, Fantasy Press, 1954, revised edition, Hawk's Well Press, New York, 1959), *The Sense of Movement*, Faber, 1957, *My Sad Captains*, Faber, 1961; Ted Hughes, *The Hawk in the Rain*, Faber, 1957, *Lupercal*, Faber, 1960; Philip Larkin, *The Less Deceived*, Marvell Press, 1955, *The Whitsun Weddings*, Faber, 1964; Charles Tomlinson, *Seeing is Believing*, O.U.P., 1960.

I

OF EROS AND OF DUST

*This was our pleasure, to climb among loose stones, to cut
    steps in ice,*
To find a new alternative to the mauvais pas . . .
Perhaps we were right:
A man should use every nerve and muscle,
A man should puzzle out the hardest questions,
A man should find words for the thoughts that no one knows.
At any rate, there was no room for us at the big hotel.

MICHAEL ROBERTS

I THOUGHT at first of sub-titling this book 'a liberal testimony'. *Testimony* evokes an adventure of ideas under what Mr T. S. Eliot has called 'conditions that seem unpropitious'. It also suggests, first, that the adventure was made possible by other, better men's testimonies, and second, that the adventure is perhaps worth witnessing about. There has been a disturbing moral recession in England; during the writing a phrase of Albert Camus—'I rebel, therefore we exist'—was constantly in my mind. If, within and beyond politics, liberalism is to regenerate itself and us, we must revise orthodox assumptions, re-open questions of principle, cease to be on the defensive and learn to attack. For me, works precede faith. And testimony stresses ideology rather than critique. The bulk of the book is a demonstration, making no claim to scholarship or to be more than an attempt at criticism, of how liberalism has fared in the work of differing artists. I concentrate on the significance of Mr Eliot as stylistic prodigy or aesthetic phenomenon.* Yeats and Eliot, moreover, have been grouped with Rilke as leaders in the polemic against liberalism. William Empson seemed indispensable to the debate about the Two Cultures; W. H. Auden posed the question of how, provoking some disapproval, a poet may yet exert a potent attraction; it seemed possible to divorce Robert Graves from his White Goddess; a number of writers struck me as suffering an undeserved neglect. In the last chapter the examples are again chosen for their peculiar interest, their telling differences; together, I believe, they compose a portrait; but many another poet is interesting and individual. They are *en plein développement,* and you have to choose between saying little about many or something about a few. The books are there; they reflect a predicament; they characterize a period.

By giving extended accounts I try to eschew the P.R.O. Method of Quoting or trick of turning writers into ventriloquists' dolls in order to prove a thesis. I write against the sly timidness and pompous delivery of much criticism. That almost extinct exotic—the liberal critic—chooses his subject for the odd reason that he likes it, or, if he dislikes it, he pays it the compliment of zest in saying why. A critic is simply a reader with an incurable evangelistic drive; he plays fair by his subject chiefly by *reading* him. The fallacy that poems must be seen through a mist of cosy benevolence is due to a parochialism which is hostile to general culture and social concern. Poetry is very important, but it is one way among others in which the civilized mind is made known—and those ways must be taken into

* An uncollected Eliot essay (1922) quoted by Enid Starkie, *From Gautier to Eliot,* 1960, p. 167, yields this avowal: 'The lack of curiosity in technical matters of . . . poets of today is an indication of their lack of curiosity in moral matters.'

account when we consider poetry. The only *idée fixe* I have about criticism is that it is the memory of the artist: whereas the creator lives fully in each of his phases, the spectator has to appreciate his integrity. The liberal critic aims—he owes it to himself—to explain his interest in certain artists and to initiate, or revive, the same in his readers: to quicken art's best justification, that it should be vivid and forceful in a man's life.

The anger which distinguished the last ten years is quiescent. Politics were distrusted as organized self-interest, or (the motives to Socialism for Mr Kingsley Amis) psychological duplicity; growing up under the mirage of Left idealism, the *enfants terribles* preferred to abide in radical disgruntlement, content to rail at convention. It was a kind of rude good manners: for one of the signs of moral good breeding is that it can interrupt gossip when a crisis makes this necessary. The mood was distasteful to hedonists and schoolmarms of both sexes. One liked the tough independence, the hatred of the 'phoney'—of 'pusillanimous' relationships, of careerist philistinism, of the 'ecstatic wind' of ersatz uplift and modish, religiose optimism. If in the end one was disappointed, it was because the anger failed to follow up. The rebels reject the attitudes of the middle class as faked, inhibiting, harmful, at the same time that they—or their heroes—covet and make sure of obtaining the privileges which support those attitudes. What was alleged to be a living down, outside politics, of a scandal—the capture of the half-realized Socialist state by Tory-run affluence—meant in practice to exploit the situation to your advantage. Vitality, aware that power may go with vice of a plausible sort, was happy to make the material best of it. A failure of imagination, of prescience, a certain relaxation of vigilance, a disregard of ends and theory, could this have prepared the gutless climate of today? One prefers the frank, if futile, anger or even the heartfelt if frivolous non-conformism of the 30's to our smart satiric consent.

My belief is that our dilemma can be expressed as ends and theory, roughly as follows: for many poets, and most readers, poetry today has no religious, metaphysical, or even moral excuses. Its status is threatened by nihilism in social habits and pragmatism in public affairs, which may be mitigated, but cannot be transcended, by A Change of Government; the rise of technology and specialization (equating 'standard of living' with money and ethical 'goods' with acquisition); psychiatric accounts of creativity, and (to the chagrin of liberals) material affluence. These are dissolving in triviality, conformism and greed the traditional incentives—suffering, anxiety, indignation, danger, action, to name a few—which, as late as the Second World War, inspired the intensity of living which is vital to artistic creation. Whatever works, whatever succeeds, is good to a limited extent, yet as nothing can be obnoxious, nothing can excel; whole fringe professions keep the farce in business, while 'sociological facts' feed curiosity about the only cohesive force which people have left in common—their 'society'. Behind a camouflage of inter-party *noblesse oblige*, the pressure is to distort the citizen into a contented wage-slave, to disguise the fact that so long as mediocrity retains a vested interest in vulgarity, both will boom. We are in danger of an aesthetic of assent which acclimatizes itself to nihilism. At this point I must own up to an alarming literary perversion: I am not a don, a journalist, an official, but a thinking adult attempting to earn a living in what the old Evangelicals would have called 'the world'. From this eccentric standpoint I suggest that if poetry is to be more than a drawing-room ornament, if it is to do anything in our limbo, it must renew its conscience on liberal grounds and discover humane procedures to implement the spiritual force it carries.

Liberals are accused, however, of blind optimism, anti-social delinquency, spiritual cowardice, ignoring evil and pain, and dilettantizing the arts by draining them of intensity and imagination. Liberalism is vulnerable because it is not a dogma or a system. It is a creedless style, a vigilant stance, a responsible and discriminating tone. Both conservative and exploratory, it visits the past, keeps open the avenues into Lionel Trilling's 'variousness and possibility' (for which Mill urged liberals to read Coleridge). It dislikes obscurantism, restrictive practices, and vested interests whether social or aesthetic. Liberalism is aroused about communication, about relationships, about action. It may unite disciplines in an ethos of conduct and offer a club where specialisms can talk the same language; a critic like Arnold was followed by all thinking people. T. S. Eliot describes humanism as 'general culture'. It need not exclude, though it must not include, religious belief, and is not concerned with theory but with criticism and persuasion through taste. I shall argue that the confinement of liberalism to taste, the cutting it off from action and idea, is too limiting for an effective practice, but the point is that Mr Eliot's *détente* is a counterblast to a truculent, indisciplined life, which ignores evil and trusts in the mechanical perfectibility of man, and which the neo-vitalists rightly oppose (Colin Wilson anthologized better men). Worse is the fifth column within. Liberals are threatened with decadence from their own shibboleths—tolerance, compromise, moderation. A shot is fired across the bows of the pleasure steamer; are they able to fight back? Too often, when they have not made fools of themselves through gullibility, they have relapsed into sentiment or cracked the jokes of the cynical spectator.

As Henry James said—'he had a private vision of reform . . . to reform the reformers' (*The Bostonians*). Today, unregenerate liberalism
is amiable hedonism and smug goodwill, the type of hypocrisy which
Camus pilloried in *The Fall*.

There are pioneers who offer a revisionist liberalism together with
a reprimand to the convention. Some have one foot in exploded
myths or vitalist philosophies; others strikes censorious attitudes to
'what liberal democracy has declared respectable' (Lionel Trilling);
most generate an affirmation going beyond the orthodoxy; they
awaken us with a recall to first principles, a proclamation of incentives, an espousal of unwonted energies. Rilke diluted experience
into feeling in the effort to deify an immanent world; his vision was
predatory and he erred by introjecting the historical process; but he
realized, in the end, that he did not want to—or at any rate could
not—systematize feeling, and he gloried in this naturalism. Rimbaud's anarchy became a 'vocal mysticism' uniting imagination
with altruism. W. B. Yeats's quest for wholeness of being was van-
quished in a splendid poetry, transforming the transitory into an
eternal heroism and embattling the revivification of opposites. He
refused to pacify his tensions in mysticism or the supernatural, and
we can learn from his hatred of merely sloppy tolerance, his love of
improvised action which was a technique for sincerity. In E. M.
Forster an ethical earnestness (stronger than that of *avant garde*
divines) is freed from religious dogma; in Gide a cross-fertilization of
our forces enlarges our field of action to destroy complacency.
Forster's doubts about reason match D. H. Lawrence's distrust of
egalitarianism; and Gide lets the Devil—destructive aspects of his
personality, which elsewhere pursues a model development—into the
garden of innocence.

Isaac Rosenberg and Wilfred Owen are the hero martyrs of commitment: they visit evil, condemn it, retrieve any good it secretes.
The vision of Auden was damaged by his drive to omniscience, his
attempt to empower poetry as a social instrument, Dylan Thomas's
by a liberality of the unconscious which sinks his poetry in gorgeous
incoherence. Thomas Mann (who subjects Settembrini, in *The Magic
Mountain*, to an ironic grilling) and D. H. Lawrence reclaim myth
for humanity. Applying ancient wisdoms to problems of liberal
democracy, for a Mann type—a humanist—myth is a rediscovery
through fiction (the *Joseph Saga*) and renovation of what was once
conscious, for a Lawrence type—a vitalist—an existential revelation
that myth is present and embodies truths serviceable for life. Gide's
Theseus fuses the historical into the present: seeing himself anticipated in the myth, the wily protean who made himself *persona non
grata* with gaga capitalism, bureaucratic communism and the Holy

Office is able to give a civic ethic the power of authenticity. Albert Camus, banishing nineteenth-century nostalgias and inhibitions, defended the simple values of conversation, limits, fortitude, involvement and risk, lacking which any subtler or more glorious living will be ruled out or die of inanition. He demonstrated that we must 'create dangerously'; nothing can come of comfort and security.

If poets are to prosper I believe they must realize six qualities. First, a wider arc of exposure, more commitment to the open world where anything can happen. Second, more interest in what can be done to experience when it gets into a poem, and what a poem does to a reader when it gets into his experience. Third, without dogma, ways out of individualism into responsibility (without the stimuli of war and economic crisis) to restore the public prestige of verse. Fourth, a play of complexity, fructifying the over-simplified formulae which liberals have relied on in the past; an intelligent emotionalism is needed as a foil to the worship of reason. Fifth, a divining, then reclamation, of what is valid in myth, which remembers for the present the valuable emotion of the past in a dramatic *précis*. Sixth, avoiding absolutes, daring challenges within verse which, by injecting dialectic, tension and struggle into the static water of liberalism, will generate the new 'incentives to creation and appreciation' to redeem our society. The poet must make himself (to adapt Mr Eliot's verdict on Baudelaire's contemporaries) *man enough to be damned*. He must frequent the 'boredom, horror, and glory' of which Eliot accused Arnold of experiencing the boredom, live fully within Arnold's 'spontaneity of consciousness' and the Hebraic 'strictness of conscience'. Reconstituting our sanity, we prove that the imagination is forceful, that art is found in unheard-of places and unearthed in inclement conditions. If the danger is that of idealism there is a puritan discipline in this guardianship of consciousness.*

*   *   *

The creative faculty is a sensuously percipient unit, which can judge the effect of technics on behaviour; art is an exercise of the whole man which no specialist can dissect without surrendering his humanity before the challenge. Progress is not an idol to be worshipped by vandals, it is a means to the increase of leisure for the

---

* See Noel Annan, *Leslie Stephen*, 1951, p. 118. 'Stephen's thought was hewn in Evangelical rock. He relied on experience . . . He was not shy of preaching because it was the most natural of all duties. He was certain that he ought to make judgments when he criticised. And he looked to his conscience to guide him when doing all three.' But he rejected 'the Evangelical distrust of the intellect and the emotions'.

cultivation of ends. In its effort to be a unifying centre whence these ends may be radiated—an open city where feelings may be exchanged in an inarticulate world, where kinds of behaviour may be observed—the Republic of Letters is threatened with annexation by greedier nations. Yet the essential humane content of a poem remains operative and irrefragable: elaborate bids have been made, e.g. to interpret Yeats symbolically, but there is nothing in (say) the Byzantium poems which is not an emotional fact, an intelligible event in the story of the poem. Rilke's Angels, again, have been called 'pseudonyms for God'. In fact, they are characters in the plot of a feasible argument, and as such are more likely to be perfect harmony. Art sidesteps a metaphysic to ask questions in the light (or darkness) of what we have been and to suggest through revelation and criticism what we may become. The task of art is realistic, limited, *therefore urgent and intense*, never absolute; a retreat into the mental slum of vitalist and mystagogue is a betrayal of the artist's vocation to speak to our condition with urgency and intensity in a world of realism and limitation.

If we accept that art is no more (and no less) than a mode of knowledge in itself, we can talk about poetry with a chance of being right, which may not be original or exciting but is better than being obviously wrong. Poetry, often defined in terms of the emotion it causes, is a remarkable way of using language. It is indefinable because it has no essence; it has attributes and needs. Poetic language is concise and intense (though it may choose to expatiate) and is most versatile, complex, intimate. It conserves and directs energies, is a place where concepts may be demonstrated, as well as tested, in practice, and gives evidence more cheerfully than opinions. It fulfils an emotional task—enlarges frontiers of feeling—by exercising the associative faculty and vitalizing forces of volition which might die of inanition and impoverish the mentality of the race. We gain from poetry neither message nor mystique, but exceptional information, sharpening our faculties of recognition and prescience. Our experience is made vivid, we are empowered to alter our habitual feeling, to act in certain ways. Art heightens or depresses our vision of the ordinary by giving the sense of awe, urgency and vigilance, or points the meaning of moments when we enjoy deeper communion with nature or the self. Taking us out of ourselves as by a shock, it returns us to ourselves at a deeper awareness. The artist's success in communicating the horrible and the ugly is a mode of extrication—he climbs towards value on the icefall of anxiety and unbalance; and each stage in the ascent is relevant and is best illustrated and argued. (A weakness of verse is when it escalates from dejection to facile generalized optimism.) On the regulation of the ambivalence mental health depends. A condition of simultaneity is created which people would like to enjoy in life: the poem is a forecast of what we would like to be, and may be if we allow the work to operate on our awareness.

But the artist is not just interested in mental health; he is agitated for the quality over the average—what is *done* with the mind; he holds that art is a revolutionary force. We should pay attention to the area of immediacy poems unveil. Poetry is existential in the sense that its impact is present; one might amend Arnold's criticism of life (implying a privileged stronghold from which you judge coldly) to appraisal of life, implying frank affirmative celebration *at the same time as* inspection and judgment. Form, however subtle its ramifications, offers a moment of equipoise which balances us. Our response to long 'organic' structures like *Duino Elegies, Le Cimetière Marin, Four Quartets, The Twelve, The Quaker Graveyard in Nantucket** is always at once, a condition of simultaneity is evoked, a sensation of presence, a harmony of complexities which, momentarily held in the mind, seems to demand to be perceived in, and acted out through, reality by the reader. It is a strange, deeply moving and—luckily in view of the transitoriness of the event—unforgettable experience. It is not illuminist, since it reveals nothing beyond the worldly evidence it has gathered, nor is it Roger Fry's significant form, since it is not insulated from the worldly contingencies in which the reader is involved. One might call it programming power. It leads straight to the felicitous generalization: when a good poet generalizes, he converts into community value—into natural law, so to speak—a collection of lived instances; that is his way of prolonging the moment, making it unforgettable. If poetry is a muddle, extracting and juxtaposing memories, it also revives valuable sensations, associates these with immediate, maturer feeling and suggests that this selection of data is possible for us in the future.† We are capable of it; it is virtual action.

Poetry is vulnerable, no doubt from lapses of energy, but usually from abuses of diction which are either meaninglessly ecstatic or records of inertia which take the place of shaping. I argued that poetry is not a means to vitality, nor a proof of ascertained beliefs, but a liberal investigation which is concerned with the personality rather than specialist accounts of it. Poetry is sensitive to improvement

---

* The long poem has a future, if not in symphonic form, as an 'outflanking' of obdurate themes by examining them from different angles. (Robert Lowell gestures towards this.) It—or any poem—could explore the analogy between individual psychology and historic events, or use history as an allegory for perceiving the same interaction in our present.

† The 'propositional symbol' of Wittgenstein is helpful here—'assembling reminders for a particular purpose'.

or deterioration of its rivals in the field of communications. Our intake of print in one day is the most frightful bombardment of raucous, garish, aimless ephemera (the way advertising enforces attention to some trivial 'still') which exacts dilution of feeling, blunting of insight, and squandering of concentration. The need is to affirm the remedial and directive functions of intelligence at a time when language is diffused and debased by advertising, entertainment, journalism, and propaganda (obviously barbarism is closing its ranks), whose aims are profitable and persuasive, and for whom 'dialogue and personal relations are replaced by monologue and public relations, which are two kinds of lies' (Albert Camus).

The ideal of orthodoxy is to go all the way to meet the reader and put him in the picture, in despite of modernism which stands for: the revelatory and/or shocking power of *selected contrasts*, the *suggestivity of insights*, the importance of *peculiar individual vision* as a justification for the *sense of comparative values*, and the preference for complex *structures* over exhaustive statements. Mr Stephen Spender throws light when he says that the moderns create the idioms and forms of new art by not 'writing within a fragmentary part of a fragmented situation, instead of comprehending the situation in a single picture which restores wholeness'. Liberals looked this gift horse in the mouth. The modern envisages life 'as a whole complexity enclosed within individual consciousness . . . invents a new style to express deeply felt change'.* This became the troubleshooter for a neo-classicism hostile to liberals. Yet if orthodoxy goes too far, verse ends up as indistinguishable from prose, a cloistered pastime, freelance journalism and musical short stories. Post-war verse did recapture the virtues of good prose; and it has been known to resemble a prolapsed mannerism. Rigorous workouts in the gymnasium of language, verse which is not a graceful record of experience but a communication of enacting experience, does not mean a poetic equivalent of action-painting: that would be spiritual defeat, masquerading as beatnik brio. It does mean including what Camus calls the 'alteration' asked by judgment—to give the plot in the expression while subduing it to a moral argument in the organization. Assembling a poem from fragments, the maker may tell what the episode is like and also, through the assembly, what he hopes for it, what he thinks about it. The reader may compare the treatment to his own knowledge of a like episode, this suggests fields of action, the pattern of the poem becomes a strategy for life.

The natural voice, oblique wit, literary allusion should be spontaneous; raised on idioms, poets should make them breathe in a

* Stephen Spender, *The Struggle of the Modern*, 1963, pp. 79–97.

humane, emotive context, use them for fun or to heighten or muffle an effect,* even if this appears obsolete to the Enemy. (Eliot gives a philosophical boost to that platitude of the media, 'home', Yeats glorifies archaisms such as 'ebullient' and 'beget', purges journalese such as 'world-famous'.) Mr Francis Berry has shown how style can be the seismograph of the physical voice: it is a clue to the poet's background, temperament, and assumptions. But in the thrust and play of speech and spaces, the designs of ambiguity and association, the complots of rhythm and syntax the mind can be watched *administering the pattern of feeling in the telling*; there the changes mooted by the poet's free choice are partially formed, distinctly indicated; the poet sides with Coleridge, for whom technique was a provocative force, or Wordsworth for whom it was a therapeutic agent. One closely argued, emotionally packed, liberally endowed poem will do because poetry is a device for communicating feelings—interpretations of feeling—which cannot be given in any other way. The way is the avoidance of diffusion, the gain of vividness and penetration. Like a medical demonstration, a good poem reveals the facts with ruthless frankness but has a charitable aim. The reader may be shown that insights and images which he apprehends separately—is forced by the Enemy to apprehend separately—may act in unison to produce simultaneous states of mind of high complexity and thus more useful as ethical tools than dispersed states of mind. The best poems of Meredith, Hopkins, Empson are such passionate ideograms,† and there is a hint of it in Graves, Rosenberg, and Norman Cameron; to such a poetry the notion of 'elegant moral instruments' is a contradiction in terms.

Law (the 'enforcement of morals') takes over when manners break down; but art is to do with a kind of amateur law-giving in this extra-legal sphere. Our ideal, fertilizing that law, should ensure that institutions are refreshed by imagination, corrected by intelligence, and braced by concern. And the prospect for institutions might be brighter if we ceased categorizing people as types. To accept the compromise overtures of C. P. Snow is to deny that the cultivated man may exist in England, to doubt that literature is the spokesman of liberalism. One is offended at Snow's view that the boffin is doing 'an honest technical job' (don't Auden and Empson, scientifically literate both, do just that?) whereas the artist is backward, perverse, and odd (Snow's officials are odder when it comes to moral funk or forming a privileged group), and his derision of T. S. Eliot's line

---

* See Christopher Ricks, 'The Resurrection Men', *The Listener*, June 1st 1961.
† Disillusioned yet intransigent, emotionally radical yet culturally 'late', in Baroque there is a hint of artists, themselves infected, taking measures against decadence. The objections to Baroque are just as instructive: its propagandist bias, un-English exaggeration, moral tactlessness.

'this is the way the world ends / Not with a bang but a whimper' as preposterous (in the age of the H Bomb) without admitting that it heralds a terrifying truth: man is able to die a coward's death in the bosom of plenitude. Snow won't read these backward fellows: there is a sense in which birth control, conservation of resources, and automation will save us—and there is a sense (to start with) in which the poetry of Kathleen Raine and Ted Hughes is a plea for conservation of resources. Against (Lewis) Eliot, the bureaucrat-cum-writer who hazards a timid foot in both camps, we require secular ascetics who recognize that their function, their status as types, is a means and that literature is a judgment of means as well as a witness of ends. Culture is not a co-existence of aptitudes, it is a quality: and for the adjustment of ends and means, G. M. Trevelyan's autobiography (see 'The Call and Claims of Natural Beauty' and 'Milton's *Areopagitica*'), the autobiographies of Leonard Woolf and the memoirs of Bertrand Russell seem better than the corridors of power, however draughty.

As Valéry showed in *Monsieur Teste*, what divides the artist from the manager is choice. The artist does not co-ordinate the work of others nor administer the *élan* generated through action; he acts out the idea, he incarnates it in works. His arena is his art, where he rehearses the changes which reform should inspire. Admirers of Isaac Babel, Malraux, Hemingway will not need to be reminded that ideas have been practicable. The symbol of poetry in society dates back to Madrid—John Cornford defending the Faculty of Art and Letters behind a barricade of philosophy books. Commitment is to 'cast your life upon a hazard', to declare your interest, not to let your case go by default. The fighter pilot, that redundant symbol, was the arbiter of his destiny through control of the machine (instead of being controlled by it). Will the frightfulness of the *entre deux guerres* be recalled as an episode? We cannot wish back the wickednesses of that period, while to hanker after the era of wars is to will the end of civilization. The apotheosis of violence in recent verse has a different tone from the purgation by violence of poets who have undergone violence in physical form. Some is furtive and sadistic; some is beginning to look like a tough ethic or a muscling of a man's reason by his animal nature: such poets offer a one-man compensation for torpor, at a time when prosperity transcends ideological divisions. Excellent: only note the caveat of Camus about the frenzy of production, god of all the ideologies. It is a colossal challenge to art. What we can do is confront the horrible, the agonizing, the depressive, to counteract those facile optimisms which are fathered on liberals and which lead all too seductively to academicism and comment. Through making themselves worthy of tragedy liberals will discover the delightful, the constructive, the sensitizing, and forward the meaningful.

Kierkegaard's hope that his anxiety and delight should set a standard to emulate—a hope renewed in every generation—will be regarded as reasonable. The power of example, as distinct from dogma, militating against nihilism, will convert the incentives into ideas to be recognized, to be priorities, to be at least discussed as authoritative. The spur of action, ever in readiness, will be raised when required. We may realize in the world and enact (or perceive) within the poem, humane values—the faith of relationships, of lyrical precept, of disconcerting honesty, of forthrightness of feeling whatever it may reveal, and rational and joyful rather than chthonic reconstruction of the symbols and myths of the past. (Ortega y Gasset's mass-man, the 'spoiled child' of history, who thinks he can get on very nicely without inherited wisdom.) In the life of individuals, in the living death of organizations, the dignities fought for will become affirmation and resistance. The poet will be quite a character. Inherited quirks, present moral priorities and future spiritual objectives will through him remind consumers of their potentiality, basic enough to live down distractions and incite a sense of purpose. If these prognostications strike the reader as eccentric, he should remember that the encroachment which diminishes our freedom is a faceless one. The living down process—the introduction of weight into the void, of adventure and peril into the ennui, of imagination into the self-sufficiency—is the task of the liberal artist.

> *Defenceless under the night*
> *Our world in stupor lies;*
> *Yet, dotted everywhere*
> *Ironic points of light*
> *Flash out wherever the Just*
> *Exchange their messages:*
> *May I, composed like them*
> *Of Eros and of dust,*
> *Beleaguered by the same*
> *Negation and despair,*
> *Show an affirming flame.*

W. H. Auden

2

FORBEARS

. . . not to beautify or to give a characteristic expression, but to separate the lasting from the transitory, to sit in judgment, to be just.

RILKE Rodin

We mean all sorts of things, I know, by Beauty. But the essential advantage for a poet is not, to have a beautiful world with which to deal: it is to be able to see beneath both beauty and ugliness; to see the boredom, and the horror, and the glory.

T. S. ELIOT

TRAGIC JOY: W. B. YEATS

. . . what is Whiggery?
A levelling, rancorous, rational sort of mind
That never looked out of the eye of a saint
Or out of drunkard's eye.

WHIGGERY catches it from both sides; the first, though not the last, lines might be from an essay by T. S. Eliot. In Yeats's hands they denounce compromise rather than arrogance. Out of wisdom, Yeats brought forth rebirth, in Dryden's fine phrase 'a series of new time'. He ushers out the old and monotonous and heralds a fresher, more demanding epoch. His feat of self-renewal, in essence pagan, unites with his cultural ideal, in effect aristocratic, to banish that stuffiness which is the core of fashion. Yeats is allied to the traditional 'not yet' which Ortega laments as superseded by the 'at last' of pragmatic conceit. He *is* old in the sense of rooted: for all his airs and graces, the emotions he exalts are democratic, fundamental, 'in widest commonalty spread'. His lyricism is profound, his Cassandra voice is young; he personifies the paradox of Thomas Mann that 'democracy is timelessly human, and timelessness implies a youthfulness' and his request for 'the reform of freedom in a conservative sense'.* More than of Symbolism or romanticism, Yeats is a child of the Enlightenment: hard, reckless, quick to seize the logic and the passion of ideology. In spite of his longing for a system, when he embraced causes he did so on his own terms, and although every cause failed his own standards he reached fulfilment not in splendid isolation (albeit an honoured outsider in his own country) but surrounded by a concourse of works.

Sligo, a rocky, austere terrain as if 'from mountain to mountain ride the fierce horsemen', quickened by a dazzling green and salted by the influence of the sea—'the commonness of thought and images/ That have the frenzy of our western seas'—gave Yeats that lore which, emerging first as fantasy but later as the prodigious, composite symbol, was a rudiment of his art. The folk phase gave way to the Dublin phase—'When grey gulls flit about instead of men / And the gaunt houses put on majesty'—and that gave way to a crusade for wholeness of being. The integrity which Yeats missed in public life was revealed in him, for it was vital to 'ascend out of . . .

* Thomas Mann, *The Coming Victory of Democracy*, 1938, p. 79.

the thoughts of the newspapers, of the market place, of men of science, but only if we can carry the normal, passionate, reasoning self, the personality as a whole'. He came to glorify the many-faceted man of the Renaissance, at once active and contemplative, as his ideal type, and the Italian city state as his Utopia. In the Dublin National Gallery, Yeats found portraits of a Venetian gentleman by Strozzi and of President Wilson by the inevitable Sargent. Yeats says the Venetian's thought feeds upon his body as a flame upon the candle. Wilson, the modern liberal, 'lives only in the eyes, which are steady and intent', and his clothes reveal no characteristic movement but the mere attentions of the valet.* It was the conviction that the man who refuses to sell his soul to specialization and standardization must *fight* against loss of ground, the knowledge that he must create a myth not out of legend but out of experience resolving into legend, out of friends, love, events in the raw; divine in this, inform this with, vital values, and ennoble them as timeless symbols promising wholeness, that transformed Yeats from a soothsayer into a leader.

The debris he could salvage from romanticism being inadequate, Yeats had the luck to get embroiled in a time of turbulence, to have an aptitude for ordeal and indignation, and to be in a position to react against the rationalism of his father's generation. The modern liberal lacks occasions of concern, yet is deficient in inwardness, nor feels threatened by any ideology unless it be the compromise of C. P. Snow. Yeats has been accused of fascism, mainly because the old warrior wrote songs for General O'Duffy at a time when his juniors were playing ping-pong for the Anarchists against the Communists in Barcelona. Fascism is built on the idea of group efficiency. Loyalty goes to a nonsense disguised as a tradition; lip service is paid to roots, meantime the herd is conditioned by exhortation which reflects the lunacy of the Leader. It is the climax of anti-intellectualism, the denial of personal responsibility, the collusion of technological and vitalist determinisms, without any but a propagandist obeisance to the past. The worship of power as an absolute, the hatred of wit and satire, the fear of informality and the imitativeness even of the dispossessed and the conquered, makes fascism above all an opportunist weapon, tarted up by its capitalist paymasters.

I waste this space because such tendencies threaten us today. Yeats, as he never fails to remind us, was the sworn enemy of the anthill. His chances under totalitarianism were zero; his chances under our expurgated edition for U.K. readers are a little better. Yeats is not *efficient* enough to be fascistic or careerist; he is

* For discussion of the portraits, and much else, see the catalogue of the exhibition, *W. B. Yeats: Images of a Poet*. University of Manchester, 1961.

too imaginative, obstinate, dignified, unprofessional, erratic, ill-informed, and amorous; you will never get Hunchback, Saint and Fool to march in step. His cult of honour and his feeling for 'heroes' are the side-effects of his drive to reconcile his inner conflicts in action. Impulsive disinterestedness, seeking a mould, was his reply to the educated savage who betrays liberalism by aggrandizing himself. The anarchy Yeats attacks is the incubator of reaction, and fascism is a burlesque of the order he admires. Yeats did have a cult of background, manifesting in admiration for decent landed families and the relics of their life. He hoped to see tradition transmit a health over the heads of mercenary classes and apply this as a corrective to decadence. We may jeer at this as a delusion: what counts is that Yeats made beneficial hieratic verse out of his belief. His notes on his poem, *Upon a House Shaken by the Land Agitation*, express his ideal:

> One feels that when all must make their living they will live not for life's sake but the work's and all be the poorer . . . This house has enriched my soul out of measure because here life moves within restraint through gracious forms. Here there has been no compelled labour, no poverty thwarted impulse.*

Not exactly fascist; hardly democratic either. This signalizes the message of the liberal mandarin. As the century moves on, more must 'make their living'; the reactionary innuendo is thus a lament over a *fait accompli*; like much of a poet's 'system' and 'politics' we must swallow his arrogance as a form of Poetic Licence which he needs to enforce his assertion of what *is* desirable: that we should live for the life's, not the work's, sake, and that life should 'move within restraint through gracious forms'. We have to ensure that leisure is not frivolous recuperation or exploited amnesia, that it does not become a coda to 'compelled labour'; and we may find Yeats's drive to single-mindedness a stimulus in that pursuit. Mr G. S. Fraser has written that 'there is an element of appeal to perhaps brutal and perhaps sensible popular prejudice in all Toryism', but for Yeats 'the mob was essentially . . . something to be defied'. His hatred of British royalty reminds us of an aristocratic semi-republicanism, going with a feeling for style and courage in public life (the courtesy and bravura of his poetry is the model) which was on guard against the horde, just as likely, in his view, to deny personality as the abuse of government. Imbued with a respect for law, a horror of anarchy when 'the night can sweat with terror as before / We pieced our thoughts into philosophy', Yeats felt that the grace of nobility—as much as acquired excellence as an inherited trait—could refine

* Quoted by A. N. Jeffares in *W. B. Yeats: Man and Poet*, 1949, p. 151.

A VISION OF REALITY

law and sustain a man when fighting for his rights. This is the world of 'Be secret and exult', 'in scorn of this audience', 'delirium of the brave', and 'What if excess of love / Bewildered them till they died?'

Yeats seems not archaic, but most topical, as a believer in ideas at a time when debate has declined, government is utilitarian and secretive, and policies are becoming a competition in public flattery. As a 'last romantic' he seems most histrionic when he declares his 'traditional sanctity and loveliness' to be allied with 'the book of the people', and offers the 'dream of the noble and the beggar-man' *as the balanced society* instead of a spur to individual effort. The mediaeval velleity, deteriorating through three romantic generations, here becomes certifiably unbalanced. Like Tolstoy at the fair, in much of his 'fascist' balladry and marching songs Yeats seems ill at ease in his bonhomie. Endowed with the anti-conformist instincts of the old middle class, Yeats grew anxious about this inheritance and projected its virtues above (when he rages through the aristocratic loud-hailer—'riches drove out rank') and below, without understanding what new material pressures were changing his world. What burgeons is not the revolutionary liberalism of Tom Paine, nor the Benthamite utilitarian liberalism, but the paternalist ideal of his hero, Burke. He looked for the creativity of individuals within an order of priorities, which would accept reform, but was fearful of commercial gun law ('money's rant is on'), of monolithic socialism, and what Yeats considered the politics of ambition. The rule of the best men within a parliamentary framework is not altogether dumb to our condition.

Good-headedness—the conversation with Ezra Pound, the discovery of Sir Herbert Grierson's edition of Donne—and public provocation, such as the Lane picture scandal, 'theatre business, management of men', helped Yeats's transition from the Celtic Twilight to the 'hard, bitter' style. Dublin was a blind bitter place. His skirmishes over the *attentats* on *The Countess Cathleen*, and on *The Playboy of the Western World*, were preludes to battles with wrongheadedness—including the timidity of the tolerant as well as the fanaticism of bigots—which had as maturing an effect as the revelation of Donne or the gadfly of imitators. Critics have taken his hint in comparing his approach to Swift's; and the forthright psychological incision of Yeats's wit is that of one who has passed 'through Jonathan Swift's dark grove' and there 'plucked bitter wisdom that enriched his blood'. But the intimacy of his admonishments—I am going to tell you in spite of yourselves, by purgation of mockery, for I know you well—is more English than Anglo-Irish, and connects Yeats with patrician liberal wits like Sydney Smith and Henry

28

Labouchere—both of whom, it is worth noting, were of Huguenot descent. Like Swift and Sydney Smith, Yeats is the veteran of urban culture, of the way capitals set the tone of a nation by collecting people of talent and of the institutions through which tone is radiated, just as Eliot is the veteran of urban decadence, of *civis* dissolving into atonal chaos. There is a purely Augustan core in Yeats, the patrician as citizen. He is adept at transforming the talk of the town—or at any rate the talk at the club—into terms of High Tragic Civility (or virulence) but we miss that fusion of intimacy with ubiquity which creates a moral climate.

*　　*　　*

That Freedom of the City which Baudelaire enjoyed is exercised by Yeats in the country; there his sense of vigour and recreation has more scope. His physical myopia helped him to omit, rather than amass, nature images and to arrange them in relation to what is nearer the eye—to wit social textures. (When Yeats laments the fall of the country houses he does so by the same tokens which he prizes in the city states.) In his Preface to *The Oxford Book of Modern Verse* Yeats remarks that at the end of the eighteenth century 'man became passive before a mechanized nature' but nature revolted and became a 'flux' and the time had now come for poets to cry 'the flux is in my own mind'. This is said apropos the modernists and it joins his purged style—'beauty like a tightened bow'—to bring Yeats close to that aesthetic. In the town Yeats operates within an Augustan code of civility; in the country he is dealing with flux, reluctant to gape. There is a skilful use of invigorating discord between the poet's mood and what he sees, as when Yeats watches the wild swans at Coole in the still water beneath the autumn trees. He *watches* them; the scene is passive and present; over it the tinge of a grand finale. Memory strikes—'The nineteenth autumn has come upon me / Since I first made my count'. At once there unfolds a tableau of past action—the magnificence of swans ascending ('I saw, before I had well finished') which circulates a remembered power superior to the set-piece of the first stanza. The poet's heart is 'sore':

> All's changed since I, hearing at twilight,
> The first time on this shore,
> The bell-beat of their wings above my head,
> Trod with a lighter tread.

The depression is stated within the balance of power, between present, static regret and the reserve of remembered energy; it is hinted that the 'lighter tread' may walk in reality; as Yeats said 'in Greece the tragic chorus danced'.

Unwearied still, lover by lover,
They paddle in the cold
Companionable streams or climb the air;
Their hearts have not grown old;
Passion or conquest, wander where they will,
Attend upon them still.

(The Wild Swans at Coole)

This is the 'lighter tread' of the swans' present—the stanza is charged with potentiality at variance with the impressionism of the first. We feel this to be an emergent mode of *his* present: the lighter tread walks in the rhythm, the poet surrenders to the tone; like the swans, the mood has ascended to the point where power and regret come together to beget a serenity the reverse of sterile. Why should the poet envy the swans? Their qualities exist by virtue of his discernment—'lover by lover', 'paddle', 'companionable streams', 'hearts', 'Passion or conquest . . . Attend upon them still'—they are as human as animal. The poem recollects itself in the end. The swans, 'mysterious, beautiful', dwindle to the affective impressionistic creatures of the first verse. We remember that they are wild, like harbingers in the poet's life. He seems to wish them away, to speed the parting guests, in blithe anticipation. Flown away, they will 'delight men's eyes', but this seems a flippant politeness of farewell after what the poet has been through—a triumph of the mind. At other times nature may operate *upon* the observer, to be welcomed with openness: under neither dispensation is there inertia, wishful thinking, or illusion:

What motion of the sun or stream
Or eyelid shot the gleam
That pierced my body through?
What made me live like these that seem
Self-born, born anew?

(Stream and Sun at Glendalough)

Yeats moved into an ancient tower in Galway in 1919, not far out of hailing distance from the scene of his poem, at Coole. The Tower became the abode of 'the lonely light that Samuel Palmer engraved', the totem, steeped in the delirium of the brave, of that triumph of the mind which Yeats craved and feared. What is perfected may be a threat to civilization and sanity because a destiny is a kind of end; it may breed sterility ('Is every modern nation like the tower / Half dead at the top?') or some barbaric recoil. His energy asserted itself as if in defiance of the tower:

TRAGIC JOY: W. B. YEATS

Never had I more
Excited, passionate, fantastical
Imagination, nor an ear and eye
That more expected the impossible—
No, not in boyhood when with rod and fly,
Or the humbler worm, I climbed Ben Bulben's back
And had the livelong summer day to spend.

(The Tower)

He will compel his soul to study 'in a learned school' and 'make' his soul in the face of the 'slow decay of blood'. But there was always some challenge, some choice calling him to ride his 'mysterious wisdom' into the lists, to banish his repose. Unity of being was not to be the plenitude he envisaged in youth; it was an ordeal in form, of climax and recapitulation—'I am content to live it all again' even if that meant 'a blind man battering blind men' in a ditch, of guilt and absolution—'When such as I cast out remorse . . . we are blest by everything . . . everything we look upon is blest'. The confidence which this commitment brings is not the same as compromise; it is on guard against complacency; it instinctively probes danger:

Greater glory in the sun,
An evening chill upon the air,
Bid imagination run
Much on the Great Questioner . . .

(At Algeciras)

A few months before the Civil War flared up to distract Yeats again, R. M. Rilke, whose genius had been paralysed by the 1914 war, took over his own tower in the Valais. Rilke's myth was subjective, demanding a recurring state of ecstasy, the poet being at the mercy of his environment though merciless in his means of obtaining the right environment. Yeats 'made himself up' not by wooing the ecstatic but transforming himself into symbols; his myth has more historical content and substance than Rilke's. Yeats's tower was an ivory tower *and* a stimulus to plunge into the arena. His Elegies complete, Rilke had little use for his tower except as a retreat where he could commune with the Swiss spring; having concentrated a cosmology of feeling in an atom of time and inspiration, that was that. Feeling surprised Yeats in unlikely places: in a crowded London shop with a book and a cup on a marble table, his body 'blazed' and he 'was blessed and could bless'.

Yeats, in *A Prayer for my Daughter*, pits his prayer against the sea-wind which 'screams upon the tower'; she is to have beauty, though not the kind which causes pride and loses 'natural kindness';

31

courtesy, for 'hearts are earned'; she is to be a 'flourishing hidden tree' rooted in 'one dear perpetual place', doing all through merriment, and she is to avoid the conceit of opinions; her bridegroom is to bring her to a house where all is accustomed, ceremonious, for 'arrogance and hatred are the wares / Peddled in the thoroughfares'. The innocence which, for his daughter, he hopes will be socially guaranteed, was a discipline which Yeats learned in the thick of the fray. By achievement in thought and action, he believed, men regained an innocence born from the fulfilment of their deepest nature in the work. The spirit relaxes in joyful tranquillity, and this has virtue in proportion to the integrity of motive which inspired the exploit. When he says 'Considering that, all hatred driven hence / The soul recovers radical innocence' he proposes that dross, whether exiled or put to work in the course of endeavour, may be harnessed to clear the way for that gay, unsullied fecklessness, found in and beyond anguish, which upholds us in struggle.

Prize of creativity, innocence was 'the highest achievement of the human intellect'. The innocent and the beautiful 'have no enemy but time'. Danger, though, lurked in moments of joy: Yeats perceives what the magus fails to perceive: a consummation prevents a repeat of the process which brought it into being. The value was in the struggle; when the angel wrestles, he grants no privileges. 'I, through the terrible novelty of light, stalk on, stalk on / Those great sea-horses bare their teeth and laugh at the dawn'. The novelty, with all that it means of suffering in the effort to create, is set against that 'desolation of reality' which is the inertia of innocence, of fulfilment. Rimbaud, the *mystique sauvage*, crying 'True life is absent', disordered his senses, made them a bridge to felicity—it broke, there followed his putsch against God, his belief that he was omnipotent and could dictate reforms. Yeats saw the eternal irradiate man here below; and insights gained from these annunciations were to be ploughed into life. He portrays the Virgin as any woman, and the antagonism between her humanity, which he portrays, and the superhuman, which he imagines, generates a blend of pity and terror. The theological virtues are ignored; the pains of birth are emphasized; the amazement felt by Yeats that woman can accommodate the future:

> *What is this flesh I purchased with my pains,*
> *This fallen star my milk sustains,*
> *This love that makes my heart's blood stop*
> *Or strikes a sudden chill into my bones*
> *And bids my hair stand up?*
> (*The Mother of God*)

In *Meru* the process is mystic in the hermits ('Caverned in night under the drifted snow'), the mystic being more concerned with the result than with the values created *en route*, and spiritual where man, terrified, struggles to think through things, to surpass himself, until he come 'into the desolation of reality', and nature finally surpasses man, 'His glory and his monuments are gone'. The warning—that fatalism ('Egypt and Greece, goodbye, and goodbye, Rome!') and opting out can do no more than *contemplate* the life of tragic conscientiousness—comes from a poet who has been tempted, and whose innocence is not bought at the price of frustrating his energies. On the other side of the Irish Channel, T. S. Eliot washed his hands of fallen man and became a spokesman of Anglo-Catholic conservatism. Having ransacked towns for images of degradation, later he used natural images as supernatural symbols. On this Yeats pronounced 'Mr Eliot remains a poet, he is unhappily in love with God'. Grounded on the rock of Blake's 'I must create a system or be enslaved by another man's' and perhaps with some memory of people restraining desire because theirs was weak enough to be restrained, Yeats felt a vital tension between 'the cold blown spray in my nostril' and 'I hail the superhuman'; if we shirk this tension, the inhuman will rush in.

Was the poet's nightmare of gargoyles—'they do not even feel, so abstract are they / So dead beyond our death / Triumph that we obey'—a mirage, reflected off 'the grey rock of Cashel'? We can see these lines captioned under advertisements, sky-written over cities, banner-headlined above the casuistry and the commands. Between a Sphinx and a Buddha—avatars of wisdom and forgetfulness—a girl dances. Her début spells out hope, she is the embodiment of 'the cold blown spray in my nostril', sharpens our sense of 'Man is in love and loves what vanishes, What is there more to say?' In that swashbuckling address there is an ironic invitation to the dance. 'He who sings a lasting song / Thinks in a marrow bone'. In this Yeats saw the force which binds friends and enemies together (what Eliot refines into 'folded in a single party'), for it is love for the creation which makes them bitterly contrary about it. Or the outcome may be civil, when the 'sixty-year-old smiling public man', who is simply an old man, visits a school where the children remind him of Maud Gonne's youth. A reputation is set against human feeling, and found wanting. Tempted to celebrate the ideal of the nuns, or the sexuality of 'a mother's reveries', Yeats makes the contenders lose self-consciousness and enhance each other—'O chestnut-tree, great-rooted blossomer / Are you the leaf, the blossom or the bole? / O body swayed to music, O brightening glance / How can we tell the dancer from the dance?'

33

The Byzantium poems are working models, dramas in miniature of the poet's tragic myth. They are mythical in their expression by symbols rather than thought of a relation between the human and divine, 'transcendental', superhuman—everything which delights and alarms man because it is unaccountable; the poet's pitting of desires and qualities against each other does not aim at balance, extinction, or even synthesis, but at cross-fertilization: the sowing of the seed into new life; and they are tragic because conscious of the difficulty of the heroic life, threatened by human stupidity, biological decline, complexity of choice. Mr G. S. Fraser has said that Byzantium is 'a symbol of the permanence of art' and that Yeats looks forward to 'a kind of immortality in his poems'.* I find no evidence, in the 1927 poem, of art being permanent; on the contrary, Yeats was conscious of the transience of art, a victim of the juggernaut of history—'all things fall and are built again / And those that build them again are gay'. The duration of art is included in the idea of man—the transient thinking animal. The 'sages standing in God's holy fire / As in the gold mosaic of a wall' are the masters of understanding, ablaze with vision, who *have* achieved 'such a form as Grecian goldsmiths make', who *are* 'out of nature'; and Yeats yearns towards this consummation. He is *sailing to* Byzantium, an envoy from the West, and has hove to outside the harbour, half envious, half afraid, dazzled, and is *tempted by what it would be like* 'to sing to lords and ladies of Byzantium / Of what is past, or passing, or to come'.

The being 'out of nature' is, it appears, a delusion. The old are 'a tattered coat upon a stick'; only rebirth of soul renews man, the influx of power, the 'transcendental'—'soul clap its hands and sing, and louder sing'. The first stanza is not a lament, it is a passionate ironic apprehension of 'whatever is begotten, born, and dies'. If Western Ireland—why cannot the Jungians take the place for what it manifestly is?—is 'no country for old men' it is because *nature disregards her admirers*; nor is 'unageing intellect' the changeless work of art, it is the still labouring spirit, Blake's 'true man, the imagination which liveth forever'. Yeats is 'sick with desire', afraid that the 'dying animal', the integument of the spirit, will sap the *intellect's power to admire nature*, to make sense out of the multiplicity of objects of perception. So he sends an embassy to the sages, inviting them to be his 'singing-masters'—the stress is on spontaneous, ephemeral utterance —and gather him 'into the artifice of eternity'. 'Artifice' is ironic— eternity constructed, not vouchsafed—and it refers to something beyond the poet: the structure of culture, an order of wisdom which indeed *seems*, in its concentration, prestige and intensity, to be be-

* G. S. Fraser, 'Yeats's Byzantium', *Critical Quarterly*, Autumn 1960.

yond the reach of change; but remember 'artifice'. The poem depicts the moment when Yeats knew that he was a spiritual adept, and then was smitten with an unrequited love for nature. He could have climbed Olympus and haughtily reviewed the world; he sailed to Byzantium, prepared for anything; the poem is a parley before the alarums and excursions of battle.

In the basilicas of Ravenna, a majesty of figures expressing divine, absolute values, seems to fertilize a wondrous parade of birds, beasts, streams and flowering shrubs. This is the world of *Sailing to Byzantium*, where Yeats wants his two poles, 'the artifice of eternity' and 'the fury and the mire of human veins', kept apart at their utmost intensity; celebrating the seasonal, he augments (as it were) the absolute; eternity is the confrontation of recurring value with the energy which sustains it; the eternal is earthed in the best productions of time. In *Byzantium*, he is there; this is like the Theophany in San Vitale, where transcension is all. Mr G. S. Fraser ('I take the night-walkers to be prostitutes') informs us that the lines 'A starlit or a moonlit dome disdains / All that man is / All mere complexities / The fury and the mire of human veins' involve astrology and Yeats's occult system. Why? Yards of shelving are devoted to the 'sources' of these poems. In fact, there is nothing in their plot which is not an act or scene, an intelligible factor in the play of the poem.

The Dome of Santa Sophia reflects the night sky, and that sky, simple, changeless, dumb, and vast, is unmoved by history and character; the city of understanding, of consummation, and of art is not so far 'out of nature' after all, even though the soldiers and the whores have cleared off the streets; Byzantium is in league with nature. As well it might, the next stanza falters into occult reverie, rising to a face-saving rhetoric; the next, a more realized assertion of art's power to triumph over mutability; but it lacks the hidden elation of the 1927 poem. The spellbinding and magnificent descriptiveness of 'At midnight on the Emperor's pavement flit / Flames that no faggot feeds, nor steel has lit / Nor storm disturbs, flames begotten of flame' stuns the mind (literally the flames are the flashing particles in the interstices between the tesserae). This art is a vital stasis, awesomely compelling, yet if it consumes complexities, it is also self-consuming, and finally overthrown. Although the last stanza shows the 'smithies' breaking the flood, the mosaics triumphing, in fact the spell *is* broken: flesh and blood (dolphins) with spirit up, rides the ocean of flux, procreation, and possibility, and 'fresh images' are signalled across the agitated sea.

Jean Cocteau, speaking at Oxford in 1956, compared the poet to Marco Polo returned from a China where only he had been to tell

amazing stories and be derided as a lunatic.* The Byzantiums are
not symbolic puzzles; they are stories. Naturally they secrete a
magical, wondrous element; they are also perfectly comprehensible
and practicable, embody a fierce anvil-wrought wisdom, to everyone who reads them in the way one reads *The Brothers Karamazov*.
Byzantium is Yeats's China; our men of straw would dismiss him as
the Marco Polo of our time. Rotten with contentment, how should
they feel the call of spiritual extremes, the need for a Byzantium as a
focus of possibilities, and of limits? Whereas *Sailing to Byzantium* is a
true story, *Byzantium* is a fiction, eked out with the occult. 'Human
kind cannot bear very much reality' said Eliot, and Yeats might
accept it for epigraph; but when Eliot makes this the basis for a be-
littling of humanity and the creation of a supernatural myth including organized religion while repressing in his verse lyricism in favour
of concepts, Yeats would have gone away and written 'For beauty
dies of beauty, worth of worth . . . We that look on but laugh in
tragic joy'. Our deficiency of perfection, our revolt against it when
it is gained, is to Yeats peculiarly inspiring whether to truth or
fiction, realism or reverie, but not a stigma of sin—in fact, a call to
arms. Apprehensive of evil, he was too conscious of a mixture of
motives, an ambiguity of impulses, too proud of an innocence regained through an objectification of the inner life to allow himself
to be stultified by guilt.

*   *   *

The Irish Troubles were enough of a family affair to convulse the
individual. This sense of the person, with his values and his choice,
counting, had been difficult for Owen and Rosenberg and was not
felt again until the Spanish war. Yeats felt in violence a liberation
from the stagnant self, a dismissal of complexities, a revival of will
and decision: even the 'wisest man' must know violence before he
can 'know his work'. If violence could be made the dynamic to
meritorious acts, so much the better; he celebrated the patriots—
'Yet they were of a different kind / The names that stilled your
childish play / They have gone about the world like wind'. Yeats
had his share of practical brawls, but chiefly he cherished the
spiritual fury of men of unusual perception. Anger can guarantee
the depth of our concern, it may be an actuated form of good faith.
This is a truth which our era of TV get-togethers and good-mixing
is unable to understand; our neglect of it condones too much false
reticence, slick talking and invertebrate assent. Yeats is the enemy of
the P.R.O. ethos. For him, to rage implies a standard, a wrestle and

* See Jean Cocteau, 'Poetry and Invisibility', tr. Jean Stewart, *The London
Magazine*, January 1957.

almost a communion with the *bête noire*. 'I study hatred with great diligence' is a beautiful line; he throws a gauntlet at the deity—'Hatred of God may bring the soul to God'. Proper pride is another means to self-respect, which is a means to respect of others. Proclaiming our singularity, these provoke a response and furnish a principle which spurs the play of values; the qualities, repellent in the egotist, may nourish that continuity lacking which no spiritual initiative may come to fruition, or keep up the morale of some cause. Continuity, demanding that things last long enough to be judged, and causes, upsetting convenient fixtures, are repugnant to people for whom lines like these will have a nuisance or curiosity value:

> *Pride, like that of the morn,*
> *When the headlong light is loose . . .*
> *Or that of the hour*
> *When the swan must fix his eye*
> *Upon a fading gleam,*
> *Float out upon a long*
> *Last reach of glittering stream*
> *And there sing his last song.*
>
> (*The Tower*)

The statesman of *Death*, 'a great man in his pride', confronts 'murderous men' in no boastful, and 'casts derision upon' death in no mystical, state of mind. He 'dreams and hopes', this places him above the 'dying animal'. Man has 'created death' in man's own image; it is the supreme test of whether we prefer the pathos and tragedy of reason to the dumb acquiescence of instinct. The assassin is worthless because he is the tool of blind historic and neurotic forces; the victim is majestic because, doing his work, he 'knows death' as a constant presence realized at the moment of assassination. At the extreme of emotion, Yeats reaches self-knowledge; in this mood sober judgments are made, and pity arises. For in Yeats there is always a reaction *against* merely brutal and stupefying violence—'All the folly of a fight / With a common wrong or right / The innocent and the beautiful / Have no enemy but time'. Yeats remembers two girls in silk kimonos, great windows open to the south, and imprisonment and death. Compassion: in concert with his dislike of the abstract fanaticism for which a woman has stood:

> *When long ago I saw her ride*
> *Under Ben Bulben to the meet,*
> *The beauty of her country-side*
> *With all youth's lonely wildness stirred,*
> *She seemed to have grown clean and sweet*
> *Like any rock-bred, sea-borne bird:*

37

Sea-borne, or balanced on the air
When first it sprang out of the nest
Upon some lofty rock to stare
Upon the cloudy canopy,
While under its storm-beaten breast
Cried out the hollows of the sea.

(On a Political Prisoner)

The unity a man seeks, he verifies in action. Half-determined, he is yet *taking place*, incarnating himself in the places he loved, the friends he admired, the events he helped to foment. In art he escapes from mechanism to record and watch the process, like actors in a Japanese mime who observe their acting with superb consciousness. Performing a role men deform themselves in time, though extricated from it by virtue of the values they justified, available in works. They may have been people whom Yeats considered boring, unmannerly, and nearly always misguided, but in the decisive moment when they unmasked, risked all, and did the ultimate unretractable thing their essence was revealed; the clumsy chrysalis casts the shard, airs its wings, and soars into a 'terrible beauty'—terrible because it shakes the validity of judgment, shows how unique, how unaccountable, a man may be, and what rare, dire conditions may be required to provide the new, strange value with its element.

Was it needless death after all?
For England may keep faith
For all that is done and said . . .
And what if excess of love
Bewildered them till they died?
I write it out in a verse—
MacDonagh and MacBride
And Connolly and Pearse
Now and in time to be,
Wherever green is worn,
Are changed, changed utterly:
A terrible beauty is born.

(Easter 1916)

Unpopular heroism which is defeated, the heroism of causes which make no stir in the world, or a fine subjectivity which breaks down (the appreciation of Lionel Johnson) are as moving to Yeats as the heroism which writes history. One thinks of the poems about Mabel Beardsley's death ('Matching our broken-hearted wit against her wit'), on the fall of Parnell, and to Sir Hugh Lane, or *To a Shade* which is reputed to amalgamate thoughts about both men:

> *A man*
> *Of your own passionate serving kind who had brought*
> *In his full hands what, had they only known,*
> *Had given their children's children loftier thought,*
> *Sweeter emotion, working in their veins*
> *Like gentle blood, has been driven from the place,*
> *And insult heaped upon him for his pains . . .*

The 'beauty' of tragic action remains there. Proceeding from the impassioned conscience, it is like Albert Camus's conception of revolt, the 'you are going too far' moment, when a man defends his individuality at such risk that he displays qualities more general than his selfhood; and if the qualities are institutionalized for the benefit of society, a limit must be respected which preserves that personal freedom (revolt distinct from revolution). With Yeats, freedom fraternizes with the unpredictable senses; abstract thought, divorced from genuine revolt, leads to the destructiveness of blind faith or dogmatic reason:

> *What if I bade you leave*
> *The cavern of the mind?*
> *There's better exercise*
> *In the sunlight and wind.*
>
> *I never bade you go*
> *To Moscow or to Rome.*
> *Renounce that drudgery,*
> *Call the Muses home.*
> *(Those Images)*

To people who find 'terrible beauty' a more agreeable 'social hope' than the short-cut of C. P. Snow, the *dramatis personae* of Yeats's poems are like the noblemen of Shakespeare's History Plays, 'familiar in their mouths as household words'. Symbolic of constants like passion, idiosyncrasy, and renunciation, Yeats's friends were courageous—acclaimed by him as such—for their championship of value in situations which it was hard to remedy, and tragic because forever bedevilled, like Yeats himself, by inner division. We prate of 'personal relationships' and think it sufficient to have met someone on the strength of chatter at a party; the *friendship* of which Montaigne speaks has been almost lost. To Yeats it meant a communion which was sealed, confirmed in some action in which the friendship became objective, inalienable, legendary. 'Character isolated by a deed / To engross the present and dominate memory'. The poems to Maud Gonne reflect in one mirror, 'her form all full /

As though with magnanimity of light', his development from illusion
to a brave exposure to the world. At first she was a Celtic incarnation
of Heine's Lorelei. Later, as he 'withers into the truth', the old age
which withers her transforms her into a symbol:

> *A young man when the old men are done talking*
> *Will say to an old man, 'Tell me of that lady*
> *The poet stubborn with his passion sang us*
> *When age might well have chilled his blood'.*

(*Broken Dreams*)

In the end she is a quality involved in time; she gives proportion to
memory; her 'present image' might have been fashioned by 'Quat-
trocento finger'; she ennobles and redeems the present, for by the
standard she embodies the age may be judged 'as though a sterner
eye looked through her eye / On this foul world in its decline and
fall'. The stern eye completes the earlier 'beauty like a tightened
bow / That is not natural in an age like this'. That is a perfect prediction of what Yeats's style became. Byzantium is belied. In this
foul world 'that sensual music' does not neglect 'monuments of
unageing intellect'. It is as though a Platonic alchemy, at work in
the man and the woman, has caused the unity of being, the uncom-
promising distinction, and the moral stamina which Yeats dimly
divined in Maud Gonne's youth to infect his development and to
reach apotheosis in his style; for these lovers soul claps its hands and
sings for every tatter in their mortal dress.

In *Beautiful Lofty Things* Yeats sculpts a metope where the friends
are motionless in the posture of characteristic action: O'Leary's
noble head, his father pacifying a mob at the Abbey, Standish
O'Grady stuttering drunken wisdom, Lady Gregory defying an
assassin, 'All the Olympians; a thing never known again'. For Maud
Gonne's archetype Yeats went beyond Ireland: she was 'Pallas
Athene in that straight back and arrogant head', waiting for a train.
Thus friends are memorable—immemorial—because a rare character stamped itself on a unique event and created a myth. Yeats as
'biographer' judges his friends according to their consummation,
their final meaning for him. He eschews the Victorian method of an
exhaustive list of events, and the progressive method, inaugurated
by Lytton Strachey, of selecting events to fit the biographer's interpretation. The one degrades man to a social cog, the other to a
psychic puppet, and though Yeats was prone to examine himself in
the light of ancestral precedent, he has more confidence in the
person, to him the core of character is one and indivisible—'. . . I
am in despair that times may bring / Approved patterns of women
or of men / But not that selfsame excellence again'. Their qualities

kindled his; friendship is not a matter of luck but a discipline and a ritual.

Robert Gregory had been 'our Sidney and our perfect man', the many-sided humanist quickened in gifts but enslaved by none. Here the contrast with the landlocked poet Rilke again works in favour of the sea-girt poet Yeats. Of Rilke's death cult, we may say that if a poet must walk in graveclothes, let him not pretend that he is re-hearsing for the fancy dress party. To Yeats's Gregory, death was a vulgar nuisance—'that discourtesy of death'; in arduous play,* in mutual trust, in a landscape charged with memories death is out-witted—'for all things the delighted eye now sees / Were loved by him: the old storm-broken trees . . .' As a symbol—and these people must create priorities to respect—Gregory was the magnanimous man of Aristotle made a citizen by the honest man of Voltaire: the streak of Augustan intransigence, of reason fulminating against the machinations of unreason ('What fanatics invent / In this blind bitter town'), in Yeats must be appreciated. Such men are bound to look incongruous, and be inefficient, in the world's eyes until their peculiarity has become undeniable in deeds; Castiglione making his

---

* Gregory is the hero of *An Irish Airman Foresees his Death*; the Yeats-Rilke clash recurs. The *Sonnets to Orpheus* hold that:

> Only when some pure Whither
> outweighs boyish insistence
> on the achieved machine
> will who has journeyed thither
> be, in that fading distance
> all that his flight has been.

In spite of his cult of the instant, Rilke disregards the fact of the machine, deni-grates the prowess which produced it. Yeats accepts the moment in the context of the material fact, on a basis of rejection of ignoble motives. Single-mindedness rules all:

> Nor law, nor duty bade me fight,
> Nor public men, nor cheering crowds,
> A lonely impulse of delight
> Drove to this tumult in the clouds;
> I balanced all, brought all to mind,
> The years to come seemed waste of breath,
> A waste of breath the years behind
> In balance with this life, this death.

In Wilfred Owen, the 'lonely impulse' is removed from the 'pure Whither', and the 'those that I fight I do not hate' of Yeats, to become an ethic of reproach:

> The scribes on all the people shove
> And bawl allegiance to the state,
> But they who love the greater love
> Lay down their life; they do not hate.

A decade later the mind puts the machine in its place by control; then men 'left the vivid air signed with their honour'—or dishonour. Rilke's 'pure Whither' leads to, is reproached by, lines in *Little Gidding* and poems by Dylan Thomas, MacNeice, and Spender on the London Blitz.

presence felt through admixtures of Machiavelli. Yeats's later poetry is a testament of the tension between them; to know it is a liberal education, since it teaches that in this century art, which means a turning inwards—towards Castiglione—may be both the redoubt and the legacy of the Renaissance man, provided it orients the 'turning inwards' towards deeds.

* * *

When Yeats eyed the scene he was filled not with admiration for Henry Ford and compulsory fun and fellowship but with a towering contempt. These aims encouraged (in his view) a degradation of feeling, of concern for the condition of man rather than his appearance. Conscious of weakness and insecurity which he was transforming into works and strength, pugnacious in public, amused and amusing in company, with his capacity *to see history in the making*, to see *the present as if it were history*, and to divine the role played in both by 'unity of being', Yeats must have felt his talent and way of life threatened by scientific determinism. He looked into the present and saw the disorder which makes progress ugly:

> *Mere anarchy is loosed upon the world . . .*
> *The ceremony of innocence is drowned;*
> *The best lack all conviction, while the worst*
> *Are full of passionate intensity.*
> (*The Second Coming*)

He looked into his past with its engagement and unrest; into his heredity of Protestant parsons, master-mariners, scholars, artists and 'hard-riding country gentlemen', 'cold and passionate as the dawn'; he looked into history, to Greece when 'measurement began our might' and ancient Japan when Sato's jewelled, changeless sword was forged before Chaucer drew breath, to the amenity of Italy, the court of Duke Frederick at Urbino, where an exquisite intellectual refinement was emboldened by a barbarian vitality, to Coole Park, that sacked Urbino where the tradition of patronage was extinguished in a sunset glory, amid 'the unperturbed and courtly images'; and everywhere he looked he saw 'that ancient sect . . . thrown upon this filthy modern tide'.

The way to save the tradition was for the poet to celebrate it. To exorcise the deterministic bogey, Yeats formed his cyclic view of time. Political theories, concepts of leadership, systems of ideas are made corporeal and yoked to the reality of human types, who to all historical intents and purposes die and resurrect; and Yeats diversifies his description of beings, not just in his 'system', but in observation of contemporaries and the tormented antinomies he acclaims in himself ('out of our quarrel with the world we make rhetoric, out of our quarrel with ourselves we make poetry') with such verve and tenacity that determinism ceases to interest us, becomes a crashing bore. The effect of Yeats's exaltation of personality is to deflect us from the analysis of trends, statistics, fashions, and confront us with the centrality of men. As with most poetic philosophies—Rilke's 'transformation' fad and Robert Graves's White Goddess infatuation are examples—the system Yeats offers us in that gallimaufry of theosophy, folk-lore, E.S.P. and temporal guesswork, *A Vision*, is neither credo, nor hypothesis, but *agenda*: an emotional prolegomena, and in its dogmatic aspects a sensible stock-taking, before doing confident and original work. This work short-circuits the system because it is based on selections; and to associate the selections, the poet participates in, and draws on, emotional and objective worlds opaque to the system. The result is a new force, practical myth rather than dogmatic system.

In the case of Yeats and Graves, you have the Irish gift for magpie-like connexions and the regurgitation of information in a remarkable form. They display a gallant insouciance which warns us not to be too solemn; the more seriously the world takes him, the louder the practical joker laughs. Of those fructifying actors, the Hunchback, Saint and Fool, Yeats was stage manager—and unity. Art partook of sainthood and foolishness, for to verify his feeling and justify his vision the poet must put them to the test, always experiment, though seduced by the attractions of contemplation and quietism. To refuse 'a heavenly mansion, raging in the dark' may prove that 'those who love the world serve it in action' and disprove that 'a man in his own secret meditation / Is lost amid the labyrinth he has made / In art or politics'. Of the tortured, rancorous Hunchback of terrifying insights, the innocence of the Saint, and the unworldliness of the 'deep considering' Fool Yeats was never ashamed. The antithesis of C. P. Snow telling the *Sunday Times* about Magnanimity, he offers the rarity of a wise man unafraid to seem ridiculous—'the unfinished man and his pain / Brought face to face with his own clumsiness'.

Ritual became a barricade for the defence of values. Here Yeats meets Eliot, but the latter's rightist Anglo-Catholicism, a prepared system imposed on the problem, is worlds apart from Yeats's dream of the aristocrat as the free man, above fashion, who chooses of his own volition and is never compelled by prudence or ambition. If Yeats is a snob, it is in the tragi-comic Byronic sense of one who does not see why he should imitate the values of anyone else; the author of *The Leopard* might have said for Yeats 'to rage and mock is gentlemanly, to grumble and whine is not'.* If we dislike the 'go, go, drive

* Giuseppe di Lampedusa, *The Leopard*, tr. Archibald Colquhoun, 1960, p. 162.

a trade', 'in scorn of this audience' aspect of Yeats, if orthodox liberal shibboleths were lost in his transition into the leisured glades where 'life overflows without ambitious pains', that is a fair escape from the soul-destroying jungle of conspicuous consumption, where 'fashion or mere fantasy decrees'. Yeats was, no doubt, mischievously unappreciative of the benefits of science (his operation prolonging his sexuality) and the sheer relevance of science as a framework for humane thinking (the poetry of William Empson). What infuriated him was the farce of science being used, by professional manipulators, to promote a profitable ugliness and apathy. As an antidote unity of being, the Yeatsian values, must remain available; the question of *where* they take sanctuary is immaterial.

Yet the incorrigible flamboyant disdain of Yeats, full of force and furore, is anchored in a kind of humility. He was forever apt to change, to renew his art, to dive into sources of energy, and he surfaced with a vision of the delicacy of civilization which rests on a volcano of barbarism. Yeats never fell for the fallacy that a peaceful era is its own justification, unless it is also a creative era and a decent era. 'Those masterful images because complete / Grew in pure mind, but out of what began?' and realizing that culture may be explained, though not explained away, this genius was not afraid to see himself as a stupid old man fussing with squalid images in 'the foul rag-and-bone shop of the heart'. When delight came, Yeats exulted with the same candour; then like Dostoevsky's Alyosha he was 'not afraid of that ecstasy'. Yeats was quick, quicker than anyone this century, to see history in the making; and to cherish the events in a tradition because they had once been present. He does not like Eliot exorcize time, nor like Miss Kathleen Raine does he see in it 'a reflection of fallen man'. In Yeats a civilization—'that civilization may not sink' —is wafted on a lyrical articulation into the heart of obdurate reality. Only when he declaims is he boring: he impresses most in that mastery of the delicate, minute image which, resonant and composite, opens up perspectives. What else is the Yeats stylistic miracle, but the fruitful marriage of youthful virtuoso lyricism with an old, long-sighted, ripe, yet belligerent wisdom? Beneath civilization runs the quenchless transience of art, redeeming man out of dumb nature and blind time into creative self-recognition:

> *There on that scaffolding reclines*
> *Michael Angelo.*
> *With no more sound than the mice make*
> *His hand moves to and fro.*
> Like a long-legged fly upon the stream
> His mind moves upon silence.
>
> (*Long-legged Fly*)

'Man may embody truth but he cannot know it. I must embody it in the completion of my life.' If the Chinese mandarin cries with aroma in his nostrils 'Let all things pass away', banners choke the air, armoured horses neigh in the battle in the pass, 'all things remain in God'. What man can do is to forge potent symbols immobilized in time which remain salutary for the unborn. A man is not the creature of 'environment', he is a compound of qualities drawn from tradition; in his myth his forbears are revived. 'An old man's eagle mind' will beat in frenzy for the truth, and though art—'picture and book remain / An acre of green grass / For air and exercise'—is accorded grateful deference, the mind at the quiet of life's end 'consuming its flesh and bone' cannot compass truth. So 'all men live in suffering'; those who accept it will find that 'some stream of lightning' from the skies has power to burn it out. Rilke confuses the world with his introspection, Valéry sees it through a fastidious analysis of consciousness, Eliot in fear of sin and pantheism anathematizes it, Rimbaud is burned on his own bonfire. In Yeats's myth all these time-honoured solutions are transitory, for the spirit must experience them all until it come 'into the desolation of reality' and thence to 'radical innocence'.

> *Everything that man esteems*
> *Endures a moment or a day.*
> *Love's pleasure drives his love away,*
> *The painter's brush consumes his dreams;*
> *The herald's cry, the soldier's tread*
> *Exhaust his glory and his might:*
> *Whatever flames upon the night*
> *Man's own resinous heart has fed.*
>
> (*Two Songs From a Play*)

T. S. ELIOT, ALAS?

On the ridge where the great artist moves forward, every step is an adventure, an extreme risk. In that risk, however, lies the freedom of art. A difficult freedom that is more like an ascetic discipline? Like all freedom, it is . . . an exhausting adventure, and that is why people avoid the risk today, as they avoid liberty with its exacting demands.

The freest art and the most rebellious will therefore be the most classical; it will reward the greatest effort. So long as a society and its artists do not accept this effort, so long as they relax in the comfort of amusements or the comfort of conformism . . . its artists are lost in nihilism and sterility . . . today rebirth depends on our courage and our will to be lucid.

ALBERT CAMUS: 'Create Dangerously'

Et Saint Apollinaire, raide et ascétique,
Vieille usine désaffectée de Dieu, tient encore
Dans ses pierres écroulantes la forme précise de Byzance.

T. S. ELIOT: *Lune de Miel*

IN the T. S. Eliot symposium of *The Review*,* Mr Michael Hamburger described the early Eliot as 'already a mystic'. If so, he was an uncommonly *conscientious* one—Mr Eliot makes his bow with his features in the clerical cut of a revolutionary puritan. His rebellion is both provoked and thwarted by the imbroglio of a bourgeoisie whose material assurance and spiritual *laissez faire* has reached *reductio ad absurdum*. Everything is either there, 'known already', or can be anticipated, 'there will be time'. Prematurely ageing, addicted to depressing obligations, the young puritan rebel is perplexed by a dispiriting sense of accumulated inbred complexities, destructive of energy and incentive. Horror at so much as the likelihood of bad behaviour, fear of expressing the emotions, leads to an obsessive concern with the filigree of conduct, so that 'personality' becomes the decisive factor in a milieu where:

There will be time, there will be time
To prepare a face to meet the faces that you meet . . .

* *The Review: T. S. Eliot Special Number*, November 1962.

T. S. ELIOT, ALAS?

Time for you and time for me,
And time yet for a hundred indecisions,
And time for a hundred visions and revisions,
Before the taking of a toast and tea.

Phrases like 'the latest Pole', 'you will see me any morning in the park', 'I remain self-possessed' evoke an eternity of habit well known to be boring but still adamant. Subjective verbs like 'feel' and 'mean' take on a kind of baffled portentousness. Inability to stop thinking about one's 'personality', and neurotic interest in the degree of credit one enjoys in the eyes of other 'personalities', entangles one further in the snares of convention ('the eyes that fix you in a formulated phrase'), reticence ('Do I dare / Disturb the universe? / In a minute there is time / For decisions and revisions which a minute will reverse'), covert knowledge ('I know the voices dying with a dying fall / Beneath the music from a farther room'), and uncommunication ('And turning toward the window, should say: / 'That is not it at all / That is not what I meant, at all'). One's feelings oscillate between 'a slight sensation of being ill at ease' and promptings to 'have the strength to force the moment to its crisis', but between these states, and without any field of force to mediate between them, yawns the gulf of convention, reticence, knowledge, and uncommunication. One may dramatize one's reticence as Hamlet in the idiom of Shakespeare, or one's baffled knowledge as 'I am Lazarus, come from the dead / Come back to tell you all, I shall tell you all', one may yearn towards a standard of worth, yet for all one's fine intentions worth remains unknowable—'among some talk of you and me / Would it have been worth while . . .'

Not knowing what to feel or if I understand
Or whether wise or foolish, tardy or too soon . . .
Would she not have the advantage, after all?
This music is successful with a 'dying fall' . . .

The Prince Hamlet's 'attendant lord', 'full of high sentence but a bit obtuse', who vivisects so conscientiously his spiritual cowardice in *Prufrock* and *Portrait of a Lady* is a kind of gifted failure, rather as Eliot must have seemed—indeed was—a helpless original. Socially accomplished, the puritan rebel is gravelled by a sense of moral gaucherie; his 'would it have been worth while' festers on a guilty denial of 'some overwhelming question' which has too often been shrugged off with a jaunty 'Oh, do not ask, What is it? / Let us go and make our visit' in the streets that follow like a tedious argument of insidious intent. His guilty protest manifests as elegant, startling conceits, poking fun at rhyme ('smoothed by long fingers . . . or it malingers')

47

and farouche associations which disconcert conventional vision without challenging the *status quo*. Such is the quality of failure: the disenchantment and prescience of the hypersensitive liberal are the gift. Without fully knowing it, perhaps, the poet has plumbed a depth of disillusion; he has yearned after, he has almost apprehended, a redemptive vision beyond 'are these ideas right or wrong' and the 'overwhelming question'. But he burkes the issue, he is constitutionally incapable of taking the plunge. All he can do is demonstrate in his *style* the truth of Oscar Wilde's 'the pagan miracle is the work of art'.

Imagism is employed as a tactical device to *make sure of the enemy*. The ideal of classicism adumbrated in 'Tradition and the Individual Talent' (1919) extricates language, at least, from the toils of 'personality'. It dismisses romantic reliance on the poetic impulse as a panacea, since the 'Inner Voice of Whiggery' does not utter valid universals out of individual depths; it multiplies the chaos. The last gasps of European romanticism, exhaled by the Symbolists, are inhaled with discretion by Eliot when he amends 'pure poetry'—the poem as itself a sensation—to mean a steady clarity of objective vision; and in larger gulps when he adopts the subversive twist inflicted on romanticism by colloquial or grotesque poets like Laforgue and Corbière. In his final phase Eliot will remain in the Post-Symbolist tradition, but with important differences: though he uses the personal symbol (as distinct from emotion) to point a universal meaning, he lays the ghost of the creative impulse as a redemptive value and uses poetic perception as a gateway to religious illumination, so that his symbols in the end correspond to a traditional hierarchy of beliefs which transcend the subjective. The distinction between observer and observed is restored, and the poetic impulse, no longer confused with the poetic mind or 'medium', is dethroned from the status of a good in itself. Wordsworth and Coleridge experimented with the changes of substance an experience may undergo when recreated in rhythm and versification, but this became moral delirium, so Eliot drives the invalid, like a scapegoat for Mr Prufrock's own latter-day romantic impotence, into the wilderness of 'I have seen the moment of my greatness flicker / And I have seen the eternal Footman hold my coat, and snicker / And in short, I was afraid'.

Words no longer find their place according to the sequence of the metronome. The deployment of the word is to correspond to the rigour and timbre of speech, and to the fits and starts of thought as it 'spells out' just before speech. Fluctuation of pattern and layout prove that by implying judgment, and inviting our participation, the literary Bolshevik had method in his madness, and changes of rhythmic structure are like geological fissures to reveal the upheaval or decline of a profound moral implication or sub-conscious release. The so-called 'borrowing' which at times looked like plagiarism masquerading as a fine art is a way of enfranchising tradition by showing that past spiritual sureness, once felt, is alive once and for all; 'retwining' the threads of 'dissociated sensibility', Eliot renovated epithets by depicting the changes which time, viewed through his end of the telescope, had wrought on their 'static' historical context. The style—the task force of this revolutionary puritanism of the medium—eliminates the importunings of private emotion because it aims to cope with chaos without imposing a pattern.

One must combat the canard that Eliot is a sort of bardic Monsieur Teste, always 'killing his puppet'. His anti-emotionalism is, paradoxically, the requisite to an honest *use* of emotions; he hates romanticism because it never questions them, allows them to sprawl, mixes them up. Romanticism, posing as the conscience, represents the bad faith of the emotions. Eliot represents the good faith of the emotions. The trick of playing off antinomies, often ending in a *dennoch preisen* affirmation, would strike Eliot as burking the issue or whistling in the dark. Isolating each perception, he studies it as if his intellect was a magnifying glass which concentrates the sun's rays until the perceptions catch fire. It is vital to appreciate what Eliot's religious faith, and his later devotional poetry, owe to *the guidance he accepts from extremes of emotional perception*. Or rather: Eliot's two extremes of emotional perception—intolerable horror, and saving beatitude—become the starting point for disinterested spiritual research, in which the associating 'medium', free from preconceived ideas, plays the role of assessor of evidence. Eliot loathes moralizing poetry because it postpones the crisis of the emotions, the point of no return when we must ask the *meaning* of an extreme finding; and poetry will be fit to moralize only when it owns up about its motives. Hence his dislike of Arnoldian morality and his approval of blasphemous or perverse poets such as Baudelaire, Marlowe, and Villon, who made different myths—accompanied by different life-goals of which Eliot is bound to disapprove—out of perceptions which both they and Eliot have experienced to the full.

Eliot's style reflects hallucination; and it refracts the promise of renewal. The chaos it confines polarizes into hysteria and redemptive insights. It is a point of honour that the hysterias be corrected; at the end of the *Portrait* the reluctant hero is caught out in an insincerity; he breaks down, he loses face:

> *And I must borrow every changing shape*
> *To find expression . . . dance, dance*

Like a dancing bear,
Cry like a parrot, chatter like an ape.
Let us take the air, in a tobacco trance—

Thus he recovers his *voyeur* poise, his tranquillity, and his humanity. At times the panic gesticulates as a delusion of grandeur, associated with the 'worth it' yearnings and the tired prognostications of a
dubious apocalypse—'You will go on, and when you have prevailed
. . .'—before relapsing into reminiscence and nostalgia. The milieu
is one of inverted liberalism, plagued by misleading historical echoes.
Art, mixed up with such states of mind, is cherished for its curiosity
value—'Among velleities and carefully caught regrets / Through
attenuated tones of violins / Mingled with remote cornets / And
begins'. Or the panic strikes, intimate, unattainable, instinct with
the far-flung sensual pungency of an unimagined otherness—'I
should have been a pair of ragged claws / Scuttling across the floors
of silent seas'. No wonder the poet feels *hors de combat* in rooms where
women come and go talking of Michelangelo; no wonder he feels
older than the others. Then something compassable, yet still peculiar
—the most he can do is mention it—is the focus of disturbance, 'the
smoke that rises from the pipes / Of lonely men in shirt sleeves, leaning out of windows'. These alarming 'butt ends of my days and ways'
are so firmly contained (in the military sense of 'containing a break-
through') in the style that they might be mistaken for abortive
redemptive insights. Rarely, and then with unbearable impact, do
they declare themselves without equivocation. When Mr Apollinax
—Bertrand Russell in the incognito of the god of reason?—visits the
United States:

His laughter was submarine and profound
Like the old man of the sea's
Hidden under coral islands
Where worried bodies of drowned men drift down in the green silence,
Dropping from fingers of surf . . .

I heard the beat of centaur's hoofs over the hard turf
As his dry and passionate talk devoured the afternoon.

The upsurge, gratuitous and resistless, of the—Dionysiac?—
creates a desperation which evokes a state of being unknown to the
academic tea-party; and that state is the more urgent because the
poet marvels at it in secret. *Rhapsody on a Windy Night* gives us the
anatomy of hysteria. Its collocation of precise timing, discursive
vividness, and unrelated exactitude makes the injunction to 'prepare
for life' itself 'the last twist of the knife'—the knife dissecting at a
depth, with a degree of pain, which seems perfectly adapted to the

improbable operating theatre of a London street in the small hours
of the morning:

> *A twisted branch upon the beach*
> *Eaten smooth, and polished*
> *As if the world gave up*
> *The secret of its skeleton,*
> *Stiff and white.*
> *A broken spring in a factory yard,*
> *Rust that clings to the form that the strength has left*
> *Hard and curled and ready to snap.*

The trouble is that the ordinary, the charismatic, and the hysterical refuse to meet. If T. S. Eliot is 'already a mystic' he is a heretic
who dwells in a fragmented world—a mystic turned worker-
priest?—who will not and probably cannot move towards that unity
which is the mystic's reward. But if a vital stage in that progress is
the ejection of distractions from the mind, the undeviating regard of
quotidian torpor, a sense of the automatism of most behaviour, and
the painful, daily, ratiocination of the conditioned reflexes which
most people perform without awareness or question, this revolutionary puritan is a secular mystic. His anti-emotionalist aesthetic in any
case militates against the indiscriminate. For him the duty of the
'medium' is to *collect the necessary*, to distinguish between the vital and
the superfluous, and to create an *œuvre* which convinces by the
justice of its sentient reasoning.

What makes 'His soul stretched tight across the skies / That fade
behind a city block' a great poem is this blunt confrontation of
unflinching ordinary regard with a force which, isolated as necessary, remains unassimilable. Like the damned poets of France, Eliot
accumulates the circumstantial until it becomes obsessionally intense. 'The conscience of a blackened street / Impatient to assume
the world' has the workaday visionary rectitude, gifted to people
disciplined in the art of discernment in such matters, which burgeons
more imaginatively in Blake's *Auguries of Innocence*. 'The notion of
some infinitely gentle, infinitely suffering thing' prolongs the mood
in the same tone; yet two worlds veer apart; the poet's mind is the
place of reconciliation. That way lies escape, evasion. With 'Wipe
your hand across your mouth, and laugh / The worlds revolve like
ancient women / Gathering fuel in vacant lots' the poet disarms
impending ridicule; he anticipates derision, and projects the pessimism upon a more desperate plane than could be imagined by the
mockers. Minds able to conceive the possibility of reconciliation will
appreciate that, in placating 'the world', Eliot has paid the homage
of contempt to the importance of the laughable notion.

As secular mystic, Eliot withdraws from the American satires; he refuses to speak for his characters and treats the situation clinically; he is professional, aware of his public. Cousin Nancy who 'smoked / And danced all the modern dances / And her aunts were not quite sure how they felt about it / But they knew that it was modern' has made a fool of Arnold's and Emerson's 'army of unalterable law'—liberal high seriousness, later Eliot's 'substitute for religion'. Not only that: she has broken out of the ossified dissatisfaction of the Prufrock generation, vitiated by the decadence of the seriousness, and is acting out a dress rehearsal of the Scott Fitzgerald era. Her emancipation is at least vital. Like Gatsby's Daisy, she has 'money in her voice'; to Matthew Arnold, she would be modelling the latest fashion in anarchy. Eliot declines to judge (Gatsby, we remember, will admit in his fall that 'it was all very personal') and accords Nancy the same stylistic and ironic treatment as his drawing-room denizens. The lesson of 'they knew that it was modern', usurping the 'guardians of the faith', is that modishness will always be *in motive* the same. Through technique, through the separation in art of the lasting from the transitory, the chaos may be contained; 'modernity' in art is more meaningful than its social equivalent. Compared with the fetching futility of Nancy, acting her historical role, the frail Pre-Raphaelite of *La Figlia che Piange* seems little more than a figment of a girl around whom the poet weaves a premature philosophizing. A fantasy of conduct—'some way incomparably light and deft', the fear of losing 'a gesture and a pose'—still motivates the lover. But his loss is now sublimated in the 'autumn weather' which 'compelled my imagination many days'. A new element, amazing the troubled midnight and the noon's repose, diverts the 'cogitations' and hints that the fantasy is evasive.

A more truculent voice speaks in *Gerontion* (1920). In contrast to Prufrock's, the tone is clipped, emphatic, accustomed to deference, though hardly mellow. This poem looks like a recovery of confidence. The speaker has distinct views—'My house is a decayed house / And the Jew squats on the window-sill, the owner . . .'—a proud stoic bluntness ('I have no ghosts'), a rather self-pitiful mock-modesty ('a dull head among windy spaces'), a judicial discriminating vision ('Signs are taken for wonders') which is inhibited by sensual fatigue ('I have lost my sight, smell, hearing, taste, and touch / How should I use them for your closer contact?') and a most articulate sense of the psychological futility of arguing from historical precedent. He is living in straitened—rather embittering—circumstances, and appears to have not only missed the war ('neither fear nor courage saves us', so this may have been deliberate) but to regret the salubrious pleasures of the Kipling burden. He is that creature

for frightened irony to Mr Prufrock and for ridicule to Cousin Nancy
—the benighted liberal idealist in an advanced state of decline.

Because he is a learned cynic, he is able to see clearly, even into
the far future ('We have not reached conclusion, when I / Stiffen in
a rented house') with the lens of the intellect. The power of regeneration, flashing on the retina of his consciousness, dazzled him, to
become schematized, to be contemplated or simulated—'In the
juvescence of the year / Came Christ the tiger / In depraved May
. . .' In weary reminiscence he has seen one source of unity and
effort dissipated by sophisticated individualism, 'by Hakagawa,
bowing among the Titians . . .' Rilke lost 'beauty in terror, terror in
inquisition' because he was too receptive, too vulnerable; Gerontion
is too intelligent; he has *known* what Prufrock 'felt' might be 'worth
while'. As the rhythm hurries to its bleak catharsis he clutches, melo-
dramatically, at the impersonal, abandoned relief proffered by the
inhuman, 'Gull against the wind, in the windy strait / Of Belle Isle,
or running on the Horn / White feathers in the snow . . .' In this
great poem Eliot has harrowed a certain seedy modern intelligence;
indeed, he *is* that intelligence; more lenient in method, Eliot remarks
the qualities which, employed in a different spirit, with different
emphases, restraints, and objectives, might recruit liberal culture.*
The fate of 'leaving disordered papers in a dusty room / Living first
in the silence after the viaticum' may yet be transcended; from signs
may come forth wonders.

Gerontion may be living in wretched lodgings—given his foreign
contacts, has he been deprived of shares held in St Petersburg?—but
he is proud of his remaining private property: his sense of a special
cultural election. Whom does he consider his inferiors in this world
where he still feels cantankerously at home? The answer follows in
Eliot's poems about the mass man, poems of entranced exaspera-
tion; tired of the ingrate business of playing the devil's advocate, he
prefers to scrutinize people as specimens.† One cannot read *Burbank
with a Baedeker, Bleistein with a Cigar* with its Princess Volupine,
money in furs, and moth-eaten coat of arms without revising one's
opinion of Rilke's *Late Autumn in Venice*; one suddenly sees Rilke,
oblivious of people, covetous of history, expatiating in his space-
world by gracious permission of the decadence which offends Eliot,

* Miss Iris Murdoch has written: 'Mr Eliot is . . . an anti-Puritan Puritan,
invoking the evil-conscious Puritanism of Hawthorne and James against the
"decayed protestantism" of the present. Mr Eliot is notably not in the English
Conservative tradition. He is an eclectic moralist.' *T. S. Eliot: A Symposium for his
70th Birthday*, ed. Neville Braybrooke, 1958, p. 157.

† I use 'mass' in the classless sense defined by Ortega in *The Revolt of the Masses*:
people who, rejecting standards, have 'no more to worry about'; and I am aware
of the Raymond Williams view that we are all, in some degree, mass.

poet of time and humility. *Sweeney Erect* exhales the atmosphere which must have encrusted itself, like smog, on Eliot's brain: the 'one-night cheap hotel', venue of isolated restless consciousness, *pace* Mr Thom Gunn 'on the move'—an ordeal perhaps undergone by the poet on landing in this country from New England or in the jungle of London. Three voices, literary, authentic, and semi-burlesque, concur in thinking badly of Sweeney. But Eliot is less uncharitable than critics who, posing as the Galahads of fellow feeling, impute to Eliot a hate of mankind which they have obviously searched for themselves. The 'contrast' between maritime splendour and urban squalor is not malicious, for it has no pejorative intent. Eliot uses literary diction, classical allusion, because he wants to show that other people, other literatures, have divined in the 'snarled seas' an emblem of cleansing and vitality; if anything, the poet laments their impotence in this case! Again in *A Cooking Egg* it is not the splendours of history which disdain the miseries of the multitudes in the hundred A.B.C.s. History exists for *what we make of it*: if we make it a fantasy to enhance fashion and vice, we humiliate ourselves. Far from satirizing us, time is degraded by us to our level of peculative corruption:

> *I shall not want Capital in Heaven*
> *For I shall meet Sir Alfred Mond.*
> *We two shall lie together, lapt*
> *In a five per cent. Exchequer Bond.*

Thus the 'penny world' of fish and chips bought to eat behind the screen promises, before the image fades in squalor, a fruition of desire and will beyond the comprehension of decadence. *A Cooking Egg* is, agreed, morally tendentious; in *Whispers of Immortality* mannerism is a device for playing fair to both sides. Grishkin is not condemned for rejecting 'a substitute for sense' any more than the *memento mori* is censured for distrusting 'pneumatic bliss'; distanced through mannerism, the dichotomies are commended to our mercy; the nearest the *poetry* can get to being 'expert beyond experience' is to force us to recognize Eliot's categories. A ritual vulgarity, in *Sweeney among the Nightingales*, co-exists with the ritual sublime. Each has its own code and emblems; each subtly modifies the other; we are left with the 'overwhelming question' echoing in the nightingale-soiled air. There is more than contrast, there is enigma and impartial justice in Eliot's summing up. Like a good judge, he has an opinion, but he wants the reader to compare the evidence. We are invited to think: and this is the highest compliment an artist can pay his readers.

*   *   *

T. S. ELIOT, ALAS?

Eliot must have been tempted to turn professional satirist. He had unique technical weapons, a most propitious background, moral indignation. England has a genius for breeding the benevolent moralist who turns professional: Mr John Betjeman is the choicest exponent of this brand of consent. But Eliot's technique is a going concern. The fecund mobile shape it weaves, full of presageful and admonitory alignments, enticing lacunae, and question-begging non-sequiturs, is oriented towards the future. We know that for Eliot the best Whig subjectivity can do is make false public virtue out of emotional necessity. Imagism helps us to see life clearly, association helps us to see life whole; despite Arnold, this reflects no moral credit on the seer, nor is it a valid stand-in for any discarded inconvenient supra-personal allegiance. The poem is new knowledge: a reunion, presided over by the poet, of delegates from far-flung parts who are more likely to pass effective resolutions in conference than in unruly and often wretched isolation.

We admire in *The Waste Land*, not the growth of a poet's mind, but the passion, flair and authority of language as it goes about the task of generalizing insights, giving them a universal application. *In proportion to the poet's self-effacement* the poem is an event of public interest. Artifice is not there for the fun of it: the vanguard of a strategy of value, inimical to pragmatism, it is a tactic of communication which aims to control chaos, then to recommend, through a subtle infusion of emotional desiderata, a principle of generalization to compose chaos. Technically the poem is a crash programme, an emergency law rushed through by Eliot to cope with 'an overwhelming question' which was getting out of hand. This enacts in an open world: no handholds; it is the acid test of modernism. Since a cancer is suspected in the poet's soul, he has reason to undertake a prognosis for the body social, but when the poet offers to examine other souls the cry of 'spiritual fascism' goes up. What has injured the poet's soul? It does not greatly matter. The curious may look up the 'New Interpretation of The Waste Land' of Mr John Peter* who has pieced together a plot for the poem—the poet's sense of loss about a friend drowned at sea. Mr Peter neglects, I think, the technical advantages of this: inhibition makes the poet invent androgynous speakers, psychological factotums which make the feeling still more ungainsayable. I would say the 'plot' is a substratum, but that is not the point. The point is that the 'objective correlative' here refuses to sublimate emotion in the manner of *In Memoriam*. In *The Waste Land* the aspirations drawn from private emotion are searched for, lost, apprehended, found and lost again in the purgatory of *civis*, 'a heap of broken images'. In its deceptive way this

* *Essays in Criticism*, July 1952.

compelling vision of London–Europe is a work of courage, subsuming grief.

Orthodox liberals swear by Instant Ethics: add hot water to the coffee and you get conviviality; one forgets that the water is lukewarm. Lacking the courage of their convictions, such critics are dismayed by the delayed-action puritanism of *The Waste Land*. E. M. Forster, whose essay on Eliot is still the best, regards the poem as 'a personal comment on the universe'. Eliot has 'seen something terrible, and underestimating . . . the general decency of his audience, has declined to say so plainly . . . the horror is so intense that the poet has an inhibition'.* An Old Liberal, Forster thinks in relationships where Eliot thinks in technique (in his later development Forster acutely observes 'well-turned compliments to Divine Grace but no trace of religious emotion') and it is significant of the ambiguities of Forster's position that he distrusts *The Waste Land* yet acclaims in the early poems (read when doing Red Cross work in Egypt in 1917) 'people who seemed genuine because unattractive or weak . . . the waves of edifying bilge rolled off me . . . he who could turn aside to complain of drawing-rooms preserved a tiny drop of our self-respect, he carried on the human heritage' where a Christian like Mr Michael Hamburger can discern only despair. I. A. Richards justifies *The Waste Land* by his psychological theory of value; the ineffable or mythical puzzles are units of emotion; harmonizing pessimistic units, Eliot imparts 'a peculiar liberation of the will'.

Both liberals compliment the poem at the level of their subjectivity: it works, but whereas for Mr Forster the 'personal comment' presumably fails, for Dr Richards it merely succeeds; works of art are being judged by commercial standards. Neither old nor new liberalism perceives that Eliot goes beyond 'sensibility' and 'therapy' into a new ethic of authority; avoiding institutions, dogma, rhetoric, Eliot plays a one-man 'you ought' card against the pragmatic hand of materialism. As he speaks from the table, is adept at the history of the game, and lets veterans lean over his shoulder to give advice, it is difficult to debate his ought away, and this is bound to be a stumbling block to the C. P. Snow type of utilitarian gambler. Games are won by men who act most unpredictably within a given plan; that is the meaning of initiative. To change the metaphor, Eliot's disjunct collage is like combat: a continuation of private diplomacy by extreme means. The poet defends his vision on the social plane, just as society invades his vision; on that battlefield the collage harmonizes. An Internal Censor fructifies Eliot's work when it errs towards the didacticism of narrative, or some lucidly intimated memoir, alerting the reader, will remind him of the poet's

* 'T. S. Eliot', in *Abinger Harvest*, 1936, p. 87.

56

standard of judgment. Then, lest we relax, we are turned back, trapped again in the materialism of 'fear in a handful of dust'. No; it hardly flatters the assumptions—this moral Pavlov technique— of the consenting liberal.

Mr David Craig would turn in his grave were he labelled a con- senting liberal. Even so his essay* is the most adroit fifth-column operation since the Two Cultures. Excess of zeal is his downfall. The golden rule of they who surfaced in the wake of the angries, the New Left, and the Eng. Lit. sociologists is that acquisitive technocracy is buzzing with creative potential; what prevents that potential is organizations rather than individuals. It is not the bourgeois who devotes his leisure to television, gambling and the golf course; it is those distractions which violate his innocence. Any radical who mutters that he puts his faith in the revolutionary guts of people, transforming an abuse from within, or through persuasion, or exemplary abstention, is dismissed as an amateur, a paternalist, and ignorant of the Second Law of Thermodynamics. Thus far have we fallen since Orwell. To this Critical Calvinism, the common man is determined in virtue; an academic elect will lead him; the artist in the field is damned; the idea of reforming *ourselves* will throw us deeper into hell. Hence from Ceylon University Mr Craig informs us that: Eliot's London is a defeatist depression masquerading as a picture of society; favourable critics spread the infection; and 'real- ity is manipulated . . . to fit an escapist kind of prejudice'.

Mr Craig is especially upset by the seduction of the typist. This is the result of his need to prove that Eliot distorts history into an ideal to denigrate the present. The narrator, though, has *foresuffered all: in the narrator's mind*—and this corresponds to the way people at all times ('I who have sat by Thebes below the wall / And walked among the lowest of the dead') in fact apprehend the past—history is either a curtain-raiser to the present, or a sublimate: felicity, desired yet elusive, being displaced and imputed to the past. Is felicity therefore invalid? The 'Sweet Thames' of The Fire Sermon, the 'sweet ladies' of the Cockney Pub, 'Elizabeth and Leicester / Beating oars / The stern was formed / A gilded shell . . .' and the other juxtaposed dazzlements are not pomps to overawe our squalor. They are late ironic commentaries on those pomps: as things are, so they were, we are deceived. In the age of nakedness, we are content to be gulled by costumes. Conversely, as things were, so they could be: for appearances, extant or remembered or imagined, often *are* splendid; translated into ideal images, far from gloating over ugli- ness they create symbols which generate hope, teach us to recognize splendour in improbable places. As for their literary flavour, Eliot

* 'The Defeatism of The Waste Land', *Critical Quarterly*, Autumn 1960.

has said that the revival of tradition, the *use* of tradition, means a modification to fit a changing pattern. The man of letters is equipped to testify, for he is most conscious of the way the past was once the present, the present soon be past, just as his predecessors were most conscious of that quality of life-giving imagination (it exists in *The Waste Land*) which is bequeathed to us in literary evidence, however sordid.

To revert to Mr Craig and the typist. If Eliot is wrong in condemning her and her security-sanctioned paramour (why on earth should the latter *not* betray 'one bold stare' and be 'one of the low on whom assurance sits / As a silk hat on a Bradford millionaire'—surely an Acute Sociological Point is made here?) he is equally wrong in condemning his neurotic demi-mondaine, 'Mr Eugenides, the Smyrna merchant', the leisured drifter who 'went on in sunlight, into the Hofgarten', and the sterile Fisher King—the impotence of myth—himself, and insincere when he acclaims popular exuberance in 'a public bar in Lower Thames Street / The pleasant whining of a mandoline / And a clatter and a chatter from within / Where fishmen lounge at noon' and associates it with 'Inexplicable splendour of Ionian white and gold' of a city church. Left critics would be delighted if Eliot attacked the mass media. They whine when he sets about the poet's job of witnessing, and cites the 'gramophone' as the accompaniment of a typist's automatism. Do they object to the parody of *chic* philistinism in 'O O O O that Shakespeherian rag / It's so elegant / So intelligent / What shall I do now / What shall I do . . .?' and his dislike of luxury and misconduct? Nor can I see that the Cockney Pub patter is literary slumming. The fruit of good listening, it contrasts favourably with the affected grandiloquence of the sophisticate ('I read, much of the night, and go south in the winter') and the parodistic-ironic *Rape of the Lock* elegance of the Game of Chess—literary triumphs all, the last another rehabilitation of tradition whose present relevance enhances its past validity.

The ethos is classless: method, mentality, and factotum framework guarantee this. Mr Craig being oblivious of the positive content in the juxtapositions we must forgive him when he ignores the prophecy. I do not mean foretelling the future. I mean a sensation of *what might be* whose enfranchisement in the world is frustrated by adversities. We observe it in D. H. Lawrence, Joyce, and Rilke. It therefore *expresses* the world with a kind of impatient heightening or compressed generalization—a mixture of reported horror and frustrated acquaintance with its antidote. Such prophecy always *foresees* more than the historically predictable; the concern makes it a warning, a case for the spirit. It comes upon us in 'After the torchlight red on sweaty faces / After the frosty silence in the gardens / After the agony in stony places / Prison and palace and reverberation . . .' which is partly telescoped reportage, partly prediction (the date is 1922) kindled into prophecy by concern. One is not necessarily contemptuous of the October Revolution ('the Russian armies were defending themselves on twenty-three fronts' says Mr Craig with glorious irrelevance) to discern prophecy in 'Who are those hooded hordes swarming / Over endless plains, stumbling over cracked earth / Ringed by the flat horizon only . . .' The what might be is often intimate, yet elusive:

> *Your arms full, and your hair wet, I could not*
> *Speak, and my eyes failed, I was neither*
> *Living nor dead, and I knew nothing,*
> *Looking into the heart of light, the silence.*

When they fuse, opposing foci may evoke a desperate longing—'Not the cicada / And dry grass singing / But sound of water over a rock / Where the hermit-thrush sings in the pine trees . . .' They are transcended once, in Death by Water, so that we 'forget the cry of gulls, and the deep sea swell, and the profit and loss'. This ominous lull, the epicentre of the poem, is prophetic because its finality is like an alienation which must point forward since it is fatal to turn back.

*   *   *

Eliot has stated that 'the great poet . . . in writing himself, writes his time'. His drive to 'extinguish personality' by giving the medium a free, administered hand solved in circumstances of public interest the problem of 'perpetual work' which afflicts poets like Rilke. If Eliot was in danger of fabricating a *voulu* development, he was saved by *The Hollow Men* (1925). The puritan's 'overwhelming question', just put, is answered. Liberalism was incapable of this. For the puritan is a revolutionary: it is intrepid honesty which brings him to 'death's dream kingdom' where 'the stone images / Are raised, here they receive / The supplication of a dead man's hand / Under the twinkle of a fading star'. One thinks, at once, of Stonehenge, and hence of E. M. Forster's Wiltshire, just as 'voices are / In the wind's singing / More distant and more solemn / Than a fading star' blends with Leopardi's *L'Infinito* to make each of one's solitary landscapes a school of meditation—it is a proof of Eliot's unique gift for crystallizing a generalization in a 'thing'. Dramatic monologue, the community of self-defence, puritan social conscience desert him; his objective correlative is himself. At the end of *The Waste Land*, nature heralded rebirth, the thunder shook our solipsisms—'thinking of the key, each confirms a prison / Only at nightfall, aethereal rumours / Revive for a moment a broken Coriolanus' and granted that 'the boat responded / Gaily, to the hand expert with sail and oar / The sea was calm . . .' Now the immediacies depart; nature tortures the soul with its animal affinities—'behaving as the wind behaves' (three years after the sublimated animism of Rilke) and reminds us (contemporary with the hero myth of Yeats) that we are 'not lost / Violent souls'; flotsam from *The Waste Land*—'sunlight on a broken column'—floats away. Writing himself, the poet has called out, as his medium will, an unsuspected truth *about* himself. Played out metres, like a death rattle, breathe their last will and testament: they utter essentials. 'Between the desire / And the spasm / Falls the Shadow'. As in Bergson's theory of humour, or like the Fool in *Lear*, to relieve the horror he must turn it into an infantile pantomime—'this is the way the world ends / Not with a bang but a whimper'—and in the age of the H Bomb we accept the respite with thanks.

'Consequently I rejoice, having to construct something / Upon which to rejoice' is the human *cri de cœur* after the whimper. 'Let these words answer / For what is done, not to be done again' affirms the faith of the poet in the efficacy of art. 'Teach us to care and not to care / Teach us to sit still' announces a purposeful humility which will subordinate humanity and art to an ascetic discipline. *Ash Wednesday* (1930) abandons the ellipses and dislocations central to the testing of imagery in the world, replaces outer-directed association with the subtler, more fluent association of an inward wrestling. The experiment is as candid as before, and more limpid; never will Eliot's diction come nearer to a mathematical lucidity. Earnest, punctilious rhymes, mournful and translucent cadences, a hopefully expatiating, apprehensively withdrawing line, metres arrested, like an intake of breath before some hazardous but inevitable confession or acceptance, followed by delicately ornate, resting, or refreshed sensuous progresses of imagery—these echoes (Prufrock, who envied Lazarus 'come from the dead to tell you all', sees his conceits mellow into spiritual exercises) infuse a new rhythm into devotional poetry.

It is not nature which saves, but the Virgin who makes 'firm', 'strong', 'cool', and 'fresh' the desert, and who heals awareness—'the new years walk, restoring . . . with a new verse the ancient rhyme'. An atmosphere in fact abstract, tentative, is decorated by the diffusion of occasional, muted sense impressions. Although the mood is reticent, the thought is often antithetical. Horrors—'an old man's mouth drivelling', 'the devil of the stairs', 'the toothed gullet of an aged shark'—are answered by felicities drawn from nature, often subliminal. They may be tempting—'Blown hair is sweet,

brown hair over the mouth blown / Lilac and brown hair / Distraction, music of the flute . . .' or erupt with unsought, vivid force—
'From the wide window towards the granite shore / The white sails still fly seaward, seaward flying / Unbroken wings . . .' which has to be broken off with the aid of William Blake (rather *hors de milieu* at the shoulder of the Lady of Silences)—'And smell renews the salt savour of the sandy earth.' The Virgin prays for the benighted; but when the poet responds, his truth, though accurate enough, is inhospitable—'Not here, there is not enough silence . . . no place of grace for those who avoid the face / No time to rejoice for those who walk among noise and deny the voice'.

Ash Wednesday alerts us to E. R. Curtius's complaint that 'Eliot proclaimed that England was a Latin country'.* English religious poetry is reserved about the actual throes of conversion. All the better that Eliot should write it, but do his apologetics ignore the English passion for works? We either have—well, the Blakes, 'minds naturally Christian' whom Eliot's orthodoxy dislikes, or sequences of poems which explore a unified state of mind in reaction to a spiritual crisis (*In Memoriam* is an echo of this). Donne's Holy Sonnets defy dissolution, in Hopkins's Terrible Sonnets the spirit is assailed by disappointment, fear of hypocrisy, and temptation. The authority of their rhetoric, the earthy resonance of their faith—Donne's 'And soonest our best men with thee doe goe / Rest of their bones, and soules deliverie / Thou art slave to Fate, Chance, kings, and desperate men . . .' and Hopkins's 'England, whose honour O all my heart woos, wife / To my creating thought, would neither hear / Me, were I pleading . . .' owes to this dramatic clash of the dark powers against the tried body of belief; the poets put forth all their strength, as it were, within their virtue. We examine Eliot's conversion for such qualities—or for the liturgical good manners, the gentleman's witty sober reverence of George Herbert, the visionary nurture which Vaughan derived from the seasons, or even the Baroque sensuality of Crashaw—and we find this imperturbable casuist operating in an allegorical and symbolic fairy-land; it is like an embellished garden in a mediaeval Book of Hours, enclosed in text.

The Ariel Poems benefit from the hesitancies of *Ash Wednesday*: they go beyond them. They journey into a redeemed sensuality, not defending the faith but exploring alternatives to illumination. Eliot is aware of having missed the fullness of the Dark Night of the Soul; the master of *Gerontion* wastes no time repining about this. In the poems of this phase we detect an oblique desire (explicit and in my view unsuccessful in the *Coriolan* satires) to reflect the world crisis of

---

* See *T. S. Eliot: A Symposium for his 60th Birthday*, ed. Richard March and Tambimuttu, 1948.

the period, together with a feeling of voyage, resignation, and return, which is also a discovery in the sense that it secures something vouchsafed at an earlier stage of life. The pressure is off, technical rigour modulates into an amazed and tranquil virtuosity. Even in the Biblical poems we are conscious, in the description of the dangers of the Journey—'. . . the lack of shelters / And the cities hostile and the towns unfriendly'—or the prediction of the sack of Jerusalem, of social analogies known to the poet beyond the literal story. In these very beautiful poems Eliot is being kind: he is creating feasible spiritual experience for those who are incapable of undergoing even his attenuated Dark Night.* His Magus is a man of the world, conscientious, enterprising (hobby—travel), and speaking in a stilted, embarrassed diction. Because of his readiness to 'voyage', to suffer by his own standards, he may look forward to 'another death'. Simeon, on the other hand, is the charitable, patrician, stay-at-home citizen; fearful of the future, denied the 'ecstasy', he yet 'sees salvation'. Salvation comes to both by accident, but they are none the less sincere; the will is towards perfection.

Both poems look death in the eye (see the consummate overture to *Simeon*) and generate, through redeemed images of daily life, a foretaste of eternity. *Animula* is Eliot's hell-fire sermon about unredeemed images of life, and gives the stench of death. The greatest of these poems, *Marina*, is also the most enigmatic, in spite of the confidence of the poet's surrender to this gentle, fertile loveliness, freed from old contingencies, granted at last. For the first—and last—time it describes the 'infinitely suffering thing', once done to death in London, *in extenso*, and its success must be remembered by those who find the 'epiphanies' on which *Four Quartets* relies tenuous, retrospective, and cursory. There may be psychological reasons why the poet selects *this* set of images (they are not mystically ordained) but the operative fact is that the 'living to live in a world of time beyond me' comes to us in purified natural images, such as anyone, in a prepared state, might receive. Ploughing them back, Eliot makes peace with nature —witness the thoughtfully enjoyed, finitude conscious, affirmative lines of the *Landscapes* cycle. Eliot has moreover purged himself of puritan anxieties about 'positives'; the *Marina* experience is a-moral, a-religious, and if recognizable in literary terms at all, aesthetic. But he is quick to condemn other behaviours which exploit the *same naturalistic images in the wrong way*—'those who glitter with the glory of the hummingbird, meaning / Death'.

*   *   *

* Eliot tells us why (though perhaps not how) he was converted in the crucible of his development. Auden announces (in effect) his conversion and juggles with his other knowledge accordingly. Auden is regarded as the franker poet.

To the oracular staginess of late Yeats, the bombastic filigree of *La Jeune Parque* (in contrast to the athleticism of *Le Cimetière Marin*), the tiresome earnestness of *Duino Elegies*, is it too irreverent to add the calculated humility of *Four Quartets* (1935–1942)? Testing out insights in the open, fallen world ceases; composing a multiplicity of experience around one dominant, guiding 'moment in and out of time' begins. I say compose rather than systematize, for Eliot is at pains to ward off dogma: he hopes to carry the doubters on the strength of their emotional consent. As the thought starts from where *The Waste Land* ended, the technique has to be a development of *Ash Wednesday*'s. The good old fits and starts, foreshortenings and shocks, which contrasted forms of behaviour or evaluations of sense data, give way to easier transitions between rival states of being: the internal censor, indicating an open secret between poet and reader at the expense of the subject, is displaced by passages of argument which convict us of invincible ignorance. Eliot has ridiculed I. A. Richards's 'ritual for heightening sincerity'—he trumps each of Richards's mournful procedures ('consider the isolation of the human situation' etc.) with a spiritual ace, and his final position *re* Poetry and Belief seems to be that, provided poetry *is* poetry, criticism must be completed from a definite religious standpoint. The 'timeless moments' of *Four Quartets* are poetry all right, in fact the whole cycle tells us what it feels like to be a sensitive believer* —one halts there, advised by (Edmund) Wilson's remark that Yeats betrays 'an instinct to . . . check up on the supernatural which is disastrous to genuine mysticism'. These 'moments' are of paramount importance. Begotten of heightened consciousness, equated with 'reality' ('human kind cannot bear very much reality'), they are allied to, if not identified with, 'heaven and damnation', accredited theological concepts from which 'the weakness of the changing body' protects us. And the moments rescue us from the traditional incentives to creative endeavour—'the inner freedom from the practical desire / The release from action and suffering'.

What we *make* of our literary, emotional consent, must depend on the degree of existential credit the moments enjoy in our experience. Whether we have missed or known the moments—before deciding that—we should pause to relish what the *poet* makes of them, the fruitful reformative commination Eliot launches against the pharisaic liberal: his attack on the hubris of knowledge ('. . . imposes a

---

* There is one review of *Four Quartets* which one would like to see—the Bishop of Woolwich's. But would he, any more than the most mystic commentators, accept the literary fact, which is that the value-system is justifiable, in detail, as *formal poetic organization* alone?

pattern, and falsifies / For the pattern is new in every moment / And every moment is a new and shocking / valuation of all we have been'); the cult of speculation, self-advertisement, commentary ('pastimes and drugs, and features of the press'); posing as the detached observer, hiding ulterior motives ('you are not here to verify / Instruct yourself, or inform curiosity / Or carry report. You are here to kneel / Where prayer has been valid'); the belief in happiness as a criterion of worth, both for oneself and others ('. . . not the sense of well-being / Fruition, fulfilment, security or affection / Or even a very good dinner, but the sudden illumination . . .'); the egotism of securing one's security, henceforth to relax, which is breached, and swept out into chaos by the tremendous river and sea music of *The Dry Salvages*; and the bitch goddess success—lady of situations?—confounded, in the Dance of Death of *East Coker*, by the treason of motives and the annihilating frown of the darkness of God. 'The sea has many voices / Many gods and many voices.' But one goddess. And she does not smile on success . . . 'Lady, whose shrine stands on the promontory . . .'

> Repeat a prayer also on behalf of
> Women who have seen their sons or husbands
> Setting forth, and not returning:
> Figlia del tuo figlio,
> Queen of Heaven.

> Also pray for those who were in ships, and
> Ended their voyage on the sand, in the sea's lips
> Or in the dark throat which will not reject them . . .

It is encouraging to see that even bureaucrats are—to exploit Mr Eliot's essay on Baudelaire—men enough to be damned. 'And dark the Sun and Moon, and the Almanach de Gotha / And the Stock Exchange Gazette, the Directory of Directors / And cold the sense and lost the motive of action'. That Eliot speaks in the language of Milton, 'O dark dark dark', is a more eloquent tribute to the puritan than the subsuming into a symbol of the English Civil War (*Little Gidding*, III, 180–200) or the constrained Recantation Lecture.

Those who have missed the moments will applaud Eliot and, being unregenerate liberals, do otherwise. Those who have known the moments will have strong views about their status, use, and implications (for they do imply) in the poem. We are unlikely to forget that Mr Eliot is the eternal puritan; he is also the eternal imagist. The type of prestige which the moments claim is the legacy of imagism: the belief that, once a perception has been pictured with entire clarity—freed from obfuscating relative emotions—it has an authority which its context must defer to or be damned. Once the King has unfurled his standard, the rest of the chessboard is in check. It takes time, no doubt, to get adjusted to the *particularity* of *any* set of images which 'bisects time'; our surprise at the texture of the conquering images over—they seem retrospective, subliminal—we are free to note the way the poet reiterates these brittle runes, like a charm, at key crises. But while the moments are fortified by steady argument, they are not necessarily maturing—or, if that seems derogatory to their essence—diffusing an influence. The rest of the chessboard is mobilized: Eliot pulls out all the stops of his naturalism to create diapasons in aid of timeless moments which retort on the very nature they reflect. Before 1930 the establishment of the image was a valid spur to social criticism; it overthrew the special pleading of 'personality' and 'inspiration'; it spoke the truth. The disapproval of free love in *The Waste Land* was understandable because Eliot opposed, in a liberal society, a one-man 'you ought' opinion to behaviour which he thinks is destructive. We can obtain evidence on both sides, and if with Mr David Craig we burn Eliot as a Savonarola, no worse fate can overtake us than to be asked why. But you are at a loss for words when the aesthetic establishment exists *sub specie aeternitatis*; open your mouth—the direst punishments may follow.

In *Burnt Norton* Eliot treats us to a jeremiad against the London tube. Nature is made to clinch the point, and it is clinched with a grave beauteous authority which is almost unanswerable:

> *Here is a place of disaffection*
> *Time before and time after*
> *In a dim light: neither daylight*
> *Investing form with lucid stillness*
> *Turning shadow into transient beauty*
> *With slow rotation suggesting permanence*
> *Nor darkness to purify the soul . . .*

The commuters are 'filled with fancies and empty of meaning', tumidly apathetic, inept for concentration, 'unhealthy souls'—as null and void as the mass media they have to look at, 'men and bits of paper'. The ant-heap is a misery to all who crawl in it; if one is a man and a fighter, one resists being 'driven on the wind that sweeps the gloomy hills of London' as much as one resents being compared to the capitalist press. Force of circumstance might be conquerable, but Eliot destroys our morale by adding force of super-nature. We cannot appeal either to a 'propositional' literary technique or to the tribunal of other opinion; nor is Eliot the man to hold the Evangelical adage that you should hate the sin, not the sinner. We await, in the funereal hush of the *memento mori* lyric which follows, the answer. We are given the image of a kingfisher's wing. 'After the kingfisher's wing / Has answered light to light, and is silent . . .'

The imagism of *Four Quartets* approaches hypostasis. Consider phrases of summary or reference—'home is where one starts from', 'playing cards', 'popular mind', 'containing laughter', 'the gloomy hills of London', 'an open field, or a factory, or a by-pass', 'an underground train, in the tube', 'in my end is my beginning'. Ratiocinated in context, these phrases open windows in the mind, aerate their context, refresh ours; our sense of what we really mean—or should mean —is wonderfully sharpened; we are handed precision tools. It is when Eliot repeats an image cluster to fit an emotive specification that we feel that language, worked to the last decimal point of purity, does duty for actual communication:

> *Whisper of running streams, and winter lightning.*
> *The wild thyme unseen and the wild strawberry,*
> *The laughter in the garden, echoed ecstasy*
> *Not lost, but requiring, pointing to the agony*
> *Of death and birth.*

We are lost in arrested fascination; the moment absconds. The fact is that imagism puts a colossal premium on consciousness: the pressure must be relieved, rather palpably, by pointing with the definite article or listing phenomena; and the clusters then burgeon and resound amid a powerful flow of physical magnificence—the forward spring of *Little Gidding*, the ocean music of *The Dry Salvages*. Or isolated vision—'Dawn points, and another day / Prepares for heat and silence. Out at sea the dawn wind / Wrinkles and slides. I am here / Or there, or elsewhere. In my beginning'—gains power from the inherited earthiness of what has gone before.

Eliot's will to bring order out of multiplicity, made more urgent by his avoidance of dogmatic sermonizing, reminds one of . . . Prufrock, half out of love with decorum, shirking commitment. His creator is now an aesthetic, as distinct from a revolutionary, puritan. If rectitude is lacking in life, it shall exist in poetry. Look at the Quartets at a distance of six feet—out of reading range—and we admire at once a perfectly modelled and jointed, self-supporting formal structure, vibrating firmly, like a mobile, in the paper air. The poetry *does* matter: the thematic curve of each quartet echoes the grand design. Aesthetic authority lends to moral authority; the debt is manifest. If the 'quiet-voiced elders' have *not* 'bequeathed us a receipt for deceit', we can thank an ideal of art ('Only by the form, the pattern / Can words or music reach / The stillness . . . Not the stillness of the violin, while the note lasts / Not that only, but the co-existence . . .') which comes near to being identified with the

Word of God—the 'Word in the desert' barracked by raucous voices, so that 'music heard so deeply / That it is not heard at all, but you are the music / While the music lasts . . .' may almost enjoin the ascetic ideal of 'prayer, observance, discipline, thought and action'. There is an almost Gnostic mystique of language in late Eliot whereby the sum of words formalized in the art order is a higher dimensional design, a vision of simultaneity transcending time. To liberalism, culture is a virtue fought out in the historical process, to Eliot an effort towards wholeness of being which protrudes beyond history, provided culture remains faithful to classicism by refusing to act as a *locum tenens* for detritus and orders the 'signs' set in existence.

All that, the delicate moments, the thin Trinitarianism, the negatives and latinities make Eliot's Christianity curiously incorporeal, and that would be diagnosed as a deviation from the English tradition were it not for his famous English rootedness. This is based, partly on British sentiment about the American who comes home; partly on the poet's own sentimentality, on which E. M. Forster comments '. . . there is never all this talk about tradition until it has ceased to exist . . . we suspect that Mr Eliot is romanticizing the land of his adoption . . . what he really craves is *stability*'; and partly on the topographic and English-historic passages in the Quartets—'History is now and England'. Of Eliot the rustic, we feel that he is fine as far as he goes, but that Blake, Thomas Hardy, and Edward Thomas go further, into the corporeal. Eliot does not easily reconcile his 'time of the coupling of man and woman / And that of beasts' with his 'Earth feet, loam feet, lifted in country mirth'. As provocative is his use—his ironic praise?—of landscape as symbol. He buys permanence, for the profound *naturalism* of these canticles will make them endure, it will be long before technology despoils the ocean, the Spring, and the shires, at the price of the equivocal. The 'midwinter spring' of *Gidding* is presented as 'not in time's covenant'. As a symbol for a spiritual mutation, it is perfect, and its intense beauty makes us retort that this particular 'pentecostal fire' is as grounded as Shakespeare—'short summers likely have a forward Spring' (*Richard III*). We recall Mr Eliot's lifelong vendetta against the Spring; we wonder what he is up to. The same slight unease plays over our awe at the elegy for the four elements, 'this is the death of water and fire'. The groundswell is and was from the beginning.

It would not be the first time that a rebel, of course, has ended in the odour of sanctity. The paradox is that Eliot gains tension from this weird connivance of innovating reputation with espousal of authority. There never was much of what Mr Stephen Spender has called the 'theme of hope' in Eliot's modernism—the artist framing in microcosm the changes he desires in the wicked world; the artist putting first, in his art, the spiritual changes which a revolution might procure. Eliot is as alien to the Apollinaires, Mayakovskys, and Eisensteins as he is to Swinburne and Pater. Blok in *The Twelve* aimed to produce a revolutionary state of mind in the reader: for example, the shock tactic of presenting Christ as a Bolshevik insurgent. *The Waste Land,* and all early Eliot, is a defensive operation, a policing of panic, an injection of individual values into a decadent community. In the end the poet's will to order is central to his need for reconciliation; in *Gidding* he expounds the unification in symbols —institutions, blends of thought—of rival historical factions who are 'folded in a single party' and 'accept the constitution of silence'; the prodigal son makes peace, rather late in the day, with the party of his ancestors—the puritans. At the same time that he wants people to 'fare forward' into new 'moments', and calls on Oriental mysticism to point the way, he embraces that (now) unmystical stability the Church of England and its acolyte the Tory Party; elsewhere, he feels, is the lunatic fringe or chaos. Had Rilke had a comparable drive to order, he might have embraced Eastern Orthodoxy with its stress on Resurrection. Valéry rose before dawn to study the advent of consciousness; Yeats, revolving tragically on the Wheel of Becoming, played with magic and the occult; Eliot prays through a winter's afternoon 'now and in England'.

Valéry alone faced negation and returned to life on the same terms; a humanist might argue that *Le Cimetière Marin* is a braver poem than the others. But to Valéry consciousness was a profession: he tamed it on a tight rein, so that it seldom strayed towards the grosser problems which outrage sensitive minds in our time. Much of what is precious in Valéry, morbid in Rilke, and extravagant in Yeats, is made philosophic, the first step to being civilized, by Eliot in the Quartets—the pacification of 'old age', the placing of 'the backward half-look / Over the shoulder, towards the primitive terror.' Against fashionable augurs I predict that liberals will give thanks for T. S. Eliot. In any competition to be decadent, the materialists are bound to win. The legalistic Christianity of Eliot stands foursquare against the drift of pragmatism, the worship of happiness, the whole aimless charade of improvising in the vacuum while the vandals take over. His timeless moments are precisely what is difficult to procure, and most easy to misconstrue, in a technocratic society. Equivocal and challenging as they are, his pastoral symphonies remind us that the ground of being is earth as well as God. Beyond the discipline which he has chosen, Eliot's work of containment, of salvage, of renovation has won respect for the *idea* of disciplining one's freedom to some purpose beyond self-gratification.

T. S. ELIOT, ALAS?

He makes an idea—in England—aesthetically and morally presentable. In the words of Rilke about a statue by Rodin, Eliot is above all 'the Thinker, the man who realizes the greatness and terror of the spectacle about him, because he thinks it. He sits absorbed and silent, heavy with thought: *with all the strength of an acting man he thinks.*' Such strength is needed in a world where still with a vengeance:

> *Sweeney shifts from ham to ham*
> *Stirring the water in his bath.*
> *The masters of the subtle schools*
> *Are controversial, polymath.**

---

* The reaction to Mr Eliot's death, which occurred while this book was in the press, was controversial though hardly subtle. It revealed a clash between hedonists like the *New Statesman*, who want him to be a tonic for those tired after the party, and stoics for whom he makes positive demands on our moral and spiritual faculties. Mr Connolly's quote about *The Waste Land*—'thoroughly decadent, it will ruin your style'—confirms one's secret theory that Mr Eliot was, if not a believer, a convicted visionary from the start, a spy for a higher truth, and that his early work was a deliberate sabotage of the morale of humanist self-regard. (This might account for his possibly ironic encouragement of the 30's movement, which is comprehended, predicted and finally transcended in his own work.)

Mr Eliot's 'extremes of emotional perception', noted by us on p. 49, become the starting point, *not for another indulgent little poem*, but for 'disinterested spiritual research'—including an appraisal of society as well as the un-British but not unreasonable (his perceptions being deeper and subtler than anyone else's) belief that one man's findings can be relevant to other men; as the *Spectator* said, 'to reject Eliot was to welcome anarchy'. From high and low vision Mr Eliot derives a rule of life, which he recommends (no more) to a blind age. It is a simple point, but one which may have to be made quite often in future: Mr. Eliot believed that, provided poetry *is* poetry, its values are important.

Mr Eliot brought off the fusion of 'innovating reputation with espousal of authority' (p. 67) because he was at heart *an English patrician liberal who escaped an English education,* i.e. an emotionally mature leader. In this matter, he was not unlike Winston Churchill.

3

WAR AND PEACE

The right of every man to life is correlative with the duty to preserve it; his right to a decent standard of living with the duty of living becomingly; his right to investigate the truth freely with the duty of seeking it profoundly.

JOHN XXIII *Pacem in Terris*

When security has been achieved, the task will be to find for these dangerous and powerful instincts neither merely restraints nor the outlets that make for destruction, but . . . the outlets that give joy and pride and splendour to human life.

BERTRAND RUSSELL *Authority and the Individual*

There are times which resemble the coming of spring . . . The activity of applying external forms to life, hides from men . . . the activity of a change of consciousness, which alone can improve their lives.

LEO TOLSTOY *The Kingdom of God is Within You*

THE EMBATTLED TRUTH: WILFRED OWEN AND ISAAC ROSENBERG

> *It seems just possible that a poem might happen*
> *To a very young man . . .*
> <div align="right">T. S. Eliot: <i>A Note on War Poetry</i></div>

> *This book is not about heroes. English poetry is not yet fit to speak of them . . .*
> *Above all I am not concerned with Poetry.*
> *My subject is War, and the pity of War.*
> *The Poetry is in the pity . . .*
> *All a poet can do today is warn. That is why the true Poets must be truthful.*

THE Preface to the Poems has sovereign value as a declaration of Owen's aims, a secular pastoral theology about force, and the attitudes which a man of moral intelligence can strike towards it. For to dub a man 'war poet' is unhelpful: it does not excuse his deficiencies or enhance his qualities; good poets who have been killed in war—Edward Thomas—decline the title. In the Second World War, Sidney Keyes, Keith Douglas, and Alun Lewis wrote about war luminously, but they were, in a sense, detached; they aimed to maintain their integrity amid the fighting. It is better to speak of war *poems*, when the individual talent is embroiled in force, danger, and combat. To young poets shocked into maturity by Munich, the Hitler thing was both justifiable and embarrassing: since, in Day Lewis's phrase, they must 'defend the bad against the worse' they were determined to 'live by honest dreams' in the process. The point of the Kaiser thing was vague: a glorious *fait accompli* to some, it became Antichrist to others, taunting the 'honest dream' into protest and suffering.* Herbert Read is gifted at the

---

* The same issue of *Penguin New Writing*, April 1946, carries memoirs of Alun Lewis, by J. Maclaren Ross, and of Wilfred Owen by Sir Osbert Sitwell. The difference between the wars comes out. Lewis (1942): '*this* was what he hated: the paper-work . . . red-tape . . . while the poems, the stories, remained unwritten'. It is the *cri de cœur* of the artist in bourgeois organizations.

Owen (1918): 'War had become transformed . . . into something so infernal, so inhuman, that only the poet could pierce through the armour of horror to the pity at the human core . . . steadily contemplate the struggle at the level of tragedy.' Osbert Sitwell adds 'his compassionate heart could have been moved by other matters to the same profound and poignant expression'.

satirical-diagnostic attitude; Siegfried Sassoon, whose compassion and power have not yet been honoured, is a master of the polemical attitude; while of the heraldic attitude, Péguy's 'heureux ceux qui sont morts dans une juste guerre', Rilke's *Five Hymns* and Brooke's 1914 Sonnets are religious, pseudo-philosophic, and private variations. Péguy wanted Holy France to crush Apostate Germany; Rilke was wallowing in Nietzsche; Brooke divined in war some force to transform the individual.

Of Brooke's 'Now God be thanked . . .' Sonnet we may say that it is a morbid aberration of the lyric impulse. It imputes to God motives which are disclaimed by Christ in the Gospels. Had Brooke any comprehension of history, of Tolstoy's Peace Essays, or altruistic imagination of the Rimbaud kind he could not have written those poems. He dismisses his friends, all who worked for peace and who foresaw tyranny followed by moral collapse in the wake of a European war (and Bertrand Russell had done that as early as 1896),* as 'the sick hearts that honour could not move'. He cannot see war as soul-destroying boredom or dreadful Armageddon: in a biological regeneration of man, his own beauty will be imposed upon a world 'grown old and cold and weary'. He fell for the delusion of a narcissistic mind. That Rosenberg liked Brooke's verse but found his war work 'reminiscent of flag days' we know from his letters; and Owen has a sardonic 'Funeral March' which begins 'Not one corner of a foreign field / But a span as wide as Europe . . .' I hope to show *why* these allegations about Brooke are correct in this study of Owen, who wrote in *Bugles Sang*:

> *Voices of boys were by the river-side.*
> *Sleep mothered them; and left the twilight sad.*
> *The shadow of the morrow weighed on men.*

Wilfred Owen was diagnostic and polemical, but he was also more passionately involved than others; and he was only heraldic in the mock-heroic mood. When seeing a revival of the film of *Richard III* I was struck by the contrast between Bosworth Field and a display in the newsreel of missiles at some proving grounds. Olivier has made Richard's death a bloody business, but it was the result of man-to-man combat, a flourish of chivalry; the rockets were ghoulish, downright ugly, and expensive. Nor was I consoled by the thought that medical science had kept pace; it would pace further if funds were available. The war god, as Mr Forster has written, had 'turned chemist'—to propitiate him needed no moral choice before or (unless you were A Neurotic like Major Eatherly) pangs of guilt afterwards and no exercise of imagination. Owen

* In *German Social Democracy*.

worked under conditions—the mechanization of force—which were unique; he spoke out of war, not from a daydream about it. War presented in an urgent form those peccadilloes of peace which we ignore. In war the senses, though violated, are sharpened; familiar problems become drastic; we are given object lessons in the hardness of charity. For Owen, because war is not a set of conditions outside 'ordinary life' we cannot judge it from armchairs; indeed, the *truth* about peace is disclosed in war, the caged beast escapes. His accent, sinewy syntax, his power of follow-through are mounted to display the grand image of encounter; it is the muscle, never the gesturing, of a situation which attracts him.

Throughout his development Owen dramatizes physical images, making sight, touch, and hearing (stronger in him than smell or temperature) force repose into action. Already in those days called halcyon, Owen wrote a poem, *From my Diary: July 1914*, where the current of energy leaps at once, without impediment, to its effects: each scene, charged with strength, blazes in unison with the active senses; and the aim is made crystal clear in the structure. *Training*, a late war poem, energizes through exact rhyme, unadorned contrast, and resolute endings:

> *My lips, parting, shall drink space, mile by mile;*
> *Strong meats be all my hunger; my renown*
> *Be the clean beauty of speed and pride of style.*
>
> *Cold winds encountered on the racing Down*
> *Shall thrill my heated bareness; but awhile*
> *None else may meet me till I wear my crown.*

Owen's colloquial mode relies on speech idioms, not contrived rhythm; his dramatic monologues, his reported speech, are based on talkative phrasing rather than irregular syntax; had Owen been *known* five years earlier would the campaign of Eliot–Pound in that sphere have been viable? The design of *The King Ghosts* is to expose romantic indifference to the fact of war: echoes of Victorian myth writing are heard. The method is a contrast between those who stay and those who fight, and the difference is so imperceptible, the images are so interwoven in the woman's dream, that Owen, having made his point with some subtlety, shocks us back to reality with the harsh 'keep down'—a popular usage, a battlefield idiom which contains enough menace to ruffle the tone:

> *She dreams of golden gardens and sweet glooms,*
> *Not marvelling why her roses never fall*
> *Nor what red mouths were torn to make their blooms.*

The shades keep down which well might roam her hall.
Quiet their blood lies in her crimson rooms
And she is not afraid of their footfall.

In *Hospital Barge at Cérisy* there is predicament as well as state of mind. The barge 'budges' the 'sluggard ripples' of the Somme; its engines 'chuckle' with 'contented hum' and its bell's 'fairy tinklings' conduct its 'bulging amplitude' gently into the 'gurgling lock'. A pleasant scene; less ruggedness and it might be Proustian. In the third verse Owen looks up from a book (*sic*) to see the sunset. The funnel screams. In a trice the genial verbs, the homely adjectives of the opening, fuse with the sunset, the scream to evoke the 'long lamentation' of the queens who bear kings in agony to Avalon in Merlin's barge. Myth is not satirized: one of the most potent and poetical of English legends is brought to life, regarded as real—and the shock gives a thrill of seriousness.* If sarcasm is there, it is directed at the chauvinists who pervert myth into propaganda.

It degrades that masterpiece, *Anthem for Doomed Youth*, to quote in part:

> *What passing-bells for these who die as cattle?*
> *Only the monstrous anger of the guns.*
> *Only the stuttering rifles' rapid rattle*
> *Can patter out their hasty orisons.*
> *No mockeries now for them; no prayers nor bells,*
> *Nor any voice of mourning save the choirs,—*
> *The shrill, demented choirs of wailing shells;*
> *And bugles calling for them from sad shires.*
>
> *What candles may be held to speed them all?*
> *Not in the hands of boys, but in their eyes*
> *Shall shine the holy glimmers of good-byes.*
> *The pallor of girls' brows shall be their pall;*
> *Their flowers the tenderness of patient minds,*
> *And each slow dusk a drawing-down of blinds.*

At first sight it fulfils its title. But it is more than characters in an anecdote. It conjures, by deep sleight of hand, a disturbing *volte face* of mood. Although the odds seem against the dead, the real question is, who are the gainers, who the losers? In verse one the foreground is humanity dehumanized. A subtle play—perhaps sarcastic—transmutes the tokens of religious observance into instruments of torture. In verse two the plot comes home; the setting humanizes; the evidence has been provided; yet the atmosphere is ethereal, and the

---

* Edmund Blunden, in his edition, quotes Owen to the effect that *Barge* followed a reading of *The Passing of Arthur.*

question is asked—'What candles may be held to speed them all?'
Answer: not acolytes' candles, but the light in living eyes which may
soon be dead. This is a 'holy glimmer': the note of dignity is there.
By the end, bells, orisons, choirs, candles, pale brows and flowers
have baleful associations which prowl around the poem. They put
the romantic lie on trial: they evoke the marriage service and the
Eucharist. These types of fertility and sacrifice are tending to the
ironical. They also exist as holy glimmers in eyes quite apart from
any literary tradition or religious rite. In the last lines the well-
meant homely acts of remembrance, keeping their echoes, are seen
to be—images of sterility. Back in Britain a chill has befallen the
senses: who are the gainers, who the losers? Even the sedate accomplished movement is a challenge blending inescapable fact with the
deceit of the plot. This accomplishment manifests in tenderer form
in *Futility*:

> *Move him into the sun—*
> *Gently its touch awoke him once,*
> *At home, whispering of fields unsown.*
> *Always it woke him, even in France,*
> *Until this morning and this snow.*
> *If anything might rouse him now*
> *The kind old sun will know.*
>
> *Think how it wakes the seeds,—*
> *Woke, once, the clays of a cold star.*
> *Are limbs, so dear-achieved, are sides,*
> *Full-nerved—still warm—too hard to stir?*
> *Was it for this the clay grew tall?*
> *—O what made fatuous sunbeams toil*
> *To break earth's sleep at all?*

The order 'Move him into the sun' establishes the nature theme,
leaves us in no doubt where we are: where they handle flesh to plan.
The second and third lines—reminiscent of fertility, hinting at
impotence—sober the command. Loved and hated, blamed and
praised, 'the kind old sun' is meant, I think, as a gibe at the pathetic
fallacy. Armed with facts, we are sent beyond recorded time with the
second imperative, which restoring the sun mounts a bitter creation
myth which harks back to the scarcely breathed hope (it is not
certain that the casualty is dead) of the first stanza; together they
embrace in one present, pointed crisis the whole of evolution. The
human adventure ends in a question mark; one man and his fate
are the accusers of creation; we non-combatants want an answer,
because of the dialectic of evidence. The anxious tone changes; the

cease of life is less a tragedy, than a scandal, staggering the imagination, provoking disbelief; the departing life seems so real, so near compared with the vastness of the before and after. Reading this poem, I fail to understand what Mr Thom Gunn meant by saying that 'Owen was a wet'. The human-natural, factual-cosmic balance is played out with proud subtlety. There is no complaining, no railing, rather the protested treaty between incompatible equals. It is the fecklessness of nature and the dignity of man in nature which is insisted on.

Owen did not live to develop the blend of conflict and intensity which older poets appease in symbols. His sensibility, impelling him to indictment on the spur, rejected the moralizing choice of symbols of a Tennyson. The insights of the Post-Symbolist visionaries appeared to correspond with the meaning of the symbol. Owen is not a visionary, though he approaches vision through his intense physical awareness. His method is more fictitional: whenever verse is recalled to the prosaic, his example will deserve pondering. The poet is attracted by the variety and mutations of feeling, the novelist's vision is in the round—and gains in range what it loses in depth. Poetic language is exposed, suggestive, though not inaccurate; a poetic statement is usually taken as a proposition of the truth. Fiction does not jump to conclusions so quickly; it plays with feeling by putting it in action and describing the effects. That younger art, the novel, has technical leg pulls which enable it to deceive us; when poetry follows suit we still look for a degree of concentration, of complexity and approximation to truth. 'Above all I am not concerned with Poetry.' Owen aimed to express poetic truth in the novelist's context. His is not the symbolism of cult objects in which feeling reposes, or escalates into the supernatural: the rose, star, cross, stream, angel, or charismatic hero. In his chronicle of events, such mystery as exists is involved in his sense of *what might be* amid the sterility *that is*. The physical, enchanted world explicit in the peacetime lyrics is implicit as something threatened in the war poems. He offers the positive and condemns the negative at once; shows how the former is cruelly modified, until it is perverted into a painful velleity, by the latter. The integrity of the double vision may be verified by observing the transference from home to war conditions:

> *From off your face, into the winds of winter,*
> *The sun-brown and the summer-gold are blowing . . .*
> *When paler beauty on your brows falls snowing,*
> *Through those snows my looks shall be soft-going.*
> *(Winter Song)*

This corresponds with the frank, direct approach of 'Dim, through the misty panes and thick green light / As under a green sea, I saw him drowning' (the gas attack in *Dulce et Decorum Est*) and 'Dawn massing in the east her melancholy army / Attacks once more in ranks on shivering ranks of gray . . .'

> *Since we believe not otherwise can kind fires burn;*
> *Nor ever suns smile true on child, or field, or fruit.*
> *For God's invincible spring our love is made afraid;*
> *Therefore, not loath, we lie out here; therefore were born,*
> *For love of God seems dying.*

(Exposure)

The looking the reader in the eye remains. The sinister reacting on the baulked felicity, accented by the effort to impose an ironical explanation, disturbs and colloquializes the tone and makes it eloquent and intimate.

* * *

If *Exposure* echoes the peace tone while ironizing about it, it is because in this poem the modern consciousness becomes aware of itself. Georgian observation and wise passiveness are present in *Exposure*, and *appear* to be coping with the visitations of technics— 'low, drooping flares', 'Northward, incessantly, the flickering gunnery rumbles / Far off, like a dull rumour of some other war'— with aplomb. This is partly due to the fact that nature herself has turned traitor—'sudden successive flights of bullets streak the silence / Less deathly than the air that shudders black with snow' —causing the brain to 'ache, in the merciless iced east winds that knive us'. More, it is because gripping the heart of this poem— Owen's greatest—is the cold hand of shock. The effort to control, to transcend a shock is the inspiration of much modern verse: as vital to work as prolonged concentration. Terror stampedes the poet out of our predicament of dullness; the poet, rough riding, struggles with the bridle and creates art. Roy Campbell thought too much bridle meant no art: there must be the 'bloody horse'. The shock is normally to vision—Rilke, Rimbaud, Eliot—or it may be biological: Yeats's dread of old age, Dylan Thomas's panic at sex, Mr Hughes's bewitchment at our nearness to the beasts. With Owen, and his followers of the 30's, the 'horse' is material—in *Exposure* a realization that *homo faber*, maker of munitions, and nature are in a moronic collusion which baffles understanding because it eludes a crisis. All the poet knows is that 'The poignant misery of dawn . . . massing in the east her melancholy army / Attacks once more in ranks . . .' and that 'the mad gusts tugging on the wire' are like 'twitching agonies of men'.

The poem lives on its nerves. The jumpy complacence and frustrate, wilful rhythm, kept on the alert by the foiled purposefulness of the half-rhymes, is a device for framing stasis; it allows time not for 'a hundred visions and revisions' such as Mr Prufrock was prognosticating at home, but to ask leading questions—'What are we doing here?', 'Is it that we are dying?'—and judge old, peacetime assumptions. The reverie of home (sixth verse) creates ominous, suspended animation: no source of glory, no point in escape. With the help of nature a crime is about to be committed against nature; thus is born that sense of cosmic outrage, of perversion of nature which grows on us in Owen, where it binds together those who undergo the shock in a guilty secret which sets them apart from *voyeurs* as hero-victims. But this is not Original Sin; nor is it Yeats's 'crime of being born / Blackens all our lot'. (Later Owen gives us 'one of many mouths of Hell / Not seen of seers in visions'.) The stanza I quoted explains the alienation between profane love and the Love of God—that sacrificial 'love pure' of 'Red lips are not so red / As the stained stones kissed by the English dead'. Enigmatic to the point of sterility though the home values are, there is no other source of regeneration, for 'God's invincible spring' making 'our love afraid' seems to be compromised in the 'dying'. We think of the forward spring of Eliot's *Little Gidding*. But this spring is too much for mortal men to contemplate; the roads of escape are closed to home and eternity; and the wit becomes sarcastic in 'Tonight, His frost will fasten . . .' So, in this agonizing hiatus in time, the purpose of life is to wait upon crisis, and to hope ironically that thereafter 'suns will smile true'.

Within the negative plot of *Greater Love*, however, there is an assessment of value. The subject looks like 'love pure', the Platonic or sacrificial love dear to patriotic orators. But we perceive behind the grave progress, the controlled sense content, forward swing of outriders, sharp fall of alliterated centres, a delicate yet relentless logic drawn between 'love pure' and 'the fierce love they bear'— the readiness to renounce comfort in order to defend what good it may contain. This is not the last refuge of a scoundrel: it is a weighing of the value against the risk. Negative grammar reproaches the peace values—physical love, song, country life—but they are exalted to the same pitch of force as the dreadful: the poet is doing his best to vindicate and commend them! 'Love pure' is lost sight of, because it becomes an excuse for indifference; the grim inertia of the dead is the price paid for the gratification of the living. The dead triumph over 'love pure' and horror; the emphasis on grief insists that the dead be taken seriously, not etherealized. And the seriousness again connects the ideas of courage and barrenness—'you may touch them not'—for these dead, who gave up dubious comforts, have known pain and tasted life more deeply by virtue of their peculiar love. It is the love at home and its trappings, which the dead question by defending, which is abandoned to sterility.

The motives of sacrifice, brotherhood, and suffering operate in Owen's account of war. They form networks of insight in his monologues: soldiers speak them or Owen drops an aside; and they inform the lyrics. In *The Send-Off* the posting of recruits to the front figures as a bungled sacrifice. Song, decking with flowers, public acclaim is punctuated by ominous obscurantism—'so secretly, like wrongs hushed-up, they went'—followed at once, as if the sureness of the result abolished the discrepancy in dramatic time, by the return of a very few, creeping, up 'half-known roads'. In *Arms and the Boy* an incantation is pitched; one remembers the passage in *The Golden Bough* about iron being taboo. The instruments of injury —bayonets, steel, bullets—are pointed out in a mastery of malevolence. *Dulce et Decorum Est* describes a gas attack, changes to a poetic attack like the stark, grotesque realism of a Bosch on the myth of heroic war. *The Last Laugh* makes its point by its mercilessly *normal* choice of verbs, one of the most overwhelming lists of verbs in the language. The weapons grin, guffaw, 'leisurely gesture'—it might be a scene in a pub. Only the victim's last, extreme utterances suggest an apocalypse, and then the verbs are heard to be jeering, to almost receive the poet's imprimatur when the gas, dropping the pretence, hisses. Owen is not, if a critic may say so, all Pity. He often affects this jeering tone, especially when he writes about individuals, and I think he had two reasons: to preserve his sanity, a condition of his 'pleading', and to give the reader no chance to escape, to salve his conscience, by siding with a poet's sympathy.

Owen gets an angle in every dimension: the boredom of blasted landscape, fertile for evil, natural law turned inside out; or a trek through war's underworld, different from the classical, as in *Mental Cases*. The poem shuns patronage, puts a finger on the pulse, looms behind the poems of hope as the ultimate threat. *Spring Offensive* illustrates what Winston Churchill has called 'the scene that will forever haunt Western civilization'. A heaven and hell, finite in origin, oppose and details gesture in a vast perspective. It captions the photos of battle-fronts—pocked land, acrid cloud, tiny figures moving. Raising them from the dead, poetry makes the figures larger than life, puts a word in edgewise in the din. The heroic is protest not resignation; and sacrifice in Owen is not an ethic; in three poems at least he proclaims its perversion. Abraham *slays* Isaac (and half the seed of Europe) in *Parable*; the hopes of the recruit's family in *S.I.W.*—'proud to see him going, aye, and glad'—and *Inspection*

where the world 'washes out its stains' by red cheeks, objecting to
'young blood'. Death is an expiation of the evil created in the leering
tone, evil pertaining to the ruling caste and 'Field Marshal God'
who desires to 'inspect' white-washed humanity. In poems on the
Ancre crucifix and the Virgin of Quivières, admiration for the
Christian sacrifice accompanies doubt about its relevance; Owen
is not a casuist of time or of the redemption of the present in time.
In the fragment *It is not Death** he proposes that death is a release to
those whom E. M. Forster calls 'the benighted' and for the martyrs
and saints; it is intolerable for those who are alive in the present.
The otherness of the neighbour is adventure, tension, challenge.
Involuntary death is a deprivation of mobility, contrast, mystery.
What survives is the otherness—a vanishing by people into their
undiscovered being which faintly echoes value and inspires hope.
At the instant of death Owen watches the 'magnificent recession of
farewell' which is 'like a Sun': the cosmos is dumbly resentful of its
divorce from man:

> *And in his eyes*
> *The cold stars lighting, very old and bleak,*
> *In different skies.*

> *(Fragment)*

Owen grappled with the unnerving fact that barbarism augments
vitality, may be a constructive force. *Apologia Pro Poemate Meo*
catalogues the benefits of war. It may promote comradeship, tolerance, deep emotion, and a sense of duty. Spectres of Stefan George,
or Brooke, arise. But the poem ends amazingly: no *hypocrite lecteur*
must share these benefits who does not share hell—the pain,
butchery, suicide, insanity, and fear, 'Whose world is but the trembling of a flare / And heaven but as the highway for a shell'. We,
owing them tears, are not worth their merriment. Again the flames
which illume the lyrics and flicker like winter lightning in the
grimmest narratives burn. A demand for at least imaginative sharing
—D. H. Lawrence's 'follow the agony through to the hearts of the
individual fighters'—now democratizes the defiant privacy. Taken
to catharsis in the *Sonnet on Artillery* ('Be slowly lifted up, thou long
black arm / Great gun towering towards Heaven, about to curse')
Owen appeals through that prodigious vocabulary ('thy vast mali-
son') for a renunciation. The 'spell' must be 'cast' until arrogance
has been obliterated, and Yeats's 'radical innocence' may be discerned through the clearing smoke of battle; then God must intervene to root out violence from the soul. The word 'cast' having

---

* Printed in Edmund Blunden's edition, this is a later version of *Has Your Soul
Sipped*, printed in full in C. Day Lewis's edition, 1963.

associated iron-founding with the black magic of 'spell', in a prophetic stroke the poet urges the expulsion of offensive weapons from
'the bosom of our prosperity'.

The classic on the commitment-withdrawal theme is *Insensibility*.
Now it is the combatants, not the home front, for whom ignorance is
bliss. The metre aggravates the meaning, a willed heave and a
malevolence. The muted tone, like a tolling bell, but quick, vigorous,
fusing taciturn space with the minutiae of 'cauterized' feeling, moves
irresistibly to 'cursed are dullards whom no cannon stuns'. Im-
munity to pity, meanness, pettiness masquerading as 'ordinary'
behaviour is identified with the inanimate. This was by choice. But
it was no short cut: it was the far side of involvement. And because
the cannon fodder *are* involved, the 'intellectual' feels a pitiful guilt
in their regard (the key fifth stanza); he will not think above them,
and the last world-wide verse hints that the 'dullards' are scapegoats
for the poet's hatred of more refined cowards. Two alternatives,
forever at odds—isolated comfort, and suffering fellowship—are
brought before the bar of what of nature they have in common.
'The last sea and the hapless stars', which cannot opt out anyway,
join 'the endless reciprocity of tears' in an alliance between the
natural and the human in spite of man's refusal to suffer and
communicate. Inspired by a colliery disaster, the 'peace' poem
Miners is less intense, just as telling:

> *Comforted years will sit soft-chaired*
> *In rooms of amber;*
> *The years will stretch their hands, well-cheered*
> *By our lives' ember.*

If we require for partisan ends Owen's 'opinion' of violence we
must go to his letters, where we find a reference to business men
reading *John Bull* on Scarborough sands. Violence was evil because
the Gospels say so: it was derogatory to nature (if not to sterling) and
favourable to pain. Owen wanted a Forster dispensation based on
the values of a single poem, on complex rich feeling, the regulation
of tensions, creative give and take. He would have detested anything
to do with laurels, but there is a sense in which he is the laureate.
In a notorious scandal W. B. Yeats, taking his cue from Arnold,
threw Owen out of the *Oxford Book of Modern Verse* because 'passive
suffering is not a theme for poetry'. Coming from the author of
No Second Troy, this was odd, but he may not have read *The End*.
Its structure, eloquence, and morality can only be called Michel-
angelesque. Like Renaissance sculpture it seems to demonstrate,
though still. It is mock-heroic satire in the tragic mood, because the
real courage, latent and undeclared, marks the poem with its

marmorean stoic grandeur. Sheer experience dictates that that abuse of nature, which is war, shall be unredeemable, nor is there any supernatural recompense. Old men—symbolic of a too gnarled civilization?—will be left, preferably to tell the truth, but their truth will be narcissistic and unfeeling because they lack the experience of the young. Irony ceases when the creation, like the poet, in admitting her mortal wounds and refusing false comforts shows the best compassion, and affirms what does remain of the energy of being:

> *After the blast of lightning from the east,*
> *The flourish of loud clouds, the Chariot Throne;*
> *After the drums of time have rolled and ceased,*
> *And by the bronze west long retreat is blown,*
>
> *Shall Life renew these bodies? Of a truth*
> *All death will he annul, all tears assuage?*
> *Or fill these void veins full again with youth,*
> *And wash, with an immortal water, Age?*
>
> *When I do ask white Age he saith not so:*
> *'My head hangs weighed with snow.'*
> *And when I hearken to the Earth, she saith:*
> *'My fiery heart shrinks, aching. It is death.*
> *Mine ancient scars shall not be glorified,*
> *Nor my titanic tears, the sea, be dried.'*

As for *Strange Meeting*, the gravity, the deep bass tone, the *terribilita* of this poem's high seriousness—there is no other phrase—is like a gage flung in Arnold's teeth. The poem cannot be excerpted, so I will finish by quoting from Edmund Blunden's assemblage of variant readings, which seem to me among the most powerful fragments in literature:

> *With a thousand fears that creature's face was grained.*
>
> *Miss we the march of this retreating world.*
>
> *Beauty is yours, and you have mastery,*
> *Wisdom is mine, and I have mystery.*
>
> *Let us fall out from them that trek from progress.*
>
> *Let us forgo men's minds that are brutes' natures.*
>
> *Let us turn back to beauty and to thought.*

*   *   *

I should like to do something—but how can one think or write, after a day's dull stupefying labour? When will we get on with the things that endure? (Isaac Rosenberg to John Rodker.)

It is the brain succumbing to the herculean attempt to enrich the world of ideas. (Isaac Rosenberg to Miss Seaton.)

I don't think there should be any vagueness at all, but a sense of something hidden and felt to be there. (Isaac Rosenberg to Edward Marsh.)

Among the hypocrisies of criticism is that of paying lip-service to Isaac Rosenberg, while refusing to advocate his virtues in the field. Rosenberg has found generous champions but he has never found the kingmaker he deserves. The B.B.C. condescended to him; *Scrutiny* favoured him to little public avail; Mr Jon Silkin staged a Rosenberg Exhibition at Leeds University in 1959;* but he has never emerged into fame in the manner of Owen (a parallel case in the Second World War is Keith Douglas).† His art is not obviously striking nor is he altogether a 'war poet', but his work is founded on rare gifts and will prove to be as permanent as Owen's or Edward Thomas's, and more permanent, I believe, than that of any other poet of the Georgian period.

At first sight Rosenberg is cliché-ridden: a sitting target for the marksmen. Words like sweet, strange, and aeon, themes such as Spring, the ravages of time, the distresses of love proliferate. Yet an echo vibrates in the memory. A whole harmony rings back which is the resonance of a peculiarly inventive movement. On examination we find that he seldom mounts a theme which is unmotivated or a word which is not justified by its context. In a poem in which he contrasts his position as soldier artist with that of the historical heroes, Rosenberg says of himself:

> *Let them shrink from your girth,*
> *That has outgrown the pallid days,*
> *When you slept like Circe's swine,*
> *Or a word in the brain's ways.*
> *(Soldier: Twentieth Century)*

* See the catalogue of the exhibition, *Isaac Rosenberg 1890–1918*, with letters, reproductions of Rosenberg's paintings, critical preface by Jon Silkin. University of Leeds with Partridge Press, 1959.

† Douglas is the only poet to have affinity with Rosenberg, whom he hails in *Desert Flowers*. The 'repose at a point . . . of great strength' which Ted Hughes praises in his preface to *Selected Poems of Keith Douglas*, 1964, was a force behind the 'creation of ideas' of Rosenberg, noticed by Mr D. W. Harding—'he brought language to bear on the incipient thought at an earlier stage of its development'. For both poets 'death at the moment when life was simplified and intensified' was

The last line, sobering the affirmation of strength with a dignified humility, suggesting linguistic order proceeding from mental chaos, is typical of his power of using exact images to announce comprehensive implications. His moulding of form is agile and incisive. He bristles with distinctions, paradox, and surprising changes of mood. A comparison would be to the lyrics of Blake: like his, Rosenberg's naïveté is a grace of sublime deception, for the internal twists and shifts of his structures are forever 'at work'—each stanza a mode of contrast, or of worthwhile reversal or consolidation, with the preceding one. His art is at a remove from narrative: it has purposeful variation within the given form. The lyrical, idealistic, ecstatic strain in Rosenberg is not decoration to edify or to deceive; built into the scaffolding of the poem as a functional strut, it would win the approval of Ruskin, since it is also beautiful. The visionary streak is a natural reflex of a sensibility used as an aid to living, for the enhancement of beneficial, encouraging situations, and not to evade by a leap into metaphysics but to endure with nobility unpleasant happenings. No innocent starry eye, his clear sight derives from a long tradition of hard looking; in him, the astringent is bathed in the lambent, the lapidary is made to dance.

In *On Receiving News of the War* he presents the South African summer landscape suddenly whitened by winter. (Rosenberg had gone out for his health and to paint—but he was poor, no luxury tourist.) 'Snow is a strange white word' fixes both the 'news' theme and the abnormal transformation—another rogue variant on that 'not in the scheme of generation' of Mr Eliot. Next the emotion is made impersonal *beyond* the poet. Ice and frost 'from earth to sky' is 'known' by the summer land, but 'no man knows why'. The play on know is a psychological stroke expressing the ominous, inevitable, calamitous size of war which at the same time bewilders the individual—'in all men's hearts it is'. It is daemonic: some 'spirit old' has turned our lives to mould with a 'malign kiss'. In the penultimate verse the colour symbolism changes from white to red. God's face is 'torn' and the 'crimson curse' is urged to purge our squalor and restore the land to innocence. Although resistance to force gives way to acceptance, this may indicate a deeper wisdom, for there is no complacent surrender; it is as if a mind attuned from old to inevitable suffering has uttered its hopes and fears, glimpsed a chance of revival through ordeal, and gravitated towards hope. The texture with its amalgam of political and ritualistic elements could only have come from a poet with Rosenberg's religious back-

---

'no more than the immortality of the possibilities of life'. See D. W. Harding, 'Aspects of the Poetry of Isaac Rosenberg', *Scrutiny*, March 1935.

ground. His family had, in fact, emigrated from Russia to the East End of London—Rosenberg admired Trotsky. We are not surprised to find a different, virile and urban, note in Rosenberg's narrative mode which relates a poem like *A Ballad of Whitechapel* to the Dickensian realism of Davidson's *Thirty Bob a Week*, and the visionary realism of Eliot's *His soul stretched tight across the skies*, and looks forward to Larkin's *Deceptions*.

His skill in verbal organization is crowned by victories on the structural plane; the whole is qualified by a rugged though confident rhythm. In *Returning, We hear the Larks*, a war poem, the overtures add up the detail in narrative:

> *Sombre the night is.*
> *And though we have our lives, we know*
> *What sinister threat lurks there.*
>
> *Dragging these anguished limbs, we only know*
> *This poison-blasted track opens on our camp—*
> *On a little safe sleep.*
>
> *But hark! Joy—joy—strange joy.*
> *Lo! Heights of night ringing with unseen larks.*
> *Music showering on our upturned list'ning faces.*
>
> *Death could drop from the dark*
> *As easily as song—*
> *But song only dropped,*
> *Like a blind man's dreams on the sand*
> *By dangerous tides,*
> *Like a girl's dark hair for she dreams no ruin lies there,*
> *Or her kisses where a serpent hides.*

Two clear statements—'sombre the night is' and 'a little safe sleep'—are kept apart by longer lines which contain the aggravating phrases—we are alive, we know the threat, but we are so tired, that all we effectively know is that a blasted track opens on our camp. These lines put the sure statements in doubt, mutually alienate and physically distance them. The economy of description, the sinister ebb and flow of movement, the surprise lurking round the edge of the *enjambements* create a sense of expectancy amid menace. Then 'But hark! Joy—joy—strange joy / Lo! Heights of night ringing with unseen larks / Music showering on our upturned list'ning faces.' The change is forceful. The thankful impetus and communal spirit informing the exultant images is centralized in the poem with zealous wit. Last a coda passage fuses the tone of the overture with the central scene; narrative becomes reflective monologue; death might have dropped from the clouds, but song dropped instead; it was like (a reminder of menace) a blind man hearing the tide or a girl's kisses where a serpent hides. There is a fundamental joy of life in Rosenberg which looks credulous but is deceptive, the fruit of that instinctive wisdom of the senses which triumphs over adversity.

The bulk of Rosenberg's peacetime work is lyrical. He concentrates on personal identity and personal relations. A poem in which both fuse felicitously is *In the Underworld*, the underworld being Valéry's limbo of non-being, Yeats's 'foul rag-and-bone shop of the heart'. For Rosenberg it loomed up at the point where a sense of one's inadequacy and guilt coincides with a decrease of consciousness. It is clear from a couplet in *Moses* that he suffered under the burden of awareness—'All day some hoofed animal treads our veins / Leisurely—leisurely our energies flow out'. The first verse of *In the Underworld* engineers the meeting of a 'creature of light' with 'I have lived in the underworld too long'. It is a poem on a theme made famous by Demetrios Capetanakis, 'The ageless ambiguity of things / Which makes our life mean death, our love be hate.' Yet the pessimism of 'I am a spirit that yours has found / Strange, undelightful, obscure . . .' is made to seem sensible by the optimistic disillusionment of 'I have lived in the underworld too long', a sort of hard-won maturity which earns a reward. This is confirmed by the sober confession, amounting to a challenge, without self-pity, which follows the 'too long':

> *For you, O creature of light,*
> *To hear without terror the dark spirit's song*
> *And unmoved hear what moves in night.*

The encounter of incompatibles is good, it generates a blend of illumination and apprehension tending to a union of opposites—'underworld' with 'light', 'undelightfulness' with 'happiness'. There is a brotherhood which diminishes the otherness of the neighbour, a shared plight and common responsibility. In spite of 'bound / In terrible darkness impure' implying the paralysis of volition, there is motion in the underworld which may move sympathy in the light:

> *Creature of light and happiness,*
> *Deeper the darkness when you*
> *With your bright terror eddying the distress,*
> *Grazed the dark waves and shivering further flew.*

Suffering followed, the darkness thickened, the union of brightness with terror was imperfect but opposites did meet to prove the worth of communication. The poem is remarkable because written in a

Nineties convention (accounting in part for the mephitic décor) into which the poet injects a profound idiosyncrasy of his own. This exercise in chiaroscuro, purged of embroidery and ornamental sensuous impressions, recalls Donne rather than the Decadents and has the sombre force of a Dürer etching.

Rosenberg can use sense and decoration when it is demanded. He can inject surprise into familiar themes. He does not try, for example, to escape from time, transcendentalize it, use it as an emotional trumpet, but revels in its existence, its way of framing the pleasure of relationships. He writes of a chance meeting that 'We walked our way / Our way hewn for us from the birth of Time' and a poem on timorous love ends with 'What dread, dark seas and perilous / Lie twixt love's silence and love's speech?' He commands a stern wit which is informed by a sensitive intelligence, rock with diamonds in it. This is plain in his extended imagery. The spring of 1916 is a masquerade stumbling 'through granite air'; the poet's girl is a star—but one which can be trapped in a rock pool; our delusions of desire are a sky reflected in a moving stream on which petals fall *which cannot reach the sky*. A skit on the edifying subject of lice in an Army greatcoat is called *The Immortals*: it begins 'I killed them, but they would not die' and ends with the comparison of Beelzebub to a louse. The poem is funny in itself. It prompts conjecture. The subacid humour is typical. It is a perfect philosophy for peril and informs much of his satire. In *Break of Day in the Trenches* he commends 'a queer sardonic rat' whom 'they would shoot' if they knew its cosmopolitan sympathies—for it trots between the lines. It is asked 'What do you see in our eyes / At the shrieking iron and flame / Hurled through still heavens?' We have the tripartite vision of no-man's-land, a clandestine hit at the jingoists, while the ugliness and bombast of war is made to look absurd when set against exact, natural life, the ancientness *and* freshness of this world—'The darkness crumbles away / It is the same old druid Time as ever'.

In his treatise on *The Poetic Image* C. Day Lewis has deplored the decline of metaphor in favour of simile in modern verse. Metaphor helps to retrieve the structure of personality. Rosenberg excelled at them:

> *And Nature, who would never let*
> *A sun with light still in it set,*
> *Before you even reached your sky*
> *In inadvertence let you die.*
> (from *Killed in Action*)*

* Printed in *Colour* in 1919, this poem is excluded from the 1949 edition, but appeared in book form in *Poems by Isaac Rosenberg*, ed. Gordon Bottomley, 1922.

The sun, lord of fertility, becomes host to Rosenberg's anticipation of death. He does not rail at nature, he catches out her fecklessness. The splendour of solar symbolism and the classical-modern idea of reaching the sky are made to co-operate in a tragic assertion of free wit in the face of necessity. *Per ardua ad astra*, man and nature are not confused (as they are in a greater poet, Rilke, when he faces this theme). But Rosenberg achieved nothing like the set-pieces of Owen. The challenge and response of inner life, the obstacles to this which occur in the external world fascinated him. In *Chagrin* the horsemen of thought are caught like 'hair of Absalom' by a sudden depression apparently reaching from the skies. 'We are lifted of all we know / And hang from implacable boughs.' The 'choked soul' remembers Christ, who is invoked to end the endlessness of a hanging death. A force blows the flame apart in *If You are Fire* so that 'desire eludes desire', yet it is the same flame with a 'central heart' whose law is reunion (compare Eliot's different 'crowned knot of fire'). *A Girl's Thoughts* is an implementation of his ideal for poetry 'where an interesting complexity of thought is kept in tone and right value to the dominating idea so that it is understandable and still ungraspable'. The title looks ambitious, but the treatment is subtle. The plot is the tension between the virgin, contemplative world of 'this quiet hour' and the instinctive 'need whose hauntings terrorize'. In the middle of the poem the 'dim apprehension of a trust' holds uneasily, contended for, and flattered by, auxiliary and ambivalent emotions (fear, pride). The tension breaks in a burst of awareness: former 'life' seems to have 'shrunk' but in fact instinct, the 'founts of being', has been provoked and 'dreads surprise'.

Rosenberg could retort on Nietzsche—'God is alive, who can be responsible for him?' Like Spinoza he was a 'God-intoxicated' man, his God was evolving and, because immanent, was most demanding, rather an example to the Bishop of Woolwich's in fact. The wholeness of God had to be realized in detail, through word and image, by the observing intellect; by living fully in the present Rosenberg strove to create the future, peering forwards, seizing things which (otherwise) might be overlooked in future. God was a body made up of human actions ('Your elbows in the dawn, and wrists / Bright with the afternoon / Do you not shake when a mortal slides / Into your own unvexed peace?') This obligation towards a God who has been, is and will be is where our poet abandons Rilke, who considered that the Lord of Space should be obliged to him. Granting that it lacks the religiosity of the late verse drama, it is a mystery why tge play *Moses* is not performed by groups interested in verse speaking. Moses, charged with vigour, his own fulfilment at one with the liberation of his people, gives a poet's God's-eye view of the world. His thoughts stand 'like a mountain' behind mists; he is sick of 'rigid dry-boned refinement' and senses 'voices of deeds not done' and 'songs more secret than desert light'. His rootedness, which qualifies him for leadership, forces him to ask 'Is their unbeing my choice?' For if we neglect his works and his future, God may turn cruel and malevolent. Feeling the weakness of his time, and an artist's lost spiritual opportunities, to be the 'miasma of a rotting god', Rosenberg knew a 'fury' or impulse to 'fill the veins of time / Whose limbs had begun to rot' . . .

> *Ah! Let the morning pale*
> *Throb with a wilder pulse . . .*
> *Thin branches whip the white skies*
> *To lips and spaces of song . . .*

Our wealth is God's 'cunning' to make death harder, to break our 'iron sinews' more painfully. Yet the words of Moses are 'fleets of treasure' sailing 'treacherous seas'. His girl's father is a toad who, shifting its belly, revealed a diamond, and would be 'more interesting as a mummy'. The language is full of vivacious dramatic devices. It ends with the captivity being likened to a night which dreams of the sun, abolishes the dawn and, mixing itself with light, creates a 'new thing'—the image of rebirth.

In his war poems, everything that burnt finely in Isaac Rosenberg was consummated at the moment that it was quenched. He is too involved in examining his feelings to become the voice of a group. Yet he is involved—'I will not leave a corner of my consciousness covered up, but saturate myself with the strange and extraordinary new conditions of this life'. There is no divination of the causes, no self-pity, not even the magnificent protest of Owen. The method is the same as in the peacetime poems: the descriptions are transcended by the pressure of feeling and turn into a type of insight.*

---

* With Owen, we feel a sense of shock, of complete difference, between his peacetime and wartime experience; in his letters, the lyrical and pastoral felicities of peace contrast with the affrighting realism of his despatches from the front. Owen's war letters, for all their frightfulness, show a stiff-upper-lip element: Owen seldom complains, he confronts the iniquitous as ordeal.

For Rosenberg the waste of war was a dramatization—a macabre *legalization* of what he had undergone as a struggling artist in the East End. He does complain, yet he is not less brave than Owen: it is the stoicism of candour. Hence the strong pathos of *Girl to Soldier on Leave*:

> *Pallid days, arid and wan,*
> *Tied your soul fast.*
> *Babel-cities' smoky tops*
> *Pressed upon your growth . . .*
>
> *It held you hiddenly on the Somme*
> *Tied from my heart at home.*
> *O must it loosen now?*

Dead Man's Dump is the descendant of Rimbaud's *Le Dormeur du Val* and the ancestor of Dylan Thomas's poems on the London Blitz, one of the best war poems ever, because it refuses to do what war poems are expected to do: it reveals the normally concealed. (At the Imperial War Museum you find no photographs of carnage such as Wilfred Owen carried on him.) Immediacy of promise denied, waste setting in, of an evil too big for man's considerable ingenuity and compassion to grasp or to explain, with nature, source of energy, impassively receiving her dead, is potently evoked:

> *The air is loud with death,*
> *The dark air spurts with fire,*
> *The explosions ceaseless are . . .*

> *A man's brains splattered on*
> *A stretcher-bearer's face;*
> *His shook shoulders slipped their load,*
> *But when they bent to look again*
> *The drowning soul was sunk too deep*
> *For human tenderness . . .*

'The blood-dazed intelligence' is 'beating for light'. If this poem is frightful it is lightened by the elegy on the poet's brother (*In War*) which offers this amazing image—'Untuned air shall lap the stillness / In the old space for your voice . . .' The tranquil unrelenting fall, resolute though broken, of lines testifies to a determination to perceive the meaning of the death. Reported at a time when 'we thought of alien things, irrelevant' it makes the poet ask 'what are the great sceptred dooms / To us, caught / In the wild wave?' The death is sadly celebrated: its stature is equated with 'sceptred dooms' and disregards, rather than denounces, its cause. The creation will witness to the death forever, and it is not a degradation for the 'motion of your spirit', whether in anger or joy, will 'fret the nonchalant noon', will be present, a reminder, *because* of absence and silence.

Rosenberg has no truck with the vulgarity of patriotic uplift. His love of England flashes in the line 'England—Time gave them thee'. But 'their blood is England's heart' is answered by the disturbing pathos of 'We cannot give you water / Were all England in your breath'. With Owen he knew (in *On Receiving News of the War* he anticipated) that barbarism may be a stimulus to gaiety and revival, but he was never hoodwinked by this in the manner of Brooke. *Soldier: Twentieth Century* astounds us with 'I love you, great new Titan!' and 'cruel men are made immortal'. Rosenberg is praising the influx of energy which war has given him, which enabled him to write *Dead Man's Dump* and the memorial to his brother, which ushered in one of the legends of our age; and the trouble is that cruel men are made immortal. The poem ends with the stanza I quoted on page 85, a definite claim to have outgrown historical villains in a personal renewal which involves responsibility. *Louse Hunting* —'nudes . . . yelling in lurid glee', 'gargantuan fingers . . . smutch supreme littleness' yokes the energy to a democratic context. In *Troopship* and *Marching* it becomes a dramatic irony within the lyric convention. 'We husband the ancient glory' in the backs of necks and hands, but they are suspended on 'automatic feet'.

The Judaism in Rosenberg's thought is manifest in his respect for justice, his moral fibre which is never stuffy, and the ambivalence in his estimate of God. For him (here, again, he resembles Blake) as for Owen, God can be a jealous, cruel lawgiver, His Son the numinous rebel of David Gascoyne—'Christ of Revolution and of Poetry'—or as Rosenberg puts it, 'O think, you reverend shadowy austere / Your Christ's youth was not ended when he died'. We have seen, however, that he was disinclined to blame God for rottenness which he (the poet) could not set right himself. His spirituality is aware of the plastic and tangible body, sensitive to any privation of beauty around him, cognizant of the transience of objects which would otherwise have a terrifying power. Some lines sound the note of physical intensity heard in Jewish mystic literature:

> *Divine—divine—upon my eyes,*
> *Upon my hair—divine—divine,*
> *The fervour of the golden skies,*
> *The ardent gaze of God on mine.*
> (*Night and Day*)

The rub is that the poet is not parroting 'divine' in the patois of the West End sophisticate: he means what he says, he could defend his point of view. Such insights go to subtilize his irrefragable humanism, as expressed in *Creation*—'Your roots are God, the pause-less cause / But your boughs sway to self-windy laws'. Rosenberg had no time to achieve major form; his admiration had no time to settle on symbols and charge them with significance. If we define major form as a nourishing amount and complexity of material communicated in the most meaningful variety of structures, which are finally unified, it is clear that his work is fragmentary. Yet he had conflicts, he could suffer ensuring development, he knew that the value of a praise is to do with the overcome ordeal behind it. Consider the use of 'unthinkable' here:

A VISION OF REALITY

Taut is the air and tied the trees,
The leaves lie as on a hand.
God's unthinkable imagination
Invents new tortures for nature.

And when the air is soft and the leaves
Feel free and push and tremble,
Will they not remember and say
How wonderful to have lived?

(*Moses*)

He is not a master of the strong line of the Metaphysicals. His method is to energize imagery and distribute it in a pattern. Owen's mighty 'these are men whose minds the Dead have ravished' is in the royal lineage, a blood relationship with Donne's 'And made the darke fires languish in that vale'. Rosenberg is less inclusive, less 'central', more delicate and translucent—'None saw their spirits' shadow shake the grass'. Brought up on Swinburne, Francis Thompson, and Rossetti, he discovered Donne, though the effort to imitate him in *Spiritual Isolation* is a failure. There was a lack of distinction in his aesthetic between 'the bone taken from Adam remains a bone. To create is to apply pulsating rhythmic principles to the part; a unity, another nature, is created' and the Swinburne orientated 'we know infinity through melody.' But considering the transformative gift of sensibility there is no doubt that the New Adam would have triumphed. His grasp of form was resolute to master the checks and desolations which dog the path of older poets. His art, which was to prove that our Judaeo-Christian heritage is more than a platitude, would have gone on making Jewish history alive in a time of terror: not like Mann's *Joseph Saga* a reconstruction, but a lyrical enactment. The death of young poets is usually a matter for sorrowful acceptance; it is idle to speculate about their promise. The death of Rosenberg is one of the few cases among young poets where one can speak of a definite loss to the future of literature.

*   *   *

. . . born in this century, tempered by war, disciplined by a hard and bitter peace . . . let us struggle against the common enemies of man: ignorance, poverty, disease and war itself.

John F. Kennedy: *Inaugural Speech*

Isaac Rosenberg was killed in action in April 1918. Wilfred Owen was killed a week before the Armistice in the attempt to cross the Sambre Canal. Are Owen and Rosenberg 'pacifists'? A poet's business is to get feeling into words; any views we derive can at best be generalizations on the results of our appreciation. Any artist who does not herald war—anyone who *thinks* critically about force outside war—argues for peace. Violence was cultivated as a dynamic by Yeats and Rimbaud, they expected it to be a spur to transformation and they mourned (as we saw in Yeats's poem about assassination) its victims. Rilke sobered up after the *Five Hymns*, refused (literally) to write propaganda; Edward Thomas corrected his proofs;* D. H. Lawrence saw the hysteria of robots; war arouses Auden's humane logic and Dylan Thomas's compassion. You do not need to be a 'sociologist', but a sensible person with his eyes and ears open, to see that in war a complex of jingoist ('prestige at the conference table') and economic factors is governed by the psychological factor; it is the interaction of millions of death-wishing, competitive, or cruel minds which allows the junta to plan for aggression. That, one hopes, is an academic statement: but major war, probably obsolete, is local violence writ large, and has to be provided for to the neglect of problems which are by no means obsolete. Violence (I include the Space Race and so on, the motives to which are similar) hides the seeds of its own mitigation, but frustrated in peace, energies become destructive. War poetry comprehends it, and will appreciate in value.

Paul Claudel called Rimbaud 'a mystic in the savage state'. Owen and Rosenberg are pacifists in an active state, that is to say in them heroic reason—altruistic intelligence—descends into the asylum of politics, a secular Harrowing of Hell. They transcend 'pacifism' and reach one of the strangest, and to the creative mind most indispensable, truths of life: the only way to convict evil with any authority worth respect is to suffer it yourself. The sainthood of pacifism is to undergo cruelty in order to affirm the good while denouncing the destructive, or, most difficult, to unravel the entanglement of both. For to make the body, straining in war, strengthen the muscles of peace, is a desperate endeavour. Reading Herbert Read's *Poetry and Anarchism* I came to the conclusion that all arguments against (and for) force were wanting, because they are overwhelmed by man's ubiquitous cruelty—it is probable that pacifists and aggressors are motivated by comparable drives. Decent taste has to appeal to physical abhorrence: to have undergone pain, or to fear retaliation, we must hope, will be sufficient to prevent people inflicting pain. Yet not one of Herbert Read's experts so much as mentions the scandal of pain—it is all quack psycho-biologic *realpolitik*. Presumably it takes a poet to be articulate about suffering. In him, the moral courage of the pacifist is dignified by the physical

* See the letters quoted by Eleanor Farjeon in *Edward Thomas: The Last Four Years*, 1958.

courage of the sensitive thinker. The fibre to undergo, to separate, denounce and then affirm, belongs to men with a poetic degree of vision. The artists and those who feel with them constitute the 'figure in the carpet', though hardly in Henry James's aesthetic sense. They are the suffering and resurrecting heroes (through their art) who form the harmonious strand in a carpet of lurid colours and conflicting tones.

In Tolstoy's *War and Peace*, Pierre visits Prince Andrei Bolkonski on the eve of Borodino. 'Why are you here?' 'Because you cannot hate something you do not know.' How often, facing the bickerings of historians, or the peevish, and usually vainglorious, memoirs of Great Soldiers, does one long for a single line by these poets who know death to the bone. For those who administer force are the last to suffer from it and the first to reap its macabre glories. As peace lengthens, war poetry remains a standing reminder—a crucifix in the summer fields—of what violence is like and why it must be prevented. The remainder goes for *all* violence—civil, domestic, as well as militant; Adenauer and de Gaulle worshipping in Rheims cathedral, Moscow and Washington banning tests make no difference to the harrowing of hell in English verse. Since 1945 the entertainment racket, the corrupt press, and the Ian Flemings have permutated the formula sex-sadism to popularize an image of violence. As we have barbaric chaos disguised as booming peace the sub-conscious preconditions for violence are more propitious than we realize. Against this stand Wilfred Owen and Isaac Rosenberg.

FORMS OF FLIGHT: HERBERT READ, EDWIN MUIR, KATHLEEN RAINE

SIR HERBERT READ'S lyrics, in Parts I and V of his 1946 volume, affirm admirably his own cherished belief in 'spontaneous form'. They justify the emphasis he places on mobile personality as distinct from fixed character. The poems are not inert hosts to experience. They show a strong pictorial quality, revealing with limpid vividness the surprises of perception. The quizzical, breathless rhythm of *The Even Skein*, about the inconclusive effort to cope with multiplicity, and the anguish of interrupted initiatives, creates well the tantalizing experience. *Day's Affirmation* uses careful contrasts of tone to denote, first the influx, then the questioning, of sensation, so that we accept the balancing veracity of the first and last stanzas:

> *Emerging at midnight*
> *To cool my aching eyes with the sight of stars*
> *I hear the nightingale*
> *Throbbing in the thicket by my garden gate. . . .*
> *Sing on! The night is cool.*
> *Morning and the world will be lit*
> *With whitebeam candles shining and O the frail*
> *And tender daring splendour of wild cherrytrees. . . .*

In *Night's Negation* well-judged transitions give the sense of refreshment and relief mingling:

> *Trees*
> *have held these flecks of light*
> > *these brittle stars that in the night*
> *flash*
> > *on the unfolding fans of space*
>
> *Blue fans*
> *that bring me peace*
> > *and nerves that cease*
> *to feel*
> > *the torture of day's lease*

The stanzas are sharp, faceted: few poets swoop on sensory immediacies with the boldness of Read, or exhibit such inordinate skill in juxtaposing them. A meticulous earthiness, constant in Read, adores nature as the donor of swift joys which appear to compensate for all other anxiety and woe. But the poems give hostages to directness: they are static idylls, beautifully focused snapshots posed by an expert intellectual photographer. They are not suggestive, animated wholes which provoke new responses in the mind when read; like photographs, they are enjoyable in retrospect; for all their stress on country matters, they lack roughness and disturbance.

Read's best lyric work was produced after the First World War, the decisive and traumatic event in his development. One of his cleanest-cut works, *Logos* ('Suddenly he began to torture the flowers . . .'), looks back at the war, but succeeds because it has a unifying personal plot which is projected on a humane scale. It ends with one of Read's desperate, unexplained optimisms, but this seems honourable when 'the carnage at the Menin Gate' has been so powerfully recalled. I emphasize this seriousness and sincerity, for criticism of Read's war verse must be limiting. Of the two great poets of the front, Owen speaks *for* the private soldier and Rosenberg *is* the private soldier speaking. Herbert Read observes the private soldier; in *Kneeshaw Goes to War* and *The Execution of Cornelius Vane* he does his thinking for him. In *The End of a War* it is the officers who philosophize; apparently the men are denied this consolation. A sincere yet treacherous German, the Englishman who kills the betrayer, and a mysteriously murdered girl give good (if not 'valid') accounts of themselves; and the injury to civil life is compassionately brought out. The interesting idea, unique in war poetry, lacks dramatic tension and tragic intensity. Read's cogent forensic essays on the motives of war and peace, put into the mouths of combatants, are weak on why bad violence must be cured, because they are not (they do not feel as if they are) genuine apprehensions of what it feels like to be crippled, condemned for desertion after attempting suicide, or subjected to atrocities: they are at times arch and patronizing. Not that Read himself is insensitive to the ghastliness and the fleeting mitigations. He horrifies with all the force of minutely studied images—witness *The Happy Warrior*. His gift for extraordinary instances triumphs at moments like these:

> Going to the Brigade with my prisoner at dawn,
> The early sun made the land delightful,
> And larks rose singing from the plain.
> In broken French we discussed
> Beethoven, Nietzsche and the International.*
>
> (*Liedholz*)

* A curious trio—and a tribute to the brotherhood of man.

In *My Company* Read speaks of the sense of enhanced community felt in the virile group. Like Owen and Rosenberg, he faces up to the fact that combat may be a help to vigour, song, kindness, and humour. A hellish battle scene follows. Read admits that, through his 'intellectual's' power of detachment, he can rise above these terrors, is thus privileged above his men: then he remembers that all 'are of one species' and bows his head to 'share their doom'. It is impressive, graphic, undergone. But there is little real sympathy (in his poem); the detachment is what enables him to write; the final grace is willed rather than given. In Owen this subject is a technique for sharing (remember what he makes of the 'wise thinker' theme in *Insensibility*) and a mode of invective (in *Apologia Pro Poemate Meo* he rounds on the reader and declares that only the sufferers have the right to enjoy the comradeship). His theme is stated in terms which suggest that its true consummation is in time of peace.

Part III of Read's collected volume brings us to the Spanish Civil and Second World wars. *A World Within a War* depicts Read fortified by nature (his own farm) and pitting this, rather innocently, against the public bedlam. There is attractive anarchist argument; there is vintage bucolic writing. *To a Conscript of 1940* shows a resurgence of social passion—'We think we gave in vain . . . there was hope in the homestead and anger in the streets'—but its message is that to fight without purpose or reward is honourable: it is no doubt better than to fight with hatred or ambition, but in no circumstances can fighting be gratuitous, or it will become the mindless instrument of some anti-cultural ideology; one should fight for an honest cause or, like Owen and Rosenberg, as 'a pacifist in an active state'.* The *Ode during the Battle of Dunkirk* mobilizes Read's aesthetico-moral philosophy to defend a romanticized humanism against militant unreason. There is some mordant satire —'One of the dazed and disinherited / I crawled out of that mess / With two medals and a gift of blood-money'—which outclasses the mannered conceits of his satires on the English Jazz Age (Part IV). The poem founders, however, on an inverted form of the same hiatus which fractures his poems of the Western Front. Instead of the leap from detachment to community, we now have the 'leap of faith', simply interjected without any transitional dialectic of evidence, from depression to ecstatic praise of spiritual values. And certain faults of style grow on Read as (ironically) his theoretical

---

* An honest cause is described by Edward Thomas in *This is No Case of Petty Right or Wrong*. Out in the country, he hates 'one fat patriot' and thinks the Kaiser colourful. To defend a way of life—'all we know and live by'—is not to traduce an enemy's; for each, 'what is good and must endure' is all they have.

interest in 'organic form' increases. If the ground plan of his style was constructivist—from prefabricated blocks of images he built poems which were habitable—he still had harmonious qualities, but later he loses even interlinear attributes. Each image tends to be a climber leading a concentrated life of its own; when it falls it drags the rest into the abyss. Part VI contains ideological poems. Of a violent idealist, Read told us that 'this beautiful assassin is your friend / his action the delivery of love', and yet:

> Lorca was killed, singing,
> And Fox who was my friend.
> The rhythm returns; the song
> Which has no end.*
>   (*The Heart Conscripted*)

They are autodidactic: even when Read puts up a celebrity (*John Donne Declines a Benefice*) or a leader (Starr in *The Nuncio*) he is still, more palpably than his form permits, putting words into the mouth. Rejecting traditional aids:

> Reason prevails
> Against all symbols;
> Symbols are idols of mind's darkest level:
> Live in light immune from evil. . . .

He is forced to rely, to enliven his narrative, on purely formal devices and the genuine collusion between experience and style which distinguished his lyrics is lost: instead, we have arbitrary line lengths; capricious, unjustifiable acrobatics of rhythm; incongruous injections of sensual imagery into the Teutonic discourse. Of the images many are beautiful and meaningful, but they are, as so often in Read, brilliant instances; they fail to resurrect the whole into permanent life. The old 'leap of faith' is framed in futuristic imperatives which seem anti-cultural. 'New children must be born of gods in a deathless land':

> Sense and image they must refashion—
>   they will not recreate
> love: love ends in hate; they will
>   not use
> words: words lie. The structure of events alone is

---

* See Stephen Spender's *Fall of a City*—'All the names of heroes in the hall / Where the feet thundered and the bronze throats roared / FOX and LORCA claimed as history on the walls . . .'

comprehensible and to single
perceptions communic-
ation is not essential.
Art ends;
The individual world alone is valid.

(Beata L'Alma)

Art ends. The individual world alone is valid. The dogmatism and facility are related to weakness in the poet's views. Anarchism may be a blessed personal ethic but it is unlikely to be a public leaven unless Read can explain how anarchism is to be implemented. If this begs sociological protests, we can invoke art and say: he should be able to found the anarchy in the verse. Yeats wrote poems in which he divined the mind of rebels, who had not experienced anything like the society for which they were fighting. Is it absurd to ask that Read should do the same for the anarchist ideal? His nearest approach is *Hymn for the Spanish Anarchists*; where this convinces, it is derived from permanent, visitable, geographic, and temperamental traits—elsewhere Read has to rely on idealized fiction. Perusal of the work suggests that the sane, redeemed selfhood, based on logical cerebration and trained sensualism, which Read would substitute for the mortmain of bureaucratic technocracy would die of boredom unless it admitted the hostilities, tensions, and anxieties of that depth psychology which Read has banished from his poetics (though not from his aesthetics and art criticism).

The penultimate chapter of Read's book on Wordsworth is called 'The Self Annulled'. In 1955 Read brought out *Moon's Farm*—poems written since his collected volume. The self is certainly annulled here. According to Read, Wordsworth broke down because he allowed his inhibited 'character'—his compounding with the Establishment, his repression of his revolutionary and philandering youth—to kill his mobile 'personality'. As the chances for anarchism recede, as his immersion in aesthetics deepens, and as he compounded with the Establishment a similar hardening of the arteries afflicts Read. The disjunct constructivism of the middle phase is abandoned; he aspires to the interlinear; but it is not toughened and sharpened by that swiftness and angularity of observation which characterized the early style: it is more like those Georgians against whom Read was reacting. The diction is blurred, slow, a bit coy; the movement prosaic, based on plodding metres with little rhythm; one grows accustomed to 'the sense of endless space' and 'the mystical solitude of the oaks'. There is an ominous descent into classical myth: the 'anarchist' quest for moments of grace, equipoise, lightness, baffled on the plane of reality, will irrupt into some atavistic theme. Of Sappho we are told:

A VISION OF REALITY

Confidently she will carry
these essential glories
these trophies from the wellhead
her conquest absolute.

The lyrics are a curious blend of the fictitious with the mythical, a feint to conjure, through magic, what might be. *The Death of Kropotkin* is the best poem: where good, it gives Kropotkin the qualities of the early Read; where bad, it is a wistful lament not over Kropotkin, but over a lost cause. 'A prophet's dead face', 'the eternal intelligence on his brow', snow falling 'gently', the sun 'staining' the plain, and the gibe at Lenin following the awful cliché—'poor humble people—Lenin had let them come'—produce the aura of melodrama. The poem ends with the idea of Kropotkin 'travelling eastward into rich lands / Where many will follow you'. No sign of people, or of poet, following into rich lands enlivens *Moon's Farm*.

The evidence suggests that the 1914 war shocked Read into intense clarity of vision, the more passionate because endangered. When the risk in this vision faded, the poet was bored by the formlessness of peace and fell for what Amiel, who should know, termed 'the malady of the ideal'. If a vital aim of progressives is to reduce working hours while raising the standard of living, achieved through automation and the fair distribution of property, their final aim is, one hopes, what is done with the mind, *the way we live*, when the new leisure arrives. We can rehearse that living now. Our exercise of the Read virtues—rational prowess with educated sensualism—is best kept on its moral toes by what he ignores: the exposure of the self to its own depths *and to other selves*. A task of poetry is to moot the incentives to inspire fullness of life, the balance of quality with equality, of the convivial with the individual, which is needed to distract the egalitarian society from the old egotist greed. In *The Nuncio*, Starr, anarchist-architect-aesthetician, delivers a lecture full of orders like this:

> *Each to his cell:*
> *The individual*
> *Is the pivot of our plan.*

Result? The fulfilment of prophecies like this:

> *The evil and the ill*
> *Tamed and all*
> *Spiritual corruption*
> *Given absolution.*

Starr is an engaging type—frank, adroit, quixotic—yet the impression he gives is that reformed individuality is a panacea.

Sympathy, disagreement, and dottiness, which are often maladroit, unfrank, and obsessive in their operations, get no honourable mention. Read's verse labours not under the contempt of concern but under a too limited, too naïve, practical idea of it. It is philosophically and politically urged more than shown in existential terms. One feels that Read is offering a private literary ideology which tends to become a fiction when applied. But that is no reason why we should not be grateful to him for sketching what a genuine commitment might be:

> *We have known that a certain way of life was good*
> *the easy salutation, the open hand*
> *the sober disquisition, the frank eye*
> *the unfailing satisfaction*
> *of water wine and bread.*

*   *   *

Herbert Read's imaginative vision inspires a semi-moralistic social ideal. Edwin Muir's is found in a set of mythical facts which, to his great credit, he makes no attempt to systematize or impose, but rather discovers in all circumstances; his myth is humble enough to remain a myth. Behind the 'Story' of our lives, subsists the 'Fable' —we enact recurrent patterns of behaviour. These are announced in prehistoric symbols such as The Age of Innocence, The Fall, The Journey, and the myths of Greece and the Bible. These symbols correspond to mutations of the individual spirit as it labours through Time; they guide us back to our roots, refresh, chasten, and instruct us, and affirm our kinship with animals and with nature. (Muir's poems should be read side by side with Mann's *Joseph Saga*.) Marmorean and costive though his vision has been known to be, there is no strain, no attitudinizing; it is a good taste—'terrific, sad and simple', as Muir characterized the Scottish imagination —which succeeds in the virtue of being modest unawares.

It was also a lifetime's effort: is it easier for Celts to resurrect with age, to make *themselves* new? Like Yeats when old, Muir grew young —young to outgrow the ponderousness of his earlier work and project the eloquent, pristine forms of *Soliloquy, Adam's Dream, The Transfiguration, The Annunciation,* and *One Foot in Eden.* Muir finds the right words, the one poise and tenor for what he evokes—'the source of all our seeing rinsed and cleansed / Till earth and light and water entering there / Gave back to us the clear unfallen world'. He keeps up a rigour of description to illustrate his concepts— 'Sometimes they paused / While one stopped one—fortuitous assignations / In the disorder'. He creates atmospheres of suspense, in which his feeling flowers with vivid force—'See, they have come together, see / While the destroying minutes flow . . . So great a wonder that it makes / Each feather tremble on his wings'. He throws surprising light on well-worn generalities—'I have picked up wisdom lying / Disused about the world, available still'—or revives attention with some counter-stressed, thought-provoking aside, 'Deep in the slaughter once I watched / A madman sitting happy in the sand / Rapt in his world'. He exerts a true peculiarity which reverberates beyond the self—'One foot in Eden still, I stand / And look across the other land / The world's great day is growing late . . . Yet still from Eden springs the root / As clean as on the starting day.' Felicities of high degree become the characteristics of his style. Formerly, they were the exceptions. Moments of the order of 'An echo caught / From the mid-sea / On a still mountainside' and 'listened half the night to hear / The spring wind hunting on the hills'; poems like *To Anne Scott-Moncrieff*, where the compassion unifies the poet's often meandering reveries; *Suburban Dream*, where he makes a sociological point without prejudicing the timelessness of his myth; and *The Prize*, where he concentrates on the perceived, giving it full weight, before summing up, had to compensate us for moribund diction, contrived syntax, and what one can only call premature middle-aged spread of thought.

Although it is fashionable to decry the imagists, Muir is an example of a good man fallen among non-imagists: he would profit from the alacrity of the word-placing of the young Herbert Read. Muir had the equipment to have remedied this defect had it been a matter of technique only. But it was ordained by his over-receptive vision; his mind became passive under the bombardment of myths, dreams, and symbols, forfending reality. One pauses to avoid some unexploded bomb—'the invincible shade', 'man's long shadow', 'endless', 'millions', 'great' (the use of 'great' is a mania in Muir), planted by the poet in a context of resonant verbs and rhetorical flourishes to suggest that he is contending with Time, and that the issue is important. Vigilance about images is often accompanied by an impulse to select experience and mould it to express a viewpoint; lording it over selected images, the poet revels in his free choice. Muir has been the victim of his experience; his mind is too much on the stretch; he is all-seeing without being fully conscious. The oddity of his symbolism, the incongruity of his effects is due to the enormous time-scale of the poems being framed in easy, prefabricated rhythms which pre-digest any attempt the themes might make to contour the form by their pressure; and into these categorical metres—at times ruffled by an irregular lilt—Muir will inject some colloquialism or archaism as grotesque as heckling at a funeral oration. Remarks like 'material things will pass', 'love gathers all', 'the elected joy', 'his vastest dreams were less than six feet tall', and 'break and *remould* the heart' (Mr F. W. Bateson's italics) do little but gesture without striking.

Muir's best poems anticipate, or later transcend, those of his middle period when he seemed, like Penelope at her loom, his favourite symbol, to have lost himself in the labyrinth. Three early works, *Horses, Childhood,* and *When the Trees grow bare on the High Hills* are moving sensory evocations of his Orkney upbringing; they are visionary, imparting the feel of ancient strength behind common phenomena, of future felicity beckoning through the interstices of the present, 'something ever more about to be'; they are not fabulous, for Muir is not yet transforming remembered fact into present fiction. In middle poems like *The Stationary Journey, The Fall, The Recurrence, The Voyage,* and in episodic poems written under their sway such as *The Child Dying,* I myself feel that it is a question, not just of the gaucheries, but of 'all or nothing'—the mystery is so confident that it ceases to be incarnate and becomes indulgent; the 'great non-stop heraldic show' overawes or bemuses; we either submit or revolt, as to a dictator. 'A week refutes a prophecy / Which only ages can make true'. The 'week' element, refuting 'prophecy' in Muir's sense, emerges with strengthening effect in *To J.H.F., The Wayside Station, The Confirmation,* personal poems articulated by drama, which approach fully realized dramatic allegories such as *The Bridge of Dread, The Interrogation, The Combat.* And these announce the wonder of the last poems—one thinks of *Abraham, Day and Night, The Difficult Land,* the luminous clarity of *The Brothers*—where metrical torpor gives way to masterful blank forms whose visionary birth is like a second youth.

*   *   *

One of the oddities of the weather is that the sun which shines on Edwin Muir has not reflected on the poetry of Kathleen Raine. Chronologically, she is of the 30's generation; as a poet, she is a cat who walks alone. Her use of dream, myth, and the unconscious relates her to Muir, and to a lesser extent Herbert Read, but her use is more considered than Muir's and, to my taste, more rewarding. Yet in the Preface to her *Collected Poems* (1956) Miss Raine goes further than Muir into outright anti-historicism. She omits 'personal love poems' and 'poems descriptive of events in place and time as such, mostly from the war years, that seem now as dead as any other journalism'. According to Miss Raine 'whatever in love is personal and not imaginative matters not at all' and 'the ever-recurring forms of nature mirror eternal reality; the never-recurring productions of

human history reflect only fallen man'. Well, the nature poems
which follow are a tribute to the scope of Miss Raine's version of
Negative Capability; 'vitiated' is the last word one would invoke.

Kathleen Raine has the scientist's wariness before emotion and
his impertinence before the unknown. She controls, from the centre,
her unruly material where Muir disperses his powers by straddling
his. Her use of scientific terms—'retina', 'alembic', 'chromosome',
'metabolism'—has more practical relevance than Auden's: where he
is a bit of a playboy, Miss Raine is relating a scientific appreciation
of nature to a moral enthusiasm about its meaning for the enhancement of personality. Her insights are produced as evidence in an
often impassioned, always enunciated and sometimes original, poetic
argument. Each poem is a felt experiment; as they accumulate we
feel encouraged to accept them as truth, attuning ourselves to
unfamiliar insights as if we had always known, not just in our
emotional wits, but in our perceptive common sense that 'air filters
through the lungs fine branches as through trees' etc. Even lines
which appear less forensic, more poetical—'the baroque assumption
of the clouds'—have a terse, authoritative correctness.

The virtue of the poems is: this scientist is feminine in a rare sense.
Women poets too often run to ecstasy or gentility, the *Magna Mater*
or Bride of Christ pose. Miss Raine has the wisdom, basis, and tact
that one associates with Emily Dickinson and Frances Cornford.
She is more cautious in the sense that she evades metaphor (Dickinson's strength) and the robust domesticity of Mrs Cornford.* Her
learning is fertilized by feminism. Her femininity consists in magnanimity—her readiness to entertain her experience; to her, science
is not a *weltanschauung*, nor is nature a mine of symbols awaiting
exploitation. Science is a means to sympathetic understanding and
nature is to be invited, rather than forced, to enrich the personality.
She considers what T. S. Eliot adopts as symbolism and Edwin
Muir relegates into fable. She remains juridical: her poems are full
of natural breaks, moments when she seems to stop or deflect the
action when it threatens to run away into some emotional orgy or
facile absolute. Admitting the maximum of emotion—and it is
feminine emotion, taking more and staking more than masculine

* Like most poets who anthologize easily, Mrs Cornford had the bad luck to be
identified with her indiscretions—chiefly 'O fat white woman . . .' This sport is
dropped from her collected volume, which should be relished in full.

At the time of writing, I did not know the work of Lilian Bowes Lyon (*Collected
Poems*, intr. C. Day Lewis, 1948) to which I was introduced by Anne Treneer's
article in *The Poetry Review* in 1964. Superfine strength, technical agility, and considerate brain put Lilian Bowes Lyon high on the roll of honour. She is near
Rosenberg in her power to render elusive, far-sighted perceptions as it were corporeal and imagistic. To face death with such good faith and taste, and to remain
completely sensitive, was to make tragedy a fine art.

affection or feeling—she knows, by a sort of matriarchal good sense, how to accommodate it.

Miss Raine's first book, *Stone and Flower* (1943), displays some of the temptations she has overcome. There is a note of virginal savagery, of plangent yearning and emotional pronunciamento. In *Invocation* she woos inspiration by offering herself as a sacrifice; the orgy of dismemberment comes over as a petulant masochism; the psychological motif is valid to the point of being trite, nor is the treatment complicated or impersonal enough to make it interesting. It is the landscape of her native and ancestral Northumberland, 'the strength of the hard rock / the deafening stream of wind / that carries sense away / swifter than flowing blood' which endows the poetess with staying power. 'Since I must love your north / Of darkness, cold, and pain . . . let me love true worth' (*To My Mountain*). 'Loving' is the initiative which makes nature an agent in the development of personality. Our identity is defined by the difference of pace and potentiality between ourselves and the world:

> *O lovely earth, with richer life than mine,*
> *whose teeming seas and blooming fields decline*
> *slowly into stillness, yet remain!*
>
> (*Desire*)

Yet language is not a helpless echo: it is (my italics) 'the *authentic* utterance of cloud / The speech of flowing water' which articulates the natural and thus, while remaining near to it, translates it in a moral sense:

> *Words say, waters flow,*
> *rocks weather, ferns wither, winds blow, times go,*
> *I write the sun's Love, and the stars' No.*
> (*Night in Martindale*)

The imagination is neither alienated from nature nor displaced in society (as it often is when these ideas are treated by Rilke) and man's capacity to 'dream' becomes, not so much traumatic or magical, as an enlargement of consciousness as natural as the breathing of the fish in the stream:

> *Against the flowing stream, its life keeps pace*
> *with death—the impulse and the flash of grace*
> *hiding in its stillness, moves, to be motionless . . .*
>
> *It lies unmoved, equated with the stream,*
> *as flowers are fit for air, man for his dream.*
> (*In the Beck*)

The masculine urge to differentiation is offset by a return to the feminine. The end of male technological curiosity is the attempt to rape the cosmos—the waste of funds which could be devoted to medical research, the poisoning of the earth in the lunacy of competition. Kathleen Raine is free to create in the knowledge that nature is neither an enemy to be outmanœuvred nor an exhibition of symbols to prop the failing intellect: it exists in her, as gravid stasis as well as the 'difference in pace and potentiality':

> *The memory of earth is like a burden*
> *Of waves and islands, in my blood and bone*
> *The heavy substance of my incarnation.*
>
> (*Azrael*)

Dichotomies and nostalgias which vex the male intellect are relished, as things in themselves, in her vision; they lose none of their force and sharpness. There is a critical demand that to be 'good' a poem must juxtapose antinomies and then resolve them in a *dennoch preisen* affirmation, a demand which inherits great prestige from poems like *Le Cimetière Marin* and *Among School Children,* but is not necessarily valid for lesser poets and has been known to sponsor evasion of difficulties and disingenuous exhibitionism. Miss Raine tends to keep the antinomies apart for a deliberate purpose. *The Sphere* looks like a lament over change—'the certainty of being . . . ourselves, perfect at last, affirmed as what we are'. The world 'stands still while lovers kiss' and moves on, leaving us questioning the validity of the felicitous moments. Because there is 'no end, no ending' and the hours 'succeed each other' the job of the poem is to resurrect the incidents—'steps of a dance, petals of flowers, phrases of music' and remind us that *they* constitute 'our single soul'. The poem shows a won, integral confidence founded neither on the exploitation, nor the banishment, of what threatens, but rather its contemplation from a source of defended strength. *The Unseen Rose* (in the second book, *Living in Time,* 1946) depicts a phase of alienation in love. Although 'five wide deserts of the senses open' there is no point in repining, rather a resigned wholeness of the senses, unmaliciously rendered here, which can abolish sentiment and give courage—'If you were near / It would not change this peace / Or break the living silence of my house / Where no sense stirs to tell me you are distant'.

Love Poem may be compared with Edwin Muir's 'Yours, my love, is the right human face'. Muir equates the girl with an ideal person in a world of (presumably) defectives, he hails her as a clue in the labyrinth. Miss Raine's lover is 'the face that the earth turns to me', no respite or ideal. The lover stands for an immediacy—

'when your hand touches mine, it is the earth / That takes me'—
which mediates the past and future, 'the green graves / And children still unborn, and ancestors' and even the creation—'those
paternal fingers, streaming through the clouds / That break with
light the surface of the sea'. The meaning of this 'presence' is endurance—'where I trace your body with my hand / Love's presence
has no end'. Miss Raine's ability to regain the past, master the
turbulence which specified it, and then modestly withdraw is clear
in *For Posterity* (on a drawing of Patterdale in 1830):

> *All life, tumbled together in a storm*
> *And the crags stand out clear in the lightning.*
> *The wind, like a bolting horse, pounds down the valley,*
> *The sheep, like vegetation, draw to earth,*
> *And trees, like animate things, tear at their roots and groan.*

> *That was in 1830. That storm long since was over.*
> *So, my tempestuous love, closed in a quiet book,*
> *And in a quiet grave, disturbs no heart but yours,*
> *Reader, stretched on the summer grass*
> *Waiting for tea-time, and shadows growing longer.*

Pusillanimous variations on the last lines would fill much *bien
pensant* verse. The poetess exposes the violent forces lurking behind
a genteel scene; gives full rein to the thusness—the presence—of the
vanished storm; invites the reader to balance between the 'tempes-
tuousness' and the 'quietness' of her closed book; then leaves the
whole experience in the reader's hands. The key verb is *disturbs*:
by speaking with such self-effacement from (as it were) beyond the
grave the poem makes the situation provocatively elusive *and*
immediate; the reader may not realize that he, still living, is being
challenged about his faith in the power of art (even at two removes
—a poem about a drawing) to transmit the force of the transitory;
and he may miss the irony of the last lines.

Miss Raine's eye for mutability, her consciousness of attrition,
her urge to classify phenomena means that when she attempts a
social theme she is prone to indulge in a gloating lament over fallen
man ('the never recurring productions of human history reflect only
fallen man'). The London Fire Raids evoke 'a storm of hours has
shaken the finespun world'; this seems too general and too precious
to be relevant. (One turns from this to Dylan Thomas's and Louis
MacNeice's poems on the London Blitz, which voice the heightened
heroic compassion and the spectacular vitality which do exist in
these tragedies and are best recognized.) Miss Raine tends to see
people as types rather than characters. In *Heroes* she revels in

dissolution—'Who sifting the Libyan sand can find / The tracery
of a human hand . . . the fade-out of a soldier's daydream'. Miss
Raine cannot resist reminding war widows that 'you'll know your
love no more', nor such Sitwellian afflatus as 'the seed of man is
ravished by the corn'. Her categorical thinking as a scientist, her
spontaneity as a poet, here scorn the individual and the particular.
Her third book, *The Pythoness* (1949), is perhaps too open to arche-
typal symbols, dream and the unconscious. But if Miss Raine is
pedantic about dead soldiers, she is equally harsh on herself:

> *God in me the four elements of storm*
> *Raging in the shelterless landscape of the mind*
> *Outside the barred doors of my Goneril heart.*
>
> (*Storm*)

A kind of indirected pantheism goes beyond gentility into
paganism; that discipline of accuracy, Miss Raine's emotional
scholarship—'the four elements of storm'—is strict enough to contain
the threat of chaos and the conviction of guilt. In *The Journey* there
is a frankness of abandonment to the menacing macabre which,
coming from such a proud, meticulous sensualist, is honest:

> *At nightfall in an empty kirk*
> *I felt the fear of all my deaths:*
> *Shapes I had seen with animal eyes*
> *Crowded the dark with mysteries.*

The mesmeric terror arouses a harping on the image—'I was
the dying animal / Whose cold eye closes on a jagged thorn /
Whose carcass soon is choked with moss / Whose skull is hidden by
the fern'. At these crises the angel, the dream, nature in (now)
impartial aspect—'birds sing their phrases from green places'—and
the 'mute things of home that anger has assailed' may restore the
sense of sanity and roots; they absolve one from the secular error of
having frequented the morbid. Such 'radical innocence'—Yeats's
sense of what is left as invincible after superficial happiness has been
burned away—implies a freshness, a change, both in the psyche and
in the out-there arrangements which it contemplates (see *Absolution*).
Miss Raine feels no need to transgress her limits; having affirmed
her kinship with nature, she looks to it for an answer. Far from
descending from on high, her 'angel' is the moment of conscious
enjoyment of enjoyment (or admiration, a pleasure of intelligence)
and her 'dream' refreshes her roots by exposing her to the unsettling
influx of her own past, that of her ancestors, and, dubiously since
it entails Jung, that of the race. The dream may be traumatic as
well as delightful, but it is beneficent—for it opens a window upon

the past and makes it available to contemplation, and this, of course, throws revealing light upon the present. In *The Invisible Spectrum* the poetess justifies the dream as 'a mode of being', illumination not escape. After the 'seventh colour' lies darkness; beyond sound exists 'silence audible to bats / And deep-sea fish that feel the throb of waves'; beyond sense are 'the spinning spheres'. The dream should be as natural, as expected. And as the dream refines the past, it is the task of the word to read the open secret of nature—'hieroglyph in whose exact precision is defined / Feather and insect-wing, refraction of multiple eyes . . . myriadfold vision of the world'. The danger of murdering to dissect is banished at the point where man overtakes his environment, responds to it, and makes it perform services for himself alone:

> *Word that blazes out the trumpet of the sun,*
> *Whose silence is the violin-music of the stars,*
> *Whose melody is the dawn, and harmony the night.*
> (*Word made Flesh*)

The responsibility before truth, the exactions of imagination, are reconciled in the word's 'statement of mystery'. 'A spirit clothed in world—a world made man'.

Winter Fire shows Miss Raine accepting natural law and quietly dominating it. Fire is 'the presence of nature in my winter room', it is 'older and more wild' than the lakes, fells, and clouds the curtains hide. It will outlast them all, take them all—'spring blossoming is the slow combustion of the tree'. The flamboyant history of fire, its power as example, its beauty—'flames more fluent than water in a mountain stream'—make the poem an eloquent celebration. *The Human Form Divine* applies the same honesty to the analysis of structures; it might be sub-titled 'the research scientist examines her conscience'. It begins with 'The human contours are so easily lost / Only close your eyes and you seem a forest / Of dense vegetation' and develops into an excited—yet still punctilious—vision of dissolving forms and analysed metabolism. 'Science applies its insect-lenses to the form divine' until for man there is nothing 'but the will of love to uphold your seeming world'. Honesty inheres in the bareness of this statement; no rhetoric ekes it out; the 'love' has been indicated in the sober verve, the respect for the object delineated in the tone of the preceding stanzas. *Isis Wanderer* orchestrates Miss Raine's urge towards a reintegration which will not debauch the facts. 'This too is an experience of the soul' it declares (note the conjunction of nouns) summoning the archetype into the arena of the present—'the dismembered world that once was the whole god'. The firmness, the topicality of the recognition stanzas echo, deliberately, the love poems and endorse the fact that the regenerative forces are *given in the situation*, and though the poem ends with an unfortunate rush into the Jungian posture—'I piece the divine fragments into the mandala' etc.—Miss Raine's female scientism (her 'experience of the soul') has presented us with enough similitude in dissimilitude to make Jung the merest sequel. The poem voices the promise of rebirth:

> *I trace the contours of his hand fading upon a cloud,*
> *And this his blood flows from a dying soldier's wound.*
> *In broken fields his body is scattered and his limbs lie*
> *Spreadeagled like wrecked fuselage on the sand.*
>
> *His skull is a bombed cathedral, and his crown's rays*
> *Glitter from worthless tins and broken glass.*
> *His blue eyes are reflected from pools in the gutter,*
> *And his strength is the desolate stone of fallen cities.*

Almost alone among her generation, Miss Raine's opening towards myth has meant that she has not been stranded by a failure of social inspiration. Her latest book, *The Year One* (1952), shows that her listing of images in sequences, the translucent, bold nominalism of her style is a bodying forth, a consolidation, of the perceived, embattled against the blurring virus of easy sentiment, totalitarian emotions, and the grandiloquent imponderables of the unconscious. Her robust, grammatically impeccable yet flexible sentence layouts, her (not always) subdued, discursive yet versatile rhetoric are above all communicative; they first unify the disparate by collecting and describing it, then evaluate it by projecting it in a variable format. In the 'Spells' and 'Incantations' nature is commanded to do things; instead of starting with a condition—love, sorrow, estrangement, sleep, anger, the need for roots—and ransacking the environment for illustrations, Miss Raine singles out those qualities of nature which are going to promote the desire or cure the problem; the pressure of multiplicity is received—and ordered into action.

Within its thematic limitations (the Rainean exclusion of 'fallen man') *Northumbrian Sequence* is one of the more interesting attempts since late Eliot at what used to be known as an 'organic' statement. Its selective basis, fluctuations of mood and unified immediacy make it more compelling than the retrospective summaries of Edwin Muir. For epigraph, it takes the Saxon myth of the bird which 'tarries for a moment in the light of the hearth-fire, then flies forth into the darkness whence it came'. The first movement evokes the poet's kinship with the materials of the creation; she feels nourished by the potent, anonymous life 'before the world began'. In the second movement she is the focus of unity, enjoying to the full the centrality of consciousness—'his radiance shines into my darkest place'. Clashing ideals, crossed lines of life, a sense of bewildering ramification, localized in finely instanced detail, ruffle the tone of the third movement. Then a resistless, incantatory rhythm heralds a tremendous storm; creation rebels against consciousness; the ghosts of ancestors walk, the unborn wail, nature rages in malevolent aspect:

> *The storm beats on my window-pane,*
> *Night stands at my bed-foot,*
> *Let in the fear,*
> *Let in the pain,*
> *Let in the trees that toss and groan,*
> *Let in the north tonight.*

Although the 'nameless formless power' opposes her 'virgin fingers' and 'fearful form', it is partly understood in the observation, and human consciousness will have to 'take pity on' the storm when the time comes to hold 'the lonely stars at rest'. Unrest keeps the mind for ever on duty; though frail, it is old in the ways of the world. In the fifth movement, an unstressed four-beat line carries the pacified elements as they unfold in the dream of the sleeper at a tree's foot on a hillside; the dream calls up, in particular images, eternal recurrence; it releases our tensions. 'As sleeper wakes from sleep, I wake from waking' announces the change to a speculative rhythm, the anticipation of death, in the last movement. Like the Saxon king buried on the moor, and 'the finer dust of his dead queen', the poetess must lose 'the house that has sheltered me since I was born' and the 'body that was imperfect from the first'. The frailty of the body is compensated by wonder, the renunciation by a sense of abundant life, creating new being for others as it 'shatters every form'.

The tactful acceptance of declining power—no moaning—is a constituent of dignity which Miss Raine repeats in the life of sensation, where most masculine poets have by this stage relapsed into nostalgia or self-pity. What harm is there in asking 'where are those dazzling hills touched by the sun?'; it is vital to relate the facts:

> *O storm and gale of tears, whose blinding screen*
> *Makes weather of grief, snow's drifting curtain*
> *Palls the immortal heights once seen.*
> *Hidden is the heart.*
>
> (*Lament*)

A model of rhythmic control, *Rock*, states 'there is stone in me that knows stone / Substance of rock that remembers the unending / Simplicity of rest / While scorching suns and ice-ages . . .' This condition of arrest endues patience; it must not importune 'the pulsing, the awakening, the taking wing'. The theme is repeated— 'all that is in me of the rock'—with such veneration that it creates a natural rightness equal in value with the 'awakening'. *Introspection* is a confession of guilt, fear, regrets, 'the unbidden anguish, when the fair moon / Rises over still summer seas, and the pain / Of sunlight scattered in vain on spring grass'. In the same tone of discovery, she adds that 'sense endures no extremities', and that death is 'the deepest knowledge of all you will ever unfold'. The timing of the reflection symbolizes the refusal of extremism, the readiness to research a passion for knowledge. Both qualities animate that faith in conscious union which is Miss Raine's special gift— 'Because I love / The iridescent shells upon the sand / Take forms as fine and intricate as thought' (*Amo Ergo Sum*).

Kathleen Raine's most startling poem is *The Holy Shroud*. This has the same topical, almost journalistic background as a poem we discuss later—the *Church Going* of Philip Larkin.* The origin of *The Holy Shroud* was the report that Cardinal Montini preached about the alleged shroud of Christ. Where the seriousness of *Church Going* depends on the proposition that organized Christianity is obsolete, the seriousness of *The Holy Shroud* depends on the *fact* that, if not 'true', Christianity is still an awesome force which demands to be reckoned with. (William Empson treats the same idea with more virulence.) As Larkin resists the temptation to administer the *coup de grâce*, so Miss Raine resists the temptation to dramatize the awesomeness. Nor is it necessary to invoke a Keatsian suspension of belief or disbelief, for the poems themselves, operating within their terms of reference, constitute the seriousness of their themes, so that the issue of belief gives way to the poetry—to perceptions subtler and more important; we are given clear sharp lessons in what poetry is. Both poets pay their respects to Christianity: that of taking it seriously, Miss Raine the mystique, Mr Larkin the institution. We are led to feel that religion, in its decline, is more meaningful than in the days when we thought we knew all about it. Dozens of vatic ranters could enjoy a not very classical *walpurgisnacht* on Miss Raine's subject. Her virtue is to be crystal clear, yet mysterious: thus terrifying. The features on the shroud are indescribable *because the imprint is vague*. Miss Raine does not dream up a 'description' of the

---

* Readers may care to look up p. 232. I try to indicate the range of different effects which may be won from an apparently unpropitious theme by good poets who, by average criteria, seem to have little in common.

ineffable: she gazes at a face which could be divine; her thoughtful concepts equal an emotional description, distinct yet reserved. The probing, attentive rhythm of the first eight-line sentence, at once respectful and inquisitive, is a technique for communicating the *effort* of comprehension, an honest yearning; the theme is presented with a resolve which distances both faith and scepticism:

> *Face of the long-dead*
> *Floating up from under the deep waves*
> *Of time, that we try to see,*
> *To draw towards us by closer looking, that fades*
> *And will not become more clear than shadow,*
> *Mist gathering always like dusk round a dead king,*
> *That face, however closely we look, is always departing,*
> *Neither questions nor answers us.*

The second movement evaluates the research in the same tone of cautious deference, but the rhythm is a little fractured, as it were disturbed from within by a growing terror which has to be accepted with dignity although not fully conscious; at last, the ineluctable and tragic drum-beat of the caesura:

> *It is still,*
> *It is whole, has known, loved, suffered all*
> *And un-known all again.*
> *That face of man*
> *Un-knows us now; whatever being passed*
> *Beyond that holy shroud into the mind of God*
> *No longer sees this earth: we are alone.*

Awe, profound enough to be religious, is balanced by candour, brave enough to be human. An awareness more provocative than either denial or belief is distilled: the frightening sense that something has been, perhaps *still is*—something akin to the echo in *A Passage to India*—a sort of blind power between the undiscoverable and the certain, the stable, 'the mind of God'. This makes the 'we are alone' discharge great force: life is very important, it is also utterly trivial; and whichever sphere we inhabit we make the choice alone.

This excursus into *ultima thule* breaks new ground; it is the transience of the trained mind contemplating the known which is Miss Raine's normal habitat. *The Moment* ('Never, never again / This moment, never / These slow ripples / Across smooth water / Never again these / Clouds white and grey') seems more tragic because the mystery subsists in what our senses confirm—our compulsory removal from a world we enjoy, and the transience of those moments of enjoyment. To know that nature, also, is in Rilke's phrase 'always taking leave' brings a resolute acceptance which, precluding lament and rhetoric, raises the status of man: for it is man's privilege to be the *only watcher*. The moments of analysis ('here coincide / The long histories / Of forms recurrent / That meet at a point / And part in a moment') are reintegrated by the episodes of attention ('White gulls / Leisurely wheeling' etc.). And we are told why this vigilance dignifies man:

> *The sun that rose*
> *From the sea this morning*
> *Will never return,*
> *For the broadcast light*
> *That brightens the leaves*
> *And glances on water*
> *Will travel tonight*
> *On its long journey*
> *Out of the universe,*
> *Never this sun,*
> *This world, and never*
> *Again this watcher.*

HOW NOT TO FLY: ROBERT GRAVES, NORMAN CAMERON, WILLIAM EMPSON

IN a poem on the angular flight of butterflies, Robert Graves commends the creature and himself for 'a just sense of how not to fly'. Graves rejected the mindless harmonies and pointless forms rampant in 1914, but he never rebounded into experiment for its own sake. The reason was emotional, not strategic: Graves had something to say and got on with saying it, so that his hard, flexible line, his rebarbative tone, and his richly suggestive, on purpose adult vocabulary, vivified by his appetite for idioms, articulate perfectly his vagaries of feeling and contours of thought. They articulate rather than reflect it; his poems are not pictures of experience but voice poems which follow the tonal variations of vital, educated speech. His work is hewn in an abrasive grit which renders it the reverse of soporific. We are made to try. We are conscious, in the act of reading, of difficulty just overcome, of a reined anfractuous quality which is most flattering to the effort of comprehension. His strict forms, though variable, are *chosen*, as a climber chooses a rockface to prove himself on a problem judged to be just within his prowess. The Gravesian voice seems to be talking about values in crucial situations created by the exigencies of his style. Bold verbs, capacious nouns, and true adjectives are sited on idioms which are timed with wicked cunning—'this night-seed knew no discontent', 'a single heart that grieves / For lost honour among thieves', 'the wit well-timed', 'wise after the event, by love withered', 'Socrates and Plato burked the issue'—or known literary, or even scholastic, imagery—'By love we disenthralled our natural terror / From every comfortable philosopher / Or tall, grey doctor of divinity'.

Graves declares that his poems 'have never adopted a foreign accent or colouring; they remain true to the Anglo-Irish poetic tradition into which I was born'. Graves is as disabused as Yeats of the pixilating style still known to cross the water. Both poets share the same all-defences-down pride—'proud remnants of a visionary race'—as if they were wooden-wall flagships, bombarded by ironclads, going down with colours flying, a carriage which seems to invite allies but is in fact severe, aloof, a little crotchety, because founded on a minority code of behaviour. Yeats and Graves dramatize situations—they manœuvre sensibility into contexts where it must act, behave, or throw in the sponge; both fix the essence of an incident by making it hieratic and ceremonial; and this, as in all rituals, honours the subject while it asserts the apart-ness of the celebrant:

> *The North Wind rose: I saw him press*
> *With lusty force against your dress,*
> *Moulding your body's inward grace*
> *And streaming off from your set face . . .*
> *O wingless Victory, loved of men,*
> *Who could withstand your beauty then?*
> *(Love in Barrenness)*

Lovers become adepts, or fallen angels, beliefs become principles, a quarrel may illustrate some general truth and be recalled years later:

> *Green things, you are already there enrolled.*
> *And should a new resentment gnaw in me*
> *Against my dear companions of that journey*
> *(Strangers already then, in thought and deed)*
> *You shall be advocates, charged to deny*
> *That all the good I lived with them is lost.*
> *(Fugitive Firs)*

Yeats, borne forward by his late-flowering lyric impulse, sings the pride and drama until it becomes a tragic assertion of doomed values. Graves ironizes: not against himself, but to outwit external threats; and his values seem far from doomed. Decadence may hide the principle of continuity from which a vital future may derive; in *Ancestors* he attacks the dipsomania of forbears with Jonsonian largesse; though wise to his knavish tricks, Graves is of the Devil's party. In *A Country Mansion* wit about the guilt-ridden absentee heir is checked by instinctive pounce on the focus of growth; if the house *is* Britain, so much the better:

> *A smell of mould from loft to cellar,*
> *Yet sap still brisk in the oak*
> *Of the great beams: if ever they use a saw*
> *It will stain, as cutting a branch from a green tree.*

Graves is an eccentric in the true sense that the juggernaut of popular capitalism must recognize as inimical. When all beliefs have gone, only the upsetting individual is left to remind the con-formists that standards exist. 'The pavement-feet', 'lift-faces' and "sick words' in parliament 'rule a dust-bin world', yet when 'healthy words or people' dine 'there is love-taste' and understanding is real. Graves is eccentric because he achieves maximum personality *within the limits of the sane* without resorting to artificial aids (if he did he would be a fraud or a crank—his White Goddess rig-up, like Yeats's Vision, is a set of instructions for a poetic do-it-yourself kit). The eccentric makes singularity noticeable because, being sane, he wins the hostile respect of the less daring; the dilettante is accepted because lack of what it takes absolves him from threatening the conformists. (In *It Was All Very Tidy* death the bourgeois is 'unexceptionable', discreet, timid, a model bureaucrat shocking because so invincibly characterless.) As congenial as Graves's eccentricity is his amateurism. One hastens to add that the poems are craftsmanlike to the letter—there is no genteel reserve, unless it be the reserve of the guardian who is not going to waste his time with fools and cowards. By amateur one means a blend of seriousness with informality, that for Graves poems are by-products of private thought, which is the quest for understanding, and the business of living, which is the quest for maturity. His *Collected Poems* represent a development, not a 'career'. For him the act of creation calls for the most subtle, rigorous, and discriminating use of language different in effect from other uses, but this is not driven by his desire to write or belief that he can do so: the resort to verse is commanded by some occasional crisis which Graves wants to investigate in terms of what poetic language can do. He talks about his material in the tones that he would use in life; it is the treatment, the demeanour which is revealing.

A vivacious poem, full of virile impressions and sensitive charity, is *The Last Day of Leave*—'Our tragic day, bountiful from the first' full of 'our braggadocio under threat of war'. ('The basket had been nobly filled'.) Graves has written that the war, in which he fought in the trenches, 'permanently changed my outlook on life'.* It made Herbert Read determined on social reform, and to use, in the end, poetry as a substitute for Arcadia. For ornaments of the Establishment it was an invite to an egregious love-affair with the Edwardian façade the war destroyed. Graves is more liberal. From the outset he has been conscious of the void and what can fill it—as late as 1961 he knew 'pain, that unpurposed, matchless elemental / Stronger than fear or grief, stranger than love'. The

---

* Asked to speak at a War Memorial service, Graves relates in *Goodbye to All That*, 1929, how 'instead of Rupert Brooke on the glorious dead, I read some of the more painful poems by Sassoon and Wilfred Owen . . .'
Most autobiographies by poets (in this century) read like farewells to art or over-written apologias. Graves is the poet off the job, relaxed, still truthful. His premature tempering, his trench life, is a cause of the classlessness, anti-prudery, and spiritual fortitude of his later poems. The earlier—mainly public school—chapters prove that these qualities were not inculcated.

abominable is never scotched; it lurks under complacent surfaces—
'Be assured, the Dragon is not dead / But once more from the
pools of peace / Shall rear his fabulous green head'. In *Mermaid,
Dragon, Fiend* he tells how he laughed at the fables of childhood,
but 'had cause indeed for fear' for the monstrous was 'bound by
natural laws'. In woods he apprehended 'old gods almost dead,
malign / Starving for unpaid dues'. Jesus Christ wanders in a
haunted wilderness accompanied by a 'guileless young scapegoat';
in *An English Wood* 'small pathways idly tend / Towards no fearful
end' yet it is Graves's art to put this over in a breathless, apprehensive, nervous rhythm; *A Frosty Night, The Country Dance, Unicorn
and White Doe* mix the delightful with the macabre in the innocent-
seeming manner of nursery rhymes. The war matured, perpetuated
and democratized Graves's sense of evil destiny. 'He becomes dull,
trusting to his clear images / I become sharp, mistrusting my
broken images'.

Graves aimed 'to manifest poetic faith by a close and energetic
study of the disgusting'. The motor of this 'study' is that facts, in
their obtuseness, cannot be spirited away, glamorized or by-passed;
they are themselves terrifying; Graves will communicate alarm in
the most steadfast of descriptions:

> *The full moon easterly rising, furious,*
> *Against a winter sky ragged with red;*
> *The hedges high in snow, and owls raving—*
> *Solemnities not easy to withstand:*
> *A shiver wakes the spine.*
>
> (*A Love Story*)

But this menace is the spur, an ironic rationale, to activity, to
work, to physical transcension of the disgusting. The prospects may
be discouraging, but what we have to do, since there is nothing
else to do, should be done consciously and decently:

> *Trudge, body, and climb, trudge and climb,*
> *But not to stand again on any peak of time:*
> *Trudge, body!*
>
> *With no more hours of hope, and none of regret,*
> *Before each sun may rise, you salute it for set:*
> *Trudge, body!*
>
> (*Trudge, body!*)

He has the tools to finish the job. In poems of sexual guilt and
revulsion such as the *The Succubus, Leda,* and *Down, Wanton, Down!*
obsession with the facts is relieved by a brazen stock-taking and

unrepentant self-examination. The fantasy—whether it be idealiza-
tion or recoil—is acted out, as always in Graves, so that depression
is transformed into adventure. And all the poet's historical imagination and sensual prowess is mobilized to set the stage for this acting
out. For Graves, dread, conflict, the simplest daily worries, disgusts,
and irritations are experiences to be tamed in allegory, personi-
fication, happening; then civilized by irony, so that the evil is
neutralized and we are left with its power to shake complacency,
to stimulate. *Lollocks* gives us the anatomy of the heartache and the
thousand natural shocks—'nasty together / In the bed's shadow',
'Dreams of vexation suddenly recalled / In the middle of the
morning' and so on. The spiritual rogue's gallery is reviewed with a
genial wariness, as if the poet was greeting old but untrustworthy
friends; we are then urged to apply the 'Sovereign against Lollocks'
—disciplined daily action. *Certain Mercies* uses prison conditions to
symbolize the sly triumph of spirit over body in introspectives;
minor favours and respites 'pamper' the spirit with 'obscure, proud
merit' till it forgets 'each new indignity' humiliating the body.
Doubts, dualities, paralysing feebler minds, are taken in charge by
Graves; they are made tolerable:

> *A view of three shires and the sea!*
> *Seldom so much at once appears*
> *Of the coloured world, says heart.*
> *Head is glum, says nothing.*
> (*To Walk on Hills*)

Later the legs 'sprawl in a rock's shelter' and the head is 'at last
brought low'. From this position it distorts the view into fantasy,
so Graves goes one better by putting (we feel) his tongue in his
cheek with 'have you known shepherds? / And are they not a witless
race / Prone to quaint visions?' *To Evoke Posterity* and *To Bring the
Dead to Life* are satirical working models of a hollow future which
end with cheerful renunciation; a man who has declined to air
himself 'along the promenade' in life will not covet a stained
statue in death; by concentrating on a dead man, blowing on his
'embers' you may start 'a live flame' but will have to lie in his
graveclothes (literary critics take note). There is no imposed system,
no instalment-plan philosophizing. The poet's 'factual universe' is
austere and ill-disposed: it distrusts the luxury of summer—'the
windows frame a prospect of cold skies'. Practical values are
mooted, rather than ordained, by the gradual amassment of
apprehended episodes. Because Graves never exploits rhetorically
the nasty, any more than he decorates sentimentally the nice, he

is justified when, after admitting his failings, he tells us of his triumphs:

> *We were in love; he with her, she with him,*
> *And I, the youngest one, the odd man out,*
> *As deep in love with a yet nameless muse.*
>
> *Deep water and a shelving bank.*
> *Off went our clothes and in we went, all five*
> *Diving like trout between the lily groves.*
>
> (*The Last Day of Leave*)

The exhilaration of sexual emancipation (of the beneficiaries of the collapse of Victorian *mores*, Graves is one of the few who retain the splendour while relinquishing the taboos); moments of happiness when the imagination, having traversed horror, basks in a vision which is reward rather than escape, when 'the untameable, the live, the gentle' stir 'my loving admiration, that you should travel / Through nightmare to a lost and moated land / Who are timorous by nature'; quickness to divine the imaginative drama, the operative good, in dubious situations, 'For love it shone, never for the madness / Of a strange bed— / Light on my finger, fortune in my head'; those rare, total communications which justify friendship, often sponsored by landscape, 'O the clear moment, when from the mouth / A word flies, current immediately / Among friends'; and an aptitude for repose, for equilibrium, in a semiwakeful, yet attentive and fertile state:

> *O gracious, lofty, shone against from under,*
> *Back-of-the-mind-far clouds like towers;*
> *And you, sudden warm airs that blow*
> *Before the expected season of new blossom,*
> *While sheep still gnaw at roots and lambless go—*

All these are built-in stabilizers in his Emergency Poetic Economy whereby, converting feeling into experience, he evokes the wonder in the act of experiencing. The wonder beats deep in the heart of a poem, 'sister of the mirage and echo', beneath the gristle of phrase, the flesh of an adjective, and the bony structure of verbs we cannot escape. Graves's pagan spirit of poetry, 'wild and innocent, pledged to love / Through all disaster' is a demi-goddess, sojourning on earth without divine favours, reviled by 'other women' and most men, trusted and dangerous—and offering, to the poet of all people, more than human gifts. One outcast challenges another to prove himself; through encounter the poet forgets himself, becomes what he is—'the just man justices / Keeps grace . . .' as Hopkins put it in his way. Casually overheard the talk, being vehement, sounds like rhetoric, but *listened* to it is no vulgar stunt to catch the eye, just astute, thewed speech which dazzles as it thrills the mind's eye.

In *Rhea* the 'mother-mind', a kind of headstrong calm amid the storm, views the destructive flux as 'mishap'—yet 'she nothing cares' since she reserves a greater power to do harm and give pleasure. 'In a half-smile archaic, her breast bare / Hair astream'. Despite Mr Graves's anathema ('poor, sex-starved D. H. Lawrence') it is a picture out of Lawrence's praise of Etruscan painting. The enclosure of repose with vigour in 'astream', juxta-placed (more than 'posed') after the wise, abandoned passiveness and the placing of *that* athwart the uproar of the elements is what generates the strength. The complete word in the compelling place, and both unusual, is Graves's way of making it new.

When the episodes jostle each other Graves obviates muddle by introducing a crisis, felt in the present. The *Pier Glass* depends on this method. Its locale, the 'lost manor where I walk continually', is distanced enough to seem legendary, yet the poet is 'drawn by a web of time-sunk memory' which the legend reinforces; remembered fact and childish reverie unite; and this forms a rich contrasting background, pregnant with suggestion, for the announcement of truth:

> *Is there no life, nothing but the thin shadow*
> *And blank foreboding, never a wainscot rat*
> *Rasping a crust? Or at the window-pane*
> *No fly, no bluebottle, no starveling spider?*
> *The windows frame a prospect of cold skies*
> *Half-merged with sea, as at the first creation—*
> *Abstract, confusing welter.*

That done, Graves describes, peering into the glass, the ravages of time and delivers his appeal for renewal—'true life, natural breath'. The appeal comes with a whole imaginative saga behind it. *The Presence* is another unforgettable multiple episode, culminating in catharsis. At first we are uncertain whether the woman *is* dead, 'rotted underground'; next the poet, guilty, distraught, in love, behaves as if she were alive; finally, he cannot be 'deaf or blind' because 'horror of the grave maddens the mind' with the 'same pangs' which 'altered her substance, and made sport of death'. Again the bitterness of facts, openly faced, presages real conquest; the macabre wins a Pyrrhic victory, since by forcing the poet to re-enact the past, to recreate the woman, it convinces him of the justice of his grief and pays tribute to the dead.

Compared with Yeats, Graves lacks civic passion, self-transformation, and the epical symbolizing and dramatizing power.

Compared with Eliot he lacks range of thought, ethical finesse, and the gift for simile and analogy. Compared with both, he has no need of the supernatural, the superhuman, and the esoteric to make his ripeness all; he is less of a great poet in the inaccessible sense, he is more of a recognizable being. He has mastered a generous humanism through a self-education in poetry as ascetic and passionate as Paul Valéry's. Thanks to his refusal to create a world fit for heroes to swagger in, he creates a world where venturesome modern men—with their not ignoble limitations and opportunities—are doing distinct things in contexts we all share, or could share if we had the audacity to shake the dust from our feet and strike out on 'the heavenly causeway'. And it is a generous humanism, which can comprehend the next man's insights without perforce accepting them. It is a form of greatness to be able to own, in our time, lines like these:

> *Though in what listening horror for the cry*
> *That soars in outer blackness dismally,*
> *The dumb blind beast, the paranoiac fury:*

> *Be warm, enjoy the season, lift your head,*
> *Exquisite in the pulse of tainted blood,*
> *That shivering glory not to be despised.*

*　　　*　　　*

The poetry of Norman Cameron (1905–1953) is a variation on a theme of Robert Graves; the use of real-life, historical, and geographic 'hosts' for elucidating spiritual states and moral questions. Facts become the outward and visible sign of an inward and spiritual grace or disgrace. Cameron's narratives are faithful to the host material, and the moral, as in fairy tales, is partly a riddle which awaits the degree of level head and imaginative acumen we devote to construing its meaning. Nor are the poems primarily metaphoric, since they do not create a unity by reconciling disparate elements; Cameron disregards the emotional denominator between incompatibles: he tells an anecdote, embroils the mind, erects difficulties, lays traps for the unwary, nonchalantly provides a clue, sometimes indicates a resolution. The poems are like a modern *Pilgrim's Progress* or spiritual obstacle race. Cameron's attraction is a blend of sardonic geniality with respect for the reader, who is left free to jump the obstacles in his own way and congratulate himself, more or less self-righteously, on safe arrival.

This raconteur objectifies dualities, complexes, weaknesses, of the type which are potent yet elusive and thus intolerable. (The enemy broke Cameron's defences in the end, for in 1950 he consented to psychoanalysis, became a Roman Catholic, stopped writing.) The alternative with such material would be to exalt it into tragedy, as Hopkins did in the Terrible Sonnets, or shrug it off with frivolous conceits, but Cameron, bereft of binding moral criteria or systematic beliefs, refused to fake the absolute, ideal standard required to see his problems as tragic; and he had enough self-respect and social conscience to decline to bury his head in the sand of a foppish inwardness. Finding hosts for his beggars, he transfers them to the democratic arena, addresses us in the *lingua franca* of common sense and common knowledge and challenges us, with a wink in his eye, while avoiding the embarrassment of intimacies.

Many of Cameron's hosts enjoy a reputation. His art is to persuade us to apply his themes afresh, to new hurdles, to guess new meanings. The fun begins with this last, which can tell us a lot about the man who guesses. In *Virgin Russia* a scorched earth policy repels the invading armies. The joke is that the invader also crushes his own 'rich cornlands', the lesson is that rash strivings after the unattainable ('Eldorados in the snow') boomerang on the credulous. *Decapitation of Is* depicts the 'Protean visage' of 'Is' as so disturbing that 'the axe of reason and the block of fact' are employed to execute him ('the deed is most humane; Is never feels') only to find that his neck is undiscoverable. (Cameron admits that 'Is' is vulnerable and sensitive—'Is face was working horribly'.) To save *their* face, the executioners plead that they 'had not aimed to turn him into Was'. Cameron pokes fun at logical positivism, semantics, the cult of analysis—or what you will. In *The Voyage to Secrecy* 'those in idleness' follow, *aided by instruments*, the explorer's progress. 'How many days the voyage to secrecy?' The explorer may get out of range— 'When shall their compasses strain wide and crack / And alien milestones, with strange figures / Baffle the sagest of geographers?' Intuition, adventure, research, and perhaps art, can still have the manners and skill to elude the mob of onlookers, cynics, and robots who try to explain them away.

The Thespians at Thermopylae points out that the bravery of men of business, the Spartans, is compulsory and thus not admirable; the real scandal is that of mental workers of 'sober-witted judgment' who 'chose the Spartan way' instead of the 'many roads', who surrendered to convention instead of faring forward. *Fight with a Water Spirit* is about the comedy of moral initiation. The poet first detects, then tackles, the 'jeering water-ghost' that 'denies' his 'true conquest of the stream'. In this fight, he is the first traveller in the ring; he wins, but the opponent resurrects. The incident is maturing because it brings a sense of disillusionment consoled by a challenge accepted, an ironic fulfilment, a triumph within; there are no spectators. 'No use to fight / Better to give the place a holy name / Go on with less ambition than I came'. *Rhinegold* likewise modernizes myth: the answer to *Virgin Russia*, here effort, though wasted, tilts against phoney pretence—the cheats who 'peddle their gold-bricks in the streets'. The dive is a consummate expression of solitude, anxiety, ratiocination:

> . . . *refracted angles shine;*
> *Not all the Rhinegold in the Rhine*
> *Could tempt me further downwards. Dazed*
> *By weight of water, almost crazed*
> *By tilted and perplexing planes*
> *I seek the surface.*

Central Europe—'fat peasants winterbound'—warns of the danger of allowing habit to harden into neurosis. 'They need a wind bringing up gulls and salt / Sailors and nabobs with new foreign gifts / To blow their crannies free of ancient fear'.

Robert Graves writes in his Introduction to the poems that

> Norman called himself a part-time poet, perhaps because he was a divided character—alternately a Presbyterian precisian and moralist; and a pagan poet and boon-companion . . . he never became a schizophrene, but learned to watch the internal drama and politely introduce the irreconcilable characters, giggling: 'I'm afraid you're bound to quarrel; still, please remember that you are all me, or should one say "I"?'

Cameron's puritanism was a means to self-knowledge, rooted in a melancholia which relished the ironies of evil ('. . . set a stone and write on it / *Hic Antichristus obiit* / The verb is nothing, but the name / Remains triumphant all the same') and its tenacity ('It was taken a long time ago / The first pressure on the trigger'). The money-changers' temple, locked up since the 'scourging prophet' had cursed it, becomes a charismatic, baleful object of curiosity—'Disquiet makes us sleepy; shoddiness / Has come upon our crafts'. The perils of emancipation are painted in *Naked among the Trees* where the 'booted Puritan magistrate' did right to whip the 'naked devotees' of the sybarite who, before he was perverted into 'the drinking bouts, the boasting and the bets', had been a well-loved god.

In *The Dirty Little Accuser* the obnoxious domestic troublemaker is evicted 'to go on the parish'—and the poet misses the self-satisfaction of refuting his accusations; guilt, in *The Compassionate Fool*, causes the poet to be so nice to his 'enemy' that he attends the banquet with his eyes open and 'pities' his enemy for his 'small strategy' while he is 'stabbed through and through'. His masterpiece, *A*

Visit to the Dead, calls up a landscape of 'subtle practices', 'strict observances', 'movements faint, sparing of energy', of mock battles which 'turn inches into leagues', which is bourgeois convention as well as the limbo of the puritan conscience. The poet is sharp enough to know that he 'aped' all this 'crudely'; a cause of embarrassment —and of hope. 'A passage to the dead one's habitat / And learnt, under their tutelage / To twitter like a bat'. At the point of defeat 'the innermost resource', laughter, comes to the rescue, and the poet returns 'like Marco Polo, traveller' to tell the tale of this modern Divine Comedy. (Is it fanciful to catch in the Polo image an overtone that the hearers will deride the tale, refusing to believe that such things exist?)

Cameron stakes everything on his story; when he fails, it is because the story is too unprovocative to intrigue us and generate the meaning which transcends the story; then his poems suffer from low-pressure discursive monotony and an over-staid tone. There Cameron is no worse than much that passes muster; at best, he declares a whole reverberant judgment in terms of one focal image; it is his exhaustive, dauntless pursuit of this image's potentialities which makes the meaning reverberate. *A Modern Nightmare* shows how Satan, finding 'a rebel in his realm', tortures the rebel, makes him scream, *distorts his evidence*; the poet mocks, in *A Hook for Leviathan*, the zeal of the Super Hook manufacturers who are shocked by the suggestion that no ship can carry the Hook—'that's not our affair'; *The Firm of Happiness Limited* sees Britain as a randy, peculative corporation. While Auden's report on this theme ('Get there if you can' etc.) seems brisk to the point of being insincere, Cameron's allegory has angles teaching us a lesson which sticks—'the customers noticed the difference—to judge from the way they behaved'. These poems make shrewd comments on three emblems of our time: the hazards of conscientious revolt (could Orwell have been in mind?), the hubris of specialization, and the corruption of *laissez faire*; and they talk the same picture language as well as offering purely spiritual interpretations to those who prefer it that way. If we must have anecdotes, let us have these ideograms which are more than diary jottings. They are the products of altruistic intelligence nurtured in individual integrity:

> *'Simply as common men we came'.*
> *'How dared you, by the heroes gate?'*
> *'We purposed no heroic claim'.*
> *'But you disown it now too late'.*
>
> (*By Leave of Luck*)

*   *   *

In the 1930's W. H. Auden had his say about the failure of nerve of the Cambridge humanists—the 'Cambridge ulcer', reducing the wicked world to 'mind events', 'mental pictures', and amity. William Empson hit back in *Just a Smack at Auden* where the activists of the 30's are mocked as panic-stricken shooters in the dark, mooting hilarious courses of action because incorrect in their analysis of the facts. Empson's genial reserve is now seen to be a delayed-action tactic for the realization of something immensely significant: for Empson embodies a poetic acclimatization of liberal empiricism in a manner vital to the debate about the Two Cultures; in fact Empson, of whom C. P. Snow never appears to have heard, has anticipated and solved many of his cherished worries. Rejecting the reverberant commitment, occupied with knowledge, especially the knowledge of crisis—like Paul Valéry 'above all an intelligence'—Empson is yet orientated towards a certain, ultimately philosophical, idea of ethics and relationships which carries him through and beyond aestheticism. Bothered about what ought to be done, how, why, and when, Empson is never dogmatic; he will recommend action, seldom command it; he points out the strengths and deficiencies in given evidence, then leaves it to the reader to adjudicate without detracting from his own preferences. Empson is busied, in short, with that non-utilitarian adjustment of ends and means which ennobles the work of E. M. Forster. It could be argued —has been argued by Mr Noel Annan in his book on Leslie Stephen —that it was this spiritual probity and free-thinking puritanism which motivated respecters of science when they rescued the aesthetic movement from followers of Pater and related it to social conscience and rational disciplines.

In his poetry Empson has steered a liberal course between the 'revolutionary romp' and the neutral moral alienation of poets who came later, who should have remembered his 'it struck me trying not to fly / Let them escape a bit too far'. John Wain's essay on Empson signalled the counter-attack on the 'punch-drunk, romantic scribblers' of the 1940's. Wain quotes a forced scientific flight from Thomson's *The Seasons*, then observes:

> Who cares? It is useless merely to describe in verse the things of which science tells us, while to introduce them in the form of simile and metaphor when the poem is really about something quite non-scientific is not much better. The only way to treat such material is to form it into a series of conceits on which the general meaning of the poem can be made to turn. This was Donne's way, and it is Empson's.*

* John Wain, 'Ambiguous Gifts', *Penguin New Writing*, No. 40, 1950.

At the time this was a brave statement; it is hardly Wain's fault if some people perverted it into an excuse for turpitude.

Empson, indeed, takes the longest and closest look at science which has yet been taken in verse; and as I like to be looked in the eye, I find his level gaze more honest than Lord Snow's. By longest one means that Empson's science is not fodder for the varieties of space fiction: for him, science is here below, will outweigh party strife, condition our lives whether we like it or not. *To think in terms* of science, then, as opposed to throwing the scientific dice, may liberate science from both distrust and misuse; it may improve on acquaintance, we may begin to like it. By closest one means that Empson has taken poetry as his province for this acclimatization of science: he is the Francis Bacon of verse, and if his ideocritical books are his *Novum Organum*, his poems are his *Essays*, where his forensic concerns are not imposed upon, but found enacted in, our natural experience. New learning is judged before the bar of common sense.

One goes through three reactions to the poems—an instant general communication, preceding full understanding; trouble in construing passages; areas which remain unintelligible. The first communication is due to the thematic audacity of the poems (the 'And now she cleans her teeth into the lake' attack), the speed and timing of the syntactical footwork, counterpointed by a supple rigour of movement which keeps us on the *qui vive*, and the poet's siting of incentive: the versatility and precision whereby he prepares the swim, baiting the hook of the unfamiliar with the morsel of the mundane, gratifying our understanding while stimulating our curiosity. The 'trouble' reminds us of the readjustments of convention which the naturalization of science demands; in fact they *produce* these readjustments in the mind in a memorable way. The obscurities are irritants, question marks, escape clauses which make us see that the gap between theory and action, prejudice and knowledge, mind and nature may be absolute, or, when tackled, fruitful, but whether we shirk or try, the choice is voluntary; and the requisite to all won comprehension is effort.

The 'Why cannot the poems be simpler?' brigade fasten on the Notes, seeking to prove, in effect, that the poems equal their paraphrasable content. The Notes are not of course paraphrases but local elucidations; the distance between the Notes and the Poems is the gulf between the Two Cultures, and to use the Notes as a stick to beat the Poems is merely to aggravate one's fragmentation. What appears as learning in the Notes transmutes, through selection, abridgement, and amalgamation, into emotional drama in the Poems; and this drama is focused on a human centre—a relationship, situation, or event. The Notes aid our understanding, first through explanation, second through the ineluctable *difference* between the virgin knowledge they express and the fertilizing of this knowledge in the Poems, the transcension of science expressed in the immediate human impact. New research becomes operational, it leaves the drawing-board; assembled in one mind, for a definite purpose, at a given moment, tempered on tests, impregnated with particularity, to ask for more 'simplicity' is to broaden the paraphrasable content at the expense of the urgent human complication. Empson has provided his motto for his aesthetic—'You don't want madhouse and the whole thing there'. ('It is this deep blankness is the real thing strange / The more things happen to you the more you can't / Tell or remember even what they were.')

In *To an Old Lady* Empson equates the point reached by astronomy and physics with the paradox of old people: their frailty belied by their alarming power and confidence, the way they seem to invite help yet repel intimacy; this becomes the basis for a sort of respect with tragic undertones. From the start ('Ripeness is all; her in her cooling planet / Revere; do not presume to think her wasted') to the finish ('Strange that she too should be inaccessible / Who shares my sun. He curtains her from sight / And but in darkness is she visible') lay and professional images, coloured with a kind of pathetic grandeur ('Whose failing crops are in her sole control'), are alternated with compelling skill; as for being Audenesque this poet is capable of an astute charity (giving wit to the decadent hint of 'Ripeness is all') which moves us because it suspends judgment; the whole breathes the spirit of Graves's *A Country Mansion*:

> *No, to your telescope; spy out the land;*
> *Watch while her ritual is still to see,*
> *Still stand her temples emptying in the sand*
> *Whose waves o'erthrew their crumbled tracery;*
>
> *Still stand uncalled-on her soul's appanage;*
> *Much social detail whose successor fades,*
> *Wit used to run a house and to play Bridge,*
> *And tragic fervour, to dismiss her maids.*

Camping Out—teeth cleaned into the lake—shows how Empson galumphs through a whole argumentative paragraph, then before you can round and shout 'obscurity' he infects you with his enthusiasm, gratifies you with the pleasures of the chase. Although the sky's 'vaults are opened to achieve the Lord'—Empson elsewhere excels at this rhetorical dubbing of dubious myths, offering us, tantalizingly, a vision of lost romantic aspirations—the girl, creating *her* star-pattern out of toothpaste in the waters, reminds the poet that 'it is we soaring explore galaxies'.

The immediacy of *Camping Out* may be credited to the daring of the episode which, echoing on, predisposes us in favour of the argument in the speculative second stanza. *Legal Fiction* owes its immediacy to its authoritative pitch. This reinforces the awe inspired by the theme: our mental prospects reviewed in terms of the law of property. The symbolism is redeemed from pomp by a mephitic empiricism, a trademark of these poems (the 'You own land in Heaven and Hell' touch) and topical documentation ('Your well fenced out real estate of mind / No high flat of the nomad citizen / Looks over, or train leaves behind'). But you get more than a professional bargain: you go 'under and above' your 'claim' into a spiritual underworld where you are at one with the species—Hell, 'where all owners meet'. In the last stanza the rhetoric holds, but 'Earth's axis varies'. 'You are nomad yet' and intelligence is both a flashing lighthouse beam and a candle's shadow. Our response to the poem is unified, like the law, yet an area of freedom has been reconnoitred.

The title of the poem is doubly ironic, for there *is* a relation between man's spiritual reach and the restraints of law, a relation in part educative, since it emphasizes our responsibility for our independence ('your well fenced out real estate'), and in part cautionary, since law offers us a redoubt into which we may retreat when the mind ventures too dangerously far into Hell's 'pointed exclusive conclave'; and it is implied, with some subtlety, that if we ignore that caution we will be punished. As in Baroque art, as everywhere in Empson, intense feeling is *utilized* by splitting it up into a diaspora of intellectual detail; the impact is of a planned explosion; the nearness of the explosion enjoins a sense of balance between the counter-thrusting forces; and a metaphor about civil law attains the authority of a moral law. *Aubade* shows us a third, less ambitious, perhaps more engaging type of immediacy. The conflict between the tie-lines, 'the heart of standing is you cannot fly' and 'it seemed the best thing to be up and go' creates, like a vibrant high-tension wire, a suspended animation, and in the grotesque seriousness of his predicament the poet masters a wry candour which is meaningful because Empson is the type of man who finds words in a crisis *as it occurs*. By the end, extremes become a matter of reasonable choice, since they partake of each other's virtues: the words are far from panic-stricken: Mr Empson is not dumbfounded, he has much bizarre wisdom to impart—'the language problem but you have to try'.

Critics have complained that Empson's style is 'a splendid

weapon for avoiding commitment of any sort'. Yes, he avoids the public espousal of a system or a cause, he prefers the registry office to The Social Page. Devoted to the naturalization of science, Empson lacks the wordly-wise canniness of the lords of the Two Cultures. Snow's recipe for State success in general and his careerist in particular, becomes in Empson an inner-directed harmonization; he offers pure knowledge at a deeper level than his applied science. From this integrity, the poet moves outwards: his commitment is to people; the fact that company is present, invoked, or deferred to in many of his poems has been overlooked. That royal plural 'we' —usually a defence against insecurity—seldom mars Empson: he is the poet of 'you, your, one, I, she, it', of the primacy of the objective 'thing', his favourite word. Norman Cameron used history and geography as hosts for states of mind; Miss Raine builds herself up through a many-sided response to nature; Empson defines and evaluates other people, out there situations, with the aid of a rational discipline. Starting with the impure, he ends with pure knowledge; he takes a specialism—law, physics, astronomy, mathematics, medicine, theology, engineering—and puts it in perspective, composes it around the neglected centre of human concern without detracting from its integrity. The justice of Empson's cause is recorded in the equity of his method: in *Villanelle* ('Your chemic beauty burned my muscles through'), with *Arachne* a great love poem, and *Missing Dates* ('Slowly the poison the whole blood stream fills') the specialist images are so acclimatized that they function at parity with 'Poise of my hands reminded me of yours' and 'It is not the effort nor the failure tires', valetudinarian refrains which, unrelated to contingency, would be catastrophic; they cease to be romantic souvenirs, are emotionally decisive.*

Somewhere in the Notes, Empson identifies 'a body of people without fundamental beliefs as a basis of action'. Elsewhere reflections on Christ and 'the official and moneymaking cult of blood sacrifice' lead him to posit a cultural hope beyond nihilism—'the way earlier societies seem obviously absurd and cruel gives a kind of horror at the forces that must be at work in our own, but suggests that any society must have dramatically satisfying and dangerous conventions'. His poems are such conventions, the drama and the danger lying in the fluent style which is stressed against the strict forms. Mr Wain, in his 1950 article, discussed the form and meaning of *The Teasers* separately, and adumbrated the weakness of those who dilute empiricism into flat tones while ignoring the moral

---

* For a sceptical, and intricately argued, view of the 'naturalization of science', by Ian Hamilton, as well as much else, see *The Review: William Empson Special Number*, June 1963.

rationale of Empson's empiricism: that he works in a tradition, that of the interdependence of studies, and that in him form and content are more than usually inseparable, since his vision is dynamic—his 'style' being 'learnt from a despair'. In fact the 'crumbling' of contour, which Wain berates in *The Teasers*, reproduces the sensation of loss—'Not but they die, the teasers and the dreams'. The third half-line athwart each stanza is a rallying point, reflecting the genuineness, the irrevocableness, of the loss, isolating the 'colder lunacies', 'our claims to act', as equally real, thus endorsing the poet's claim that they 'appear so small' compared with the teasers, and enriching the command to 'make no escape' by including both claimants in the final reversal of fortune —'build up your love'.

With Thomas Hardy and the Meredith of *Modern Love*, this style explores the maximum of adventure within the limits of convention, conflict, pessimism, and the disheartening enormity of the world *per se* (see *Homage to the British Museum*). *This Last Pain* opens with one of Empson's archaic theological *trouvailles*, but now he is not tantalizing us with old wives' tales, he is introjecting the concept to leave us in no doubt about the psychological odds we face:

> *This last pain for the damned the Fathers found:*
> *'They knew the bliss with which they were not crowned'.*
> *Such, but on earth, let me foretell*
> *Is all, of heaven or of hell.*

The language game may let in a little ventilation, ' "What is conceivable can happen too" / Said Wittgenstein, who had not dreamt of you' but the draught it ushers is likely to chill the distracted individual; the best hope eschews both ancient and modern games; it is an artefact:

> *All those large dreams by which men long live well*
> *Are magic-lanterned on the smoke of hell;*
> *This then is real, I have implied,*
> *A painted, small, transparent slide.*

Such moral paradigms 'the inventive can hand-paint at leisure', or buy in 'emporia', we must 'feign then what's by a decent tact believed', 'act', 'build an edifice of form', and 'learn a style from a despair'. Once more Empson reclaims, through tactics of style, minutiae of value which the systems ignore but we cannot do without, yet is free of aestheticism because cognizant of the theory of knowledge, the history of ideas, the contingence of things, and last but not least the social world; unlike many masters, this tactician has a profound grasp of general strategy. His *confidence in the possible* is a guarantor of a refreshing amateurism, akin to Graves's (in *Sleeping Out in a College Cloister* and *Flighting for Duck* he delights us by doing his cerebral exercises in the wrong clothes, quite naturally) and justifies the throwaway, libertarian tone, ranging from the associational acute—'It is the trigger of the literary man's biggest gun / And we are happy to equate it to any conceived calm' (*Ignorance of Death*), 'It is Styx coerces and not Hell controls', through the informal incisive, 'Man, as the prying housemaid of the soul', 'Verse likes despair. Blame it upon the beer / I have mislaid the torment and the fear', to the sudden, overwhelmingly found colloquial—the 'we miss our cue' of *Villanelle*. All combine in *Arachne*, which is Empson's early *summa*. In *Long-legged Fly* W. B. Yeats saw the gay, the heroic, and the creative borne away, unawares, on the silent senselessness of time, yet opposed to the flux a flamboyant rhythmic affirmation of their finest moments. Empson accepts a limit: the renunciation of the tragic. To compensate for that loss, he digs his heels in. Man, the King Spider on 'the velvet roof of streams,' is above all *aware* of ambiguity, paradox, annihilation, their omnipresence and likelihood. He must avoid 'bird and fish . . . god and beast'—animism, barbarity, and beatitude—and 'Dance / like nine angels, on pin-point extremes'. All that unifies man is 'mutual tension', the tribe-membrane; two may enjoy 'full tension'; reduce to one, and there is chaos:

> *We two suffice. But oh beware, whose vain*
> *Hydroptic soap my meagre water saves.*
> *Male spiders must not be too early slain.*

4

BIRD'S EYE AND WORM'S EYE

Is not all life the struggle of existence, naked, timid, un-armed, but immortal, against abstract thought? All good art is experience, all popular art generalization.

W. B. YEATS

. . . some shall say So What *and some* What Matter,
Ready under new names to exploit or be exploited . . .

LOUIS MACNEICE *Epitaph for Liberal Poets*

ENGLISH AUDEN AND THE 30'S ETHOS

Last the tow-haired poet, never done
With cutting and planing some new gnomic prop
To jack his all too stable universe up:
Conduct's Old Dobbin, thought's chameleon.
Single mind copes with split intelligence . . .

C. Day Lewis: *Transitional Poem*

EVEN to begin to think about W. H. Auden is financially embarrassing, thanks to the camouflage operation which the poet has mounted to cover his retreat. When Yeats revised his early poems, he did so as a 'remaking of the self' after a lifetime of experience. Like all great tragic poets, Yeats knew himself at the end; he had no need to falsify his development because all his poems could be reviewed as steps towards integration. Auden does not know himself yet; by issuing in middle age his *Collected Shorter Poems*, replacing their anarchic and rebellious features with religious faith and the sense of sin, shuffling their chronology, and trying to impose on a fragmentary *œuvre* the stamp of organic integrity he has shown that he is aware of his weaknesses without being able to correct them. *Collected Shorter Poems* is the fiction on which all those who were not around to buy *Poems* (1930), *Look, Stranger!* (1936), and *Another Time* (1940) as they appeared, have been brought up.* Unless one is content to think badly of English Auden at the behest of American Auden, one has to buy them now.

As a young writer Auden was renowned for wearing a journalist's eyeshade and sporting a pistol on his desk—not that Auden had practised as a journalist or fired a shot in anger. Only the associations—of observation, leading to action—are telling. Technological progress, the imbroglio of class values, the malaise of democracy, and the possibilities of rejuvenation and growth revealed by new learning had reached a degree of mutual alienation, as well as individual complexity, which made it imperative for them to mix and heal in poetry. The first task was to bring the dilemma to light, to unearth it through spade-work. Auden vivisects his time differently from Yeats, for whom history was a series of mutations

---

* For discussion of the revisions, based on the factual record in J. W. Beach's *The Making of the Auden Canon*, see John Mander, *The Writer and Commitment*, 1961. I rely on the original texts, but have christened poems with the names supplied in the collected volume.

reviving the same human powers over and over again, which, to gain fulfilment, the individual must objectify in acts; and from T. S. Eliot, who having opted out mystically from the dilemma persists in judging it. Auden discovers the past influencing the present; he is interested in the future so long as it is demonstrably likely to be affected by the present, which he aims to master not by 'making up' his self like Yeats or judging from a supernatural height like Eliot, but by a creative detachment ('Consider this and in our time / As the hawk sees it or the helmeted airman') in which modern aids like psychiatry and social science are used to analyse the situation *as accessible to common sense.*

Yet these observant, athletic poems, centred on a most acute appreciation of facts, show little grasp of essences—of motive cause or remedial agent. *Let History Be My Judge* gestures vaguely towards revolution; to provide the poet with an excuse for crocodile tears and mock heroics it has to assume that the revolution is already lost. Like a lantern lecture, *The Watershed* shows memorable, almost nostalgic slides of industrial case-history which live, as poetry, because they perpetuate the transient—'Snatches of tramline running to the wood / An industry already comatose / Yet sparsely living. A ramshackle engine / At Cashwell raises water'. The lecturer then taps his stick and shouts the rhetoric of command— 'Go home, now, stranger, proud of your young stock / Stranger, turn back again, frustrate and vexed'. The land is 'cut off, will not communicate'. This interval of pointless *frisson*, of concocted crisis importing the atmosphere of the Nordic Sagas, is followed by another slide, which does give the sense of suspended urgency and waiting menace:

> *Beams from your car may cross a bedroom wall,*
> *They wake no sleeper; you may hear the wind*
> *Arriving driven from the ignorant sea*
> *To hurt itself on pane, on bark of elm*
> *Where sap unbaffled rises, being spring.*

In *Consider* we feel a constructive detachment: the 30's hero, incarnated as the hawklike 'helmeted airman', surveys the distracting details of society like a scientist or mountaineer who operates on the frontiers of experience, concentrating the will in order to return and apply the knowledge for the amelioration of life. We feel a comprehensiveness in Auden's vision, a pleasure at the unmasking of pretension and vacuity, a relief at the spectacle of one mind mastering the symptoms of crisis. We assent to 'insufficient units' dangerous and easy in furs; we are instructed by the idea of 'handsome and diseased youngsters', financiers leaving a room where 'money is made but not spent', the game being up for people who pace in slippers on lawns, 'seekers after happiness' following the 'convolutions of your simple wish', and giving prizes to ruined boys. We are instructed, up till now, because this way of life is still with us. The poet postulates a 'supreme Antagonist' capable of 'visiting', 'summoning', 'mobilizing', and starting a rumour; the Antagonist is credited with apocalyptic powers; and his methods of work are melodramatic, which makes the chasm between abuse and reform more glaring. Although the 'old gang' in a world of silted harbours, derelict works and strangled orchards must go, it is only by looking up more integrated poems that we obtain any light on the programme. According to *Petition*, their riddance must be justified by an influx of love and charity—'send to us power and light, a sovereign touch / Curing the intolerable neural itch'—and the effort to create 'New styles of architecture, a change of heart' must be directed by the emotionally saved whose business is to rally their own and the public's positive forces—'Publish each healer that in city lives / Or country houses at the end of drives'.

The last line sounds paternal in a period when psychiatric treatment and social welfare have been recognized, however meanly, as a charge on the State. For Auden psychiatry was more than a medical aid (which is all it is)—it was an infallible key to understanding! Except for that literary exploit *Petition*, an intricate linguistic weave (revival becomes a single revolutionary hope), the key, inserted into classes and proclaimed in society, is a failure. It unlocks too many of those curtly sinuous, nervously abrupt, riddle-me-ree assemblages of aperçus which look so assured but are really so evasive, meanderings of thought around a fictitious object. Sometimes they come into focus—'touching is shaking hands / On mortgaged lands'—or materialize because penetrated in depth:

> *And what was livelihood*
> *Is tallness, strongness*
> *Words and longness,*
> *All glory and all story*
> *Solemn and not so good.*
> (*Such Nice People*)

When Auden takes a person, he goes deeper. In *A Free One* observed traits—gesture, habit, presence—are netted, accounted for in terms of their motivation, put on view, tagged, and restored to the aquarium. Informality of statement makes an aloof subject accessible. A bluff is called—the poise of what *The Times* terms a top person is apparently a defence against depression, an ignorance of limitations—and the balancing of fact with insight makes us realize the *interaction* of psychology with environment: there is no question of the one usurping the other; we are free to draw appropriate conclusions:

> *Watch any day his nonchalant pauses, see*
> *His dextrous handling of a wrap as he*
> *Steps after into cars, the beggar's envy.*
>
> *'There is a free one' many say, but err.*
> *He is not that returning conqueror,*
> *Nor ever the poles' circumnavigator.*
>
> *But poised between shocking falls on razor-edge*
> *Has taught himself this balancing subterfuge*
> *Of the accosting profile, the erect carriage.*

1929 associates all Auden's flairs—meaningful reportage, arresting simile, introspective wit, the revolutionary myth, the viciousness and hyprocrisy of the 'old gang'—but fails to integrate them into a convincing diagnosis or a feasible argument to support the call for action. Conceived under the shadow of *The Waste Land*, the poem aspires to a total account of the 'changed' conditions of the late 20's. But there are no built-in epiphanies concentrated in intense personal vision; and the organization of material *per se* is insufficient to provide grounds for hope. We are left with the cartoons of a man who has seen something drastic, intolerable, but is too impatient, anxious, and informed to be able to deal with it; a man who knows his enemy, but whose weapon is the endless parley:

> *It is time for the destruction of error,*
> *The chairs are being brought in from the garden,*
> *The summer talk stopped on that savage coast*
> *Before the storms, after the guests and birds . . .*
> *The falling leaves know it, the children*
> *At play on the fuming alkali-tip*
> *Or by the flooded football ground, know it—*
> *This is the dragon's day, the devourer's . . .*

It looks as if the ancient British trust in tradition has at last made its fatal mistake, has been brought to book. But the avenger is an upper bohemian rebel, and his dual inheritance—belief in reason, concern for community, embarrassed by prior emotional loyalties and love of privacy—stultifies action. He can only end with a vague appeal to 'more love', death of the old gang, 'the hard bitch and the riding master'. We are left guessing who exactly the redeemer is—'the lolling bridegroom, beautiful there'.

The Oxford hope to make verse a result of action, which was to include topical images, led Cambridge to plead through Michael Roberts and William Empson for less journalese in verse, more rigour and finesse, and cooler and more precise inspection. Auden and his entourage were less interested in understanding the facts, more concerned with illustrating and curing the sickness. Kathleen Raine, in her essay on Roberts, writes that for the hero 'every act is conscious, voluntary, the outcome of choice, of free will carried to its extreme point . . . the hero has to heed a chorus of imperatives which are the antithesis of the imperatives of nature'.* Such a life is rooted in moral conflict; neither animals nor saints are beset with alternatives. The poets agree that the fragmentation of knowledge is a scandal; deeds are to be guided by a co-ordination of disciplines, the poet a maverick university whose faculties interact. Empson makes treatment do the unifying; Roberts illustrates symbols to dispel murk; Auden tends to select his field and scatter his seed on that stony ground. Offering to frighten us, his protagonist is a puppet going through the motions of leadership in *ultima thules* we are asked to believe in; his heroes seek Gothic ordeals in landscapes removed from the English alarums—'Doom is deeper and darker than any sea-dingle' is their watchword. *Taller Today* is full of melancholy memoirs about a figure whose efforts to 'break through' and 'fight' have failed. The Adversary, a sort of abominable iceman coming out of the North (always for Auden the birthplace of beckoning, superhuman forces), has triumphed. At the end, the poem rallies: local 'period' imagery is contrasted with a minimal statement of what good faith and friendship can do:

> But happy now, though no nearer each other,
> We see the farms lighted all along the valley;
> Down at the mill-shed the hammering stops
> And men go home.
>
> Noises at dawn will bring
> Freedom for some, but not this peace
> No bird can contradict: passing, but is sufficient now
> For something fulfilled this hour, loved or endured.

* 'Michael Roberts and the Hero Myth', *Penguin New Writing*, No. 39, 1950. 'For those who lose themselves in the darkness of nature, or in the light of vision, death is no longer tragic . . . neither, perhaps, is life.' She admits that Yeats excelled at the heroic although 'the alertness of the hero is opposite from the certainty of those who "dance on deathless feet" '. According to Miss Raine 'Roberts suffered to the full that anguish which the mystic hardly knows'. Miss Raine shows how

Poem XXII ('Shut up talking, charming in the best suits to be had in town / Lecturing on navigation while the ship is going down') is unnameable because Auden has excluded it from the collected volume. He probably bowed to the conventional criticism—that from the angle of later economic progress, this inventory of the slump is outmoded. If so late Auden suffers from myopia as well as failure of nerve; since there is nothing in his jeremiad—or, for that matter, in the bitterer invective of the young C. Day Lewis—which is not perfectly valid today. The old gang has become the new swim, recommends its habits to the area of affluence, and looks like prospering. The fault lies with Auden, who attacks the corrupt *dolce vita* of his time with gusto, yet mistakes permanent vices of manners for a transient economic setback.

*   *   *

The Post-Symbolist poets tried to endow personal feeling with a universal validity. In his poem on the statue of Apollo, Rilke appeals for a self-transformation by the beholder in response to the work of art—'Here there is no place / That does not see you. You must change your life'.* W. H. Auden appeals for transformation in activity. Throughout *Look, Stranger!* (1936) we feel that poetry is not ectoplasm clowning in the void, but the result of a humane set of causes—'For men are changed by what they do / And through loss and anger the hands of the unlucky / Love one another'. The intent of fascism was manifest. The rationale behind the verse is: when external evils overwhelm private goods, poetry must claim its prestige as a public art by exploring the connexion between our values and their environment. This phase of concern lasts until 1939; it is consummated in the sonnets at the end of *Journey to a War:*

> *Ideas can be true although men die*
> *And we can watch a thousand faces*
> *Made active by one lie:*
>
> *And maps can really point to places*
> *Where life is evil now:*
> *Nanking; Dachau.*

Historically transient, Nanking and Dachau are eternal symbols of the operation of evil, as valid for verse as the Angels of Rilke and

---

mountains symbolize for Roberts the reaches of knowledge, and the constellations the unknowable which can only be marvelled at.

* Tr. J. B. Leishman, *R. M. Rilke, Selected Works: Poetry*, 1960.

the Byzantium of Yeats. For Auden, politics was a forceps which enabled him to 'hold' a multiplicity of events while investigating their causes. His *politique* is dictated by his judgment of history and his interest in psychiatry, which show him institutions consolidating themselves against the individual. To get the hang of one individual in a group makes it easier to deal with the rest, and Auden fills out his polemic against bad politics with a critique of such perennial everyday vices as careerism, domestic or business greed, grovelling towards office, genteel wills to power and peculative or subtler kinds of mendacity. These remain here—and so, when one comes to think of it, does bad politics.

Prologue is a tuned-up restatement of *Poem XXII*. The remedy is to be 'love' and 'some possible dream'—the realizable ideals of left-wing politics. The Freudian probing of motives is enhanced by a broader historical perspective, but this is called up in romantic terms. The best passages are marvellous evocations of England as she is (or was), 'Alive like patterns a murmuration of starlings / Rising in joy over wolds unwittingly weave'. The poem ends with an elaborate 'hero' aspiration, rendered mythically—'into the undared ocean swung north their prow' etc. Refreshment and hope breathe in the geographic and evolutionary rhetoric; factual analysis, and the clever glimpses of psycho-biologic anomalies, vanish in the verve of the vision. *XIV* ('Brothers, who when the sirens roar') starts by soliciting the support of the wage-earner, goes on to attack the 'Cambridge ulcer'—X-rayed by us apropos William Empson—and ends with well-drawn, cordial abuse ('. . . till they resemble / Cartoons by Goya') of the mindless athletes, leisured dreamers, careful compromisers ('proud of your nicely balanced view'), and effeminate 'gifted' egotists whom the poet knew all too well in his generation. As lampoon the poem is as valid as *XXII* for the best of reasons— that *its targets are still targets*; it is vulnerable at the points where Auden thought he was original: his notion that the bourgeoisie would die of emotional impotence, or, failing that, be swept away by irresistible progressive forces. Our English Lenin seems jovial; there is no *anger* in the poem; he is half in love with easeful death; and the mixed-up quality of the puritanism (for it is none other) is itself touchingly middle class.

Macspaunday's judicial attitude to landscape, and its effort to humanize the machine, appeared then to be subordinate to its vision of reform. Today, this aspect seems honester than the baffled and abortive revolutionary yearnings, more central to the needs of poetry. Auden's *Look Stranger!* is a worthy title-giver to his 1936 book. Its sharp, stark fall of lines, clever turns of syntax, startling dispositions of pitch and phrase make good technical use of Eliot, without demanding any reach of vision, awareness of contrasts or superior philosophy; the altering perspective, the reproductive visual and aural images correspond to the quirks and sinuosities of the sense-arranging mind. It is not just the subject, but the rhythmic cast of the poem which makes it inimitably English. Nearing 'nature poetry', it is muscled by the resolute intellectualism and adroit execution of its structural plan. Normally Auden tutors his land-scapes; he distrusts the pastoral for what it excludes; helped by his knowledge of geology and agriculture he enlists with Edward Thomas and Robert Graves to rescue England from the week-enders. *It's So Dull Here* was no doubt dismissed, in 1936, as a relapse into reactionary romanticism; today, it looks prophetic. Auden seems to be really aroused about 'the sham ornamentation, the strident swimming pool / The identical and townee smartness' and 'a licensed house for tourists / None too particular'. His involvement is so declared that it is more vulnerable than sentimental:

> *True, the hall*
> *With its yews and famous dovecot is still there*
> *Just as in childhood, but the grand old couple*
> *Who loved us all so equally are dead . . .*

In a poem called *The Climbers*, Auden takes the heroic mountain symbolism of the age, makes this a comment on the failure of re-lationships:

> *Climbing with you was easy as a vow;*
> *We reached the top not hungry in the least;*
> *But it was eyes we looked at, not the view;*
> *Saw nothing but ourselves, left-handed, lost:*
> *Returned to shore, the rich interior still*
> *Unknown. Love gave the power, but took the will.*

A gravamen in his nature imagery links him with the reluctant optimist Tennyson who saw the otherness of nature as a stimulus and a threat. Patriotic systems, religious dogma, and technocracy direct the earth into a means (to vitalistic nationalism, the redemption of generation, property rackets and so on). Auden approaches nature with the deferential strictness of his hero, the scientist, the moun-taineer, the explorer. Of course he digs for ironies, as in the sexual allegory of *The Climbers*, but often the episodes illustrated are in part induced by the environment. When he visited Iceland he was charmed by the fable of the man who fell off his horse and refused to budge because the mountain was beautiful; he also devoted three stanzas to the 'indigenous figure' whose blood 'moves also by fur-tive and crooked inches'. With music ('pour out your presence, O delight, cascading / The falls of the knee and the weirs of the spine') and intense affection ('in my arms till break of day / Let the living creature lie . . .') landscape is one of the sources of those redemptive whirlwinds which seduced Auden—witness the bucolic philosophical importunings which 'reconcile' that polymath essay, *New Year Letter*. Much of the purpose of Auden, and not in the futuristic mood, appears in *The Malverns*. For once, the collected volume is on the ball: the excision of the patter ('Out of the turf the bones of war continue . . .') was wise, though the garrulous thunder, no doubt related to the same preacher in *The Waste Land*, still mars the poem with its Freudian sermon—'Has not your long affair with death / Of late become increasingly more serious'. As in *A Free One*, interest is withdrawn from open society and applied to units within it. Panoramic though the scale is, the observer accounts for himself very carefully; the findings inhere in the facts or are appended near them; the knowingness is subordinated to understanding. When Auden says 'for private reasons I must have the truth, remember / These years have seen a boom in sorrow' it is not a manifesto but a wish arising in a pause of a helpful review of man's condition, the poet being himself 'a digit of the crowd'.

The sweep is broad enough to be representative, precise enough to be memorable (*Dover 1937* runs it close). The interplay of psychology with society, neither dominating the other, is favoured by the adjustment of good faith, of instances, to the collective. The purpose—verse the result of action, verse to cope with intractable phenomena, verse to be an intelligent, inquisitive, informative means of investigation, no longer cold-shouldering other means such as history, geography, political science—seems to justify itself in this poem and about twelve others. There the bedside manner is more than a confidence trick, the surgeon does his job.

The machine had been exhibited, or sniped at, since the Industrial Revolution, but Hart Crane was perhaps the first poet to break his vision (in *The Bridge*, 1930) in a bid to accommodate a mechanized community. A pioneer where poets had been ecstatic (Verhaeren), hostile, or like Rilke, afraid, Crane had announced: 'unless poetry can acclimatize the machine as naturally as trees, cattle, galleons, castles and all associations of the past, then poetry has failed its contemporary function'. Crane insists that 'a program of lyrical pandering' or even 'the specific mention' of machinery is otiose; we require 'a surrender to the sensations of urban life'.* At their worst the 30's poets avoid 'lyrical pandering' by going one better and embracing the machine with open arms, adoring it as a fertility god; they ignore the human problems of industrialism, let alone the

* 'Modern Poetry', in *Collected Poems of Hart Crane*, ed. Waldo Frank, 1946.

unpoetic bureaucratization of the Russian Revolution. At their best, C. Day Lewis assigns the machine a place in the hero myth by getting it under control, either for valorous play (the Flight to Australia choruses in *A Time to Dance*) or in the service of an ideal (*The Nabara* is the best poem about the Spanish war from the pen of one who did not fight in it).

In Spender there is a vein of juvenile enthusiasm; other poems—*The Express, The Pylons, Landscape near an Aerodrome*—do 'acclimatize' the machine by divining the meaning of its design in relation to its environment. The promise of the pylons—'There runs the quick perspective of the future', 'Dreaming of cities / Where often clouds shall lean their swan-like neck' is not so far, emotionally, from his 'Eye, gazelle, delicate wanderer / Drinker of horizon's fluid line' or even 'Ear that suspends on a chord / The spirit drinking timelessness' since Spender connects the quickness and fecundity of machines with his own brand of aesthetic idealism (viz. *Beethoven's Death Mask*) which is itself crucial to his hope for a transformation of the community; the poem which flourishes the 'aesthetic' lines above ends with a denunciation of armaments, 'that programme of the antique Satan', a misuse of the machine which a poem like *The Nabara* corrects. Louis MacNeice gets inside the mind of the machine-users with his spirited poems on bicyclists (could he be an ancestor of Philip Larkin?), car-tinkerers, ships at sea, air-raid wardens; such human concern is natural to the man who warned in *Autumn Journal* that 'the nicest people in England have always been the least / Apt to solidarity or alignment / But all of them must now align against the beast . . .'

Auden invokes machinery less, yet is more prescient: his sense of the machine as a conditioning factor is weighed by the evidence yielded by his other interests. If industry now flourishes this does not debunk the fact that Auden annexed that terrain for art. He weaves technics into traditional themes, he relates it to a human foreground. *The Unknown Citizen*, hilarious as well as minatory and prophetic, anticipates the atrophy of the individual in the all-provident State. The hero has all mod. cons. except a rocket, and television has not been marketed; the question of whether he is free or happy is thus, in part, rhetorical; though the Bureau of Statistics can be trusted to find out. If this banter was just a recluse's attack on 'progress' it would be negligible; its distinction is that it airs a problem—the advances are relished, yet their effects are questioned; the epigraph might come from Simone Weil—'in the most prosperous society, there will still be a gulf between those who dispose of the machine and those of whom the machine disposes'. And if we think that automation will refute this, Auden hints that JS/O7/M/378 will remain at the smothered end of the administrative process. In rumbustious mood Auden is more helpful (more likely to be listened to) than when he retreats into the bizarre extravaganza or hallucinated dream of poems like *Paysage Moralisé* and *1st January 1931*.

The Unknown Citizen (in the 1940 volume) is a liberal's reservation about progress. Those who disposed of the machine were the legatees of Victorian *laissez faire*. Auden's 'we' and his 'old gang' —gerontocrats of all age-groups, always around—are factions within the bourgeois class, E. M. Forster's eternal row between the Schlegels ('the inner life shall pay') and the Wilcoxes ('telegrams and anger'), a quarrel more crucial now when the growing bourgeoisie is in a state of moral chaos. Mr John Mander argues that *Look, Stranger!* is Auden's 'Supremely Fortunate Occasion'; he believes that Auden was at his best *because* he was addressing a coterie of like-minded artists. To my mind Auden's group-conspiratorial pose is jejune. Too scornful of motivation to be able to act, guilty about his advantages, detecting an ailment throughout the body politic, his confidence was sapped and his diagnosis rendered quixotic. The strength of English Auden is not due to his audience but to initiatives which at the time looked incidental—the new attention paid to landscape, science, industry, the bird's eye comprehensive view, the insight into types in their environment, the attack on ugliness and privilege, the democratic curiosity and mobility ('maps and chaps'), the hero myth, associating the chances of action with the primacy of the idea, and all this enlivened by alfresco individualism—that gregarious 'but your lust for life prevails / Drinking coffee, telling tales' touch.* (The sheer cheek, wit and exuberance of *Letters from Iceland*—most unpompous travel book ever written?—seems to me a rewarding antidote to official fustian.)

Confusion and strength rub shoulders in *Our Hunting Fathers* and *A Summer Night*. Our hunting fathers patronized the animals 'raging for the personal glory / That reason's gift would add / The liberal appetite and power'. The first stanza is a fair attack on facile optimism, the egotism of reason. The poet asks who 'nurtured in that fine tradition' could have predicted that love is 'suited to the intricate ways of guilt', that indulgent 'southern gestures' are shallow, and that 'mature ambition' will, following Lenin, 'hunger, work illegally, and be anonymous'. The second stanza is based on allegation and fantasy: 'mature ambition' overbears; *when did Auden* (in his verse) 'hunger, work illegally and be anonymous'? The 'intolerant', 'glorious', 'raging' animals—that absoluteness of instinct which Ted Hughes welcomes—lend nothing of their intensity to the

---

* From *Epilogue*, one of Louis MacNeice's contributions to *Letters from Iceland*, 1937.

subversive stanza; the suffering and vitality of the animals are rejected, as they are not in Hughes.

A Summer Night calls up the country holiday, free, casual, disinterested, 'equal with colleagues in a ring'. John Mander finds 'ease
and sureness' here, and in a way he is right. Etching with subtle
sensory and evocative power, the poet seems confident of a delightful
experience—happy, amused, alert. He faces up honestly to the
contrast between his own perquisites and the cruelty gripping
Europe, and asks what 'violence', what 'doubtful act', allows 'our
freedom in this English house'. This tradition which the poet 'loves'
is failing, though he would gladly give 'the Oxford colleges, Big
Ben and all the birds in Wicken Fen' as the price of rejuvenation.
The triumph of unreason is envisaged as an apocalyptic deluge;
then reconstruction will follow the subsiding of the waters. Although he admits that his ethic is feeble, his way of rendering
catastrophe is bathetic; were I Coleridge, I would say it is fanciful
but hardly imaginative. One feels no stress, no alarm, in Auden's
foppish style at this point; how the poet hopes to ally the old
privacy with the new strength is uncertain. And if Auden sees no
future in the values, why bother about their survival? The poem is
too nice to be true, too easeful, too sure; an atmospheric triumph,
we want the more thrilling and the more troublesome.

In spite of some flat lines, *A Bride in the 30's* is more modest and
robust. The girl is unequivocally there. 'Love' is invoked, it is true,
but the abstraction is counterpointed with physical facts—'easily,
my dear, you move, easily your head', 'the pool of silence and the
tower of grace', 'a pine tree shadow across your brow', 'you stand
now before me, flesh and bone', and these, distributed evenly, govern
and qualify the exploration of the 'sombre sixteen skies of Europe'—
the barbarism of propaganda, force, and greed which is destroying decency, 'Hitler and Mussolini in their wooing poses'. But the
poem does not end on that simple opposition. The poet detects
a threat, first at home, coming from the cowed, 'the lost in their
sneering circles', hatred with her 'immediate pleasure' and fashion
with her 'fascinating rubbish', and second, from the devious nature
of love—of optimistic energy—itself, forever tempted towards self-
sufficiency: 'that power to excess / The beautiful quite naturally
possess' may be as dangerous as 'ten thousand of the desperate
marching by' if it leads to indifference about, or fascination by, the
odious. The spiritual toll of growing up, limiting the field of capability, is treated as part of the problem, and 'love' is seen as the supreme
individual act: only through 'our private stuff' is born 'his public
spirit'. That is the point of departure; the road is as voluntary as
demanded; it is for us to decide:

Wind shakes the tree; the mountains darken;
And the heart repeats though we would not hearken:
'Yours is the choice, to whom the gods awarded
The language of learning and the language of love,
Crooked to move as a moneybug or a cancer
Or straight as a dove.'

The not world-shattering theme is given loyally; its prospects are strengthened. *Not All the Candidates Pass* is about teaching, as frequent (and less deleterious) an employment for the impecunious poet of the 30's as advertising is today. Again the poet is in the thick of things: the delineated detail is alert, present, and profound; the fears and hopes, petty but genuine, of Britain's future tone-setters are fully entered into, and the teachers and examiners—the mandarins of British liberal culture, still unaroused by 'Hitler and Mussolini in their wooing poses'—metamorphose, due to their weapons of discipline, apartness, and moody sensitiveness into eccentric prison guards. The Freudian comments are subdued to the plot. One of Auden's least didactic works, it has what he often lacks —unity of mood; we are left with a feeling of disturbance and concern which involves a lot beyond the deceptively limited scene.

Auden's contrite frankness and readiness for amendment fuse in *Birthday Poem* into benign persiflage, followed by an oath of allegiance. The English coastal resort, attracting 'all types that can intrigue the writer's fancy', is treated to a rueful yet loving analysis; this high noon of popular relaxation, just before the war, wins Auden's good cheer as well as his chuckle. He girds at himself. Products of 'the stuccoed suburb and expensive school', Auden's and Isherwood's folly—their silliness and intolerance—has been rudely shaken by the unrest: 'private joking in a panelled room', freelance gallivantings, must give way when 'the wireless roars its warnings and its lies'. Desperately, the poet asks whether 'love'— 'one fearless kiss'—could cure 'the million fevers'; at this period he is not so certain. A rogue's gallery follows: the corrupt leisure class feeding on the innocuous pleasure-loving public of the opening. This malediction has been disliked, mainly because of Auden's craze for inventories, but it seems to me thematically just—the precision of the early 'public' stanzas is set against the big sprawling bogey of established coarseness; each villain is equipped with his or her material prop:

Slim Truth dismissed without a character,
And gaga Falsehood highly recommended . . .
Greed showing shamelessly her naked money,
And all Love's wondering eloquence debased

A VISION OF REALITY

To a collector's slang, Smartness in furs,
And Beauty scratching miserably for food,
Honour self-sacrificed for Calculation,
And Reason stoned by Mediocrity,
Freedom by Power shockingly maltreated . . .

1930's, or 1960's? At any rate a time of 'crisis and dismay' when the 'strict and adult pen' must 'make action urgent and its nature clear'. Auden has come into the open. He is involved. We ignore him at our peril.

From the narrow window of my fourth floor room
I smoke into the night, and watch reflections
Stretch in the harbour . . .
And all sway forward on the dangerous flood
Of history, that never sleeps or dies
And, held, one moment, burns the hand.

*   *   *

As the hands of the clock moved from the eleventh hour to midnight, Auden's desperation and bewilderment worsened as his intelligence increased; all three jostle in the 1940 volume, *Another Time*. 'Love' makes its début as a panacea, together with 'Justice', 'The Just', 'Man', 'The Good Place', 'Time', 'The Unexpected' and —ominously—'The Godhead'. Auden holds that liberal civilization is poisoned by narcissism, as at Oxford where 'without are the shops, the works, the whole green county' and 'thousands fidget and poke and spend their money' but 'Eros Paidagogos / Weeps on his virginal bed', let down by his 'box of lucky books'. Liberals run away from their inwardness, their code militates against self-knowledge in favour of success cloaked by conscience-salving ideals. A deep dive would reveal panic and muddle, but confrontation is the only way to rebirth and the release from inhibition. Matthew Arnold, the liberal patriarch who scourged his age but produced no art to transcend it, is 'a dark disordered city' who could have won through had he refused to become his 'father's forum'; alas, his generation 'saw itself already in a father's place'.

The state of being of 'holders of one position, wrong for years' must give way to 'felt their centre of volition shifted', our conflicting wills be mobilized to assist 'the birth of natural order and true love'. In an age when many poets have praised frustrated, unrequited, or repressed love as a gift from the gods, Auden has sung out in lyric after lyric for the boon of spontaneous relationships. There is a creaturely frankness, a beautiful sanity, about *Fish in the unruffled lakes, Lay your sleeping head, my love, May with its light behaving, Warm*

are the still and lucky miles, and *O lurcher-loving collier, black as night*
which places them near Graves and Yeats among the finest love
lyrics of this century. Yet the asperity of Auden, his respect for
'the slow fastidious line / That disciplines the fell' and the distrust
of uplift that made him banish 'we must love one another or die'—
the line which won E. M. Forster—from his collected volume,
maims even these lyrics. Many of the Ballads, Songs, and Musical
Pieces are as distasteful as cabaret smut. Their excuse presumably
is that only by utterance can the oddities of relationships be raised
into consciousness, set free from a conspiracy of silence. This sub-
limation-defence is worth considering (for example, when he lists
modish pleasures, then sabotages the lot with 'there is always a
wicked secret, a private reason for this') but why doll up the pieces
in *chic* Hammersmith Palais metres and cynical frivolity? When
Auden is not crowing over freaks or haggling about love, he is
lauding it with grotesque optimism. In the poem dedicated for the
wedding of Elizabeth Mann, he hopes that 'this quiet wedding' will
plant human unity, reconcile hostile truths, begin modern policy!
After this, all Auden can manage is a slick analysis of history; the
poem peters out, gamely but innocuously, in a roll-call of the Great
Creators and an appeal for their blessing.

'New styles of architecture' was Auden's totem of revival, whose
dynamic was to be 'a change of heart' in people. Unable to create
any character or situation where this miracle happens, still less
conjure it in himself, his desire that it should happen brings him
down from his bird's eye vision of interaction to the earth of particularity. He cherishes the individual not as a romantic hell-bent on
fulfilment, but in self-defence, being perturbed about the harm
which maladjusted mediocrities can wreak in a community, especially when they entrench in organizations. A dictator can laugh and
be applauded; when he cries 'the little children die in the streets'.
In *Gare du Midi* a dedicated official obeys orders and sallies out to
'infect a city'. Conversely, people may be disregarded ('battered
like pebbles into fortuitous shapes') in cities, or humiliated like the
servants in *Hong Kong 1938* who 'enter unexpected' and count for
their masters to the sole extent that 'their silence has a fresh dramatic use'. Nobody is committed to his neighbour except as a means to
self-approval or profit; all bask in the General Will, hoping for the
best; nobody understands cause and effect, communicates his love
and realizes his ideals: 'for what we are, we have ourselves to
blame'. The good-timers of *The Ship*—clearly a State symbol—are
meretricious; their life is subhuman *per se* and in what it ignores—
'the beggars sleeping in the bows have never seen / What can
be done in staterooms'—while their shattering mistrusts are tiny

distractions which concern only their own circle. Somewhere beyond this calm 'progression' (a subacid term) there is a 'War' and a 'Tomorrow' which is planning a test. No one guesses 'who will be most ashamed, who richer, and who dead'.

The inertia of ordinary life is deceptive, our indifference to our neighbour is the equivalent, in microcosm, of frightful abuses and much suffering. Auden's instinct for the changes wrought on men by suffering, his detection of the factors which deprive people of happiness, is serviceable. We must magnify our sympathy until we achieve harmony with another—for men crave 'not universal love / But to be loved alone'. Entangled in a web of connexions, we cannot fail one value without detracting from another. Since the 'knowledge of the world' of the 'wounded' (of the *In Time of War* sonnets) is restricted to 'the treatment that the instruments are giving', then 'truth in their sense is how much they can bear' and the initiative must come from the healthy, the lucky, the more abundantly aware, who live 'in the common world of the uninjured, and cannot / Imagine isolation'.

When Auden wants a simile, he goes to people. 'Observant like a beggar', 'patient as a peasant', 'hinting at the forbidden like a wicked uncle'. Averse to romantic metaphor, he chooses enterprising social connexions—'all Love's wondering eloquence debased / To a collector's slang', 'the millions in whom the wish to be one / Like a burglar is stealthily moving', 'noble emotions organized and massed / Line the straight flood-lit tracks of memory', 'far off like floating seeds the ships'—which serve as reminders of the existence of each, even the humblest, link in the continuum; they enhance tension and vigilance. Auden notices consequences—'printing presses turning forests into lies'—he sets ideals against facts, personality against background, and can achieve a Chekhovian light tragicomedy—'O dear white children casual as birds / Playing amid the ruined languages'. When Auden likens Freud to Dante—'Of course they called on God: but he went his way / Down among the Lost People like Dante'—he signifies that the humility, the self-abasement of the mental worker, has taken its place in the continuum side by side with others who had different motives and beliefs and cannot be cried down by partisan groups.

Auden is quick to vindicate MacNeice's 'integrity of differences', that sense of sane proportion which made 'the greatest figure of his day' of *Who's Who* ('A shilling life will give you all the facts') prefer the eccentricities of private life. He portrays a veteran who won self-confidence after a lifetime of vicissitudes; give her any surround and she will 'compose them all / Centring the eye on the essential human element'. Such centring is vital to Auden's dispassionate eye for texture of life in given contexts. He admires consummation in activity: Rilke at Muzot felt 'the gratitude of the completed'. Fulfilment may come arbitrarily, as when Edward Lear, depressed and ill, found that 'children swarmed to him like settlers. He became a land.' Auden warns that a group may falsify a man's authentic image; the sequel to the agonized life of Rimbaud was 'his truth acceptable to lying men'. However acclaimed or misunderstood a man may be, he is engrossed in a web of circumstance which permeates his being; in a sense Freud was just 'an important Jew who died in exile'. And Voltaire enjoyed 'gardening' as much as 'the fight against the false and the unfair'. Our sense of the integrity of differences heightened, tragedy would be more vivid to us; the Old Masters knew how tragedy occurs when someone else is 'eating or opening a window or just walking dully along'.

The reader will protest that, in order to sketch a pattern in Auden's ethic of love and responsibility, I have had to piece together extracts. This is indeed the point: no pattern emerges, nor are the poems, as wholes, uniformly successful. Just before and after his removal (it was not a flight) to America in 1939 (since 1947 he has been an American citizen) I believe that Auden underwent a cataclysm of feeling and that his insatiably developing intellect was unable to tolerate it. For long the poems seem stunned. Contrast of abstractions is the method; out of the blue flights are the thought; the rhythm is that of the metronome. The vignettes about people—mainly artists—may be perceptive but they betray: a flight from the self, so that he tries to suffer and understand through others; a claim to be arbitrator, as if having the last word on others was a substitute for developing one's self; a predatory critical faculty —Auden gets away with gobbets about Great Writers which would be challengeable in less eloquent mouths than his own. In poems like *In Memory of W. B. Yeats*, *Refugee Blues*, *In Memory of Ernst Toller*, *1st September 1939* pity and terror seem baulked in the expression—paralysed by the appalled intellect, stylized by that tone which mars the Songs, Ballads, and Musical Pieces. Because the rhetoric in these poems is so plausibly quotable—'with the farming of a verse / Make a vineyard of the curse / Sing of human unsuccess / In a rapture of distress'—we suspect its place in the whole; Auden is whistling in the dark, it is pre-Apocalyptic. The horror is *felt intellectually*: fair enough. The antidote, the specific, would have to be felt emotionally, in the man.

The *Journey to a War* poems teach us much, since in them we are aware of Auden's unique gifts and of his loss of direction; and as regards the former we must all hope for another *Auden de nos jours*. A train of sonnets in lilting monochrome is followed by a homily in buoyant tercets, drawing on the ethos of science manuals, in which history evolves towards a glorious but unspecified triumph. Auden lets reaction have its say, but ends with the 'voice of Man' declaiming to Himself in a minatory sublime.* The work gives the measure of our epoch: insight into key behaviour, understanding of causation, sensitiveness to events and their repercussions. But the whole disappoints; Auden, having raised the curtain, temporizes; this drama lacks excitement. Instead, there are anticlimaxes of style. In return for the attack on leaders—'we know them now / For humbugs full of vain dexterity . . .' or 'Evil is always personal and spectacular / But goodness needs the evidence of all our lives' —we have the tearful gaucherie of 'We wander on the earth, or err from bed to bed / In search of home, and fail, and weep for the lost ages . . .' or party-game precocity like 'that Catholic country with the shape of Cornwall'—which is there as a pacemaker to the rhythm. In the sonnets, a tenebrous 'he' imports the enigmas of myth in 'his' endeavour to develop; next comes a medley of situations which Auden interrogates, and very sharply. We have the news made flesh in 'Behind each sociable home-loving eye / The private massacres are taking place', 'He will not be introduced / When this campaign is tidied into books', '. . . cousins in the city / Pursued their rapid and unnatural course', and 'Remote like savants, they can only see / The breathing city as a target . . .' We have Auden's charisma for conjuring poetry out of the disparate: the way he involves the savants and the tidying into books with the practical, collective guilt is vintage Audenesque. Again, though, this play fails to catch our conscience. Some parts miss their cue, such as the hollow Kiplingesque of 'that our daughters be fit to love the earth' and the crystal-gazing of 'can future ages ever escape so far . . .' Nor does it help, with 'violence successful like a new disease', to be recommended to the hermit Rilke.

*   *   *

As we move with Auden through mid-century what is this flippant cleverness, this facile accomplishment, except riderless brilliance galloping over a vacuum of hysteria? Many of his 'saved' poems jump from adversity to triumph without telling us how or why. Others brandish hope as a happy ending to a cautionary tale, or betray uncertainty with self-defensive irony, or mount an overponderous theme and laugh it off with a feigned light touch, or give unasked-for advice, attitudinize and comment, proliferating ideas. Auden's successes are verbal and imagistic: what he will not do

---

* The re-touching of the last stanzas, in an attempt to brazen out the argument in a Christian light, is the most staggering of Auden's revisions.

is control the elements of a ramifying theme, engaging our interest in each aside, while satisfying us at the end with the impression of a single moral drive. Auden is becalmed in a doldrums; until the poet whistles up a breeze, his admirers will prefer the bracing ozone of the earlier poems. He broke his roots in English earth, lost his urgency about the crisis, while the pertinence of his values has been deformed by a growing sense of regret and frustration which verges on the sentimental. The moving lyric gift, now sobered by nostalgic pessimism, remains; the satiric sword is still unsheathed, if blunted; though Auden has become a beneficiary of institutions he is not subservient to them. But the lines are less arteries to transmit life in the organism, than limbs of a corpse; the surprising imagery is less original, more gnomic; the allusions and personifications are jaded; the phrasing lacks piquancy; the refreshing vein of fantasy is degenerating into operatic floridity. The effect of the conditioned structures of which he is fond is to petrify his thought in repetitive, cryptic patterns. To triumph he must manage a consummation of style in a late period, a process achieved by Hopkins and few others, or a feat of self-renovation as radical and dynamic as that of Yeats in middle life. His emergence from the *selva oscura* would blaze the trail for us all.

The impasse of American Auden has made people think twice about English Auden. That pin-table on which he whirled colourful balls of thought is felt to have been rigged: the props that set the stage for a revolutionary drama—martyrs, airmen, spies who break out into pantomimic lyrics—were premature, perhaps superfluous; those commands resemble squeaks of bewilderment as much as battle-cries. In particular there has been resentment, from the wage-slave writers of our day, of the 'easy lives' led by the men of 1930, while the Welfare State, gilded by the affluent society, has realized the first instalment of the 'new styles of architecture' in forms which have bred a 'change of heart' not altogether reassuring. Gas and water planning for real, abetted by, or alternating with, free material enterprise, threatens much of what the poets cherished. The weakness of Auden is his failure to see that poetry like his may be a symptom as well as a solvent. In this maverick puritan we detect guilt, without suffering; a cult of kindness, without much idea of how to adjust it, through action, to the collective; a clash (often fruitful) between bohemian and don, libertine and preacher—in Auden Iconoclastes there is always the offspring of Midland yeoman stock, of Icelandic extraction, and Church of England grandparents struggling to get out (see the *curriculum vitae* in *Letter to Lord Byron*). Governing all is what I call the *pretension to omniscience*, not to be confused with the experience of multiplicity as it evolves in poets like Rimbaud, Rilke, Yeats, and Eliot. Intensity and the instinct for development drive these artists into more anguished and ramifying awarenesses, which demand to be lived out, tested, correlated; their exposure is total. Auden chooses his ground, marches forward behind slogans. His maw is always demanding new fodder, always cooking it in different ways: he can be charged with quixotic Alexandrianism.

To be fair to the ethos in general, we must distinguish between the intention of the poets and their meaning for us today. One source of injustice has been the fallacy that radical verse is insincere unless it is enjoyed by the masses; Macspaunday is ridiculed for failing to be Yevtushenko. The erstwhile Pink Liberals have reiterated that they were generating, from the standpoint of privilege, mainly for the literary reader, a 'revolutionary mythos'. This believed that improvement, cultural and industrial, would stem from below: the leisure class was sterile and replete, so unless its poets were content to be parasites on a carcass, its morally conscious faction must go over to the future, presenting to the new life what was good in the old and abandoning the bad. They may be censured for glamorizing, for meddling in, worlds they knew nothing about—for patronizing the workers in a manner inexcusable then, certainly unthinkable now, when flattery seems the order of the day—but not for failing to communicate to them. The horseplay of the verse reflects, rightly, the confusion of these who wrote it. But after all, the return to plain statement never approached a Yevtushenko: its prosy diffidence and thumping obviousness is just as unmarketable as the radical enthusiasm which it disdained.

One must insist that our official 'sociological' keenness was pioneered with warmth before the war by Mass Observation, *Left Review*, the progressive cinema, the Group and Unity theatres, and the poets, who took up the tradition of egalitarian-cultural Socialism which R. H. Tawney had kept going in the forlorn Twenties. These amateurs were insecure and guilty enough to discern individuals where our professionals prefer to juggle with statistics; all the topics of with-it journalism were aired in verse before the war *in the interests of a moral idea*: for the last time so far, English poets used all their knowledge to grasp their society as a whole, keeping the experts at bay. (They also showed a love for what is stale and unprofitable to the experts—alongside industrial advance: rural preservation: Spender's *Pylons*, Day Lewis's *You that love England . . .*) Having stressed the faults of the 'revolutionary mythos' I must underline the cogency of that aspect of it which chastised the unregenerate middle class—Day Lewis's *The Magnetic Mountain* still reads like a guide to a world of malefactors always with us. The mythos departs; or was it superannuated by an increase of wealth? Everyone in the new, collective bourgeoisie is tempted to don the commercial uniform whose merits are loud-hailed at us by those who hope to recreate us in their image; and the *élan* of 30's non-conformism should act as a time-bomb under the mood of meek doubt which is the Englishman's response to our super salesmen.

People cavil at Auden. Yet he remains central to literary discussion.* The reason, in my view, is that Auden doubles the parts of scapegoat and avatar in our sub-conscious. We envy, to the point of nostalgia, the poet who enjoyed a social stimulus; we imagine how much more efficient as heroes and revolutionaries we might have been. There is a desire to revive Auden's *jeu d'esprit* and unsolemn concern in an epoch when the Enemy appears to have made peace with imagination because his teeth have been drawn: he still has his boots and biceps. Social urgency, which drove Auden, has eased; moral passion, which Auden reserved, we desperately need. Auden's vocation is to be a tragically didactic poet. Deprived of transfiguration himself, he instructs others on the way to fulfilment, warns them of the obstacles, enhances their pleasure in their enterprise, and explains their false starts. His anti-authoritarianism is not an invitation to frivolity but a device for vitalizing a void with activities more genuine and intense. His critique of idealism is salutary: that is why his characters are often buffoons and sages, Utopians and iconoclasts, at the same time. His art is a guide to enjoyment, naming, scourging, and above all accounting for a great deal of vulgarity, hypocrisy, and pretension. Where formerly we were ignorant, unaware, and gullible, Auden makes us conscious, sensitive, and responsible. His liberal vision is as much a warning and an example today as it was thirty years ago:

> *So many try to say Not Now,*
> *So many have forgotten how*
> *To say I Am, and would be*
> *Lost, if they could, in history.*

* See *The Review: Thirties Special Number*, Nos. 10–11, 1964.

DIRECT ACTION: JOHN CORNFORD
AND THE SPANISH CIVIL WAR

THE protest of William Empson on behalf of foresight and rigour was reinforced by a counterblast from John Cornford and Julian Bell, two poets killed in the Spanish Civil War, Cornford as a fervent Marxist and Bell as an ex-pacifist liberal who demanded some response to a challenge. Michael Roberts, then impresario to the movement, foresaw some of the objections to liberal poetry. He complains of 'Utopian lyrics', that 'we are deluged with good advice, but nobody can act on it', and that 'if your writing about a new world is to mean anything beyond buttercup lyricism, you must know how that world is to come into being and what sort of world it will be . . . not intelligence is lacking, but control'. Roberts predicts that the old gang may, by hook or by crook, survive: he prophesies Midas turning all to tinsel with his embrace.

> The problem of leisure may be solved, but it will not be solved as we would wish. Shall we watch our children hypnotized into buying machines? Daily our efforts as scientists, poets and teachers are wasted and turned against society. How can people be their most kindly, sensitive and intelligent selves when the competitive system forces the lowest level of standardization?*

We must oppose to this free-for-all, says Roberts, a constructive act—an 'ethical communism' fulfilling the individual through his participation in a cause bigger than himself. Some poets 'found this in the Great War'; Roberts finds it in mountain climbing.

John Cornford found it in Spain. The son of a classical don and a talented poetess, his first name was Rupert—after Rupert Brooke; later he was to write 'in the next war there will be fewer Rupert Brookes and more Wilfred Owens'. Outspoken, a fanatical organizer, ruthless to all complacency and weakness, the letters and essays in the Memorial Volume reveal him as the last person to read lectures to poetry.† He opposed the bellicosities of Cambridge and helped to rally liberal elements behind the Hunger Marchers; in everything he did, he searched for 'the essential element, the key to action'; and he found time to make himself a first-class historian. Cornford's early

---

* See the Preface to *New Country*, ed. Michael Roberts, 1933.
† *John Cornford: A Memoir*, ed. Pat Sloan, 1938. This contains the letters, essays, and poems.

poems are Audenesque, apart from their clear-sighted aim, bravura, tough common sense:

> All this half-felt sorrow and all this unfelt laughter
> Is the question to be decided, and I am the answer.
> Wherever the vague sea wanders in the blind, cold, useless dark
> It shatters itself on the coastline, my purpose, heavy as rock.

They are notable for an absence of petulant attacks. The philistines are ignored; Cornford is unconcerned with manners; the moral consequences of the millennium are no bother to him. Cornford's leftism is not the guilt atonement, symbolic patricide and power-lust of Mr Amis's sensitive,* but the result of clear thinking about history, powered by the instinctive need his personality had, if it was to stay fertile and efficient, to feed on the collective. Cornford was too consumed by the essence of his belief to waste his time on propaganda. This lucid constructive drive, this refusal to accept any proposition which could not be tested, makes Cornford a damaging critic of dilettantism. In his essay, 'Left?', mainly levelled at the future editor of *Encounter*, he castigates the 'Utopian wish-fulfilment'. Artists, 'playing at Revolution', reject the sacrifice, hardship, and suffering of struggle. 'It is the poetry of revolution as a literary fashion, not as a historic possibility.' Spender is the darling of the Old Liberals because he revives their mirage without giving them cause for fear. The future is with 'the revolutionary participator and not the impartial observer'. Cornford raps the lesson home in a polemic of a kind rare in England: tranquil hatred outside all the conventions, and all the innovations. For the new conventions are half-measures or crank escapisms, paying lip-service to progress, essentially defeatist, ill:

> Wind from the dead land, hollow men,
> Webster's skull and Eliot's pen,
> The important words that come between
> The observant eye and the difficult scene.
> All the obscene important names
> For silly griefs and silly shames,
> All the tricks we once thought smart,
> The Kestrel joy and the change of heart,
> The dark, mysterious urge of the blood,
> The donkeys shitting on Dali's food,
> There's none of these fashions have come to stay,
> And there's nobody here got time to play.

* See Kingsley Amis, *Socialism and the Intellectuals*, Fabian pamphlet, 1957.

A VISION OF REALITY

All we've brought are our party cards
Which are no bloody good for your bloody charades.
      (*Keep Culture out of Cambridge*)

Within a year of this poem, Cornford was in Spain. The first Englishman to fight on the Republican side, he returned for the purpose of organizing a British section for the International Brigade, rejoined the front at Madrid University, where he helped to defend the Faculty of Arts and Letters behind a barricade of philosophy books, fought at Boadilla, and was killed near Cordoba at the end of 1936. It was during his freelance bout in Aragon that he wrote, as a convinced Communist, the *Ode Before the Storming of Huesca*, on which his claim to liberal significance rests. The only earlier poem to approach it in maturity is *As Our Might Lessens*, which is, rather surprisingly, about his fear of pain—the possibility of torture, the inevitability of violence. Pain and sexual love are not seen as polarities but as incompatibles; pain, 'the blind goddess born in dark of mind', is equated with introspection, madness, reaction; sex, 'a naked girl, the future, at our side', with enlightenment and motion, the banishing of Old Liberal nostalgia, worry, and inhibition. 'No abstraction of the brain / Will counteract the animal pain'—only 'action intervenes', the intellect giving form to biological chaos. There is no dogma or theory. It is the poet communing alone, facing the ultimate penalty of risk.

In the *Huesca Ode* the poet is embattled against pain. Echoing the Pyrenees, that rampart-gateway to 'the hot plateau beneath the night's grave manifold of stars', the first movement likens the 'past' to a glacier gripping a mountain wall, about to break, we cannot deflect it—'and time was inches, dark was all'. The 'present' is a torrent *eroding its banks*; this we can 'swing to its final course'. The 'future' has no 'image in space'; it is *with us*—it is *up to us*—'crooked as the road that we must tread / Straight as our bullets fly ahead'. The second movement localizes this topographical imagery. Moonlight floods Huesca: the 'innocence' of the plateau is pitiable, for it is threatened by pain. 'The barren hills of Aragon' is not a cliché, because it underlies the idea of matter about to be fertilized—humanized, raised in the scale of creation—through ideological conflict, and can justly 'announce'—a bare mountain terrain does precisely that—'our testing has begun'. It is the ideal—'if true, if false, is live or dead'—which is to be tested, and which, realized in part, speaks 'in the Oviedo mauser's tone'. The 'dragon's teeth' of an isolated hero like Dimitrov (who made a fool of the Nazis at the Reichstag Fire trial) has 'sprouted' into an army. We feel the vibrant tension, the expectancy; the outcome is in the balance. Avoiding exhortation and manifesto, the 'testing' is not just of political rectitude, but of integrity, of the status of the idea—whether true or false, the idea must be put to the test, its durable quality must be verified—and exercised intelligence, 'we studied well how to begin this fight / Our Maurice Thorez held the light'. The third movement does what propaganda abhors: it plunges us into Cornford's subjectivity, his fears, his doubts:

> *Though Communism was my waking time,*
> *Always before the lights of home*
> *Shone clear and steady and full in view—*
> *Here, if you fall, there's help for you—*
> *Now, with my Party, I stand quite alone.*

The test is on the individual. The time-analysis, the declaration of sincerity, the tentative hopes become an examination of conscience before battle. The poet hopes that his 'private battle' with his nerves, his fear of pain, 'the love that tears me by the roots', the loneliness that 'claws my guts' will 'fuse', be tempered into purposefulness, in the welded front of combat and exhorts himself in terms of the qualities of the instruments of battle he understands rather than trite political bombast. Confidence won, the last movement generalizes. 'The impartial beauty' of the night and 'the unfeeling sky' look down on Europe, the concentration camps, those abodes of pain, and 'freedom's crooked scars', of which he admits that 'we can do nothing to ease that pain'. All we can do is '*prove* that the agony' has not been otiose; we cannot waste time repining: one recalls Spender's 'my pity moves among them like a breeze'. The stars are not disdainful, pitying and so on nor do they start soliloquizing, as they would in Auden; matter's *neutrality* demands man's responsibility, the presentness of pain. The last stanza contains the only fantasy in the poem: that of the free peoples standing guard upon the plateau. It is placed as fantasy, a battle-cry whose easiness—'freedom is an easily spoken word'—recognizes that 'facts are stubborn things', and as a functional event in a man's thinking before battle, his desire that 'proof' will be given, that his comrades can 'swear' that the dead did not die pointlessly because the proof exists.

The *Huesca Ode* has more volume, temper, and purpose than genteelly cerebrating fibs which pose as poetic wisdom. It hovers on the verge of obscurity, demanding the attention of the reader just as the poet is making demands on himself. Cornford was blissfully unaware that he was integrating himself through his absorption. The question of whether one agrees with his politics—or the pros and cons of fighting in Spain, or that the Reds ruined the Republic—is irrelevant. It is his belief in his cause *and* the circumspection of that belief which unifies the poem: the virtue of free-ranging thought, crystallizing in action, which counts. (I would say the same of a Catholic poem such as *Aux Martyrs Espagnols* by Claudel.) Histrionics for the converted, the dodge of juggling with his own inconsistencies, is anathema to this poet who goes beyond doctrine to prefigure Michael Roberts's desiderata—through risk and ratiocinative honesty he discovers a common value. Initiative, decision, open speech, the brain cool in defiance, the facing up to deficiencies, eagerness to test the idea are qualities which are desirable in any society which hopes to transcend Roberts's 'lowest level of standardization'. The value in the poem burns long after its incendiary cause has been quenched; the poetic performance may be restaged in a duller arena. The proof lies in Cornford's lyric, *Heart of the heartless world*, where we find the same conquered fear, practical pride, and sensitive resolution, issuing in a modest affirmation of what *is* good in a community. Written at the same time as the *Ode*, it rehearses these qualities for action:

> *Heart of the heartless world,*
> *Dear heart, the thought of you*
> *Is the pain at my side,*
> *The shadow that chills my view.*

> *The wind rises in the evening,*
> *Reminds that autumn is near.*
> *I am afraid to lose you,*
> *I am afraid of my fear.*

> *On the last mile to Huesca,*
> *The last fence for our pride,*
> *Think so kindly, dear, that I*
> *Sense you at my side.*

> *And if bad luck should lay my strength*
> *Into the shallow grave,*
> *Remember all the good you can;*
> *Don't forget my love.*

For every reader of Cornford's work, W. H. Auden's *Spain* has hundreds. He is grandiose, omnicompetent, suspiciously plangent: without any diffidence Auden appoints himself liberal laureate to the Spanish war. Instead of speaking out of the crucible, as Cornford does, and exploring the area of freedom within it, Auden dissolves Spain in the vastness of the evolutionary continuum; he treats us to an optimistic lecture, like the instalments in the *Children's Encyclo-*

paedia, on progress culminating in 'the struggle'.* This struggle is associated with aesthetic idealism ('the poet startled among the pines'), the psychological-miraculous ('O descend as a dove or a furious papa'), and a disputed historical concept—History the Organizer—which is invoked (alleges Auden) by the poor reading the evening papers. 'Life' is apparently the instigator to participation; this is surprising because life (in its motherly way) embraces a weird, arbitrary assortment of subjective motives—it never occurs to this military psychiatrist that people like Cornford, Bell, Orwell, and Esmond Romilly could have defensible reasons for serving in Spain. On the mechanics of commitment, Auden does speak the same language as the event, forgets himself and is memorable:

> *They clung like burrs to the long expresses that lurch*
> *Through the unjust lands, through the night, through the alpine tunnel;*
> *They floated over the oceans;*
> *They walked the passes: they came to present their lives.*

He then tells us that in Spain 'our fever's menacing shapes are precise and alive'. What fever? Where is the menace, shape, precision? And why must the 'life' be so narcissistic? Perorating with a *vae victis* salutation to the defeated ('the stars are dead'—compare Cornford) and tomboyish guesses at military conditions which might have been culled from Hemingway, Auden soldiers on with a vision of the future which is Part Two of the lecture on the past; neither the prospects for, nor his hopes about, the future are affected by his feelings about the Spanish struggle. Auden sins against the Yeatsian law: he belittles the grandeur of the historical moment; he betrays Spain by degrading it into a reference in an exhibitionist monologue. Moving on a broader scale than Cornford, he rehashes the dubious Old Liberal concept of progress as a substitute for the intenser power to act on his beliefs, or even register them at pressure.

---

* Mr Hugh Thomas, in *The Spanish Civil War*, 1961, quotes Spender to the effect that Auden was, briefly, a stretcher-bearer. Mr Thomas makes impressive use of *Spain* (its 'words still irresistible') in the historical context; this should be read as an antidote to my literary reservations.

Letter from Aragon, by Cornford, is just as impressive, though Mr Peter Lowbridge finds 'formless flatness' and 'emotional detachment'. The latter is its virtue; no indulgence ('death was not dignified', 'how ugly fear is'); the message—'tell the workers of England'—*at the end*, where it is logical, even required. The refrain 'this is a quiet front' is gainsaid, violently, by the facts; the laconic tone, more and more eventful, brings 'our nerves are steady' into collusion with bombardment, burial and the wounding, creates a challenge and suspense, as the grand image of *pain* draws nearer and nearer. A *letter*, the poem has a right epistolary touch, relates the truth with such tact that consoling lies are absent, fights the horror as it greets it, so that 'detachment' is really control. The peroration is the idea, having traversed facts.

IN BUT NOT OF: E. M. FORSTER, JULIAN BELL, AND THE LIBERAL CRITIQUE

JULIAN BELL was born in 1908, the nephew of Virginia Woolf, the grandson of Sir Leslie Stephen, and a descendant of James Stephen the Clapham Sect Evangelical. He was educated at a Quaker school and at Cambridge; divided the next four years between a thesis on 'Some Applications of Ethics to Politics' and the open-air activities of a countryman; went in 1935 as Professor of English to the University of Hankow, but returned from China two years later to serve as an ambulance man on the Republican side in Spain, where he fell before Madrid in July 1937. He published two slim volumes of verse* (which were upstaged by the demonstrative work of the Auden group) and produced three incisive and prophetic essays of his own, which might be sub-titled 'a young liberal examines his conscience'. Bell had a provenance of socially anxious, culturally vigilant, educationally aware families who had been directors of conscience to the recalcitrant Victorians. He was the offspring of Bloomsbury, of which D. H. Lawrence's charges of shallow rationalism, immaturity, and debility of physique are gleefully remembered, while the book in which J. M. Keynes (himself the manipulator of means who is devoted to ends) admits these charges in respect of later deviations but defends the unworldliness of the original group, has been rather ignored.† Their hates and preferences were included in Lawrence's more dynamic either-or vision; it was a feud between factions of the puritan tradition, with E. M. Forster as heckled umpire—his 'glory of the animal' relating him to Lawrence, his 'couple of ideas' to Bloomsbury. ('Leonard had given up the glory of the animal for a tail coat and a couple of ideas.')

Bloomsbury is an imperfect example because it was too clannish to have use as a leaven. In losing the Victorian worst these reformers, who now look almost Edwardian, also mislaid much of their progenitors' best. Individuality for its own sake, or, in Bloomsbury's case, a collection of individualities, is merely factious, and may be subversive, unless it promotes a community excellence. Yet the

---

* *Winter Movement*, 1930, and *Work for the Winter*, 1936.
† J. M. Keynes, *Two Memoirs*, 1949. The commentary on this by Leonard Woolf in *Sowing*, 1960, and *Beginning Again*, 1964, is instructive. The Woolfs could see the strange and dark sides of life.

prejudices and conformities against which Lawrence and Bloomsbury set their faces have retrenched under our noses. The weakness
of Bloomsbury, infecting all thinking people instead of a leisure class
(Forster's 'piety before plenty—but plenty'), should get short shrift;
the idea of the civilizing group might be revived. At a time when
wealth has put the good life—in Arnold's sense rather than the
tycoon's—within the grasp of many deserving persons we see a recession towards pleasure-seeking and pretence in collusion with a
coarse boom. We need enclaves where character is more important
then status, and spiritual communication than professional gossip.
We need teams which relate conduct to a conception of ethics, who
have a reasoned faith in the priority of the idea, who are fortified by
trust in shared values individually pursued, and who decline to
imitate the views, accoutrements, or behaviour of any commercial
or administrative caucus. A civilizing group will always be ethical,
never utilitarian, for even though it revalue manners it will be on an
agreement of manners—a shaking of convention by manners—
rather than official fuss and bother that its worth, ultimately, will
rest.

One might restate Bell's heredity in terms of social history, by
saying that it represents the education of a middle-class clan by a
habit of cultivated seriousness, and in terms of the history of ideas,
by saying that it represents the refinement of innate puritan ideals
by ethical interests. As Leslie Stephen rejected religious belief but
inherited a moral gravity (his avowed aim being to prove 'you can
be a gentleman and an agnostic') so his inheritors rejected gravity
but exalted art, friendship, and the pursuit of knowledge as goods
in themselves. The virus came from Cambridge, more respectful of
where you are (in thought or feeling) than what you are, then under
the sway of G. E. Moore's *Principia Ethica* (1903). Over-reaching its
Clapham cradle, Bloomsbury aimed to trim the Enlightenment
lamps, to utilize new psychological discoveries, to devise purer, more
complex art forms. Attentive to the sociology of art, they disliked any
commitment by artists, and their ethos might be summed up in this
formula: enjoyment was the order of the day, but earnestness was in
the blood. A vain emancipation was tempered by an austerity, a distrust of the garish, the vote-catchers in art and conduct. There was at
first an ideal of plain living and high thinking. A good taste of the
emotions was to distinguish ends from means. The mathematical
tradition of interest in abstract truth, hard and ineluctable, was
quickened through the infusion of art appreciation with its attention
to fine shades, subtle discriminations, and emotional rarities into an
amalgam of the exact with the imaginative which was to avoid the
pitfalls of both idealism and materialism. (It was hardly the latter

which inspired the Post-Impressionist exhibitions and the Omega Workshops. The initiative of yesterday is the commercial cliché of today, but if some interiors *are* more presentable we should thank Fry more than the admen.)

All Bell's seniors had done was to change the convention; they failed to go *beyond* convention into the 'horror' and the 'glory', they upheld convention as a discipline provided it is spring cleaned. They changed the Edwardian regime of sophisticated frivolity and unmentionable greed in favour of debate and discrimination; changed the protestant regime of good works into that of quality of feeling and warmth in relationships. Relishers of that humane little classic, *The Dreadnought Hoax*, will know that these traits could embrace the practical joke, a subtler and in this country more effective form of protest than the demonstration.* The respect for ordered speech, stemming from the idolization of the Bible; the preference for reading and talk over the 'slackness' of amusements; the contempt for cash, officialdom, and pushing persons (not so difficult on an unearned income), are the birthmarks, though not the life-lines, of the protestant, and where he has compromised Bloomsbury was a recall to the milk of the gospel. The attitude which Forster divines in Roger Fry is required:

> If you said to him, 'This must be right, all the experts say so, all the Trustees of the National Gallery say so, all the art-dealers say so, Hitler says so, Marx says so, Christ says so, *The Times* says so' he would reply in effect, 'Well, I wonder. Let's see'. He would see and he would make you see. You would come away realizing that an opinion may be influentially backed and yet be tripe. Needless to add, his rise in the official world was slow.†

Equally, the vices of Bloomsbury are the inheritance, the temptation, of the nonconformist conscience *and of all groups*: private criticism—yet public admiration, both mutual; the idea of election exalting a team; the impertinence about doings and motives, disguised as anxiety about salvation (it was this which maddened Lawrence—overblown, inbred liberalism talking out the power of action); the dislike of the damned, or those outside the circle; and passionate interest in humanitarian causes provided the reforms are effected by those who know best. It was well said of Roger Fry that 'his protest against puritanism was protestant'.

---

* 'It seemed to me . . . that anyone who took up an attitude of authority over anyone else was . . . someone who offered a leg for everyone to pull . . . I don't pretend I had a moral to preach, I only felt that armies and suchlike bodies presented legs that were irresistible.' Adrian Stephen, *The Dreadnought Hoax*, 1936, p. 10.

† 'Roger Fry: An Obituary Note', in *Abinger Harvest*, 1936, p. 39.

When Julian Bell comes to reject the pacifist and permissive aspects of Bloomsbury he addresses his argument to E. M. Forster. He is not only seeking a tolerant listener; he reveres in Forster a more activist orientation; the values this poet died defending were Forster's, whose injunction to 'only connect—the prose and the passion' diagnoses the liberal anaemia. In Forster the administered, discursive morality of prose and the ratiocinative, centrifugal fervour of poetry are, to some extent, connected; and the mediator is the *idea*, God's gift to this agnostic, an ethical concern about how, to what end, without being stuffy or regimented, one should think and behave. Between a Forster and consenting post-war novelists there is the difference between a spiritual director and a haunter of the confessional; between puppets capering in a vacuum, and characters whose revolt, alienation, and even acquiescence outline a conception of conduct; between symbols 'ever in the great taskmaster's eye' which, in addition to enriching the form, alert us to standards outside it, and symbols as a technical ploy, a pretence to mystique or an objectified figment of the author's or characters' inwardness. This power of the idea is what poetry needs; failing it, verse will drift into the backwaters of culture and end as the asylum for private neurosis.

It is correct to make this novelist the moral centre of a book about poetry—Forster, with Mann and Lawrence, is one of the novelists of the period who have either written good poetry, created characters who are like the best type of poet, or upheld views commendable to bards. (His collected journalism, twin beacons in the miasma of mammon, shows a public vigilance which puts it in the line of patrician wits. Could the rot of Parliament be stopped if Forster's 'private member who is a nuisance' was a poet?) Poet and novelist meet in the conviction that rejuvenation lies in landscape; England is invincible if she keeps faith with the springs of being. Wiltshire in *The Longest Journey* is a chalk backbone, the heart of England pulsing with history. (The Marabar Caves, rightly foreign, show the power of nature to stabilize and mystify, to taunt man with the promise of nothingness and provoke him to live.) Forster's 'yeoman' may or may not be a landowner, but his inner life is a study for poets: an aristocracy not of wealth or success but of 'the sensitive, the considerate and the plucky'. These aristocrats are not ordained to walk through a fiery furnace to emerge shining. Wit is the humanist's device to expose himself to conflict and suffering and to subjugate it; irony, the shock troops of the intelligence, is a regulator of tensions; it transforms them into sane and fruitful acts.

No dynamic persons disturb Mr Forster's art; if some demagogues resent this it is because he deprives them of mouthpieces through which to harangue the public. We cannot mistake his reluctant heroes for anything other than unclubbable, evasively adapted or elusively dissenting. Fielding is a picaresque hero positive for our time; he has the same raffish detachment, offset by self-effacing, ironically sympathetic concern, his lips hovering between a wisecrack and a moralism, as the heretical liberals of Mann (Joseph in the *Saga*), Gide, and Lampedusa (Tancredi in *The Leopard*), but he speaks most clearly in the English accents of Graves, Empson, Cameron. Defiant when at bay, committed to the people he meets, the action he incites, the philosophical hares that he starts, he is yet apt to be mobile, adaptable. Immersed in India without roots, with an odd background of breakaway and renewal and a penchant for travelling light, he is saner in a row, better trained for insight than anyone in the Officers' Club where he is made an outsider (I use the humble 'o' to distinguish Fielding from Colin Wilson's ventriloquists' dolls). The abortive apotheosis of friendship between Fielding and Aziz does not disqualify the idea, it explores the limits to which a given application may go, and refuses to bluff its way further, to invoke the gods, in an alien context; it is more knowledge, more exchange, more sympathy cherishing differences which is invoked. To know when to stop, especially in an alien culture, is a liberal virtue —just as Gide in his Russia and Congo books knew when to go on.

Different habits do reflect different values, conflicts about what should be defended and promoted: Forster does not let us forget it. He judges people before the bar of his requisites for civilization, and the jury (who are often popped into the dock, nor always acquitted) turn out to be the middle classes. The idea traduced, the idea refined, in a small space: each episode is a 'minute particular' subject to 'the lost traveller's dream under the hill'. Dreamed or writ large, they result in bigger injustices and neglects ('rockets are not in my line; unfortunately I am in theirs'). As Forster portrays an obsolete milieu, those for whom sociology does duty for literature have charged that his idea is redundant. Forster admitted that he stopped writing because 'the world changed so much'; we know that he wrote about 'the person I think I am, the people who irritate me, and the people I would like to be'. The wheel has revolved from the first statement to the last. The neon-lit desert, built up, insured, of our day calls for advice from the Edwardian peace across the war-torn no-man's-land. Our difficulties—the 'cankers of a calm world and a long peace' of Falstaff—have as much affinity with those of the *douceur de vivre* as with the bitter certainties of the *entre deux guerres*. Another reason has to do with the meaning of tradition. Forster's stable critique may help to rally, to mature, to warn the broadening middle classes in a period of ferment; the Enemy has made himself more glamorous, less grandiose, more plausible, less aloof, that is all. Schlegels and Wilcoxes 'ready under new names to exploit or be exploited' dig the trenches in offices, factories, staff-rooms, and New Towns as well as drawing-rooms, suburbs, and Officers' Clubs.

In his letters to Lord Russell ('what you want to do is jab and strike . . . only you are sublimated into words') D. H. Lawrence cuts Forster's 'social passion' with 'Cure the pain—don't give the poetry' yet discerns in Forster 'something very real'.* Lawrence hated Bloomsbury because it put mental idealism before practical being. To Lawrence the spirit is just where we differ; social equality (he wanted nationalization of the mass media) is desirable to liberate spiritual differences; through equality, diversify, or die. Let the Russells 'jab and strike'—defending their vital interests, their values will be meaningful. Lawrence pierces the Achilles heel of Forster when he advocates a Moral Corporate State to correct the liberal bent to *divide* private values and public aims, private life and professional work in the hope, British and hypocritical, that they will be reconciled in respectability. According his enemies the courtesy of believing that they were sincere enough to act on their beliefs, Lawrence operates in the un-British belief that a man and his views are inseparable. If we want a community instead of a rat-race, this must be learned. Lawrence looks like a literary Hindenburg, but is really a spiritual communist, who betrays a logical, though fitful, impulse to see himself as he saw others, to make others what he made himself; therefore, he reiterates the need for differences, and he can see how power is perverted by envy and ambition—knowledge which might save liberals much fretful bewilderment. Forster turned satirist; Lawrence left the country. They meet at parting. On the eve of exile Lawrence's love of England expressed itself as that fusion of tradition with rebirth which is instinct to the spirit of poetry—'I must go as a seed that falls into new ground. But . . . these elm-trees, the grey wind with yellow leaves—it is so awful, the being gone from it . . .'

Mr Forster's delight in music reads a lecture to poets. It works to unite the themes, contrasts with the mode of Virginia Woolf who charted the currents of feeling yet lacked penetration in breadth, for the orchestra soon goes out of tune without the score. For Mann music is the food of love—or death; for Proust a luxury, steeped in nostalgia, heralding the absolute; for Eliot a harbinger of illumination, for Auden a therapy. For Forster it is symmetry of design. Like poems, his novels constitute a simultaneity; the values are there once and for all, they cannot be pilfered; reading these works we are not just passing the time for something is being established in us and in

* *D. H. Lawrence's Letters to Bertrand Russell*, ed. Harry T. Moore, 1948.

time. Although music is evoked in the Beethoven Fifth Symphony chapter of *Howard's End* (this must rank with Spender's *Beethoven's Death Mask* and Rilke's 'Music stands . . .') it is in his *montage* that Forster applies his knowledge of structure. His inviting address, confidential diction, and racy syntax have little to do with Swinburnian music, nor Symbolist-like does he embellish reality. If there is a hierarchy of values in Forster this is due to his refusal to dissolve informative in sensational modes; he resumes a tradition where music is in harmony with the discipline of mathematics. His silence is resonant. There he stands, with a quizzical smile at the self-congratulatory party, with a pin held innocently between forefinger and thumb, and suddenly the balloons of cant, hypocrisy, and blandishment go bang, deflated before our eyes. 'We must love one another or die' he extracts from Auden. It was left to a later generation to delete that line from the Collected Poems.

*   *   *

Julian Bell became intellectually conscious at a time when the conditions of leisure on which Forster thrived were under a cloud; his literary advent coincided with that of the Pink Liberals, rallying to the principle that the need for action outweighed the claims of privacy, but that the impulse to action flowed from and was intended to protect, ultimately, the values of privacy. Bell agreed to the hilt with their protest against greed manifesting as strength through joy. But he could not accept the dogmatic remedies which attracted Cornford and others. For he valued highly the amenities of liberal civilization; in contrast to some apologists, Bell was quite capable of saying what the good life was and why he held it to be good. It was the life of talk, cultural enjoyments, and the pursuit of learning recognized by Bloomsbury as good in itself. In his poem *Autobiography* he singles out 'not breeding but environment' as a value, and praises 'humane, sensible' men who follow mind, feeling, and sense 'where they might lead', with no pretence to 'fame, success, or meddling in that world'.*

Bell recognized, however, a flaw in this diamond: bourgeois life can be boring, trivial, and behind the façade of service, grossly materialistic. The merit of Bell's first essay, the *Letter to A on Roger Fry*, 1936, is that he goes *beyond* the ethos to examine problems of the implementation of this ethos in the Socialist state of the future. He believes that it 'will, with any luck, make the common citizen a free man; free economically, free to choose how he will live'. (We can read affluent for Socialist in the terms of the debate.) He then asks,

* All quotations are from *Julian Bell: Essays, Poems and Letters*, ed. Quentin Bell, 1938.

'How will he live?' Bell fears the growth of 'a material and psychological barbarity', resulting from a Gresham's Law which will operate in the absence of any respected code of values. Since, according to Bell, there are no metaphysical justifications for a dogmatic assertion of right values, the responsibility falls on the literati to maintain the highest standard of taste. This is not a democratic procedure, so it must be complemented by an unrelenting educational effort to *persuade* the mass to practise 'rational behaviour'—'conscious and intelligent behaviour towards ends judged to be valuable'.* It is typical of Bell's ideal that he cannot envisage these ends except in terms of human types; thus the Letter ends with a tribute to Roger Fry 'in a perpetual movement of emotion, sensibility, intellectual passion'. (Bell's own teaching success with working people was related to his 'solid' poetic virtues, for he avoided both condescension and an equally absurd bonhomie, and appears to have pursued the deep and extended exchange of views and experiences.)

The fruit of this judgment and foresight was that Bell was only in, not really of, his generation. Leslie Stephen had championed the judicial method against the transcendentalism of Carlyle, the aesthetic of Ruskin, and the moral imperialism of some Arnold, had fought to preserve the relevances of literary valuation from being subsumed in mechanistic schemes or dissipated in vague idealism. In Bell's account of the line of hardness we hear the chord of his grandfather's austerity: 'there is in it', says Bell of judicial criticism, 'a possibility of detachment, of unworldliness, and intellectual courage and virtue that is of the first importance. It does at least admit some of the unromantic facts about the world.' Indeed, Bell strove to exert on his generation the same moderating and chastening influence. His Letter is addressed to a scientist by a poet, and in his discussion of the role of art in the prosperous state, Bell is influenced by Fry's blend of 'the sensuousness of the arts' with the 'hardness of mind' of the scientist.

Bell sees the work of art as a relation of constructions, an exercise which suspends desire, an interval of contemplation before acting. 'Not only is our behaviour regulated, it is also enriched by these organizations; we discover possibilities, subtleties, and relations between our different activities.' The maximum of clarified emotion is

* In *Democracy and the Arts*, read to the Cambridge Fabians in 1910, published by Hart-Davis in 1946, Rupert Brooke examines the same problems. He opposes the fallacy that 'spare time' will produce a Florentine civilization, gives an exhilarating picture of the enthusiasm for adult education, looks for the extinction of dividends, and proposes State endowments for worthwhile artists, which is better than piecemeal patronage. Brooke sees the answer in economic terms. He is oblivious of the problem of incentives. He fails to foresee the vulgarization of a Welfare State by profiteering interests, the snob-appeal of those interests, and the growth of wage-status careerism in a progressive society.

subjected to the most informed control; when disconcerted by violent, ugly, and conflicting passions, the resort to art may help us to observe our conduct, envisage ends beyond the present, judge the value of states of mind and order our energy with reference to those ends. 'The arts . . . do not call for so great a precision as science, but they do call for intuitive, sensual intelligence, not the suppression, but the understanding of emotion . . . alone among human activities they satisfy both mind and senses.' Art will tap up deep emotion into a reservoir, from which it will be released into life through the valve of the intelligence, so that outbreaks of exasperated reaction or primitive violence will not wreck civilization. The discipline of applied aesthetics can focus clear vision, help to sort things out, give remedial pleasure. 'To have acquired the habit of contemplation, tragic or comic, is a main resource in crisis. It invites feeling, denies nothing, yet allows the perceived pattern to exert control.'

In his second essay, the *Open Letter to C. Day Lewis*, 1936, Bell berates what he calls the 'irresponsibility' of certain poets. He attacks the *recherché* obscurantism of their technique, childish romanticism masquerading as realism, their defective psychology, the duplicity of their discontent, and their sabotaging of the tradition with the *deus ex machina* of ill-judged extremism. A devotee of Pope, Dryden, and the Augustans, if there was one thing Bell could not stand it was 'enthusiasm'. For Bell it was a matter of controlling emotion with a view to effective action, the curbing of enthusiasm, the promotion of careful reforms and a vigilance by the cultivated for 'the establishment of ends judged to be valuable'. In some of his poems, notably *Bypass to Utopia*, he ridicules the myth of idealism, which he regards as a betrayal of the independence of the intellect. The poem reminds one of *Just a Smack at Auden*, the Empson squib which begins 'Waiting for the end, boys, waiting for the end'. In spite of his campaign for discipline and detachment, Julian Bell was not yet out of the wood. His need for action was not slaked. From China he wrote to Vanessa Bell that 'I am tired of being an intellectual on the loose: I want to do something practicable, tiresome, and involving other people . . . the only way to recover that heavenly sharpness of feeling about the quality of the world is to do exciting things that make one wake up.' This need for action was not a T. E. Lawrence mystique, since Bell shared the Bloomsbury view that 'achievement' for its own sake, or for the sake of profit, was grotesquely ridiculous and evil. It stemmed from a regard for politics, considered not as a means to advancement or the defence of self-interest, but as a call to responsibility; the confidence in his values gained by doing a teaching job; and a conviction that, although the ethos was valuable as an end, it would only gain respect and efficacy when its exponents were willing to defend it and, if necessary, die for it.

In a poem sent from China on the aftermath of love, Bell writes:

> *Escape, sea-gale winged through the cold*
> *Red sunsets, black bent trees, the steep*
> *English bird-voiced cliffs; till old,*
> *Tangled across the bars, we sleep.*

It is the note of this charismatic image—'English bird-voiced cliffs'—which echoes through Bell's poetry, and transfigures the naturalism of such poems as *Winter Movement* and *Marsh-Birds pass over London*. His mind was established, created; the letters are full of vivid density and idiomatic life. He lacks Edward Thomas's power to mature an emotion by following it through a landscape, so that it loses its enfeebling inwardness and is nourished by the observable, and Ted Hughes's power to shatter natural things by violent encounter and exhibit their properties. He does provide, without softness, the foundation of fact which is needed to support a more dynamic poetry. His work breathes the tranquil amenity, the intricately poised formal intelligence of a landscaped park, spacious, leisurely, measured—the nearest parallel is the Augustan pastoral, though Bell avoids the pentameter; he owes more to the sustained adventurousness of Dryden's formal odes. The poems are not rigid, 'elegant', they are refreshing, full of the sharpness of surprise— faithful to the colours, temperatures, noises, mobile patterns, and atmosphere of the South Downs which rise continually in this portraiture. The ejection of easy, prepared feelings, the variousness exacting hard work, the virile, chosen sensuousness is aware of what it is up against, and what can be said against it—the pressure of chaos and violent emotion. It is not messily and idly 'accommodating' the chthonic; it is distancing the destructive for civilization's sake, and admitting, quite deliberately, the degree of energy it needs. The merit of these minor poems becomes cogent when we realize that this led Bell to Spain.

Bell's third essay, the *Letter to E. M. Forster*, 1937, is a defence of his views about the virtue of action—that action which Old Liberals had spurned. He expounds the thesis that 'war is a lesser evil balanced against some kinds of peace' and explains why he has jettisoned the pacifism of his upbringing. The principle that everyone has a right to opt out of aims of which they disapprove is invalid in face of an enemy who denies free speech on principle. The need now, Bell declares, is to 'down the Fascists' with the minimum of fuss and bother; he would like to see the Left adopt the policy of Machiavelli. In a letter to Vanessa Bell just before he sailed for Spain, he affirms that 'I seem to have learned from you my attitudes to life and the sort of things to value and ways to behave', and that 'art can and does mean everything to you', but he recognizes a need to be fulfilled which is best sublimated in the defence of liberalism. For 'only a thinker can see something very unpleasant very clearly' and the urge towards violence, which is a means, can be placed at the service of good ends.* Bell had reached a point where he not only felt; he felt there was something worth fighting for:

> The best states of mind of a civilized society. To anyone appreciative of the arts . . . of leisure and love and flirtation, of sports and the beauty of nature and the amenity of a country life, of the richness and variety of the world, war must come as a black and dismal termination . . .

If we think of Bell's death as a meaningless waste of talent, remember that death was a risk inherent in the choice and cannot be isolated from it. It was a fulfilment, a meritorious action and a token for posterity. We have to consider the *symbolic* value of a commitment transcending a transitory event. The death is an affirmation of the free spirit and its wish to embrace a purpose beyond itself, to proclaim that quiet colours are to be painted on the larger canvas. We begin to see such events in the way W. B. Yeats saw them: immobilized in time, stamped on history, a signpost for the future, and the right motto springs to mind: 'a terrible beauty is born'. The comparison with Yeats may be furthered. For Yeats action was not the result of panic or muddle, but a device whereby the individual may extinguish 'all those complexities' and be reborn into new being. There is evidence that Bell suffered from depression, Virginia Woolf's 'black blood of the Stephens'; he is hampered by 'sudden fits of nervous inhibition'. Action was an inward triumph *and* the Yeatsian achievement of an external, eternal design, as calculated as the ordinary man's decision to plan a holiday or change his job. Bell proved that considered action inspired by emotional indignation is not to be dismissed as naïve by the devotees of rational detachment. He would have regarded the insistence on the verification of statements which has become a fetish among positivists as a symptom of decadence, for if thought is to have any existential in addition to its academic use it must be tested in practice, it must provide Cornford's 'essential element, the key to action'. Michael

---

* Mr Hugh Thomas, in *The Spanish Civil War* (footnote to p. 463), gives a sceptical account of Bell's motives and supports it with a damaging quotation, out of context, from Bell's letters. Mr Thomas has not read his literary sources as closely as his political ones.

Roberts, lecturing to the Alpine Club on the idea of risk of life in climbing, has expressed this admirably:

> The risk excuses itself. It is a demonstration that man is not wholly tied to grubbing for his food, not wholly tied to family and social loyalties; that there are states of mind and spirit that he values more highly than life itself on any lower level . . .
>
> Sacrifices are good because they show an excess and overflow which is really a gesture of confidence, of vitality.*

After a relapse made worse by the rise of a callow, neutral discontent, the writers of the 30's are now being, if not acquitted, at least tried again. They will emerge with unspectacular but exemplary reputations: and the example will lie in their gropings towards social commitment as an essential factor in moral intelligence. Julian Bell will be a key figure. He rests on the validity of his anticipations and the efficacy of his work. He would not have been surprised by the angry mood of British thinkers who contemplate the betrayal of the high possibilities of the Welfare State by commercial philistinism and mass entertainment, because he had pre-analysed the pitfalls of a progressive society in his critique of the Old Liberal calculus. And he would have welcomed the retreat from dogmatism towards the purpose and conduct concerns of the radical tradition. Never losing sight of the ideal of community excellence, he struggled to formulate a rational basis for the creativity of individuals.

*   *   *

Cornford went to Spain for a purpose; he found himself as a poet as a result of his action. Bell used Spain to resolve certain problems; he found himself in action as a result of thinking like a poet. These motives are reconciled in the artefact: the probity which Bell sought in art, and the integrity of Cornford's Spanish poems, are bound up with the virtues which both demanded in life—the values implicit in a single good poem. 'Romantic idealists' is the fashionable gibe at the men of Spain. Byron, no doubt, was such another. Reading them closely, you realize they were neither Luddites nor idealists, they lay stress on mastery of the machine, on gaining understanding through involvement. Their revival in modern dress of the first scenes of English romanticism should inspirit verse whenever anaemia brings it to the verge of the grave. Playing for safety, the delegation of feeling and deeds, followed by the vicarious enjoyment of them, the cult of the anecdote, discreet, tritely moralizing, and eagerness to join the swim once the next man has taken the plunge will at all times be

* Quoted by Janet Adam Smith in her Introduction to *Collected Poems of Michael Roberts*, 1958.

unable to say: this is what I feel, that is the question, the other should be done. Failing a challenge without, it should be possible to discover within everyday affairs challenges as strenuous and urgent as a war; if poets step aside, worse people will inherit the earth.

The individual in Spain could feel that his decision to fight for his ideas was a dignifying thing; two liberal fetishes—the individual and the idea—were made to acquit themselves in public. Being ideological, to do with what could be as well as what is, and being a conflict Spain produced a literature, unlike other episodes such as the attempts on Everest which have an equal potential. To visit Spain is to feel that Franco's days deserve to be numbered. But my complete point is that the lesson of Spain, as it can be learned from art, will outlive the restoration of freedom; Spain teaches us that the idea cannot be allowed to perish in selfishness and materialism; it must be fought for, not just on battlefields, but in every way; the individual and the idea march together. Nor is there any reason why the sense, beneficial to art, of inward wholeness attained in relation to outward choice should exclude the practical act. The nuclear stalemate may abolish total war; violence will seek civil outlets and ask to be converted into unfamiliar vision and unusual deeds. Poets like Owen and Rosenberg, with their balance of energy with charity, will become arbiters. Vitality will leap at tests and ordeals: then the deliberate, more cerebral commitment of poets like Cornford and Bell will be in order. It must be screened by the whole liberal conscience against the infiltration of the perverse and the opportunistic.

Two prose books of the 1930's, little known today, in my view rank as classics of the conscience in action. Esmond Romilly was a born anarchist, quite probably driven, as Mr Philip Toynbee has inferred—'I remember murmuring the word "Passchendaele" in an ecstasy of excitement and regret'—by envy of the generation who fought in the war. Not an encouraging start. Still, Romilly had diverted *les honnêtes gens* by absconding from school and publishing ('I am one of that large class of unskilled labourers with an educated accent') from his hideout in Soho a scurrilous rag, *Out of Bounds*, in which he attacked the Establishment in general and militarism in particular. (*Out of Bounds* is not to be equated with the satire boom —Romilly was the reverse of *comme il faut*.) * Romilly went to Spain neither as a journalist, nor as a politician, but in search of adventure; his book is devoid of pleading, impregnated with sense impressions. *Boadilla* shows how a feckless activism grows into a serious, tragic, but still decent and humane purpose. Romilly traces with

* See Philip Toynbee, *Friends Apart*, 1954. This features Romilly, who appears as Markham in Toynbee's *The Barricades*, 1943.

sensitivity, with humour and searching good sense the troubled yet maturing pattern of relationships in the English group of the International Brigade, 'changed utterly' in the 'terrible beauty' born at Boadilla; his friendship with the roving radical and soldier of fortune, James Gough, killed in the disaster, forms a dramatic subplot.

We read of an onset of bullets 'like a cool breeze whistling in the grass', of confessions, intended as pejorative, which are so candidly described that they win over the reader. The unawareness of the courage comes out in asides like 'knowing nothing of war, nothing surprised me in the way it was fought', and, in battle, remembering days wasted on playing fields, 'I was not the same person—I had different senses and feelings'.* The motif of change—the grotesque arrival, the growing seriousness, insights into the ambitious dogmatism of agitators and orators, the rests between battles, when sensual awareness revives in sharp bursts of description, the extravaganza of fooling M.P.s and journalists—and the tense, gradual approach to the tragedy, itself prosaic, circumstantial, yet overwhelming, is followed through with a freshness and resolve which is in my view more lasting than anything in Hemingway or Malraux (on this subject). Romilly has started from the wrong end of the spectrum: being the qualities, living the ends, for which the Left was fighting he is led to partake of the means. We understand him when he says that although the dead 'were only important for a day' his abiding impression is of 'the vastness of this thing which united so many individualities' and that it is not with 'the happiness of the convinced politician' but rather 'reluctantly' that he fights against 'profit-seeking, self-interest, cheap emotion and organized violence'.

Half an American of protestant stock, Lauro de Bosis was a poet who had lectured on Italian literature in the United States. Inclined at first to discern 'regeneration' in fascism, he later founded a resistance group inside Italy; this being repressed, he escaped to France, scraped up money to buy an aeroplane, and vanished over the Mediterranean after dropping leaflets over Rome—'a feat of great skill and daring . . . the plane seemed to be mounting the Spanish Steps'. *The Story of My Death* was written the night before the flight. The facsimile has not a single correction, the argument is not febrile but as practical as the leaflets which it justified—these urged proposals for passive disobedience which could have made the regime unworkable. De Bosis reminds liberals that you cannot be impartial about unreason—'its excesses are its logic, to exalt violence and strike Toscanini in the face'. As 'no one takes the piecemeal loss of freedom seriously' an individual must imperil his liberty for the

* Esmond Romilly, *Boadilla*, 1937.

idea, for 'we are in the fullness of the Risorgimento'.* The meaning of risk is that it unites the idea—'as one throws bread on a starving city, one must throw history books on Rome'—with behaviour. Without the clarity of this type of poetic vision—Shelley and Byron knew it—we walk blindfold. The De Bosis's unite technique with art to make history; beyond the imagination of C. P. Snow, they reconcile the Two Cultures. For De Bosis was by training a scientist, and in his verse-play, *Icaro*, Minos represents acquisitive power, Daedalus disinterested science, and Icarus the creative imagination. Acquaintance with technique, prowess at pulling the utilitarian strings, is not enough: Icarus is the man who tries to fly. If art is to make good use of material progress, and at the same time triumph over acquisitive power, it must understand the meaning of De Bosis's 'armed dream'—to stake the whole personality at the point of danger.

* *The Story of My Death*, tr. and intro. by Ruth Draper, 1933. This includes the treatise, of which there is a facsimile, and the manifestos dropped to the King and the Italian people. See also Neville Rogers, 'A Man and his Mission', *The Listener*, October 19th 1961: a version appears in *Keats, Shelley, and Rome*, by various hands, published for the Keats Shelley Memorial Association in 1949.

WORM'S EYE: DYLAN THOMAS

THE poetry of Dylan Thomas began to appear in 1934, and at first bid fair to overthrow Auden's school with surrealism. To-day, however, the alarums and excursions which skirmished under Thomas's banner in the 40's—the attempt of Henry Treece to found an Apocalypse, of Derek Stanford to Baptize the Pagan—take on a Byzantine look, while the poet's voluble friends seem to have been too amused by his antics or dazed by his brilliance to bother to examine the implications of his originality. There is a stumbling block in his development as in Auden's, but whereas Auden was swamped by a flood of knowledge, Thomas was blinded by a Dama-scene light of the unconscious which vouchsafed him dazzling in-sights but never emerged into the light of common day. Like hal-lucinations, his poetry may be made to mean anything, is thus a best buy in the Ph.D. racket—and his quarrelsome expositors either mis-construe what he did or blame him for muffing what he never tried to do. The latest is Mr David Holbrook, who blames Thomas be-cause, having failed to take Marie Stopes cum William Morris as his masters, he is now enjoyed by subtopians who are in dire need of both. As for what Thomas tries and fails to do, it is done by the mature George Barker, who conducts a thinner orchestra, with fewer pieces, in less rococo halls, and whose roll of drums, solo violin, and trumpet voluntary is well spaced, well timed, and cor-rectly audible; and who is less overwrought.

What is Thomas's dynamic? How is it constituted? What does he make of it? Albeit challenged by Mr John Wain, the custom is to accept Thomas's obscurity with amusement, dismissing it from the realm of judgment, a sort of favourite butt. One is sorry to be a spoil-sport but the obscurity is unrewarding: when penetrated, it is found to harbour either a very private truth, or a truth which (when con-strued) is commonplace but would gain if expressed in starker and less verbose terms. This is not the fetching obscurity of Meredith or Empson which promises a reward for our effort: it is a mindless obscurity which offers no incentive. The unrisen sun of *A saint about to fall, If my head hurt a hair's foot, Twenty-four years,* and *Into her Lying Down Head,* once it dawns, is hardly worth staying awake for—the poems debauch the dictum that 'poetry may communicate before it is understood'. They remind one of T. S. Eliot's retort to I. A. Richards's demand that we should meditate on the facts of birth and death in their inexplicable oddity, to which Eliot replied that there is nothing particularly odd about birth and death (in Thomas's case one would add love) unless we can devise a more natural and efficacious way of entering life (engendering it) and leaving it. The dogged vehemence of Thomas's obsession with the biologic and the unconscious becomes an *ad lib.* ululation; he makes heavy weather out of a spring day. *I, in my intricate image* is an emetic riot of unleavened images, *Do you not father me* is lent a spurious unity by ringing changes on the title-theme, in *If I were tickled by the rub of love* the flashy clowning on the idea is betrayed by the failure of such acrobatics to establish the narrative. *Where once the waters of your face* provides no documentation of symbolism; the metaphor for the deprivation of love seems a substitute for the absence of structure, so that the last stanza is a memorable lyric by itself rather than a credit to the poem.

The most confused poems give flashes of direct, thankful clarity, drawn from a reservoir of truth within the poet:

> *I knew the message of the winter,*
> *The darted hail, the childish snow,*
> *And the wind was my sister suitor;*
> *Wind in me leaped, the hellborn dew;*
> *My veins flowed with the Eastern weather;*
> *Ungotten I knew night and day.*
> > *(Before I knocked)*

Such stanzas fuse the power of inspiration with the sobriety and authenticity of—yes—reportage; this grain is the approach to a strong line founded on association rather than sequence—'I know her scrubbed and sour humble hands / Lie with religion in their cramp'—or the far-found, richly suggestive, yet identified, and graspable, overtones of 'the towering dead / With their nightingales and psalms' and 'shells / That speak seven seas'. When Thomas confides in his clarity of vision, makes it the dominant of a poem and resists the temptation to daub, he achieves a tragic diapason which, anchored in mundane causality, offers no consoling rhetoric, or comfortable fancy, to distract us from the emotional frankness:

> *And you, my father, there on the sad height,*
> *Curse, bless, me now with your fierce tears, I pray.*
> *Do not go gentle into that good night.*
> *Rage, rage against the dying of the light.*
> > *(Do not go gentle into that good night)*

Behind the possibly offensive extremism—hysterical revolt against death—there is a profound pity and an adoration of being. Thomas is saying: *this is it,* he takes our jaded sense of life by surprise, and jolts it. In a world where worship of profitable arrangements is allowed to override the need for preserving decent arrangements at all, such a poem, asserting the sheer shockingness of the difference between life and death, is invaluable. So is the acceptance of natural law in poems like *Find meat on bones*, whose dignity of observation expresses reverence for life, not a lazy surrender; the ample tone and noble, right rhythm imparts a fine understanding:

> *Black night still ministers the moon,*
> *And the sky lays down her laws,*
> *The sea speaks in a kingly voice,*
> *Light and dark are no enemies*
> *But one companion . . .*

So is the humility of the poet's fulfilment in a recognizable world, where self-sufficiency of the senses is free from the rant which often disfigures the theme in Thomas:

> *My one and noble heart has witnesses*
> *In all love's countries, that will grope awake;*
> *And when blind sleep drops on the spying senses,*
> *The heart is sensual, though five eyes break.*
> *(When all my five and country senses see)*

Of these and about sixty lines or passages like them—'God speeded summer's end', 'the blinding country of youth', 'her flesh was meek as milk', 'my wine you drink, my bread you snap', and even the publicity-soiled 'and death shall have no dominion'; 'the flying rant / Of the sky, king of your six years', 'In the beginning was the mounting fire / That set alight the weathers from a spark' we may affirm that they do conceive that rejuvenation of being for which W. H. Auden could only argue. On such platforms Thomas stages his production of the hero myth: himself. He was quick to parade himself in a number of roles. The child:

> *And the twice told fields of infancy*
> *That his tears burned my cheeks and his heart moved in mine.*
> *These were the woods the river and sea*
> *Where a boy*
> *In the listening*
> *Summertime of the dead whispered the truth of his joy*
> *To the trees and the stones and the fish in the tide.*
> *And the mystery*
> *Sang alive*
> *Still in the water and singingbirds.*
>
> *(Poem in October)*

Less attractive, the emotional Hercules—'my hero bares my side and sees his heart', the puppet-master of a many-faceted 'modern' personality—'I, in my intricate image, stride on two levels', the devil-may-care sensualist—'When I was a gusty man and a half / And the black beast of the beetle's pews'. Thomas needs these heroes, who need this victory psychology, to give the lie to Auden's deconsecrated world: they are the harbingers of a great influx of new wonder, of amazed enchantment, of delighted self-remembering. For a moment—at instants within poems—we share with Thomas a domain where are no problems of what to communicate, how, and to whom, only 'the word flowed up, translating to the heart / First characters of birth and death'. We are reborn into a world where 'sleep navigates the tides of time', of 'the dark-vowelled birds', 'I dreamed my genesis in sweat of sleep', 'a calm wind blows that raised the trees like hair' and 'Acquainted with the salt adventures / Of tides that never touch the shores', where exist:

> . . . *animals thick as thieves*
> *On God's rough tumbling grounds*
> (*Hail to His beasthood!*) . . .
> *O kingdom of neighbours, finned*
> *Felled and quilled* . . .
>
> (*Prologue*)

The motto for this world might be 'we in our Eden knew the secret guardian / In sacred waters that no frost could harden / And in the mighty mornings of the earth'. Here Thomas, like Rilke, 'leaps the chapter of mankind'; both are limited by their deification of instinct; for them, Freedom and Sincerity lie in emotive individualism; actually they are in thrall to their own, self-willed, automatism. Where Rilke swings incense at the hardness of experience, Thomas accepts rival categories without bothering to examine them—'The wise men tell me that the garden gods / Twined good and evil on an Eastern tree'. This leads to testimonies so direct, so pristine, and naïve that they avoid sentimentality and almost disarm criticism—'There was a Saviour / Rarer than radium / Commoner than water, crueller than truth' is an inspiring, almost sybilline, utterance. His follow-through, though, does not traverse the delicacy and intransigence which it gestures towards; the poem ends with another confession as beautiful but extempore as the first—'Exiled in us we arouse the soft / Un-clenched, armless, silk and rough love that breaks all rocks'. And the grand gesture we looked up to becomes a fabulous velleity. Lacking symbols to house the testimonies, they become inverted; then Thomas is his own self-adulating hero with a vengeance—the 'dear, daft time I take to nudge the sentence', 'heart leads helplessly', and 'lovely gift of the gab' dictator seizes power, and the muscle-bound strong-arm tactics follow, heralded by such addictive bromides as 'innocent', 'heaven', 'vows', 'love', 'rant', 'thigh', 'dry', 'holy', 'prayer', and, last but not least, 'seed'.

Auden's hope was that revival should be a dynamo of social power. This demands that at some point the 'genius' of poetry—the fundamental quality of added force it carries—should accept relativism and become, like certain verses in the Bible, 'a very present help in time of trouble'. To insist on this would be pedantic, but Thomas deliberately excites, with all the genius at his command, our expectations; and he never crowned his inspiration on this untheatrical plane, to the end he stayed an umbrageous *prima donna*. Edward Thomas, knowing that people are qualified by their environment, by their labour in nature, their endowment at birth, the ramification of their love, their meditation on death and the consequences of that for their life, and that the exploration of birth, love, and death *per se* becomes silly and tedious, wrote poems which, similar in temperament and locale to Dylan's, have a searching relevance absent in Dylan's pyknic world, where everything is confiscated by the poet at sight; his *trompe l'œil* wrings every mixed-up, minuscule fancy out of sex and the unconscious. *The seed-at-zero* is very trying, in more ways than one; in *A process in the weather of the heart* the bumptious rhythm hides with grandiloquence the infantilism of the thought; *When, like a running grave, time tracks you down* muddles through by muscularity, relieved by lucky shots at purple passages; before and after these orgies the words drift away or conglomerate in blocs; and this is a besetting vice in Thomas. The so-called Welsh *en masse* vitality is, often, the scream of panic in the face of something which can only be yielded to, never regarded; the lines blunder forward in short and long gasps, we drag on unflagging—but we are accumulating glaring and contradictory images rather than expatiating into one complex, ordered impression.

Thomas is best when he forgets his Bardic status, his paraphernalia of myths, and allows his physical imagination full play—lets a physical episode accentuate a memory or kindle a vision—'forever it is a white child in the dark-skinned summer . . . Scales the blue wall of spirits'. In *The force that through the green fuse drives the flower, Light breaks where no sun shines*, and *This bread I break was once the oat* we observe a metamorphosis of the Dionysiac into man's self-regulating physical powers. Now a passive copy, now a mere auxiliary, of natural forces, the poet emerges as in kinship with them—free, yet nourished. In *The hand that signed the paper felled a city*, a most mature poem, Apollo has become too powerful; the sacramental bond with nature has been broken:

> *The five kings count the dead but do not soften*
> *The crusted wound or stroke the brow;*
> *A hand rules pity as a hand rules heaven;*
> *Hands have no tears to flow.*

When the connaturality asks to be dramatized, Thomas excels. It may be the struggle to articulate:

> *Some let me make you of the vowelled beeches,*
> *Some of the oaken voices, from the roots*
> *Of many a thorny shire tell you notes,*
> *Some let me make you of the water's speeches.*
> (*Especially when the October wind*)

Or the struggle to do justice—no mere lip-service—to a human complication in *The tombstone told when she died, We lying by seasand, Lie Still, Sleep Becalmed, The Hunchback in the Park*, and *After the funeral*. These poems typify, as wholes, distinct moral states—compassion, bitterness, remorse. Tension is achieved, as in the poem where he 'longs to move away' from the 'half convention and half lie' of religion, but is still enchanted by 'the thunder of calls and notes'. In poems which seem recondite or fantastic—*The Conversation of Prayer, Ears in the turrets hear* are the best—the poet is still present, because the plot seems a reflection of what he once underwent, and is disfocused in order to be united anew. If the human entanglement absconds from *Why east wind chills, Poem in October, Fern Hill*, and *Over Sir John's hill* it is compensated by the poet's manifold delight in *doing* something to his material, outwitting it, borrowing the energy he needs, exerting control when it becomes obstreperous. As a rule Thomas relies for unity on the method of the mob orator—he hopes that the impact will make the outpouring seem integrated. In these poems there is a real unity of mood, for Thomas is interested in the experience and is willing to present it carefully.

> *The country is holy: O bide in that country kind,*
> *Know the green good,*
> *Under the prayer wheeling moon in the rosy wood*
> *Be shielded by chant and flower and gay may you*
> *Lie in grace.*
> (*In country sleep*)

Although the unity breaks down and the poem rants along, the endurance of *In country sleep* and *In the white giant's thigh* is higher than the ornamental talent displayed in works like *Ballad of the Long-legged Bait*—'the sun shipwrecked west on a pearl / And the moon swam out of its hulk'—or the evocative felicities of *A Winter's*

Tale—'the stars falling cold', 'the mousing cat stepping shy', 'the bird lay bedded / In a choir of wings'. Yet these wondrous moments of otherness are alien to the phantasmagoria of the early poems.

As a classic on the theme of home-front suffering, *A Refusal to Mourn the Death, by Fire, of a Child in London* will go down to history; with the war poets he rebuts the Arnold charge that passive suffering is not a theme for poetry. It has the Owen quality of austere *terribilita*, the glowing sombreness, the sense of the omnipresence of nature in 'the still hour is come of the sea tumbling in harness'. In *The Casualty*, Ted Hughes honours the apartness of the burning airman because he energizes the watchers. Thomas is aware of his *kinship* with the burning child. The poet must enter again 'the synagogue of the ear of corn'; he knows this, and has no fear of the 'fathering and all humbling darkness'. Conscious of his destiny, for once he is not a slave to nature: accompanied by humanity—'the mankind of her going'—he is in comradeship with it. The quietness of consent is enough for dignity: there is no need to abuse the mind with fantasies, 'elegies of innocence and youth'. The dead girl, alive in the poet's mind, has shocked him into sobriety. 'London's daughter' is mentioned for the first time in the last stanza. Unidentified, she is typical; the charity lies in the reticence of the poet's respect for one who has undergone 'the first death'. The next may be the poet's—but she is an adventurer, worthy of tribute. 'There is no other' death for beings; the ordeal of suffering will not have to be repeated; 'there is no other' death in nature because the 'fathering darkness' begets new life.

> Deep with the first dead lies London's daughter,
> Robed in the long friends,
> The grains beyond age, the dark veins of her mother,
> Secret by the unmourning water
> Of the riding Thames.
> After the first death, there is no other.

Ceremony After a Fire Raid could have been a subtler sequel, but though it retains the brotherhood ('myselves the believers', 'forgive us your death') it will declaim. The child is movingly lamented, but the ululation is too facile, an excuse for bombast which has more relevance to the poet's literary aims than the burned baby; and the deafening peroration, as often in Thomas, is the crescendo of an orchestra which has played too long and too loudly.

Let us hope that the memoir-vultures who fed on Dylan Thomas are satiated; their gossip was vulgar, their criticism parasitic. The views which see Thomas as a kind of suicide courting death through his weakness, or as drunk to death on the toasts of his 'hypocritical' admirers, are equally false. He was simply a prodigious and sensitive man benighted in a madhouse which he kept at bay through a mixture of posing and buffoonery. His *Collected Poems* are like a box of cunningly cut jigsaw-puzzle pieces which throw up the same glorious colours again and again but never interlock into a pattern which we may live with. His deepest urge was towards expression: this either intensifies our sense of life or reduces it to dazed automatism. He foresaw his death in *Poem on his birthday*, expiring in a machine in New York, hundreds of miles from Wales—'as I sail out to die'. In the large trusting naïveté of these lines his essence is revealed; his martyrdom by our society accounted for:

> *And freely he goes lost*
> *In the unknown, famous light of great*
> *And fabulous, dear God . . .*

> *But dark is a long way.*
> *He, on the earth of the night, alone*
> *With all the living, prays,*
> *Who knows the rocketing wind will blow*
> *The bones out of the hills . . .*

The 'this last blessing most' for which Thomas prayed was the enhancement of consciousness through union with nature, coaxing from man that flash which vanquishes the darkness for a moment, then is lost:

> *Four elements and five*
> *Senses, and man a spirit in love.*

*   *   *

The aim of Auden was to make poetry an instrument, to revive its function as an instructive and didactic power; Thomas was, as it were, a natural who enthroned his imagination as a free power. Auden, predatory, overstrained his intelligence with a profusion of subjects, Thomas, narcissist, forced his to abdicate. Owen was involved in a situation—war—which monopolized his vision and demanded choices which affected all his life. Auden and Thomas had more elbow room; no challenge was forced upon them; the most they could feel was engagement. Auden's brand was at bottom satirical, lacking in intense emotional conviction. Thomas's brand was sub-satirical, too surrealist. Thomas mistook the relation between the *creative impulse* and *poetry* as a community power. Auden, for all his poised rational penetration of crisis, tried to solve this by imposing a series of formulae which pleaded for more creative impulses, but he has not (yet) embodied these impulses in his art. Lionel Trilling discloses Thomas's Disease in this passage:

> For the unconscious mind works without the syntactical conjunctions which are logic's essence. It recognises no *because*, no *therefore*, no *but*; such ideas as similarity, agreement and community are expressed in dreams imagistically by forcing the elements into a unity.*

This also hits at Auden. In his verse there is too much logic, too much community, because, therefore, and but. And the failure of Auden and Thomas to strike the harmony requested by Trilling is a symptom of our failure to adjust the order of daylight to the night of chaos and emotion. Yet the effort of these poets will be salutary for a long time yet; it is their justification, and a guarantee that liberal poetry, aided by collaboration from an intelligent public, may achieve that fusion of common sense with depth which Julian Bell discerned in his *Open Letter to C. Day Lewis* as the hallmark of true classical art:

> Their art (the eighteenth-century masters) was to submit to reason in the imitation of nature, to take for subject the world, society, as they knew it, *never to depart from the accepted good sense of society, but to penetrate to the essentials of human nature*, and to exhibit these impartially, with a full sense of their tragedy. Such a world should be accessible to all human beings—it was the avowed object of classicism to transcend bounds of time and place by reason and generalization, but to be invariably exact; to abandon all mystification; and to start from bare, human facts.

* 'Freud and Literature', *The Liberal Imagination*, 1951, p. 53.

5

THE WINTRY DAWN

Now they ride the wintry dawn . . .

W. B. YEATS

EXILE, VIGOUR, AND AFFLUENCE:
PETER PORTER

And I Tiresias have foresuffered all
Enacted on this same divan or bed;
I who have sat by Thebes below the wall
And walked among the lowest of the dead.

(*The Waste Land*)

PETER PORTER is an Australian living in London. While the Tory Britain malcontents were reaching their advertised *apogée* in the late 1950's, Porter was getting on with the poems which appeared in his first volume, *Once Bitten, Twice Bitten*, in 1961. Instead of cashing in, raving to the converted or agonizing over class distinctions, Porter settled in London and exposed himself to the one thing genuinely new in the *après guerre*—the affluent society. He is sweating it out, moreover, in the West End, where wealth may be countenanced in its most insolent, pretentious, and influential guises. Mr A. Alvarez was wrong when he publicly advised Porter to leave Chelsea, for it is precisely the West End saturation which makes Porter (and his outrageous Sancho Panza, Mr Martin Bell) such a deadly analyst of metropolitan manners, and also an inverted, cantankerous, yet in the end edifying, moralist. Referring in the 1930's to D. H. Lawrence's removal *to* Australia, John Cornford stated that 'the working class is not in a position to go half way round the world looking for an escape from industrialism. That is why it does not read Lawrence.' Porter has come from Australia into the golden heart of commercialism—a heart which beats in the breasts of all classes.

Porter's 'colonial' extraction is enviable: it has proved a source of strength and relevance. In *Forefathers' View of Failure*, *A Christmas Recalled*, *Phar Lap in the Melbourne Museum*, and *Tobias and the Angel* he examines his background. He impeaches the narrowness of his forbears but hails a quality of unthinking energy, of Old Frontier purposefulness. This is not the improvised vitalism of a freelance like Thom Gunn: it derives from a tradition. These tough Scottish puritans were 'men with religion *as their best technique* / Who built bush churches six days a week', who 'had no life but the marking time of work', who 'climbed to bed with a bottle'. Lost in the pioneering anonymity of a land where 'on any visitor the same / Wind trespasses ashore from a wailing sea' it would 'seem failure' to them 'to have knowledge a Scottish textbook never gave'. They were constructive within the framework of the functional:

> *After drinking the sun down into the bay*
> *Their gulps shake out time, their health*
> *Is in country roses, a hard red wealth.*

As pioneers, as *homo faber*, they are admired; there is neither revolt nor adulation, only the earnest of a more sophisticated value to be attained in the future. *Phar Lap* brings us forward in time: the pioneers are now urban sportlovers, but the nation's enthusiasm for its 'top patrician'—a racehorse—is still an expression of uncomplicated, anti-phoney self-affirmation. 'It is Australian innocence to love / The naturally excessive . . .' An almost poignantly graphic poem, *A Christmas Recalled*, evokes the poet's home town, Brisbane, in the mid 1930's—the time when W. H. Auden and his English associates were cavorting under the threat of war. To Porter it is the memory of a mildly unhappy, bewildered day in a vanishing childhood, made memorable by an uncle who talks of the next war 'not the way / Men talk of the Last War but as prophets do / Of retribution'. In the last poem in his book, *Tobias and the Angel*, he uses religious allegory as a means of generalizing what looks like an apologia for compromise. He is ironically reconsidering the Australian ambiguities on the basis of the Chelsea knowledge (Eliot's 'After such knowledge, what forgiveness?'):

> *I shall get home one day or if I die instead*
> *An Insurance Angel will tell my waiting wife*
> *His grave is furnished by his good upbringing,*
> *His habits were proper, his doubt all to the good;*
> *From his warm orthodoxy melancholy shrinks,*
> *He did what he was told, obedient and sane.*

The exile's burden, the contradictions of the Australian inheritance, are not found wanting. There is a hint of the stormy coalition which Thomas Mann divined between philistine conscientiousness, the *virtu* of the man of action, and the moral intensity, the inwardness, of the man of ideas. Concerned artists are often the cadets of declining lineages; and there is a congruity between the associative mental processes which are required in both administration and creativity. Like his father 'closing his Day Book on his trade', the poet now has 'an inventory of praise'; his father 'starves for light' but the poet does not 'tire of the simple entering in'. The poem resolves on a note of what Giuseppe di Lampedusa calls 'profitable altruism':

EXILE, VIGOUR, AND AFFLUENCE

> *Our house*
> *Is not a tabernacle, miracles are forgotten*
> *In usefulness, the weight and irony of love.*

Like Thom Gunn, Porter is the poet in exile. Unlike Gunn his energy is not the flight from roots of the spiritual nomad. It is the endeavour to convert a genuine but irresponsible energy into a moral critique. For the theatre of this endeavour he has selected the place where the odds seem most weighted against any concern. As Gunn left England for the American Far West, Porter left the Commonwealth to undergo his exile in the place where the dehumanizing pressures are most efficient. He is judge and victim. His tone is so distinct, so declared that it cannot conveniently be filed as 'colloquial', Jacobean idiom. It is less complex in structure, essentially vernacular, an urgent speaking voice: at the instant of reading the poems demand our verbal reply. This tone is different from the studied reserve of Gunn, the super-charged engine of Hughes, the unerring guardedness of Larkin, and the gracile niceties of our aesthetes. These are valid devices to give edge to an ascertained view of life, literary aim or emotional orientation. Porter's tone is the frank articulateness, rather didactic because tense and observant, and susceptible to changes caused by circumstances, of a man who has not yet decided, who is still with us making up his mind, but is neither uncertain of his motives, nor unaware of what he does possess.

Porter's poems create a horrifying sense of the power of money to actually determine questions of value and the fate of individuals. The lust of lucre has been mitigated by a tacit acknowledgment of other priorities; this, though we prefer to forget it, was a principle in the concept of the gentleman. In Porter's world, cash is the great *arriviste*. Nobody bothers about *how* it was amassed or how it relates to drastic economic problems. You either have it, in which case everything is added unto you, or you lack it, and the devil take the hindmost. In relationships 'the gold is at the mathematics of our several hates', in religion 'the faithful work for a merchant God who deals in souls', a London party, with its nuances, becomes 'splendid value for a pound', and even the suicide (who can stand the racket no longer) requires—thinks in terms of—'a shilling's worth of gas'. *Made in Heaven* with resistless forward-lilting line and pert rhymes distils an odour of inevitability. Money *vincit omnia*. A magician makes marriage profitable and senseless, with miraculous promptitude brings, *contra naturam*, the 'fruits' of the union across the 'dog-paraded' street on 'workmen's feet'—a glossy mag. dream of the earthly paradise. 'From Heals and Harrods come her lovely bridegrooms / One cheque alone furnished two bedrooms'. The poem digests, in the same tone, echoes of class idiom, 'as the relatives said, she was living in clover', of the bride soliloquizing, 'found nothing more exacting than my own good looks', and the poet's untactful reminders of 'the massive years ahead' and 'the apotheosis of the young wife and mediocre dancer'. Yet her selfishness exults in 'at least I'm safe from everything but cancer'. Subtract the conjugal element which will probably be dissolved anyway—you are left with the Denning Report, not exactly Yeats's Dream of the Aristocrat.

Lament for a Proprietor depicts the property after the owner has died. The sustained rhythm suggests an immortality; we feel the weight, the inertia, of possessions. But they are dead 'because he had lived for them'—the only thing which outlasts the irony, like some biological organism, is 'the pots of cash he will inherit'. The detail may be what Mr Philip Toynbee has dismissed (anent Porter) as 'fashionable realism'. Balzac, too, fixes with tutelary precision the objects and activities which many excellent people live by and for; and these poems confirm warnings of Tolstoy. By contrast, *Euphoria Dies* works on an insouciant line, artificial and superficial and full of abrupt, aimless transitions. It is, indeed, about a 'party'. 'You are the figure to whom the lights allude / Your charming grace, such standard turpitude.' *Who gets the Pope's Nose?* applies what one might call an inquisitorial device by alternating five- and three-beat lines and making each stanza episodic. 'It is so tiring to look after the works of God'; yet man's weakness is infinitely exploitable; odd that Death the Leveller isolates as it unites us all. 'High above Rome in a room with wireless' the Pope also 'waits to die'. The last stanza suggests—'God is the heat in July'—a pantheism which cuts down to size religious dogma; it enlarges our sense of potentiality and shocks us, through fear, into the awareness of universal brotherhood. 'Of all God's miracles, death is the greatest.'

For this exile, the urgent need to define his identity—to understand his motives, to discover his beliefs—is at one with his assessment of the identity of others and his adjustment to them. This is difficult when personality, trapped in materialism, becomes a chameleon which assumes whatever colouring circumstances dictate. In *Conventions of Death* the poet walks up Bond Street under the 'stately mushroom shadow', 'a cliché to walk with'. He is 'isolated by what I feel, calling it love', and feels that the loneliness of bored, modern individuality is a madness which turns him into a freak. His 'snake of brain' may be 'scotched' but 'waits in phone calls, letters, clocks'. Tempted to become (in this event) a conformist, he realizes that appeasement is a defeatist escapism verging on self-pity:

> *So give up thinking, work hard, buy a car,*
> *Get married, keep a garden, bring up kids—*
> *Answers to all the problems that there are,*
> *Except the love that kills, the death that lives.*

In *Metamorphosis* he attempts rebirth in a utilitarian way—buying 'a new Daks suit' on the instalment plan. For two jaunty stanzas he feels 'stuffed with recognition', confident, the embodiment of the adman's ideal. 'I wait in the pub with my Worthington.' His girl, *chic*, dominant, arrives; they exchange cynical gossip on the level of the advertising slogan; suddenly she seems 'real' and the poet is assailed by dreadful anxieties—'if only I had a car' and so on. His new suit has betrayed him: he is an outcast, a werewolf, reverting to a primitive state. The point is that Porter accepts the false identity, tries to live with it, frankly confesses the consequences. Nor is the reversion condemned. It may be a move towards genuineness.

It is no use retreating into dream, into unconsciousness. Somnolence, in *Death's Morning Shadows*, arouses fantasies of patricide, childhood guilt, sex and pain, but these are side-effects of the strain of responsible choice; just as well, the poet implies, that the alarm clock 'bursts my head' and drags him into wakefulness. The drive to falsify distorts the literary act: *What a Lying Lot the Writers Are* satirizes our need to 'make metaphysics' out of our bored limitations; it is an attack on the thinker's crime of chewing opium. A 'good income', of course, solves everything; meanwhile we must resist the temptation to accept a complacent model of the world—'Great events are remembered as History / Science understands us, we are free' heralds a train of ironies. Instead of groping in the cul-de-sac of introspection, Porter moves towards encounter, estimating others with a shrewd charity born of self-knowledge. His most moving poem, very skilful metrically, *Sick Room at Home*, avoids the maudlin because it blends his pity with his guilt. We have had uxoriousness, sweet gentility, and nursery bluster from what Mr George Macbeth has termed 'our potent young domestics'. Porter writes like a sensitive adult:

> *Your stomach, darling, is upset.*
> *Your head runs its cold, yet*
> *From your bed you smile on the room*
> *For love of love; your head assumes*
> *A bright sickness and your eyes*
> *Flavour our dry temerity.*
> *Our quiet is the spoken words of fear . . .*
> *Ours too this waiting, healthy on chairs*
> *For further lovers down the stairs . . .*

Does art bridge the gulf between egotism and kindness? The poet answers with a tale about himself. *For John Clare From London* provokes groans—we expect a bucolic 'to one who has been long in city pent' homage, no tribute to Clare! We receive an urban non-idyll, a summoning of strength; our routine being our fate, Porter posits a residual courage akin to that of the old Australia; all delusions discredited, such saving non-grace—not so different from Clare's—is the most we can expect and probably all we deserve:

> *Brimming with its torpor, step out and resent*
> *A weak tea sun on brick and cement,*
> *But stifle resentment again for the sake*
> *Of the passionate cough and the proud headache.*

For this poet the art which nearly pierces the clouds, which verges on the transcendental, is music. *Walking Home on St Cecilia's Day* is one of the best poems about music (as distinct from evocations *of* it in the Symbolist line) written since the war. Porter does not treat music as a therapy, as Auden does, or a donor of yea-saying as Spender does in *Beethoven's Death Mask*. He reconciles the real with the aesthetic: music is 'sublime adjustment', 'beautiful impermanence', and 'a miracle on the ground'. It 'won't make tomorrow other than' the nastiness of the cash nexus. None the less music 'befriends the ear' like 'useless, impartial rain on desert'. By 'conjuring' the listener to be happy, it puts the responsibility *on the listener*, who must make from this art of limits 'what he can'. A poet who regards music as more than a solace raises one's respect for music more effectively than a eulogy from the ecstatic. *A Vicious Vignette* shows that the privilege he accords to art cannot be extended to the artist. He invokes Freud to prove that the Great Composer was not such a Tolstoyan lover of nature after all: having shot birds, he went in to make 'music of his guilty childhood's peace'. (It is typical of Porter that it takes the Biographer, who is really after the heart of Mr Jacques Barzun—'his grant spent on rococo treasures and rich food' —to unmask the Composer.) Porter exorcizes I. A. Richards's phantom; he rejects art for art's sake; he implies that, if art helps, it is because it is a salutary gift of a character and both can be judged.

The narrator yields to another in *Beast and the Beauty*. The girl, 'twenty-one and experienced', comes of a truculent type of Woman's Page milieu—'Her sophistication was his great delight'. If accelerating social mobility encourages this life we can do with it in verse:

> *The unhappy marriage, the tradespeople on Christian*
> *Name terms—all the democratic sexiness—mornings*
> *With the Pick of the Pops and the Daily Express*
> *And yet the sudden itching despair, the wonder in King's*

College Chapel, the depth that lived in her soul
Of which this raciness was only the worldly covering.

The last lines argue another case of mistaken identity. The family
are snobs and vulgarians. The narrator is jilted, he becomes 'a beast
again'. Yet his beasthood is more propitious than their sophistication. When a person has dominated us, we may in language and in
justification avenge ourselves. *Mr Roberts* personifies the educational
system. Writers of the lost generation would have panicked—e.g. Mr
Connolly's 'I was a stage rebel'. Porter is worried by the damage
done to character by bad education, maximized in 'later a man shot
himself, a man went mad'. Mr Roberts 'owned them for four years',
they 'wore their fear to match his moral frown'. 'The sweaty jersey
kept / Faith with the Silver Age, the men of old'. The attack, developing inside the facts and blending with Roberts's own ludicrous
fantasies, makes this a classic on the educational theme, which is
hardly an unimportant one. *Sick Man's Jewel* is a recitative of
defeat, on a theme which the Mr Roberts's despise: mental breakdown, loss of identity. The art is to make the milieu of this breakdown seem familiar; perhaps we have got the wrong word? The
victim 'for his statistics becomes lovable' (again the inhuman idealism) though at least 'the stratas do not matter in this Hell'. As for
music, it can be used as a therapy. As we congratulate ourselves on
being sane, informed moderns, the affair boomerangs. The neurotic
is degraded into a type, yet the *content* of his neurosis has been evoked
in terms which any sensitive reader will recognize in himself. The
patient remains an 'embarrassment', misbehaving in restaurants
when we are about to Go To The Theatre or Away For The
Week-end.

Porter works best in what he calls arias—spacious, resonant forms
which leave room for documentary manœuvre. Some poems are too
undigested, they brag and posture, complicate a theme without clari-
fying it, rely on an argument which is unmotivated and unresolved.
In modester forms he brings off a haunting versatile cadence where
the intent, sometimes, founders. *All Other Time is Peace* has a wry
flexible music, but is obscure, too homiletic. Poems like *Jack and Jill*
and *The Smell on the Landing* waft us through on the strength of telling
insights, asides, and innuendos scored in a poised pace. One lives in
the ambience of the poems. Only later, thinking them over, one feels
that the poet is absent from these skilful reportages. In five poems he
is fully present, though not in the first person. He finds objective
correlatives inclusive, interesting, and known enough to fuse a description of facts with an attitude towards them. *John Marston Advises
Anger* employs the Jacobean legend, for Eliot a means of knocking
the specious present, for Thom Gunn a parade of symbols. Porter

simply displays the charade of smart 'culture' and assures us that it fits Marston's stage. Invited to meditate on salvation, we observe that if the flesh is weak, the spirit announces vigour, opinion, purpose. It is the poetic voice which makes the spirit resound. Then, we accept the Marston assurance, we recall the Antipodean vitality, that 'radical innocence' of Yeats which, itself amoral, thrives on *dégringolade* and can help to redeem it. In *South of the Duodenum* Porter expresses it thus:

> *Keeping alive in jealous pools of eyes, astir*
> *At windowings of Vogue and such*
> *A conniving click of a car door, this innocence*
> *Is life's.*

The Historians Call Up Pain is an excuse for our day. A warning against historicist despair, and the crimes of the credulous, it refuses blame for the past, yet affirms men's creaturely unity on a foundation of what they have, or should have, spiritually in common. Sympathy and reserve aid understanding:

> *Yet if we keep*
> *Our minds on the four last things*
> *And join the historians on their frieze of pain*
> *We may forget our world of milk gone stale,*
> *Cancer touches in the afternoon, girls in Jensens,*
> *Gramophone records scratched and warped,*
> *Managers fattening tumours of ambition.*
> *We cannot know what John of Leyden felt*
> *Under the Bishop's tongs—we can only*
> *Walk in London, our educated city,*
> *Wishing to cry as freely as they who cried*
> *In the Age of Faith. We have our loneliness*
> *And our regret with which to build an eschatology.*

The structured resonance, braved dualities, and ascending, counter-stressed emotional rhythms of *Death in the Pergola Tea Rooms* gives it the quality of tragic music. An old rationalist is dying near a tea house in a storm: that is all. Opposition of will and fate, man and nature, tragedy and the trivial are the ingredients. There is no 'leap of faith'; the storm will not abate. At the epicentre of the poem, like trumpets sobered by drums, is a bloc of impassioned reasoning. We are taught the meaning of rational work and its continuity in time through the famous images of man's revolutionary past, here personalized, and assimilated in the only way they can be in a period which has rejected the heroic:

198

EXILE, VIGOUR, AND AFFLUENCE

The blood is roaring
In his head, the carcinoma commune, the fronde
Of pain rule in his brain—the barricades have broken
In his bowels—it is the rule of spasm, the terror sits.
He knows he is dying, he has a business of wills,
Must make a scaffolding for his wife with words,
Fit the flames in his head into the agenda.
Making up his mind now, he knows it is right
To take the body through committee meetings and campaign rooms,
To wear it and patch it like a good tweed . . .
There is no God. It is winter, the windows sing
And stealthy sippers linger with their tea . . .

If the pre-war exaggerated the role of reason in public affairs and underrated that of psychology, our phase is tempted to withdraw into a detachment which exaggerates psychological knowingness —'You can't take me in, I know better'. The danger is that the occasions of heroism, both spiritual and practical, will be missed in both cases. Dividing the generations is the shame of the concentration camps, uniting them the scandal of armaments. Porter's *Annotations of Auschwitz* is unelegiac. Approaching a subject which most poets should avoid, he shows respect in trying to 'outflank' this most baffling of themes from different angles—how the guards see it, how the public sees it, how nature—'the bee made free by work'—could not care less. Another way of seeing it is by projecting yourself, through audacity, into the condition of victim; this can be done 'on Piccadilly underground'; and Porter throws light on the meaning of sadism in persons and in nations, then returns us to London, 'full of chickens on electric spits' where 'all poultry eaters are psychopaths'. In *The Conservation of Energy* the horror is world-wide, but the idea of perverted mind controlling science (C. P. Snow technological optimism?) is the same. The H Bomb is 'part of the state', 'something to believe in', 'a rigour for slack times'. 'No monster raving on mankind's sins', it provides no incentive to the bravery called for in Yeats's *The Second Coming*. Science gives the means to good and evil, so the will does not matter. And the gross gulf between our moral and technical maturity is burlesqued in:

> *To have caught God up is something. He said*
> *His patience would thin out. We have more tact*
> *And grow more tolerant every day.*

If we ask for **Peter Porter's** positive values, the answer lies in his *complicity* with his material. He is incapable of Audenesque laughing off, analysing out, or tidying up with a formula. His workouts on the treadmill of 'careers', parties, profits, his dossier of on-the-make types is deceptive, for it looks like callous approval. It is a mode of participation which brings knowledge:

> *One girl undressed because she thought it right;*
> *Another, trained in truth, watched what she did*
> *Loving her mirrored love, her second sight.*
> *A judge of conduct gasped to see the fun,*
> *A valued impotence safe in his head.*
>
> *(Party Line)*

Although some knowledge may strike us as funny, confusion of values must be stated truly or our thinking will be both partial and priggish. It is the absence of pompous moral opinion that wins our confidence. That done, Porter makes *us* do the judging, has a knack of implicating us in his complicity! He is less a blind rat in the race than a private detective—primed with a joke, eyes and ears open— of the cult of material success. To 'construct something upon which to rejoice' from the ruin upwards is more expensive than conjuring castles out of the air; thus Porter appears on the verge of bank- ruptcy. But his worldly-wise asceticism is a prelude to the heroic, a reorientation of what was once objective courage. He may retain only a period interest—though his book, due to the pertinence and immediacy of its revelations, will have value as testimony.* The reader will decide whether, in future books, the 'complicity' becomes acceptance; will fifth column tactics give way to collaboration? The evils of over-ripe capitalism, and the ravages of divided conscience, are here for a long time, we have got to live with them and they demand every better quality we can mobilize.

At this point one could offer some drug like 'the poems of protest are all very well, but one prefers the lyrics in which love shines through'. That would be charming, but in Porter's world love is unlikely to shine in any recognizable form until the reasons for pro- test have been registered. Our silliness—the mad harping on con- sumption, going with a contempt for tradition, the artificial stimula- tion, followed by the rapid obsolescence, of plausible fashions, the worship by educated people of material means as ends in themselves —will become more swaggering, and impose more strain on the sensitive and the decent before it is remedied. I. A. Richards says 'the vanguard must go forward before the mass is extricated', and it is precisely to this vanguard—the constructive workers and seekers

* The trick of Prince Henry—'I know you all, and shall awhile uphold / The unyoked humour of your idleness'—is perhaps an essential ingredient of agit- prop.

—that the Porters are likely to appeal. His complicity, then, is a base for action, a sort of pilot scheme. This poet's refusal to abandon the Headquarters of Goliath to its fate is as rallying as the Paris addiction of Baudelaire.

PEACETIME CONSCRIPT: THOM GUNN

*The John Cornford hero has been replaced by just as aggressive
and positive a hero . . . irreverent and uneasy . . . behind the
impatience there is the consciousness of a malaise.*
*There are no ready-made values. The agony of the time is that
there is no agony.* *

THOM GUNN comes of the same generation as Peter Porter,
but his development starts in the early 1950's when the Welfare
State aspect of Britain was more noticeable than the affluent society.
By the time he arrived at Cambridge, Gunn had done two years'
National Service without firing a shot in anger. The legacy bequeathed him by the bandwagon of progress, by the peace, was to
be the liberal ordered about in the interests of the British way of life
and the cold war. True, there was a Welfare State: it hinted towards
meritocracy (which is no answer) and it eased the lives of the poor.
By the time Gunn left Cambridge in 1954, entrenched guile, rejoic-
ing in better brainwashing media, had condescended to adopt the
Welfare State and anaesthetize it into ennui and opportunism;
'damn you, Jack, I'm all right!' became the password for both the
meritocrats and for those having it so good. As late as 1961, safe
in America, Mr Gunn felt bound to remark of standard verse that
'it is directed towards the typical Englishman . . . it conforms to
its public, it is easy to read, it is full of accepted attitudes, and it
leaves you exactly as it found you'. A genuine poet would 'think
out his attitude to experience and embody it in a style'.

The poems in *Fighting Terms* (1954) narrate the Adventures of
the Peacetime Conscript in search of Genuineness. *Lofty in the Palais
de Danse* shows the protagonist determined to cut his losses, call the
bluff, start at the subsistence level of what may be clearly felt and

---

* Letter by Thom Gunn in *The London Magazine*, June 1957. For Gunn, a subject is 'one that Chaucer or Stendhal wrote about, and it is not very important
whether the approach is political or not'. 'For the 30's there *were* clear-cut political
issues to shout about . . . but the values were naively perceived and recklessly
applied.'

Gunn fails to appreciate the validity of the invective against vices of manners,
which was based on psychiatric as well as political knowledge. Because the politics
are obsolete, it does not follow that the invective is redundant. Living in America
has given Gunn an idyllic view of England. 'The village squires are all dead.' Or
did they move into the City? It is still a case of Auden's 'what do you think of
England, this country of ours where nobody is well?' not to mention Mr Martin
Bell's 'the old gang born again in young careerists' (1963).

known. 'Like the world, I've gone to bad / A deadly world: for, once I like, it kills.' Therefore 'I kill the easy things that others like' and for a purpose, 'to teach them that no liking can be lasting'. So it is surprising that in *Captain in Time of Peace* the seducer's inferiority complex should be bothersome. 'Pity a lumpish soldier out of work / And teach him manners with a look.' Excessive self-awareness is usually a drawback in courting. Not with Mr Gunn, who prefers to appear in control. His ideal is 'honour in the town at peace' and he admits that 'tactics commit me falsely'. 'Tactics' are a foray against sentimental scenes, absolute claims which may be made, and the Captain's own proclivity to self-pity. ('Tactics' also lectures, like most of these poems, the extra-mural world, the hypocrisy of educated society towards its creative members, who in order to operate, or even to maintain themselves, are forced into stratagems.) Going through the motions of gentility, the poet is mocking those motions in favour of more strenuous *emotive* transactions. For the habit of soldiers 'is to loot'.

The demobbed conscript's bitterness is short-lived. He sits at the feet of history—that performance which cannot be spirited away—and admires the techniques of the Metaphysicals and Mr William Empson. Result: a not always successful penchant for using historic or legendary themes as allegories of relationships, and for conceptualizing facts to fit inner conflicts. The focus is often blurred and unstable, veiled in allegorical demotic. The predictable frames, the casually fastidious metres are less Gunn's homage to the Metaphysicals as his contribution, filtered through Empson, to the trend away from afflatus towards cool, calculated logic. In Metaphysical poetry the conceits, strong lines, and daring images are the motors of the action and, often, the directors of the form. With imitators they are *included* in a discursive tone which is partly a narrow reticence, partly a sophistication, partly a literary gambit. In *Lazarus Not Raised* the climacteric points—'he had chosen to stay dead' etc.—are so undifferentiated as to be more laughable than decisive. In *Carnal Knowledge* the poet dismisses his girl with 'your intellectual protests are a bore'. The poem is such a protest. Its unity is debauched by the sudden injection, from the nervous observer, of comment into the action, and if we reject these isolated, technically indistinct 'strong' pronunciamentos as contrived, the plot is not gripping enough to save the poem. These faults beset *Fighting Terms*. But the good poems are important. For long history had been humiliated in the 'moment', by Jungian sorcery and *ad hoc* living it up. In poems like *To His Cynical Mistress* and *Tamer and Hawk* he talks about modern love in historic images which are meaningful in both contexts. *Tamer* deploys the Elizabethan-Shakespearean metaphor so adroitly that the zestful freshness of that period seems to collaborate in the point, which is that rivalry is good because it provokes a crisis:

> *You but half-civilize,*
> *Taming me in this way.*
> *Through having only eyes*
> *For you I fear to lose,*
> *I lose to keep, and choose*
> *Tamer as prey.*

The Beach Head compares a girl's body to a Welfare State, then symbolizes the sex war in terms of court intrigue, mediaeval soldiers of fortune, etc. The Welfare State and the Middle Ages— strange bedfellows!—interact to conceive a vitality which seems available now:

> *Shall I be John a Gaunt and with my band*
> *Of mad bloods pass in one spectacular dash,*
> *Fighting before and after, through your land,*
> *To issue out unharmed the other side,*
> *With little other object than panache*
> *And showing what great odds may be defied?*

Gunn exploits history on a more generous scale than men obsessed with topical images ('the pylon poets'). He liberates time from mystic abolition, and political pleading; he mixes the periods, he makes time a continuum shaped out by the individual intelligence. *As images*, everything is contemporary; thus an advance like a Welfare State is made proportionate, reclaimed in time, for intelligence. *The Right Possessor* takes a prestigious modern theme—the revolutionary who, recalled from exile, meets a tragic fate. The 'nation' may be a prevaricating girl; the sexual analogy is explicit. The poem also illustrates: intellectual adventure, the trials of the mind gaining maturity. Or it may be taken at its face value, as a political anecdote. What it really discloses is an imaginative cross-fertilization between the lot; it is an anti-atomistic and anti-specialist poem, liberating and enlarging in the best sense. *The Court Revolt*, on the other hand, has a mediaeval setting, yet manages to refer to 'a manual job' and 'write his memoirs in America'. The active, 'generous' king is overthrown, not by 'system or idea', but by the 'worst'—the greedy, bored, jealous. Expected to rule a society where 'his natural magnanimity would appear / Insulting charity to the subject now', his citizens' *real* subjection is 'self-subjection' to accidie. We accept this crack at ourselves because there is no hint (*pace* the pylon poets) of ideological side; the relapse finds its place in the continuum, is a plea for will power. 'How can a man hold office in these days?' The king explains: his 'human flames of energy had no place' in this *galère*. America and the 'manual job' beckon, for loyalists rescue him, yet he still 'loves his country' in spite of its self-betrayal. The trials of statesmanship, and the question of loyalty—the fact that in our time conscience often outbids State allegiances—is remarkably adduced.

Mr Gunn's Utopia is reflected in *A Mirror for Poets*. Quick pace, vivid density of detail, comment subordinated to action, and a ruffled line, swashbuckling and rather breathless and pausing only to sharpen itself on some pivotal image, diminish Gunn's faults. Literary allusions—'Hacks in the Fleet and nobles in the Tower: Shakespeare must keep the peace, and Jonson's thumb / Be branded (for manslaughter)'—join speculation:

> *In this society the boundaries met*
> *Of life and life, at danger . . .*
>
> *Yet the historians tell us, life meant less.*
> *It was a violent time, and evil-smelling . . .*

And presages of modernity—'Jonson howled: Hell's a grammar-school to this'—to become vitally fused into, indeed protagonists in, the enacting story; life and culture are unified in the poem as they were in the period. What is praised is a quality which acts, seeking opposition, in order to realize and thus relish its potentiality; and this in a society observed as coherent ('Winnowing with his flail of comedy / He showed coherence in society') because mindful of and accessible to reason:

> *The faint and stumbling crowds were dim to sight*
> *Who had no time for pity or for terror:*
> *Here moved the Forms, flooding like moonlight,*
> *In which the act or thought perceived its error.*
> *The hustling details, calmed and relevant.*
> *Here mankind might behold its whole extent.*

Gunn judges the Romantics by the same token. Shelley 'fell submissive' through the waves, arms at his side; he was 'but a minor conquest of the sea'. Byron was 'worth the sea's pursuit. His touch / Was masterful to water, audience / To which he could react without an end.'

Since 1954 Mr Gunn has lived and taught in America. The poems in his second volume, *The Sense of Movement* (1957), are lived in that Gunn finds real-life symbols to express his quest for vigour; they are taught in that he pedanticizes the quality of controlled energy he seeks. *Lines for a Book, To Yvor Winters,* and areas elsewhere abstract into didactic tirades certain antinomies which are sublimated, in the better poems, into behaviour, so that we feel the forces as operative and are encouraged to appraise their effects. As poets increasingly do, Gunn issues P.R. handouts about his own aesthetic ('Rule and Energy in view / Much power in each, most in the balanced two') and is not above a suspicion of briefing his critics. (The idea of Mr Stephen Spender being thrown into the ring with 'all the toughs through history' arouses a sympathy with the author of 'My parents kept me from children who threw stones' which otherwise one might not have felt.)* In *Birthday Poem* Gunn congratulates himself, too elegantly, on being a dauntless mental Blondin; this is corrected at the end where he confesses to 'bewilderment', but the modesty rings false; the tone of dandiacal panache is not rescinded.

The 'plan' of *A Plan of Self-Subjection* is so vainly described as to seem otiose; and the tongue-twister literary posturing is less Jacobean than muddied: 'In sex do I not dither more than either / In verse or pose, does not the turncoat sense / Show itself slicker, lither . . .' In *The Unsettled Motorcyclist's Vision of his Death* the solemn pomposity of the argument sorts oddly with the wilful childishness of the event, as if dashing old Walt Whitman, out for a joy-ride, was moralizing into the youth's ear. I am not attacking Mr Gunn's yen for motor-bikes and leather jackets. *On the Move,* his best poem, counterpoints each concept with its physical equivalent; in this superbly unified work the diction is at once vital and telling, suggestive and exact, while the syntax, in relation to rhythm, contracts, expands and throbs like muscles in a bony structure. There is no question of first looking, then lecturing: it is the immediacy of the action compelling interpretation, the interpretation provoking immediate action. In the end the thought is so infected by the rhythm of events that it persists, as if dazed, under that momentum:

> *A minute holds them, who have come to go:*
> *The self-defined, astride the created will*
> *They burst away; the towns they travel through*
> *Are home for neither bird nor holiness,*
> *For birds and saints complete their purposes.*
> *At worst, one is in motion; and at best,*
> *Reaching no absolute, in which to rest,*
> *One is always nearer by not keeping still.*

* For a deeper and more demanding and exciting treatment of the 'rule and energy' theme, see George Macbeth, *The Broken Places,* 1963, David Wevill, *Birth of a Shark,* 1964, and Nathaniel Tarn, *Old Savage/Young City,* 1964.

Mr John Mander complains that Gunn, seeking a rationale of action, plumps for a philosophy of crude *activism*. The evidence proves that the urge to action is a priority, a *donnée*, with Gunn. What resembles a 'search for a rationale' is the system of checks, balances—what Isherwood calls 'tests'—which Gunn sets up in order to overhaul and improve his faculty of action, keep it in trim, train it up to maximum efficiency. Once the instrument has been perfected, it must be kept in readiness: its value lies in its availability, through the will, to turn any idea or feeling into works. There is no question of making a policy of activism; it is the faculty of action which liberalism desperately needs. 'Hardness', 'discipline', the search for a 'counterpart', a penchant for 'uniform', the sense of touch, and images of domination recur in Gunn's verse. As these have sinister connotations, it is important to see that Gunn does not systematize, or impose or glory in his interest in these things. On the contrary, he believes in aloofness as the *sine qua non* to honest self-control and the exercise of common sense amid the neuroses. He goes out of himself to discover the same apartness, the same readiness for difficult action, fulfilling yet unpossessive, in people and the multiplicity of events in an open, mobile society. Attending to himself, he encounters others. To them he speaks, like Lorca's bull-fighter, with 'a hard clear Roman accent'.

In *Market at Turk* the youth's uniform is 'a reminder of the will'. In the moving poem, *At the Back of the North Wind*, it is sensual awareness which breaks in more acutely because it penetrates the sheltered mews:

> *The ostlers knew, but did not tell him more*
> *Than hay is what we turn to. Other smells,*
> *Horses, leather, manure, fresh sweat, and sweet*
> *Mortality, he found them on the North.*

In *Human Condition* the poet, enveloped in fog, is *condemned* to be an individual, and 'the test more hard' emphasizes 'that which makes me man'. *Autumn Chapter in a Novel* secretes, like the first chapters of *Le Rouge et Le Noir*, an explosive violence just below the mannered surface of restraint; there is discontent, disturbance, even genteel action ('the husband comes discussing with his bailiff'), a sense of frustrated force and muted menace ('sap draws back inch by inch'). These tentatives are quintessential, not trivial: they prepare the final promise: 'Names to her son the deserts on the globe / And leaves thrust violently against the pane.' Here, 'sweatless as watercolour under glass', limitation seems propitious. In *The Beaters* it turns into that cannibalism of sado-masochists who envy liberty as they devour it. Man appears conditioned—

'condemned to be condemned' (*Legal Reform*) yet there is no case for 'legal reform', for the sentence 'stipulated exercise'. The flamboyant poem, *The Wheel of Fortune*, depicts energy embroiled in inexorable fate. There is no question, here, of choosing one's future. The value lies in the acceptance, the exuberance, conveyed in the pulse and infectious verve of the writing. Free will is flaunted in the sense of variation generated in the structure:

> *Deeper they dream, disorder comes: high, low, are flung*
> *Faster, limbs spinning. As the great Hub cracks they peel*
> *From off the Felloe of that even round.*
> *Bishop and lover sprawl upon the ground,*
> *And Lambert Simnel stirs the under footman's porridge.*

In its movement towards choice the will may tap deep forces, is fertilized by them. It appears that the pop-song idol, 'our likeness', epitomizes the 'limitations' where we find 'success', and through his talent 'turns revolt into a style . . .'—that phrase is an example of Gunn's gift to transmute the zeitgeist into *concepts* which make us think beyond our time. Even if he is a poseur, the creator develops his free choice, builds something within determinism. The Roman centurion, of *The Silver Age*, appears to be the man of action defeated, abandoned. Yet when he speaks 'mark how his ancient wording / Is hard with indignation of a lover'. He is still holding out, still defiant. There is a subdued stoic grandeur, a sternly sculptured quality in this poem. *Thoughts on Unpacking* and *During an Absence* distil a sense of the hurried, the casual, they aptly catch the atmosphere of modern restlessness and improvisation—'We for whom time draws out, visas expire'. Both episodes, subject to the Wheel of Fortune, celebrate activity—'In sunlight we are free to move, and hold / Our open assignations' and 'I realize that love is an arranging'.

Gunn's acceptance of limitation as a challenge means that his response to the city is saner than that of most poets. Gunn sees town (*In Praise of Cities*) as a mistress, to whom he makes love more proficiently than in *Fighting Terms*. Through her the poet realizes his abilities, his lacks and what he must reject, so that in the end the city, 'extreme, material and the work of man', seems built within the poet; intellect and matter cohabit, like a blasphemy of the Interior Mansion. The development of the metaphor is subtly exhaustive. *The Inherited Estate*, on the other hand, I take to be a hail and farewell to the old landed England. Dedicated to the American who has inherited the estate, the poem is relaxed yet alert, stylized yet colloquial; the poet is not soliloquizing, he is talking *about* what is happening in the same breath as he describes it. The decayed estate, its 'Follies and façades', shows taste without passion, intelligence without purpose; only the trees, keeping 'vigour within the discipline of shape', assert 'the old virtues'; no 'dreams' or 'ornaments', they gesture towards creativity. One remembers the 'Honour in the town at peace' of *Captain in Time of Peace*. Gunn is reviving an almost Victorian admiration for the English virtues. A strange iconoclast!

Thom Gunn's third volume, *My Sad Captains*, published in 1962, is a technical advance: the shift to syllabics and simpler forms would be gratuitous were it not enlivened by daring transitions, versatility of address and a fast sensual precision. The instant leaps forcefully from the poems, unhampered by philosophizing; the poet limits himself to defining the area of 'felt thought' within the ambience of sense; this suggests a provisional wholeness. It is present in *Flying Over California*, with its 'lean upland / sinewed and tawny in the sun' and 'valley cool with mustard'. The 'Mediterranean and Northern names' can 'make you drunk':

> *on fogless days by the Pacific,*
> *there is a hard cold light without break*
>
> *that reveals merely what it is—no more*
> *and no less. That limiting candour,*
>
> *that accuracy of the beaches,*
> *is part of the ultimate richness.*

One feels it in *Lights among Redwood* where the descriptive stanzas mediate a perception of the out there in its fullness, quieting the mind. This is the opposite of the urge, reaching its overweening apotheosis in Rilke, to seize and interiorize phenomena. Gunn is adventurous and equitable:

> *constant, to laws of size and*
> *age the thick forms hold, though gashed*
> *through with Indian fires. At once*
> *tone is forgotten: we stand*
> *and stare—mindless, diminished—*
> *at their rosy immanence.*

One feels it in the breathless wait, the graduated abruptness, of *Blackie: The Electric Rembrandt*. The art of the tattooist, the respect for his skill, the 'equal concentration' on all the faces, the exploit which sets the boy apart—'now he is starlike'—become ritualistic and engage adult interest. Sinister undertones fuse with the 'hard' Gunnian innocence to make the poem striking; one is delighted by the spectacle of people doing something in common and obtaining unaffected pleasure therefrom. *Considering the Snail* develops sensual observation cumulatively: the forward thrust, sharp termination of the syllabics accentuate 'the slow passion / to that deliberate progress'. 'I cannot tell / what power is at work, drenched there / with purpose, knowing nothing.' This ignorance does not tempt the poet into surplus speculation; it leads him to defer to the object. Gunn's perception of purpose in nature, and the outgoing of spirit it brings, is a gain: it displaces the vigour from the solely human sphere, where it was too exacting and tended to inflate the facts, it dispels the morbid physical oppressiveness, the concocted violence, of earlier poems. One finds Redwoods, California, and Snails just as congenial, less mawkish, and more refreshing than motor-bikes, bars, and leather jackets. Gunn's move into the middle-distance of thought—neither too near nor too far—is a strength in lines like:

> *they withdraw to an orbit*
> *and turn with disinterested*
> *hard energy, like the stars.*
> *(My Sad Captains)*

The strong, Roman assurance is imparted. We visualize the scene, we are chastened by the idea, we are brought to earth again; we find our feet. It is questionable in lines like:

> *Calmly, perception rests on the things,*
> *and is aware of them only in*
> *their precise definition, their fine*
> *lack of even potential meanings.*

There are shades of Charles Tomlinson here. The vignette is inert, too reported. Other danger signals—'seeking merely all', 'able to see them / as they are', 'it wakes me, and my eyes rest on it', 'there is a tangible remoteness'—suggest that Gunn is too anxious to use the correct terms, to give a running commentary, to arouse intellectual interest before the intellect has been aroused—still prone to brief the reader. The move into the middle-distance, even when it does justice to the object, is a precarious stance in danger of facile detachment. A liberation, but into what? The epigraph from Scott Fitzgerald ends: 'It's startling to you sometimes—just air, unobstructed, uncomplicated air'. Compare with our poets' Home Counties, where vestigial airspace is consumed by the latest office block; one hopes that the 'crest of the foothills' of California ('the air so clear you could see the leaves on Sunset Mountain two miles away') will not serve Mr Gunn in the capacity that Zen Buddhism did for Mr Isherwood. Sad to relate, aesthetic advance equals emotional arrest, as if the dropping of the philosophizing meant a loss of direction and impetus. We miss the panorama of real-life symbols, the amplitude of observation which formerly compensated for thinking out aloud. *Santa Maria del Popolo* is an accomplishment, faultless within the poet's terms. It forces one to ask, can poetry live by accomplishment alone? Doubts arise from the strained, mechanical accent, as if the poet was weary of his terms and disinclined to invent new ones:

> *Waiting for when the sun an hour or less*
> *Conveniently oblique makes visible*
> *The painting on one wall of this recess*
> *By Caravaggio, of the Roman School,*
> *I see how shadow . . .*

Dutiful, plodding, accomplished. Later it turns into a parody of itself:

> *I turn, hardly enlightened, from the chapel*
> *To the dim interior of the church instead,*
> *In which there kneel already several people . . .*

Finally we are informed that the arms of old women are too tired to hold anything except 'the large gesture of solitary man / Resisting, by embracing, nothingness'. This is a formidable notion and we should like to know more in terms of tension, dramatization, tone *why* the poet inserts (in the most obvious and easy place—the end) this conjecture. Other poems are so accomplished that our assent is automatic—pleased though not surprised, we pass on to the next without bothering to think. Grand pronunciamentos— 'the heroic fall or climb', 'endless potentiality', 'infinite finitude', 'a grief defined or realized', 'every magnanimous device', usually thieving their effect from some inclusive, resonant adjective—rear their ugly heads, unjustifiable in context. In *A Map of the City* (remember *In Praise of Cities*) he claims town through excellent description, including comments like 'potential', 'potentiality', 'a malady's advance', 'my love of chance', 'I would not have the risk diminished'. This is tantalizing, but disappointing: no sensation of danger or horror has been given (what is the 'risk'?). There is too much wishful thinking in the poems, too many dress rehearsals, still some Napoleonic attitudinizing. *From the Highest Camp* draws on heroic climbing associations without being in the least heroic. We are told about the 'dazzling abstract drifts', 'the last camp of experience' and asked, in the same tired, lecturer's tone, what are 'the sudden yelp upon the air' and 'the malformed purposeless tracks'. The questions are academic: apparently 'we know'. Then comes the moral—'the abominable endures' enlists, with painful obviousness, the Abominable Snowman in a malapert bid to generate *frisson*; and to hear that the monster is 'born of rejection' adds insult to injury. The poem annoys because the idea—that frightfulness exists, always, just beyond the reach of reason—is important; and it should be unnecessary, in the course of our response, to have to unravel the idea in non-poetic terms.

Four poems—*Rastignac at 45*, *Modes of Pleasure* (Marks I and II), *The Monster*—concern the tactics, irony, and remorse of sex. Compared with the pounce of the demobbed conscript, these exhale an inverted, premature cynicism and sterility. T. S. Eliot described himself as 'an aged eagle' at the age of forty-two; Mr Gunn, in his middle thirties, with the advantage of not exactly suffering from shyness, appears fascinated by the glum futility of Rastignac at 45. I have met people who enjoy these poems; I grant that their urbane ripeness is the decisive factor in one's reaction; it is the reaction which is questionable. That admitted, I hope that as the Fallen Rake makes the poet 'jump with terror'— 'rigid he sits, brave, terrible / The will awaits its gradual end' the intention may be ironic: these besotted saurians may be anti-heroes like Ted Hughes's Famous Poet, scapegoats for banishing a temptation. Against this: the devoted skill of the hypnotized descriptions, and the fact that much of the enterprise of Gunn's libertarianism has gone to roost in these libertines. And the leather-jacketed lot are boring the poet; they overstay their welcome. *Black Jackets*, about youths in a bar, is a static poem, lacking the verve and purpose of *On the Move*; this wouldn't matter if the stasis was weighty or pointed, but it is hopelessly descriptive, straining after drama—'remote exertion', 'the heroic fall or climb'—and ends with crude pathos—'The group's name on the left, The Knights / And on the right the slogan Born to Lose'.

Gunn has exhausted his wild ones apparatus, its disciplinary and *épater* function is now a hindrance. Three maturer poems generalize his peculiar values—examine them, dramatize them, relate them to effects and further aims. Gunn is moving towards the more altruistic and responsible humanism, not less intransigent, which is in order in the future. *The Byrnies* is about ancient warriors trekking through virgin forest. As such, it is credible. Full of the atmosphere of consciousness differentiating itself, hazardously, from the primitive, there is no need for allegory because event and idea are matched; they function at parity, communicate, are efficacious:

> *Thus for each blunt-faced ignorant one*
> *The great grey rigid uniform combined*
> *Safety with virtue of the sun.*
> *Thus concepts linked like chainmail in the mind.*

Claus von Stauffenberg (of the bomb plot on Hitler) is less integral; the interpretative lines sheer off. Impregnated with Gunn's values, Stauffenberg is a hero we respect: he 'takes lessons from the past', prizes lucidity, is above all 'the rational man' poised 'to break, to build', finds choice difficult but vital, is limited—'maimed'. The poem celebrates a lonely courage, akin to that of Yeats—this modern Brutus is beholden to no man, '. . . motives neither / Of doctrinaire, of turncoat, nor of spy'. The last stanza echoes the 'Honour in the town at peace' of *Fighting Terms*:

> *And though he fails, honour personified*
> *In a cold time where honour cannot grow,*
> *He stiffens, like a statue, in mid-stride*
> *—Falling toward history, and under snow.**

In the guise of biography, *Innocence* sums up, brings to a climax, and abandons to our judgment many of the poet's themes. Plain style helps the generalizing function, heightens the final shock. The 'he' of the poems might be 'we'; we don't resist it, as we do the 'we know' of *From the Highest Camp*. He, with 'the egotism of a healthy body', hardened to 'an instrument', disciplined to obedience, encased in uniform and aware of 'a compact innocence', watches indifferently while the Russian partisan is burnt alive. It is a shock: tension builds up in the relentlessly aiming lines with slow, withheld inevitability, but we expect something assimilable, not this catastrophe. The poem is neither recantation nor manifesto; to some extent, perhaps, a criticism of credo. It states a paradox; it leaves us at the point of judgment, to go forward alone; its end does not have to be in its beginning; it makes us think to some purpose. Mr Gunn has travelled a long way since he was the demobbed conscript, but he has not ceased to be a forceful humanist:

> *Ran into manhood, ignorant of the past:*
> *Culture of guilt and guilt's vague heritage,*
> *Self-pity and the soul; what he possessed*
> *Was rich, potential, like the bud's tipped rage.*

* A criticism of the 1944 plotters has been that they were too saintly, thoughtful, and idealistic to achieve unified action. Gunn's poem justifies the effort which was made.

THINKING ANIMAL: TED HUGHES

There is a wagtail sitting on the gate-post. I see how sweet and swift heaven is. But hell is slow and . . . viscous and insect-teeming: as is this Europe, now, this England.

D. H. Lawrence: *To Ottoline Morrell*

TED HUGHES was born in 1930—again, the generation of Gunn and Porter. He is not interrogating a comfortable era or defining his apartness by taking tests. He prefers to go beneath and beyond society. A Yorkshireman born and bred, he is like D. H. Lawrence aware of a conflict between townee smartness and rural strength. He is not a seeker: he embraces the given. He has plunged into the abundance of his background and become a richer Douanier Rousseau, a case of the well-trained primitive.

In his first volume, *The Hawk in the Rain* (1957), there is a vehement expressionism which sometimes bawls itself out—the merciless amassment of hectoring physical images either batters us into insensibility or wins our dazed assent; we feel like a punch-drunk boxer, conceding victory to Mr Hughes. Poems like *The Hawk in the Rain*, *Egghead*, *Wind*, and *Phaetons* deliver blows like 'rain hacks my head to the bone', 'bloodily grabbed dazed last-moment-counting', 'wind that dented the balls of my eyes', and 'drags him on fire / Among the monsters of the zodiac'. Hughes is *talking the energy out*; when the full range and depth of a situation is available, when all sophistries of response are banished we find our true bearings in it. And the fine meticulous image, provided it is deeply felt, is vital to the whole. A 'glass half full of wine' left out 'to the dark heaven all night' dreams 'a premonition / of ice across its eye', and this is 'a skin, delicately here / Restraining a ripple from the air'. Later 'Mammoth and Sabre-tooth celebrate reunion'. The minuscule takes its rightful place in the ancientness and vastness of this world. The exuberance of *Roarers in a Ring*, about farmers roistering in a pub, refers to 'faces sweating like hams' yet 'the air new as a razor'. In *September*, Hughes holds disparate natural facts in equipoise. He withdraws from the foreground into the middle distance. But the vision remains rooted:

It is midsummer: the leaves hang big and still:
Behind the eye a star,

Under the silk of the wrist a sea, tell
Time is nowhere.

Hughes can be as subtle as the reader, and is not averse to
sensitives. What he demands is that emotion should be complete,
that it should never exclude, withhold, prevaricate. Animals, the
weather, landscape, gregariousness ('company' is a favourite word)
are felt in their most provocative and dangerous moments. Nature
advances on the poet: she is not solicited, and is treated with all the
objectivity and deference of a person. The intelligence lies in the
way Hughes goes out to meet nature, struggles with it, arranges it
in his mind, enriching his imagination. When he compares the
nocturnal movements of the fox to his own creative process (*The
Thought-Fox*) the word 'compares' is a critic's falsification of what is
happening: the fox is 'coming about its own business', the poet is
equally going about his. The word 'like' is redundant, for the fox is
out there; its instinctiveness and finesse is at one with the mind in
creation; it becomes actor and inspiration:

> *Till, with a sudden sharp hot stink of fox*
> *It enters the dark hole of the head.*
> *The window is starless still; the clock ticks,*
> *The page is printed.*

Hughes's animus is against the intellectual who has disabled the
improvement of feeling by selecting and systematizing the facts:

> *A leaf's otherness,*
> *The whaled monstered sea-bottom, eagled peaks*
> *And stars that hang over hurtling endlessness,*
> *With manslaughtering shocks*
> *Are let in on his sense . . .*
> *(Egghead)*

It is not a case of one impulse from a vernal wood being worth
more than the egghead's wisdom. The poet insists only that when
phases of enhanced imagining come they should be welcomed,
allowed to cleanse the mind. In *Famous Poet* Hughes has produced a
kind of anti-manifesto: the monstrous 'famous poet', the 'near-
finished variety artist' who 'slumps in his chair / like a badly
hurt man, half life-size' is a scapegoat for the banishing of one of
Hughes's temptations. If the poet ever expressed 'the vital fire . . .
that puts the gloss on a normal hearty male' this has ossified into a
formula—'Repeat that!' still they cry. The poet is a caricature of his
essence, a 'Stegosaur' echoing a time when 'half the world still
burned'. Emotion, more than reason, because it looks 'easier' may
degenerate into a convention.

Because Ted Hughes gives himself utterly to the given, his art is generous. The moment of vision, the eruption of feeling, is treated as seriously as Empson would treat a concept or Auden an event: and, since vision and feeling are often an excuse for dropping seriousness of any kind—they are, in fact, treated with contempt—Hughes has made a great leap forward. Ideas are guided towards ends through the motor of feeling, and the health and quality of the feeling, resulting in action, bears a relation to the chances of arriving on target. *The Horses* describes how the poet watches horses grazing on the moors under a foggy sunrise. The unrhymed couplets welcome as much interplay of syntactical and metrical variation as is possible within the form. Full of enthusiastic information which the poet could have withheld for technical reasons or through fear of appearing sentimental, the occasion is offered in a hesitant, antithetical idiom, which shows respect for its intrinsic force; we are put right in the picture, but in no exhibitionist or vainglorious spirit:

> *Slowly detail leafed from the darkness. Then the sun*
> *Orange, red, red erupted*
>
> *Silently, and splitting to its core tore and flung cloud,*
> *Shook the gulf open, showed blue,*
>
> *And the big planets hanging—*
> *I turned*

The poem ends with a request which, in the current state of cynicism, is risky:

> *In din of the crowded streets, going among the years, the faces,*
> *May I still meet my memory in so lonely a place*
>
> *Between the streams and the red clouds, hearing curlews,*
> *Hearing the horizons endure.*

There it is, impregnated with the poet's personality: no taking advantage. One hopes that his request will be granted and one's trust that it will be proves that the poem has communicated, has become partly our own. Hughes applies his generosity to people. Love is 'so like a fire' that it must not be 'let out into strawy small talk', so like a flood that a trickle would make the whole crack. The lovers regard each other speechlessly, relishing the plenitude. (In Thom Gunn the reserve would be a defence against giving oneself away.) A circumspect girl secretary, apparently rejecting sex, has the instinctive innocence, the commitment to domestic obligations which seems an enhancement of sex. 'All / Day like a starling under the bellies of bulls / She hurries among men, ducking, peeping.'

Is man, as an intelligence opposed to nature, kept out of these poems? Hughes has the reverence for the historical continuum that we noticed in Thom Gunn, for whom the chosen act begs the same questions whenever it occurs; Gunn is inward with the Jacobean legend—ambition, poses, calculated ends, the ins and outs of intrigue, simulated emotion. Hughes harks back to a mediaeval world: the baleful naturalism of the Border Ballads, the rude, vivid communality of Chaucer and Langland, the aristocratic virulence of Shakespeare's History Plays; and he points forward to the loamy richness of the eighteenth- and nineteenth-century country parish, the habitats of Crabbe, Cowper, and Tennyson and still a living thing today.* *Soliloquy of a Misanthrope* yields 'when I am got under my gravestone', 'praise God heartily', 'old acquaintance', 'the smirk of every man', 'every mouth confessing its crude shire'. I am not suggesting that Mr Hughes is the village idiot; he projects tried and known and rich imagery in enacting contexts because, in fact *or analogue*, these contexts have always existed and reach their full strength in that way. *The Decay of Vanity, The Hag, A Modest Proposal, Vampire, Fallgrief's Girl Friends, Two Wise Generals*, and *Invitation to the Dance* infer a cocktail party, the sex war, puritanism, diplomacy and atrocities and all employ archaistic and historical images. Because the generals compromise, don't say what they feel, they 'find their sleeping armies massacred'. The condemned prisoner, persecuted by an 'inquisitor', still despises 'the shy and idle'; his private courage augurs well for the future of human courage—witness the tremendous line which should stand as an epitaph on all the victims of oppression—'the light of his death's dawn put the dark out'. A possessive mother and her college daughter are 'a cajoling hag' and a 'pretty princess'. A party gate-crasher is a 'vampire', giving nothing, only taking. Voracious lovers, fighting like wolves in a forest, are quieted when 'the great lord from hunting' appears; one thinks of Donne's 'else a great Prince in prison lies'; a vivid tableau, as from an Uccello, follows and symbolizes the glory of requited desire:

> *His embroidered*
> *Cloak floats, the tail of his horse pours,*
> *And at his stirrup the two great-eyed greyhounds*

* '. . . England is perishing, and he was English. He was not British or enlightened or far-sighted or adaptable. He was English, and most so when he forgot his nationality and took a country walk.' E. M. Forster wrote this of Cowper in 1932.

That day after day bring down the towering stag
Leap like one, making delighted sounds.

In *The Decay of Vanity* the woman is the 'Queen' who crowns the poet King; he embalms her remains 'heart-brokenly', then forgets. Years later another man 'looms up' and, 'by the majesty in his stride', 'dreams he sweeps some great queen towards his bed'. The man's conceit is a confession of inferiority, for the woman is still beautiful—'a royal trophy'—and in 'a world of pride' this makes the man the poet's scavenger. The weighing of personality, the apportionment of justice, in this poem is magisterial. The woman being beautiful, all the characters are in the right. But it is unequivocally a contest: the best man wins. Pride of this order is disapproved of today, so the royal analogy gives an unfamiliar value some historical colour. The 'disfocusing of contemporaneity' in these poems vindicates unpopular sources of strength by exposing their roots.

Hughes's vivacity owes little to the Lawrentine 'lapsing out' into blood consciousness. He greets the intellect as in league with, though not subordinate to, nature, and his poems are often models of the ordering of experience. Hughes's poems are reared on the objective. This is clear in *The Casualty*. Farmers and housewives 'wait with interest for the evening news' before rushing out to find the crashed, burning airman. We see the victim react on his environment and become a new creature—'a snake in the gloom of the brambles or a rare flower'. Despite the terror which all share, there is reticence in the poet's approach. He does not make the man speak, nor does he mention the pain he must be feeling; the man is a natural object, doing what everybody will have to do in a particularly dramatic way; the watchers are rightly 'greedy to share all that is undergone'. Individuality is irrelevant for the watchers, for what is pain to the man is recharged reality to them, yet his humanity is crowned at the moment it returns to the general. The victim is set apart, honoured, for this. In a poem called *Bayonet Charge* a recruit sees a hare die violently; this wipes out vague idealism and he sees himself as mature amid 'the cold clockwork of the stars and the nations'.

Griefs for Dead Soldiers isolates three griefs: mightiest, that of the Cenotaph; secretest, that of the mother who 'cannot build her sorrow into a monument / And walk away from it'; and truest, that of the burial party. Mr C. B. Cox has asserted that Hughes separates the griefs to avoid irony about the public grief. I take the poem as an *ironical commendation* of future public grief—for the 'mightiest grief' is in the future tense, presented apocalyptically; and the 'crowds' who constitute 'the national sorrow' *know of no other wound.* By contrast, the 'secretest' grief is movingly sensitive, the 'truest' is grimly realistic. The thing is a fact of nature; this realism has been, therefore it is, and to complacent generations it will not be an excuse for vulgar nationalism but an almost super-natural reminder of the lost meaning of tragedy. Wilfred Owen might have written poetry like this had he lived. *Six Young Men* is about soldiers photographed against a landscape which the poet knows well—'I know / That bilberried bank . . .'

> *From where these sit*
> *You hear the water of seven streams fall*
> *To the roarer in the bottom, and through all*
> *The leafy valley a rumouring of air go.*
> *Pictured here, their expressions listen yet,*
> *And still that valley has not changed its sound*
> *Though their faces are four decades under the ground.*

Then he tells us about the deaths. The man 'you confront', 'see hale', is not 'more alive', nor is 'fabulous beast' more dead than these soldiers, since the intensity of life recorded in the photograph continues in nature; it is the human expression of that life which is tragically (he leaves us in no doubt about that) superannuated. In another poem a push-buttoner, agent of cold-blooded, administra-tion ridden war, hears the 'heart-beat' of an ancient warrior in his room. Time vanishes; war at least becomes a matter of spectacular risk. 'When archaeologists dig their remainder out / Bits of bone, rust / The grandeur of their wars humbles my thought'.

In Hughes's second book, *Lupercal* (1960), animals outnumber men. This is deceptive, for Hughes's intelligence refines the poems about animals, while the men gain by having their animality appraised intelligently. Hughes has been taunted with hiring animals as gangsters to indulge his primitive drives. Does he dis-gorge human impulses at a subhuman level? Disgorge sounds bad because we are trained to sublimate, to lose in pretension what we gain in refinement. Yet there remains an automatism of naturalism as dangerous as the automatism of material progress; and Hughes is not guiltless of the former, though he could teach a few things to the latter. (Mr Vernon Scannell upbraided Hughes's 'anthropo-morphic fallacy' in *Encounter*, in a skit called *Ruminant*, where a particularly bovine cow is caught in the act of 'composing a long poem about Ted Hughes'.) First, it is arguable that a modern poet's obsession with nature is needed to compensate for indifference, and this in a country which is notoriously sentimental about animals provided they are tame or comical and do not read a lecture to

humans (how many animal addicts care about natural conservation?), and second, I think the poems are more objective, more
complex, than the Vernon Scannells allow. Take *View of a Pig*,
where the animal is dead; any attempt by the poet to 'work out' his
aggression would be lunatic. He is intensely preoccupied with the
deadness—'too dead now to pity'—of the pig as a quality worth
exploring; the distinction between man and beast is riveting—'I
stared at it a long time'; the enacting life is his remembered life,
'once I ran at a fair in the noise . . .' Now beasts alive are very
wicked, they affirm themselves; their rejection as literary pets
makes these poems as original as Lawrence's. The tension he feels
between the otherness, and the nearness, of the beasts makes this
poet realize his own strength. The violence of a frustrated era is
attracted away from cruel, destructive outlets and returned to
source, where it can be appreciated and, energizing us, put out to
graze.

In *Hawk Roosting* the animal is alive, it alone speaks, but in two
voices: a descriptive voice, telling the reader what he sees—'my
feet are locked upon the rough bark'—and the instructive voice of
the poet which utters what is seen at the same time that it cross-
examines the reader by implication. It claims that 'there is no
sophistry in my body / My manners are tearing off heads', 'no
arguments assert my right', 'I am going to keep things like this'.
Quotes from Hitler? Hughes has not raved violent nonsense through
a microphone; he has written about a hawk; by engaging our
interest, he exposes our fear of instinct, our bent for apologia, our
postponement of choice—the 'falsifying dream'. If our kinship
with the hawk is demonstrated, it is because we share—or should
share—its adjustment as both expression and controller of its
environment—'It took the whole of Creation / To produce my
foot, my each feather / Now I hold Creation in my foot.' Less
emblematic, more puzzling, is the Otter—versatile, endearing,
'neither fish nor beast'—an English eccentric, apt to give the hunt
the slip. His affinities with man are of the order of imaginative
simile (he crosses the sea in three nights 'like a king in hiding.
Crying to the old shape of the starlit land') or of half satirical
inference ('the self under the eye lies / Attendant and withdrawn').
Pike is physically and sensually triumphant, a marvel of visual
images communicated aurally, the menace of the tactile lurking in
the incisive splendour of the language. The pike—'a life subdued to
its instrument'—is clearly other than we, the gauleiter of a police
state:

> Or move, stunned by their own grandeur,
> Over a bed of emerald, silhouette

Of submarine delicacy and horror.
A hundred feet long in their world.

When the poet comes on the scene, he participates as enemy—
'silently cast and fished'—and victim 'with the hair frozen on my
head'; he is the object of aggression. It is an aggression which does
him good. *Bullfrog*, also concerned with effects, divides man from
beast through technical mastery; Hughes abandons quatrain in
favour of a flexible form. The bullfrog, at first sight alarming, is an
engaging character, worthy of affection, and the delighted poet
wants to talk about, and to, the bullfrog at the moment when it is
in action. The result is a lively example of what syncopated rhythm
can do to harmonize events through the controlled diversification of
texture:

> *With their lithe long strong legs*
> *Some frogs are able*
> *To thump upon double-*
> *Bass string though pond-water deadens and clogs.*
> *But you, bullfrog, you pump out*
> *Whole fogs full of horn—a threat*
> *As of a liner looming. True*
> *That, first hearing you*
> *Disgorging your gouts of darkness like a wounded god . . .*

We find there is no assault on our emotion nor any attempt to
abdicate from consciousness into merging. Nature is distanced, as
in Shakespeare, precisely *through* intense intricate response (see
Bullfrog) to the point where it throws into relief the tragic isolation
and irrevocableness of articulate being:

> *The deeps are cold:*
> *In that darkness camaraderie does not hold:*
> *Nothing touches, but clutching, devours.*
> (*Relic*)

Because we feel the pity and terror as repugnant we remain
outside; because we apprehend its truth and revolt against it, the
assertion of free will is born. 'Time in the sea eats its tail', mindless,
repetitive, and casts back upon the shores from which they came 'the
spars of purposes'. Ted Hughes knows an alternative: neither to
exclude the tragic, nor to frustrate the will. Just as the Pike was
'subdued to its instrument', and the Hawk expressed and controlled
creation, the Intelligence is not asked to grovel, it is urged to admit
and exercise its kinship with nature. *Thrushes* opens with a breath-
taking dynamic insight into birds pecking on a lawn; that domestic

familiar, the thrush, metamorphoses into a monster of instinctive efficiency, all 'bounce and stab', 'a ravening second', overtaking 'the instant' and inimical to 'procrastinations', 'yawning stares', 'sighs', and 'head-scratchings'. In an aside, we are told that 'Mozart's brain' had this power of purpose; but most men are content with sitting at a desk, 'outstripping' their diaries. Emphasis is on intelligence—he singles out 'Mozart's brain'—and on kinship (not plaything of nature).

The feeling of brotherhood brings charity and amused understanding. The tramp, asleep in 'the let of the ditch' (when was that term last incarnated in English?), is adrift in the rain-sodden November countryside, yet he is the reverse of alienated, for he too is 'subdued to his instrument'. 'I thought what strong trust / Slept in him.' The hermit, believing that he can commune with God better from a position of security, abandons his exile to be greeted by a bourgeois chorus of 'I'd be delighted', 'Yours sincerely', and 'Thank you very much indeed'. In this poem we mark the disfocusing of contemporaneity again; in *The Retired Colonel* we are reminded of the historical continuum. That diehard of defunct Empire who caused Macspaunday such distress in the 1930's is treated with the amused charity of a *specimen*: to reverse Mr E. M. Forster, he retains the 'glory of the animal' even if he has given up 'the tail coat and a couple of ideas'. Unnecessary to judge his fall; he is a man; he is a trophy:

> And what if his sort should vanish?
> The rabble starlings roar upon
> Trafalgar. The man-eating British lion
> By a pimply age brought down.
> Here's his head mounted, though only in rhymes,
> Beside the head of the last English
> Wolf (those starved gloomy times!)
> And the last sturgeon of Thames.

Dick Straightup, the Yorkshire villager, 'eighty winters on the windy ridge / Of England' shames others specimens—the 'scholar' and the 'thin clerks' who exercise in their bed-sitters at midnight. Just by 'surviving among hills' he has rooted himself so deeply in his environment that he sits 'full of legend and life'; he baffles reporters (we can imagine) for the continuity he represents is 'bigger and deeper than the village'. His old age, being a natural event, is as glorious as youth; his death is consummation.

Reverence for the historical continuum, the sense of interaction, free from merging, between intelligence and nature, and the fact that animals are World Citizens means that Hughes is far from being a regional poet. Mr R. S. Thomas has taught us that regional poetry may vivify the rudiments on which national tradition is founded; it may also be the alibi of fugitives from justice. Democratism, I have implied, is Hughes's habitat, and within democratism, England. For the first time since Kipling, an English poet names his country straightforwardly, without partisanship, disarming ridicule. *Nicholas Ferrar* inherits complex overtones—Anglicanism, our Civil War, Eliot's later poetry—but its mood, atmosphere, and imagery are in simple English; as in Gaunt's deathbed speech, essence transcends association. When the poems have announced locales—*Pennines in April, Mayday on Holderness*—nothing is put in to make the poem sentimental; their enthusiasm includes general reminiscence along with regional observation; it is a far-sighted world of 'measuring the miles of silence / Your eye takes the strain'. In the 1930's they made inventories out of social abuses ('smokeless chimneys, damaged bridges, rotting wharves and choked canals' . . .) *Mayday on Holderness*, absolved of that, puts the clock back: towards complexity and roots:

> *From Hull's sunset smudge*
> *Humber is melting eastward, my south skyline:*
> *A loaded single vein, it drains*
> *The effort of the inert North—Sheffield's ores,*
> *Bog pools, drags of toadstools, tributary*
> *Graves, dunghills, kitchens, hospitals.*
> *The unkillable North Sea swallows it all.*
> *Insects, drunken, drop out of the air.*

Infected by the 'motherly summer' rather than the slump, confidence and love unfold as inventory, image added to image until 'the stars make pietas. The owl announces its sanity' and the scene travels beyond Yorkshire, beyond the recall of war (' "Mother, Mother!" cries the pierced helmet. Cordite oozings of Gallipoli') to vanish in the jungle.

Hughes's technique is original, his attitudes are instructive—the reader is intended to learn, to admire (or condemn) and do otherwise (or likewise). The poems give us the emotional jolt we need, yet leave an area between evidence and reaction which we may bridge by taking thought. Adverse criticism must fasten on the zones where Hughes seems to be faking the evidence. In certain poems and in riot spots within poems there is technical delinquency, as if Hughes, taken aback by abatement of inspiration, was trying to foment it by roughening the texture with the aid of muscle-flexing, grotesquerie, and the gnomic. This malpractice is not so much offensive as irrelevant—we know and like him, he ought to relax! Or the inspiration works at such pressure that it transmutes into vision. We define vision as feeling operating so intensely that it expels all the normal compromises and reticences, reveals the entire point: the interest of the vision depending on the extent to which it includes in a single unit—vision—a multitude of affairs normally apprehended apart. In *Crow Hill, Crag Jack's Apostasy, The Perfect Forms*, and others there is an absoluteness of feeling which is visionary. In *Crow Hill* it is robust, serious, simple—'what humbles these hills has raised / The arrogance of blood and bone'. In *Crag Jack, Forms*, and some uncollected verse there is a touch of obsession, of goggling not inclusion, of too earnest *grand guignol*, of the primitive exalted over meaning—'the undying tail-swinging / Stupidity of the donkey / That carries Christ', and 'pray / That I may see more than your eyes / In an animal's dreamed head'. There is no denying the strength of the verse, but the impact is of sterile frightfulness and morbid impasse. In hypnotic episodes this poet seems to be bewitched by the vortex in a sinister sense.

Praise of animal as example becomes obsession with animal as tyrant in *The Bull Moses*. True, nothing human is imputed to the bull's intentions, but there is a comically prudent deference in the poet's approach; we are no longer captivated by the way the poet treats the theme. (A Latin poet—Lorca for example—would intellectualize the bull, treat it as at once challenge and transcendent symbol.) *Witches, Strawberry Hill*, and *Fourth of July* make the mistake of abandoning precept and evidence for admonishment. 'Small psychology would unseam it', 'has licked the stylist out of their skulls', '. . . the few jaws / Piranha and jaguar' are eloquent but the case is presented too brazenly; the instinct of witches, stoats, and the fauna and flora of the Amazon are not allowed to correct, yet are a bizarre alternative to, scientific research, Augustan polish, and the plight of wage-slaves who 'lean over headlines, taking nothing in'—not that one fails to see Mr Hughes's point. This 'take it or leave it' strain in Mr Hughes is at variance with his argumentative mood.

As Ted Hughes has plumbed the maelstrom to the point of hysteria, as he knows in his flesh with what intimacy our creative and destructive impulses are allied, he is able, in a panic, to write a compassionate poetry of knowledge. This is why his H Bomb poem is one of the few which will survive nuclear disarmament. Sense-impregnated *knowledge*, unifying a complex statement, rather than juridical intelligence 'containing' crisis, pervades *A Woman Unconscious*. The threat to man embraces the whole of nature ('the toil of all our ages a loss / With leaf and insect') but the fact that 'Russia and America circle each other' does not diminish individual being; destruction would be 'a melting of the mould in the mother' (the stress on kinship) and man is central. Thought 'shies' away from the dreadful 'playing shadow', knowing that the menace is not unique, but 'a malingering of now': the *timor mortis conturbat me* that horrified men always. The death of a woman—explicitly cited as 'one'—is not a 'lesser death' than the death of all mankind. Her 'last of sense' divorces her, not from herself, but from 'the world's evidence'. To bring intimate ('one') and compressed ('last of sense') and far-flung ('the world's evidence') data into such fruitful proximity, to honour the need of life for all through the death of one, to resist the temptation to localize the panic and to distil calm by setting it in the perspective of time, and to outlaw complacency, is a feat of honour.

As in 'a slumber did my spirit seal . . . earth's diurnal course / With rocks, and stones, and trees' this is an art of life-ennobling fear.* At worst the threat *reminds* us of 'the mould in the mother', 'the quick of the earth', 'the toil of all our ages', 'leaf and insect'. Thought, provoked, *suggests* that 'malingering of now' is better than 'calamitous change', and calms us. We *feel* the 'lesser death' to be greater than the threat. 'One', gathering into itself 'the mould in the mother', could be a near relative, or any stranger, or the unity of mankind invoked against 'all mankind wince out'. The 'malingering' *is* now 'the world's evidence', all we have, pregnant with value, and the 'last of sense' is a tragic loss. The reader has been guided, by the poet, to make the vital responses himself. For philosophic integrity sweetened by imaginative strangeness, for the acceptance of fate lightened by future hope, this poem may be ranked not too far below Wordsworth's Lucy Saga. As always with excellence, it is the life in the poems, however grim their context, which makes the life outside the poems also worth preserving.

* The element of a tragic practical joke is comparable to the satiric practical joke in *William Empson at Aldermaston* by Alan Brownjohn, where the colourful gaiety of the fortress, a parody of life, is answered by the eccentric gaiety of the marchers, and the point is clinched with a relevant quotation from an unlikely poem—'That deep blankness / Was the real thing strange'—by the man with the Chinese beard.

NO ONE ACTUALLY STARVES:
PHILIP LARKIN

There aren't any good, brave causes left. If the big bang does come, and we all get killed off, it won't be in aid of the old-fashioned, grand design. It'll just be for the Brave New-nothing-very-much-thank-you.

John Osborne: *Look Back in Anger*

PHILIP LARKIN is an older poet than Porter, Gunn, and Hughes. His first book, *The North Ship*, was published in 1945, and, since it opposed rational syntax and mundane observation to the prevailing other-worldly garrulousness, was greeted with derision. Larkin followed Mr Roy Fuller in anticipating the trend which threatened to erect rational syntax and mundane observation into a dictatorship as obnoxious as the banished government. Thanks to his indifference to aesthetics Larkin never had, like Dr Donald Davie, a penchant for the 'purity of diction' of the Augustans, nor like Mr John Wain a cult of William Empson. One never suffers, in Larkin, from the monotonous, presumptuous, foreseeable thump of average pentameter: Larkin's lively episodic themes, his eye for objects, his novelist's feeling for variety of narrative effect, and his sheer enterprise in inventing colloquial lyric structures of his own gives his work a fructifying informality and versatility of tone. He also has a most congenial—though not in the least brash —poetic presence.

Larkin is the antidote of an exile. Where Gunn seeks enfranchisement in America, Porter salvation in London, and Hughes genuineness in the zoological gardens, Mr Larkin has stayed put in Hull. His dislike of Continental Holidays, his liking for jazz, his preference for the bicycle, another of Larkin's tell-tale and endearing affinities with Mr Betjeman, and his opinion that the so-called sources of light, not to mention the Culture Annexe of the Sunday papers, that incorrigible oracle, are neither corrupt nor brilliant but just off the beam are well known. As Librarian of Hull University, Mr Larkin struck his more bohemian co-believer, Mr Brian Higgins, as a traitor to the cause—'a sad-faced poet all Kodaks and lost chances'.

Mr Higgins jumps to conclusions. There is a rationale behind Larkin's provinciality which must be distinguished from the parochial. The parochial is the glorification of prudence, chosen through self-interest, mediocrity or fear. A dirty word to the mass media, the provincial is the trust in roots, the refusal to be gulled, the *reservation* of respect and enthusiasm before the glamorous and the seductive, which characterizes the man who is determined to start from the minimal, the known, the dependable in his own thought and experience. As Jane Austen showed, it is an attitude especially for the British, who prefer to 'know' (a verb which has no exact foreign equivalent) each other than decide through literature or hearsay: we work through judgment not ideology. Whether this be good or bad—and it permits grave errors of commission and omission—it balances us, gives most a hearing and demands a stability of which some complain. Larkin likes the Welfare State *because* it offers a basic security to all without making any of the old grandiose demands—sacrifice, patriotism, service. If middle-class idealists campaigned before the war for a 'new country' where the poet could write sane verse without worrying about injustices (what Erich Heller, reacting against the Post-Symbolists, calls 'a poetry of simple civic virtue')* their ideal has been realized in the lower-middle-class verse of Mr Larkin; and perhaps they find him uninteresting. Larkin is the poet of Kodaks, kiddies, 'packets of letters tied with tartan ribbon', 'golden tits' (on the figurehead of a sailing ship), 'tinned sardines', bills, bed-sitters, walking in the municipal park, 'his bag of samples', 'couples', 'places', 'family hols', third-class compartments, jazz sessions, washing-lines, and—most alarming—'a Grecian statue kicked in the privates'. (One faintly recalls Stephen Spender on 'the decline of a culture / Mourned by scholars who dream of the ghosts of Greek boys').

Born Yesterday is dedicated to the daughter of the author of *Lucky Jim*. Larkin shows that average situations, the virtues of the minimal, are his native heath. He wishes to Sally Amis the gifts of the 'ordinary'—not the 'usual stuff' about being beautiful, innocent, loved—and 'the average of talents'. The poet is not being cussed: he looks for an enhancement of personality. The 'uncustomary' pulls people off balance, becomes unworkable: it is better to be dull and harmonious and thus happy and giving happiness. In *Places, Loved Ones* the poet laments—or rather accounts for might be more accurate in this poet's case—the fact that he has never married and settled down. The latter can be, he feels, an evasion of challenges, a denial of choice, a canny egotism—'so that it's not your fault / Should the town turn dreary / The girl a dolt'. The last stanza argues that we must accept ('what you settled for'—the *double entendre* deposited with a guffaw) independence as the type of alienation it is, but avoid any *arrière pensée*, the yearning after Utopias. We are given an

---

* Erich Heller, *The Hazard of Modern Poetry*, 1953, p. 38.

unassuming plea for sanity; the right of choice and movement is reserved, yet no privileges are claimed for individualism.

Poetry of Departures (note his avoidance of the French phrase) reads like a good citizen's epitaph on the leisured to and froing of an older generation, indeed the whole romantic myth of renewal through change. The development is subtle. Larkin agrees that to 'chuck up everything' and 'just clear off' is audacious, purifying, elemental. One's ordered life, one's bed-sitter with its 'specially chosen junk' is hateful. But flight only appears a panacea in anticipation: it is simply the indulgence of an impulse, like a seduction, or fomenting a brawl; the feeling that 'surely I can, if he did' may just as validly be an inspiration to remaining 'sober and industrious'. The knowledge that we can uproot, like our reservation of free choice, is too important to be squandered; it is better to abide in potentiality, fulfilling the daily task, than sell out to an illusion. The hopeful excited suggestivity of the last verse is typical of Larkin's *fairness*, his determination not to conceal just how attractive the prospects are:

> *Yes, swagger the nut-strewn roads,*
> *Crouch in the fo'c'sle*
> *Stubbly with goodness, if*
> *It weren't so artificial,*
> *Such a deliberate step backwards*
> *To create an object:*
> *Books; china; a life*
> *Reprehensibly perfect.*

The phrase 'no one actually *starves*',* from *Toads*, is Larkin's minimal tribute to the Welfare State, imputed to all who 'live on their wits' (including, it is encouraging to note, 'lecturers'), who having opted out of the toad's 'six days a week' tyranny and rejected its 'sickening poison' favour a life of freelance improvisation. The Welfare State may diminish the need for wits but it at least relieves the anguish of the wit-livers. The poet might like to join the 'stuff your pension!' chorus of the professional bohemians; he approves of their faith and pride. At bottom, though, he feels it is 'the stuff that dreams are made on', for the real toad is the inward one 'heavy as hard luck and cold as snow'. Our weakness will prevent us obtaining 'the fame and the girl and the money' (it is a moot point whether he considers this a good thing) through 'blarney'; the public toad, E. M. Forster's 'telegrams and anger', co-exists together with the subjective toad, diabolically mocking the ability of Forster's inner life 'to pay';

---

* One is tempted to add: tell that to OXFAM. C. P. Snow has a case; literary men do seem selfish. But their duty also lies where their lot is cast.

true maturity, real citizenship, stem from our learning to live with both toads. But this solemn exegesis makes the poem too serious. It is a bizarre extravaganza, giving the (rejected) case for opting out the full rein which it deserves.

Does Larkin write the poetry of genteel assent? No, the man who has renounced exile to make the best of roots—one doesn't do much more with Larkin—is visited by intimations of mortality, present dualities, future threats. A strain in Larkin of discreet lyricism, of dry *vae victis*, is the disapproved nostalgia of the late developer, reconsidering without regrets a youth which may have been blunted by circumstance, vitiated by anxiety, or simply missed through social and psychological unawareness. In *Coming* the 'fresh-peeled voice' of the thrush astonishes the brickwork, presaging spring; the poet recalls the 'forgotten boredom' of childhood and feels like a boy 'who comes on a scene / Of adult reconciling'. In *Going* the confidence is withdrawn; he is abandoned; the evening is menacing, unexpected; it brings no comfort, only the apprehension of some incomprehensible otherness. The sensibility of Rilke has resurrected in the Midland suburb. The hostile elusiveness of this poem initiates the sense of resisted, questioned transcendentalism which sometimes impinges on, though never invades, Larkin's immanent world. *Next, Please* shows that the refusal to opt out, the sureties of 'what you settled for' don't automatically bring any reward, they don't endorse complacency. Our hopes—'We think each one will heave to and unload / All good into our lives'—cherished through the years of sobriety and industry look like 'an armada of promises'. We are wrong:

> *Only one ship is seeking us, a black-*
> *Sailed unfamiliar, towing at her back*
> *A huge and birdless silence. In her wake*
> *No waters breed or break.*

The allegory, nurtured through five stanzas, points no moral. Functional, cheerful, assured, the maritime imagery has been so vivid and attractive that the illusion seems a happy one, like that 'life lie' Ibsen advocates through Dr Relling to help the depressed and defeated to soldier on. We are so engaged by the warmth of the development that the final revelation of the void comes as a grim surprise. Yet there is nothing of the grovelling before death, the courting of nothingness, which is so repugnant in Rilke and his co-death-wishers. Mr Larkin has uttered a warning; he at least is going to make the best of it. He reveals horror at the heart of daily living, reminds one of Henry Reed's parody of *Four Quartets*—'Idle to hope that the simple stirrup-pump / Can extinguish hell'. What the parochial—opposed to the provincial—refuses to do is admit that the fabric of security is fragile. In *Wants*, the poet blows up the fabric. Beyond the 'invitation cards', 'the printed directions of sex', the family photograph under the flagstaff runs 'the wish to be alone'. We all know this. Well, it leads farther to 'beneath it all, desire of oblivion runs', in spite of 'the artful tensions of the calendar', 'the life insurance', and 'the costly aversion of the eyes from death'. Larkin starts from what we know, what we *bank on* (in more ways than one), and unmasks the utilitarian—let alone the Prudential —as the idiot barrier we erect against anxiety and fear. The more efficient the barrier, the worse the repression, the more vicious and uncaring the complacency. If we admitted this the pompous impotence of our material defences, embattled like concrete blocks between the refrains 'beneath it all, desire of oblivion runs', would resign their obsessive importance; we might cease to 'wish to be alone' and stop abetting the death-wish.

Admitting the reality of anxiety and fear is exactly what this poet does. It is the downright honesty (the 'I was not brave, I was just honest' of Yevtushenko) justifying his admiration for the average and the dependable. In a speakingly graphic piece informed by a grave compassion, *Deceptions*, inspired by Mayhew's *London Labour and the London Poor*, Larkin shows an affinity with Dickens—the Dickens of disconcerting psychological realism as much as the Dickens of documentary realism. A phrase from this poem, 'suffering is exact', pinpoints the centrality of Larkin's psychological realism: his quickness to apply it to himself, his aptitude for visualizing it as affected by local conditions. A poem called *Spring* exhibits, amid the placid municipal scene, Mr Larkin threading his 'pursed-up way', 'an indigestible sterility' across the park. 'Earth's most multiple, excited daughter' has no use for him, yet he sees her 'best'; I think 'best' here means truest as well as clearest. To know your 'paths grown craven and circuitous', your 'visions mountain-clear', your 'needs immodest' is to spurn the short cut to being 'less deceived' (from *Deceptions*—*The Less Deceived* is the title of Larkin's 1955 volume) and to explore the North West Passage of alienation. Another poem invites the poet's girl to 'jump, like Alice, with floating skirt into my head'. Here she discovers, not a glossy magazine home, but a mental slum, filled with viscous rubbish and rotting spiritual detritus, looking as if it was decorated by some collaboration between the early Sartre and the painter Francis Bacon. This would 'knock my darling off her unpriceable pivot'. One sees more clearly why Larkin doubts the power of 'blarney' to secure 'the fame and the girl and the money'.

At moments of vision Larkin situates himself in time with admirable poise. *Triple Time* analyses an autumn street scene in terms of the present, 'unrecommended by event', the future as the child sees it, 'lambent with adult enterprise', and the past 'that we insensately forebore to fleece' ('a valley cropped by fat neglected chances'). Astute, balanced, lucid in the management of different tenses and their emotional associations, the poem donates simultaneity; the impressions, extended in time, seem to mingle on the present plane, in a state of equipoise. The poem provides its antidote to our 'threadbare perspectives': if we keep calm, active, and thoughtful we realize the *reasonableness* of time and this precludes regret and expectancy. Mysticism is eschewed; the three rival times are fully weighed. And the theme of loss-and-recovery in time may be traced in relationships. The 'five light sounds' of a girl's maiden name 'no longer mean your face'; 'confused by law with someone else' she is no longer 'semantically the same as that young beauty'. Needless to add Larkin avoids the cliché about the girl being the same. She is fingermarked, he admits. The maiden name equals 'what we feel now about you then'; enthusiasm is indestructible. The anti-literary overtone (feeling exalted above the 'semantics' which communicate it) is countered by the language itself: it is *there* all right, enveloping a private event, exploring and eternalizing it. The moments of recognition, shared equipoise, and exchanged emotion are sufficient for Larkin; he distrusts merging. In *Latest Face* ('so effortless, your great arrival at my eyes') it is enough that:

> *Admirer and admired embrace*
> *On a useless level, where*
> *I contain your current grace,*
> *You my judgment; yet to move*
> *Into real untidy air*
> *Brings no lasting attribute—*
> *Bargains, suffering, and love,*
> *Not this always-planned salute.*

'If no one has misjudged himself. Or lied' concludes *Reasons for Attendance*, where the poet excuses his *voyeur* status at a party by protesting that 'I too am individual'. The 'lion's share' of happiness is not necessarily 'found by couples'. Where Peter Porter, whose subject is man in society, nags at himself in his exposure of manners, Larkin's subject is rather man and man: live and let live. After all, no one actually starves. Larkin agrees that people *can* misjudge ourselves and lie; and times may come when we have to revoke the benefit of the doubt. *No Road* is about a broken friendship. The idea of nature encroaching on the space between two houses, the eerie 'eroding agents'—space, silence, strangers—the laboured, mournful rhythm counteracted by crisp diction and fastidious rhymes, the note of ruminated action in the tone causes, when applied to the infidelities of modern life, the estrangement to be rendered memorably. It at least *counts*. None the less, the final self-critical lines are common sense; he is pointing out how things are:

> To watch that world come up like a cold sun,
> Rewarding others, is my liberty.
> Not to prevent it is my will's fulfilment.
> Willing it, my ailment.

Pace the average politician, this poet can make a general statement without ulterior motives—witness *I Remember, Lines on a Young Lady's Photograph Album, Church Going*, and *At Grass*. The first is about the poet's home town, Coventry. It reads like a mature riposte to the life of country house-parties, halcyon travelling, shirt-open-at-the-neck camaraderie familiarized by memoirists like Philip Toynbee, John Lehmann, and Stephen Spender. Mr Larkin 'coming up England by a different line' finds himself in Coventry and denies that his 'roots' are there; it was merely 'where his childhood was unspent', where he did not 'invent / Blinding theologies of flowers', had no 'splendid family', no febrile love affairs, met no celebrities, was not acclaimed as a prodigy. To his friend's suggestion that he wishes 'the place in Hell' Larkin replies that it is 'not the place's fault' for 'Nothing, like something, happens anywhere'. Bitterness, enthusiasm, attempts at diagnosis would destroy the delicious irony of facts. For all its provincial emphasis, this is the poem of a State citizen rather than a native son, a citizen whose roots are adaptable, practicable anywhere, because he accepts the responsibility which follows the loss of busy idealism and exaggerated expectations. What contemporary could take a tear-jerker of the media (*At Grass*, about retired racehorses) and turn it into impeccable verse without adopting an avuncular or folksy pose, without sermonizing or patronizing, so that the *real* poetry of the situation is brought out unadulterated and entire; or conjure a whole ambience, as Larkin does in the *Photograph Album*, without amplifying it into some proposition about life or rarefying it into solipsistic 'sensitive' jottings? Larkin subdues himself, as observer, completely to his subject, so that the girl's past is legitimately affirmed as her past, a living past which the poet may enjoy—'I choke on such nutritious images'.

The seriousness of *Church Going* depends on the proposition that organized religion is obsolete. The poet does not rush in to gloat over the likelihood, plead for a revival, wallow in a sense of sin, deny the crisis in a hysteria of mystic ecstasy (nor with our *avant garde* divines does he pretend that glory and horror are gone). He is concerned with evidence; he catches himself *removing his bicycle-clips in a church*; why so? At first he is abrupt, clowning, full of the usual gruff Larkin disclaimers—'there's nothing going on', 'up at the holy end', 'much at a loss', 'someone would know: I don't'—and the usual affable Amisite anti-cultural quips. Still, he took his cycle-clips off in 'awkward reverence'. The church is vaguely interesting; at any rate not positively repellent (phoney); it provokes speculation about ends and impulses and matures, through the poet's admission that he is 'bored, uninformed', to the status of an antidote to the instability of our time. The church gathers up, attempts to understand, the disparate infidelities and fragmented aspirations of secularism. At least it accords the erring sheep a decent burial, and if there is virtue in the shell there may be value in the institution. The last stanza relaxes, expands; the slangy opening, the visit itself, *is to do* with the seriousness the church is felt to be about! Hankerings after a substitute religion are lost in the search for a rationale which can respect religion without going to extremes of belief and disbelief. This liberalism, tapping deep roots, is vital whether we are Christians or not in the *paradis artificiel* of today.

Mr Larkin's third volume, *The Whitsun Weddings*, appeared when this book had reached the point of no return—a happy mishap since Mr Larkin consolidates, but does not refine or elaborate, earlier themes. (He still hints at magnificent prejudices; no Nice Liberal is allowed to have prejudices.) Is his failure to fare forward a destiny, a reluctance to tell lies, or a limitation? By simply floating off from where he touched ground, the poet has left his imitators high and dry. His style is more than metrical thinking out loud; akin to Eliot's in kind, though not in method, his structures 'argufy', they convict through intonation and bearing rather than explain themselves through repetition. The title poem, with its amalgam of regional, class, and period imagery, is typical, and shows up the 'aesthetic idealism' of (say) Stephen Spender's *The Express*. Larkin's rhythm more than echoes the train, it prevents, as it accentuates, the tremor of resistless contingence which he sees undermine the members of the weddings. Older, and envious, the late developer is an artist: he feels their 'travelling coincidence' as a climax, lets it grow on him until he thinks the long thoughts they would think could they relax. (The idea of London's postal districts 'packed like squares of wheat' is a refreshing fusion of the disparate: it reminds the town of its near ancestor and relative, the agricultural community—one of the poet's Halévy echoes.) The poem is disenchanted charity in a setting, and perhaps this mood has replaced 'no one actually starves'.

One realizes how historic this poetry is—Auden's 'devastated areas' have become 'a cut-price crowd' and 'the furnace-glares of Sheffield'—in its fidelity to our present: its aphrodisiac prosperity, its cheerful non-culture, its random violence, when the girl of the *Sunny Prestatyn* poster, a picture of health, is violated by images of frustration and finally banished by a reminder of disease. *Ambulances* pass, and the poet is aware of 'the solving emptiness / That lies just under all we do'. *Afternoons* is typical of poems whose kindly stoicism is British and provincial in its refusal of *angst*, its observance of the pessimistic proprieties (although *Here* and *Essential Beauty*— about urban advertising—over-state their facts and suffocate their conclusions for the same reason, and *Love Songs in Age* is almost lachrymose). Larkin speaks up for the stragglers, as unwitting as they are undramatic—*Mr Bleaney*, like Ted Hughes's retired colonel, is a human specimen, not a museum piece, and Larkin can share the quality of his happy limits because they mirror his own disillusionment. He notices the thrivers, the purposive; and perhaps it takes a professional anti-hero, like the narrator of *Dockery and Son*, to see that Dockery was not a villain but a natural man, who fulfilled 'a style / Our lives bring with them'. As natural for the poet to be devoid of family and property; no need for him to be a Tolstoyan or a crank. To renounce the will is to be less deceived, to be immune from sophistication. Honesty comes 'not from what / We think truest, or most want to do' but from style 'hardening into habit' and used for understanding.

At moments we feel that Larkin catches the tone of his time, is ephemeral, but unlike Auden's his time is likely to enjoy a long innings. This is sheer luck, since it raises the chances for that 'central core of personality' which Mr A. Alvarez thinks Auden lacks.* There is going to be time for Eliot's 'evening with the photograph album', yet Eliot commands us to be 'still moving' into another intensity, and it would be sad if Mr Larkin were to end as the John Betjeman of Little England. There are signs that he might. But he has come up England by a different line: lament gives way to earth and acceptance. Throughout this book there is an air of recuperation. Three or four generations of loss, of anguish, of turmoil, here receive their quietus. In *MCMXIV*, the doomed innocence, children 'called after kings and queens', tin advertisements and pubs open all day stand against a vista which is only partly destructible:

> And the countryside not caring:
> The place-names all hazed over
> With flowering grasses, and fields
> Shadowing Domesday lines

* See A. Alvarez, *The Shaping Spirit*, 1958, pp. 105-6.

NO ONE ACTUALLY STARVES

Under wheat's restless silence;
The differently-dressed servants
With tiny rooms in huge houses,
The dust behind limousines . . .

A tinge of indulgent, valetudinarian despair, at odds with the
sardonic *vae victis* grin (resumed in *Wild Oats*, which makes it clear
that the gauche, in fact, are lucky), seems related to a certain technical abandonment: some *coups de main* are evident, one sees how
he does it. It is one thing to be sympathetically bored, another to
threaten suicide. This is probably the result of that renunciation
of will which colours the atmosphere—relaxed, classless and popular,
'the unique random blend / Of families and fashions'. Poems like
Broadcast, Faith Healing, and *Home is So Sad* show that his philosophy,
the exactness of love, the hugeness of death, and the misunderstand-
ings in between, may be simple; his pictures are precise, clear, and
complete. *Toads* said live and let live; its sequel carries distrust to
the point of the death-wish; and this taxes the tolerance. *Self's the
Man* apologizes: the poet intends to remain sane, single and, though
self-doubtful, free of guilt. When he praises *An Arundel Tomb* we
know that he got there on the excursion ticket:

> *The stone fidelity*
> *They hardly meant has come to be*
> *Their final blazon, and to prove*
> *Our almost-instinct almost true:*
> *What will survive of us is love.*

*   *   *

In a talk with Dr Donald Davie published in *The Review*,* Mr
A. Alvarez advocated a bout with the 'difficult and destructive'—
outside pressures and conflicts must be faced. Our age is one of
'intolerable neurotic stress . . . neurosis is very prevalent and men-
aces us all' and a new seriousness is needful to 'express the complexity
. . . of being human'. He summarizes his position in these memorable words. 'We must be sure of our identity because of the
movement to destroy individuals . . . we've all got these self-
destructive tendencies, tendencies to give up . . . you can do it in
your personal life, you can do it in your working life.' Dr Davie
defends the idea of aestheticism. He believes that excess of exposure,

* *The Review*, April–May 1962.

of tasks, 'all this burden of anxiety and responsibility' will paralyse imagination, poison the springs of truth; the artist must keep faith. 'We all have our jobs to do.' Concentration on things in themselves will reveal our true relation to them and to each other. 'You are finding your true self through the process of writing a poem . . . to see things in this way affords a model which you can then apply to human relations.' The state of mind during composition and the account of reality arrived at are indeed often different. A poem's ends are not in its beginnings, yet it remains sincere when, being the product of hard work, it mirrors a truth of the poet's experience: something new, something recognizable. State of mind is now account of reality; what is new to the poet is a modification of what is other than the poet; for the reader, the poem is both a surprise and an orientation; it initiates a revival, it suggests a state of affairs. The *sine qua non* is that the discoveries be verifiable by the reader: not just palatable to his fancy but nutritive to his life.

To avoid malnutrition himself, the poet has to keep the beginnings multitudinously aware, lest the ends starve. Mr Alvarez's specific for getting 'beyond the gentility principle' (in the preface to his anthology) could, if swallowed whole, result in paralysis. A fanatic streak in his a-gentility suggests that, in the urge to Ensure his Identity, he may forget that suicide may be achieved with pep pills as well as with sleeping tablets. In his zeal to get the 'intolerable stress' dealt with this critic almost consigns poets to the mental home (formerly they had fallen from high stools in pubs). Gentility can mean laziness, deceit, pretension, yet the belief that 'life is always more or less orderly, people always more or less polite, their emotions decent and controllable; that God, in short, is more or less good' is typical of the conformist element in all groups in an age of value blurring and erosion of liberties, to which the weaker brethren adapt themselves by more drastic, less conscience-stricken, self-emasculation. The union of intellect with character, drawing from the deep the energy for a dynamic, which may rise to independence of judgment (in face of mob passions), power of initiative (freedom from fashion), and drive to responsibility, is in order if people are to make anything out of raw psychic material; we are back where we started, with the question of what literature does. To Mr Alvarez the advance of Eliot–Pound was a technique for impersonality, an antidote to romanticism. He argues that in our time Robert Lowell and John Berryman have developed what is fresh in the technique while banishing the impersonality. Verse begins to approximate to the condition of breakdown. But these Americans are, I submit, only cousins of Eliot: they are a case of style as gesture not style as conviction.

The 'advance', moreover, was a bid to make spirit authoritative. The modern differs from the contemporary (to use Mr Spender's distinction) by receiving as rapture or terror, the modern experience, and projecting it upon the world; the image becomes prodigal. The real question is: will poets accept the status of second-class spiritual citizens, cogs in the machine, which the zeitgeist forces upon them, or will they envisage wholes from the vantage of their status? Failing that the little they do have may be taken away. The 30's did halt Eliot's innovations, to direct into modester forms the energy he liberated for a purpose his beliefs forbade: to heal the fragmentation of knowledge, to relate that to the world *as accessible to common sense*.* Yeats caused surprise by noticing their 'refusal to multiply personality . . . they combined the modern vocabulary, the record of the facts learned from Eliot, with the suffering of the war poets, no longer passive'. (The author of *Easter 1916* demanded colourful action; he failed to see how the war poets distil their heroism gradually into art, their discipline a patience felt at every inch of the way.) The sins of the fathers are chastised by the sons, but without the 30's, the return to good sense could never have built its flats on the ruin left when the Audenesque house-party broke up—in the words of Brian Higgins 'in the forties they burgeoned with innocent power' while squatters moved in until, with arcane wails, they were evicted. The subversive and ungainsayable whisper of poetry is manifold. It renders Mr Eliot's intense response, the duty of the individual to champion wholes, the *sturm und drang* of the war poets and the closeness to life since recovered.

The glass of the aesthete, Mr Charles Tomlinson, seems to obfuscate the vaunted medium. In spite of his advertised descent from Pound and Stevens, one suspects that the inheritance of French Symbolism counts more for Mr Tomlinson: essence outlaws existence, certain arrangements of feeling are more poetic than others. Colour formations, the suggestivity of volume and shape, transitions of light and shade, the permanence, composure, and wholeness of architecture, still landscapes which appease and do not vex the

---

* Louis MacNeice, the least political of his group, was best at the total evocation. *Autumn Journal* (1939) has more unity of mood than Auden's ambitious pieces. MacNeice receives the world as 'incorrigibly plural'; lacking Auden's nose for causality and interaction, he relaxes in the multiple, building it into wholes with a scaffolding of worthy (he is for gregariousness, reconstruction, individualism) if heretical (he is against suicide, Hellenism, pacifists) liberal attitudes. These spring from a sensualism which unifies and *limits* the poem.

The Kingdom recommends a view of life in terms of admired types, but remains 'private'; *The Casualty* sketches the same through a friend; *The Stygian Banks* shows what happens when this poet renounces sensual abundance. The poems lack the tension between inwardness and concern which makes *The Waste Land* imperative. Hence a certain tonal monotony, a certain facile humanism.

mind, the dumb, changeless life of paintings, are his constant pre-occupations. He aims to see everything for what it is, and not some other thing—to extricate things, in their singularity, from the fuss about politics, economics, psychology, religion, and all the rest of it. This is laudable. Too much bother about contingencies may pervert out of decent recognition, or liquidate, the cherished essences; there can be a spiritual Stalinism. Artefacts, natural phenomena, and ourselves can and should be appreciated apart from questions of ownership, the market, motivation. To adapt Dr Davie's image: facing a wall we should study it before trying to vault it, or we may break our necks—considering the 'neurotic stress' it would be tantamount to suicide; if there were complete social collapse objects of contemplation would remain to console us (on second thoughts I wonder); and in an age of strain the imperative is to 'keep the neurosis at bay'.

This staying of the mind on the object is done well in Tomlinson's best work. Matthew Arnold, suffering from lukewarm belief, made morality a substitute for faith. Tomlinson labours to make aestheticism a substitute for morality and thinks it will save us. *Icos, The Hawk, On a Landscape by Li-Cheng, Encounter, Aqueduct, Sconset* are excellent poems. The fluent, nervous plasticity, the clear contour, the dextrous movement, the sense of a circulated breeze—bodeful of the future—and the freshness, as of something renewed, combine to project an instant picture, a breathing pattern on the paper-space. The poet may have seen something old, established, irrefragable, but he has seen it clearly in the mould of its first youth. Speculation, if it exists at all, is uttered in terms of what *is*; the tone speaks in the accents of a surprise which is capable of precision:

> And the mountain: each day
> Immobile like fruit . . .
>   . . . it is not
> Posed. It is. Untaught
> Unalterable, a stone bridgehead
> To that which is tangible
> Because unfelt before. There
> In its weathered weight
> Its silence silences, a presence
> Which does not present itself.
>   (*Cézanne at Aix*)

Comment is superfluous—this resolves the tension we feel between the mountain's impassivity and our unrest. Tomlinson's power is lyrical: he excels at arabesques, alert, revelatory, and harmonious. He fumbles in discursive and meditative forms, for there he betrays his compulsion to broaden his insights into an interpretation of experience; it appears that sensibility is not enough. The poems are named after places, art-heroes, phenomena—*Fire in a Dark Landscape, On the Hall at Stowey, A Meditation on John Constable*. The titles are frames: the poems are abstracts, on whose clogged surface the poet scratches with an explanatory palette-knife. He preaches a sermon, sorrowfully correcting the sins of his material and the reader; or relaxes and gives us a fable, 'multiplying variety in a wilderness of mirrors', striving to reveal a universe of significance in a wine-stopper, a peeling apple, a jam-trap. He tells us what to think in the same flat tone as he describes what we are meant to think about. Aesthetic clichés, humourless and sophistical, abound: 'the sea laps by the railroad tracks / To have admitted this also defines the sea', 'You will concede that they have gained it whole', 'Distinctions? That, but not that in sum. Think of the fugue's theme', 'it is of moment', 'as many lost greens as one will give glances to recover', 'We do not / Doubt this veracity—we can only / Fear it', 'the effect is nature's / Who ignores it, and in whose impoverishment we domicile'. This gait is inexcusable:

> *A blurred shadow detaches itself hovering*
> *And cannot decide whether a green or blue*
> *Will the more grace its momentary existence*
> *Or whether a shot-red could invade*
> *Decorously so impoverished a kingdom.*

It is maddening to be informed that 'art exists at a remove', 'only we are inert', and that bridges do not exist for their own sake but 'command vacancy'. When he has to be concrete Mr Tomlinson writes a hypersensitive gloss on what Mr John Betjeman does better, *The Castle*, spoiled by its guardian who has 'risen by the scale of talent / Into the seat of blood'; *The Crane*, remarkable because it resembles a praying mantis; *Ploughing at Fiesole* (work is 'necessary', one must be 'content to remain content'); *Tramontana at Lerici*, where—wait for it—'Constitutions / Drafted under this fecund chill, would be annulled / For the strictness of their equity, the moderation of their piety'. Tomlinson excels at flashes of insight, feats of balance, the pace, weight, and mood of impressions, the attrition or purging of the mind as it waits, tense and observant, on external change. But all these transactions, so terribly important to Mr Tomlinson, are too tentative, rare, and inconsequential, to arrive with us. And his world, excluding man in the sense that his best contemporaries include man, is static: his themes are there for the asking. One looks for the humanizing of his gift, for there is integrity in his faith in the power of clear vision, the near-sightedness of his thought (his book is called *Seeing is Believing*).* His rationing of warmth, his lack of opinion is more candid than the filtering of matters through a stained-glass window of Miss Elizabeth Jennings, whose anecdotage—but this anaemia is common—shows the virtue of Tomlinson's effort to make it new.

An alternative is provided by men like Mr Alan Brownjohn.† At first he looks like a suburban Peter Porter: he owns the same Audenesque influence, plants the same decoys of complicity and subversion. Allotments, retirement, funerals, golf-clubs (not a member), and the local Tories are his beloved prey: a weekender refusing to believe that an earthquake is undermining his allotment is a symbol of the public in the nuclear age. When it comes to H Bomb verse, the astute veracity of Brownjohn's *William Empson at Aldermaston* deserves comparison with the forensic chuckle of Porter's *Conservation of Energy* and the rich virile sympathy of Hughes's *A Woman Unconscious*. Brownjohn is too busy grappling with effects to think up refinements about essences. In *A Teacher of the Deaf* he uses mountain symbolism better than Gunn in *From the Highest Camp*. Each stage in the ascent is an advance in the children's literacy; the summit is the comprehension of abstract words; the mountain is only dramatized to the extent that it reflects the teacher's skill. Brownjohn is occupied with the prolegomena to culture; he does not start from Gunn's cultured premisses; his poem is beneficent where Gunn's is pedantic. Brownjohn has an aesthete's eye. The difference is that he is powered (*Respects* is the test) by a subdued eloquence, a rhythmic wisdom—subtle not dithyrambic—which propels him towards the arena. Walking on cliffs, washing up, snowstorms, an untoward draught in his home summon Brownjohn into intriguing adventures.

> The people I admire most are those who are sensitive and want to create something or discover something, and do not see life in terms of power . . . They found religions . . . or they produce literature and art, or they do disinterested scientific research, or they may be what is called 'ordinary people' who . . . bring up their children decently, or help their neighbours . . .

* *A Peopled Landscape* followed in 1963. The reader should not be briefed by the title.

† Alan Brownjohn, *The Railings*, 1961. That the alternative need not be solely realist is proved by Taner Baybars (*To Catch a Falling Man*, 1963) being a poet of presences, of the unexpected; in his world where nothing happens—full of presage —or anything happens, it is not the fact of happening but *that* it happens that intrigues. Open forms, patterned by what he means, are as aware of what is left out as much as what is put in. See also Christopher Middleton, *Torse 3*, 1962.

NO ONE ACTUALLY STARVES

So Two Cheers for Democracy: one because it admits variety
and two because it permits criticism . . . there is no occasion to
give three. Only Love the Beloved Republic deserves that.*

Of that ideal E. M. Forster says elsewhere, 'in came the fat
dividends, up rose the lofty thoughts, and . . . all the time we were
exploiting the poor of our own country and the backward races
abroad'. When we enjoy the memoirs of the *douceur de vivre* before
1914 we are conscious that 'civilization' was the torch of a few
devotees. But we note with amazement the shock which greeted
the discovery of the irrational springs menacing progress. Between
the wars the liberal conscience tried to come to terms with those
springs; it muddled through in a creditable way or invented new
forms to vindicate its vision. Adrift in a tense calm, today we would
like to speak the language of E. M. Forster. If the fat dividends are
fatter, and there is a dearth of new lofty thoughts, at least the old
thoughts are available to more people. Yet our moment of truth is
hesitant, there is little singularity and outspoken conscience, in our
genial vulgarity and tolerant empiricism there is a shrill note and
a harsh selfishness. One advantage of progress is that 'concern' may
be turned, though not too much, upon the self.

A permissive society cannot be truly liberal, if it rejects the living
values of the past. It has been said that *Othello* may become lost on
audiences which do not know the meaning of the plot; it will, surely,
live as drama in the care of good actors. The attitudes of the artists
in this book may become lost on otherwise public-spirited folk.
These attitudes—the fighting gaiety of Yeats, the high and low
vision from which Eliot derives an ethic, Muir's civilized, rooted
naturalism, Porter's disgust at the power of money, the social acumen
of Empson, are the ones which need help most—will live as objects
of research; there will be well-paid archaeologists, but few good
actors. Luckily, for the most interesting poets today the tension and
the demands are great. Aware of the method of modernism, designed
to justify an individual value, they have learned from the intelligence of the best poets since and avoid an obscurantism designed for
ostriches. They explore a purpose for action or that emotional
integrity which makes action worth while, give to verse moral direction and physical basis. The violent, the primitive, and the unusual
are regulated by provinciality and ungullible rootedness. When
Peter Porter describes thinking people as 'secular saints who do
without power' he speaks for them and us and helps on the idea
of the poet as humanist and hero.

* E. M. Forster, *Two Cheers for Democracy*, 1951, p. 79.

INDEX

'Brilliant – a passionate and poignant story of a glittering family on the precipice of a vanished world. Spellbinding, gripping and beautiful – a must-read'
Lisa Hilton

'An all-encompassing, sweeping epic. It's a book to get immersed in for hours at a time ... a wonderful achievement'
Katherine Webb

'A wonderful evocation of a family torn apart by war, packed with drama and written with a sensitive warmth and fantastic historical insight'
Imogen Robertson

'Kate Williams paints a spellbinding portrait of a family clinging on desperately to their privileged way of life'
Good Housekeeping

'A beautifully conjured family saga. Fans of *Downton Abbey* will love it'
Alison Weir

'Richly detailed, light of foot, Williams tantalises with loose ends and disturbs with shocking shadows'
Independent

'This terrific saga comes with a fascinating twist ... Williams has a gift for showing how great movements in history affect the lives of people caught up in them'
Kate Saunders, *The Times*

'Williams has a sharp eye for the contradictions and mysteries of human nature and a vivid turn of phrase ... she uses her historian's knowledge to brilliant effect'
Daily Mail

'Shades of *Downton*, with a dash of *Atonement*'
Tatler

'Williams draws expertly on mysterious, flawed characters coming of age in a displaced world in this gripping period novel ... A haunting piece of historical fiction'
The Lady

'Her insight into the aftermath of the First World War and shattered society shines out of every page, enriching a powerful family saga'
Sunday Mirror

'Gripping from the first page, I absolutely loved this novel. Following the journey of Celia, whose life is shattered by the First World War, it combines suspense with history and fascinating characters ... It's a must-read'
Grazia

'An epic, romantic read set in the roaring '20s'   *Fabulous*

'Rich in sumptuous detail and full of twists and turns'
                                            Isabelle Broom, *Heat*

'A vivid portrait of a perennially fascinating period of history'
                                                    The Observer

'An epic story about a young woman whose idyllic world is shattered by
the First World War'   *Sunday Telegraph, Stella magazine*

'The de Witt family's struggles are a compelling, vibrant and poignant
fictional reflection of living history and if the next chapter of their story
unfolds with the same emotional power and extraordinary resonance, then
we are in for another treat'   *Lancashire Evening Post*

'Williams has created a resonant and nuanced evocation of life in the
aftermath of the First World War in which the shadows of the conflict
loom large ... But her novel also explores the deep psychological and
emotional worlds of the individual'   *The Press and Journal*

'Historian Kate William's epic about the First World War starts in the
idyllic country mansion of the wealthy de Witt family ... [She] outlines the
tragedy of war but also reveals ... how this first modern conflict changed
British society beyond recognition'   *Sunday Express*

'Kate Williams is a vivid writer, conjuring atmosphere through scents and
tastes as well as period props'   *The Times Literary Supplement*

'This book has more firepower than *Downton* ... Powerful storytelling'
                                        Peterborough Evening Telegraph

'One of the queens of historical fiction'   *The Guardian*

The
HOUSE
of
SHADOWS

KATE WILLIAMS

ORION

First published in Great Britain in 2018 by Orion Books,
an imprint of The Orion Publishing Group Ltd
Carmelite House, 50 Victoria Embankment
London EC4Y 0DZ

An Hachette UK Company

1 3 5 7 9 10 8 6 4 2

A CIP catalogue record for this book is
available from the British Library.

ISBN (Hardback) 978 1 4091 3995 9
ISBN (Export Trade Paperback) 978 1 4091 3994 2

Typeset at The Spartan Press Ltd
Lymington, Hants

Printed and bound in Great Britain by Clays Ltd,
Elcograf S.p.A.

MIX
Paper from
responsible sources
FSC® C104740

www.orionbooks.co.uk

Also by Kate Williams

FICTION:

The Pleasures of Men
The Storms of War
The Edge of the Fall

NON-FICTION:

England's Mistress: The Infamous Life of Emma Hamilton
Becoming Queen
Josephine: Desire, Ambition, Napoleon
Young Elizabeth: The Making of Our Queen
Rival Queens: Elizabeth I and Mary

'We're explorers,' he whispered, reaching for Lily's thin hand. And so they were, passing deep into unfamiliar land, looking for dragons, treasure, except they weren't looking for things but freedom. Pulling the branches aside and entering the forest they had been so consistently forbidden. *Don't go there. Promise me.* He could almost feel the blueish light burn his cheeks, fluttering like flame on a stove.

He'd thought she would be afraid. As they passed over a branch, she let go of his hand and then she was moving forward, her dark hair swinging down her back.

'Come on,' she said. He followed her, even though inside he was crying out. *Let me go first.* She was going on, jumping over the knotty branches on the floor, as if it was a game. *It's not a game!* The whole wood was silent now. You couldn't hear the noises they'd left behind, the adults, drinking and talking and laughing in the warm late summer air even though it wasn't funny, none of it was ever funny. They lied, pretended, didn't live for the truth. He and Lily would never be like them, not ever.

He caught his ankle on a branch, almost fell. The damp ground dipped towards a stream, fast running, faster than it should be for September. The dashing water filled his head. He'd drawn a map but he hadn't put in a stream. He couldn't think where it had begun, it would have to start in the Stoneythorpe garden, but there was only that stagnant pond in the place where he and Lily had sat and made their dreams – until the adults had come in and everything had been spoiled. He thought of his mother, holding tight to him in those early days, telling him she'd never leave him.

His heart lurched and he threw his mind into the rushing dark water, staring at it until the thought of his mother went away.

'We have to jump,' said Lily. 'Come on.'

A few years ago, they'd played explorer games. Arctic, Africa, India. It had to be the Arctic first, he said. Start at the top. They fought polar bears, skipped over icebergs, chased the woolly mammoths. The worlds had been divided by the stream and when they grew weary of one, they were supposed to leap to another. Lily would always mark out the stream in the garden. 'Jump,' she said, already weary of polar bears, keen for new beasts, capturing lions in Africa or wrestling snakes. He didn't want to, he wanted to stay where they were. 'We haven't finished!'

'Yes, we have. Come on.'

And so he did, leaving the world unfinished behind him, waiting for them to return.

Lily leapt over the stream. She waited on the other side, hands on hips. 'Why are you so *slow?*'

That pierced his soul. He stared at her, dark figure against the tangled branches on the other side. The trees were like strands of a woman's hair. Lily had pulled her hair down as they had run together and now he wanted to beg her: Put it back! Tie it up before it gets tangled in the hair of the tree and girl and tree become one.

He took a step, felt his foot slide in the mud. He grasped at a branch. I don't want to fall, he wanted to say. Lily was already turning away.

He'd jumped over a million streams, surely. He'd jumped into the sea, swimming ponds, a river or two. His mind filled with his aunt, who'd fallen from the cliff and died on the rocks. But why did his mind do that? If he fell in, he'd only get wet. Aunt Louisa had died, looking at the sea. Uncle Arthur had held out his hands to catch her but he couldn't stop her fall.

He shook the thought away. They were leaving all that behind, all the secrets and boxes full of letters and all that talking but no one ever telling the truth.

He landed in the mud on the other side, reached out and held tight to Lily.

'Finally!' she said, shaking off his hand. 'Let's go.'

Now they were together. They could never be parted. He moved forward and his foot caught. He looked down at the spiral of small vines and pulled it free.

He had been in charge of the planning. Weeks of hiding from the adults, writing lists in his room. He drew a map and hid it under her bookshelf. Every day, one of them would steal some type of foodstuff from the pantry, a box of something, a packet of sugar, a tin of meat, food that wouldn't spoil. They took sheets and blankets from the cupboard, packed them up into his bag, along with other things they really needed, like toothpaste and soap, their notebooks.

They'd spend the first night in the woods, so that no one would find them, and then head towards the road, where they'd find someone to take them in a car along the way. No one would guess his real age, they'd think he was quite grown, not eleven at all. He would draw and she'd write stories for money – and then they could travel, live in France, Italy, places by the sea. They wouldn't be like the others, bowed down by work and home and money, never seeing what really mattered.

They'd stolen from their grandmother. One day, she'd beckoned him into the room where she lay on the pile of pillows. He didn't much like her room, the air hung heavy, full of scent that smelt of forced flowers. On all the sides of the room were vases, of wobbly, wavy, marbled glass, pale colours, pink, mauve, turquoise, green, with cut lips like fancy tulips.

'No one likes my vases,' she said to him. 'They say they're ugly. My mother said they were ugly, even then. Do you think so?'

'I think they are nice,' he said. 'And you like them, that's all that matters.'

Verena lay back, smiled. 'I knew you'd understand.' She held out a finger, heavy with its gold ring and sharp-shaved jewel. 'Come here.'

He went closer, into the jungle leaves of scent, the pink silk cushions.

'Closer.' She pointed at the floor and he knelt.

He was by her bed now. The scent was cloying, like cotton wool in his nose. He held his breath.

'It's all money,' hissed Verena. The sound rushed around his ear like when you hold a seashell to it. 'Money! They all laugh at those vases but they're full of money. All my money. That's where it is.'

She fell back against the pillows, as if exhausted by the effort. 'And when I die you shall have all of it. Don't forget. Come here and take it.'

'Thank you.'

'You deserve it. You deserve everything.'

He'd stayed kneeling, not sure what to do. And then he looked up and her eyes were closed. He'd crept backwards then, so she didn't notice, out, the scent clinging to his hair and eyes.

And then he'd gone in and taken it. All of it. When she was asleep, he'd swept it into his hands and however wrong he'd felt, it hadn't stopped him.

Lily too had stolen. She'd taken all the money from the box that her mother kept under the bed – a whole twenty pounds.

'I'll go back,' Lily said. 'One day. Explain she didn't really need the money like we do. She won't mind.'

Would Verena feel the same? He didn't know.

'Come closer,' she said. 'We need to go deeper!' The thicket was dense around them, close on their shoulders.

'I wrote on the map we should go around. Not through.'

She shook her head. Her black eyes glittered against her bright cheeks and he wanted to touch her hand, the two of them against the world. Even though he was plain and childish next to her. He felt he could never reach her.

'You never know what we might find.'

'Aren't you afraid?'

'I have you! Why would I be afraid? I'll go first.' She ducked her head, moved forwards. He watched her.

And then there was a sound. A branch cracked. A bird fluttered, flew to the sky. There was someone there. Someone behind them. Michael swung around. The shadows skittered away. Mice, voles maybe.

He turned back for Lily.

He cried out, reached forward, looked frantically. Nothing.

The air was closing around where her shape had been. He reached out to stop it but it was no good. Too late.

Lily had gone.

PART ONE

ONE

Manhattan, January 1929

New York shone. The sharp brightness of it gleamed on your face, behind you when you weren't looking, loomed high over you and glittered down at your head. Even in wintry January, it was alive. Celia had never seen anything like it. London felt low and scrubby in comparison. She could hardly believe she was actually there. It didn't look real, false high buildings, shimmering windows and people rushing along the sidewalk, the roads full of cars. The whole place was always being rebuilt, she thought. She sometimes went out in the street and did nothing but stare above her head at the buildings, new great masses of apartments and offices and hotels being constructed. The city was all energy, building, talking, hurrying, making anew. The whole of America full of things bright and improved, not like the old world. And underneath all the new buildings, the glass and stone, was a different world, where you could buy the alcohol that was banned, dance hard and fast to music that beat in your mind.

They'd stepped off the chill boat into the freezing port to make their fortune ten days before, taken eye-wateringly expensive rooms in the Plaza on Central Park, they'd had appointments – three, four, five a day, hour-long meetings in large, dark-panelled, overheated rooms, with men, dozens of them, tall, dark, pale, thin, fat, all of them in grey suits, expensive shoes, their faces and bodies saying 'money', even if their mouths never did. Celia stared at them as Arthur talked – for no one expected her to speak – not a woman. But she was there to help him – for getting the Americans to invest in Winter Meats was their last chance. And Arthur said she looked the part. 'We're selling the family,'

9

he said. 'Stoneythorpe and the English country home. And you look exactly it, nice family girl, English rose.'

Not true, of course. She was half-German, full of dark secrets she could never tell. And Stoneythorpe was falling down, the great Jacobean house Rudolf had bought them when they were rich, before the war. He'd dreamt of being lord of the manor – and now they were desperate, dependent on Americans to give them money. Their time in America had to succeed.

Looking at Arthur, it made you think he'd be kind: handsome, a chiselled face, tall and broad in his suit, moving with that easy grace that made people want to look at him, men and women. Arthur and Emmeline had got all the looks. Celia had the fair hair and large eyes, like them, but she didn't have their smooth shell. Her skin seemed to have been designed to hide nothing, flaming with cold, heat, embarrassment, love. Her hair was fine and she didn't have Arthur's clean movement, but legs and arms too long, like a bird, and often when she looked in the mirror, she had a startled look in her eyes. At what, she didn't know. But she doubted that it charmed the bankers in the same way as Arthur's face did. He looked like he was always about to host a party.

'My sister,' he said, introducing her, and they all shook her hand politely, offered her a drink, sometimes told her their names. Otherwise, she sat there, tried to listen to what they said. She tried – but, really, as it was today, at Messrs Morgan and Co. on Fifty-Second Street, her mind was elsewhere. It grew and flew, high up out of the room, up past the windows into the cloudy sky – so high that it hovered above America, and there, looking down, it saw Michael, spotted her son's little, seven-year-old face, outside a house somewhere, captured him and flew him up, back to New York and the dark panelled room, where Celia was waiting for him. She took him in her arms and held him for ever. She filled his room with toys and they built a life together.

When he said, 'Why did you give me away?', she told the truth, said she'd been put to sleep and he'd been taken from her, spirited away because her mother, Verena, didn't want the blot of an illegitimate child. She'd sent him to America, believed all the advertising that life was better there – and Celia had never known where he was, didn't even know he was alive – until her father, Rudolf, started talking after Arthur's trial. 'I'll keep you forever.'

But she didn't promise to tell him the whole truth. When he asked, 'Who was my father?', she'd tell him he was a soldier. *Father unknown.* 'You don't need a father,' she'd say to him. 'We have each other.'

But, instead, she sat there, her body present, mind far away, until the meeting ended and the younger men came to show them to the stairs and the way out into the street. 'That went well,' Arthur said. 'Didn't you think?'

She nodded, but he barely needed a response, went leaping off into his own ideas, talked of how well they'd do, how Winter Meats would take over America, what it would be like to watch investors falling like ninepins, if they could just get one bank to start things off.

Everyone was busy. Shiny, icy cars – so many shiny cars queued in the roads, their bright fenders pushing into each other like a line of impatient school children. Carriages waited on the streets near Central Park, the Upper East Side, but by the shops and the theatres and town, it was all cars. Business, business! And money. So much money – women flashed by in furs, men in the new suits, double-breasted, pinstriped, loose around the waist, their shoes sharper on your eyes than the sun.

When they'd arrived, Celia had realised that she and Arthur weren't dressed correctly, that their English clothes were outdated, but she'd had no chance to visit a shop, only to stare in windows that were sometimes so highly glazed that they reflected nothing back at you but light. Their days had been all meetings, cool men with piles of papers in dark panelled rooms, talking numbers, zeros, tens, thousands, customers, products, sales.

She could see the truth. The men in the banks were polite – but they would give them nothing. How naive they had been! They had come over thinking that Winter Meats would be wildly successful, seized upon by America, factories bursting to make their pies. Coming to America was their last chance to save the family, for if they failed, then the business would crash, they'd have to sell the house and they would have nothing. Their parents near destitute, nothing for her sister, Emmeline, and her children, Lily and Albert, still so young. And their brother Michael, dead in the war, and Louisa, who fell from a cliff when she was happy – they would be left alone in the churchyard and all of their history would be forgotten.

Celia knew she had to do it. Arthur was growing angry, blaming the new fad – lady vegetarians and their fretting over baby lambs. He was impatient with the men in the banks, and that wouldn't get them anywhere. And she had a plan. She would go to one of the grand new stores, find the floor where they sold the food. She imagined it not looking like a shop back home, but a wondrous museum of things – with space, surely, for Winter Meats. She'd work out exactly how their pies and meats would fit in and then the men would listen.

She crossed over the road and fell in behind two small boys walking together. They were shabbily dressed, without an adult. Some of those they passed swerved to avoid them, thinking they were pickpockets, she supposed. She moved closer. They must be so cold without coats. The larger would be about the same age as Michael now, maybe a little older. He was talking animatedly to the other one, a thin child with gingerish hair. She longed to step nearer still, hear what he was saying. She always wondered what children talked about, especially those around Michael's age. She found herself following children, searching for him in their faces, staring until their mothers hurried them away, casting suspicious glances at her over their shoulders.

The two boys drew ahead and she hurried to catch up with them. She wanted to reach out her hand for them. She grew closer, forgetting the department store now.

The boys paused at the edge of the road. The older one put his arm round the younger. He must be afraid of the road, great roaring cars hurtling past them, buses, men dodging in between, carrying crates of bricks, parcels, deliveries. She wanted to hold their hands, help them over. She was just about to touch the elder's shoulder, tell him there was a better place to cross further down, ask them if they didn't have scarves when they pitched off into the road. Two cars flew past before she could move out – and then she saw them.

They were still walking forward, holding hands.

A black car was coming towards them. The driver couldn't see them. Things were winding around her, the cars, the people. Someone behind her was talking. Celia's eyes blurred. She couldn't see. Only the two of them holding hands. People were still passing, not understanding.

What if he were Michael? He could be.

She had to save them.

Celia threw herself forward and it felt to her as if she were jumping further than she ever could, halfway across the road, as if a car had thrown her forward. She grasped the children with a strength that felt like it was someone else's and pulled all three of them back. Then they were lying there in the freezing road, in front of the car, and the cold sun was burning her eyes. People were crowding around her, so many that she could see nothing but clothes. All the cars had stopped and she could hear horns beeping behind. 'Move on!'

'There's been an accident!' a man shouted.

'Are you all right, Miss?' One was trying to help her up.

'Don't move her! She might be injured!'

She gazed up into a woman's face, matronly, dark hair. Her head hurt so much. 'The children.' The driver she had jumped in front of was out of his car, head between his legs. The front of his car shone bright silver.

A man who looked like a fireman leant over her. 'All right, Miss. We'll take over from here.'

'Well, they can't be hers,' said a voice. 'Look like pickpockets to me.'

Celia tried to speak the word, 'No,' but her voice wouldn't move.

'We need a doctor. Is anyone a doctor?' The word rippled around the crowd. Doctor. Doctor. She heard it in the back of her lost mind. A man was leaning over her, feeling her forehead and her wrist. His hands were on her sides. 'Where does it hurt, Miss?'

'My head,' she managed. He touched it. She lifted her eyes, tried to see the children. The elder boy was sitting up, drinking from a tin cup. A woman had her arm around him. The other one was still lying on the floor.

The doctor looked again. 'I think she is fine. No broken bones.' He gestured to the woman and they both helped her up. She leant against him, wanting to fall again, feeling as if she was made from a ball of wool. 'They're not yours? That was a brave thing you did. Foolish, some might say.'

The words were lost. Her face hurt. She nodded.

'You could have died, don't you see that? You should go to the hospital.'

She felt a strength rise in her, pulled it up to speak. 'They would have died. That car would have killed them.'

She leant against him. 'Don't fall,' he said.

She looked at the children, tried to reach out her hand to the eldest. The youngest was sitting up now, looking around. Of course, neither of them was Michael. One was too old, the other too young.

'They're fine,' the doctor said. 'You took the weight of the landing. They'll be running around in a minute.'

'Oh of course they will,' said a woman behind him. 'Off robbing more like. Turn out their pockets and they'll likely have stolen something.'

She heard people nodding, agreeing. She looked around. The crowd was changing. Nobody was dead and their emotions had been wound up for nothing – they had to put them somewhere. The accents, thick and unfamiliar, wrapped around her.

'Turn out their pockets!'

'Easy enough to see why they were running.'

One of the men had hold of the older boy. Another one was seizing the younger.

'Stop it!' She pulled loose of the doctor holding her arm. 'Leave them alone. Why don't you search my bag!' She looked down and saw it on the floor. 'There! Search that bag! Maybe I was a pickpocket. Just because they're poor doesn't mean they did wrong.'

'What is she saying?' said a man. 'Is she some sort of tourist?'

'If you want to search anyone, you search me!' Her head didn't hurt any more. She was so determined on shouting that it took up her whole body. 'You check *my* bag!' She stamped her foot. And then she looked over to the boys and nodded. The elder one seized the younger and they began to edge away.

'You look at my bag!' she cried. 'You search me!'

The man who had been complaining reluctantly picked up her bag. A woman pushed through and said, 'A lady should do this!' and started pulling out the things with enthusiasm, purse, mirror, throwing them into the hands of the man next to her. Celia's pencil clattered to the floor. Celia stared hard at them, resisting her desire to look away.

And then she glanced to the side – and the boys had gone.

The doctor followed her line of vision. 'Look!'

A man shouted, a woman screamed. 'Find a policeman!'

And then they were all flustering about the boys, saying they were criminals. She picked up her bag and limped across the road, leaving them behind. She walked past a shoe shop, dragged herself around the next corner and then leant against the wall. The boys weren't there. Of course they weren't. They'd run far away. She'd lost them.

She felt a tear slip down her cheek. She'd never see them again, not in this great city of thousands.

Probably, on these roads, it happened every day, children fell and were injured in front of cars. Those great, terrifying cars. 'It's wrong,' she said. A man walking past raised his eyebrow and she looked away.

She breathed deeply. Her hands were bloodied, her face was probably scratched, her dress was torn. She wasn't in a fit state to go to the department store. They might not even let her in.

But she had no choice. This was her only spare time. They had meetings with men in banks all day tomorrow. She reached up, straightened her hat, scrubbed her hands on her dress, walked forwards. She made a bargain with God. *Because I saved those boys, please let somebody save Michael. Make them keep him safe.* Someone, somewhere, must leap out for him, just as she had for them.

She passed Lord and Taylor and Bloomingdale's, then to Bergdorf-Goodman's, through the great gold-tipped doors as the doorman held them open for her and the heat blazed on her face. The perfume hall opened out to her, giant bottles that looked like they could barely be real, beautiful women with bright lipstick holding out presents. There was so much gold. And probably frankincense and myrrh as well, the whole lot.

She smiled politely at the women wielding glass bottles – who were themselves so polite, they didn't flinch at her, when she was dirty and probably even had blood on her face. She asked for directions to the powder room and saw that her face was even worse than she'd thought, sooty smears around her eyes, grazes on her chin and her forehead. She dabbed at her face and hands. The dirt on her gown would have to be left as it was. She sailed out, holding herself high, pretending to be her mother in the old days, before her world got old and sad.

'Food Hall, please.'

She walked down the stairs, holding the golden bannister, passing women who looked like housekeepers and office girls looking for lunch. She stepped into the hall and the place dazzled her eyes, bright piles of boxes, a great mountain of perfect red apples, glowing like a leftover Christmas tree, towers of fruit cakes arranged on tables, glistening dried fruit, dates and figs in tree-like stacks, a beautiful array of chocolates that you couldn't dare to touch. She walked in further, as if into a forest of beautiful arrangements – and saw heaps of vegetables, the meat counter, a whole cabinet full of cream puddings, chocolate eclairs and little sponges topped with strawberries, horns made of pastry, tiny chocolate cakes. She trailed a finger across the glass front. The food in New York was more brilliant than that in London. Most of the cakes she'd never even seen before, large glistening chocolate-covered things, round doughnuts glossy with pink and red icing. Meringues were stacked so high in windows that she wondered if anyone ever got to the bottom of the pile.

So much food. So many people wanting it. An office girl pushed in front of her and bought a chocolate eclair, packed up by the man behind the counter into a pristine white box.

The girl smiled, briefly, a flash of lipstick, bobbed hair under the smart hat.

'Excuse me,' she said in a thick Brooklyn accent. 'In a rush.'

Celia nodded. Her mind turned and then flew back to the boat over, a fleeting memory she had all but forgotten. She had been sitting on the deck when a group of girls had sat down nearby, not one over twenty-five. They were giggling and talking at the same time. Something about the face of one, the curve of the mouth, the cheekbone, was like the office girl with the eclair.

The boat had been full of girls. 'What are they all here for?' she'd asked one of the officers who had got talking to Arthur at dinner. He and Arthur had been laughing, calling them the ship of girls. 'They're like the ones going out to India last century, would-be wives,' he'd said.

'They're all going over to work. The shopgirls of New York are coming from England. Hundreds of them. Wouldn't you?' he shrugged. 'You're young, no men at home?'

'We're all going over to make our fortune.' Arthur grinned. 'Them and us.' He wrinkled his mouth. 'Not everyone can succeed.'

Celia had stared at the group of girls. *The shopgirls of New York.* They were talking non-stop, smiling, met on the boat, but now they'd maybe even take rooms together, always remember each other. The one who made them all laugh, they'd exchange Christmas cards with her and her husband and children, a memory of the old days.

'In New York, we'll have a restaurant under our flat so we never have to cook,' one was saying.

'We won't even need a kitchen. We'll never stay in.' The taller blonde was laughing. 'My ma spends her life in the kitchen. No fear I will be like that.'

The smaller blonde tossed her hair. 'And how will you eat? You can't afford restaurants every day on a shopgirl's salary.'

'My Prince will come. Or I will invent a way to replace meals with some sort of pill. Buy a pill, then you've had a meal.'

'No! I like eating!'

'But not *cooking*.'

'What if your Prince is hungry?'

'Then he can cook for me!'

Celia looked around the Food Hall. There was something in it. All these girls, shopgirls, office girls, waitresses, clerks. *Not wanting to cook.*

She had briefly been one of those office girls, living in a flat after she'd had Michael, when she thought he was dead, worked as a secretary, handed all her money to spiritualists and fortune tellers to contact him. What had they eaten? She tried to remember. She had shared rooms near Baker Street that had a tiny kitchen, but they'd never turned the oven on for fear of how much it would have smoked the flat. Not that Celia really knew how to cook. Tom had mocked her when they'd been children, saying she'd never made a cup of tea.

The girls she had lived with ate at Lyons' tea houses and picked at cake, a full meal only rarely, if they'd been paid. There must be thousands of girls like them, in London and New York, not cooking, not dining out, living off scraps of cake and strong tea.

And then she thought: it wasn't about serving up great stacks of meat to cooks in large houses like Stoneythorpe, it was about the modern girl in a flat and what she might buy for herself.

Living alone. That's the future. She thought back to herself: what would she like to have eaten? She imagined vegetable pies, other foods in jars, soup, a lot of soup. And puddings, so many puddings, chocolate cakes, jam sponge, jam tarts, biscuits of chocolate and jam, delicate ones. Could you put a mousse in a jar? Meringues? Her father had served canned meat – but it was mere fuel, nothing attractive and New York didn't want it. Her jars would be beautiful, things that women would buy because they had to have them.

She stood there and her mind flashed with new ideas, food for flappers, lovingly cooked by her in a kitchen in New York. Or overseen by her, since she couldn't cook. She'd have cooks to help her, other women chopping and making sauces, creaming butter, kneading shortbread. Her heart soared, her mind flew across the shop, creating displays, imagining satisfied girls leaving with baskets of food in jars, the excellence of the future cancelling out the misery of the past.

She cast her mind back to the time that she thought they had Stoneythorpe forever, in those last days before the war. She'd been fifteen, Emmeline had been about to marry Sir Hugh, Michael was back from Cambridge with his friend, Jonathan. In the days, she'd been riding with Tom and thought they'd stay friends forever. Instead, everything around her changed – Michael ran off to war with Tom, Emmeline eloped with her tutor, Mr Samuel Janus, Rudolf was taken away and interned, Verena let the house crumble around her. Celia couldn't bear it, so had lied about her age and drove ambulances in France, cradled her friend Shep when she died in the bombing, kept going until the news came to her about Michael's death. And then Tom – whom she loved, had thought she would always be with, because they'd loved each other as children – told her that wasn't how he saw it at all, that he would never love her and so she had to find a life without him.

Now she imagined great stacks of glass jars, luminous, boxes filled with rustling silver paper. She put the memories that made her cry out at night into the glass pile, the towers of fruits and jams and chocolates. Wrapped up in the beautiful glass, they would be safe, unable to hurt. She'd find Michael and create a business her family could be proud of – and then they could all live together in Stoneythorpe, mended, back to its own glory, and there would be money for Emmeline, Lily and Albert, so they could have a proper home of their own, and even though Michael and Louisa were dead, the rest of them would live and little Michael would carry their dreams forward.

Celia walked back towards Central Park, the wind slewing grey across the streets, her mind whirling with ideas. They'd start with a small kitchen, just a few women in Brooklyn busy weighing and stirring and baking. Then they would expand out, build factories, take the jars to shops all over the country. They'd go to California in the sun, then the prairie land of the Midwest, Kansas, Ohio, all the way right to the very edge, Michigan, Montana. Boxes and boxes of jars on the trains, criss-crossing America, taking the food to the modern girls so they could keep working, dancing, do what they liked.

In the boardroom, Arthur was standing at the front, talking to a table of men in suits. He went through the list of facts and figures, talked about the company's heritage, the excellent taste. He came to the end and stood expectantly. Celia hurt for him.

'We've heard all this kind of thing before,' drawled one. 'Nothing new.'

The man sitting at the head of the table nodded. 'Mr Witt, you seem like a good guy. So let me be honest with you. We don't need the British coming here telling us how to make meat. We have plenty of meat in America. We're looking to invest in something new. American customers are searching for novelty. We're straight talkers at Broad and Brothers. The truth is that there's no market for this.'

Celia looked from the man to Arthur. Her brother was almost falling against the wall.

Celia leapt up. 'I have something.'

The man – Mr Broad, she supposed – raised an eyebrow. Then he moved to stand. The others followed him.

'Wait!' Celia hurried to the front. 'Just listen. Please! I have something. I know.'

And so she started talking and conjured for them the piles of glowing jars, the modern girl dancing at cafés with no time to cook, bread and pies in jars and cans, cakes they could take away. She didn't stop. She didn't look in their eyes to see if they were bored, she just kept going. Something in her said, *This is your last chance*. It was different this time. She had the girl in her mind, going into the store. She talked and talked, about the girls in their flats who were never going to be like their mothers, the trains crossing America full of jars and tins, the girls buying dozens of them at a time.

'It's the flapper girls,' she said. 'So far, everybody has been trying to sell them make-up and films and clothes. But what about *food*? The modern girl has to eat!'

She stopped, breathless, excited as if she'd been running. The dark clock in the corner ticked.

The man at the head of the table nodded.

'Miss – Witt, is it, too? Well, Miss Witt...' He paused. He looked at her. The time in the room stood still. The air fell around her, tiny pieces of dust. Then he raised an eyebrow. 'I think there just might be something in this.' He smiled. 'I do believe you have struck on something here.'

And so the others broke in, began nodding and agreeing.

She looked over their heads and smiled at Arthur. He gave a smile back, just about.

TWO

———

Manhattan, January 1929

'*Psst.*'

Celia looked up but couldn't see anything, drew her coat closer around her. She lit the match by the moon and tried to light the cigarette. The thing smoked. She breathed in, started coughing. The smoke was up her nose, at the back of her throat, her eyes were watering. She wished she'd brought water with her, coughed violently again. She was sitting at the back of the hotel, on the dustbins. It was the only place she could think. She looked around for the source of the noise, but it was all bricks and darkness. She must have been imagining things.

'You need to breathe it in,' said a voice.

She looked up, both sides, could see nothing.

'I'm up here,' said a small voice. Brooklyn accent. Probably a boy.

'Who are you?'

'You know!'

'Where are you?'

'I said, up here!' There was a shuffle and a boy jumped down from the dustbins. His clothes were ragged, the ginger curls around his face needed cutting. He tugged back his hair, and grinned.

'It's you!' The smaller child she had rescued from the car. 'Is it really you?'

'Of course it's me!' He grinned. 'Why are you trying to smoke that thing?'

Close up, she saw the freckles dotted over his tanned nose and cheeks. His brown eyes were bright under tiny eyebrows. He almost crackled with energy in the cold.

She looked at it ruefully. 'I thought I might enjoy it. I can't understand why anyone would. It's horrible.'

'You just have to get used to it, I reckon. Practice!'

She raised her eyebrows. 'You shouldn't know. You're a child. Anyway, what are you doing here? It's too cold for you to be out. Where's your brother?'

'Oh, he wasn't my brother. Just a friend. Well, sort of a friend. Anyway, he's gone. I think he went off North.' He scraped his hand through his red hair.

'He's gone? You don't know where. And what about you?' Her head was spinning. 'How old are you?'

'I'm not sure. People have tried to guess. Maybe eleven? Twelve? Can I have one of those?' He pointed at the cigarette.

'I think you're a bit young.'

'Oh, come on, miss. Anyway, I can show you how to do it.'

He probably smoked to forget he was hungry. She couldn't not give him one. 'Here you are,' she said, passing it over. 'I have a match as well. But you know you shouldn't. Aren't you worried about fire? It's not safe.'

He lit it, experienced, and breathed in. 'See this is how you do it, miss. Breathe it right down then blow it out.'

He looked even younger than twelve to her, but that was maybe because he was so small and thin. 'How long have you been smoking?'

'Oh, for years!'

'And you live on the streets?'

He shrugged airily. 'All kinds of places. Now, miss, to business. Lots of people wouldn't try to help children like us. So I'm grateful. I came to see what I could do for you.'

'What's your name?'

'Red,' he said. 'The hair, you see. And you?'

'Celia.' She held out her hand to him and he shook it solemnly. 'But how did you know where to find me? Do you live around here?'

He shook his head. 'Oh no. I live all over. At the top, these days. I followed you, of course!'

'You followed me?'

'You bet! After you saved us from the car, I wanted to know where you were, in case I could ever help you.'

'I looked for you after the accident,' she said. 'You know you should have a coat.'

'Oh, yes, we saw you looking. But you didn't do it well. You fine people. You wouldn't see what was going on, right under your nose.'

'Well, that's probably true enough.'

'We hid behind the wall and then we followed you. You do a lot of wandering round shops, miss, don't you? Looking at all that food and not buying. John said you were maybe mad in the head but I said maybe that's what they do in wherever it is you come from. You lost ladies,' he said, shaking his head affectionately.

She had to smile. 'Listen, have you eaten tonight? Today even?'

'I had a spot of bread. I don't need much, you know, miss.'

'We need to get you more than that.' Perhaps she could get some food from the hotel kitchens. 'What about I bring you a coat?'

'No thanks, miss. They slow you down. I don't get cold. But I wouldn't say no to food. I can't now. I've got business. Tomorrow, though?'

'I'm supposed to be working tomorrow.'

'Oh, work. You don't need to do that. You're rich, if you live in a hotel. Actually, I might have things to do. I'll come back when I can.'

'I don't have my purse with me. But if you wait here, I can go and get it and give you some money.'

He waved his hand. 'I don't need money, miss. We live our own way.'

'I might as well give you these then. Perhaps you can trade them.' She passed over the cigarettes and the matches.

He stowed them in his pocket. 'Not your thing anyway, are they, miss?'

'Probably not.'

'I'd better go. Things to do.'

'See you – when?'

'Maybe tomorrow. Or maybe next week!' He hopped back onto the dustbin. 'If I'm not too busy.'

'If you're not too busy. Do you want to walk out with me?'

'I don't walk, Miss! Not on the pavements. Well, not often, anyway. I was when you saw me but usually I'm not down there. That's for you ground people. You never see us.'

'Where are you, then?'

He waved up at the roof. 'I'm there. I go along there!'

'Over the roofs?'

'You should look up there, sometime, Miss. You'd be surprised.'

She grinned at him. 'I think I would. Listen, are you sure you don't need any money?'

He shook his head, patted his pocket. 'These are better. See you, Miss!' He turned on his heel and jumped off the bin onto the wall, climbed the pipe swiftly and was on the roof. She gazed up to see his shadow but there were only blurred shapes lit by the moon. She stared up again, tried to see. Maybe there was a whole tribe of lost boys up there. Running over the roofs, looking down on her and the other adults shuffling around like ants. She gathered her coat around her and walked back to the hotel, wondering where he'd sleep.

Celia often thought of how Emmeline would like the shops, the excited bustle, the plenitude. Her sister was the sort of beautiful person that the shops were there to serve. Sometimes she missed her sister and little Lily and Albert so much that she thought she was bursting. She'd be walking along next to Arthur and see something to point out to Lily and realise that she wasn't there. The children would be changing every day and she couldn't see it. She thought too of Euan, born just before Arthur's trial, who had been weak and died before he'd even got to a year. They'd had a sad little funeral at a church off Russell Square – Emmeline's husband Mr Janus refused to let him be buried in the church next to Stoneythorpe. Emmeline had been broken, and Mr Janus had thrown himself into work. Celia's heart had smashed for

Emmeline, too, but deep inside she had felt anger towards Rudolf and Verena and their pity for Emmeline. *You made me feel the same grief and it was all a lie,* she wanted to say. They'd told her Michael was dead when he was alive. The feeling scalded her – and she was glad to be away from home. Her parents had sent Michael from her, sent him to America and told her he was dead, all for the good of the family, they said. And now here she was in New York, near to him she hoped – but she might never find him again.

She wrote to Emmeline but not her parents. Emmeline had written her one letter – which crossed hers, she supposed. She'd said that Mr Janus had been acting oddly, talking about travelling to Spain. Celia didn't pay too much attention. Mr Janus was always having crazes, fresh ways to change the world. Otherwise, there was little from Stoneythorpe. Rudolf's brother, Heinrich, and his wife Lotte, the children Hilde and Johann, wrote sometimes – they had little money, and life in Germany was hard. Celia blushed reading about them – her visit just after the war, their dream she would marry Johann. They'd laid so much hope in her. The terrible meeting between Tom and Heinrich. Tom had expected the older man to want to see him because he was his father, but Heinrich wanted to forget it, the indiscretion with the maid employed by his brother, and Tom was all pain at being rejected by his father. Then came the night with Tom by the lake in Baden – and everything was changed.

Celia had tried to tell Arthur about Emmeline's letter, the few bits of news. But he wasn't interested. 'You can write the letters,' he'd said. 'That's women's work. I prefer just to go back and surprise them.'

So in the evenings, she had written letters. There wasn't much else to do. Arthur often went down to the bar and he wanted to drink alone. Although alcohol was supposed to be banned, it was easy enough to get it to drink in your room at the Plaza. You could often drink it in the restaurant too – they said the champagne was lemonade. He'd spent the last of their money on the Plaza. 'We have to have the right address!' he'd said. It was a handsome room, the size of the parlour in Stoneythorpe, with a big bed she could lose herself in, a sofa and even a dark wood desk with gold painting on the edges. The carpet was so thick that she had even lain on it, to test it out. There were dark wood panels on the wall, so you could never hear a thing from the neighbouring rooms, all entirely silent. It felt anonymous to her, so she'd strewn it with her things, books, notebooks, shawls, like a bird stuffing its nest with favourite twigs. She looked out onto Central Park and there was a balcony to stand on – dark wrought iron. Sometimes, at night, Celia stood on it and gazed out at New York glittering below her. She wondered if anyone could see her, a shadowed lone woman, looking down. Arthur had an even bigger room – for doing business in, he said.

'No one here cares that we're German,' Arthur said to Celia. 'They can't tell. Here we're just English.'

He was right, Celia thought. She wasn't half-German, half-English, she was British, European even, and no one questioned more. Americans didn't care that Germans like them had been the enemy in the last war, that their father had been put in an internment camp, the rest of them reviled.

'What about Louisa's money?' she had asked, cautiously, one night.

Arthur shrugged. 'You wouldn't begrudge me that, would you, Celia?'

She supposed he had spent it all. And it was true, how could she criticise him? Not after he'd been wrongly accused of her murder, imprisoned, trialled. If it hadn't been for their lawyer, Mr Bird, and his patient checking of the words of the witnesses, Arthur might be in prison still, or even worse, sentenced to hang. He had been Louisa's husband and so what was left of her wealth was his, as it should be. And yet, still, her heart lurched when they went to restaurants and Arthur said, 'Have what you like!', and when she looked at her giant hotel room, gazing over Central Park.

And she and Arthur had spent money. The room, the food, new suits they had bought from the department store. Hers was a bright blue, cost more money than she could imagine. As he said, though, they had to look the part. Magazines called her the modern woman: single, with money, educated, travelled. But she felt none of these things; instead, shy, out of place in America that was so confident, so new. American women were so shiny clean: spotless dresses, scrubbed skin and white teeth – how did they get them so white? And she was twenty-nine and all the fashion was to be nineteen, twenty. Her skin was a little thinner around the edges of her blue eyes and her hair was still just about golden, but parts of it growing darker. She saw the New York girls passing her, hurrying off to work or lunch or meeting friends – colourful coats, short skirts, heeled shoes, bright hair that moved as they walked, full lipsticked mouths.

But, she told herself, who cared about looks? She wasn't in America to find a husband. She'd come here to find Michael. She stared at herself in the mirror, wondering which features of hers he had, whether he had her eyes or Rudolf's, or Tom's – or those of someone else, far back in all of their history, someone they had never seen.

On the second day there, she'd been walking Fifth Avenue, studying her map, when she saw a toy shop. Lily and Albert had begged every Christmas to go to look at the windows in Harrods, just to gaze at the toys. There was a shop nearby in Bloomsbury that sold handsome dolls Lily adored. She couldn't imagine what the twins would think of toy shops in New York. The one Celia saw, beckoning to her past the dress shops, was huge. The gigantic windows were piled high with soft toys, cloth ponies, bears, dogs, dolls, a multi-coloured rainbow of plush bodies, faces with sewn-on eyes. Who could ever want so many? She walked through the gold swing door into the first room, smiling staff dressed in black and white. There was an elephant the size of a pony and a bear at the front almost five foot high. They must be for a rich sultan's child, a prince.

Just as she came in, she saw a tiny model farm in the corner. Wooden sheep and cows were dotted around the buildings, tiny hens pecked at the ground, ponies nibbled on hay in a pen. At the front was the farmer carrying a pail, his wife in a red-and-white-checked dress and an apple-cheeked boy and girl were playing by a tree. She bought it in a moment, knowing she had to have it.

'It's a present, madam?' the man at the counter asked.

She nodded. 'For my son.' She revelled in saying the word, ignored the drift of his eye to her naked ring finger. She took her prize back, her great blue-wrapped present, hid it in the bottom of the wardrobe.

Arthur asked her to come to the bar with him, where he drank glass after glass of golden liquid.

'Maybe you've hit on the answer,' he said, slurring his voice. 'The modern girl who can't cook, wants pretty things in jars.'

'They seem to like it,' she said, cautiously.

'Well, clever you! You got it in the end. Their little golden girl. They're going to lend you money for your idea. And then where does that leave me?' He drummed his hands on the top of the bar.

'But—'

'Where does that leave Winter Meats? The business that keeps us all afloat? If we can't sell in America, we are lost.'

'But – maybe—'

'Have you forgotten? I was in prison. I almost went to *hang*.'

Arthur's trial catapulted into her mind, her brother's pale face as he stood in the box, watching the proceedings, gazing as the barristers argued back and forth about whether he was a bad husband, a bad man, if he'd killed Louisa in Margate because he'd never loved her, wanted her money. And they had all been wrong, and now he was innocent, free.

She swallowed. Arthur had nearly died. She was selfish. She gazed at him, and her heart turned. There was no need to remind him of the truth – that the banks said Winter Meats had no future in America.

'Well, when I receive the money for Flapper Foods, or whatever we're going to call it, then maybe we can do something with it.

I could lend you the money for one factory and then you could borrow on that?'

He smiled broadly. 'Would you? Would you really?'

He was family. She had to help him. And what did those banking men know anyway? The answer danced in her head. They looked at the figures. She shook it away.

He put his arms around her, held her close. 'I knew I could rely on you! What about tomorrow?'

Celia shook her head. 'I want to go to the agency tomorrow.'

'What agency?'

'The adoption agency. Where Michael was sent.' He'd known that her reason in coming in the first place was to find Michael. It had been at the dinner held at the Ritz to celebrate Arthur's freedom that the whole story had come out. She had told her family, told Arthur that she was coming to find Michael and he'd nodded, agreed. Now – she saw in his face – he thought differently.

'You're never going to find him, you know,' he said. 'They won't give you the address, even if they have it. Not unless you give them millions. And you don't have millions.'

She felt as if he'd slapped her. 'I'll tell them the truth. I will tell them that he was taken from me.'

'Don't you think all girls say that?' He shrugged. *I didn't mean it! I've changed my mind!*

'It's the truth. Mama took him from me. It was a criminal act.'

'So call the police. But you can bet this agency won't give you a thing.'

'Of course I can't call the police. It was years ago.'

Probably, if she called the police, they would agree with Verena. *It was the best thing for the boy. A loving family. Not brought up with the shame and stigma of illegitimacy.* The whole of society would agree.

'Well, that's it then. You'll never find the boy. He's gone. Get a new life, a husband and have babies.'

'I only want him.'

He shrugged. 'Take it from me. Time is running out. You're a pretty woman, but you're not getting any younger. You need to find yourself a man before you lose your looks.'

'I'm not listening to this any more.' She stood up.

'You know it's the truth. Don't you? Don't look like that. If you ask me, you're just using this whole Michael thing as an excuse. "Oh, poor Celia. Searching for her little boy!" If you can tell the world you are searching for your child... then you can avoid meeting a new man.'

'Arthur. No more.' She started to walk away.

'Selfish. That's what it is.'

She spun around. 'Selfish? Selfish to search for my child who was taken from me?'

'Yes. You have duties to your family. You need to find a husband to make our fortune.'

'Me? What are you talking about?'

'Yes, you. Emmeline is married and even if he died tomorrow, who'd have her? She's like wet washing, always fussing over those children. I've done my bit, I had my rich wife and there aren't that many to go around. So it's up to you. Marry well.'

Every word burned.

'I'm going, Arthur. We'll make our fortune the honest way, through business, rather than me hunting out a rich husband.'

Arthur narrowed his eyes. 'That's you, Celia. Live as a spinster, mourning a child who died long ago.'

'What?'

'He's probably dead.'

'No. No.'

'Look at the facts. He was weak when you gave birth to him, everyone agrees. Then sent off to London to a baby home where so many of them die. And then the sea journey that even made you sick. He died on the way over here, I wager.'

She bent over. She wanted to crouch, as if he'd punched her. 'They would have told Mama.'

'Of course they wouldn't. She signed him away. He wasn't anything to do with them any more. And even if they did, do you think she'd have told you?'

'What?'

'She'd never tell you. You'd never forgive her. Far easier for her to let you go on this wild goose chase, let you always be hoping. Let you blame yourself if you couldn't find him. But if he'd died, you'd hate her. But I say he died at sea. Too weak.'

She held her head. 'No. He's alive. I know he is.'

'You delude yourself.'

She couldn't listen any longer. She fled from the room, found herself in the lobby but that was too full of people, too much. She hurtled out of the front door of the hotel, into the New York street. She flung herself against the wall. Her legs wouldn't move. She put her face up to the sky, the grey, overcast sky, dark with buildings, all of them ready for another day of people making money. Then she began to cry, weeping great, soaking tears, even though she tried to force them back because she knew how ridiculous she'd look, sobbing in the middle of the street. She stuffed her hand in her mouth not to cry out loud, but she couldn't help it. Arthur and his words dug hard into her soul. *Dead. Your fault.* She tried to clutch to the old imagining, the dappled, sunlit dream of Michael and she together, but it was faint, indistinct. She had to go to the adoption agency, and find out the truth.

THREE

Manhattan, February 1929

'Please,' said Celia. 'Please.'

'I'm sorry, Miss Witt. It is really quite impossible. There is nothing we can do.'

Miss Bellenden was talking but Celia didn't want to hear the words. She was sitting upright behind the pristine desk, pictures of landscapes behind her. 'New Lives, New Hope', read the sign over her head.

'We have to think of the children,' she said. 'You cannot just come in and out of their lives.'

Miss Bellenden was tall, thin, official-looking. Her grey hair was piled on top of her head, as it would have been in the Victorian era, as if she was not letting the new age in. It moved as she talked, side to side. Maybe she would relent, have mercy on her. Celia told her that she had come all the way from England to America, just to find him. It was better for Michael that he was with her. She was thinking of his best interests! He would be happiest with her. She was his mother.

The name of the agency gave her hope. Bluebells were beautiful things, growing in sunny forests in May like fairy spells; they meant happiness, *children running through them.*

The woman carried on. 'You signed for our sister agency in London to take the baby. When you did so, you gave away all your rights. You cannot come back on a whim.'

The chair was too small, rickety. It was probably weak because so many girls had sat in it, weeping, begging, rocking back and forth. *I didn't mean it. I want him back.*

It was because of shame that Rudolf and Verena had taken

33

him away after birth. She said she'd never forgive them. But after Arthur's trial for murder, she'd forced herself to feel compassion. They had lost their niece, Louisa, nearly lost a son – a second son, since Michael had died in the war. The family had been splashed across the papers, hated, discussed as degenerate Germans, Arthur as a cruel chaser after money, such terrible lies. She'd reminded herself that one day they would die and she would be alone. And although she was still filled with pain, she told herself that if she found him again – and surely she would – then so much would be forgotten. Her heart told her she was half a person without him, and he couldn't be whole either.

When she'd made the appointment, she'd said she was a girl hoping to give up her child for a better life in the country. And then, when she arrived, she'd told Miss Bellenden the truth. The woman hadn't seemed too surprised. Celia supposed she had women like her every day, weeping in her office.

Let me have him.

Seven years ago, her body wracked with pain, the monster of it riding her as she held on to the bed at Stoneythorpe. The nurses taking the baby from her as he needed medicine. Then she woke up after being sedated – and they told her he was dead. So she'd believed – until Mrs Stabatsky the medium told her he was alive, not through hearing his spirit voice but because she showed her the whole episode barely made sense. And then, after Arthur's trial, her father had shouted out, 'You need to go America.' Because Michael was alive and he was there.

Miss Bellenden put her chin on her hand. Her hair fell even more alarmingly to the side. 'Miss Witt. If I could only tell you how many young women I have in here. They say – too – that they never signed, or if they did, they didn't understand what they were doing. Our forms are perfectly clear. And what we do here is give children a better life.'

'I've only just found out he was here. I would have come straight away if I'd known.' Celia leant over. 'Please, Miss Bellenden, can you just tell me he's healthy.'

'All information is strictly confidential now. Please understand, Miss Witt.'

Celia looked at the clock. She'd been in this tiny, white office, piled high with files, for twenty minutes. Miss Bellenden had said the same things over and over, was beginning to cast glances at the clock herself. Celia guessed she only had a few more minutes.

'But I'm his mother.'

'You chose to sign away your rights. You cannot change your mind.'

'But I never agreed to send him away. Like I said, my family did it without my knowledge.' She stared around the room, desperately looking at the walls, the paintings of mountains, the peeling paint, trying to cling on to it. Her eyes darted across the curtains, clenching her hands to hold a little of the air of the room, trying to keep it. Somewhere on the bookshelves was a file and in it were details about Michael. She could only be feet away from it. And yet, she couldn't find it. She gripped her hands again.

'That couldn't be the case, I'm afraid, Miss Witt. We always have the mother present. You said you were ill after the birth. Is it possible you have forgotten signing?'

'Of course not.'

Miss Bellenden sighed, put on her glasses, reached into a drawer and pulled out a brown cardboard file. There was the file! That was it. It looked to have a whole sheaf of papers in it. Miss Bellenden covered the front with her hand but it was too late. Celia had seen the writing. *Michael Witt.*

He was alive. He was real.

Celia wanted to reach up, grab the woman and seize the file off her. Michael's file. His life.

'Let me see. Miss Witt, it says here – very clearly – that you were in attendance at the meeting. You agreed to hand over your child. My colleague in London discussed this with you and you said you understood. There is no note here that you looked particularly ill, just a little exhausted, which is to be expected for a lady who has just delivered a baby.'

Celia stared at her. 'But that's not true. I wasn't there!'

Miss Bellenden put down the file. 'Miss Witt, I see little worth in continuing this conversation. You signed away your child. As I said, I see a lot of young ladies in here. What they – and you – must remember is that the child has a better life. He no longer has the stigma of being illegitimate. He is part of a family.'

shook away her words. 'So he is still alive then. That's what you mean.'

Mrs Bellenden shook her head. 'I told you, Miss Witt. I cannot give you any of this confidential information. You are fortunate that I have even entertained you here at all, after your false representation of why you came. Now, if you will forgive me. I have other people to see.'

Celia gazed at the file on the desk. Two feet. So close. All she had to do was bend down. She stretched her fingers. Miss Bellenden was old, weaker. She could seize it. It was so near. She stretched out her fingers. Miss Bellenden saw her, snapped the file shut and pushed it onto the shelf.

'The interview is over, Miss Witt.'

Celia stood there, two sides of her pulling, one half of her sympathy for Miss Bellenden, sticking to the rules, the other half longing to throw her aside, grasp the file, run with it.

'Please,' she said. 'Please give it to me.'

Miss Bellenden shook her head. 'I will call for the police. The interview is over.' She drew herself up. 'I will call for the police.'

Celia backed away, slowly, looking at Miss Bellenden, hoping for one word, one gesture that might suggest that they could talk more, a chink she could edge through, talk to her, find her humanity. Miss Bellenden turned away, adjusted her hair.

'Good day, Miss Witt.'

'I understand,' said Celia. She smiled. She had to smile. She had to try to make the woman like her, to see that she was really someone respectable. Miss Bellenden was looking down at her papers. *Give it to me!*

Celia turned for the door. She paused. Miss Bellenden did not look up. She pulled it open, burst out through the waiting room, into the street beyond, desperate to breathe.

Celia looked around her, then turned, pacing towards the hotel, feet hitting the ground hard, walking, thinking. She wouldn't tell Arthur. Not yet. But she needed to tell someone. She needed *someone* to help her through, as Miss Bellenden wasn't going to let her go any further. She put her head in her hands. The world in front of her eyes flamed red.

FOUR

'Hello.' A woman's voice. 'I saw you go into Bellenden's, didn't I? Yes I know they call it Bluebells, but she calls the shots.'

Celia was leaning against the wall, a few doors down from Bluebell's. She'd been trying not to faint. She opened her eyes and a small woman with short black hair and a mauve hat was standing in front of her, very close. Her eyes lifted when Celia looked at her and the hope was one Celia recognised.

'I saw you. What did you think? She's a dragon, isn't she? From the way you look now, I guess you were trying to find your kid, right?'

'It was Mama,' she said. 'She'd told them I'd signed him over. I don't know how. Maybe she paid them a lot of money.'

'Well, maybe. Or maybe she had someone pretend to be you. Paid an actress or something.'

Celia stared at the girl. 'Really? They'd do that?'

She nodded. 'You bet they would.' She had a pretty, rather moon-shaped face, a heavy oval, a great smile, large dark eyes, inviting. She had a soft, laughing voice, and a look about her face that she was keen to be surprised, amazed. Her body was small, like a dancer's. She was beautiful really. In another life, Celia thought, she'd like to be her friend.

'Listen!' said the girl. 'Let's walk together. I'm Violet, by the way.'

Celia knew she shouldn't really, knew she was better going back to the hotel to work on plans for the business and trying to think of some legal way to get Michael, with lawyers and letters. But something about Violet's eyes, entrancing, pulled her in, and so she nodded and, in a minute, they were side by side and anyone looking at them would have thought they had been friends forever.

Violet, she told Celia, worked in the Primrose ladies' store on Fifth Avenue, specialising in gloves. She said she'd been engaged and thought she was safe – then her fiancé died and she was pregnant. She'd hid it at work with scarves and the rest – lucky it had been winter – and no one suspected her because they all thought she was such a good girl. Celia thought that she wasn't lying. Celia didn't think she'd really know how to lie.

'It's only mother and me,' she said. 'Without my wage, we'd starve.' Her mother was ill, delicate, sometimes couldn't get out of bed. Violet did everything for her – came home from a long day in the shop and cooked and cleaned, brushed her hair, remade her bed, read to her, stroked her forehead until she slept. 'She needs me,' Violet said.

So when she fell pregnant, what could she do? She'd tried not to think about it as she'd grown bigger, prayed to God to bring her a solution. But He didn't. 'He couldn't hear me,' she said. 'I prayed to him but He couldn't hear me. I'd hoped that mother might get well and be able to look after the baby. But even if she could, the neighbours would have talked and I would have lost my job.'

She had the little girl at home, pulling on a rag for the pain, her mother fretting from the bed. A little girl. She called her Hope. She took the child to Bluebells. 'I wept all the way. But I believed everything they said in the literature that it is a better life for a child. They'll live happily ever after in the country. I wanted to help her. I thought, what sort of life does she have with me, shushed and secret in our one-room apartment?'

'And now you want her back?'

'I don't know. I want to know she's happy. I want to know that the people she is with love her as much as I did. Do.'

'I know she's happy,' said Celia, not sure she was convincing. Because if she didn't believe that Michael was happy with his family, why would little Hope be any different?

'Why did you end up getting pregnant then? You look like a clever enough girl.'

39

Celia shrugged. 'I didn't think straight.' That was true enough, for she didn't, she hadn't, that night in Baden with Tom, eight years ago. She'd met him by chance there – she was with her cousins and her aunt and uncle and he was there after finishing business. He'd been pleased to see her and that had thrilled her soul. He'd told her that there couldn't ever be anything between them, that there never had been really. *I was the servant*, he said and the painful undertow of it all hit her. He had never had any choice, stuck in the house, imprisoned really, he hadn't truly wanted to spend hours riding with her or playing games. But it hadn't been like that, she was sure! They had really been friends. No matter what he said. When he had told her that he believed Rudolf was his father, she had been shocked. He'd said it was because she was disgusted by him, would never want someone so poor in her family. And when she tried to explain, it didn't come out right, it was because her father wasn't *like* that, he'd always been loyal to her mother.

And then she had realised, through working back, the dates of visits, what she'd been told – his father had to be Heinrich, her uncle. Tom had been furious with her. He wanted it to be Rudolf, had admired him so. He had said he would never speak to her again. And in Baden, when she'd sent him to Heinrich, it had been terrible. Her aunt had screamed and the whole restaurant had stared and Tom ran from there, her following after him. They'd drunk wine that night, and then in the cold grass near to the lake, he'd turned to her – and she'd thought, yes. No more talking. Just the two of them, close together, one of them really, and nothing else mattered. But afterwards, he'd been shocked that she had been a virgin and she had felt shame, ran away.

'I couldn't tell him. I told my family it was a soldier.' They still thought it.

'Was he married?'

She shook her head. 'No. He just didn't love me.'

'But he'd manage to do whatever with you? That was *fine*.'

'It wasn't like that.'

40

'Oh, it was. Men do what they want. And we have to deal with it.'

'That's not always true.' But then, Rudolf had always told her mother what to do, and then Arthur, ordering Louisa around. But Tom hadn't been like that. Nor had Jonathan. The name rang in her head like a small stone dropping into water. *Jonathan.*

Violet clutched her hands. 'I need to go to the store now. But we must help each other. We need to get your Michael back and find Hope. See she's happy.'

'How do we do it?'

She smiled. 'We'll do it together! I'll meet you back here in a week.' She turned and dashed down the street. Celia watched her go, a tiny, mauve-clad whirlwind. She didn't know how. But they'd succeed together.

FIVE

Manhattan, February 1929

Whatever she did, wherever she walked, her mind returned to Bluebells. She went to see a solicitor and he told her that Michael had been signed away and she could not have him back. She took out the farm set from the bottom of her wardrobe, touched the miniature animals, perfectly carved, imagined handing them to her son. She put a horse into her pocket and told herself she would keep it there until she could give it to him.

At the end of each day, she went out to the back of the hotel, hoping to see the boy, Red, again. No luck. She had to fill the week until she saw Violet. The banks had offered her enough for her to start up a small kitchen. If she made a success of the business, she told herself, she might gain a position, a status in America that could win Michael back. Every morning, she scribbled up the figures, conjured pictures of glittering tins and jars, and finally she had nearly a hundred pages of plans. Supplies, transport, labour, packaging. She found a comfort in methodically working through it all. Tom's voice came to her, from their childhood. 'You couldn't even boil a kettle for tea!'

Well, she'd show him. Not that he was watching, she reminded herself. But still. She showed Arthur the ideas she had written out.

'The puddings seem quite English,' she said, doubtfully.

'Do you think it's not too filling?' said Arthur. 'The girls I used to know never used to eat a thing.'

'Plenty of girls eat. Especially working girls.'

Jars like theirs would make Violet's life so much easier. Instead of having to shop after work, then cook for Mother and clean, she'd be able to buy a few jars and then just go home to heat them up. And maybe, once Flapper Foods was established, Violet would come and work for them.

She carried on writing down the recipes, rough guesses of ingredients. 'You have to put in a bit extra,' she said to Arthur. 'I think. That way people think they are getting something special. Onions and leeks in the macaroni cheese. Little bits of chocolate in the cake.'

'What about an advertising campaign?'

'A what?'

'We need an advertising campaign, Celia. Something to show the world what we've done. We can't just hope that girls will happen to see the things in a shop.'

He was right. She had seen all sorts of advertisements since she'd been in New York. Beautiful, white-teethed ladies in summer dresses smiling out of billboards, holding raisins or ice cream or gesturing at new apartments in Florida.

'We need a modern girl,' Celia pondered, 'as a model.' She had to be a girl like one of those on the ship. Short hair, not too much powder and lipstick, a smile.

'What about a competition to find her?' said Arthur. 'Everyone could send in photos. Then we could get a lot of publicity.'

'That's an excellent idea. The Flapper Foods Girl!'

They conjured ideas: the competition, how they'd advertise it, newspapers across the land, how the competition would be on the radio news, talked about everywhere. How could it fail? They took their dinner in Celia's room, the waiter coming up with trays of food and a note he said was for Celia. She put it aside, too busy thinking about their ideas, supposing it was probably something about the laundry. They kept on writing. Finally, at ten, they agreed they had everything.

'Tomorrow,' he said. 'We will take it to the bank tomorrow.'

Arthur kissed her goodnight and she felt flooded with affection for him. As she fell into bed, exhausted, she remembered the note.

She lay there for a moment and swung herself out of bed. She wouldn't have time to deal with it tomorrow, as it was an early start.

She picked it up from her desk and opened it.

Telephone Message: Mr Jonathan Corrigan Telephoned from Connecticut.

Then an address. A phone number.

Celia stared at it, blood beating hard at her face. He must have called home to Stoneythorpe and they'd told him she was here.

Jonathan. She had all but forgotten him. When he'd said goodbye after the trial had ended, he'd told her to come and see him. 'You'd like America,' he'd said. 'People can do whatever they want. It's not like England where they're always trying to hold you back.'

They'd been in a restaurant near King's Cross station, windows steamy with the breath of dozens of travellers hurrying in and out, the sort of place that would have been full of soldiers in the war. Handsome, tanned, confident, American Jonathan, making the English people around him look shabby. Everything she'd said sounded shy and stiff. When the trial had been adjourned, when she'd gone back with him to his hotel and she'd tried to forget that Arthur might be found guilty and hanged, and to remember her brother Michael, who had been with Jonathan at Cambridge before the war, when they were young, on the brink of possessing the world. She and Jonathan had held tight to each other, forgotten it all. Perhaps they could be free together. But then, in the restaurant, her world had been stopped by the news she'd just heard from her father – that her child was alive and had been sent to America. After that, nothing anyone said had any meaning at all.

She had smiled at him, barely making her voice heard over the hubbub. 'I'll come,' she said, telling him it was for the business, for she'd never mentioned her son to him. 'I promise.'

And yet she'd arrived and hadn't contacted him. All her thoughts had been about her child. But he was Michael's best friend from university. Her link to her brother's past.

She looked at the clock on the wall. Half past ten. Quite late. But there wouldn't be time tomorrow. She had to do it now. She dressed hurriedly, putting her gown over her nightgown, pulling on stockings and shoes, hurried down to the concierge. She thought she saw Arthur just through the door in the hall, sitting at the bar. Drinking. She shuffled behind a pillar.

'I need to return a phone call,' she said to the concierge. He was her favourite – Alberto – a small man, fifty or so, grey hair, round, trustworthy face. She was glad it was him, not the tall dark-haired one who made her feel nervous. 'Please could you dial through to Connecticut for me?' She blushed even asking it. She held out the paper and the address.

Alberto nodded. 'I'll try the operator, madam. When do you wish to place the call?'

'Now, please.'

He raised an eyebrow. 'It's late.'

And he was right, of course, the hotel lobby was full of well-dressed people leaving after dinner. The evening was over.

'It's important. I must do it now.'

She waited by the desk as he walked away. The dark-haired one came to stand in his place. She stared at the people going past, a handsome man and a woman who looked like they were pretending not to be lovers. She gazed out at them. She might brush past people who had seen Michael – and she'd never know.

'Madam?' The voice came through the fog of faces in her mind. 'The call is connecting.' The tall concierge gestured her towards the door behind him.

Alberto held out the receiver. 'I have the house here for you.'

She reached out, tentatively. She'd never used a telephone, not really. They'd had one in Stoneythorpe, but she'd only lifted it to hear the sound, speak down it to the crackle. At the few office jobs she'd had, she'd never been senior enough to answer the telephone. It sat, polished and handsome, on the head secretary's desk, treasured. She asked the reed-thin voice in the receiver for Jonathan, gave her name.

'Hello, Celia.' Jonathan's voice was incredulous, she could hear that even over the crackling of the line. 'Is it you? How are you? Are you really in America?'

She breathed. She should have told him she was coming. She had been caught up in Michael. 'I'm sorry,' she said.

'How long have you been here?' He was telephone-distorted, slower and deeper than he normally was. He sounded older.

'Quite a bit of time. I – I came with my brother...' The line was flinging crackles into the air, burning. 'I did mean to tell you,' she began.

'We promised that if you came to America – I, I could have helped you. It's my home. Why are you even staying in the Plaza? The service is bad.'

Celia thought of Alberto, helping her with the telephone. 'They are very nice.'

'I've dreamed of you coming,' he said. 'I'd meet you at the boat, take you to your hotel.'

'I'm sorry.' Her mind had been caught up in finding her lost child. She couldn't tell Jonathan about it. She flushed hot, red, ashamed. How she had hurt him. But then, if he had always been there, she might not have been able to look for Michael. Arthur wasn't curious, she could carry on a whole secret life without him even noticing. But Jonathan would have cared, asked questions.

'Could we meet?' she asked. 'Are you coming to New York?'

'You're probably too busy,' he said.

She listened to the line flame. 'I am not busy. Please.' The sound of his voice pulled hard on her heart. He was kind, generous.

Jonathan sighed. 'How long are you here for?'

'I'm not sure. It's up to Arthur and how the business goes.' *Until I find Michael*, she didn't say, but that was the truth.

'So we have time, then. I'll call and let you know.'

'When?'

'When I can.'

'I wish we could meet!'

'Do you remember that time when I saw you in the garden at your house? You were so young.'

The memory made her blush more. How different things had been then, before the war. So simple. Everything had seemed so straightforward, as if love and family and the bonds they had together would last forever, and Celia would always be safe within their branches, never having to hold the tree up herself.

He was still speaking, as if he hadn't heard her. 'The light was coming through you. You came over with your sister and the light was behind you, flowing through your hair.'

We've grown up, she wanted to say. She'd been in her dell, at the bottom of the garden, and she felt that her future was in front of her, that she was on the verge of reaching out, touching it and then everything would glitter, shift and change and the world would never be the same again. She looked back on herself, incredulous about the selfishness of youth, simple, wishful. She'd thought all the change would begin and end with her, that all the others would stay the same. As if the point of her life was discovering herself and the years would be taking her through doors, and behind one waited her own self, predestined, certain.

His tone grew clipped. 'I don't know. What's the point of holding on to the past? None of us are the same any more. Why pretend?'

'Yes, we are! Inside we are!' They had to be. Otherwise, all of her brother was lost, if the parts of them that had known him before the war were gone.

'I don't know, Celia. Listen, I'll telephone you another time. Perhaps in a few weeks when you say you're free. Or whenever it is.'

'I'm sorry I waited.'

'Me too. It's getting late. Goodbye, Celia.'

He put the phone down and she listened to the breaking line hiss. If he picked it up again, she'd still be there. She willed him to. Nothing happened. She put down her receiver on the table, still burning. She gazed at it again, then put it back on the hook.

47

She wanted to race up to see Jonathan this minute, beg his forgiveness. But what if he turned her away, or was angry with her for her presumption? What if she made things worse? She rushed upstairs and scribbled a letter, would post it the next day.

SIX

Manhattan, February 1929

Celia couldn't sleep. Even the street lights scored into her mind. She gave up, dressed quickly and walked downstairs for some air. She sat at the back of the hotel, wishing that she might see Red.

'Hello, Miss,' came a voice from above her. 'How have you been?' She looked up and saw Red peering down at her.

'I was wondering if I'd see you again.'

'I've seen you a lot. You don't go out much, do you, Miss?'

'If I knew when you were coming, I'd have some food for you. I have some money upstairs.'

He shook his head. 'I don't want money. I want to repay the favour. You saved me. So I should do something for you.'

She hesitated. It was too much, impossible. He was only a child. But she had no one else to ask. 'There is something I need. I don't think you could get it for me.'

'I can get anything. Try me.'

She couldn't ask him. Telling him her problems would be a burden to him. But then. Someone had given him up too.

'I lost my little boy. He's only a few years younger than you. My parents gave him away when he was just a baby. I need an address for my little boy. It's in an office.'

'That one you went to and were talking to that lady in purple outside?'

'You followed me there.'

'Of course, Miss.'

'Well, there's a file in there that I need. It's a piece of cardboard with papers in. And I need another file for a friend of mine.'

'And you want me to take them for you?'

49

'Could you do that?'

'I can try, Miss. We could definitely get in. The thing is – I can't read so I wouldn't know the right files.'

'I'll come with you.'

He shook his head. 'No, Miss. No one sees us. Everyone notices you. Give me the names and I'll ask the others. We must know someone who can read.'

She fished her notebook from her purse and wrote down the names. 'Could you match them up, perhaps?' But if they were in alphabetical order, even that was no use.

'Maybe,' he said, doubtfully.

'Let me come with you.'

He shook his head. 'You'll get us arrested. We'll find a way. Must go, Miss.' He swung himself up, disappeared.

She didn't want to wait a week. Next morning, she rose and took a cab to the Primrose ladies' store. She needed to see Violet, her gentle smile, her pretty oval face. She wouldn't go near her counter. She'd just stand and watch nearby. And Violet might guess what she was thinking: that they were closer than they'd ever been.

The Primrose department store was laid out like all the rest. The glove counter was near to Hats and not far from Scarves, on the ground floor. Violet wasn't by Gloves – it was two smart-looking girls and a stern woman of fifty or so. Celia stationed herself by Scarves, easier to be unobtrusive there, she thought. She told the girl behind the counter that she was merely looking.

'Here on holiday, madam?' she asked politely.

Celia shook her head. 'I live here.'

She was on her third scarf (all such wild colours, who would buy them?) when Violet finally came out. She must have been down to the stockroom because she was carrying a heavy box. Celia's heart leapt.

'Oh, finally,' said one of the smart-looking girls, the taller one with dark hair. 'Here you are, *finally*.'

'Sorry,' said Violet. 'I couldn't find the box.'

'You can never find the box, can you? You can never find

anything. I don't know why Miss Adams sends you there. Except I do – it's because you make so many mistakes with the customers. Unless it's a handsome man, of course.'

Violet continued to lay out the gloves. Celia felt as if she was swelling with fury.

'And you're not even pretty. Miss Adams? Don't you think? Miss Betts is not even pretty.'

Violet didn't answer again, busied herself with a display.

'When did you last make a sale, Miss Betts?' The smart girl, the blonde one, was joining in. 'Tell us.'

Violet's head was bowed. Her hands fluttered over the pink gloves on the display case. She didn't look up. Celia remembered school, a girl who was cruel to the younger ones, how they'd used to flatten themselves against the wall. You thought you had to hide yourself from bullies. But that only made them come out more. But how could she tell Violet that?

She couldn't stop herself. She marched over.

'I'd like to look at some evening gloves, please?' she said. The smart girls were standing upright, all smiles now. 'And I'd like this lady to show me.'

Violet's face was pure shock. She mouthed something at Celia but Celia didn't know what.

'Well, get to it, Miss Betts,' said the stern woman. 'Evening gloves.' Violet flushed red and Celia felt guilty.

Violet brought out tray after tray of gloves. They were all rather ugly, Celia thought, thin material, not much quality, but she expressed interest, asked Violet her advice.

The smart girls tried to intervene and Celia ignored them. She turned to Violet, looked at her only. The other girls hung back, stood resentfully behind the counter.

By the third set of gloves, Violet was no longer red and mumbling. She was smiling, expansive. She recommended gloves and textures and Celia pretended to be fascinated. Net flowers and silken fingers, bead embroidery, tiny pieces of glitter, white, pale blue, cream. She asked Violet to put aside three of the most

51

expensive, elaborate ones – what on earth was she going to do with those?

'Yes, madam,' said Violet, nodding.

Violet rang them all up perfectly – ridiculously expensive – and Celia took them in a bundle.

'Thank you, Miss,' she said. She turned to Miss Adams. 'I must say, I really must compliment you on your staff's excellent service! The levels of service are practically *European!*' She gave Violet a beaming smile. 'I shall be sure to come again.'

The smart girls stood holding the counter as if they were being buffeted by winds.

Celia took the parcels under her arm and set off towards the door. She had taken a risk. She knew she had. But it had been worth it, every moment of it. As she headed to the hotel, she passed an old woman begging on the street.

'Have these,' she said. 'Sell them on the market.'

She hurried on, leaving the old woman taking the evening gloves out of the paper, net and silk and flowers fluttering.

She still held the list of prices in her hand. At the bottom, in Violet's handwriting:

You shouldn't have come. But thank you.

When Flapper Foods was a real business, she'd employ Violet. And they'd both have their children back.

Eventually, Red came once more. She was ready for him with chocolate and cigarettes; she'd waited every night. 'I have what you want,' he said. 'One of the boys could read.' He passed over a hefty paper bag. They'd taken the whole files. Miss Bellenden would surely realise. What if she called the police?

'Can you take them back after we've seen what we need?'

He shook his head. 'Don't think so, Miss. It was close.'

'Did you break in?'

'I wouldn't ask, Miss. I won't go back. None of us will. We nearly got caught.'

Her mind rang with the panic he must have felt and she felt filled with guilt. 'I'm sorry.'

'Don't apologise! We enjoy it. But it took Sun a long time to read the names and the bells were ringing. We thought they'd catch us.'

She stared down at the brown cardboard files. Michael De Witt. Hope Pennington.

'Thank you,' she said. She'd have to hope that Miss Bellenden would think she'd lost them herself, or even if she guessed what had happened, would never admit it.

'Don't go back there, Miss. Better not raise any suspicions.'

'No, I won't. When will you come back?'

'In a night or two, maybe. There's a lot of business at the moment.' She watched him bounce away into the night, while she held tight to the papers.

She stared at Michael's file, back in the hotel room. She was almost afraid to open it. She kept staring, took a breath, put her hands on the pale card. A signature that wasn't hers. Birth certificate. Age. Address. The light from the lamp slipped through her fingers, broke into a thousand stars.

'Twenty-two Upper Eighty-Seventh Street'. Michael's home. *New York*. He lived there. Not so far from her. She might have even walked near it, on the odd walk she had taken to Central Park. She might have passed him. She'd thought of him on a farm Upstate, picking apples, helping with the crops. Not in some great apartment in a new building on the Upper East Side. Perhaps his family was poor, was in service. But something in her told her that they were rich.

He had a home, an address. He probably had a new name. The truth of it all hit her, hard. If she went to him, she might bring such discord into his life. He might be happy, in Upper Eighty-Seventh Street.

Was she being selfish? Wanting to take him from people who loved him. Maybe she should only observe him from afar, check he was happy, not go further, come back when he was an adult.

She closed the file, her heart on fire.

SEVEN

The next day, Celia walked to the department store, but Violet
wasn't there. Thinking she was on a break or an errand, Celia
waited outside, her hands growing painful with cold. Ready to
give up, she ventured back inside. The stern woman, Miss Adams,
had shooed her away, but one of the other girls had come forward
when the others weren't looking, slipped her Violet's address. 'I
think she needs someone to look out for her, Miss,' the girl had
said.

She found a cab and the driver headed north quickly. He let her
out at a ramshackle house, the roofs built across, windows falling
in. Celia knocked at the door. A pale woman in a dirty flowered
apron opened the door, one child clutching at her side, another
behind her legs. She looked as though she was always tired, as if
all she could tell you was that she was tired, great purple smudges
under her eyes.

'I'm looking for Violet,' Celia said.

The woman raised her eyebrows, gazing at Celia's hat and bag.
'Upstairs.' She pulled open the door and Celia squeezed past her
and the children. 'Second staircase on the right.'

Celia balanced her way up the rickety staircase, watching where
she put her feet. The wood was splintered, cracked, broken across
the sections. Children were standing in the corridors, men leaning,
a couple smoking. There were doors everywhere, names on doors.
It must have once been two great houses and now the rooms that
had been bedrooms, grand salons, were housing whole families.
She walked across the corridor and came to a door. Betts. Violet

and her mother. She leant against the door frame, listened, heard low voices talking.

Celia knocked on the door. There was silence behind it. Quickly shuffling feet. She knocked again and stood back. No response.

'Violet? It's Celia.'

She approached the door again. Then it opened, just a small crack. Violet's eye peered out.

'What are you doing here?'

'I came to see you.'

Violet sighed. 'Well, you'd better come in. Quickly.' Her pretty face so sad now, the moon lost all its light. There were broken veins on her cheeks as if she'd been ill.

Celia looked around, took in the low bed, older woman lying seemingly asleep under a lace coverlet, the walls broken and splintered like the stairs. There were a few pictures, scraps of material to decorate, empty bottles of what must have been hair stuff arranged on the shelves. There was a worn-looking table and a rickety chair.

Violet stood back, against the wall, face pale. 'We have to keep our voices down,' she said. 'Mother's sick.' She shook her head. 'Why did you come?'

'I have something. I think I have Hope's address.'

'How?'

'Never mind. But I do.' She handed over the file. 'Now I can help you find Hope. We could do it together.'

Violet shook her head, pushed the file back at her. 'I don't know why you're here. I don't know how you got this and I don't want to know! If you stole this, do you realise what this could do to me? Mother and I could lose everything. But I suppose you didn't care. I'm the kind of girl who'd be a servant to you. Don't you expect everyone to be your servant?'

'No!' Celia tried to move forwards but her legs were locked, cramped. 'I don't want anybody to be my servant. I – well – we had so much in common. We had both lost a child. I thought—'

'You rich people, you're all the same.'

'All?'

Then something struck her. 'Your fiancé. He didn't die, did he?' The words they said in the shop. *Unless it's a handsome man of course.*

Violet looked away. 'Don't talk to me.'

'It was a rich man. He left you.' Celia's legs released but she didn't move forward. 'Why didn't you tell me?'

Violet shook her head. 'I was stupid. Wrong. He said he loved me. Of course he did. I thought he'd rescue us. What stupidity. Still, I wonder every day if he's written me a letter. And I wonder if he might come to the shop and find me. Save me from all this.'

Celia had thought of the same. Tom appearing, saying he loved her after all.

Violet shrugged. 'And what do I get instead? You. You following me round. Stealing things for me.'

'We won't get found out. I promise.'

Violet closed her eyes. 'Your sort makes promises.'

'Why aren't you at the shop anymore? I went to find you there.'

She shrugged. 'Got above myself, they said. And so they asked me to leave. And that's when I understood that I had to keep away from you. You see, people like you remind me of what people like me can't have. I thought of myself as your friend and all the rest of it. How wrong I was.'

'They were horrible to you at that job. And I'm not like him. I want to help us.' She and Violet had talked so happily that day they'd met. It couldn't just go.

And then, even though it didn't seem the right time, she couldn't stop herself; Celia started talking of her dream. 'I wanted you to come to work for us. You're so good with figures. The business will need someone to deal with the accounts. We need you to help us.'

Violet shook her head. 'You need to go. Mother will wake up soon.'

Celia's head swam. 'But Violet. It would be a good job. Proper money.'

'He made me promises too. If mother was awake, she would say – better to do honest work.'

The sick woman on the bed stirred. 'Violet?'

'Go back to sleep, Mother.' Violet shot Celia a furious glare, hurried over to the sick woman, tried to soothe her.

Celia watched her, thoughts turned in on herself. She tried to see it from Violet's point of view. If they both got arrested for the stolen files, no doubt the courts would be harder on Violet. She watched her try to soothe her mother back to sleep.

But the woman was sitting up now. Gazing at Celia. 'Who are you?'

'She's no one, Mother. She's looking for one of the neighbours.'

The woman wasn't old, maybe late forties or so. She didn't even look so ill. She was just lying there, under her crochet blanket, making Violet work so hard, earning, cooking, cleaning. No wonder she had believed that man and all his promises.

Celia moved over. 'I hear you're ill,' she said. 'I'm sorry. What exactly is wrong with you?'

'Celia!' said Violet. 'Why can't you just go?'

The woman reached out her hand. 'I just feel so tired. Tired all the time.'

Celia moved towards her. 'I could send a doctor. When did you last see one?'

'Not for years. They're too expensive.'

'You need to go.' Violet picked her bag up off the floor.

'She needs to see a doctor.'

'We don't need your help. Do we, Mother? We don't need you.'

'Please,' she said. 'Take the file.' Violet shook her head and then she was pushing her towards the door, stronger than she looked. The door was opened and closed and Celia was outside. A wide-eyed child sat on the stairs, fiddling with a doll.

Celia leant against the wall, then took a piece of her notebook from her bag, scribbled her hotel address on it and pushed it through the door with the file. *In case you change your mind.*

She meant to travel back to the hotel. But she couldn't bear it, staring at the empty walls. She thought of the address she'd taken from the file, crammed in her purse. She could go there. She could just see where he lived. Then she'd act on it, later, when she felt sure Miss Bellenden had not gone to the police.

Celia got out at Lexington and changed trains to go north. She'd head up to the Upper East Side and find the apartment building. She'd look. She wouldn't do anything else. She'd just see that he was safe.

EIGHT

Manhattan, February 1929

Celia jumped out at the subway and walked up, heart beating hard against her blouse. She turned a corner, walked through a small green space dotted with plants and up in front of a large, red-stone building. She stood outside, gazed up at the spotless windows.

She walked to the other side of the road, tried to work out which window was Michael's. 'Come to me!' she wanted to cry. 'I'm here.' After half an hour or so, a well-dressed man walked out of the building. Two maids came next. A tradesman with boxes knocked at the door and what looked like a concierge in uniform let him in.

The door, opening, closing. She could pretend again – say she was a maid – but how far would she get? She could try saying that she was Michael's new governess, say she had come for an interview, but surely they'd check.

Perhaps she could just tell the truth. Go in and say she was his mother. But they would tell her she was wrong – and how could she prove it? And what if Miss Bellenden had told the family about the break-in? Then she would be exposed and perhaps bring Violet and Red down with her. But there had been nothing in the newspapers and she felt sure that Miss Bellenden would want to keep such a thing quiet.

She couldn't steal him away. All she could do was see if they might take pity on her. Maybe let her see him, just once. Tell him about her when he was grown up. She stepped forward and pressed the bell.

The concierge answered. 'I'm here to see Number 22. I have an appointment.' She gave her name, the real one, trying to

59

sound confident. She had to hope that her English voice, the fine upbringing that Verena had planned, destroyed by the war, would be something to let her through.

The concierge nodded. 'I will ring up.' He went to his office, picked up a phone, returned and told her to enter the elevator. She sat on the bench as he stepped in with her. The metal grille closed across, he whirled the handle and they were going up. She couldn't turn back now.

He let her out at a grand, dark-wood door. A maid dressed in black and white stood there. Her eyes were sharp, would surely see through Celia in an instant.

'The name is Miss Witt. I have an appointment,' she said. 'With the – er – Mistress.'

The woman nodded. She drew back, let Celia past. Luck, pure luck. Perhaps the lady of the house was often receiving people without telling the maid. 'She should be back in about ten minutes,' she said. 'Please wait here.'

The maid ushered Celia through the hall full of dark oil paintings. She opened the door to a cool room with great windows that Celia could just see looked out onto Central Park. There were fine sofas, a grand piano, beautiful rugs. There was nothing for a child, no toys, just handsome furniture, all pristine surfaces. She thought with a pang of Stoneythorpe's old, shabby curtains and rugs, splintered sofa legs, nothing they could afford to repair. Michael's life here was completely different. He had money.

Then it struck her: if he was here.

Perhaps they had moved.

But, surely, people who lived in a place like this would pass on their address. They wouldn't just disappear in the middle of the night like they might in other parts of the city. She sat down on the sofa and tried to still her beating mind. The apartment was entirely silent, muffled by carpets and rugs, no sound of the traffic outside. But still, perhaps she might hear a child. Please. She begged. Michael. Come to me.

She heard the front door open, conversation with the maid. Steps in the hallway. The door swung open and a finely dressed woman, arrayed in navy-blue silk, walked through, the maid behind her. Celia stood up hastily, then thought that might have been a mistake. The maid closed the door and they were in the room together, airless and cold.

'Do we have an appointment, Miss Witt, is it? I don't remember it.' Her tone was not unfriendly. Perhaps, Celia supposed, if you were a very rich woman in New York, you met all sorts of people who might attend you, never needed to remember them.

She could offer her the chance of investing in Winter Meats. That would seem legitimate. She could say she'd read about her in the newspapers and thought she might be interested. She almost opened her mouth that way, let the words flow out. But she didn't. Couldn't. The truth was pushing at her.

'Do you have a child, Madam?'

The woman looked confused. 'We have four.'

'A young boy. Seven. Seven and a half, exactly.'

'Yes. Sebastian. Is this about him?'

He's not Sebastian, Celia wanted to cry. 'I'm sorry if this sounds shocking to you, Mrs—'

'Mrs Whetstone.'

'I'm sorry if this sounds shocking to you. But what did the agency – the Bluebells agency – what did they tell you when you adopted the child? Sebastian.'

The woman's face turned cold. 'We didn't adopt him. He's ours.'

'That is not what the agency told me.' The lie came easily to her. 'You adopted him.' She was betting that Miss Bellenden hadn't contacted the clients. That she'd kept it secret.

The woman took a step back towards the door. 'We did not.'

'I'm sorry if this is a great surprise. But they told you lies. I expect they said the mother was unmarried, ruined. But he was mine and he was taken from me. I hired a private detective. He found it all out for me.'

'This is madness.' She stepped back again.

'Don't go! It's the truth. I just wanted to talk to you.'

The woman reached for a bell on the table by the door and

rang it hard. 'Merden,' she shouted. 'Get Edward. This person is leaving.'

'I just wanted you to hear the truth.'

'You are here for money. You are here for blackmail. Well let me tell you, it will never happen. Mr Whetstone receives such threats often, as a wealthy man, and we speak directly to the police. If you don't go, I will call them now.' The maid appeared at the door with a burly man in a suit.

'Make her go, please. You should never have let her in, Merden. I blame you for this.'

The burly man advanced. 'You don't need to force me,' said Celia. 'I will walk out. Don't send the maid away. It was my fault.'

'How dare you tell me what to do? You are a criminal, Madam. You must leave immediately.' Merden stood there, her face frozen.

Edward seized her arm and started propelling her forward. 'You don't need to,' she said. But he was pushing her on and there was no point protesting. 'Just let me do one thing,' she said. 'Please. I left my notebook.'

He must have pitied her, let her dart back to get it from the chair. Then in a moment she had picked it up, was scribbling on the paper, tore it off and left it on the table.

'My address,' she said. 'If you reconsider it. I am at the Plaza Hotel.'

Mrs Whetstone looked at it, then her, eyes all disgust. 'This is disgraceful. You are disgraceful. Remove her from my house, Edward.' She hurried from the room, her skirts flouncing behind her.

He pushed her forward.

'I'm sorry,' she said to Merden. 'I didn't know this would happen.'

Edward moved her out of the door, into the hall, past the paintings, to the lift in the hall. 'Will she be fired?'

He looked at her and she saw something like pity in his eyes. 'No. She knows too much about the family. But don't come here again, Miss.'

'Just tell me, please. Is Sebastian happy?'

Edward stared at her, sizing her up. He shook his head. 'No. He should stand up for himself more.' He raised his voice. 'Now, I don't know who you are or why you came, but we'll never see you again. I have friends who are much quicker to anger than I.'

He pressed the button and the elevator and the concierge appeared. 'I'm sorry about Merden,' she said. 'I didn't mean to get her in trouble.' She opened her purse and took out a note.

Edward shook his head. 'You don't need to worry. Like I said, the lady will never let Merden go. She's been here too long.' He ushered her into the lift.

She sat against the wood wall of the elevator. Michael was back there in the apartment. Called Sebastian. She had been so close to him. But in her quest to find him, she had got Merden into trouble. Her heart overflowed with guilt.

Outside the building, she stood against the wall, buried her face in the bricks. Mrs Whetstone would never see her. Women like her didn't look out of the window. She was probably tearing up the address right at that minute. She spun the day over and over in her head, how she might have done it differently, approaching Mr Whetstone first. But he would have probably sent her away too, whatever she'd said. *He should stand up for himself.* She needed to think. Her thoughts were too much, rising, threatening to engulf her. She needed to be out of the New York streets, sitting quietly in her room. She hailed a cab, clambered in, closed her eyes as it bumped her to the hotel.

'There you are!' Arthur's voice. She turned and he was behind her in the lobby. 'I've been looking for you. Where have you been?'

'I went—' But already he wasn't listening, he caught her arm and started talking.

'I've been to the bank. They love everything. They said we need to launch the competition now. And what they said is that they think you should be the face of the competition. You will advertise the Flapper Foods Girl.'

'Me? What do they mean? I can't do that.'

'Yes, you can. You will inspire all the girls across the country to send in their pictures to become our Flapper Foods Girl.'

'But this can't be possible. I'm not a flapper! There are a hundred girls on the street who'd be better than me!' And I'm exhausted and all I want is my son back, she thought. If Mrs Whetstone loved Michael, then yes, she should leave him. But if the family hated him, she needed to save him. But how? She couldn't just take him. He would be terrified and he might even protest anyway. Just because they didn't love him – he might still love *them*.

'But we don't want some girl off the street. We want you. It's your idea. You will be the face of the competition. That's what they said at the bank. Businesses like ours need faces.'

'I'm too old.' She thought of Edward's face as he'd said, 'No.'

'You look twenty-one.'

He was excited, all talk. It could save them. Her parents could live and die in the house they loved. Emmeline wouldn't be destitute. They could guard Michael's and Louisa's ghosts, be near them. Flapper Foods would rescue them all.

'I don't know,' she said. 'Let me think about it.'

'But we don't have time to spare. We need to strike while the iron's hot.' He stopped at the top of the stairs. 'Listen, Celia. I've been looking after the business for years now, and I've never seen anyone as excited as this. We have the chance to make it. We can succeed! I don't want it to slip through our fingers.'

He was right. They were so close. But Michael was locked up in a tower and she didn't know how to get to him.

NINE

Manhattan, February 1929

'Just turn to the right!' Celia tipped her head up and moved as the photographer said. The lady who had come to do the make-up jumped forward to brush back her hair. They'd cut it to make her look the part.

She doubted she could see a lawyer again, since she'd had no right to find out the address and by all accounts had signed him away. And even if she could prove she hadn't – she knew that any judge would believe it in the better interests of a child to stay with a rich family like the Whetstones, rather than an unmarried woman like her. The Whetstones probably knew all the judges!

She'd sat in the salon as the woman picked and plucked at her hair, talking on about young girls today. She'd tried not to look in the mirror, watching her hair shorn away. Bobs suited girls with sharp chins, cheekbones that came out as if they always had shadow on their faces. She suspected that short hair would make her eyes and cheeks look even more round.

Arthur had found a dressmaker with two gowns, pale green for summer, red for winter. They were exquisite, lace edged, just past the knee, delicate fabric in the green, fine wool in the red.

So she stood there with her new hair, unfamiliar make-up over her face, so much of it that she felt her skin was almost suffocated, smiling for the photographer. Arthur couldn't stop talking.

'You know, Celia, I never thought you would have the answer to all our problems. Little Celia saving us all.'

He jumped forward in a photograph break. 'But are you happy? This is what I want to know. Are you happy?'

She almost started. Michael. The Whetstones. Jonathan. Violet.

She opened her mouth. But then he started talking again, on and on about how he was lonely now and needed a wife; where could they meet anyone when they only knew each other? He hoped that one of the bankers might have a sister or a friend. The words came tumbling out, so fast. She was glad she hadn't spoken. He wasn't really interested – he had only been asking so he could talk. Don't forget Louisa, she wanted to say. But it was over two years since she died.

She smiled for the photograph, wishing she could make everything stop, but things just kept moving on and there was nothing you could do to stop them, time was taking them all and everything that had happened yesterday was already gone. Back in her room, she unwrapped the toy farm at the bottom of her wardrobe and cried.

The days proceeded. Celia tried to fill them. She attempted to telephone Jonathan, to tell him she was sorry, but each time she was told by a sharp-sounding man that he wasn't at home. Red didn't come even though she waited outside with cigarettes and chocolate every night. Sometimes she worried that he had been caught by the police but she scoured the newspapers every morning and there was no mention of the break-in at Bluebells. She supposed that they'd kept it secret, not wanting their clients to know. Violet didn't write. Mrs Whetstone didn't write either – but at least she hadn't contacted the police and sent them to the hotel. Or if she had, they were biding their time. She tried to throw herself into work. She bought cookbooks from the bookshops and wrote up ideas for foods, wrote plans, stood in grocers' shops surveying flour, sugar, bought samples of meat in the butchers' and fish from the fishmongers'. They advertised for a cook to try out the recipes for them. She added up numbers, went to the studio where they were drawing and painting pictures of her to be advertisements, put on her best dress and sat with Arthur through bankers' meetings. Twice she did what she promised herself she would not do and went to Upper Eighty-Seventh Street and looked up at the windows. Sometimes she told herself that she saw a shadow, but she couldn't tell if it was anything more than a trick of the light.

An agent, Mr Martinez, found a few restaurants for sale that he judged to have big enough kitchens for food preparation and cooking. She chose the first one she saw – a long, light kitchen in Brooklyn. She imagined it full of women making cakes, puddings, pickling fruit, rolling pastry for pies.

So this was her vision – eight girls and maybe a man or two working in the kitchens, baking, cooking. She thought of Mrs Bell in the old kitchen at Stoneythorpe, the warm steam coming from the oven, gathering pieces of biscuit dough from the table. It was all gone now – they had no money for a cook, so the ladies from the village Rudolf and Verena could manage to pay brought in ready-cooked food from the bakery. The Flapper Foods kitchen would be like the old Stoneythorpe kitchen, but bigger. And Celia wouldn't be like the rest, paying the lowest wages, sacking people when they were ill. They would have a good wage, a high wage, maybe as much as a man, and she'd pay when they got ill and give them some days of holiday. They'd set a new standard and soon all businesses would be like Flapper Foods. She told Arthur her plan and amazingly, he agreed.

'You and your high ideals. But if things start to drop and we need to cut wages – we'll have to? Do you agree?'

It seemed a fair compromise. She nodded, vowing that if it came to it, she wouldn't give in.

TEN

Connecticut, March 1929

'I've come to see Jonathan. Mr Corrigan, I mean.'

The man on the step, the butler she presumed, raised an eyebrow. 'He is at home. But he didn't tell me he was expecting anyone.'

Celia smiled. 'Might you tell him I'm here? It's Celia de Witt.'

'Will he know who you are, Madam?'

Arthur had gone to see Mr Martinez and she'd said she'd stay behind and go through the applications of the cooks. But walking past the telephone where she'd spoken to Jonathan struck at her heart. She rushed to her room, hunted through her address book for Jonathan's address, caught a cab to the station, crossing her fingers that he would be there, taken another cab up a long drive past trees that looked as if they had been growing there for two hundred years.

Celia recognised his sharp voice from the man who answered the telephone. Her hope sank. He would never let her through.

And then he nodded. 'I will ask him. You can wait in the hall, Madam.'

The butler ushered her into a marble hall with a grand gold clock on a marble table. After fifteen minutes in which she tried her best not to look around, not to touch the clock because who knew who was watching (Red had taught her that), the butler returned to usher her into a beautiful library. She gazed out of the window at the grounds full of sheep, touched the wooden globe on a stand, looked at the books on the shelves. She stared at them behind the glass fronts of the bookcases. She tried to open a door, but it was locked. She traced her hand over the smooth glass.

Lucky Jonathan living here, this beautiful parkland, the library full of books. His lucky wife to be mistress of all this.

The door opened. Jonathan stood there, against the frame.

'Celia,' he said. He didn't move forward. He hadn't changed. Still radiating health, blond hair, ruddy face, tall and broad, wide almond brown eyes, everything about him shooting energy and a heart strong enough to bear them all. He was wearing clothes for golfing, she supposed, casual.

She smiled at him. Her heart warmed, sent the fire up to her face. 'Your family have a beautiful house.'

'You look different. You've had your hair cut.' She wondered what she really did look like to him, her skin flaming red from the New York cold and the late nights, her hair dried out.

'Oh, yes.' She held her hand up to her fringe. 'Arthur – we – we have this idea for a business. Who knows if it will work.' She was gabbling, she knew, but she couldn't stop herself. Everything was coming rushing back – dancing together in the Ritz in wartime after he'd seen her in the street, his arms around her. Then that night before the trial when they had held each other close, and she had felt not just that he was rescuing her from it all, because he was, he was, but that she was rescuing him, too.

He took a step forwards. Then he stopped, leant against the bookcase. 'Celia—'

She had to get in first. 'I'm sorry I said the wrong thing on the telephone. I should have told you I was coming. It was all such a rush, Arthur was coming, I came too, and—'

'You didn't think about me.'

'No – I…' She stopped. It was true. She hadn't really thought about him. Her mind had been full of Michael. 'I'm—'

'I've told myself that I need to stop this,' he said, looking at the globe. 'It's been going on too long.'

Celia gazed at him, watched his hand on the globe. And then she was flung back, so hard it almost made her breathless, to fifteen years before, 1914, when she'd first met Jonathan. Michael had brought him home from Cambridge. They sat on the lawn and talked about boats and people she didn't know. She'd been awkward, not really popular at school, always running away at home to be with Tom or hide in her dell, seek out her imaginary friends. Michael and Jonathan had seemed impossibly grown up, the promise of what she might have if she studied, went to Cambridge too, jumped with both feet into the world. And here she was, nearly thirty, having never jumped at all. The one thing that she did do – spend the night with Tom – had only tied her even more strongly to Stoneythorpe and her parents.

Jonathan had shone with promise then. Michael, too. But Michael had died without dignity and Jonathan did everything instead: joined the Air Force, finished his degree at Yale, lived in a house that was whole and handsome, not like crumbling Stoneythorpe, the castle in *Sleeping Beauty*, falling to bits, covered in moss, while everyone slept inside.

He'd kissed her, the night the war broke out, out on the lawn, and her body had coursed with shock. The ornamental garden Verena had been so preoccupied with, the false canal, the fountain, the perfectly symmetrical flower beds, and beyond it the garden billowed up, overgrown rose bushes and hedges, flowers so interwoven you didn't know where one ended and another began. The garden Verena had hoped would be the seat of culture, refined behaviour. Instead, Jonathan and she, Emmeline with her tutor and Arthur and Louisa walking. A place of secrets.

'I'll always remember it, you running out of the door, your hair loose from its plait. Michael laughed and said you'd come back. You didn't. Then later, after I'd greeted your parents and your sister, Michael and I came to look for you. It was my idea, you know. But he said he knew where you would be. We walked down to the bottom of the garden and there was a cut in the hedge. We looked in – saw a small pond with a willow tree. You were sitting on a stone. We came through. I wasn't sure – I thought we might be invading. But Michael said you wouldn't mind. He called you and you wouldn't come. He laughed and said you had to. But you shouted back that you were staying there and you weren't moving. I looked at you sitting there, and your hair was so bright. It was as if you were all light.' He looked up, gazed at her.

Jonathan spun the globe, hard and fast, bitter. 'So long ago. Of course you were so young. But I said to myself: that's it. The light was flowing from you. It was a *sign*, that's what I saw. And then the war came and Michael left and what reason was there for me to stay? With everything that was happening to you, I was just making it worse.'

She remembered. Sir Hugh breaking off the engagement with Emmeline. Suddenly they were Germans. And then in the garden, the lit end of Jonathan's cigarette burning as he swooped down. *Little German fräulein.*

'I know it was wrong of me to kiss you. I shouldn't have. If it hadn't been for the war – I thought I might never see you again. I tried to write all through the war, but the words wouldn't come – and anyway, I knew I'd have to wait. Then I saw you in London – and—'

'I know,' Celia said, her head bowed. 'I remember every moment.'

'The world turned,' he said. 'You were an adult, then, driving your ambulance. We went for tea, we danced. I asked you to marry me. And then Burlington turned up and told you everything.'

You would think there were enough Fritzers killing off our chaps without the Brits doing the same to our own men.

Jonathan had bundled her out and she'd begged him, forced him to tell her. Michael was ill, he'd said. He couldn't go over the trench. His legs wouldn't take him.

They make the officer stand in front of his men. Each of his men has a gun. Then they are told to shoot.

It had all been a lie. Michael hadn't died bravely, as they'd been told. An officer in charge had known him at Cambridge and covered it up 'for the family'. He'd been shot as a coward.

I hate you! She'd stood in the street and shouted at Jonathan. *I hate you! How could you not have told me!* Then she'd fainted and woken up in her bed in Emmeline's flat, her sister scolding her.

'You didn't say this at the Ritz. You'd said you'd liked me at Stoneythorpe. You hadn't said you'd loved me.'

Jonathan looked back at the globe. 'Well, I'm telling you now. It's true. I thought it would only frighten you away. Anyway, I thought I'd lost you. I came back here. I tried other women. Nice women, pretty women. But I thought of you. I read of the trial and I came back for you.'

Celia blushed hard.

'We were together that night. You and me. I thought that – despite everything that had happened to you, I was helping you.'

'You were!'

'And then you forgot me.'

She felt tears at the back of her eyes, tried to push them back. 'I'm sorry. But with Arthur being freed and the rush and I ...' She broke off. If she went any further, she'd have to tell him about Michael, him being taken from her and he'd ask, but whose was it? He'd think badly of her, going with him and another man before marriage. He might think she'd been with dozens. Or he might tell her, as she always expected people to do, to leave Michael where he was. Say that he was better off in a real family. She blushed, miserably.

She wanted to say, 'You can't love me! I have a son! What makes you want to love me when I already have a child?' Jonathan's wife, the mistress of all this, would have to be pure. She should tell him the truth. At least he might understand why she'd been so distracted. But then, maybe he'd say, why didn't you tell me before? He'd be disappointed in her. The tears were billowing at her eyes.

'I can't explain,' she said. 'But I promise, there is something important. I can't tell you.' Everything was rushing through her head now: the war, Michael's death, his few belongings sent back to be buried, later her nightly imaginings of Michael's end, shot by his fellow men. Shot by *Tom*. No matter what he'd said, that he hadn't wanted it to happen, that he had no choice – he had fired shots forward, along with the other men, and her brother had died. Maybe he'd shot him. She couldn't blame Tom – he'd had no choice – but how could she love him after that? It wasn't possible.

'You're in love with someone else.'

She jerked her head. 'No!'

'Celia, don't say that. You're trying to make me feel better. But you're not free for me. I can see that.'

It's not a man, she wanted to say. It's my child!

'Would it have made a difference? If I'd said before, *I loved you since the moment I saw you.* You were thinking about your family, just as you're always thinking of your family – that brother who was never worthy of you. He pushed Louisa, didn't he?'

'No! They found him innocent.' The barrister, Mr Bird's words at the end of the trial came back to her. He'd questioned the witness who said he'd seen Arthur push her. 'Are you saying you cannot be sure?' He'd taken his assistant, Miss Sillen, to the spot, reproduced the distance in the court. It was too far for anyone to see clearly – and Mr Bird was proving them wrong. 'He is no murderer and there has clearly been no crime.' The men of the press rushing to file the story.

'No, Jonathan. Arthur and Louisa had walked to the edge. They stepped out too far. And Louisa fell. It was a terrible accident.'

'I was watching in court. A clever lawyer proved him innocent. But you can't tell me – Oh, anyway.' Jonathan shook his head. 'You're – how old? – thirty? And you're still obsessed by your family. Perhaps there isn't another man. Perhaps it's just *them*.'

Celia looked at his finger, on top of the globe, tracing out the lines of a country. 'Jonathan—' But she couldn't speak. She tried hard to bite down the tears. 'I had a—' She stopped.

'You know,' Jonathan said then, taking a step towards her, 'I always thought you looked exactly the same, still that runaway girl. Even at the trial. But now, we're all older. You've changed.'

Celia stepped back towards the window. He was right, she knew. Her face wasn't the same. In the same time, Jonathan had only grown more handsome – his healthy, tanned face, pale hair. He looked even taller. She was about to nod – and then a streak of anger ran through her.

'People grow older. Women do! I like it. I'm independent now. Arthur and I are making a business and it's my idea. I don't want to be eighteen any more.'

Jonathan shook his head. 'Sorry, Celia. I didn't mean it like that. You're still beautiful. You still look like that girl. I was just – I was just trying to get free of you. I was just trying to tell myself that I don't love you any more. I have to. My father wants me to marry. He introduces me to girls of good family all the time. The country club, the sailing club. All the rest of it. But it isn't honest to marry if you're in love with someone else, is it?'

'I don't know.' *Yes*, she'd said to him, that night in London, pretending that Tom didn't exist. 'Maybe everyone is. A bit.' Perhaps love was always mixed, traces of other people you'd been in love with, a cocktail, like the ones the flappers drank.

He wasn't listening to her. 'I was doing well, getting free of you. And then you turn up in New York. I think – well, here she is, perhaps we can begin. But then I find you've been here for ages and I know you are here because you want something.'

'No. I just – I just want to be friends again.'

'That's not true. Why did you really come to America? Was your man an American soldier and you've come here for him?'

Her head whirled. She was on the edge, her feet either side of the fall. She could do one of two things. She could throw herself forwards, tell him she loved him, too, that it had all been a misunderstanding, that she wanted to try together. When she was sure, she'd tell him about Michael and he would be kind to her, say it was in the past – and he was right, it would be, since Mrs Whetstone would never let her have him. Or she could tell him the truth now and the whole house of cards might come tumbling over her.

She felt the air speed past her. Time waited.

'I had a baby. After the war. I came here to look for him.'

'A what? A baby?' He stared at her and then he began to stammer something.

She shook her head. 'Not yours.' How much easier if it had been. Jonathan would never have allowed his child to be taken away. He'd have got solicitors and policemen, the full force of his money and power.

'Whose was it?' She saw his mind working. 'When?'

'After the war.'

'So, after we met in London, went out. But before the trial.'

She nodded, miserably. She hadn't told him there had been a

man before. They had been so caught up talking about the trial, it had seemed such a big thing, so much bigger than anything else, nothing else seemed to matter.

'Who was the father?'

She couldn't get the words out. 'I don't know. It was after the war.'

'Did he take advantage of you?' Jonathan's voice was softer. She wanted to catch it, hold on to it, the tone of a man who cared. She wanted to agree with him, so the softness didn't stop. But she had to tell the truth.

'No. I probably persuaded him.'

Jonathan raised his eyebrows. 'You didn't tell me before. I suppose your family don't know either.'

She shook her head. 'They know. I had him. They gave him away, told me he'd died.' She should stop there; she could see it in his face. But she rushed on. 'When I found out it was a lie, I tracked him down in America, I tried to see him but they sent me away. I've lost him forever.'

There was silence. Jonathan looked at the globe.

'And this man. You aren't trying to find him?'

'He never loved me. He would never want me.'

'But you don't love him?'

She couldn't speak. She couldn't tell him the whole truth, tell him it was Tom.

He gazed back at the globe. 'So you adore your family, who took your son from you. You forgive them. And you maybe love this man who deserted you. But not me.'

'I'm sorry. I did. I do! I just. I'm confused. My mind was caught up in finding Michael. I should have telephoned you. If only I could turn back the clock.'

'You called him Michael?'

She saw his face change and she thought he too was remembering her brother, young with him at Cambridge, before the war. He shook his head. 'How we miss him.' And then his eyes were cool once more.

'And you're here with Arthur. After helping him dodge his—'

'He didn't do it!'

He shrugged. 'Whatever the truth is. Anyway, you should go. Before my father returns. I'll ask them to call you a cab.'

'Will I see you again?'

'I don't know. I need to think. This – I didn't expect any of it.'

'You think less of me for having a child.'

'No! I'm not that sort of man. Or I thought I wasn't. Those men who take as many girls as they want but expect their wives to be pure are hypocrites.'

'I'll be at the hotel. If you want to write.'

'Celia. I need time to think.'

She stood still, watched him as he left the room. She stared at the back of the door. She couldn't move. She was like a broken plate after you'd balanced all the pieces together – and then, if you moved it a tiny spot, they'd all fall and shatter and nothing would be left.

INTERLUDE

Lily had decided what the answer was. She needed a friend. All girls her age had friends. After all, she was nearly ten now! In every book she read, little girls had friends. They told each other secrets, wrote letters to each other, it was the *two of us against the world*. They spent hours together. And she had no one. Albert wasn't interested in her, he only wanted to make trains and engines and read books about them. It was strange how people called them 'the twins' as if they were two parts of the same person, when Albert and she seemed so very different!

It was typical of Mama to not understand. She'd never have any friends and if Lily ever asked, Mama just said she didn't want any. She said her family and Papa were enough. Papa, of course, before he went away, used to have dozens of friends, always coming over to talk, all day, all night. That was going too far. She wasn't going to be a girl who had too many friends so that she could never go to sleep.

She just wanted *one* friend. One little girl. At night, she lay awake and dreamt about her. She called her all sorts of names: Jenny, Sarah, Ruby, Rose. She had their story entirely worked out. She would meet her in the square where she and Albert were sent to run around and get their exercise while Emmeline watched from above. Usually, the square was deserted, but this time, there would be a little girl there, alone too. And they'd look at each other shyly, walk towards each other. They'd talk. And then every day, they'd meet up. She'd give Ruby a bracelet made of beads that she'd taken from one of Mama's broken necklaces (she had so many broken necklaces. She should really throw them away, you could never fix them now and they were years old). Ruby smiled and then next day bought her a card that she'd coloured and made herself, a pin-and-red heart with flowers around it.

Best friends forever.

She clutched the soft purple cat that Papa had made for her, trying to show how even men could sew. It had tiny holes in the mouth so the stuffing escaped. She loved it, though, even though it was worn, made her wishes on its gentle cloth face.

She said it to Papa, but he wasn't really listening. 'I have to have a best friend! Maybe if I went to school?' A proper school with other girls, rather than the boring room in Mrs Kinle's house where she and Albert learnt history and wrote out sentences that never started with And or But.

'School is repressive,' he said. 'It teaches children to obey, be factory cogs in the wheel.'

Mama said that female friends were a waste of time. 'Mine all stopped being friends with me when the war broke out and everyone said we were German.'

They didn't understand. But Mama once had friends. And if you didn't have a best friend, then you had no one to practice being in love on and *you would never have a husband.*

Lily didn't care what her parents thought. She was going to find a friend. She had to save herself.

ELEVEN

Red bit into one of the apples. 'Why are you interested in that rich house up near the park?' After a week of waiting, he had finally come. She'd asked him if he'd heard that there had been any report to the police of the break-in and he said he thought not. He barely even seemed to remember it. He had a new pullover another boy had grown too big for, red and yellow with holes on the shoulder. It suited him, made him look like a small, bright elf.

'What?'

'That rich house near the park. Why do you stand outside?'

Celia shook her head. 'I can't hide anything, can I?'

'I just wondered what you were looking for. Do they owe you money?'

'That's where my little boy is.' She shook her head. 'The address you found. I'm looking for something I can't ever have.'

'I can get it for you, Miss. I got the files, didn't I? I can get *anything* for you.' He took a huge bite of the apple. 'You don't know what I can do.'

'I told the woman that he had been mine. I only wanted to see him.'

He nodded, chewed on the apple. 'So let's go and get him for you.'

'No, no. We can't do that. It would be a crime. We can't kidnap him. He's theirs. I just want to see him. And how can you do that?'

It was ridiculous, placing her faith in a child. He couldn't help her. He had enough problems, surely.

'I just want to see him. That's all I want.'

He patted his head. 'I'll be back when I can.' He picked up the bag of food. 'Any more smokers?' he tried.

He raised his eyebrows and jumped up onto the bin lid.

She watched his legs disappear upwards and then he was gone.

Two nights later, he was back.

'I told you I'd find an answer! We've worked out how to get onto his house and through his window.' He wagged his finger. 'One of us – Jamie – he got in through another window and managed to get round and get the key for your little boy's. He has opened it up so we can push through. But it's only time before they find out and lock it again. So we need to move fast.'

'We?'

He blew out smoke. 'You're coming with me! Tonight. You need to climb through that window, Miss!'

'Climb through the window? But I can't.'

'Yes you can. You ladies! Then you can see him and talk to him, well you'll have to wake him up first. We'll stand guard.'

'I can't go into his room in the middle of the night! He'll be afraid.'

'Jamie said you should just say you're an angel or something. Then the parents won't know.'

'Say I am an angel?' Her mind was reeling. 'I—'

He put down the cigarette she'd given him. 'Don't you like our answer, Miss?' His face looked hurt. 'We've been working it out.'

Her heart rushed. 'No – no. I like it! I just worry that – we'll get caught. We all might. And you've found me the address. You don't need to do more.'

He blew out more smoke. 'Oh no, Miss. The decision is made now. We are helping you. No going back.' He patted her hand. 'None of you ground people has ever done anything kind for us, you know. They just shoo us away, usually. Come on, Miss, no more talking. Let's go. I'll see you there.'

And then she was in a cab to Upper Eighty-Seventh Street ready to meet him there. She clambered out and waited. It was only ten minutes or so before she heard a whistle and looked up to see Red surrounded by five or six shadowy figures, little boys too. In a moment, they were clambering down the side of the building, jumping next to her. 'Hello, Miss,' hissed Red. 'This is Jamie.' He waved at a bigger boy. 'And the rest I'll tell you later. Come on! They're all asleep.'

She followed them. 'I can't climb up there,' she said, flatly. 'I just can't.'

'Easy,' said Red. 'Easy measy. Just follow me. There's a staircase at the back.'

They walked around and then she was at the back of the house and being pushed up to get onto an iron flight of stairs. She clambered up, watched Red pulling himself up onto the window ledges above her. When she got to the top, he reached down for her. 'I can't climb on the ledges,' she hissed, but already Jamie was pushing her up and she was balancing on someone's iron balcony; then Red was tugging her hand and she was being pulled up, feet flailing onto another. *Don't look down.*

'Up there,' hissed Red. She gazed up, and one storey above was a window, slightly open. He nodded. 'There you go.' She hoped he was right, was too dizzy to count.

He jumped up ahead of her and perched on the sill. She heard the traffic behind her, the sound of someone drunkenly shouting maybe a few streets along. She could never get her feet on such a narrow piece of wood. It was impossible.

'You won't fall,' whispered Jamie behind her, as if reading her mind. 'We'll catch you.'

'I don't know.'

'Go on,' whispered another boy. 'We can't wait around.' And so she had to. She had to push herself up and try somehow to manoeuvre her foot onto the ledge, as Jamie pushed her from behind and Red held her hands on the ledge to steady her. He reached across, nimbly, caught her and hauled her up by the waist. It felt strange to have the child's hands on her, holding her close on the ledge. He was bearing her weight, she couldn't help it, felt too dizzy to hold herself up. The curtains were closed, she couldn't see in and yet behind that window was Michael. Or Sebastian. He was there. 'You've got the right window, yes?' she hissed.

'Hope so.'

If they hadn't, she hoped they would burst in on a maid or a store room – rather than Mrs Whetstone.

He shuffled her along, opened the window to his side, pulled it out. 'Through you go. Lucky you're not fat, Miss.'

He pulled her hand and she bent and ducked and balanced herself and then she was pushing through thick material and putting one leg down on the other side of the window. The ledge was hard on the back of her legs as she put down the other foot.

A room, darkened. Not large – it might be a maid's room. Her eyes adjusted to the lack of light. Shadowy shapes, a chest of drawers, a chair. Not much else. Any toys must be all packed away. She looked across to the single bed. There was a figure under the covers, hunched up in a ball. It had to be him. Michael. She moved across the room, tiptoeing, reached the bed. The figure didn't stir. She bent down, her hand hovering over the covers. And then the figure sighed, turned onto his back and she looked at his face. Pale skin, long eyelashes, round cheeks, dark hair over his forehead. Small nose, large forehead. She had imagined him, thought of his face so many times. She'd searched for him in the faces of different children. He hadn't looked like this – not quite. She'd imagined him blonder, more ruddy, thick hair. His was fine, looked as if it would feel shiny if you even touched it, his skin looked delicate too, would go red with wind, rain, show up embarrassment, emotion. Skin like hers. He was biting his lip in his sleep, small white teeth. He sighed. He looked so tranquil. She could hardly bear to wake him. And what if she did and she scared him? He might scream – he surely *would* scream. And then he'd wake everybody.

She wished she could just sit by him, watch him sleep. She'd engrave the contours of his face onto her mind. She'd never forget him. She'd come back every night, sit by him until morning. But she couldn't, of course not, she couldn't ask Red to spend every night helping her – he had business to attend to, whatever that was. It would be impossible to get into the window without him.

She knelt by his side, reached her hand out for his forehead. She extended a finger, touched. His eyelids fluttered a little. She put the fingertip on his forehead, warm to the touch, fine as she had thought. *Hold yourself back.* She wanted to seize him up, never let him go. 'Michael,' she whispered. He didn't stir.

'I love you,' she whispered. Maybe he would hear it in his dreams.

She couldn't pretend to be an angel. Ridiculous. Angels didn't wear navy day dresses and sensible boots. You couldn't touch them and feel flesh. She reached for his hand on the coverlet. The fingers clenched back, lightly, as if they were truly holding hands and her soul soared. He knew her. Even in his dreams, he knew her. He let go of her hand, turned over.

She couldn't wake him. It would be too much for him. She turned, gazed around the room. No toys, as she had thought. No toys on the bed, not even a bear, so fashionable because boys could have them as well as girls. It could be anybody's room, she thought, nothing there to indicate it was a child's. *Is he happy?* Her words to Edward by the Whetstones' elevator filled her soul with dread.

There was a shuffle, a movement. She turned back.

And then he was turning over again and his arms moved, his hands up in the air. He was breathing faster, harder. He was beginning to sigh. He was moving, tossing, then crying out. 'Stop it!' She turned to him, couldn't stop herself, put her arms around him. She held him close. He cried. 'Sssh. Don't cry. You're safe. Don't cry.' His warm body against hers, his hair under her hands. She held him close. Her child. She wanted to call him by name, held herself back. His blue pyjamas were threadbare, nails unkempt but all of him was true. He was *real*. She stroked his hair. He was still mostly asleep, his eyes fluttering. She willed him to wake. To see her. Her soul catapulted, afraid again that he would wake up and scream. She rocked him, back and forth. *Don't cry.* Although it was she who wanted to cry, weep for all those days missing, the days and nights she would have done this for him, when he was ill or sad, toothache or nightmares.

'Do you have many nightmares?' she whispered.

And then his eyes opened and he looked up. Her heart skipped. She froze.

He blinked, opened his mouth. She felt her hands on him grow slack. Her heart filled with dread.

He blinked again. 'Who are you?'

She wasn't an angel. Of course she wasn't an angel. Her heart, blood was beating as she held him close. She gazed down into his beautiful brown eyes. Not her eyes. Maybe Tom's. She couldn't bear to think about it. They were beautiful, whatever they were, whosever they were.

'I'm—' she stopped.

'Are you a new maid?' His voice. Once she had heard him speak, *how could she ever leave him*? His voice was curiously high, clear, a little like Michael's had been when they were children.

'Yes! Yes I am. I'm the new maid.'

'Oh.' He settled back into her arms, close to her. Their warmth, the two bodies. They might be one. *I am your mother*, she willed through, wouldn't say it.

He sat away again, opened his eyes. 'Is your room up here?'

Was he on the same floor as the maids? 'Er. Yes.'

'You must be very new. You know you're not supposed to come in to me when I'm crying or having a nightmare.'

Jamie's voice at the window. 'Miss. We need to go.' But she couldn't.

She didn't think he'd heard it. She squeezed him close. 'I think children should be held.'

'Well, Mother says it's fine for my brothers and sisters to be held. They're strong. But I'm weak and I need to learn. The first time I cried all night. But I've got used to it now.' He was sitting up, talkative now. 'I wish I had a doll or something but mother says they make me weak too.'

'And the others?'

'Well, they're different. They're naturally strong!'

84

'Ah.' Her heart was swelling, blood rising.

'Miss!'

There was a step outside the door. 'Sebastian?' A woman's voice. She looked at him in panic. He pointed to the area under the bed and she scrambled down, slid herself under, pushed to the side near the wall. She saw feet visible through the gap at the bottom of the door.

'Shouting in your sleep again? What is wrong with you?' Mercifully, they stopped and didn't come in.

Then Jamie was in the room and he was grasping her. 'We need to go. Now!'

She reached behind to Michael. 'Come with us!' He looked at her in shock. 'Please.'

He was staring at the child behind her, his face terrified. 'Who are they?'

'My friends. Come with us.'

He began to back away from her. 'Who are you?'

The fear on his face broke her heart. 'Please, we want to help you,' she said.

'Come with us. I promise we'll look after you. They aren't kind to you here, are they?'

'No.' But she saw it in his face. It was all he knew.

He shook his head. 'I can't. I live here.' She couldn't lift him, even if he'd wanted to let her. Her heart was wrenching. Quickly, she took the toy horse from her pocket and thrust it into his hand. He clutched it, barely looking, staring into her eyes.

'Please! Please come.'

He wouldn't. He couldn't. He loved them. Probably despite everything, no matter what they did to him, he loved them. The woman was shouting for someone else to come up. Michael's face was terrified. Jamie grasped her and she scrambled out. 'I'll come back!' she said. And then Jamie was pulling her out and she was running down the staircase and they were all hurtling along the street.

TWELVE

Manhattan, April 1929

How could she have been so stupid? She had put him in such danger. He could be beaten, punished. All because of her. Back at the hotel, she'd given Red the food she had and all the money in her purse.

A feeling seized her, washed over her, emotions pulling at her. 'Come and live with me. I'm not like the others. I can look after you. You can even go off wandering if you like. I won't stop you. I won't make you do anything. I just – it's not safe out here. Someone could kill you. Bring Jamie too, if you like.'

Red reached down, patted her hand. 'That's very kind of you, Miss,' he said, indulgent. 'But we like things this way. We know you're different. But other adults might make you send us to school and all the rest of it.'

'But what if you get ill? And it's dangerous here.'

He grinned through a mouthful of chocolate. 'Why don't you come and live with us? You're a good climber. We could teach you. Once you've lived outside, you'll never go back.'

'I can't.'

'Like I said. Adults are afraid.'

It was true. 'Wait. I have something in my room. I bought it for Michael – but – I'd like you to have it. It's a toy farm.'

He shrugged, looked pleased. 'I've never had a toy.'

She hurried inside, ran upstairs, took the farm out of the wardrobe, took it back down, wrapped in a shawl. Red opened it up, looked quizzical.

'What do we do with this?'

'You play with it.'

He cocked his head. 'I don't think we'd have time for that.'

'At least – take a few animals. Please. For me.'

'If you like, Miss.' He picked over, selected horses, pigs and the farm dog, lifted them up high, inspected them. 'These are swell.'

'Please take them. And the money. And if you ever need me – here's my home address, if I'm not here, you can write to England. Or ask your friend who can write. If you're ever in trouble, I can help.'

He grinned. 'We never get in trouble. That's for you adults! I'll take it though. Maybe I'll learn to read one of these days.' He tapped his head. 'I'll see you again, Miss. I can almost guarantee it.' He scratched his nose. 'Fate. That's what this is. It's fate. I might tap on your room one day. You'd better watch out!'

'Would you go and check on my little boy, from time to time? And maybe tell me? Or don't tell me. Just see he's all right?'

'I'll do it. I'll see what I can do.'

'Thank you. Come down. Please.' He clambered down from the bin and she hugged him hard. He wriggled out, laughed. 'Must run! Goodbye, Miss!' And then he was gone.

That night her mind was restless, visions of Michael, cruelly beaten, crying out for help. How wrong she had been. She'd ruined things for him and made his life worse, perhaps nearly unbearable – all from her own desires. Or perhaps seeing her, being held by her, the offer of friendship, of coming with them had been a help. At least he knew that someone liked him, wanted him.

But still, she thought. She should have left him alone.

She turned her head into her pillow. How could it hurt so much? And this wasn't like death, the pain she'd felt at the loss of her brother. This wasn't wartime, it was peace. She wept for him, for everything, for her own love for him and because it was hopeless, there was nothing she could do.

*

87

The next three days were busy with Flapper Foods, looking at advertising, the arrangements for the kitchen, looking over the lists for suppliers. Celia threw herself into it so Arthur wouldn't suspect the anguish inside. The photographs were being made up into advertisements. They interviewed six cooks and chose a Miss Salm, who had trained at a cookery school in New Jersey and was working in a department store restaurant – but had so many ideas for her own recipes that Celia fell in love with her on the spot.

'Once you've been here a month or so and we have the recipes, you might start recruiting the under-cooks. We need six or so to help you, I think.'

She had three orders – from Macy's and Bloomingdale's and Bergdorf's – as soon as they were ready, they wanted a display of cans and jars. Mr Goodman had been first and once she had told the rest that Bergdorf's had agreed, all the others wanted the same. Four more were considering the numbers.

She checked at the desk for messages – from Jonathan, Violet, even from her family. Nothing. She didn't allow herself to hope for anything from the Whetstones. She wondered after Albert and Lily, Lily particularly, missed her sweet smile, laughter. She wrote to her sister, asking if Mr Janus had stopped talking about Spain, and saying how well Arthur was doing. She even wrote to her parents at last. *We both like New York*, she said. The words felt stiff and hard. She couldn't help it. She couldn't help but blame them for Michael's cruel situation. She longed to go to Miss Bellenden and shout, 'Look what you have done! You said he'd be in a happy place. Loved. Wanted! That you shouldn't disturb him because he was settled. But you gave him to these cruel people.'

Why had they taken him if they hated him so much? Maybe they had thought they couldn't have children and when they did, preferred their own. Or he didn't turn out as they thought. She didn't know. But she prayed and she wished and she begged any god she could think of, even though she knew it wouldn't do any good.

The burgeoning business couldn't fill the void inside her. After a week, Celia went to the local church. 'I'm here for a few months,' she said to the weary-looking priest, Father Crisp, after finding him in his office. 'Maybe longer. I want to help. I wonder if I might help with children.' He relented, eventually, sent her off to the Sunday school attached to the orphanage, where a Miss Breadker told her to start cutting up triangles of blue for the children to use to make pictures of the Virgin Mary. When they finally let her play with the children, she was immediately struck by one little boy, Ethan, red-haired, big blue eyes, about eight or so, she thought. Their heads were bowed. Except him. He gave her a giant smile and winked – boldly. She almost jumped. He was skinny like the rest of them, but unlike them, he was sparking with energy, his limbs fizzing. He couldn't sit still, always jiggling his leg or wiggling his hand. She smiled at him and he grinned back. When she went around to help them cut out paper, he gave her another great smile. 'Where are you from, Miss? My family are from Ireland. Have you ever been?'

'Not yet.'

'If you go, will you take me?'

Miss Breadker looked on disapprovingly.

'They've got pixies in the hills.'

'Ethan!' Miss Breadker looked positively shocked.

'If I plan a visit, I'll let you know,' Celia whispered into his ear.

Miss Breadker had told her that the children's names weren't their own, they were re-named when they arrived at the orphanage. 'New name, new life,' she said. Celia wondered if Ethan or any of them might know their real name – whether they kept it at the back of their minds, to hold on to, return to. Or whether it meant nothing to them, just another word given to them by parents who had died, left them, not cared enough, just another of the many names they might have, along the way.

Michael stayed hidden in her heart, waiting for her – and when she came out of the door of the orphanage, he came back to the fore and she could think of nothing but him.

*

Over the next days and weeks and months, Celia tried to devote herself to Flapper Foods. Miss Salm and the cooks she had hired created the recipes, and Celia costed each of them. She and Miss Salm spent two days trying to perfect the tying of the red bow at the front of each jar, throwing away yards of ribbon after they'd tried and failed to get the bow exactly correct. They created a whole range – six savoury, six sweet – and packaged them up into the jars. Celia bought a new suit and took them to show to the bankers. They smiled and nodded and signed off more money. The third bank even brought out forbidden champagne to share. She sipped at the yellow liquid, honeyed, sweet, felt the bubbles dance down her throat. She interviewed companies about creating packaging, looked at designs for labels, debated whether they should feature flapper girls or hats or flowers. They made final plans for the advertising and the competition. On one walk back from the kitchen, after a particularly rewarding day in which all the biscuits in the latest recipe had been perfect, she looked up at the New York skyline and thought, Why not do more? Why spend so much time on charming Macy's and Bergdorf's when she could simply have her own shop?

She went for another meeting with the bankers two days later, sketched out her plans. She conjured visions of starting with a small food shop in an exclusive part of town. A grand opening with actresses smiling and girls dancing. Then stores across America. Chicago. Los Angeles. Detroit. The man in charge nodded.

'Quite so, Miss Witt. The female shopper is the engine of our modern economy. If Flapper Foods does well, after six months, we will invest in a store.'

Celia's mind circled the business all day and at night she dreamt of shelves and jars and shop windows and the Flapper Foods Girl up in lights.

She advertised for salesgirls, interviewed ten and chose two, Betty and Mary-Anne. Betty was pretty, dark hair, red lips, pale skin, a fast-talking Snow White from Brooklyn, had sold furniture from a warehouse before, loved food, was fun and young and could be a flapper girl herself. She told Celia that she never let a sale get away. Mary-Anne was fair, taller, quieter, from Connecticut, just moved to New York, had been to teacher-training college and worked in a dress shop in New Haven. She was the type to send to the subtler stores, because she seemed quiet, but once she began talking, she didn't stop, she wove you in and her eyes were so bright and engaged, you just wanted to agree and buy anything she offered. Celia took them to meet Miss Salm, go over the products and they packed up two cases, sample jars, tied with bows, a few boxes, jars of puddings and stew. They would start with the New York shops and then move out of Manhattan, to the stores in Brooklyn and Queens, and then past into New Jersey and Connecticut. Celia gave them the money to buy three new suits and hats, agreed the salary, said she'd go with them to the biggest stores like Bergdorf's and Macy's – but all the others would be soft clay in their perfect hands. Once they'd sold into a few shops, she'd advertise again and they could interview the next girls, to see who they'd most like to work with them.

Outside of the business, she continued at the orphanage Sunday school and tried not to favour Ethan too much, although she did give him extra sweets, found herself listening to his readings for longer than the others. She read the newspapers in the hotel lobby and scoured them first for news of the break-in at Bellenden's and then for news from Europe, although there didn't seem to be much. Every day was a fight not to walk up to the Whetstones' house.

'We need to do more with our money,' Arthur said to her, on the way back to the hotel. He grasped her hand. 'After all our work. We're making a lot now.' He had accompanied her to see Miss Salm, talked to Betty and Mary-Anne. Her happiness dropped a little, watching him smile at Betty and listen to her talk – then she chastised herself as a poor sister. He was just friendly to women, nothing more.

'We haven't got much of it. Not yet.' They had paid for everything so far – but the big tranches would come when they needed to go into proper production, hire factories and dozens of girls. 'Once we have some more orders, then we'll have more money.' Her mind was dizzied, sometimes, by the amounts they needed, bags and bags of sugar, hundreds of chickens, great piles of potatoes, as if they were feeding a king and his giant Tudor court.

Arthur put his arm through hers. 'But don't you think it's a waste, just leaving it in the bank?'

Having his arm so close to her was comforting. 'How do you mean?'

'Property. All the money's in Florida. It's a gold mine there. If we don't invest now, we're missing our chance.' And Arthur conjured up Florida as they walked along, money there for the taking, houses and land so cheap, it would double, triple in price within a year or so. America was on fire and Florida was the burning coal, pure energy, pure money. Florida was the place that bred money, created money, where there were dollars on the sun-baked trees, falling from the ever-blue sky. He talked and talked and she was swept up in it, all his words, the girls on the billboards in swimsuits smiling with their bright teeth, the houses reflecting the white light of the sun.

'Well, maybe,' she found herself saying. Because why would you want to miss out? You couldn't fail to make money! There didn't seem to be much interest in Winter Meats any more and the banks wouldn't fund it. This could be Arthur's new focus. 'Maybe we could pledge some of the money.'

Arthur caught her up in his arms. 'My brilliant sister!' he said. 'I knew you'd have the right idea!'

It was America. Investing in America. It was the land of the future.

And then Arthur caught hold of a lamppost and swung himself around it. Celia laughed, smiling. Her old Arthur back again.

'I think we should go to a ball!'

'A what?'

She hadn't been out in the evening since that night after his trial. The night where they'd been sitting around a table in the

Ritz and Rudolf had started talking about America. Then she'd understood about Michael.

'I didn't just come here to make a business. I came here to find a wife.'

Of course. He'd talked about it before, but she had put it out of her mind. Blood rushed to her head with Jonathan's words, murder, Louisa. She pushed them away. It had been an accident. Arthur deserved happiness like anybody else.

'I don't think a ball is really me.'

'Come on, sister. Imagine you're in a book, one of those ones you're always reading. Just see yourself as regarding it all with the eye of an observer. I want to meet a pleasant girl, someone I can talk to. And I've read there's a Vanderbilt girl who is free.'

'Oh excellent.'

'Look, it would do you good to get out. You're sitting here, thinking about that child and you'll never find him.'

'No.'

'So it's a yes, then.' He caught her up, drew her to him. 'Thank you, Sis! You won't regret it.'

'Just once!' she said. 'That's all.' She didn't want him to marry. Louisa seemed like yesterday.

'Splendid! I'll pay for the gown. Will you be ready enough for tomorrow night?'

'Tomorrow night?'

'No time like the present! Buy whatever you want.' He laughed, jumped towards a door.

'I'll need days!' she called, trying to laugh. But he'd gone, the door closed behind him.

'Is this the set of a play?' Celia whispered to Arthur. 'It doesn't look real.' They were walking up the stairs to the ball, through palm trees in pots on the stairs, strung with what looked like diamonds. The chandelier glittered above them. They'd arrived in a cab at the door of the great brownstone house on the park to see dozens of people queueing at the door in front of them; ladies in fur stoles and long, glittering cloaks, gentlemen in white tie.

Celia watched the women kiss each other and chatter ahead, all of them like jewels, rubies, amethysts, emeralds jostling together on a crown. A few had ankle-length gowns but most were long, trailing nearly to the feet, you'd almost think you were in pre-war times – until they turned around and you saw the bodices were cut very low or so close that they couldn't possibly be wearing a corset or even any underwear at all. Celia's dark-green dress was calf length – the dressmaker had told her it was all the fashion. But she was completely wrong, she knew it while she watched the women-jewels wait to glide in the door, hand their stoles to the waiting servants in the hall.

'Don't twitch, Celia,' Arthur said, as they walked up the stairs. 'People can see.'

He was right, she was being excessively nervous. After all, she wasn't going to dance. She wasn't looking for a husband, on show, proving herself to a dragon-like mamma. She was accompanying Arthur, she'd sit quietly with all the chaperones, enjoy the music. The only thing she had to do was not stand out. And since her dress was darker and plainer than everyone else's – and far too informal, she had no jewels and her hair was thin and looked barely styled, even though she'd spent three hours at the hairdresser – she was hardly rivalling anyone for fashion. She would watch the others, sitting in the background. Arthur had been clever, said the right thing to her: she liked the idea of being an observer, watching, keeping the secrets.

'You never had a coming out ball, did you? I suppose you never wanted one.'

'I suppose I didn't.' She'd never had the choice, of course, the war had come and by the time it was over, no one wanted coming out balls. There were no men, for a start.

'Father could have set you one up. After the war. It seems rather a rum deal you missed out. Surely he could have found the money.' Celia remembered Emmeline's; watching the guests arrive from her position at the top of the stairs, too young to go. Laughing young men, beautiful girls. Her sister the handsomest of them all. She'd watched her dancing with Sir Hugh, her eyes shining.

'You forget, Arthur. Everyone hated us then. The village wouldn't even come to our summer party. Who'd come to a ball for a *German*?'

They passed a giant arrangement of flowers, the perfume so strong that it almost knocked Celia back. 'Now come along, Celia. Smile.'

Celia did so, a bright, painted smile, and faced the ballroom. She felt as if she was looking at a great body of water, a wave of colour, blue, red, green gowns, all coming forth for her. A thousand people, it seemed, pretty women, tall men, dancing, waltzing, giant arrangements of flowers, waiters with trays of delicate glasses, giant silver bowls of drink, a table of cakes and biscuits and enough space for the fine meal to come later. 'Isn't it lovely?' said Arthur, and in a moment, he was gone. Celia gazed around, dizzily, and saw a row of older women sitting straight backed against the far wall. She started over there, dodging dancing couples, waiters and young men who already looked drunk. There was a spare chair at the end of the row. She smiled at the woman next to it and got a quizzical look in return. She sat down, carefully, steadied her head, looked up. Everyone seemed to know each other, all caught up in dancing and celebrating, kissing and talking. She watched a young couple just in front of her, dancing, gazing into each other's eyes.

The women next to her had begun to talk. Another woman, tall and rather plump, came over and stood as they continued the conversation. She threw Celia glances. Then Celia realised that they were all looking at her. She was in the way, not welcome. She stood up and the woman hastily took her chair, without smiling. They bent their heads together. She stood there against the wall, alone. She couldn't even see Arthur. But of course, she said to herself, of course – these people have known each other from childhood. It takes time to be accepted.

She leant against the wall, watched the dancing. Circling,

swirling, dancing, hundreds and hundreds of them. She wondered how Arthur would even discover who the really rich ones were.

'Do you mind?' said the woman who had taken her place. Celia looked back. 'I said, do you mind?'

They were all staring at her now. Celia looked back, unsure.

'I said, do you mind? We're trying to talk here.'

Five faces, beautifully coiffed, necks hung with diamonds, all looking at her with hostility. Celia shrank back. 'I'm sorry,' she began. But then she thought better of it. Why should she apologise? She turned her back and walked away from them, into the dancers. But as she did so, she realised she had no idea where to go. The other wall had a line of sitting women. They probably wouldn't want her either. The only women standing were those near the table, waiting to be asked to dance, pausing between waltzes. Everywhere else she saw men, lounging by the table of food, clustering by the bowls of punch. Or, at least, she supposed it was drink. The police would never come and raid somewhere like this – she supposed it counted as drinking at home. She stood and watched, but no women came to collect a glassful.

She had nowhere to stand, no one to talk to. She stepped forward – and as she did so, a dancing couple moved forwards and hit into her. She fell with them, a tangle of legs and arms, the girl's skirt on the floor. 'What the hell do you think you're doing?' said the man, furiously. *I'm hurt too*, Celia wanted to cry. The man gathered the girl up, delighted, Celia supposed, to look like a rescuer. The couples were stepping and dancing around them. 'You've ruined the whole dance,' he said. 'Look!' Celia lifted her eyes and saw all the couples staring at her as they circled. Someone laughed.

'Oh, Emmanuel,' the young woman breathed, clutching his chest, tears glimmering on her perfect, delicate cheek. 'I think I've hurt my ankle.'

'I'm talking to you,' Emmanuel said to Celia. 'What the hell do you think you're doing?'

Celia was about to answer. The words were there, waiting in her mouth. And then the room was turning and shooting and there were a thousand gowns whirling, people looking, waiters standing, faces, eyes gazing. She couldn't bear it. She pushed through the dancers, a crowd of men, new couples coming through the door, ignoring the shouts, the gasps. She flung out of the light onto the stairs, shoved through the couples coming up, threw herself past the flower arrangement, dived down the stairs and through the last block – a group of men in deep conversation by the door. There were laughs and shouts of 'Stop running, girl!' She ignored them, jumped out into the cool air. The clusters of manservants and drivers leaning by the cars stared at her in shock. She turned away from them, picked up her gown again and began running down Fifth Avenue.

Celia burst into the hotel, her hair falling around her face, her bodice stuck to her with perspiration. She meant to scurry through the lobby as quickly as she could, dive into her room. Three or four couples walking through the lobby stared at her.

'Miss Witt.' It was Frederick, the dark-haired concierge, calling to her across the hall.

'I feel rather unwell, Frederick. I really must go to bed.'

'There's someone waiting for you, Miss Witt. He was very insistent that I tell you he was here. He's in the restaurant.'

'For me? This late? It must be some mistake.'

'He was very insistent, as I say, Miss. The minute you got in, we must tell you that he was here. He is a Mr Crogan.'

'I don't know any Mr Crogan.' But the couples were staring at her. 'All right, Frederick. I'll see him.'

He ushered her to the restaurant. The lights were still on. He opened the door – and Jonathan stood up.

'Celia,' he said. There was a half-drunk cup of coffee in front of him. There was a flurry of a breeze as Frederick left, closed the door behind him.

She gazed at Jonathan, feeling the sweat on her bodice cool uncomfortably on her skin. She felt painfully self-conscious, untidy, no coat, emerald dress covered in street dirt. She held her hand up to her straggled hair. 'I went to a ball,' she said. She meant to say that she felt ill, had to leave – but then she looked at his face and couldn't lie. 'I hated it. I bumped into someone and they shouted at me. So I ran away.'

Jonathan gave a small smile. 'Still running away.' His face was swollen, his eyes red.

'How... are you?' She couldn't think. His last words rang in her mind. She had resigned herself to never seeing him again.

He stood up. 'I had to see you. I thought it would be easier if I told you I wouldn't see you again. But it wasn't. I couldn't stop thinking about you.'

She looked at him, the expanse of restaurant behind him. Her mind was muddled, on fire. She tried to speak. The words wouldn't come.

'I was unfair to you, Celia. I wish you'd contacted me. I was hurt. But I can't let pride stop me. Like you say. We were friends.'

'But – I—' She couldn't say it. The words were lost, somewhere in the back of her mind.

'I'll help you, if you still want me to. To find this child, I mean. If you'll accept my help. I understand that you must have been thinking about him. And I think of how hard it must have been to have lost him. You should have told me before. I could have – well, we could have talked about it.'

She leant her hands on the chair. Her head was dizzy.

'I think I've lost him for good.' But perhaps Jonathan could help, had another idea.

'Sorry, Celia. This is probably too much to take in. I don't mean to cause you even more pain. I just had to see you. I'll go. I've made things difficult for you. I can see that.'

He started to walk. As he passed her, she grasped his hand. She felt it, the rough whorls of the fingers.

'Don't go,' she said. 'Stay.'

His eyes were on fire, his face sparked gold.

He tightened his grasp on her hand, suggested they walk out, get some air, and she agreed. They'd walked out into the street, his arm in hers. Frederick had looked oddly at her but she'd ignored him. He's my cousin, she was ready to say, but he didn't ask.

'I'm sorry I didn't ring you up.'

The city was going to sleep around them, cab drivers on their way home, men sweeping the pavements, workers from the diners setting off home to Queens or Brooklyn.

'I spoke out of anger. I didn't mean what I said.'

She nodded.

'Let's be friends again,' he said. 'Can you forgive me?'

'Of course,' she said. 'There's nothing to forgive.'

They had been so out of time, the one wanting to forgive the other when the other didn't want to forgive, and it was almost amazing they had managed to coincide, rather than go on for years, back and forth.

'You look thoughtful.'

'I expect I'll be in a lot of trouble with Arthur. I rather wrecked his ball.'

'Him.' Jonathan held her arm tightly. 'You need to stay away from him.'

'He's my brother! He wanted to make an impression at the ball. He's trying to find a rich wife.' She was trying to put it out of her mind, how they had clasped each other before Arthur's trial, in his hotel room, holding on to each other as if they had been shipwrecked.

Jonathan's body sharpened, she could feel it. He straightened up. 'A rich wife?'

'He's aiming high. Probably one of the girls you know in New York.' She couldn't help that stab.

'Celia. You can't let him—'

'Lower your voice!' she hissed. 'Anyway, stop it. I know what you think. I'm not listening to this. He was innocent. It was a terrible accident.'

Jonathan snorted.

'And you know more than the judge, do you?' She turned to face him, feeling her eyes blazing. 'How dare you!' she hissed, still keeping her voice down. 'He's my brother. Michael's brother. How can you treat us this way?'

Jonathan looked at the street. He came towards her. 'I'm sorry, Celia. Forget I said it. You love your brother, of course you do.'

'And you know nothing about it.' Her voice was rising, but she didn't care.

'I was at the trial. Don't you remember?'

She kept on. 'You're all the same. You made your decision. Don't you think Arthur's suffered enough? He lost his wife. People suspected him of killing her. You wouldn't say it to his face, would you? You wouldn't dare.'

Jonathan put out his hand. 'I'm sorry, Celia. Let's not – look.'

'No one dares! They all whisper behind his back at home. So it's no wonder he has to come here. At least people here can see him properly.'

The door beside them whisked open. A man poked his bald head out. 'Do you *mind*? I'll report you to the police for noise.'

Jonathan grabbed Celia's hand. He pulled her as he began to run and the two of them hurtled down the street. She started laughing despite herself as they turned the corner, breathless. Then he was laughing too, and she pulled him along and they were back at the entrance of the hotel. She stood with her back to it and laughed. He stood there, across from her, leant on the wall.

'Poor man,' she said. 'I'm in trouble. With him. With Arthur. And the hotel, probably, for wandering off with strange men. Maybe they'll tell me to leave. I've been here long enough.'

Jonathan shrugged. 'Not if you keep paying the bills.'

She smiled.

'I'm sorry I said that about Arthur. I know it upsets you.'

'But you believe it?'

He shook his head. 'Let's not discuss it. We've come this far. I don't want to argue. Let's forget it.' He held out his hand. 'We've lost so much. Let's be friends.' She felt his hand around hers. 'Are we friends?'

'Of course!'

And they were then, her heart flooded with warmth for him, her friend in New York. And they held tight to each other and it was love and forgiveness, and all the rest of it was forgotten, deep in the ground, intertwined with all the deaths and the memories. His arm around her, they stood, quietly.

THIRTEEN

Manhattan, April 1929

'I can't hear you!' She was dancing to music she'd never heard before. Jonathan had taken her to a café, the tables so close that she could barely squeeze in to sit down. The people were all around them, the women in bright colours like butterflies, all of them laughing and talking as if they had never known unhappiness in their lives.

For the last two weeks, she'd seen him nearly every day. He said he was in town for the month and had plenty of free time outside of discussions about the business with his father's manager, Mr Galss, and they'd fallen into the habit of meeting up most evenings and in the daytime too. She'd shown him the kitchen in Brooklyn, taken out the recipe descriptions, discussed the artwork on the advertising. He'd had clear ideas, useful suggestions. Jonathan took an interest, said how fascinated he was, told her that they were really onto something!

He introduced her to Mr Galss, a tall man with thick glasses and a grey suit that never seemed to crease. Mr Galss set up a meeting with a lawyer, who'd acted for the family before and she told a story fudging how she'd got Michael's address. The lawyer looked at her over his papers and Celia thought he probably didn't believe her, or at least knew there was more to it than she gave, said that she didn't have much chance of getting Michael back, but he would look into it. Jonathan took her on walks about the park, but only in the afternoon, in case anyone thought ill, he said. That made her laugh – who was here to mind about her reputation? But he insisted, courtly, protective.

He'd gone with her the first time she'd met Arthur after she'd fled the ball, at lunch at the hotel. She'd rushed into an apology.

'You can't apologise enough for that, Celia. You behaved badly.'

'I'm sorry.' The words stuck in her throat.

Arthur raised his eyebrow. 'Not that you care. I danced with a Vanderbilt girl. They're a very rich family. I have an invitation to visit next week. I told her mother that you were ill.'

So it had continued, through the meal. By the time the apple pie had arrived, Arthur relented and they changed the subject. 'What are you doing here, anyway?' he asked Jonathan, as he poured cream over the pastry.

'I came to see Celia. And business. I've been looking at investments. What's your opinion?'

That was clever. Arthur started talking about the property funds. There was no point investing in Miami any more – that was all done. But Florida. Everything was in Florida! The whole place was just one giant money-making machine.

Jonathan agreed with him. They started talking about money, hundreds, thousands, piles of it, just flowing out of Florida.

'It can't fail,' Arthur was saying. 'If I put in all our money, it still couldn't fail.'

'I agree. Mr Galss is so cautious. He won't let our family. I envy you. It's such an opportunity.'

'You're right. I'm going to do it. We're going to be rich!'

They held up their glasses and drank to it. 'To a hotel in Florida! To apartments! To the sun!'

Celia thought of them all, sitting somewhere on a beach, great hotels and houses going up behind them. Was it so easy to get rich? Celia gazed down at her drink. Why did everyone want to be rich? And then she reminded herself that someone like Violet would tell her that it was important – that otherwise you would be poor, and think about money even more. Violet would say that it was fine for Celia to be romantic about it – she'd never gone hungry.

In the days after, Jonathan and Arthur didn't get on so well. When they met up with Arthur, Jonathan was cool, sometimes even argumentative. 'I was pleasant to him for your sake,' Jonathan said. 'Once is enough.' Arthur talked about the business and Jonathan looked blankly at the table. Celia felt for Arthur, trying to tell Jonathan about his latest meeting and Jonathan looking so bored.

Jonathan shrugged when she challenged him. 'He's untrustworthy. Celia, try to look past loyalty. Your love for your family was always one of your most endearing qualities. But Arthur is untruthful and cruel at best, a—'

'Stop it!'

'A murderer at worst. You shouldn't trust him. And especially not with the business! You have really come up with an excellent idea here, Celia. It could make a lot of money.'

'I'm not listening to these lies. I'm not!' But something in her was cold, as if a thick liquid was pouring around it. 'Stop saying these things!' She stood up and Jonathan followed her, touched her arm. 'Look, Celia, I care about you! I worry that he'll take it all from you, all the money, all the credit.'

She sat down, heavy against the seat. 'He wouldn't.'

'How do you know? Has he asked you to sign anything?'

'He's talked of it. I put some papers he gave me in my room. I don't like signing anything I haven't read properly.'

'I'll wager he is trying to take the business.'

'No, he's not! And anyway, even if he did, what does it matter? It's for all of us. The business is to make all our lives successful! To give money to mother and father, to rescue them, Emmeline, Stoneythorpe.'

'And you think that's what Arthur wants?'

'Of course!' But yet again, that cold, thick stuff curling around her heart. What if Jonathan was right?

'But why do it at all for that house? It's only a house. It's not even that appealing. It's an ugly old place.'

'No, it's not. Just because it doesn't look like New York and isn't all shiny! It's just different.' Stoneythorpe, the ivy tangling around it, the turreted walls and the roof sloping down over the top windows. Built for a friend of Elizabeth I, still there, unchanging.

'No, Celia. It's too big and it's falling apart. Well, it was when I saw it. God knows what shape it is in now.'

She looked down, fingered the drink, one of those New York juice cocktails that the waiter would secretly drop another spot in. 'But it's all the history, memories. I grew up there. And – it's their home. My parents'. They're too old to move now.'

'Too old? I don't buy that. They weren't too old to lie to you.'

She shook her head, not wanting to listen.

'If you're going to make money, then use it for your future. Try and get your son. Give it to your sister, the poor woman needs some luck. But your parents deserve nothing. Look at you! Your heart is broken. And that's what they did to you.'

'I'd have done anything to shield their reputation, if they'd asked. I could have gone off and had the baby in secret, brought him up in London and no one would have known. I could have kept it secret.'

'Look, Celia, I'm not saying they don't have reason. How Germans were treated, are treated. But they lied to you repeatedly – and still you'll do anything for them. I don't understand it.'

'Of course I'm angry with them! I can't write to them anything but pleasantries. When my heart aches for Michael, I blame them. I scream at them in the middle of the night. But what's the point? They did it. They said they were sorry and I have to try to forgive them. I have to hope that I'll get him back and so it will be like it always should have been.'

'Apart from the fact that you've missed nearly eight years of his life.'

She bowed her head again. 'Yes.'

'And if you don't get him back?'

And this time, what she had been withholding, the tears pushing at the back of her eyes, came forwards. One dripped and fell into her glass, dissolving in the dark liquid. She watched it, then another. 'I'll wait until he is eighteen. And I'll make sure he can be proud of me in the meantime, with the business and everything I do. One day, we will be together.'

He clenched her hand. 'I upset you.'

She shook her head. 'I was thinking some of it. Maybe you're right about the house. But it would break their hearts. They're my parents.'

He patted her hand. 'I know. I'm sorry.'

If they stayed away from talking too much about her parents and Arthur, they were almost constantly contented. She had forgotten how easy it was to be with another person. They talked, laughed, sometimes sat quietly. He introduced her to some of his friends from Yale at the club, saying she was a friend from England. They were pleasant-enough men, responsible, building family businesses to earn well.

She kept trying to confide in him her secrets: Mrs Bellenden's, Arthur's final words, Michael's real father. She longed to tell him – but the words wouldn't come. She'd written to Violet and received no reply – and when she went to Primrose's, a new girl was in her place, being spoken to maliciously by the smart girls again.

So she sat there in restaurants and cafés and bars, feeling like two people. The one was smiling, laughing at their jokes, talking about the business and everything from New York politics to the other people in the place. The other was keeping secrets, of love and death and deception. She couldn't reconcile both sides. She wondered if it would be too much to ask to see if he could too.

And then when they were both tired and Celia's head was confused over the accounts and she'd had enough, she said, 'Let's go somewhere different to dance. Somewhere we can listen to music. Somewhere small.' She lowered her voice. 'I wish we could have something to drink.' The red wine that Arthur stowed in his room, refused to give to her. The punch at the ball surrounded by the men.

'Oh!' he said. 'I see. I had some at home.' He walked along. 'I don't know New York well enough. Let me think. Someone told me about a place. I wonder if it's still open.'

'We could try it.'

'I don't know, Celia. They can be dangerous. Sometimes the police are called.'

'Well, then we can run away! It's ridiculous that you can't buy drink here, anyway. I think it's that they just don't want poor people to drink. At home, Lloyd George said that drink was the enemy in the war, but he didn't mean in the House. All the MPs were drinking. Rich men can ruin themselves through drink too.'

'That's true. Listen, I can remember somewhere. It's on West 49th. Let's get a cab.' He held out his arm, a car stopped and he helped her in. 'Number 50, please.'

When they got out the street was quiet. 'It's not really Number 50. Or at least I don't think it is. These places keep moving.' He set off towards a door, knocked hard. A face peered out of a small shutter.

'My friend Robert Vertstein recommended we come here. For an evening.'

The man moved back and opened the door. There was a dark passageway. 'Come in,' he said. The noise of music and people flooded up the stairs towards them, shouting, women laughing, trumpet music.

The man pressed another button. 'We have a system of four alerts,' he said. 'The last one drops all the bottles in the cellar so it looks like everybody is sitting around drinking tea.'

Celia followed Jonathan down the stairs and into a room not three times the size of her room at the Plaza. The crush of people and voices was like two arms, holding out to her. She couldn't distinguish them, bodies whirling, hair, skirts swinging, shoes tapping. The band was on a stage, four black men in suits, two trumpets, one double bass and a drummer who was using what looked like a brush on his cymbal. They were playing fast, energy spilling out of them, the music flooding and circling around the room. The couples – some not even couples, women dancing with women, men with men – were throwing themselves into it, so much that you couldn't see them, not as they had been, normal people, walking down Fifth Avenue, going for a drink, working. They were all dance.

'Do you want a drink?' Jonathan was shouting in her ear.

She nodded. 'I'll come with you.'

'How do you get it?' Jonathan asked the barman as they shuffled forward.

'They get it over the border. Who knows how. I once heard that it comes in egg boxes. They inject the eggs and put it in the shells.' The man handed over two glasses. 'Whisky. Our best tonight.'

She drank, quickly. 'Strong stuff,' said Jonathan.

They stood, watching the dancers whirl.

'You know, they said this jazz music would never catch on. But they look like they're never going to stop,' he said.

She nodded. The music was taking her over, too. 'I don't know how to do this dance.' She'd never paid much attention to dance lessons at school, and every dance she'd ever been to since had been simple stuff. The awful people at the ball with Arthur hadn't even been dancing, not compared to this. They'd just been stepping around each other.

Jonathan nodded. 'Nor me. Maybe we should try it.'

And then the band paused. A woman in a purple dress stood up in front and the brushing cymbals and the trumpets started again. Jonathan seized Celia's hand and in a moment they were in, deep in the throng. Jonathan had her arm and the rhythm was throwing them, back and forth, nothing else mattered but the music, beating above their heads, whirling them together as if they were one person. He shouted something in her ear, she couldn't hear, smiled, it didn't matter. They kept dancing.

'Do you like the music?' he shouted across to her, as they walked to the side for a pause. She nodded and smiled, because really she didn't want to talk, she wanted to watch the dancers whirling past, dancing, not stopping, skirts flying, feet off the floor like they were flying too. She didn't want to use words or think or any of it, just wanted to hear the music, feel it in her soul. He raised his glass to her, she took hers, drank it quickly, felt the liquor go to her head, fast, but it didn't matter, because it didn't matter what her head did, she just wanted to dance. She stood up and seized his hand and back they went, deep in the music that made you forget everything. She felt that anything was possible. She could do anything. Jonathan could get Michael back for her. The three of them would live together as a family.

When they stood back at the bar, he was talking to her. 'It's like I said, Celia. You had so much when I first saw you. But ever since, what fun have you had? Working to support your family, now here looking for your son, again spending all your time trying to earn money for your parents and the rest. Is that enough?'

'But I'm alive, aren't I? Michael died. Shep died. They all died. I'm here. Isn't that enough?' Her brother died in France and millions of others had died, and they both had life. Even dancing seemed wrong when there were so many men buried in the soil, who would never feel anything again.

He shook his head. 'There are thousands of girls out there who lost their brothers, more. And they're still grasping at happiness. Look, Celia, don't take this the wrong way. But don't you want to do something for yourself?'

'The business is for myself!'

'I think you need to travel. See some more places. More of America.'

'Maybe.' He was right. The Celia of five years ago would have leapt at the chance. 'I've never been to California.' The magazines she'd looked at, the smart girl in the swimsuit, palm trees over her head.

And the music started again and they were dancing. They were dancing through New York, again in the secret club where the music flew through her body.

On the way back, he started talking about the night of the ball, how he hadn't been sure whether to come to New York.

'I'm glad you did.' She realised how much she liked his voice. It was deep and reassuring, close up.

'If you hadn't run away, I would have had to wait for hours. And maybe you might have been swept off your feet by some railroad magnate – and by the time you'd arrived home, you'd be entirely in love with him.'

Celia smiled, tried to laugh. Jonathan was kind, gentle, funny – and fond of her. But Michael was always at the front of her mind, cutting hard into every thought, her loss of him, her failure to get him back, always thinking of what she might have exposed him to at the Whetstones', how she might have made things worse for him, for surely the woman had been shouting for men to come to chastise him or beat him. Every day, things sparked in her, toys in a window, little boys who were Michael's age. Yet, she told herself, it didn't matter how many times she replayed it. She had to face the truth. Michael was gone. She had to live without him.

She tried to talk, couldn't get the words out. There was too much to say.

He held her hand. 'When I was younger, I used to question things a lot,' he said. 'Before the war. Now I just feel—'

'I know.'

'I don't know where to start.'

He closed his hand around hers. 'Don't try. We don't need to talk.'

Michael buried, somewhere in France. They didn't know where. His grave in Stoneythorpe marked him, but he wasn't there.

'We're alive,' he said. 'Aren't we?'

And they wouldn't be, forever. Not many more years at all, really, maybe thirty or forty or fifty, no more. And by the end, they'd be too old, like Rudolf and Verena, fighting daily private battles with pain and ailments. *I promise you*, she said to Michael in her mind. *We will be together.* And then another voice, even stronger, said to her *You've lost him. You'll never see him again.* She fought it back.

She turned to him. 'Yes.'

And then every blood cell, every bone, pounding, she turned and caught his hand and they began to run together, hurtling up the road like the night when they first met, past slick cars and smart people and delivery men and maids and running made them all cross, all of them. And they were free, running not to get away but because they could, they were alive, and others weren't, they were under their feet, and if they didn't run now, they might never. She clasped his arm and they ran and ran, dodging people, old men clucking in anger, jumping past cars, they were alive and young and they would live forever. Jonathan was whirling her and smiling and her mind was laughing and he talked and she didn't want it to stop.

FOURTEEN

In August, people left New York and Celia felt as if she had the city to herself, wandering up and down to Miss Salm in Brooklyn to try the latest recipe, readjust, talk about seasoning, discuss the flavours. The artwork was ready for the advertising – they'd made her eyes rather too big but the artist said they had to, that this was what people expected to see. She sketched out how they'd create displays in the department stores, went to meetings about the figures with the bankers, made plans and spent her free time with Jonathan, talking of travel, plans, walking through New York, admiring shops. The whole, great city, which had seemed so odd, cold, unfriendly, opened itself up to her like the sun and she said, 'Oh!' and 'I see!' because it was the New York that everyone had been talking about, expanisve, beautiful, sharp-edged with expectations.

She missed Lily, Albert and Emmeline, wrote to Emmeline, who filled her in with what news there was – the house was still crumbling, Verena low-spirited, Mr Janus was out all the time for meetings, still talking about Spain. Albert and Lily were happy enough. Winter Meats was struggling on at home under Mr Pemberton, their family lawyer who they'd asked to take over in the interim. Celia tried to read between the lines, see the real truth but she found nothing. Emmeline asked after Michael and Celia wrote that she thought she knew where he might be. There was no reply from Rudolf and Verena to Celia's letter asking them to lay out the circumstances of Michael's adoption. The Whetstones wrote back to the lawyer Mr Galss had found to say that Celia must never contact them again. Celia walked past their house a few times, looked up, saw nothing. At night, she took out the brown cardboard file and looked at the words, as if by gazing at them, she could be closer to Michael himself. She knew it was dangerous to have kept it, that even though it seemed as if Miss Bellenden hadn't reported the break-in, she might change her mind and do so – and if the police investigated, the file was evidence. But she couldn't help it.

On a too hot Wednesday, she and Jonathan were walking down the street, on the way to see Miss Salm in Brooklyn and she saw a woman in front, with her familiar walk and dark hair. Celia hurtled after her, seized her arm. 'Violet!' She flung herself forward. 'Violet!'

The woman turned. It was Violet, older, thinner, sadder.

Celia clasped her hands. 'I've missed you! I've been hoping to see you, I even checked at the shop in case you went back.' Violet was wearing her usual blue dress but it looked thin, ragged. Her cheeks were hollow and her eyes were yellow at the edges. 'Where are you going? Can I come with you?' Jonathan stood aside, watching.

Violet shook her head. 'I have to go.'

'I'll come with you.'

'Please don't.'

'How is your mother? Have you seen Hope?'

Violet shook her head.

'I'm not well.' She began to waver on her feet.

Jonathan stepped forward. 'Let me help. You should sit down.' There was a bench to the side. He tried to steer her towards it. Violet shook her head.

'We could help you,' Celia stammered. And her heart struck with the thought of Michael crying out and she thought: perhaps Violet shouldn't find Hope. Because if the child was suffering, then what good was it to know? Violet would have even less chance of getting Hope than Celia had – for she'd been right, the law was more forgiving to rich women. But then, surely it was worth it, just to see her daughter. Just to know she was alive.

'I've told you. I don't want your help.' Violet turned around and

113

Celia noticed that one leg was dragging slightly. 'I have to go.' She probably had never looked at the file and never would.

Celia persisted. 'Please take some money!' But Violet shook her off, carried on.

'She won't take anything from me,' she said to Jonathan, watching after her. 'It means nothing to me, this money, but she won't take it.'

'She doesn't want charity.'

'It's not charity. We were friends!'

Jonathan shrugged. 'Not any more.'

'I suppose not.' She had been naive: her brightest, most golden dreams of she and Violet finding their children together, taking them to the park, rescuing them, being free, were ridiculous of course, but surely there had been *something* in them.

'Maybe you could go and talk to her,' she said, impetuously. 'Take her some money.'

'I don't think she'd welcome me either.'

'But she might let you in the first time. And then you could just give her the money and go.'

'You can't solve everything with money, Celia.'

'But you can solve a lot! They're so poor.'

'I will try.' He looked at her quizzically. 'Although there's a lot you're not telling me, isn't there?'

She looked away.

'I can't tell you,' she said.

'You don't have to.'

'Too many of other people's secrets.'

'I can wait. Or never.'

They sat for a while, then got up and walked on.

Three days later, Jonathan went to see Violet. He came back, saying he'd given her the money, that she wouldn't talk much but asked him questions and so did her mother, who didn't look so unwell as all that, he thought. He said he'd try again in a few months. 'Give her time to think.' Celia held his hand, grateful that he didn't ask why Violet meant so much, just did it for her, without asking.

The business carried on. Celia and Miss Salm carefully assembled the sets of sixty jars and cans for Bergdorf's and the other two big department stores, working until eleven every night, decorating jam jar lids, tying bows around the fronts. They hired a cab and delivered them, with Jonathan's help to carry them in, and then assembled them in the Food Hall, decorating the top of the pyramid with little sprays of paper flowers that Miss Salm's sister had made. Celia stood back and looked at the display in Bergdorf's and wished that Rudolf and Verena had been there too. It looked so beautiful.

'I think this looks marvellous,' said Mr Goodman, coming behind her. She jumped, surprised. 'Very attractive.'

And once they were in Bergdorf's and a few others – well, everything began. She put on smart gowns that she bought newly from Bergdorf's and Macy's and she and her sales girls went to the offices of other stores to talk about Flapper Foods. She smiled a lot to men in suits, with Arthur and sometimes Jonathan behind her (she did better with Jonathan, she thought, perhaps because he was American, too). They tested out different ways of keeping the food fresh in the jar – and even talked of buying a canning factory to send things all over America.

They all came, one after the other, dominoes, all the shops. 'Yes, Miss Witt, please do, we would take one thousand dollars, thank you, and do you have anything else?' Jonathan or Arthur would mention that other shops were interested and so the buying men would ask for more – 'I'll take it all!' one said. They all asked to be the exclusive retailer but Jonathan thought it was best not to agree to it – because if the store changed its mind and didn't like the foods any more, then where would you go? They were dizzied by all the interest, like a girl with a dozen lovers. 'Enjoy it,' Jonathan said. 'You must enjoy it while it lasts.' She tried but every day was a panic of hurrying between meetings, saying the right things and smiling. The shops bought from her, resulting in pages and pages of figures and numbers, the promise of boxes and boxes of stews and soups, cakes tied with bows, biscuits and even the bread rolls in a jar, bought it all up, promised her sums of money she could hardly comprehend. She rushed, rushed, dashed between places. She went to help at the school on Sundays but, otherwise, her mind was all hurry. It meant she didn't think about Michael.

By late September, they were all exhausted. Celia's eyes were permanently watering from lack of sleep, Arthur couldn't shake off a cold and Jonathan's back ached, nearly always. The products were flying off the shelves (most popular – chocolate pudding, sausage rolls, cheese scones, chicken à l'orange) and they had hired another kitchen, ten more cooks and three more deliverymen. Sometimes Bergdorf's or Macy's would telephone Miss Salm and demand another twenty jars – within the hour.

'We need to take a holiday,' Jonathan said. 'We've all been working too hard. You've been working too hard. We decided on California, we should go.'

She was loathe to, there seemed so much to do. But he was right, she knew. And they'd talked of the holiday, the palm trees and the oranges and the beaches.

'I'll stay here,' Arthur said, when they told him about it. 'I'm too tired even to travel. I'll stay and sneeze in the hotel room until I can't sneeze any more.' He'd been quiet of late, Celia thought, sometimes going off to meetings that he didn't tell them about. They'd knock on his door and he wasn't there. Jonathan had been walking up to his club and he'd seen Arthur go into a bank. Celia supposed he was finally investing that money he'd talked about – and he was right of course! That was where the money was now, hotels in Florida or Hawaii, sets of flats. There were advertisements for it everywhere. She had given him over half of the money he asked for, but he said that was fine, he could borrow the rest against Winter Meats.

'Unless you see something you want to buy in California,' he said, because that was where they were going, Los Angeles, the home of the movie stars and beauty and sunshine. She was going to see America.

*

She and Jonathan went by rail all the way to Los Angeles, sleeping on the train for two nights, and he took her to a hotel on the Boulevard which had a balcony. She and Jonathan stood there and looked down on the city – and it seemed like all the lights and beauty of it were just spread out for her.

Jonathan knew people and so they went to a great movie set, a giant sign under palm trees and inside the floor was covered with cables and dozens of people were watching a beautiful girl in a red swimsuit dive into a tank against a painted backdrop of the French Riviera. She dived, came out, three women in black dried her hair, and then she dived again. Then the director shouted, 'That's the one,' and the women in black hurried forward with robes for her. 'Come along now, Miss Grilt, let's get you warm.' And they ushered her away like a queen. Celia watched her go – and all of the glitter fell out of the picture, as it was only men in overalls cleaning up the water and moving the backdrop as the director and some other men pored over a script.

That night, Jonathan poured her more wine from a bottle disguised as apple juice and no one seemed to notice. She drank it because the words and the wine went together and her heart had broken out from her body and it was flying over the hotel, high above the autumn night city.

'I love you,' she said.

'Do you really?' Jonathan replied. 'Do you really love me?' His face was as if it had opened, she thought.

'Yes,' she said. 'Yes I do.' But then, she thought of what she'd done, not telephoning, getting Red to steal for her, breaking into Michael's room and probably exposing him to more ill treatment from the Whetstones. 'I'm not good enough for you. I'm not.' She was too damaged, like Verena's broken vase.

'Don't say those words again. You're Celia. You're – you're – I can't find the words.' He smiled. And then he took her hand and she moved towards him and they were holding on to each other, as if everything around them was shipwrecked and they were the only ones not drowning.

*

117

On the next day, they walked down to the beach and he was holding her hand. 'Celia,' he said, talking through the bright mist in her head. 'Celia, there's something I wanted to ask you.'

And she turned to him and said, 'Yes. I'll say yes to whatever it is.'

'You don't know what it is.' He held her hands. 'Will you marry me?'

'Yes,' and they were in each other's arms and she knew she wanted to say yes to everything from now on, because now was the beginning and Jonathan had the future in his hands.

FIFTEEN

Manhattan, October 1929

Two weeks later, they were on a train back to New York. 'We need to speak to Arthur,' Jonathan had said.

She would have married Jonathan there and then in the hotel, but Jonathan was talking about the ceremony and speaking to his father. He said he had a family ring that he'd like her to try. She nodded – but she supposed it must be a great diamond. She'd rather have something small, a simple stone. She shrank at the thought of it, such scrutiny.

'Couldn't we just run away and do it?' she asked. 'We could find somewhere to marry us quickly.' Arthur would want a big occasion too, it would help him with the Vanderbilt girl.

Jonathan shook his head. 'How would that look, Celia? Really.'

She dreamt of it, just the two of them, free and high above the city as they had been, not talking about ceremonies and money and who they should invite.

Penn Station was packed with people, even busier than it normally was. They were crowding around the newspaper kiosk next to the platform. Jonathan held her hand and pulled her through – and the other kiosks were even busier. 'We must have missed something while we were away,' said Jonathan. 'Perhaps someone's resigned.'

Out in the street, the buses were crowded and people were hurrying around again. There was no getting a taxi, so they started to walk, pushing through throngs of people.

'What's happened?' Celia said. 'There must have been something.'

They passed a group banging on the door of an office. And

then a woman weeping on a corner. A group of men in suits were arguing and one looked as if he was going to break into a fight. They looked around for a newspaper boy, but each one was shouting, 'Nothing left.'

Jonathan touched a passing man's arm. 'What's going on?'

'Wall Street,' he gasped. 'Sell everything. Sell!'

'What is he talking about?' Celia said.

'Stock. But it's riding high. Mine was worth thousands before I left.'

She nodded. 'They said it would stay high forever. Permanent plateau, that's what Arthur said.'

He looked around. 'Still no taxis. Come on, let's walk. To the Stock Exchange.'

They started walking along, heading south to Wall Street. He was gripping Celia's arm. She watched people flooding past them, women weeping, some men arguing. Others were sitting on the roadside, head in hands. She believed it now. Something terrible had happened.

They couldn't get close to the Stock Exchange. It was crowded with people shouting. They were begging people – anyone – to sell for them.

'They should close the market,' Jonathan said, staring at the crowd. 'This is terrifying.'

'They couldn't,' said the man next to him. 'They couldn't get them out. We wouldn't let them.'

'Have you seen a newspaper?'

'Sold out hours ago. Have to wait until this evening. If we're lucky.'

'How did this start?'

He shook his head. 'It just began, they say. Out of nowhere.'

'We've been in California,' Jonathan said. 'They have no idea there.'

'They don't have any idea anywhere. The President was on the radio,' a man burst in next to him. 'He said business was strong. What does he know?'

'We have to get in,' said Jonathan. 'I need to sell.'

'You and everybody else. Big business comes first.'

'What about Arthur?' Celia said, suddenly struck. 'He bought more at the last minute, do you remember? That property fund for the hotels in Hawaii and houses in California.'

'I was just thinking that. He borrowed a lot. He took money from your accounts at Flapper Foods, yes?'

'I know.' We encouraged him, she didn't say. Because it wasn't Jonathan's fault, not really, everybody had agreed on how it was the thing to do. Everybody was buying. 'Now we're all selling.' That night at the table, clinking their glasses. *It can't fail!* Arthur had said. *If I put in all our money, it still couldn't fail!*

She looked at the people surging forward. 'It's carnage here.'

'This is dreadful,' Jonathan was saying. He pulled her away, wouldn't let go of her hand until they had moved on a couple of blocks. They ran, not thinking, to the hotel.

Arthur was sitting there, in the lounge. People were hurtling around him. He sat, staring straight ahead.

Celia shook him. 'Arthur! Arthur, we're here.'

He looked to the side, down. He didn't see her. 'Everything,' he said. 'We've lost everything.'

SIXTEEN

London, November 1929

Emmeline felt as if she'd said the same words too many times. *Don't. It's not safe.*

'Please don't go to Spain,' she said. 'There are hundreds of men out there. Why does it have to be you?'

'I've told you. It's bigger than just me. We were put on earth to change things.'

Samuel was always so patient when answering her, so reasonable. It made her want to scream, throw herself on the floor, anything to get a reaction. 'Why don't you care about us?'

'I do care. But this is important.' He patted her shoulder. 'You'll be fine. You always are.'

'The children need you. I need you.' He told her not to talk about Euan, that it had been two years now and she should forget. She tried. But it made her treasure her time with her children, try and seize every scrap of their time. It seemed so wrong that he'd want to leave them all behind.

He grinned. 'I'll be back before you know.'

'To go somewhere else again.'

'Maybe. Look, Emmeline, the Crash has liberated us. It's going to mean the end of the system as we know it. We can free ourselves from the banks. They've all gone. We can make a new world without them. Free of money. But this country is cowardly. We always choose the Establishment. I have to go to Spain. Forces are rising there. The military will be put out of power soon by the people. That country will show the rest what to do.'

She put her head in her hands. She couldn't stop him.

'You go and stay with your parents while I am away,' he said. 'We'll give up the flat.'

'Don't go,' she said. 'Please.'

'I have to go. It's our chance, Emmie. Maybe our last chance.'

It reminded her of the early spring three years ago, 1926, so filled with possibilities. The flat had been busier than ever with visitors, meetings going on after Emmeline and the twins had been bundled off into bed. Lily and Albert slept while she lay there, listening to the voices rise and fall. When Samuel came to bed, finally, at two or three in the morning, she tried to speak to him, ask him what was going on but he told her he was too tired. She read the newspapers instead, poring over them, read the pamphlets handed out on the streets by men who looked like Samuel. They were going to strike to support the miners. It was time to throw off the tentacles of businessmen and politicians, who were rich because they kept so many in poverty. They would show the country how much they depended on the workers, bring it to its knees.

She felt as if she'd been spinning and the world wouldn't right itself. Everything was out of her grasp. She bought a magazine, cut out the pictures of sitting rooms, plush sofas, cushions, comfortable chairs.

The people came in and out, made plans. Emmeline opened the door to them, made tea and sandwiches. They were all hope and optimism. They had been promised so much for fighting in the war. Now they were going to take it, whether those in power liked it or not.

Things got so fervent that Samuel barely slept. He lived the cause, all the time. At the end of April, the baby Princess Elizabeth was born. Samuel said what was coming would be the end of the Royal Family, too – they would have to live like the rest of the people. Samuel banned mention of the new baby – but Emmeline brought home a newspaper for Lily. 'If she's going to be ordinary like the rest of us, there's no problem is there?'

He shrugged. 'You have a point.'

Emmeline and Lily read the article together: the little Princess, visits from King George and Queen Mary.

'She'll only be royal for a week or two. Maybe a month,' said Emmeline. 'What Papa is planning will change everything. She'll be so ordinary, she might even move next door to us!'

Lily was delighted with the idea, imagined pushing the new Princess around in her pram.

'You'd have to call her Elizabeth,' said Emmeline. 'That would be the new way.'

The planning intensified. She had never seen her husband so animated, so caught up, so genuinely excited. He said they were standing on the brink of it, just about to jump.

And then – what happened? A strange sort of doubt started to creep in. Reports that men were losing their nerve. The government bringing out middle-class men and women to staff the railways. The army were going to come out too. And then the worst blow. The head of the unions said that not all workers could go out. They said *only some*, because they feared revolution.

The day came. Samuel went out and didn't return. Emmeline kept the children inside in case the law broke down, but ran out to buy a newspaper. The transport stopped. But nothing much else. Over the next few days, buses started to run with volunteers. The army protected lorries so that they could get to Hyde Park with food. Samuel still didn't come back.

Then nearly a week after the strike began, she woke up, walked into the sitting room and found him on the sofa.

'We've failed,' he said. 'The unions have given in. They can't even get the government to promise strikers will get their jobs back.' Tears ran down his face as he talked. 'This is the end. We could have done it, made a change. Now we've lost everything.'

She tried to comfort him, sat down beside him, held his hand. He wouldn't listen. 'It's all gone,' he said. 'They've won. We can't fight again.'

No one came for discussions that night. He lay on the sofa, staring at the ceiling, refusing to eat. Deep down she was grateful. Grateful that it hadn't worked, that the government had won. Now she had her husband back.

*

How naive she'd been. To think she'd thought that was the end of it all. He'd been in what she supposed was shock for weeks, not really speaking, barely eating. Then he'd started working as a tutor once more. She hugged herself at the possibility – just a possibility – that he was going to behave *normally*. He was going about his days like some sort of machine – but she hoped, no *knew*, he would go back to his old self, the man she'd fallen in love with.

When he started taking an interest in Spain she had become so saddened by her broken husband that she welcomed it, his talk about politics and the change of system in Spain.

Then came the Crash and he was suddenly truly alive once more, the old Samuel, bursting with hope and possibility for the future. He talked of a new society, free of money. Exchange rather than markets. She worried about Arthur and Celia in New York, her parents' house – but didn't tell him because he would say it was better for them – for the whole world – to lose all their money and then begin again.

Men came over to their house once more, talking endlessly into the night. She lay in bed listening to them come and go. Albert was still preoccupied by his trains but Lily was growing more interested in the conversations. She'd become fond of one of the younger men, who seemed happy enough to chat to her. He explained to her the point of their discussions, talked about Karl Marx and communism. Emmeline had to smile to see Lily looking so serious, pretending she understood.

At night, she'd crawl into bed with Emmeline and whisper her questions.

'What do Papa and his friends want to do?'

Emmeline held her close. 'They want to get rid of money. They want it so that there's no money in the world.'

Lily thought. 'But where would they put it? Where would they put all the money? In a big hole?'

'I don't know. That's a good question. Maybe they'd melt it all down and do something useful with it.'

'But what would we do without money?' Against Mr Janus's

orders, Emmeline had been teaching Lily a little about money. The teacher at the school where she and Albert went in the mornings had told her that Lily was a little behind in mathematics, so Emmeline had been using coins for simple sums.

'But how would you buy anything?'

'Well, Papa says that we don't always need to buy so many things. They tell us we do, but we don't really. So we'd start by buying less. And then, well maybe we'd exchange or give each other presents. Papa thinks that money is wrong. It ruins our mind.'

Was she disloyal, always saying, *Papa thinks*? Shouldn't she say, *I think*? He was probably right about money. It did trap people – and what good had it done for their family?

SEVENTEEN

Manhattan, November 1929

'It hasn't changed anything, you know,' Jonathan was saying. 'We'll still get married. It just won't be quite such a big ceremony.' She'd tried on the ring – a very large diamond from his family collection and it was too big. 'I'd prefer something smaller,' she'd said, but Jonathan had looked so hurt that she'd relented, said they should get the gold resized to fit her finger and she loved it really.

Jonathan's family hadn't lost as much as they'd thought. They'd kept so much in land that it really only meant twenty per cent or so. His father's manager, Mr Galss, had said he saw something odd coming and changed a lot of the stock to gold in September – just in case, he said.

'We were fortunate,' Jonathan said, sheepishly. 'I wasn't paying attention. I was – er – distracted. Lucky Mr Galss saw prices dropping and wondered if the tide was changing. I do remember he tried to tell me. But I didn't believe him.'

'Clever man.'

Because Jonathan had been distracted by her, of course, and how dreadful it would be if he'd lost all his money because he was trying to spend time with her. She already blamed herself enough for Arthur. She knew that thousands, hundreds of thousands across the country had made the same mistake, but perhaps if she'd made the effort to research – or even to think *of course this can't last.*

'He did try to stop Arthur, while we were away. But Arthur wouldn't listen.'

'I wouldn't have done either,' Celia said, meaning to be loyal. 'The money seemed like it would never end.'

'I blame the newspapers,' said Mr Galss, when he came up for lunch. 'Telling the ordinary man to buy stocks. What did they think was going to happen? Investment should be for professionals.' He sighed and rubbed at his thick glasses. He talked about Jonathan's money and how much he had. He asked Celia about hers.

'I have the banks'. Not much of my own. But the banks are happy to lend to us, still. They think we're a good bet. And Arthur must have something. He had so much money after Louisa died. He can't have invested it all.'

It had been a week now since that awful Monday. Surprisingly, Flapper Foods was holding steady, sales were still quite good. One of the managers in Bergdorf's had told Betty that people had stopped buying clothes, toys, furniture, everything – but the one thing they were still buying was food. And women, especially, since they weren't having the enjoyment of buying clothes, wanted to treat themselves to pretty food. The orders were staying the same – and Miss Salm was considering hiring another cook.

'They'll start to ask to pay less soon,' said Mr Galss. 'I would say. Take the orders while you can.'

Mr Galss said that she was lucky to keep the favour of the banks but she needed to drop the wages if they were to survive. 'Everyone else is doing it,' he said. 'It's imperative. You need to show the banks you are making savings. And the workers would prefer to have a job paying less than no job at all because you can't pay the bills, Miss Witt.'

'But we can. We can make different savings.' She wouldn't do it.

'What? Ingredients are more expensive. Inflation.'

'We'll find another way. Rent somewhere cheaper if we have to.'

Mr Galss raised his eyebrows. 'Indeed.'

She promised Miss Salm and all the workers that they wouldn't drop the wages. The girls lined up and were meant to shake her hand but then the one at the front hugged her and they all did.

'All the other businesses are laying off,' said Miss Salm, on the way down. 'Thank the Lord you're not like them.'

'No,' she said, fighting off Mr Galss's words. 'No, we're not.' But she knew Miss Salm wanted more of a promise, couldn't get the words out. In the cab back, the tears pricked at the back of her eyes.

They couldn't persuade Arthur out of his room. Stocks were still falling. The newspapers screamed the headlines, politicians counselled calm, no one went to restaurants and half of the hotel was empty. Every bank they passed was crowded with people trying to take out their money. Jonathan had taken his. But Arthur said there was nothing left – he'd put it all into stocks. He'd said that on the first day – and now he wouldn't speak.

Luckily Mr Galss had told Arthur to get out two thousand dollars, just last week, in cash. So he had money to live on – pay the hotel, buy what they needed. Celia hadn't telegraphed or written home about it. She didn't know what to say. It would only worry them more – and Emmeline's letters about Mr Janus had been growing more and more fretful. And – she said to herself – perhaps the money news would change for the better. Everyone said markets were always swaying around. Maybe they would go back up. Hopefully, the American business would soar back and her parents would never have to know.

Celia worried about Violet, alone with her mother. If food got even a little more expensive, as the newspapers said it would, how would they survive? She sent some money to Violet, pretending it was anonymous, but she must have guessed because it came back to the hotel.

Reverend Crisp was distracted, afraid, worried there would be no more donations. She feared for the orphanage. A wild feeling possessed her.

'I wonder, Father, about the children's future. Ethan. I hope to make a life for myself here ...' Ethan's twinkling smile, the way he clutched her hand when she had to go.

Reverend Crisp looked sad. 'Oh, now Miss Witt. You know the rules. I didn't think you were one of those ladies. These children must go to proper godly families in the Catholic faith. You know that.'

'I could give him a home. I'm getting married,' she persevered, knowing she shouldn't.

'He has a home. He lives here, in the faith and if we let him go, it will be to a home in the faith. Father and mother. Really, Miss Witt. Perhaps we will have to stop the classes altogether.'

'Please! No!' she begged him. He relented a little. 'But you have clearly got too fond of the boy. It isn't good for him – or you.' The next week, she was sent to make cards with the girls. She walked back to the hotel and the covers of the newspapers burned into her mind. Central Park was full of little houses and tents now, people who'd lost their homes in New York and had set up home in the park. The churches went out there with bowls of soup. One of the concierges had said they'd seen a man taking and roasting a Central Park sheep.

'We need to make progress with the wedding,' Jonathan said that night, at dinner in the empty hotel restaurant. 'How about December? Then we can go over and have a celebration in London and be there for Christmas.'

It seemed wrong to talk about weddings when the whole world was falling apart. If she had a wedding, would Violet come? She wished she could ask her to be bridesmaid, but Violet would never accept. She would have Jonathan's sisters and cousins instead. She nodded, listened to his ideas.

The shops opened doors for them, begged them in, shops that she felt sure would have been too busy for her a month ago. Ladies in black suits showed her fabrics, tried tacked-up dresses against her, talked about flowers and veils. Jonathan took her on a tour of New York hotels to look at their dining rooms. 'I thought you said *small*,' she hissed to Jonathan, after one manager had shown them a room the size of a church. He gestured at her, helplessly. It was hard not to let the managers show them their best rooms, their eyes shining with desperation, a wild need for someone, anyone, to sample their wonderful food, flower arrangements, impeccable service.

'I can't bear to see it,' she said after one terrible afternoon when the manager had practically begged them to throw the wedding there.

Jonathan shook his head. 'We shouldn't stop ourselves. We need to put money into the economy. Even the President said it.' They decided on the small dining room in the Tower Ballroom – and Celia felt pained with guilt at all the other places that wanted them. She knew she should be dreaming of herself in a slender white gown, embroidered veil, holding flowers, but couldn't do it.

Two days later, she went up to Brooklyn and found Miss Salm in tears. There had been a spillage of water and all the flour and sugar was ruined. The girls were arguing over whose fault it was. She and Miss Salm cleared it up, then passed over the money for more, tried to settle the arguments. The girls were angry, resentful.

'They are afraid that they will lose their job even though you said they wouldn't,' Miss Salm said. Celia looked into her dark eyes and knew that she felt the same.

She found a taxi and fell into it. She was so exhausted by the day. She just wanted to lie down in her bedroom and not talk. If Jonathan was there, trying to discuss the wedding, she'd tell him she had an awful headache and say she had to lie down.

She walked into the lobby – and her heart stopped. Mrs Whetstone and a heavyset man with pale eyes who was probably her husband were sitting there on one of the sofas. With Michael. The air around her curved and disappeared. She clutched her hands. They were looking ahead, not at her. She moved towards them.

'Hello.' Mrs Whetstone looked oddly smaller, nothing like she had done in their house.

She stared at them. She couldn't speak. Mr Whetstone stood up. 'I don't believe we have met. Miss Witt?'

She nodded. Michael was looking older already, his hair grown now, flopping over his collar, trousers patched at the knees. He looked so handsome, his dark eyes against his brown skin, the eyelashes even longer. She wanted to run over to him, seize him in her arms. She stood there, gazing at them all.

'Would you like to go somewhere quieter?' She gestured towards the restaurant. 'We could go and sit in there.'

He shook his head. 'No point wasting time. Listen, Miss Witt. We're having problems. We have loans. The bank are calling them in.'

'You need some money?' She thought of the Whetstones' beautiful apartment block, thick red walls, high windows.

'We need more than that. We need a miracle.'

Michael was looking at his feet.

'So what I wanted to say was – how much?'

'How much what?' Celia was confused.

'How much to give him to you?'

The hotel lobby, the desk, wavered and fell. The air pieced around her into tiny specks. 'Give me?'

'You want him. We don't need an extra mouth. But we're not giving him away for free.'

She stared at Michael. He sat quietly, hands in his lap. He could clearly *hear*.

She stepped forward. 'I don't know what to say. I'd give anything, do anything to have him back.' She looked at Michael, staring at his feet and her soul lurched. 'If that's what he wants, of course.' A picture of him in his room, terrified, the woman shouting through the door, calling men – to do what, beat him? – flashed into her mind. 'Are you sure? He's your son, too, on paper.'

Her heart wrenched as she said it.

Mr Whetstone shook his head. His face was stony. 'You can have him. There's nothing to talk about. It's yes or no.' She gazed at him – and then he broke away. 'Sebastian,' he said, gesturing at him. 'Go and walk around.'

The boy stood up, head bowed. Celia watched him go. She swallowed. 'I was wrong to come to your home, Mr Whetstone.' Despite her actions that night she'd broken in, surely it was not right to take Michael from them so abruptly. They'd lost every-thing.

Mr Whetstone rolled his eyes. 'You don't understand, Miss Witt. We don't want him. We can't afford him. You can have him. If you don't take him, my wife says she's giving him to a home.'

'But—' Celia looked at Michael's back, painfully vulnerable. He was bending to look at something on the floor. 'You said...'

'We took on an orphan. But he's never worked. He's always been bad. You can have him. Everybody's doing it.'

'What?'

'Sending back their orphans. Charity begins at home.' He shook his head. 'You know, Miss, a lot of things fell into place when my wife told me about you. When we took him on as a baby that agency told us he was from good stock, that he'd be the boy for us. But he was never good at applying himself, always off dreaming, never right. And then you turn up – this wafty, dreamy person – and you were entirely him. He wasn't from proper stock at all, he was from you, and whatever man you found. He doesn't fit in with us. Either you take him or we send him to a home.'

Celia stared at his angry, resentful face, clenched hands.

'Yes or no.'

Her heart opened up and flew to the sky. She held tight to it, as if it were a balloon. 'Yes. Yes, of course. If he'll come.' *My son. Michael.*

'Ten thousand.'

'What?'

'We've lost everything. That's the deal, him for ten thousand dollars.'

'I'll find it.'

'How soon can you get it?'

'You want *cash*?'

He nodded.

'This isn't right!'

'It's up to you. Money or child.'

'I don't even have ten thousand dollars.'

'You'll find it. You're staying in this hotel aren't you?'

'But I don't have cash. Everything we make goes back into the business.'

'Not my problem. Pay or don't get him.'

'I'll need to talk to people. But I'll go and speak to Michael – Sebastian – first.'

She walked towards her son, carefully, putting her feet forward as if she was playing that old game – *don't step on the cracks. Don't fall down a crack. Get to the other side.* She knew they were staring at her, on the concierge desk, she ignored them, kept moving forward. *Don't step on the cracks.*

She stood next to him. He was still looking at something on the floor. She put her hand out for his back – then drew it away again. Then she reached out and touched him.

'Sebastian.'

He turned around. She wanted to gather him into her arms, pull him towards her and dash upstairs with him. She held back, looked at his eyes. Why were words so *useless?* 'How are you?' she said, feeling how hopeless they were as she said them.

'You're the maid,' he said. 'I saw you.'

'I'm not the maid. I'm sorry I came into your room. I just had to see you.'

His face crossed with confusion, questions. 'My parents don't want me any more.'

Her heart broke. 'I know. I'm sorry. But *I* do. I've always wanted you. I want you more than anything. I promise.'

He stared at the floor. 'Did they ever love me?'

'Yes. I'm sure they did.'

'They were always angry with me. And Mama told the servants to beat me. It's because I wasn't their son, that's what Papa told me on the way.'

'I'm sorry.'

'I never knew. I thought I was their son. But I'm not.'

She held his hands tighter. 'I'm sorry they've been cruel to you. It's all over now.'

He was still reluctant. 'Who were those other people with you? The boys who came into my room.'

'They were helping me. I wanted you, you see. So much.' And it all flashed into her mind, the night, the shouts, the fear.

'Why?' he said. 'Why did you want me?'

She took a breath. 'Because I'm your mother.' She said it and it was just the two of them, no one around them. The people in the hotel, the Whetstones, none of them were there. She said the words and his face flamed with confusion.

'You're my mother?'

'Your father told you that you weren't their child. That's because you're mine. I'm your mother. You were taken from me when you were just born. And given to the Whetstones. They didn't know you were stolen, of course. But I wanted to get you back.'

He said nothing. The whirl of the hotel crashed around. She made herself wait.

He stared. 'Sometimes I dreamt of another mother. A kind one.' A single tear ran down his face and she reached for his hand. 'Why did you take so long to find me?'

'They told me you were dead. When I heard you were alive, I looked everywhere for you.' She reached out and gathered him in her arms. After a minute, he was hugging her back and her heart was on fire.

Tears were pouring down her face and dropping onto his. She couldn't believe it. She felt him clutch to her and she never wanted to let him go. She never would. 'I love you,' she said. 'I've always loved you.' His body so close to hers, touching his hair, his face. 'We'll always be together,' she said. 'I'm here for you now.'

Mr Whetstone's voice. He had walked up to them while she was holding Michael. 'I'll take him with me now. You can have him when we have the money.'

Celia's heart gripped.

'No. You know where I live. You'll leave him here and I'll get the money for you. I won't let you take him away!' She stared Mr Whetstone down.

'Like I said, no money, no child.' Michael was weeping beside her.

'If you take him away, like he is some sort of used toy... Well, no deal!' She knew she was in the stronger position. She knew she might even argue down the money. But she couldn't bear to bargain. Not over Michael. She drew herself up. 'You'll leave him here with me!'

She could see him think, uncertain. 'Agreed, then. I'll come back tomorrow,' he said. 'To get what we discussed.'

Celia nodded. 'Where are his things? Where are Michael's things?'

'Sebastian doesn't have much. What he has can be thrown away. We've spent enough on him. You can buy him what he needs.'

Celia gazed at him. 'Why do you hate him so much? What did he ever do to you?'

Whetstone paused. Then he put his face closer. 'It was all his fault. Everything that went wrong with our family went wrong after him. He was like an evil spirit. My wife – she changed. The children changed. I said we just need to get rid of him and then we'll be back to normal.'

'He's a child. He's so gentle. He wouldn't hurt anyone!'

'Dumb insolence. That's what he did. Dumb insolence. I told my wife to give him back but we couldn't as everybody thought he was ours.'

'You were cruel to him.'

Mr Whetstone tossed his head. 'You'll have to watch him! If you pay, that is. Otherwise I take him back.' He turned and walked away.

Celia stood there, in the hotel lobby, with her son in her arms. He was hers, her blood. She felt a strange fear as if she'd been given a china child, and even the slightest wrong movement might break him. She stroked his hair, his forehead.

She couldn't believe it. The thing she had longed for, desired for so long, was here, given to her. She had thought it would never happen. And now it had and it was almost too much to understand. There was so much to tell him, she didn't know where to start.

She had no idea how to get the money. If she went and asked the bank for it all, they might refuse her. She had to pay, though, make herself free of them. But she didn't know how.

'They didn't want me,' he said. 'They never loved me. They loved their other children. Not me.'

She held him tighter. 'I'm sorry,' she said. 'It was your home. We'll make a new home together.'

She didn't know how to make Michael's hurt go away.

'I got hit for so many things,' he said. 'Talking too loud, waking up, crying, looking the wrong way.'

'That's over now. I won't hit you. Never. Most parents don't, or at least only when the child has been very naughty.'

'Oh.' She could see him thinking it over. 'I wish I'd gone with you then,' he said. 'In the days after, I was watching for you. I wish I'd gone. I thought I'd missed my chance.'

'I'm here now. It's all better now.' She added his name. Sebastian. She'd tell him about his true name later.

'I'm hungry,' he said. 'There was nothing to eat today. For me, I mean. They had things. I came last.'

'Do you like ice cream?'

He nodded. The ice cream shop window she'd stared through before, envying all the happy children, the counter piled high with bowls of the stuff, pale colours, pink, green, yellow. 'I know just the place!' And she caught his hand and he didn't pull away and they hurried together to the shop where she said, 'You can have anything, anything you like!' And he stood there, gazing at all the pictures of the different types of ice cream, the glittering bowls, triangle wafers and cherries on top, chocolate sauce.

He turned to her. 'How did you come into my room?'

'I broke into your house. Like a burglar. It was very wrong of me but I wanted to see you.' People were pushing past them. She drew him close to her.

'I kept watching, I wished you'd come back.' He was buried in her chest now, nearly crying. 'Why didn't you come back?'

Her heart broke. 'I couldn't. I didn't want to get you into trouble.'

'I waited for you. I looked out of the window and I waited.'

'I'm here now.'

'And you're my mother?' He was testing out the words. 'You'll never send me back?'

'Never. Never. We'll always be together now. I promise.' Her heart broke at the thought of him watching for her from the window.

'They gave me to you for money.'

'I know. I'm sorry. It's because they knew how much I loved you. They knew I'd do anything for you.'

'Tell me about when I was a baby.'

She didn't have much, told him about the early days. 'And I called you Michael,' she said, nervous of how it would be received.

'Well, I shall be Michael, then. I've always hated Sebastian.'

She hugged him hard. 'Do you think you can forget – how they were? Do you think you can try? We have a new life now.'

He nodded. 'I'll try.' Then he whispered, 'I don't know which ice cream to choose.'

Celia hugged him and whispered back. 'Just choose any one. And then we'll come back tomorrow and have another one.'

'Another one?'

'Yes, tomorrow. We'll come back tomorrow and have a different one. Or you could always have the same one if you like.'

He nodded solemnly, eyes great and round. 'Anything I like?'

'Anything.'

He held out his hand and pointed to a picture of a big sundae in a curved glass. 'That one.'

The man behind the counter made the ice cream carefully, handed out two spoons. 'Would you like to share with your mother, young man?'

Mother. That's what she was. She watched him eat it, ate a little of the cream and the chocolate sauce. She told him about her home, Stoneythorpe. He talked a little about the Whetstones and her heart pierced for him. How cruel they had been. She could see the loss in his face, the pools of his eyes, as he looked around nervously, his hands twitching, wanted to reach out, cover it all with love. But she had to let him talk through the Whetstones, listen to every time they were cruel to him or hit him.

He reached the bottom of the ice cream and was scraping for the last scraps of vanilla.

'I'll never leave you, you know,' she said. 'You were taken from me. I'll never let it happen again.'

He looked up quickly and back down again.

'I mean it,' she said. 'Whatever happens.' *I'm your mother now*, she wanted to say, worried it might be too much for him. Then with a flush of guilt she remembered Jonathan, how would he feel now Michael was real. Surely Jonathan would help her sort out the money. She'd marry him, be grateful. They'd be a family.

After the ice cream, she took Michael to buy some clothes in Bergdorf's, the one she had haunted, once upon a time, staring at the toys, thinking of her son. The shop was quiet, the assistant pleased to see them. He fitted Michael up for a suit, talking about his own son all the time. 'There,' he said. 'Doesn't he look handsome!'

Celia smiled. 'Yes, he does.'

'Would you like to wear them now?' the man asked.

Celia looked at Michael. He shook his head.

'One last thing.' And they went to the toy department and she said he could pick out anything he wanted – and he chose a small brown bear with a red ribbon around his neck.

'I shall call him Harvey,' he said. 'I will carry him.'

'Come on,' she said. 'Let's go home.' Now he was with her, she'd have to find somewhere proper for them to live. She supposed she'd have to rent an apartment.

She burned for Violet, yearning for Hope. She was lucky, so lucky, and because of money. Violet could never have found ten thousand dollars.

She held tight to Michael's arm, walking back. He clutched the bear. Her *son*. She wanted to pepper him with questions, about what he liked and didn't like, try to get back all the years that had gone. But he was gazing around him, staring at the buildings.

'I couldn't believe New York when I first came,' she said. 'I felt like an ant. You wouldn't think you could get things so high, don't you think?'

'They look like they hit the clouds. I didn't go out of the apartment much.'

'Well now you shall. Maybe we can even go and see the clouds one day.'

He nodded, craning upwards to see.

'I'm here with my brother you know, Arthur, you'll meet him. He'll love you. He doesn't have children.' And then she was talking, telling him all about her childhood, about Stoneythorpe and Emmeline and Arthur. She hesitated – then she told him about Michael and how he had died in the war. 'He was brave,' she said. 'He died bravely. And then I called you after him.'

'I like Michael. I am going to keep it.'

She wouldn't tell him the whole truth about her brother, not yet. But what she had said was true. He had died bravely. It was just that they hadn't understood him at the end. She talked a little about the war for her, trying to make it sound like an adventure, driving fast with men in the back, hurrying to hospital, playing cards at the end of it all with the other girls. Not the horrors of the men screaming, Shep dying on the road, hit by a bomb.

She stopped herself, talked about Stoneythorpe, Verena and Rudolf again. Emmeline and Lily and Albert living there too, when Mr Janus left for Spain. He'd have a friend to play with.

'Grandma. Grandpa.' He tried out the words.

'Lily and Albert are so much fun. And only three years older than you. They'll be so excited to meet you.' She thought that he might even get on a little better with Lily than Albert – she was a little delicate, dreamy. She conjured them together, playing in the Stoneythorpe garden, being imaginary explorers. 'You'll have so much fun,' she said. She talked about her life, her childhood, her world. She told him about everything except Tom. She told him a little about Jonathan, the engagement. She could see his mind was reeling, so much information, so much change.

Back in the hotel room, Celia took out the model farm from the wardrobe, laid it out on the carpet, wondering where Red and his animals were. Then she listened to her son making the remaining animals talk to each other. Harvey was sitting solemnly at his side and could barely believe she had him with her, that they had found each other and now they could begin their lives.

EIGHTEEN

Manhattan, November 1929

That evening, after Celia had tucked Michael into her bed with his bear, Harvey – realising that she'd forgotten to buy him pyjamas or a toothbrush or even a storybook – she sat with him, smoothed his hair until he slept. She wanted to sit in the chair and watch him – but she had to find Arthur. She took off her shoes, stepped noiselessly out of the room, into the corridor. She hurried to the stairs – and Jonathan was standing there.

'Oh!'

She had forgotten. She had been supposed to meet him.

'I came to your room,' he said. 'I was about to knock on the door. But I think you were talking to someone.'

She laughed. 'You're jealous?'

'Well, I am if you're talking to someone in your room! And it wasn't Arthur, you don't speak to him that kindly! Who was it?'

She moved towards him, held his hands. 'It was Michael.'

'Who's Michael?'

'You know.' She was weeping, tears at her eyes, she knew it. 'Michael.'

'Your son?'

She nodded. 'Michael's here.'

He gazed at her. 'How? What happened?'

'Come in,' she said. 'We'll just have to be quiet.' She opened the door, closed it behind him. Jonathan looked across at the sleeping child, the eiderdowns piled up on his bed.

'His father brought him here. They've – lost their money – they need more. They said I could have him for ten thousand dollars.'

'Have him?'

142

'If I got them ten thousand dollars. I have to find it. I have money in my accounts but it's due to the bank. I'm supposed to give it back if I don't make Flapper Foods work. It's not mine, not really. But I have to. Do you think they could tell the police?'

'I imagine they'd have other, bigger loans to chase at the moment.' Jonathan took her hand. 'When do you need it by?'

'Mr Whetstone's coming tomorrow to get it.'

'Otherwise he takes the child back?'

'He does.'

He shook his head. 'What sort of people do that? I'll give it to you. Don't worry. You have to have it.'

She blinked. 'What?'

'I can get it for you. Tomorrow.'

'Thank you! Thank you. I will pay you back, I promise. You must come and meet him. You'll love him.'

'But we need to make sure they'll never come back to get more from you.'

'They wouldn't.'

'You don't know that. They might. I'll ask Mr Galss to draw up a contract. That's it. We don't want to see them again.'

'Legally, they're his parents.'

'Celia. Don't be so honourable. They tried to sell him. There are parents all over the country who can barely afford to feed their children, but they're not *selling* them. These two aren't even poor, not really. They're greedy. I'll ask Mr Galss to deal with it. You don't need to see them again.'

'They're expecting me.'

'Mr Galss won't take any nonsense. They can't come back for more.'

'I'll pay you back.' She would. She'd make sure of it.

'Later. You might need that money for yourself.'

'What do you mean?'

He looked away. 'You two wanted to make money in two ways, yes? Your business. And investing money. Arthur's money.'

She didn't have to nod. He knew the answer. The billboard girls in the swimsuits were turning away, crushing the oranges under foot, their bright white smiles dimming as they moved into the darkness.

'Arthur was wrong when he said he had nothing. It's less than nothing. I saw Mr Galss today. Arthur doesn't understand.'

'Doesn't understand what?'

'Mr Galss had a letter from the bank. Or, the last of the banks. Arthur had borrowed from four to put into the property funds. Did you know?'

'No.'

'He borrowed against Louisa's money, which he'd invested. He also borrowed against Flapper Foods.'

No. She'd promised her workers that their jobs were safe. She'd promised herself that Flapper Foods would rescue Stoneythorpe. She'd told herself so much. She'd been sure. At her school, Winterbourne, their year had been dominated by a beautiful girl, Eloisa, half Russian, darkly glamorous, cool in her passions. Celia walked past and Eloisa laughed behind her hands at her. The girls on the California billboards were all Eloisa, mocking them with their beautiful, perfect faces. They had reached out their hands to them, offered friendship, love, happiness – and now they were taking it all away.

She clutched his arm. 'We've lost everything?'

'I don't know. I think so. I'm sorry. But – Celia, you have me!'

'Does Arthur know?'

'Mr Galss said he was going to try to talk to him. But he probably does, I imagine, Celia. That's why he won't see anyone.'

'I'll see him. I'll tell him it's not his fault! I understand.'

'What do you mean?'

'You were praising those funds too! He wasn't the only one.'

Jonathan's face clouded. 'Don't blame me! He wanted to. He could have put just a little in. And certainly not borrowed against your business. He had no right.'

'I'll tell him. I can make the money back. Flapper Foods will survive! I will make it so! I'll tell him about Michael, too. He'll be so pleased.'

'Celia, I don't think so. I think—' But she was opening the door, running down the corridor and up the stairs, hurrying towards Arthur's room. She banged at the door. 'Arthur! It's me!' There was no answer.

'He's probably not even there,' Jonathan said, catching her up. 'Look Celia, he'll be fine.'

She leant against the door. 'I should be with Michael. He might wake up.'

'That's true. Let me take you back.'

He took her arm and they walked to her room. Inside, Michael was still sleeping, turned over onto his back. She stroked his hair.

'He looks like you,' Jonathan whispered.

She smiled. 'Why don't you stay a while? He's asleep. We can talk.'

'If you don't mind.' He sat down.

'What will I tell the workers?' she said.

'Don't tell them he borrowed money. Just say that you are pushing through the difficult times. As long as you pay their wages, they won't care.'

But did she? Did she have the money to pay the wages? Her heart dropped.

Jonathan put his arm around her as she talked. 'Things will right themselves,' he said. 'We're just having a dip. Business will start again. Your business. That's what Mr Galss was trying to tell Arthur.'

'Trying to tell?'

'Arthur was a little upset. He wasn't really listening. I'm sure he'll be calmer tomorrow.'

She'd thought the money and the good fortune would go on forever. She'd borrowed and spent, told everyone how well it was going, she'd danced with Jonathan and laughed as they whirled to the music – and she'd thought they could dance, keep dancing and the music would never stop. She hadn't seen a thing, not really.

*

She woke, still on the sofa, having slept in her clothes. Michael was stirring. She'd sent Jonathan away when she woke earlier at four o'clock or so. 'We'll come and find you,' she'd said, as she pushed him sleepily out of the door.

'How did you sleep?' she asked Michael.

'Pretty well.'

He sat up in bed. He looked so small, surrounded by the heaps of covers. It struck her that she should find him a school. Then, once he had structure – children liked structure, she'd read – they would be more comfortable with each other. She looked at his big eyes, wondered if he felt fear that he didn't know what they were going to be doing.

'Let's get some pyjamas today,' she said. 'And then I thought we might go to the park again. And the ice cream store. I've got a friend I'd like you to meet.'

She sat down on his bed. 'How about you and I have a few days enjoying ourselves? Then maybe I can find a place to live – my brother might come too. You could even go to school. Would you like that?'

He shook his head. 'No.'

'Why not? You don't like school?'

He looked down at his hands.

'I learnt at home. They said I should never go to school because they'd be mean to me there, I was such a dunce.'

How she hated them.

'Well, they were wrong. You're not a dunce. But you can learn at home if you like. I think you might like school, though. And if you don't like the school, we'll take you out and we'll find you another.'

But then what? Were they all going to rent a townhouse together, she, Jonathan and Michael? Jonathan had always said that after they were married, they'd take a house on Washington Square or similar and divide their time between it and the country. He said that his father would like that best. But now – what?

They dressed, shyly, turning their backs on each other. Michael wore his old clothes – she didn't ask him why. Of course he clung to what he remembered.

Being with Michael was like cleaning a window in smog – each time she managed to clear a little gap and see through it to his heart, it would fog up again and she'd have to find the right bit once more, keep rubbing and rubbing. Of course, she knew, she'd never expected him to suddenly fall into her arms and talk. He was in shock, everything had turned – and no one had ever encouraged him to talk anyway. The Whetstones had taken him in, then had their own children, preferred them. The only reason they hadn't given him up was due to how they might look to society, she supposed. When he spoke of what they had said to him, done to him, it made her heart stop. She held him tight, walked next to him, followed his eyes when he looked up at a bird in the tree or down at a bug in the park. She would go at his pace, wait for when he wanted to talk. He told her about his two elder sisters, who were kind to him but even when they were back from school, their parents kept them away from him. He asked if they might see the girls but Celia knew the Whetstones would never agree. She said they could try, or if not, write a letter. He missed the servants too, he said – Edward, who would slip him biscuits and Merden who was kind when no one was looking. Merden had told him he was always the child indoors, watching from the window while the others went out: skating, to cafés, to the zoo. 'I'll write to ask,' said Celia about a meeting. And then he began to cry.

'Why did they just want to get rid of me? I tried to be good.' She took him in her arms. 'I don't mean it against you. But why did they?' She could only hold him, tell him they were wrong.

In the afternoon they met with Jonathan. He shook Michael's hand solemnly and she was ashamed of the wash of relief she felt – someone else to talk to Michael, another man. They wandered down to look at the ducks.

'Mr Galss has spoken to them,' he said. 'He's got the agreement from them.'

Michael was kneeling down, with the remains of some bread Jonathan had brought, throwing it into the pond. Harvey was clutched under his arm. He took the bear everywhere with him now, even into the bathroom.

'Why would you ever give him up? How could they have been so cruel?' *He should stand up for himself.* Edward's words in her mind.

'Some people are.'

'Should I give them an address when we leave? I'd rather not.'

'They won't care. They want – *need* money. And ten thousand – well, I had to ask my father hard. I can't give it again if they come back in the future. And they might, Celia. They might try to break Mr Galss' agreement.'

'It all feels so wrong.'

'Celia, they don't need to know how he is. They gave him up. They didn't want him. They're glad to get rid of him. We've given them enough.'

He was right. She watched the ducks swim up to her son. 'I wish I could think of what to say. To get through to him. He's been hurt so much.'

'You will. It will happen when he wants. You're his mother, don't forget that.'

She breathed, readied herself. 'We come as a package now,' she said. 'The two of us. He comes with me.'

The air shone between them. He could go. He might say, *yes, well, maybe we should rethink.*

'Of course. I know that. I always knew that might happen.'

'So, we'll all live together?'

'Of course. How could you think anything different?'

He pulled her towards him and she leant on his chest. She could feel the tears pricking at her eyes. *How could you?* she wanted to ask. *How can you love me so?*

After wandering around the park, then to the ice cream shop, they walked to the hotel. 'Come on, sport,' said Jonathan. 'Let's go to a restaurant. Eat potato fries.'

In the days that followed, she felt pure gratitude towards Jonathan. He found fun places to go – museums, parks, a car showroom,

Grand Central Station to watch the trains go in and out. They bought books at the bookstore that he'd read as a child. 'This one is the best,' he said to Michael, who held it in his hand all day. He seemed to know just what was right. A man in the shop suggested the zoo, but Jonathan thought Michael wouldn't like to see the animals in cages. They played sticks in the park and made patterns out of stones under trees.

Sometimes Celia felt a pang of jealousy, envy at how Jonathan knew exactly what to do. But she knew it was only because he had once been a small boy too. She watched them kicking a ball, Jonathan laughing as Michael shot it past him, and it led to her thinking about the children she might have with Jonathan – a little boy and a little girl, running down the stairs in the old house in Washington Square, dashing into the garden, out into the sun.

NINETEEN

Manhattan, November 1929

A week passed and Celia still hadn't seen Arthur. She'd knocked, left notes. He left her a reply at the reception saying he was busy. She hadn't telegraphed home. She meant to tell them that she'd found Michael – but then she changed her mind. Everything was too precious, unbelievable. Her mother and father might say something to spoil it. So she'd hug the secret to herself – and take him home to meet them. Emmeline had written in misery that Mr Janus had gone to Spain, and that seemed to be enough for them all to bear. She decided not to worry them about the Crash and tell them that Arthur had invested in those funds. The market would improve and everything would get better. It would all be forgotten. She went to the Sunday school, where Father Crisp said that many more children were being left at the door and they had no time to direct volunteers. Her soul cut for Ethan.

'Tell him I said goodbye,' she said.

'I shall tell all the children.'

She passed him an envelope, money she'd asked Jonathan for. He nodded, pulled the door shut.

In her heart, her wildest heart, she'd thought about taking Ethan so that he and Michael could be brothers. But Father Crisp had been right. She'd known the rules. She walked home past stores with flimsy Christmas decorations in the windows. Who on earth would buy Christmas presents at the moment? Her vision of the modern woman, stocking up on jams and jellies for Christmas, not possible now. But they still needed to eat, to survive, and some of them had the money for it, scurrying to the food counters and ignoring all the other more expensive goods that filled aisles empty of customers.

But if the shops were deserted, the streets were full of people, men wearing placards looking for work, their wives following behind with children. The newspapers talked on about failing banks, mechanisms, money. She went to a meeting of a charitable organisation she saw advertised in the newspaper and they discussed setting up stalls in the street where people could get soup for free. The woman in charge seemed exhausted by all of it. 'There are too many!' she said, at the end, when Celia tried to ask her a question. 'Too many!'

Mr Galss said that they should sell off the stock of Flapper Foods and pay back Arthur's loan. She refused. The banks didn't want their money back right away. They had been so clear, so secure. 'It would be such a waste to stop now,' she said. 'Everything would be ruined. We're still getting in big orders, making sales. We're expanding!'

Mr Galss shook his head. 'I would get out now,' he said. 'Get rid of that kitchen while you still can and sell the rest. Then they can't come for you for Arthur's loans against the business.'

'You won't need to worry about running the business,' said Jonathan. 'Not when you're my wife.'

That made her even more determined. She shook her head. 'I have to see it work!'

She wanted to speak to her brother. 'I want to tell Arthur. I wanted to tell him about Michael in person but I'll have to write – he still won't see me.' And then her mind cleared. 'We'll ask Mr Galss. He has meetings with Arthur. We'll ask when one is and go at the beginning and tell him.'

'I suppose so. He can't be having a very easy time of it.'

She saw the doubt in his face but ignored it. 'When he finds out about Michael, he'll be so pleased. It will lift his spirits.'

They left a note for Mr Galss, asking him to come and see Celia in her room that evening at six thirty. On the dot of the half hour, he knocked.

'I wanted to talk to you about my son,' she said to Mr Galss, ushering him in. 'I wanted to tell Arthur the news that I've found him.'

Mr Galss took off his glasses and held out his hand. 'Hello, young man.'

'Say hello, Michael.' The child smiled, extended his hand for Mr Galss to shake.

He nodded politely.

'So we're terribly keen to see Arthur and talk to him. He'd be thrilled to meet his nephew. I just wanted to tell him in person.'

Mr Galss sat down. 'With all the losses, he's very upset.'

'Michael will cheer him up.' And he would. Just the sight of Michael, the child that everybody – even he – had thought was dead. It would encourage him, a success gained. Michael putting his hand in his, hugging him as an uncle.

He sighed. 'Perhaps, Miss Witt. I can't tell.' But she was sure. Arthur never gave up. He bore things, even though he sometimes pretended not to care. It was only money. They'd get it back. They were selling more jars every day, the salesgirls were taking more around New York and they would get there – bit by bit! And then the economy would improve – and the modern woman would want to buy Flapper Foods across the country.

'So I wondered if I could come to the beginning of one of your meetings. I'd just speak to him quickly. Where do you meet?'

'We meet in his room, Miss Witt.'

'In his room? But I've knocked on the door so many times!'

'I doubt he's answering. As I said, he's rather distressed at present.' Mr Galss sighed. 'I'm afraid he's said he will only speak to me.'

'So if you knocked on the door now and said it was you, then he'd open the door?'

Mr Galss sighed, nodded.

She firmed her voice. 'Well, let's do that.'

He shook his head. 'Arthur trusts me to follow what we agreed.'

'But I'm his *sister*. And this is his nephew.' She was going to sort this out, make Arthur look to the future again.

'I could go too,' said Michael.

Celia ruffled his hair. 'I'll tell him first. Then I'm sure, the first thing he'll want to do is to rush to you and meet you.'

Mr Galss gazed at Michael, sitting on the floor, laying out his farmyard animals with the assistance of Harvey. 'Very well. It can't do any harm, I suppose.'

'You'll be all right on your own, won't you?' Celia asked Michael. 'You can play.'

He nodded happily. 'Then I'll meet my uncle.' They closed the door on him in Celia's room, leaving him already deep in his imaginary world.

At her brother's door, Mr Galss knocked. 'It's me, Arthur.'

There was no response.

'Are you there?' He turned to Celia and Jonathan. 'Perhaps he's gone out.' He looked relieved.

Then Arthur's voice, thin, breaking up. 'Is that you, Reginald?'

'Yes. And I – have someone with me.'

'Who?'

She put her mouth close to the door. 'It's me, Arthur! I came to see you. I've got something to tell you.'

'I'm busy.'

They'd run around Stoneythorpe together, him always ahead. His room at the top of the house was filled with his treasures. She was never allowed in. But they'd been children then. 'I'm not going until you see me! Why are you avoiding me?'

'Go back to your own room, Celia.' He was only inches away. If she were a witch, she could have reached her hand through to touch his, join fingers.

'No! I want to see you. I have to see you! You have to let me in.'

'We can come back,' Jonathan touched her hand.

She heard steps, to and fro behind the door. 'Arthur?'

'Why are you always trying to see me? Why can't you leave me alone? I don't want to see you.' His voice muffled by the heavy wood of the door.

'Look, Arthur, I know about everything, about the money. It doesn't matter. We don't need money. We'll manage.'

'You think that's right?'

'Of course. Listen, if you just let me in. Then we can talk. Please.'

There was silence. Celia waited. 'Let's go,' said Jonathan. 'We'll come back when he wants to see us.'

'That might be a good idea,' said Mr Galss. 'I'll try and talk to him.'

Celia stood closer to the door, pressed herself against it. Then she heard hands on the doorknob. She turned to Jonathan to smile – but the door was open and Arthur was standing there, staring at them all. His hair was awry, his eyes dark and wild.

'You wanted to see me?' he said. 'Come in, then!'

She edged towards him. 'Not you!' he hissed at Jonathan, and then he turned to Mr Galss. 'Not either of you. If she wants to see – then she should!'

He slammed the door behind her, his face pale, his eyes confused, maybe even crazed. The room was freezing, dark around him, smelt strong and musty as if he hadn't let the cleaners in for weeks. She could see that the bed was unmade, piles of clothes on the floor. He seized her hand and pulled her forwards – so close to him, she smelt him too, dirty, unwashed, a sickness about him. Arthur, who was always so fastidious.

'Arthur, I'm sorry. I know we've lost—'

'You don't know anything. You don't know anything at all.'

'I know that I love you. I know that you're my brother.'

'Words! Women's words. Don't you think I've heard enough?'

She breathed deeply. 'Look, Arthur, everyone's in the same boat. Everyone's lost money. We just have to pick ourselves up and try again. Things go up and down. We'll be up again once more, just you see.'

'*Just you see*,' he mocked, waving his hand effeminately. '*Things go up and down*.' She saw herself through his eyes – stupid. He had buried his face in the curtain now, had his back to her.

'I've been out there, working. I know we can do it.'

He shook his head. 'Just go away.'

'Arthur. There was something I wanted to tell you.'

'Nothing you say could interest me.'

'I've found Michael! I found my son.'

Arthur turned his face to her. 'Oh, did you?'

She nodded, ignored the bitterness in his voice and smiled. 'It's wonderful!'

'And how are we supposed to support another mouth to feed? Celia, you have to get down from your dream world. We have nothing! Absolutely nothing. I can't even pay for this room any more, my money ran out yesterday. We should be on the streets.'

'I have the business. That is still here!'

'That's too late! Who will buy that stuff now? No one has a job. It's dead, Celia. Why can't you see?'

'I don't agree. We've put in so much. The banks trust us. We still have each other. We can go back home and be with Papa and Mama.'

'*We have each other!*' There he was, cruelly imitating her again. 'Celia, you're so naive, it makes me sick.' He buried his face back into the curtain. 'There's no getting through to you.'

She stood quietly, took a step towards him. 'Why don't you try?' she said, gently. 'Tell me. Talk to me about it. We can find a solution.'

He roared and this time his face was on fire. 'Don't come near me!' he shouted. She fell back, afraid. 'You can't solve anything! You're the problem! You and your idiotic words, your stupid ideas. You've been nothing but a burden since we got here. You've ruined everything. And then you come here and expect me to congratulate you because you've found your bastard? Get away from me.'

She stared. She'd listened to him – but then 'bastard' turned the knife. 'How can you say that?'

'It's the truth, Celia.'

'Money's made you cruel.'

'You live without money then.'

'I will. We don't need to stay in a hotel like this. We don't *need* these things.'

Arthur lifted his head. She thought he was coming to her. He was going to turn around, talk to her properly. He paused. She waited. Then he started to roar again. He threw his head back and roared, like a child.

'Stop it!' The noise filled her mind, deafening. 'Stop it!' He carried on. Surely he'd stop, surely he'd cough, and his voice would fade. 'Stop it!' He wasn't looking at her, wasn't even hearing. He was staring at the ceiling, still shouting. Someone was knocking at the door, then Jonathan's voice came. 'Celia? What's going on in there?'

'Please, Arthur.'

He threw back his head again – and this time he was laughing. He was laughing, cruel, painful peals of laughter. 'Please!' he shouted. 'Oh please!'

He turned, backed against the curtain. 'I did it all for money! Everything. And now I've lost it.'

'You'll get it back. Stop this now.'

'Come here.'

Her heart was touched with fear. She told her legs to go forward, around the bed. They wouldn't move.

'I said, come here now.'

She clutched herself. He was her brother. She had to go to him. She edged along the bed, around the end. She was a few feet away from him. He jumped forward, seized her, and then he was swinging her around, through the curtain, and then they were standing on the tiny balcony over the street below.

'Arthur! You're holding me too tight!' He clutched her harder. Fear was sparking around her heart.

He pushed her forwards, her hips thrust hard into the iron of the balcony. She wanted to cry out in pain – did not. This wasn't Arthur any more, not her brother, not the man she loved. This was someone else, a man possessed and angry.

'Look down there,' he said. 'Look at all those people.' She'd gazed out of her window enough times, down at the people walking around. And now it made her afraid. The people below were tiny figures walking up and down. The dizziness seized her mind and she closed her eyes. 'Arthur—'

His mouth was close to her ear now, not whispering, for that would be too kind, but speaking quietly, cruelly. 'Don't you ever want to look down, little sister? Don't you wonder what it might be like?'

The world was spooling apart in front of her. Everything was breaking. His hands clutched her waist, his body pressed into hers – and there were thoughts bleeding in her mind that she didn't want to hear. *Stop it! Please.* She tried to move to the side, just a little, but he was holding her too hard. It was as if she was shored in iron: she couldn't move. 'Arthur—' *Please let me go. I'm your sister.* Louisa at the edge. *No!*

'Times like this really tell you the truth,' he said. 'You see the truth of everything, when you're on the brink. You understand what's important.'

'Please let me go.' But she whispered it, the wind swallowed her words. She was too afraid to shout.

'And you say that money isn't important. But what if you'd given everything in your life up for money? What if you'd done – the darkest act for money? And now you had lost it all?'

'What darkest act?' The words were out before she could stop them, because she didn't want to know, she really didn't, she wanted never to know.

He hugged her waist tightly. 'I was here with Louisa. On the cliff. I said, *Would you not like to see further?* She didn't want to. I said, go further. And she did – because she loved me.'

'Stop it. I don't want to hear any more.'

'Ah, but I want to tell it. Because then you'll understand why I don't want to talk and why all your words are useless. Because I killed her for her money – and now I've lost it all.'

'You didn't. I don't believe it.' Louisa's body crumpled at the bottom of the cliff. The trial, Arthur standing there, Mr Bird talking in court about how the couple couldn't see a thing, how they had been wrong to say that Arthur had pushed her. The dinner at the Ritz after Arthur went free, holding up their glasses. *To freedom!* Louisa's dresses, packed up and taken to Stoneythorpe, pink, green, gold, her evening bags piled on top. Her ring. 'Arthur—'

He pushed into her again so she was almost bending over the balcony.

'Please let me go. We can talk.'

'Oh, don't lie, Celia. You don't love me any more. How could anyone? I killed my wife for money – and then I threw all the money away. What was the point?'

Words ran through her head. *Arthur. Don't kill me.* She didn't want to say them, make it real by saying them. She was going to have to find some way of getting free. She couldn't fight him off, he had her pinned so tight. He pushed her again and they swayed together. She gazed at the people dizzily. They were looming at her. *Look up,* she begged. If they looked up and saw her, surely they'd send someone to rescue her. *Help me.*

'Please, Arthur. You have to let me go. Whatever you've done, it's in the past. You need to let go of me. We can help you.'

'Let go of you?'

'Yes. Please let me back into the room.'

'But I love this game. I want to get to the edge. I want to touch it. Why won't any of you come with me?'

'I don't like it.'

'You're just like Louisa.'

And then the idea came into her mind. 'But you're not at the edge. I am.'

He laughed, hard ringing laughter. 'I am at the edge. I'm always at the edge.'

'Show me.'

And then they were scuffling and he was at the front and she was behind him. She was flung back into the room, breathless. He stood against the balcony iron, back to the air.

'Show you? Here I am. Now what shall I do?'

'Come back.'

'Do you love me, sister?'

'Of course I love you. Please come back.'

'What do you think it would feel like to fall? You're dropping through the air, grabbing at it. But at the same time, you're flying. Free. Entirely free.'

'I don't—'

But he wasn't talking to her any more. He eased himself up

so he was sitting on the rail of the balcony. 'You'd be flying. And then, the moment before you hit the ground, how would that be? You'd see the truth then, wouldn't you? I bet Louisa saw it.'

Her whole body revolted at the idea of going back onto the balcony, taking his hand, trying to bring him back into the room. But she had to. She had to help him. She stepped forward, cautiously. He laughed again. He jumped back down from the railing and her heart swelled with relief.

'Come with me,' she said.

'Never.' He swung one leg, then another over the rail, so he was standing on the stone edge of the balcony, on the tips of his toes, holding the iron. 'You have nothing I want.'

She flung herself forward. 'Arthur!' She grabbed for his hand – but he pulled away, laughed again. 'See you!' Then he smiled, closed his eyes. He leant back. She screamed as his arms and legs wavered, desperately, his hands clawing. 'Arthur!' She grasped the rail. And then the noise of all the traffic horns and people and market boys shouting stopped as she heard a blow of body on stone – and she knew she had lost him.

TWENTY

Manhattan, December 1929

'I have to go back,' she said to Jonathan. 'I need to take Arthur home.'

The past week had been a miserable flurry of police, interviews, arrangements. The police wanted Arthur buried in New York – as did Mr Galss – but Celia was adamant. 'I'm taking him to Stoneythorpe. That's where he belongs.' They'd bury him in the graveyard of the church, next to Michael, where plots waited for all of them. She'd written to her parents to tell them and say she would bring him with her. It had been almost unbearable to write the letter.

'You won't come back.'

'I promise I will.' Jonathan and Mr Galss had taken care of so much. The hotel wanted them to leave after such a scandal, but Jonathan had persuaded the manager to let them stay for just a little while, at increased cost. He had taken Michael out to feed the ducks and eat ice cream when Celia was so captured by sickness and guilt that she could only lie in the dark and feel hatred for the world. He had tried to talk to her, make her feel better. At night, the darkness overwhelmed her and she couldn't be alone. He sat by her, held her.

'Don't leave me,' she said then. 'Don't leave me alone.'

She couldn't stop talking, telling him things. 'I tried to save my own skin,' she said. 'I thought he was going to make me jump. I made him change around. I was just trying to save myself. And he died.'

'You did the right thing.' They were whispering, as Michael was asleep – the only time they could really talk. She didn't tell him about what he'd said about Louisa. She couldn't.

'I pushed him to do it.'

'No, you didn't. It was going to happen eventually, don't you see? He was in a bad way. Mr Galss knew it, but thought he was improving. Galss said that a lot of men are in a bad way. Arthur just couldn't cope with the losses. He—'

Jonathan stopped himself. Celia guessed what he wanted to say. *Lots of businessmen have become suicides.* There were names reported every day, a list on the inner page of the newspaper. Celia had read that the newspapers had agreed to put the names on the inner page in case people were brought too low by seeing them on the front. She had agreed with the decision. But now she wanted Arthur blazing out of the front page, with a picture of him, a memory of his life. He'd just been a name in a list – an interesting note that an Englishman had thrown himself out of the Plaza Hotel.

'I don't think it was just the losses.'

'Of course, he'd had hard times. You all have. He lost his wife.' Celia nodded. Alone, late at night, she told herself that he was unbalanced when he said he'd killed Louisa. He was saying wild, mad things, thrown out in anger, not true. But something edging towards her heart told her that they were, that they'd all been wrong. Arthur had told the truth – and Louisa had died at his hand. That was the secret eating him, making him so terrifying, so dark in the final moments. Then the ivy furled up to her and tightened its grip on her soul and she had to stop herself from thinking, stop thinking at all.

'I can't stand it,' she said, and Jonathan stroked her forehead.

'I know,' he said.

But it wasn't just what she'd seen, it was the weight of all the knowledge, everything she had to keep from her family – Tom shooting Michael, Arthur killing Louisa.

'I wish someone could save me,' she said. 'From having to feel.'

'I'll save you.' She knew he'd say that. It wasn't what she meant.

'But you have Michael now. You have to be strong for him. He needs you.'

'I know.'

'Just pretend you're strong for him. That will be enough. And in time it will come.'

'I don't think I can. Not all the time.'

'Of course you can. I'll help you.'

That night she was restless, and woke when the men came for the dustbins. The bottles and leftover food from all the dinners, the paper she wrote on and threw into the bin. She couldn't imagine where it all went to. Things that people had once wanted. The soldiers had left their things in the trenches, bullets, bits of clothing, books, even guns. She'd read that in some places – not the ones full of tourists clutching their guidebooks – the grass had just grown over all the metal and the guns and you'd never know, now, that they were there.

They were falling on her, like snow.

There was no point fighting. The police and the authorities won, said that all they could allow Celia to do was have Arthur cremated, then take the ashes back home. A few days later, they had a funeral at a chapel near the park with Mr Galss, Miss Salm and the girls, Jonathan and a kind man who Mr Galss had invited, knew Arthur from the banks. He mopped his forehead, held his hand out for Celia's. Michael stayed behind with Mr Galss's sister, a teacher's wife from New Jersey who came down for the day to take him to Central Park. The minister looked exhausted, mispronounced Arthur's name, hurried through the words. That afternoon, the undertaker came to the hotel and handed Celia a dirty-looking jar. She sent a telegram to her parents. They hadn't answered her letter, too broken she supposed.

She put the urn on her desk in the bedroom, then waited for Jonathan to bring Michael back from the trip with Mr Galss's sister. Michael was tired and happy, fell asleep almost as soon as they had tucked him up in bed.

She whispered to Jonathan, all the same. 'I have to go. Arthur needs to be home. I need to see my mother.'

'I'll come with you.'

She shook her head. He would make it easier – she imagined him helping her on the boat, talking to people about the arrangements, looking after Michael. But then. 'I should do it alone.'

'I insist. I have to help you. You're my fiancée.'

'Look, it's not for very long. I just need to take him back. I need to do it alone. I owe my family. I owe him.'

'That's just making things difficult for yourself.'

'Maybe I want them to be that way. If you came, you'd make everything easy. I have to try.'

'What's wrong with easy?'

She shook her head. 'Look, Jonathan. I won't be long. I promise I'll come back. Michael and I will be back before you know it.' She tried to look away from the urn on her desk. It kept dragging her eyes back. It felt as if Arthur was listening, or as if she was betraying him by talking in front of him, ignoring him.

'What if you change your mind?'

'About what?' Michael turned over, sighed. She looked back at the urn, tried to ignore it.

'You might change your mind about coming back. Marrying me. You don't even have the ring yet!' The ring had come back from the jewellers, but not much smaller, so they'd sent it back again.

'Of course I want to marry you. I promised.'

'You might change your mind. Associate America with everything bad. But it's been good too. Remember?'

'I promise,' she said. 'I promise I won't. I'll come back and we'll get married. Properly, as we hoped.'

The banks were calling in the loans. She'd had letter after letter. He had borrowed so much against Flapper Foods, forged her signature on documents. She could never pay it back. She thought of Miss Salm and the girls, relying on her, the great opening they'd had in Bergdorf's, their smiling faces. All the orders they had in. They couldn't stop!

'I'm sorry,' said Mr Galss. 'You either sell or they will call on Stoneythorpe. He put that up as well, you see.'

'No. I can't sell the house. My parents!' Rudolf and Verena, Emmeline, with nothing.

'Then it must be the business.'

'If she just goes to the banks, they'll give her nothing,' said Jonathan. 'I'll help you find someone to buy the business, continue it, someone who will give you a fair price.'

'And the women might keep their jobs?'

'Maybe. I can't say. But at least there will be a business. And maybe you can come back to it, one day.'

In the following days, Jonathan hunted for a buyer and arranged meetings. She put her best suit on, pretended to smile as she talked about Flapper Foods to three bankers, a New York steel magnate who wanted a 'little business' for his daughter, and a widow with money to spend. She showed them around the Brooklyn kitchen, introduced them to the staff. The magnate offered the most money, but the widow was close – and she promised Celia she'd keep on Miss Salm and the salesgirls and see what she could do for the rest. The money she gave her was enough for the banks' demands but not much more. She cried when she said goodbye to Miss Salm and the women. She went into Bergdorf's, took one last look at their display and wept again, but hurried away when she saw a man from the store coming to move her along.

'Let's just hope Arthur didn't borrow anything else,' said Mr Galss. 'There's no guarantee this is the end of it.'

'They'll have to write me off as bankrupt.'

'Let's hope so. If they don't, they might look at assets abroad.'

'But I thought selling the business would be enough. I did that to save Stoneythorpe!'

'I'm sure you have. If he hasn't borrowed more. But I confess I am fearful that he might have. A friend of mine was telling me that he thought he had had all the debt requests in for a client – but then more arrived yesterday. If I were you, Miss, I'd encourage your parents to put the house on the market, quick. Then take the money and split it between you or put it in the children's names. They can't get at it that way.'

'And then you can all come and live in America,' said Jonathan, happily. 'Even Emmeline. She and I will try to get along.'

But Celia couldn't hear his joke. She sat back. They were in the dining room at the Plaza, still busy, despite the Crash, low conversations between businessmen. The place still had the chandelier, the fine damask tablecloths, the heavy cutlery. And they were sitting there and telling her that still there might be more ruin. The Florida beaches were covering them in sand. She felt like a shipwrecked person, clinging to a raft, owning nothing.

'Think about it, Miss Witt,' said Mr Galss. 'Persuade your parents to sell.'

Celia, Jonathan and Michael were walking through the park. She knew it was one of their last times. He gave her a bunch of gardenias as they strolled. Men passed them, looking for work.

'A photo?' said a man in a brown hat – and Jonathan said yes. So the little man arranged the three of them, Michael holding her hand, she clutching the gardenias. He pressed down the shutter and preserved them on the steps of the church, outside of time, forever.

PART TWO

TWENTY-ONE

Stoneythorpe, February 1930

'Here is your home,' she said to Michael, as they stepped out of the car. 'We'll meet your grandparents.' *The ones who sent you away.*

Perhaps if Arthur hadn't died, she would have stayed in America. But she had to see them.

On the last day, she had walked around New York telling herself she would come back. And yet still, a part of her body was behaving as if she never would, imprinting the city on her memory, the park, tall buildings, the museum, the lines of men looking for work. She and Arthur had tried to survive and they had not succeeded.

On the boat over, she balanced the urn on the floor of their cabin, propped up by pillows so it wouldn't fall. Jonathan thought she should have put it in her trunk but she would never do that. Trunks could get lost. The first night, she had barely been able to sleep for worrying about it. Michael slept in her arms, Harvey clutched to his chest and the wooden horse under his pillow, stowed together on the lower bunk of the bed. He didn't want to sleep alone. It had pleased her, that he had treasured one horse and Red had another.

In the last few nights, she'd waited for Red, left some sweets stuffed in a crack in the bricks, written to Violet, settled the business with Mr Galss, talked with Jonathan about the wedding and tried not to cry when she was alone.

On the second night, the passage turned rocky and Michael was sick, repeatedly. They sat on the floor outside the bathroom, pressed themselves against the wall of the cabin. She cradled him in her arms, holding him tight, trying to get him to drink water. Sometimes he slept. Then woke. Sometimes she wasn't sure whether he was awake or asleep and she talked to him, stories about home and the days before the war.

Also, she told him lies. 'It was another relative who was staying with us. Aunt Deerhurst.' Blushing for her untruth, the poor woman had already been dead for so long by then. 'She took you away and nobody knew. It was terrible.'

She thought he was asleep. And then he opened his eyes.

'Who is my father?' he asked.

Her blood beat fast in her mind. 'He was a soldier in the war. He died, just after. I wished you could have met him. He was a good man. Kind. He would have loved you so much.' This seemed to satisfy him. She had guessed – and it seemed to be right – that he would mind more about what his father thought about him than what he really was. But still. Soon he'd ask more questions. She held him tight on the cold floor as the ship swayed. She asked him about the Whetstones but he said he didn't want to speak of them. She heard him cry out in the night, begging someone not to do it.

'What will they think of me?' asked Michael, in the car from Dover. Jonathan had given her money, she'd changed it at the port. Still relying on him, another man keeping her afloat. She clutched the urn in her arms.

'They'll adore you, of course. They've been looking for you for so long.' How easy it was to lie to a child. He trusted her to tell the truth.

Jonathan had taken them to the port, brought them up onto the boat, rubbing their hands against the cold. 'You won't forget, will you?' he'd said, clasping her hands. They'd waited a few weeks before leaving – thinking that a passage in January would be too cold for Michael to bear. In the last week, she'd held Jonathan so much.

She'd shaken her head. 'Never. We'll be back as soon as we can.'

She took his money in her purse. They watched him walk down to the quay, the Statue of Liberty framed behind him – and she almost called him to come back.

Celia and Michael walked up to the front door. The trunk was left at the end of the drive, the urn at last tucked safely inside. She held Michael's hand as much to steady her own as to reassure him.

When she'd approached, the house looked like it had been hit by a giant storm, the roof crumbling, and the walls unkempt. The place looked nothing like it once had. The house was covered with ivy, too much of it, Celia saw now. Every spring, in the old days, men would hack back the ivy, because if they didn't it would grow into the hollows between stones, force them out and the house would start, slowly but surely, to fall. No one had touched the ivy in years and bricks had fallen out, some still lying in the front. It had been Rudolf's idea to buy Stoneythorpe. He'd put down his fork in the middle of dinner, when they lived in Hampstead, announced he had seen a house that he was going to buy. Celia had imagined a castle, thanks to the romantic way that Rudolf had spoken of it. The reality, a great heavy pale stone house, two red-brick front wings coming forward, three ornamental curved porches covered with carved stone like lace, high chimneys, grounds either side. Dozens of windows, thirty rooms, but few of them were now used. Celia's favourite room had been the library but it had been locked up because of the damp.

'It's very old,' she said, patting Michael on the shoulder. 'Not all the houses in England look like this.'

A woman who Celia didn't recognise opened the door. She'd told her parents and Emmeline by telegram from Dover that they hoped to arrive in the morning – they were already late. She walked into the parlour, holding Michael tightly by the arm.

The parlour was older, shabbier but otherwise the same: the old yellow-and-blue-striped chairs, cream sofas, pale walls with family portraits, big glass windows opening onto the garden, overgrown now. She paused by a table near the door, then walked forward.

171

'Here he is, father,' she said, gazing at Rudolf, smaller and older than ever in the straight-backed chair. 'I've brought Michael home.'

Verena gasped. 'Celia! You found him.' Michael held tight to Celia's hand, still clutching his bear.

'I did. I told him we'd all been looking for him. I said you had too.'

Verena and Rudolf were staring at Michael, two china dolls, unable to move. They had lost so much. They were bearing it so bravely.

The door burst open and Lily rushed in. 'Don't run!' Emmeline was shouting. 'Stop!'

'Who are you?' Lily said, eyeing Michael.

'This is your cousin, Lily,' said Celia. 'Michael has come all the way from America to stay with us.'

Lily jumped up to Michael. Celia wanted to reach out for her – her gangly arms and legs, her dark hair, her snub-nosed face – capture the last of her childhood. Adulthood was taking her up, winding its tendrils into her body, inevitable, changing her. Of course it was as it should be, but something in Celia pulled against it. She wanted her to be a child forever and ever – not have to negotiate the adult world, ungenerous, inflexible.

Emmeline looked the same, even in her old grey dress, as if she'd jumped out of a ladies' magazine advertisement for soap, the golden hair curling around her face, the figure that went in and out. Lily had her little nose and pink cheeks, but the rest of her was all Janus, dark hair, pale skin, the contrast that people had admired when she was a child, struck at Celia's heart now she was older. Her niece was so handsome. But part of her was like Celia as she had been when she was young, the thin, stalky bird movements of the legs, the constant look of nervousness.

'You've grown so much, Lily.'

'Adults always say that.' Lily was staring at Michael.

'Well, I don't know about you, but I am going to hug my nephew,' said Emmeline. 'Time for us to get acquainted.' She lifted Michael up in a bear hug.

'Now my turn!' said Lily. She put her arms out and pulled him up. 'Look!' she said, her face red with the effort. 'I can.'

'Now my turn to pick up you,' said Michael, when she had set him down.

Michael reached for Lily and she jumped away. 'You've got to catch me first!' she cried and fled from the room, laughing. Michael turned to look at Celia – and then ran too.

'Well, isn't that nice,' said Emmeline, hands on her hips, looking at the door. 'Poor Lily has been missing Albert – he's just started school. Now she has a friend to play with.'

'Lily is a practically a boy herself,' said Verena.

'Good,' said Emmeline. 'What use is ladylike behaviour? It's a new era now.'

There was a scream outside and then a shout of laughter. A door banged and footsteps skittered off towards the garden.

'Mind the vases!' shouted Emmeline. She turned and flopped into a chair. 'Well, Celia, surprise after surprise. Tell us where you found him. He's a handsome little boy, isn't he?' *Is his face that of his father's?* Celia guessed she was thinking.

Celia sat down on the sofa. 'Honestly? I asked someone to steal his address, then I half begged, half threatened his parents. But that didn't work. Then they lost all their money in the Crash and gave him to me.' She stared hard at her parents with the word 'steal'. *It was what you made me do.*

Verena's face was pale, crumped. 'I never thought you'd find him. Do you think he will forgive me? Us?' Verena whispered.

'He'll never know. I told him it was Aunt Deerhurst and that's what he believes.'

Celia watched the relief in her mother's face and felt a twinge of anger at it: cowardice. 'It will be our secret.'

'Yes, yes,' nodded Rudolf. 'All water under the bridge now.'

She felt another spark of fury. It was water under the bridge for him. But what if she'd never found Michael, never lied, sent Red to steal, threatened, begged?

'We were lucky he was alive,' she said, angrily. 'I'm sure some of the children sent away like this died. They beat him, mistreated him. You wouldn't believe it. He won't really talk about it.' She kept asking him about it and he said he wanted to forget. And maybe, she thought, perhaps he was forgetting. Perhaps the days with Jonathan, the ice cream parlours, the new country, might be enough to make him forget.

'Two hours with Lily and he'll forget everything,' said Emmeline. 'That child never stops with her imaginary worlds.' And she was right, that was what Celia hoped too, that Lily and all of them could make him forget – and her too, so that every time she looked at her parents, she wouldn't think: *It was your fault.*

Verena smiled. Celia looked at her – and then the portrait of Arthur over the mantelpiece, above her head. And she realised they didn't know. They were smiling at jokes, laughing. Lily was tearing through the house, giggling.

'You don't know,' she said.

'Know what?' asked Rudolf, suddenly seeming to grasp the conversation. 'Are you talking about the Crash? We hear about nothing else. I've been writing to Arthur about it but I haven't heard back. I presume the stock is lowered? I don't doubt the company is strong. Everybody needs to eat meat!'

'Was it awfully dramatic?' asked Emmeline. 'It must have been quite a shock.'

'The company has lost a lot, Papa. I don't know how much. But – didn't you get my letter? And the telegram. Jonathan and Mr Galss wrote too.'

'Who is Mr Galss? And Jonathan? I didn't get any letters or telegrams.'

'I expect she means Jonathan Corrigan,' said Emmeline. 'Is he still desperately in love with you, Celia? Anyway, what do you mean, lost a lot? I thought Arthur was setting up factories in America. *They* can't have collapsed. How much?'

'But I wrote. I sent a telegram. Jonathan said he did, too. I know he did.'

Out of the corner of her eye, she saw Emmeline sit up. 'Saying what? What did the telegram say? What's happened?'

Celia shook her head. She could feel the tears coming. 'I can't.'

'Can't what?' Outside, Lily and Michael were in the garden, screaming and whooping. 'What's happened?'

She looked at Rudolf, Verena, her sister. 'I wrote. They did too.'

'What? You tell us. Now!' Emmeline leant forward, started out of her chair. 'What's happened?'

'It's Arthur. I brought him back with me. He – he died.'

'No,' said Emmeline. 'No. It's not possible. Don't listen to her, Mama. She's just joking. No.'

'He's dead. Almost two months ago. I wanted to bring him back. To bury. They wouldn't let me. I've got an urn instead—'The tears engulfed her. She looked up and Rudolf had wrapped his arms around himself, was rocking back and forth. He was singing to himself, softly, a song she recognised – a German folk song he used to sing to her when she was a little girl. Verena was lying back on her chair, eyes closed, arms shaking.

'How?' said Emmeline. 'Tell us how. You have to! Was he ill? Did he get hit by one of those cars in New York? What happened?'

'He died. He just died.'

'He just died? No one *just dies*.'

Celia shook her head, looked down. Arthur, eyes wild, pulling her towards him, pushing her against the iron of the balcony. 'He threw himself out of the window. He wanted to die.'

Verena slapped her hand on the sofa. 'He didn't. That's a lie. He never would. Tell us the truth.'

The words flashed through her mind. *Louisa*. She pushed them away. 'We – lost a lot of money. In the Crash. Arthur was afraid.'

'He died for money?'

'You – don't understand what it was like. Everyone was afraid. Lots of people were – inviting death. He thought he'd lost every-thing.'

Emmeline stood up. 'But it's only money. Money's nothing.'

Verena was sitting forward, intently. 'He thought we'd resent him. He thought we'd be angry. That's it, isn't it, Celia? He was ashamed – of what we'd say.'

Celia looked at her mother, sitting on the sofa, the portraits of Arthur and Michael ranged over her head, her face cut over with guilt. Patches of red were rising on her mother's face, her skin flaming up with misery. She could release her – tell her the truth. It wasn't you. It was because he'd killed Louisa and then lost it all, that's why. Verena's eyes were filling up with tears. Celia could set her free, tell the truth. But the truth was worse. *You'll have to keep it*, said Louisa's voice in her ear. *Don't tell.*

But why do I have to keep all the secrets? Why me?

Verena was weeping. 'My own son! Why wouldn't he trust me?'

'He did,' Celia said, but too weakly.

Emmeline took three steps towards her. 'Why didn't you stop him? You must have known if he was feeling angry. You should have been helping him.'

'Emmeline,' said Rudolf. But he wasn't warning her strongly, not really. Celia gazed at him. Maybe he even agreed with her.

'What about when it actually happened?' Emmeline went on. 'Were you there? Why didn't you stop him?'

'I tried! I tried to hold him back. But he – you don't know what he was like. He was – terrifying.' *He was going to kill me. He said he killed Louisa.* She couldn't say that. She'd never know it was true. He had lost his reason at the end, nothing was real. She would have to bear the burden of what he had said, never knowing the truth, could not tell them because what would that do but hurt them more?

'Look, Emmeline. I'm sorry. But it wasn't my fault. He was so upset. He couldn't even be happy about Michael.'

'Michael? What did that matter if he was going to do what he did?'

It was her grief speaking, Celia knew, but still.

Celia sat back on the chair. She was engaged to Jonathan. They were getting married. She was supposed to go back. But how could she leave her family, broken, reduced.

'Emmeline,' said Rudolf. 'You're making Celia cry.'

Celia gazed out of the window. Lily and Michael were chasing each other around, rushing back and forth, dashing around a tree. Lily tripped, then Michael, and they were both on the ground, laughing. She watched them look up at the sky, still laughing.

She had done the same herself, as a child, chasing around with Tom, remembered the wonder of staring up at the sky, heart racing. And now Michael – her poor, sad Michael – was there too, laughing, without a care. She knew that if she looked into her heart, it would be a selfish one, so flooded with happiness about Michael that she couldn't agree with the words her parents and Emmeline were saying behind her: he should never have gone to New York, the city killed him and they should have stopped him. She wouldn't agree. New York was where she'd found Michael.

'Celia,' said Verena. She turned around. 'Thank you for coming back. I don't think I could lose another child.'

This was her moment to say *but I'm not back for very long. I'm going to be married to Jonathan and I need to go back to him.* She didn't. She couldn't, not then. She'd tell them later, talk about a big wedding in New York, some good news. She watched Michael, up again, running after Lily. She rested her head against the window, gazing at him. And then she saw herself, running through the gardens, dashing away from Tom. She stared at her son, watching herself racing through the gardens with him.

She watched the others grieve, feeling out of sync with them. They were steps behind, still shocked, when she was growing closer to – if not accepting, being able to say that Arthur was dead. She let them, sat quietly by them until Rudolf went to his study, Verena fled upstairs.

'Is Samuel in Spain?'

Emmeline raised an eyebrow. 'Indeed. Gone to save them from tyranny. He said he'd write. I've told the children he's taking a little holiday.'

'Poor you.'

'He said he wouldn't be long. Who knows? I've written letters. Five so far to the address he gave us. But there's been no answer. Lily has been moping about the house. Albert's at school now and she's been feeling sorry for herself. Michael might just be what she needs to cheer her up.'

'Where is Albert at school?' asked Celia, trying to be polite, distract her mind from screaming at her father. *You send one grandson to school, the other smuggled out and shipped abroad.* 'Does he enjoy it?'

'London. Harrow. He seems happy enough,' Emmeline said. 'I've had a few letters mostly just asking for more sweets to share with the other boys. Samuel probably wouldn't approve. He's learning Latin and all the tools Samuel would say were of the elite. So it's the only advantage of my husband being away. By the time he gets back, it will be too late to move Albert to somewhere else. We only managed to get him in in the middle of term because another boy was ill and had to leave without notice.'

'I'm glad you didn't send Lily to school. So Michael has a friend.'

'That would be too much. Samuel couldn't have them both learning to be cogs in the capitalist wheel. Anyway, Papa can't afford two.'

The children played all evening, protested loudly when they prised them apart to go to bed. Celia put Michael to bed in her room, lay next to him stroking his forehead until he slept. She waited to check he was fast asleep, holding tight to Harvey and his horse. Then she crept away.

That night, when everything was quiet, Celia wandered around the house with her light. The weeds hadn't just been in the garden. There were a few in the corridor near the kitchen, scratching through the stones. The ceiling of the hall was covered in a thick dark mould. The wallpaper was peeling in all the rooms she could open – and there were cobwebs thick with spiders in the corners. She walked up to Michael's room, tried the door. Still locked. She wondered if they'd changed it since her brother died, whether the little wooden planes he'd been so fond of making hung down from the ceilings, fluttering in the cold air on tiny white strings. She walked up to Arthur's room, tried the door. That was open. She slipped through. She hadn't been in Arthur's room for years. It was still as he must have left it when he eloped with Louisa, except the maids had stripped the bed. There was a pile of clothes on

178

the chair that she supposed must have been thrown aside because they couldn't fit into his suitcase.

She knelt up on the bed and touched the shelf full of things, silver ornaments, candles, old books. She didn't recognise any of them, supposed he must have bought them in Paris, little trinkets from market stalls that caught his eye. An old box of chocolates with a few crumbs inside, bloomed with white. She had not realised he was so sentimental. Something about the things hurt her heart – the intimacy of them, collected and then left behind. She held an ornamental box to her, as if by clutching it, Louisa would have never gone with Arthur, didn't fall from the cliff.

She felt the tears on her cheeks. She lay down on Arthur's bed, staring at the cracks in the ceiling, let the tears fall.

'Winter Meats didn't succeed in America and it won't survive here unless something changes.' She was sitting in the parlour with Emmeline, Verena and Rudolf. Michael was outside with Lily, chasing squirrels, probably, dashing through the overgrown grounds. It was a week since Celia had arrived and told them about Arthur. And Winter Meats in Britain was without anyone to run it now. They had the family lawyer who Arthur had appointed before America – Mr Pemberton – but they needed someone in charge.

'You can do it,' Rudolf had said. 'You manage the business. These are different times.'

'I'm not sure I can,' she said. She couldn't do it from America. And besides, even though she knew she could run Winter Meats, she didn't know if she wanted to. Not stacking up figures and going to factories. It was selfish, she knew. For how else were they going to protect the house? She looked at her family and her soul twisted because there was nobody else to help them.

'We might have to sell the house.'

'I won't hear of it,' said Verena. 'Stoneythorpe is our home.'

Celia thought of Mr Galss. Everything she had done to save the house. And yet they might still have to. As he had said, they should sell it now and put the money in trust for the children.

'I think we should consider selling. This is too big for all of us.'
'Never,' said Verena. 'No.'

'Surely you can make us money,' said Emmeline.

'We lost a lot in America,' said Celia. 'We may have to sell.' She didn't want to, wanted to keep the house for Michael forever. He'd been denied it. But if the debts came, they would all be lost.

Her mother gazed at her, pleadingly.

All she could think was, *they sent your child away!* But they were still her parents. They'd lost so much. She couldn't lose any more. Maybe she could look after Winter Meats for a short while. And she could start Flapper Foods here in Britain. She had told them all about her success. She could do it again, in Britain, try again. There were flappers here too, young girls in shops and offices who needed to eat! She thought of herself, busy again, using the recipes, buying the stock, reusing the advertising. But then. She didn't want to stay here. She was supposed to be going back to America to live with Jonathan.

She knew that Mr Galss would say they were wrong. He'd say the roof was full of holes and the walls crumbling. No one wanted to work there. If there were more of Arthur's debts, it could sink them all.

'Please,' said Verena.

Celia tore her eyes away from her mother's. She wanted to throw herself at Verena, tell her that they'd find a way. She'd sold Flapper Foods to protect the house because she couldn't bear it – seeing her old home broken up, her dell where she'd sat as a child, conjured her stories. If they sold it now, they'd have nothing left of Michael and Arthur. And she'd have sold her company for nothing.

'We just need the financial situation to improve,' said Rudolf.

Emmeline put down her teacup, crossly. 'That's not going to happen any time soon.'

'The decision is final,' said Rudolf. 'We're not moving.'

Celia looked at the painting of her brothers on the wall. 'So what do we do?'

'When your mother and I die, you can sell it. Not before. Our graves are waiting in the graveyard. That is where we'll be buried. This is our home.'

'Look,' said Celia, hating every word. 'You could go somewhere much nicer. More modern. Somewhere warm in the winter. You have weeds growing through the cracks in the hall. And there's mould.' She thought of Arthur's room, the silver ornaments on the shelves. They'd have to clear them away, stow them in a box in the loft in a new house. Verena would have to unlock Michael's room and they'd put his wooden aeroplanes into boxes.

'We want to live here,' said Verena. 'We want to die here.' She shook her head. 'Celia, we have you back here. We can all live together.'

'I can't. I have to go back to America. It's Michael's home. You could come with me!'

Her mother simply nodded. 'Our home is here. But of course you can go back and forth.'

Celia tried to hold her gaze. 'No, I have to go back.'

She'd dropped her big news about America, what she had been so afraid to say. But Verena wasn't listening, had barely heard it. Neither was Emmeline, who stamped her foot. 'Don't you care about your grandchildren? What about Lily? Albert can get a job – but what about her? You don't care. What you're saying is that we have to wait until the house is falling down around your ears before you'll move. We have to wait until the roof falls in and then nobody will buy it?'

'We'll find a way,' said Rudolf, placidly. 'Celia will help us.'

TWENTY-TWO

Stoneythorpe, April 1930

England looked no different. But Celia felt she had completely changed, that she was a new person encountering it now, the old one lost like clothes you had disposed of, tried to get back, but realised even if you did, you'd changed too much and you had to be different now.

'You can't go,' said Emmeline. They were out in the garden, tipping back their faces to catch the sun. 'You can't leave me with all this. You need to help us. You can't just go back to America.'

Celia gazed around the overgrown garden, the weeds crawling over the flower beds, a fallen tree splayed across the lawn. She'd been down to her old place, her little dell. She'd thought it wouldn't matter that the rest of the garden was neglected, for her space had always been wild. But she couldn't find the same magic in it. Before, it had always felt as if fairy people had run away just before she arrived. Once, it was her secret place. Now there was something flat about it, dull and old. And it was vulnerable, not safe, could be pulled down at any time and all of her would be left exposed.

'He seems happy enough here to me. Lily loves him. You can barely keep the two of them apart.'

What about Jonathan? she thought, but dared not say. She'd been writing to him, three or four times a week, telling him everything but not what was important. There had been so much to do. Comforting the family, another small funeral in the church for Arthur, burying the urn next to Michael in the graveyard, a reception with Verena's elderly cousins from Dorset. Then the journalists who got wind of the story and remembered about the trial and came down to knock on the windows and say, 'Don't you want to give your side of the story?' They didn't. Although, Celia had to admit, the resulting reports hadn't been too bad. There was a lot of sympathy for America and the businessmen who died. The only problem was that it meant all the British factory suppliers had written to them in a panic and Celia had had to send letters saying everything was fine, proceeding as usual and the losses in America had been minimal, just very distressing.

She had had meetings with Mr Pemberton to go over the accounts. The business was not in a good way, orders were down, there were large loans outstanding and stores had returned a lot of stock.

'Perhaps it was simply that we were in need of leadership,' said Mr Pemberton. 'You can turn Winter Meats around.' She was going to have to do it herself, head it up, visit the factories, talk to the men, make new plans. She agreed, even though her heart was reluctant. She wanted to marry Jonathan. She was *engaged*. She hadn't told the family yet, but since they had barely noticed when she said she had to return to America, she supposed they would ignore that too.

Emmeline tossed her head. 'We need you to run the business.' Every day Celia stayed at Stoneythorpe, she imagined Mr Galss telling her she was wrong to try to prop it up, Jonathan saying the same. The house was full of dust, falling apart. Rudolf and Verena sat in the middle of it, like two statues, resplendent as their temple collapsed around them, thrown open to the burning sun, beating rain. The newspapers said houses were declining in value. They'd get more now than if they waited.

She couldn't tell Emmeline about the possibility of the debts. There was no point worrying her, for perhaps it might not happen. The thought of Michael spending time in her old home was too overwhelming. He deserved it. His childhood here had been taken from him.

'Let's see if the situation improves.' The sun was shining too hard in Celia's eyes. She looked out again. 'No word from Samuel?'

Emmeline shrugged. 'Nothing. Maybe that address doesn't work. I don't know. I presume they'd tell me if he were dead.'

'Dead? Why would he be dead?'

'Who knows? I don't know what he's doing. I'm beginning to think he'll never write back. But I'll keep on sending letters. You never know. Sometimes I feel selfish, because I don't just miss him. I miss our flat in Bedford Square, living in London. I wish I had the money to rent it again. We're just getting along here.' Emmeline cleared her throat. 'What are you going to tell Tom?'

'To tell Tom?'

'About his child. About Michael.'

'What are you talking about?'

'Don't lie, Celia. I'm your sister. I always thought it was him. Well, I believed that lie about the soldier in the beginning. Then I thought better of it. You'd at least make some effort to find the man – or talk about how terrible he was. You didn't do either. And who else would you have given in to than Tom? And now you turn up with this child who has the look of him. I see his sister in his eyes.'

'You guessed.'

'Don't worry, the others haven't. He has the resemblance, but you have to look for it. So are you going to get him to marry you?'

'Never, Emmeline! He's not – he's not. He's not part of it.'

'Of course he is. He's the father. What do you think he's going to say if he hears about it?'

'He won't know.' She hadn't seen him since her terrible words to him around Arthur's trial. And then the time before when she'd told him she'd had a baby – a soldier she'd met one night – and he'd been shocked, disappointed by her. He didn't love her. Never wanted her – so how could he want her son? If she met him with Michael, he might feel obliged to try to love them both. She couldn't bear that.

Emmeline didn't understand. She couldn't. Celia could never tell her the truth, how Tom had stood in a half circle around their brother in 1916 and shot him. She'd thought she could never forgive him. But she knew that what he'd told her was the truth: he'd had no choice. Even if he'd saved Michael on that day, still the authorities would have found him again, put a hood on him, taken him out onto the grass to be shot. Only this time, Tom would be standing next to him.

Celia had to keep the secret. She couldn't tell. It would kill her parents, break Emmeline's spirit. They might even blame Michael for it now, see something of Tom's terrible acts in the child. She couldn't open up that dreadful box, because if she did, all the secrets might be set free and, after all they'd suffered, it would ruin them if they knew the truth about what had happened to her brother: that the army had condemned him as a coward.

There was a scream behind them and Michael and Lily hurtled into view, laughing. 'Get her to give it back!' Michael was shouting.

'It's mine! Finders keepers!'

'What is going on?' demanded Emmeline, turning around. But they were off again, laughing, Lily's skirts flying out behind her. 'Remember! No going to the woods.'

'I've never seen her so happy,' Emmeline said. 'Not since she was a little girl. Certainly not since Samuel left...'

'Why are you always telling them not to go to the woods? I don't think we cared much about them when we were children.'

'We ran wild. You have to be careful nowadays. You never know what's out there. Especially for girls. Well, it may be different for boys. You're far too protective of Michael already. You can't hide him from all the evil in the world, you know.'

'I know! He's seen enough, that's all.'

'So, my question. What if Michael asks about his father?'

'He asked on the boat over and I said he was dead. But maybe when I marry, I'll say he was the father all along.' Jonathan and she together in a big hall full of flowers in New York. In sickness and in health.

'He'll start asking more soon. Everybody wants to know who their father is. Your son's a bright boy. He's going to want to know.' Celia shook her head. 'Look, why were you always moping after Tom in the first place? A servant. What did he promise you?'

'Nothing. He promised me nothing. Anyway, it was all me. He didn't want me, not really. He said I only loved him because of our childhood together – and it wasn't an equal friendship anyway.'

'Well that's probably true. But Celia! Why were you chasing after a servant? Even Jonathan would have been better than that.'

'What's wrong with Jonathan?'

'He's so brash. But Tom? I don't understand it. You were just trying to live your childhood again. It's time to grow up, Celia. If you refuse to tell Tom, find a proper man. Tough with a child in tow, since there aren't many of them to be had, but if you stop being so mopey and put some make-up on, you just might do it.'

'Emmeline. Jonathan has asked me to marry him. I've accepted.'

'You have?'

'He loves me. I love him. Would you come with me to live in New York?' Her sister, so brittle on the outside, soft and afraid under it all.

'Why didn't you say about Jonathan before?'

'I wanted to save up some good news. Please come with me.'

Emmeline tipped her head back to the sun. 'What – America? Of course not. I can't do anything until Samuel gets back. And I doubt he'd want to. Anyway, we couldn't leave Mama and Papa.'

'They could come too.'

'Don't be ludicrous, Celia. They'd never leave here. They're too old. If you go to America, you go alone.'

'I'm not going to look after Winter Meats – I don't think anyone can save it.'

I'm going back to America, she should have said. *I'm going to be married to Jonathan and then I will send back money for you all.* She was about to.

'Please, Celia. You have to help us. I'll look after Michael for you. He and Lily get on like a house on fire.'

She couldn't say it. 'Well, just for a while. And then I have to go back to America.'

TWENTY-THREE

Stoneythorpe, July 1930

Britain was trying to pull itself out of the Crash, that's what everyone said. There was terrible unemployment and British exports were dropping in price. It didn't seem fair – no one in Manchester or Glasgow had invested in Miami apartments or Hawaii hotels. But, still, what shook America shook the world.

Verena and Emmeline closeted themselves away, reading. Verena had the latest Agatha Christie novels sent over from London the minute they were published. She and Emmeline swapped them over. 'She is exactly right on an English village,' said Verena. 'They are cruel places.' Verena loved Hercule Poirot, too, his neatness and precision, said that she thought Miss Christie should write more of him. Most of his success, it seemed to Celia, seemed to be in encouraging people to speak and through them learning the truth. Another royal baby was to be born and Lily said it would be a boy, the future King.

Celia told Rudolph and Verena about the engagement and they begged her to stay, just for a little while until they were on their feet. She wrote to Jonathan that they would soon be on their way, she just had to help her family with business first. He was disappointed but said he understood and she assured him she would not be long. She spent the early summer looking over the papers and taking Michael with her on tours of the country, the factories and Winter Meats properties across the Midlands, North and South East. It had taken her a long time, sorting through the papers with Mr Pemberton, to work out exactly what was what and where everything was. But she thought she understood the business now. She'd listened to managers talk about the products, she'd visited shops, talked to workers. The loans were daunting and the demand was collapsing. It was impossible to keep it alive. All she wanted to do was set up a version of Flapper Foods here in Britain. She had come so close in America – and surely she could do it again, under a different name. She and Michael stayed in hotels, looked at factories, but he yearned so much for Lily and Stoneythorpe that she felt bad taking him away and decided she would go back and send Pemberton to look instead. And the more he loved Stoneythorpe, the more she refused to listen to Mr Galss talking reason in her head and decided she would do anything to keep it.

Rudolf called Celia into his study one day.

'We haven't had much time to talk since you've got back,' he said. 'I miss my little Celia.' She edged in, pained at the sight of him looking so old, bald-headed, his stomach fat, almost like an old round baby in the chair. How could she be his little Celia now, after what she'd seen? Arthur had killed himself in front of her and she could never tell her father the truth.

Rudolf smiled. 'Why don't you come here and sit by me? Tell me how you are, Celia. I miss our talks.'

'I'm very well, Papa.' She thought of him standing up, crying out 'America' on the evening they went to celebrate Arthur's freedom. The night in the Ritz, lifting glasses. They'd drunk to truth and justice.

Hot words flamed in her head. 'Do you not think you were wrong, Father?'

'Wrong?'

'You were wrong to send Michael away. You broke my heart. And now look at how happy he is. Aren't you going to apologise?'

'Celia, Celia, it's all over now.'

'Not for me. I still remember it. I remember having him and waking up and he was gone.'

Rudolf was shifting about, uncomfortably. 'Your mother,' he murmured.

'Not just her. You could have stopped it. You were – what? Trying to save our reputation, such as it was?'

Rudolf nodded. 'It all worked out in the end.'

Celia was seized by fury. 'No it didn't! Anything could have happened. The family didn't love him, mistreated him. Jonathan paid them off – did you know that?'

'Jonathan.' Rudolf smiled. Celia could see her father was desperately clutching at a reed that would pull him out of her hot pool of anger. She looked at him, old, shrunken in the chair, and the idea of him doing something so terrible seemed cruel and impossible. He wasn't a tyrant, he was a little old man. And yet he *had* done wrong, he *had* taken Michael. He smiled at her. 'Jonathan is just who I wanted to talk to you about.'

'We can talk about Jonathan later! Why did you do it? Michael might have died. Your own grandson.'

Rudolf shook his head. 'Verena! Emmeline!'

As if on cue, Verena came through the door, Emmeline too, Lily behind her.

'What's happening?'

Celia swung around. 'We're talking about Michael. Lily, go and find him and play. This is grown-up talk.'

'Oh, *dull*,' sighed Lily, skipped out of the room.

Emmeline hurried over to Rudolf, put her arms around him. 'What's happening?'

'I'm asking Papa why he and Mama did it. Why they sent Michael away.'

Verena was sitting down now, her hand on her forehead, her body still holding a dancer's grace. 'Celia, it was what was right at the time.'

'The family in America hated him. I was just telling Papa. They weren't going to give up Michael for free. They wanted ten thousand dollars. Jonathan got it in a day. Without him, Michael would be – well, I don't want to think.'

'Jonathan gave you the money?' Emmeline was gazing at her. 'He gave you ten thousand dollars? Do we have to repay him?'

Celia shook her head. 'No. I was – am – his fiancée. He knew

190

how much I needed it. And I want to know why they did it. I want them to tell me why!'

She looked away from her sister, at her mother and father. Her father was weeping softly. She hadn't seen him cry since he came back from the war.

'Forgive me,' he croaked, looking upwards, like a small child saying his prayers. 'Forgive me.'

Verena shook her head. 'Celia, you have to believe us. Maybe we were wrong. But it's not easy for girls to raise a baby alone.'

'You love your grandchildren, Albert and Lily. You're spending your last funds sending Albert to school. Why didn't you think you might love Michael, too?'

Rudolf shook his head. 'Let us forget it. When you are married you can have more children.'

'So I must go back to live in America. But I don't want to leave you. Why can't you come too?'

'He could come here.' said Rudolf, brightening. 'This is excellent.'

'He can't,' said Celia. 'His life is there.' But then, a feeling crept up in her. Why not? If Jonathan really loved her, why could he not live here with them?

INTERLUDE

She'd realised as soon as she saw Michael that they would be friends forever.

She'd taken Michael into the garden, this shy boy all the way from America. 'Let me show you somewhere,' she'd said, took him down the garden to the place where Aunt Celia had used to like to sit.

For the first month or so, he'd slept in Aunt Celia's room. And then they'd put him in his own room, one that used to be a box room at the top of the stairs. She'd crept out of her bed, to stand just in the corridor outside, in the shadows where nobody could see her. She'd heard him say, 'I will be fine, Mama. Don't worry!' She'd heard Celia standing outside for half an hour or so. Then her footsteps walking away. Lily waited. Then, when the corridor was silent, she hurried through to the door, pushed it open, gently.

'It's me!' she whispered. 'I came to see if you were all right.'

He gazed at her, eyes wide, over the cover. 'This house is too big,' he whispered back. 'It creaks too much.'

'Oh those are just the pipes. You'll get used to them. I did.'

She sat on the eiderdown. 'I'll stay with you,' she said.

He held her hand in the darkness. 'Our secret,' he said. She held on hard, two sets of fingers, intertwined.

The house became their wonderland. The adults didn't use even half of it. They didn't see a thing. He and Lily found rooms that were supposed to be locked but the locks had broken so you could easily creep in and no one would know you were there. They stole cakes and biscuits from the kitchens and ran upstairs with them, made dens in the sheets on the old broken beds. They imagined they were everything: African explorers, magic men flying to the moon, tigers prowling for prey. They could be everything. They wouldn't be like the adults, hidebound, always talking about the dreariest subjects. 'Let's never have secrets,' she said. 'Let's always tell each other everything.'

Lily told him about her father, always plotting something if he was at home, living in Spain and creating adventures. 'He's so brave,' she said. 'He will do anything for honour.'

They imagined what it must be like for him in Spain – as he hid in trees or behind bushes, worked hard to save the world.

'One day, I'd like to be like him,' said Michael. He wasn't sure that he really did. But Lily adored her father and he wanted her to love him as much too.

She told him how sorry she felt for him. He talked about the Whetstones. But it seemed so far away from him now, almost like a dream, so he felt bad when she cried for him, the little boy locked up in the attic with no supper when he hadn't done his work properly. He found it hard to explain – that child in the attic was a different boy. Mama had rescued him and now this was his life and sometimes he had to remind himself that he hadn't always lived here at Stoneythorpe, holding Lily's hand every night when she crept into his room after Mama had gone. She put her beloved purple cat, made for her by her father, next to his bear Harvey and they were best friends too.

The only place they weren't allowed to go was the woods at the end of the garden. The nearest they were permitted was the dell where Mama had used to sit and imagine fairies when she was a little girl. Mama liked them to go and sit there but they didn't much like it – Lily found it damp and he thought it was too dark. But he told Mama that they loved it and could see fairies there like she could. It was worth the lie to see how happy she became when he said it. Privately, he thought that Mama's childhood must have been very dull if sitting on that wet rock next to a pond choked up with weeds was the highlight.

Sometimes he and Lily sat and talked about the woods, invented what they thought might be in there. There must be something terrible, if they were so forbidden.

They sat through breakfast, just waiting until the moment when Mama or Aunt Emmeline said that they had been there long enough and could leave the table. Then they went off into the garden and they were free. Their minds hurried until they were called in for dinner. And then, at night, the moment that made his heart soar, when Lily came in and held his hand until he slept, slipped out again so that Mama would never know when she came to look in on him before going to bed. Because if he went to sleep holding Lily's hand, then that meant she was in his dreams. They ran together, through his night world, holding hands and laughing.

TWENTY-FOUR

Stoneythorpe, September 1930

Celia wrote to Jonathan to say she was still delayed. They were coming. She promised they were coming. Her parents kept asking – shouldn't you have a ring? What about a wedding? She couldn't answer. She couldn't make sense of her thoughts. She wanted to be married to Jonathan yet living in Stoneythorpe, looking after her family. And she couldn't be two things, two people. She had to choose.

There was always somewhere where the business needed her. Even though it was struggling, she could not think of a way to tell Rudolf. She knew she should be straight: Winter Meats was a business for life under the old King, we live in a different world now. But it was easier to travel to the customers, the suppliers, the factories, than it was to stay at home and speak the truth.

She arrived back early one morning from a tour of department stores from London to Manchester, raced in and ran up to find Michael, not even bothering to change out of her brown suit. He wasn't in his room – and then she tried hers and found him fast asleep in her old bed, trusty Harvey in his arms. She lay down next to him and put her arms around him, listening to him breathe.

She woke up to Emmeline coming into the room. 'I heard you were here,' she said. 'You've come back.'

Celia looked up, still holding Michael who hadn't stirred. 'It's been too long. I thought it was only going to be two weeks. But – there was so much to do.'

'Well, hopefully you made a success of it. Anyway, someone's here to see you.' Celia's heart struck. 'Jonathan's been here for about a week.'

Celia jerked up. 'Jonathan? From America?'

'He's the only one I know. We tried to send a telegram but you never seemed to stay in one place long enough. He says he wanted to see you. Did you ask him to come?'

Celia shook her head. 'I'll come and see him.'

'In that? Don't you think you'd better get changed first?'

Celia looked down. 'I suppose so.'

'There's hardly any hurry. He's been waiting here for nearly a week. I'm sure he could manage another half an hour.'

She shut the door after her. Celia looked down at her son, then changed into one of the skirts and jumpers left in her wardrobe. She hurried downstairs. Jonathan was sitting in the parlour, under the pictures of Arthur and Michael. His hair was longer, his cheeks pink through a new tan on his skin.

He looked up. 'You're back. Your sister said you have no money, that the business here is ruined too. Is that true?'

'No. She doesn't really understand money. Something could be done. But it would take a lot of work. And I'd have to borrow. But I want to do my foods again.'

'Flapper Foods again? In England? I thought you'd given that up.'

'I sold Flapper Foods so we could keep this place. But I could still start it here.'

They were skirting around it, the two of them, two dressed-up dancers circling their way around the subject. It was like a dragon in the middle of the room.

'You've been here a week,' she said.

'It's been so long since I came here. I was nineteen, then. I've been walking around the grounds, remembering. Or trying to. I've been with Michael and Lily for much of it. Your parents, a little.'

She felt hot and flooded with shame. 'I'm sorry,' she began. But he was speaking at the same time. 'I wrote.' They crossed, excused each other. 'You start,' he said.

'No, you.'

He shook his head.

196

She breathed. 'I've been – busy. The house, the family. Michael. The business.'

Her mind flashed with a picture of the two of them in the speakeasy. She'd told him she loved him. He looked taller and older. Her thoughts were on fire.

He stood up and walked to the window. 'Your father said I should have asked him if I could marry you. Then he said I should move here while you ran the business.'

She nodded. Her heart was striking hard. Everything hurt. 'But you see they're desperate. They need me.'

'Michael seems to think you are staying here forever and ever.'

'Oh. That's just because he likes Lily. I told my family I was leaving.'

'But they want you to stay. Everybody wants you to stay. And you?'

'I was going to come. Michael and I. Just after I'd sorted out the business.' She meant it, the vision of herself booking the passage, standing onboard the ship. She and Michael in New York. But then, there was that other self, with Rudolf and Verena, Emmeline.

'Why can't you come to live here?'

'I'm needed there.'

'Why do you matter more?'

They were silent.

'I've brought the ring,' he said. 'I think they've finally got it right.' He took the box from his pocket, opened it. The ring was there, newly cleaned, sparkling. The diamond looked even bigger out of New York. She tried it on and the ring fitted perfectly but the whole thing was so bright and new, it was America in Stoneythorpe and it made everything around it look old. 'Thank you.'

'It looks perfect,' he said.

'They need me, Jonathan. You can see that. They're chained to this house, the business is falling apart.'

'Yes, but I need you as well. You are going to be my wife.' The word shot through her. 'Mr Galss told you to sell it. He was right. You should. They'd manage.'

And she knew what he was saying was true – she should put it on the market and they would manage, of course they would – and they would do even better if they had him and his money. Giving the money to mend the roof would be nothing to him. She wanted to put her head in her hands. The air was parting and it was tearing her in two.

'Why are you always tied to your family?'

'I'm not.'

'It's always the same. You sacrifice everything for them. When are you going to stop? They can't have your whole life.'

'They don't want my whole life.' But as she said it, she knew it wasn't true. They had done, in the war, Verena wanting her to stay with her. And now, to them she was thirty-one, not married, and needed at home for ever and ever.

'They sent your child away. Now, when you finally find him, they want to play happy families.'

She wouldn't have him without Jonathan's money. Rudolf and Verena wouldn't have had the money, probably wouldn't have given it to her even if they did.

'Please stop.' She gazed up at the picture of Arthur over the mantelpiece.

'I'm sorry, Celia. I didn't mean to hurt you. But I'm your fiancé. And you can't be with me, because of your family.'

'I'm sorry,' she said.

'What are we going to do?' he said. 'You know, I have a ticket for you and Michael. It's here. For next week. We could all go back together.'

She wanted to fall into his arms. It would be so comforting, Jonathan organising the journey, whisking her back to New York, making everything easy. She gazed at him.

'Is that a no? You won't come.'

She dropped her head to the sofa. 'I can in a little while.' She cleared her throat. 'Why don't you come to live here? With us. I just don't think I can get Papa and Mama to leave. They're so old. This is their home.'

'And America is mine.'

Everything was tearing. She couldn't say no. If she did, then that would be the end of it.

'When? Two weeks? A month? When?'

'Six months,' she said. 'Let me help them. Get the business on its feet. Then I'll come. We'll both come.'

He sighed. 'Six months?' he said. 'You promise.'

She nodded. 'I promise.'

'And you'll tell your parents that you'll be coming to New York in six months.'

She nodded. 'I promise. When things have faded here with Arthur. I promise I will.'

'Tell them they're not too old. They'd love New York. After all, what is there for them here?'

The idea entranced her in its simplicity. But it would be too much for Verena and Rudolf, surely. 'I'll ask them.'

'Good.'

He stood up and he was embracing her, kissing the tears on her face. 'I'm so relieved,' he was saying. 'I thought – I thought all sorts of things. But I was wrong. Only a few months and we'll be together. Man and wife. Just like we always wanted to be. I'll get everything ready while you're here. The house – well, I won't choose the decor. That's up to you. But maybe I can choose a summer house for us. How about Long Island? Do you like it there?'

She held herself tight into his body, listening to him talk, pressing her ear against his chest, hearing the movement of his blood.

TWENTY-FIVE

Stoneythorpe, October 1930

Jonathan had done so much for her since he had arrived, talked to her parents, looked over the accounts for Winter Meats, said he would consult Mr Galss about the plans. She'd asked him if he'd seen Violet and he had done that for her too – gone to see her twice and given her money. He agreed with her that her mother could look after herself, preferred to depend on Violet.

'Such an intelligent girl,' he said. 'But she won't leave her mother.' They'd moved house again to somewhere even smaller, cheaper. Violet had a job in a hat factory, came home exhausted, hands stained blue with the dye, coughing from all the chemicals.

'Don't worry,' he said. 'I'll help her find a better job. Something in an office.'

'That's good.'

'How did you girls meet? She won't say.'

'Oh, you know, New York.' So Violet hadn't told him. Perhaps *she* should. If anyone could get Hope back, it would be Jonathan. When she went back to America, she would explain everything to him and they would find Hope.

Celia got up, sighed. 'I'm coming!' she shouted. She'd counted to forty – now she had to try to find Lily and Michael. It was the fifth game of hide and seek they'd played that day.

She walked out into the garden, shielding her eyes from the sun. She pushed through the hedge at the back and into the overgrown garden. The fountain that Verena had put in so long ago was grown over with moss. She walked sideways to pass under the trees. 'Where are you?' she called. Her voice came back to her from the branches of the trees and the walls of the house. She called again. It was as if the garden was completely deserted. She walked up to the flowerpots by the French windows leading out from the parlour, all of them full of weeds. There had been a sundial here when she'd been a child; but somehow the dial had been broken off and there was nothing left but a stone stump. 'Where are you?' she called again. 'You'd better be in the garden. If you've gone into the house, that's not fair!'

She almost felt like the youngest again, wandering around looking for the older ones, left behind as usual. She always failed to find them in hide and seek, felt as if she was rambling around while the others watched from their hiding places, laughed at her. And now, it was the same with her own son and niece.

'You'll never find us!' they had said. 'Go and count.'

'I'll find you!' she cried. Her voice echoed back. A tendril of fear curled around her.

Half an hour later and Celia had searched every place she could think of in the garden and was beginning to feel properly afraid. She'd shouted, turned everywhere she could think of upside down. When her voice echoed back for what felt like the fiftieth time, she seized up her thick skirt and ran to the house.

Ten minutes later, she was out with Emmeline and Jonathan while Verena was searching the house. 'But they can't be in the house,' she was saying. 'They promised me they wouldn't. I worry they are in the woods.'

'Oh, no!' cried Emmeline. 'They'd never go there. Lily promised.'

'I'm sure we'll find them. Did you try here?' Jonathan gestured towards the little pathway under the trees.

'Everywhere.'

'We'll try them all again. Come on.'

And so they did, walking diligently around every tree, every rock, behind all the hedges. Jonathan looked up in the trees as well – which Celia hadn't thought of – but there was still no sign of them.

The dusk was beginning to darken the trees. The garden that

had been for so long her friend, her refuge, was thick with looming shadows, dark monsters.

'If they're not inside, then they have to be outside. Listen, we'll have one final quick search and then I think we need to get search parties from the village.'

Celia gazed at Jonathan, her heart reeling. 'I should have come and got you earlier.' They had been lost for almost an hour. Anything could have happened.

'We'll find them. Wherever they are. Come on, Celia, you need to be strong.' He took her arm and they were rushing to the hedge at the bottom of the garden.

'You looked down there?' he said. 'The place where you used to like to sit?'

'I counted there. They can't be there.'

'We should check, just in case. They could have slipped in after you left.'

Of course! They might have done. She hurtled through the hedge, under the willow and into her dell.

They were there. She was about to scream out for Jonathan – and then she stopped herself. They were curled up next to her favourite stone, fast asleep, wound around each other so she could barely tell where one started and another ended. Her hair across his face. She stared at them and her face began to flame, as if she'd walked into a secret room, staring at something that shouldn't be seen. She tried to tear her eyes away, but she couldn't. It was only two cousins, she told herself, it's nothing! And yet the intertwined bodies on the floor had something in them that made her fear. She ran out of the dell.

'They're in there, Jonathan!'

'Oh, thank God.'

'Run and tell Emmeline they're here. I'll bring them up.' She mustn't let him see them. He walked up and she rushed back to the dell.

'Wake up!' she said, shaking Michael, then Lily.

'Ah,' said Michael, looking up first from Lily's arms where he lay. 'You found us.'

'We've been looking everywhere.' Lily was stirring.

'We like it here,' he sighed. He closed his eyes again.

'No, no! Up you get.' She hauled him up. She was furious – but what could she say? That they hid too well? That they shouldn't go to sleep? She should be happy that they were so close, so eager to be friends. She hauled Lily to her feet, too, biting back words.

'Come on,' she said. 'Let's go back to the house.' They followed her, meekly enough. Emmeline and Verena were relieved, delighted, told Michael and Lily off for scaring them, said they couldn't have any pudding. Then that was that for them, the event was over, put in the scrapbook of memories that didn't matter. The jolting fear in Celia faded – but something remained, a thin, nervous misgiving.

'What do they think about Germany in America?' Rudolf asked Jonathan at the table. 'The press here say that they're creating more industry. Perhaps Germany might be an area to take the meats.' Celia's heart broke over how much Rudolf liked Jonathan, wanted to talk to him. She fiddled with the engagement ring, unfamiliar, heavy.

Celia thought of her last time in Germany – just after the war. Her cousin Johann's body wrecked by Passchendaele, his mind fogged with pain and memories that made him cry out at night. How the neighbours gossiped about Celia and so Heinrich thought it best to leave, and they all travelled to Baden Baden, ostensibly to find a husband for Hilde, really because they wanted Celia to marry Johann. And then her night with Tom, ruining all their plans. Rudolf had said that the Crash had hit them hard, they had even less money, and Johann and Hilde were still unmarried although Hilde had a job assisting in the local school.

'I'm not sure, sir. In fact, I'd hazard a guess that going into Germany now would be nothing short of a disaster. I wouldn't do it.'

'Ah,' said Rudolf. 'What would you do then?'

Jonathan began to talk and Celia saw Rudolf, slow, old, sometimes lost, capturing Jonathan into his net of plans. She watched her father, then looked at her mother. She wasn't speaking, but she too was casting a net, Celia in a white dress, marrying Jonathan, made respectable, rich.

'America might still be an excellent market,' mused Rudolf. 'If we went slowly this time.'

'Oh yes, America,' said Verena. She was weaving, they were both threading the images, Celia surrounded in flowers, a gold ring on her finger.

She knew her parents were holding back, but really they wanted to talk about the wedding, how they would have a ceremony in Stoneythorpe, how Celia might be the beginning of a re-entry into English society: 'My daughter, married to the American millionaire. The Corrigans, do you know them? One of the best families in Connecticut.'

She said nothing, watched Verena smile at Jonathan, attempt to weave a spell of charm, all desire and need.

She looked down at her wine glass, drew her finger through the cut flowers on the side.

'Are you sure you won't come with me?' Jonathan asked the night before he left. He'd been called back to America by his father. The business needed him.

They were in her room, cramped, late at night. She couldn't bear to speak to him in Arthur's room, which he'd been staying in, so she made him sneak over to hers after everyone had gone to sleep.

'I can't now. Just five more months. Let me get this lot on their feet.'

'Of course.'

The words sounded so clear as she said them, real. Cramped in her tiny room, still full of her childhood books, ornaments she'd collected, pink cushions and brass models of horses. 'I promise. Michael longs to go back to America.'

He raised his eyebrow. 'Maybe. Well, anyway. I'll tell my parents to expect you soon. I'll take a house for us.'

'I think they should all come,' she heard herself say. Verena, Rudolf, Emmeline, Mr Janus, Albert and Lily, all together with them in the New York townhouse that Jonathan was going to take. 'I'll persuade them.'

'You will?' His face was disbelieving, shot over with relief.

'Yes. There's nothing for them here. Emmeline might be harder to convince. But if we take her over before Mr Janus comes back – it would be fait accompli. Not even he could resist that. And there's lots of demonstrating to be done in America.'

'But I thought you said they'd never leave.'

'I thought that. But my father – he was so interested in Winter Meats overseas. He's perhaps not as stuck here as I thought. They have to sell this place sooner or later.'

'If you think you could convince them.'

'I can.'

She could, she felt sure she could. It was convincing herself that she couldn't vouch for. But he didn't ask her, and so she didn't have to say – and the words hung, heavy and unspoken in her mind.

'Well, that's wonderful then.'

'Isn't it?' He couldn't see through to her heart and the truth. She wished she couldn't. She didn't want to talk any more. Instead, she put her arms around him and drew him close – and then they were on her bed, her small single bed, falling together, and he was holding her close and whispering something in her ear and his words were growing louder, his mouth hot against her skin and she drew him closer to her and held on.

INTERLUDE

Michael tried hard. Did he remember Stoneythorpe? If he was born here, the place was surely deep in his bones. He walked all around the house, trying to see if his memory caught to a door, a wall, a view and said, yes, you were here. But it did not. It was always remote to him. But then, everything was when he was not with Lily. Even the adults were gauzy and indistinct when he was not with Lily. Only she made everything clear.

He held his bear tight. New York grew fainter, the outlines of the city less straight in his mind. But not his life with the Whetstones. That was painted hard and bright across his eyes, with him late at night, always there. Mama wanted him to forget and his heart sank that he could not, no matter how kind and loving she was to him, how much she bought for him, their house was always there, tormenting him, the beatings, the cruelty, the hatred. So he had to pretend he had forgotten, that it was all behind him now. 'Children forget,' he had heard his mother say to his aunt. He had to act as if those days were over – but at night, he closed his eyes and there was someone beating him again, locking him in the attic, never coming. He crept into Mama's bed and she held him tight.

He would not forget. But the only person he could tell was Lily. He told her – and she listened to all of it. And then, after a while, he didn't want to tell anyone but her – it was the stories she knew, the whole world that was only hers.

There were so many secrets in this house. That's what he hated the most about it. He knew he was lucky to be away from the Whetstones, that Mama had rescued him, and he was safe here. But still. Sometimes he wanted to say: *Why won't you tell me anything? Who was my father?* The adults thought they were playing

African explorers. And they were, some of the time. But more and more they were exploring the house. They wanted to find things. Uncover secrets.

'After all,' said Lily, 'if they won't tell us, we'll have to find out for ourselves.'

Mama said she wanted him to be happy, not think about the past. She'd told him not to talk much about what happened with Arthur because it would only upset everyone. Not that he had much to say since no one had told him what was happening. They wouldn't even let him come to the funeral.

He didn't want to talk. He wanted to ask questions. There was so much he didn't know, years to make up for because he hadn't been here. But Mama said, 'Oh, it's not worth worrying about. Go out and play!' When he asked her about her brother, who he was named after, she just said, 'He died in the war. He was killed going over to fight.' And he knew because of the way she looked up to the side and fiddled with her hands that she wasn't telling him the truth. And sometimes he even thought there was something odd with the story of Great-Aunt Deerhurst giving him away. No one would ever talk about it.

He hated Great-Aunt Deerhurst. It was wicked to say but he did. She had sent him to misery when he could have grown up here, been with Mama and Lily – and Grandpapa, who let him stuff his pipe. He hated her so much that he wanted to ask questions about her too, so he knew exactly who it was he should hate. But no one would tell him.

'We must try to forget about it,' said his mother. 'It was a terrible thing, but it is in the past.'

'Oh, the adults are always lying,' Lily said. She was obsessed with Aunt Louisa, Aunt Deerhurst's daughter, who had been married to Arthur and died. 'We need to find out what really happened to her. No one will *ever* talk about her,' she said. In one of the upstairs rooms – the ones that were supposed to be locked and never were – they'd found a bundle of things that Lily said must have been Louisa's. A photo of a pretty girl with thick fair hair, a small photo of some older people who were maybe her parents. There were two trunks of what looked like clothes. Lily pulled a few dresses out, pushed them back. There was a pile of books on the floor, novels about love that she opened, cast aside. 'Soppy stuff!' she said.

In one of the old rooms, they'd found a pile of newspapers stuffed in a corner. First of all, they'd thought they were just rubbish – and then they'd realised. All of them were about a trial involving Arthur.

'Look at that,' said Lily, sitting back on her heels. 'Amazing. They thought Uncle Arthur killed her.'

Emmeline had told Lily that it had been a terrible accident, that Aunt Louisa had fallen off a cliff. Mama hadn't told him anything at all about Aunt Louisa. He'd asked once and all Mama would say was that she had died just after the war.

'I had no idea,' breathed Lily. They spent hours reading the articles, discussing them.

'There's so much in here about being German,' he said. 'Decline of a noble family.'

'Mama always tells me to say I am entirely English,' said Lily. 'Easier that way.'

For the next few days, they stole bread and biscuits from the kitchen, sneaked it upstairs, and sat over the newspapers, read all the stories. 'It's not our fault,' Lily said again. 'If only they'd tell us.'

After that, she was even more obsessed with Louisa. One time he came up after going down to get cake and found her lying face down on a pile of gowns.

'Lily?'

'I'm trying to be her,' she said. 'I'm trying to feel what it was like to be her.' She paused. 'Mama probably knows exactly where my father is in Spain, but she won't say.'

'Really?'

'Father was always planning things and Mama would never say what. So I think she knows where he is. Maybe Aunt Celia does too.'

They wrote to an address Lily had for Mr Janus – he'd given it to her in secret before he left. They used their pocket money, gave it to Dorrie from the village who came in to clean, to take the letters to the post office and buy stamps. Michael didn't have much to write because he'd never met Mr Janus but he liked to help Lily. She wrote pages and pages to her father, all about the days at Stoneythorpe, how she did miss London, but then Michael had arrived! Michael wondered if he shouldn't really be looking over her shoulder when she wrote about him. But she didn't seem to mind and nothing made him happier than reading those words: *Michael is so much fun! We play explorers. We have found so many things in the house.*

And they had. Secrets. One afternoon, while everybody was at tea, they crept into Grandmama's room. On her bedside table were stacks of murder mysteries that she should have taken back to the library. They looked into her vases and found dead spiders, rusty keys. And a purse filled with hundreds of pounds.

Michael kept one secret from Lily: he was Grandpapa's favourite. In the daytime, sometimes, or after dinner, he'd beckon Michael into his study and then he'd talk to him about his old life in Germany, his boyhood and growing up. Sometimes he'd get out his photograph album and they'd look at all the family photos.

Michael lied to Lily and told her that Grandpapa was just lecturing him about how to run the business one day. That seemed to satisfy her.

But then, he had heard another lie. His mother saying that she would go back to New York to see Jonathan in six months. But those months were passing and there was still no mention of leaving. Not that he wanted to go. He wanted to stay here. But still. Adults said they told the truth and they did not.

Rudolf turned over the pages of the photos.

'We thought your mother might marry Johann,' Grandpapa said. 'But children do what they want to do.'

That made him dizzy. Instead of here, he might be living in Germany, the son of someone called Johann.

'My father is dead,' he said. 'Mama said my father was dead.' He had been a soldier. Sometimes, at night, when he woke up and couldn't sleep, Michael told himself about his father: he'd been a prince, the owner of a chocolate factory, a pilot who flew round and round the world and saw every animal and the pyramids in Egypt.

Rudolf nodded. 'Truly sad.'

But there should be a picture of his father in the photograph album. There should be a photograph of him, next to his mother.

'Don't you have a photograph of him?'

Rudolf shook his head. 'I don't think so. But I am very behind with the book. I haven't even got a photograph of you yet. We should have one done.'

And so they did. Two days later they went into town. Rudolf and Michael stood in front of a man with a black sheet over his head and smiled. He wished Lily was there, just the two of them with their arms around each other. She might have flowers in her hair.

TWENTY-SIX

'I don't think I can do it,' Celia finally said to Rudolf. 'It's been a year since I got here and the business is still losing money. We need to change.' She told him how she had been laying the foundations for restarting Flapper Foods. She had asked the department-store buyers what they thought – and each one had been delighted by the idea. The fact that she had made the business successful in New York was even more of a selling point.

'Beloved of *New York girls*,' breathed one of the buyers.

Rudolf shook his head. 'We have always been meat,' he said. 'That is our business.'

'Not mine,' she said. 'Mr Galss, Mr Pemberton, they all agree. Winter Meats is dying. If you want to save the house, you must try something else.' And she talked on until he was shrunken and defeated, agreeing, and she hated herself for having to make him face it, the balance sheets covered with minus signs, the stacks of meat nobody wanted to buy, dwindling orders, the loans from the banks. 'I'm sorry.'

She passed the news to Mr Pemberton. 'There is only one problem,' he said, solemnly. He looked at her hand. 'The ring will make people think you are not serious. You will marry, have children and forget about the business. Are you about to marry?'

She couldn't say yes.

'I advise you to remove it.'

That night, she slid the ring off, but she could not bear to remove it altogether so put it on the other hand.

And so she began. She hired a kitchen in town and a Mrs Craigmire, a young widow who had been a restaurant cook before her marriage, eager and energetic, said she had dozens of ideas to try. She went to the banks, talked about the recipes, and watched the men nodding and smiling, just as they had in New York.

'But what will the name be?' they asked. 'You cannot call it Flapper Foods.'

The men were right. She couldn't.

'What about Celia's Kitchen?' said Mrs Craigmire.

That was it! Something home-like. But not Celia. She needed another girl's name. She thought of all the girls she had known, Shep and the others, the girls at Winterbourne – then she thought of Violet! It was clear that all the girls in England dreamt of a New York girl.

'Miss Violet's Kitchen,' she said to Mrs Craigmire.

'Perfect,' the woman replied.

The banks agreed and there was money for her, pots of it, to start again, for advertising, packaging, developing, transport. When Mrs Craigmire had the recipes made up, they sent it to the Winter Meats factory, canned them, tested them.

'I've called the business after Violet,' she wrote to Jonathan. 'Please tell her. I hope she'll like it.'

She went for meetings with London stores – Harrods, Selfridges, Harvey Nichols, Liberty. Once they had delivered the first orders, she would put the ring back on, go to America to Jonathan.

'Come on! We'll be late for the show.'

Celia held Michael's hand tight. Already he was growing up. A month ago, Emmeline had made a decision.

'Those children have been running wild. We will get them a tutor for the mornings – so when we move to town, they're ready for school.'

'Well, I can see the point of that,' Celia said, grudgingly. Actually, she should have thought of it herself. Michael had been so happy at Stoneythorpe that she'd put his education out of her mind. He was quick and intelligent – but she supposed he did need to be taught things: Latin verbs, comprehension, algebra.

She had been remiss, so grateful to have him back that she hadn't wanted to lose a single bit of him, not even to school.

Emmeline had sent to Winchester for some tutors, ones who could cover both a boy's and girl's curriculum. Of course, as she was told, it was quite unorthodox, children of this age should have separate classes. But one tutor was all they could afford.

They hadn't had many applications in the beginning. Emmeline said she supposed all the best teachers were in school these days. They called in the last one. A tall, thin man walked in, youngish, fair haired. He had an unfortunate squint, otherwise you might call him handsome.

'Do sit down,' said Emmeline. She gave the introductions. Mr Brennan said he'd been a schoolmaster in Kent but was desiring more individual contact. 'School is like a factory,' he said, 'turning out children who are all the same.'

'Our children are rather different to the normal,' Celia said. She kept talking and Emmeline chipped in and Mr Brennan smiled and looked at them both, open, honest. He had a blob of darkness on his right eye, as if the pupil had flowed out of its boundaries, a teardrop. Celia looked away.

'We have to give him the position,' Celia said to Emmeline, after he had left the room. 'He's the best.'

Emmeline nodded. 'I like him. He's one of those people you feel like you've known forever as soon as you meet them. But the children should see him before we commit. He almost feels familiar. Lucky us.'

They called down Michael and Lily and introduced him. They watched them talk to him, saw Michael and Lily blossom under his words.

'So it is agreed,' they said. 'You start next week.'

The children had taken to Mr Brennan, working with him every morning. Michael was coming on in his studies, doing particularly well, Mr Brennan said, at mathematics. Sometimes, Celia would walk into the sitting room and Michael was so busy reading that he no longer ran to her. He was already moving away from her, as he should, little by little, going out into the world. She looked back at her own younger self, so fascinated by looking into her own soul, how her parents had only been shadowy figures in the background of her thoughts on the future, hoped that he wouldn't be the same.

'You are lucky children,' Emmeline was saying, stiffly. She disapproved of Celia's idea to take Michael and Lily to London. Albert did have a holiday from school but he had fallen behind with his work so he had had to forfeit it. 'Lucky Samuel's not here,' she added.

'He'd have taken him out ages ago,' Celia said, but without force. Pretending that Mr Janus was coming back seemed to her a ridiculous farce. He was either too ensconced there to ever come home – or he was dead. Otherwise he would have written. She had tried to suggest – gently – that it might be worth thinking of another future. But Emmeline wouldn't listen, even to the most delicate of hints. The minute Celia mentioned Mr Janus, she changed the subject – or turned furious.

'At least my children know who their father is,' she said. 'Don't you think he's got a right to know? You need to tell him. And you need to tell Tom.'

'No! He wouldn't want to know. He – he doesn't want me.'

'But Michael's still his son. You should tell him.'

'No.' Their argument circled, hopeless, resentful.

Even Celia's idea of today's trip had taken some negotiation. She had decided to treat Michael in London – after all, he'd never been. Of course, Lily had to come too. Celia had to plead. 'But Michael won't go without her. Please.'

They were going to see the whole of London: the Changing of the Guard, Big Ben and the Houses of Parliament, and go to Leicester Square to look at the theatres and eat a meal. Celia had it all planned out. They were going to have an enjoyable, pleasant day in London. Like two normal sisters and their children. That was what people did, wasn't it?

'We'll go to London,' Emmeline eventually said angrily to Celia. 'But don't think I think this is a good idea.'

Finally, on a chill February morning, they were on a train up to London, the children excitedly looking out of the window, spotting farm animals in fields, bonfires, the decorated boats in canals running alongside them. Celia looked at them, Lily and Michael, dressed in their best coats, their shoes newly shined. Michael had wet his hair to flatten it and Lily had spent extra time on her plaits. Her son and her niece, so happy together. What more could she want? She had her son. Everything else was small, little things that didn't matter.

Emmeline shook her head and turned to the window.

Then they were in Victoria station and caught up in the swell of crowds, moving forwards. 'Awful crowds,' said Celia, as she always did, but she didn't mean it really, she felt exhilarated by the movement, the rush, and the anonymity. She could be anyone. They headed out and caught a taxi to the Changing of the Guard.

'Will we see the King?' asked Michael.

'Definitely,' she said. 'Look very carefully at the windows. I am sure the King will poke his nose out.'

They watched the Guards, took a bus to the Houses of Parliament and Westminster Abbey.

'Now, time for lunch,' said Celia. 'Then perhaps we might go to a toy shop.' What she really wanted was to visit the department stores in Oxford Street and Knightsbridge and look at the food halls.

'Let's sit the children together,' said Emmeline at a restaurant she had chosen near Green Park. 'Then we can talk.'

Celia nodded. 'Choose what you'd like,' she said to the two of them. She smiled at their faces; they were delighted because they were sitting at their own table, like grown-ups. Michael patted her hand. Her heart wrenched. She would never send him to school, didn't want him to go away, preparing for the world, where his future would matter to him more than she would. Hadn't it been like that for her once, eager to leave her parents behind? She never thought she'd one day be the same, a barrier to escape, a block between the world and the freedom of it, the feeling of lightness in his bones. She'd thought it would be the two of them forever.

'Ice cream, please. I think.' Michael was so polite, it made her proud.

'Chocolate? You just tell the waiter what you want. But choose something proper, some hot food, too.'

He nodded. Soon he wouldn't even want chocolate ice cream and it would be too babyish for him. Everyone said that children as they approached adulthood were horrid, always angry. She couldn't imagine Michael like that. But still, he was growing, his voice was changing. He'd be a man. He'd grow up, make his own life. Without her.

Emmeline was talking about the royal princesses. Celia gazed at the menu. The modern girl, working in London, probably had to come to places like this to eat her supper. With Miss Violet's Kitchen, she'd be able to look after herself – and much nicer and cheaper food too. They just had to get the canning to work.

'Hello Celia.'

She looked up and Tom was standing there. Her heart stopped and she turned away, couldn't look at him, his dark eyes, smooth face, dark brows, the hair just over his forehead. She hadn't seen him since the trial, when they'd argued.

'What are you doing here?'

He didn't answer, looked over at Emmeline. Her sister looked at the ground. Celia looked back at Tom. 'What's happening?'

They both looked away.

'You arranged this.'

Emmeline didn't reply.

'What's going on?'

'Don't make a fuss, Celia,' Emmeline said, quietly. 'We're in a restaurant.'

'I thought you were both expecting me.'

'I lied,' Emmeline said. 'She didn't know.'

Celia turned to Emmeline. 'What are you doing? What have you done?'

'The best thing. Sit down, Tom.'

Celia looked over at the children. They were still gazing at the menu. 'No. Tom, you have to go.'

'Stay,' said Emmeline. 'For half an hour.'

The air stood still. It felt as if there was a battle, the air crossing. They were all holding invisible swords.

'I should go,' said Tom. 'This isn't what I thought it was.'

'What did you think it was?'

'Sit down, Tom.' Emmeline's voice was more urgent.

He looked over at Celia. 'It's been a long time. You look well.'

'Thank you. So do you.'

Tom touched his ear. He'd done the same as a child, a nervous tic. 'How is everyone?' He was still standing.

'Arthur died in America. He fell from a window.'

He nodded. 'I did read. Terrible.'

Of course.

'I wrote to your family. Perhaps they didn't receive it.'

Rudolf hadn't said. She hadn't seen Tom's handwriting. She'd recognise it, out of a million letters, she'd know it.

'How is your company doing?' She cast an eye over to Michael. He was listening to Lily, looking at other people's ice creams.

'Not too bad. 'Now I have moved into the accounts side, there is a lot of business. No company has their accounts up to date. You'd think they would.'

She stared at his hand. No ring – but not all men wore them. He could be married, have two, three children. He probably was. He was thirty-two now, handsome, rich. He could marry anyone. She imagined him in front of a series of numbers, adding and subtracting.

'And what about the rest of your family?'

'They're well.'

She wanted to tell him everything, that the house was falling apart, might have to be sold, that Miss Violet's Kitchen was on the way to success – but perhaps not fast enough to save them all. But she feared he'd say what he'd done before, when she'd poured

217

out her heart, remind her he wasn't their servant any more, that they had separate lives now.

'Do you hear much from your family in Germany?' Tom asked.

Her uncle. Heinrich. His father. 'My father's had a few letters. They don't have much money after the Crash.' That night in Baden Baden, Tom's fury, Heinrich's refusal to see him as his son.

Tom looked at her. 'Does he ask after me?'

'I don't know.' Celia had asked Rudolf about Heinrich, the week before, wondered if he ever wrote about Tom. Rudolf said he didn't. She knew he didn't really write much at all. 'He's old now.'

'I wondered if he'd died, if that was why you invited me here.'

She looked up at him and the restaurant whirled around her and was gone. 'I'm sorry for what I said last time. It was very wrong of me.'

'Last time?'

In front of the British Museum, him telling her she should prepare herself for the worst and so she'd lost her temper, incensed that anyone might not think her brother innocent.

Well, you'd know all about being a murderer. Wouldn't you.

'Oh, the trial. That was so long ago. You were upset about your brother. Only natural.'

He'd practically forgotten it. And it was seared hard on her soul, shouting at him, running from him.

'He was found not guilty, after all,' he said. 'So your faith in him was right.'

She nodded. Arthur danced in front of her, trying to pull her out to the balcony, throwing himself off. *You'd be flying. And then, the moment before you hit the ground, how would that be? You'd see the truth then, wouldn't you?*

'He was in a bad way at the end,' she said. She couldn't say more, not even to Tom.

'Stoneythorpe may have to be sold,' she then said. 'We're trying to persuade Papa. It's in a bad way, almost falling down. I was hoping my business might save it, but I don't know.'

He paused. 'That's a shame. I grew up there,' he said. 'Even if it wasn't always happy.'

'I know.' *Don't start*, she wanted to say. *Don't start telling me how it wasn't ever a friendship and you were just paid to be kind to me. And you never wanted to ride with me or hunt for tadpoles or any of it.*

The waiter approached carrying a chair. 'Sir?'

'It doesn't look quite right, standing,' broke in Emmeline. 'You need to sit down.'

'We're going,' said Celia.

'No we're not. He can sit for a minute.'

'The gentleman will have to sit or leave.'

'Just for a moment.' Lily and Michael were still deep in conversation. They wouldn't move, she thought. She couldn't let Tom go, not yet. They would exchange words – and then he'd go and never know. She drank from her tea again. 'How about you?' she managed. 'What about your family?'

'Missy is a nurse now. She's married, living in London. Maggie is married too, in Brighton. Mother lives with her. She's getting old.'

'Everybody's getting old,' said Emmeline. She flashed Tom her wide smile, the one that had worked so well on Sir Hugh and the rest when she was young. She looked beautiful, suddenly. A strange feeling of jealousy touched Celia's heart. She shook it away. She looked down. And when she raised her head, everything had crashed. Michael was at the table. 'Mama,' he said. 'The waiter asked if we wished to order. Can we have ice creams before anything?'

Tom looked at her. 'Mama?'

She flushed. 'Yes. Anything. Off you go.'

Tom stared at him. 'You're Celia's son?'

He nodded. Celia was stabbed with a desire for him to be polite, hold out his hand, impress.

'Go back and sit with Lily,' said Celia. 'No – actually, we should go. We need to go now.'

Tom looked at her as Michael trotted back. 'He's your son. You found him? You said they took him away from you.'

'I found him in America.' She couldn't trust herself to say more. 'We should go.'

'No, we shouldn't,' said Emmeline. 'I'm going to stay. Lily!' she raised her voice. 'Both of you, come over here.'

'That must have been hard. Did the father help? The soldier.'

Celia shook her head.

'Did you tell him?'

'No.'

'Why not? At least for the boy. He should know who his father is.' *I never did*, he didn't need to say.

'I know. But I thought he wouldn't care or want to know. He probably wouldn't.'

'Is he married?'

'Probably.'

'Don't you think you owe it to the child?'

Michael and Lily returned, shyly hanging back. Tom held out his hand. 'Hello, I'm Mr Cotton, but you can call me Tom. It's nice to meet you. What's your name?'

'Michael. It used to be Sebastien. Sometimes I forget which one I am.'

'Let's go to the lavatory, Lily,' said Emmeline.

'I don't want to.'

'I do. You're coming with me.' They stood up, left in a flurry of skirts.

'Oh, I see.' Tom nodded. 'So you used to live in America. How do you find England?'

Celia listened to Michael chattering on about the boat over when he was seasick. *Can't you see?* she wanted to say. *Can't you see what's going on?* Even Emmeline had seen his sister Missy's eyes in Celia's son. Tom was asking Michael how old Lily was and what they liked to play. Michael started talking about hide and seek and chasing frogs.

'Oh yes,' said Tom, smiling. 'Your Mama and I used to do that sort of thing in the garden when we were younger.'

Celia stared at him. It had always been her bringing up the memories – he always tried to push them away. But there he was, conjuring them up again.

Michael smiled and starting talking about Lily again.

'They certainly are very good friends,' said Celia.

'That I can see!' replied Tom.

But can't you see anything else? She gazed at Tom, talking to Michael so kindly. *How can you be so blind?*

Celia was back in Baden Baden, walking down to the lake with Tom, the stolen bottle of wine, telling him she'd had other men, that it didn't matter, feeling his arms around her, wanting to tell him she loved him, pulling him close. *Go on*, she said. *Yes.*

'I like chocolate ice creams too,' said Tom.

Michael said, sadly, 'I love ice creams. But they go too quickly.' She and Hilde had wandered Baden with ice creams, trying to look like girls of good family so that men might come and speak to them. Then they saw Tom. And later he'd pulled her down to him by the lake and she'd suspected, known even, that it wasn't really her, he just wanted a woman, but she had fallen into him and welcomed it and never wanted it to stop.

'Oh dear. Shall we order you another one?'

Michael nodded. Tom called over a waiter, a fat smiling one who was passing.

'Another ice cream, please?'

'How kind of Papa,' said the waiter, jovially. 'Another ice cream for his little boy.'

'He's not my Papa,' said Michael. But the waiter was already ambling off to the next table.

'He's not my …' Tom had been talking too. Then he trailed off, stared at Michael, then Celia. 'He's …' He stopped. 'Celia?'

She looked down.

Tom looked at Michael. 'You told me you were nearly nine. What's your birthday?'

Michael grinned happily. 'Well, I never knew that. Not in America. The Whetstones said it didn't matter. But Mama told me 12th April 1922. So I have a birthday now. Next birthday, Lily said she was going to make me a cake and we'll have a proper party. You can come too, if you like.'

'Thank you.' Tom's voice was strangled.

Michael started talking about his party again.

Celia couldn't look up. She knew she had to. She couldn't. Tom would be looking into her eyes.

'Celia,' he said. 'Is that right? 12th April 1922?'

'Yes,' she said, bringing her head up, finally meeting his eyes. 'That was the day he was born.'

More ice cream arrived with the jolly waiter. They all smiled. 'Eat up, sonny,' he said. 'You're a real ice-cream lover, I can tell.'

The waiter walked off. He must be used to it, Celia thought, so many people in restaurants talking over love, war, relationships ending, beginning. He must bring women their food when they were weeping, watch arguments, take away half-cleared plates.

Tom was still looking at her.

'So he was conceived in... the summer before.'

'Yes.'

'With—'

She shook her head. 'The soldier was a story. I lied.'

'So...'

'Yes. He's—'

Tom put his head on his hand. 'I – there aren't. How did this happen?'

'What?' asked Michael, happily spooning up chocolate ice cream.

Tom looked at him. Celia's mind felt as if it was crumbling, sparking into flames – *why hadn't she told him? What had she done?* She should have told him the minute she'd come back with Michael, as Emmeline said.

Tom was shaking his head. 'I should have thought. I should have guessed.'

'No.'

'Why didn't you say anything? Why didn't you tell me? Don't you think you should have told me?' The colour was rising in his face now, the anger too. She'd seen this before, in Baden when he lost his temper with Heinrich. 'Why didn't you? What's wrong with you?'

Michael dropped his spoon, his face crossed over with fear. 'Mama? What's happening?'

222

Celia forced herself to breathe. 'Michael. Go to the door and wait for me. I know you haven't finished your ice cream. I'll get you a cake on the way home.' Michael shook his head. 'Go, please.'

He gulped down more ice cream. 'What about Lily?'

'I'll buy her some more too.'

'Don't worry, Celia. I'll go. They haven't finished.' Tom smiled at the child. 'Go and sit back at your table. Lily will be back in a moment. Take the ice cream with you.'

He picked up the glass dish, nodded obediently. 'Goodbye, sir.'

Tom looked at him, dazed. 'Goodbye. No, not goodbye. I'll see you again.'

'Go to the table, please,' said Celia.

He nodded, confused, headed off back to the table. Emmeline and Lily swished past, sat with him.

Celia wanted to stand up to leave, but Tom seized her hand, hard. 'What's going on? Is he really mine?'

'He's mine.'

'Stop it, Celia. You know what I mean. How could you have kept this from me? How could you? I can't believe this of you. You told me in Paris that he was a soldier's. And you were lying to me all along.'

Her heart was rising. He was still holding her hand, hissing at her. Then her blood rushed and her heart exploded. 'Well, what did you think?' she said, trying to keep her voice down, failing because the sound billowed out at the sides. 'You know what we did. Didn't you ever think there might be a consequence? No! Of course you didn't. Because you're only ever thinking about yourself. How you've been excluded or this or that. Nothing about the rest of us. You never thought that I might need help. You just forgot all about it, carried on nursing your wounds the way you always did. And he was gone for so long, there wasn't a point in telling you. And now I have him back. Well, you never cared before, not for me or anything. Why should you care now?' She was standing now, and the people next to her could probably hear what she was saying. But she didn't care.

'Celia—'

'Don't tell me to calm down. Or whatever you're going to say. Michael's mine. Not yours. You never wondered. You didn't even really want to, that night. I just happened to be there. And it's me who's been wanting him, searching for him all this time. Not you. You probably don't want him either. I bet you've got a wife and a perfect family and this would just be an interruption. Well, I don't care. He and I – we don't need anyone else.'

'I don't have a wife. Or a child. I wanted one. I've always wanted a son.' He held out his hand to the table where Michael sat, looking out at the passers-by on the street.

Suddenly, a terrible vision loomed in Celia's head; Tom wealthy and prepossessing, giving Michael everything she couldn't, expensive schooling, toys, lessons in whatever he wanted. Michael preferring him – because he was glamorous, rich, and lived in London. The pair of them driving off in a new car, leaving her behind.

'You have to go,' she said. 'Please. Please.'

'Celia. He's my son. I need to – understand this.'

'Please go. Or I will. But I don't want to drag him away.'

He stood up. 'If you insist. But will you meet me again, just to talk?'

She nodded. Anything to get rid of him. 'Of course. I'll write.'

'Can I say goodbye to him?'

'Quickly.'

'Thank you. Thank you, Celia.' He walked away, spoke to Michael. She could see him wanting to touch Michael, catch his hand. Emmeline held out her hand and he shook it. Then Tom left and Celia went over, sat there, staring at the dish of melting ice cream.

'Come on,' she said. 'Let's go home.'

'I thought we were eating lunch?' Emmeline looked up. 'They need to eat, Celia. More than ice cream. I'm going to order them some chicken and potatoes. You can wait if you like.'

Celia looked at her sister. 'How could you?'

'Who was that man?' Lily asked.

'It's just someone I used to know. When I was young.'

'Like me and Michael.'

'Yes, like you two.'

'Except you're not really friends with him any more,' broke in Michael. 'Lily and I will be friends forever.'

'Well, you're cousins too, so you'll always be together.'

'Always?'

'That's right. Like me and Emmeline. Always together.' She glowered at her sister.

'I was right. You'll see.'

'I'm going to the lavatory.'

'I'll order you some lunch.'

'Don't.' Celia rushed off to the lavatory, filled the washbasin and plunged her hands in cold water. She doused her face, so it wet her hair, looked at herself in the mirror, eyelashes sodden. She wanted to wash it all away, everything, the last hour, everything. But she couldn't. The past, Tom, was lodged hard under her skin.

That night, there were a pile of figures to read from Winter Meats – still all minuses even though they'd sold five factories – and some from Miss Violet's Kitchen, good but not enough. Celia sat down to write to Jonathan. *I need more time. I know I promised you six months. But I have found there is so much to do. But I will be with you in a year. Give me more time. Please.* She couldn't leave. Everybody was depending on her. She asked him to come to her. *You could come for as long as you like,* she said. If only there were two of her – one to live in America and one to live here. She meant to write to Tom, couldn't.

She walked downstairs to put Jonathan's letter for posting.

'What are you doing there?' Emmeline came around the corner, her hair escaping her bun.

'Leaving my letter. Don't come and talk to me.'

'Oh don't be silly, Celia. It had to be done. I did you a favour. He needs to know.'

'Now he hates me more.'

'He doesn't hate you. He's as moony-eyed over you as you are over him. It's just that neither of you can see it. And it's better that way, if you ask me. But he had to know the truth.'

'Why? Why tell him? You told me I was wrong ever to like him.'

'You were. You are – don't try and pretend you don't still. But you should hear Mr Janus on this. Men can't escape their responsibilities. Certainly not him.'

'You didn't think he might give us *money*? You're not saying *that*?'

Emmeline turned, flushed. 'I just think he needs to know his responsibilities, that's all. Why should we shoulder it all?'

'We? What do you mean – *we*? I am. Who paid for us to go to London? Me!'

'You and Michael living here, with us, eating the food, in the house that is barely standing.'

'I'm running the business! Making it work again! I've been working for it every day! Leave me alone. Go and talk to someone else. Haven't you done enough?' She rushed upstairs, wished she could take Michael and flee from them all.

INTERLUDE

'You can tell me anything,' Mama had said to Michael in New York. They slept together in her room, cuddled up in the middle of her giant bed. Her clothes were thrown on the side and he loved that because the Whetstones had been so tidy. It was one mixed-up friendly monster of clothes and books and papers. Sometimes he perched Harvey the bear on top of it all. Then, he'd felt as if everything of Mama's was his, all shared. None of the 'this is mine and you can never touch it' like at the Whetstones'. At night, when they couldn't sleep, Mama told him everything, all about her childhood and her houses. But now they were back in England and there was nothing but unspoken words.

At first, he and Lily had been secret chasers. Hunters. They chased the secrets through the house. He had thought they were all about the past. But now – it was clear that the secrets weren't stopping. Now they were about the present as well. Jonathan wrote to him sometimes and to Mama and he tried to sound happy. Lily wrote to Mr Janus but he did not write back. If he did, Lily said, they could go to stay with him. For surely life was better there, clearer, more honest, than the net of lies and hypocrisy, small pettiness, untruths, that was Stoneythorpe.

Mr Brennan listened to their secrets. They talked about Spain and he took their letters for them. He told them about other things that the adults did not – the politics of the world, war. Lily listened. And Mr Brennan had ideas. He told Michael to draw. 'You have a talent. That will make sense of the world.'

And he drew and drew but still he had not made sense of things. New York, the past, Lily. And now the other man who'd met them in the restaurant, been so keen to speak to him. Mama and Aunt Emmeline had been so angry with each other on the way home, continued it when they'd got back. Michael had tried to ask about him but Mama said not to worry and Emmeline told him to ask Mama.

'Oh, who knows,' Lily said. 'Some adult thing.' She wanted to lie in Louisa's clothes again, draw them over her face. 'I'll make myself as beautiful as her.'

'You already are. More so.' But she wasn't listening. She didn't seem to want to listen to him at all. When he asked her questions, she shrugged. He begged her to play hide and seek and she told him she'd rather stay inside. She closed her bedroom door and only ever came to see him in his. He tried everything to please her. He even drew a picture of a drawing room for Aunt Emmeline, since she wanted it so much, but Lily snorted at it, said he was giving in to the seduction of *things*.

Then he did something to be ashamed of. One morning, he waited until she'd gone down to breakfast, then he crept into her room. He gazed around it. Pretty things sparkled and danced and caught the light, bracelets and necklaces, beads on a string, pink, green, blue, yellow, cream. He walked to the bedside table, picked up a handful of them, tangled together as if they'd been dozens of skeins of wool. There were some hung on the hooks on the wall, casually, as if she'd thrown them there. The chest of drawers had more of them, bits of bracelets and more beads. He walked over to the window ledge. It was covered in glass animals, three glass fish of different colours, a butterfly, a dog of pure black and a soft purple cat. He ran his finger over them. There must have been twenty of them, beautiful intricate little things. You could have them play and talk to each other, a little world of pretty toys. He picked up one of the blue fish. 'Please can I play with you?' it said to the purple cat. 'Don't leave me out again.' He wanted to take them out, capture the colours in his sketchbooks, but none of the colours he had were sufficiently beautiful.

'What are you doing?' He swung around. Lily was standing there. 'What are you doing in here?'

He stared at her, stammered. 'I meant, I meant to come to

look for you. Then I started looking at these. They're so beautiful. Where did you get them?'

'This is my room! I didn't say you could come in here.'

'I'm sorry.' He was still holding the purple cat in his hand. 'I just—'

'You just thought you'd be nosy, that's it, isn't it?'

'I'm sorry.' She was angry with him, so angry. Her face was red, eyes screwed up. 'I'm so sorry. I was wrong.' She was going to cry. She was going to cry in the middle of her bedroom and it was all his fault.

She sat down. 'Go away. Just go away.'

On Sunday, walking back from church, Lily caught up with him. 'I've decided to forgive you,' she said. 'But you know it was very wrong.'

'I'm sorry,' he said. 'I really am.'

'Don't do it again,' she said.

In return, he had to let her spy all over his room, go through all his things, read some of the letters he wrote in secret to his father.

'Now we are even,' she said. 'And it won't happen again.' It wouldn't. He'd seen how delicate, how breakable their friendship was. It was a glass heart, balanced on a window ledge – he had to watch it, hold it carefully, because if he dropped it again, it would always be lost.

TWENTY-SEVEN

Stoneythorpe, April 1931

About a month or so after Tom had met Michael in London, Celia had come down to the parlour and Michael was not there. She'd gone to the garden, expecting to see him running around with Lily. She gazed out, smiling. There he was, dashing about as she'd expected. But then her heart lurched. Tom was standing there as Michael showed him his favourite tree, inspecting it, running his hands over it. She threw open the French windows and rushed out into the garden.

'What are you doing here?' she panted, skirt wet from the damp grass.

'Mama!' shouted Michael. 'Look! There's a new spider laying eggs here. Mr Cotton found him.'

'Tom, please.' Celia seized his arm. 'I need to speak to you!'

'It's nice to see you too, Celia.' He was tall in his suit and smart shoes, his hair slicked back, his wide handsome face and her son's eyes looking at her. The scar of a shot wound on his cheek that filled her with pain because it reminded her of her brother.

Michael was happily peering into the tree trunk. She lowered her voice. 'What are you doing here?'

'What do you think? You rushed off so quickly we didn't have time to get acquainted.' He reached out and patted Michael on the head, the movement of his hand searing through Celia's soul. 'I must say he's a very fine young man, Celia. A real credit to you.'

'Mr Cotton bought me a present!' said Michael. 'Look, Mama.'

Celia noticed a large cardboard box at the foot of the tree. Her heart filled with dread. 'What is it?'

Michael took his hand away from the spiders. 'The most amazing thing, you must look.' He knelt down and undid the cardboard lid, reverently, lifted out a gleaming red toy car. He ran his finger over it. Celia didn't know much about cars. She supposed it must be the latest model.

'That looks very expensive,' she said. 'I hope you said thank you.' She heard her own voice, angry, pinched. She couldn't help it.

'He did,' said Tom. 'A very polite thank you.'

Michael held the car up. 'It's the most beautiful thing I've ever seen.' He rushed off, holding it high, making zooming noises.

Celia turned to Tom. 'How could you?'

'Look, Celia, I know I should have asked you first. But I wanted to see him – and I thought you'd say no.'

'So you come here and try to buy him with an expensive toy? Do you often just march into people's homes because you feel like it?'

'If my son is there, yes.'

Anger seized her. 'He's not yours! He's the soldier's. I was just trying to upset you.'

'Anyone can see that's not true.'

'You never cared about us before. Now you do. Why – because you didn't have the son you hoped? So you thought you'd have mine?'

'Celia. Be fair. I didn't even know he existed until two months ago.'

'You didn't think? You didn't think when I said I'd had a son – perhaps that he was yours?'

Tom shook his head. She thought she detected a little shame in it.

'Well, you should have done!'

'I know I should. But you could have told me.'

'And now you're here trying to take him away from me.'

'Celia – please.'

'I searched for him. I thought about him. I found him. You don't know what I had to do. And now you want to come in and get him.' Michael was running up to the French windows. Lily was standing there in a white pinafore. She was waving at him, running towards him, laughing. Michael wouldn't come back for a while now he was with her.

'I just want to get to know him.'

She drew a breath. 'Tell me the truth. If I'd have said to you, when we met, I had your child and he died, would you have been sad?'

'Of course.' But he looked at his feet.

'Would you? Or would you have said, *Let's look to the future. Some things happen and God understands.* And what about if I'd told you that they'd taken him away from me. Would you have tried to help me find him? Or would you say, *It was probably for the best.*'

'Celia. I can't say now what I would have said then. It was nearly ten years ago.'

'So I'm right. You would have thought it was right to give him away. You wouldn't have wanted a tie between us.'

'I don't know.'

'But I kept looking for him. And now I have him and he's handsome and polite and clever – you want some of him. Well, you can't!'

'Celia. Doesn't the past mean anything to you?'

'To me? You're the one who was always saying our friendship meant nothing and we had to forget about it, that you hated us for having been a servant here. You kept pushing me away.'

'I'm sorry. I know I did.'

'And now you want to be best friends again?'

'I wish you'd let me explain. I said we had to move on – well, don't you think so? I didn't want to tie you down, both of us down, to childhood – to promises then that we shouldn't keep.'

She leant her head against the tree. 'You weren't worried about tying me down. You're trying to be kind. You didn't want me.' His tanned face, the handsome flow between eyes and nose and mouth, the face that didn't love her, but still, reached out for her that night in the dark in Baden Baden, by the lake, when all time had seemed to stop.

He looked down.

'And you were angry with me over the whole Heinrich thing. That Rudolf wasn't your father. You hated me because of that.'

'Not *hated*. Celia, these words are all too strong. Why does everything have to be so dramatic?'

'Because it is! It is to me. My childhood friend tells me he doesn't want to see me again. Then I lose my child. And I get him back – and, oh! You have a change of heart.' She was back in Stoneythorpe now, in Emmeline's room and they were all screaming at her because the baby was coming. And then he was on her breast and she was holding him close and her heart surged with love for him. She felt sleep overwhelm her – and they said they'd take Michael, just to be sure. She woke up, her breasts hot with pain and Verena said he'd died.

'Celia. I just want to see my son.'

'He's my son. You can't claim him. I can deny it.'

'Celia. Can't we discuss this?'

'He's not a toy. I know what you're like. You're always so curious. You want to know things. You can't just come into our life because you feel like it then go off again. You grew bored with me. What's to say you wouldn't think the same way about him?'

'Of course I wouldn't.'

'How do I know? He's been through so much. I have to protect him. I can't have you jumping in and out.'

'You don't really think I'd do that, do you?'

'How can I tell?'

What she feared was that he'd take Michael away. Michael asking about his father, his words echoing in her mind. And those nights when she'd heard him telling himself stories about who his father was – a prince, the owner of a chocolate factory, the builder of hundreds of houses, the pilot of a round-the-world plane. She'd heard him talking about the same to Lily as well. And now here was a real-life father, who was rich and handsome, despite the faded scars, and came bearing toys. What if he preferred him?

'I wish you'd leave us alone. We were fine without you. We don't need toys.'

He shrugged. 'You win, Celia. I'll give you time. You can let me know when you're ready to see me. Will you walk back with me to the house?'

She nodded. He put his arm through hers, like any gentleman leading a lady, and his hand burnt her arm.

'The house is in a bad way. Needs a lot of repair.'

She looked up and saw it through his eyes, ramshackle back, windows broken, fallen chimneys, tiles missing on the roof, the ivy cutting into the brickwork. The house was splitting, more so every day.

'The foundations are strong. It's been here for years.'

'Don't you think you should sell it?'

'Emmeline and I did want to. But my parents refuse. And I love seeing Michael here,' she said. 'I'm trying to prop it up with the business. But even if I can't, I'm not sure we could sell it. I spoke to an agent and he said no one really wants such a big house; so much work as you say. People want a modern look.'

They continued up to the house.

'Will you let me say goodbye to him before I leave?' They were nearly at the French windows to the parlour.

'Of course. He'd be sorry not to say goodbye to you.' She shouted for Michael and he and Lily came careening out from the side of the house.

'Mr Cotton is going now,' she said, stiffly. 'He's keen to say goodbye before he goes.'

Lily jumped up. 'I like the car you bought Michael. Have you got a present for me?'

He shook his head. 'Maybe next time.' Celia stared at him and he looked away.

'When will you come back?' Michael was asking.

'I have to go away for a while. But as soon as I get back I will come and see you.'

'The minute you get back?'

'The minute.' He avoided Celia's eye.

Michael threw himself at Tom's legs and hugged him hard. 'Thank you for the car.' Then Lily was throwing herself at Tom, too. 'Thanks for Michael's car. Next time bring something for me!'

In a moment, they were both running off again, hurtling towards the trees.

'You certainly had an effect on them,' said Celia. She pushed open the door to the parlour and Verena was standing there.

'Oh! I heard you had a visitor, Celia. I thought it might be—' She broke off. 'Have we met?' She was holding out her hand to Tom, who had taken off his hat. She didn't recognise him, Celia realised. She saw the handsome face, fine clothes – and she had no idea who it was. Celia saw hope shine in her mother's eyes and her heart sank.

'Yes, Mama. Don't you remember? It's Tom Cotton.'

Verena's eyes widened – but you couldn't fault her composure. 'How nice to see you again, Tom,' she said, shaking his hand. Her manner and tone had changed, become less breathless. She was smiling in the distant way that you would to a waiter or a man in a hotel. Celia looked at Tom, and he had seen the change too. He straightened.

'Likewise, Mrs de Witt. I am glad to hear you are still here at Stoneythorpe.'

She smiled. 'Until we die. That is all we ask. Here until we die.'

He nodded. 'I am sure that will come to pass.'

'Mr Cotton has to go now,' said Celia, quickly.

'It's been marvellous to see you again, Mrs de Witt.' He gave another gallant sweep of his hat, replaced it.

Celia propelled Tom out of the room, into the hall. 'Now can you go?' she hissed.

'Why are you being like this?'

'Because I know you. You come in and out of my life. And what if you did the same to Michael, sometimes see him, sometimes not. You admitted it, practically.'

She closed the door against him, leant against it. A fat tear ran down her cheek. She didn't try to brush it away.

She would find a way to keep the house. She would double the efforts of Miss Violet's Kitchen. She would fill department stores with silver-covered jars and boxes. Wherever you looked there would be Miss Violet's Kitchen. Every girl would be eating it. She would support them all, no matter what. She would keep the family together, keep the house, keep them alive. Shops would be full of her glittering jars and cans and boxes, wrapped up like presents, held close by girls on the way home on the omnibus. She would get the business up and running and then be able to go back to Jonathan for a little while, start a new Miss Violet's Kitchen in the US and then come back here. She would save them all.

'And here is the map of the Secondary World,' a voice was saying. Celia was passing the schoolroom when she heard Mr Brennan's voice, booming out. The Secondary World? What did he mean? She stood outside, listening against the door. The voices had dropped and Lily and Michael were talking now. Could she just walk in? She and Emmeline had sat in on a few lessons and it had all gone swimmingly. Lily and Michael seemed so happy that they hadn't needed to enquire. And Michael was clearly learning something – she'd caught him deep in an algebra problem when she'd entered his room a few weeks ago. But what on earth was the Secondary World?

She knocked on the door and entered. Lily, Michael and Mr Brennan looked up – Mr Brennan smiling.

'Welcome,' he said. 'We were just deep in geography.'

Celia couldn't read the children's expressions. Lily looked almost hostile, she thought, Michael was maybe surprised. She seated herself at the back. Mr Brennan was talking about the geography of Europe. He held up his book, listed rivers, mountains, talked about plains and weather differences, oceans and currents. Michael and Lily were scribbling down the information in their exercise books. He quizzed them on what they had learnt and Lily answered more correctly than Michael. It was all entirely normal.

'Thank you,' she said. 'It has been nice to hear the lesson.'

They wished her goodbye. Lily was pleased to see her go, it was clear. Celia walked out, trying to shake off the misgiving.

Seventeen years ago, she'd walked in on Emmeline and Mr Janus reciting from *Romeo and Juliet*, seen nothing then. *Why didn't you know?* Verena asked her. *You were there.* But she didn't know, saw nothing.

And now this? What was a Secondary World? Her mind spooled into magical worlds, second lives, parallel ghostly places, the stuff of stories. She wanted to go there, wherever it was. She wanted to take all of them there, far away from reality, live forever.

PART THREE

TWENTY-EIGHT

Stoneythorpe, March 1933

Two years had gone by and the only way you could see the passage of time was on the children, Michael nearly eleven, Lily fourteen. It was as if Lily was gaining more colour every day, redder lips, black hair, like a Snow White in the midst of the forest. Her beauty blazed so hard that sometimes Celia had to look away, it was too new, scorched you with its ardour and its hope. When they went up to town, men stared at her in a way that infuriated Celia. 'She's only a child!' she wanted to shout. But she could see it in their faces, they didn't see her as a child, but a beautiful thing that had the power to burn them too – unless they seized it and made it their own. But Lily didn't seem to notice. Her thoughts were always elsewhere.

Michael too – he was no longer a boy. Every day, sloughing off the old self, becoming new, galloping towards manhood. She remembered herself being desperate for adulthood, the freedom she thought she'd get, not understanding how cruel the world was. Michael still came to her to be held – but he didn't creep into her bed any more. So if she woke up late at night, she would tiptoe into his room, watch him sleep, pleased that he still held his bear to him, kept the wooden horse under his pillow. She wished she could catch his dreams by holding him – but he lay there, serene and absorbed, far from her.

Jonathan had come over once for Christmas and he had meant to visit again – but his father had died, unexpectedly. He had been absorbed in the death and what had to be done with the house and the business for the past year. Celia had offered to go over but he said she should stay, that they were too occupied. She wrote to him twice a week. But how could she go to America, move Michael again? Emmeline and Lily would never come and her son adored Lily more than anyone.

Jonathan wrote that he'd found Violet a good job in an office. Violet even wrote a small letter to Celia, saying she was flattered that her name was there at the business but glad the flapper didn't look like her! Celia treasured it, every word, kept it in her bureau to read over again.

Miss Violet's Kitchen was flourishing, ever since Celia and Mrs Craigmire perfected the canning. All the Winter Meats canneries were busy producing for Miss Violet's Kitchen. The big shops in London placed endless orders and Celia went up most weeks to check on the displays, in pride of place in the Food Halls of Harrods, Selfridges, Harvey Nichols, even Fortnum and Mason and Liberty too. Department stores all over the country had followed suit – Norwich, Cardiff, Birmingham, Manchester, Edinburgh, Exeter. All the newspapers had run articles about Miss Violet's Kitchen and interviewed Celia about 'The American Girl'. She was grateful to that department-store buyer for giving her the tip, just as she was starting off – everyone wanted to be a New York Girl.

They put advertising in newspapers and magazines and even on the Underground. 'Miss Violet's Kitchen. For the New York Girl in You!' Miss Violet, as created by their artist, was blonde and sassy, smiling out of every poster, holding bags of jars and cans, going home to make a party for all her friends out of jars and cans. 'More time for dancing!' she cried, always smiling, always happy. There had been criticism too – it was said that Celia was feeding this *Refusal of women to be properly feminine*. Because women were there to cook – and if they did not cook, what would happen to civilisation? Some people wrote letters demanding how these young women were ever going to be able to cook for their husbands and children – were they going to give their children food from a can? But others were more afraid – said that Miss Violet's Kitchen meant that women would never get married at all – because surely women got married because they wanted to look after their husbands and a home, and if they didn't dream of this, cooking food in their own kitchen, then *Maybe they would never get married at all.*

'They're all men saying what women should want,' she told journalists, smiling. 'We know what today's woman wants and that's time. We're giving our girl more time. And if she wants to spend it cooking, then she can! We're just giving her the choice.' And they had actually found out that their buyers weren't just women. Men bought Miss Violet's Kitchen, too. They'd even had a few wives who said their husbands preferred it! 'All kinds of people buy our foods,' Celia said. 'We are giving them what they want and making their lives easier – so that they can enjoy a nutritious meal at the end of the working day, without spending three hours preparing it.' The newspapers printed profiles of her, noted as 'The Modern Woman', took photographs of her after a woman had come and painted her with make-up, made her lips red.

Celia bought an office in Winchester and rented the shop below it. She and Mrs Craigmire hired painters and decorators to paint the interior a warm yellow, put in shelves and large glass windows. They filled it with pretty chairs and fine curtains, a neat desk. A sign-painter painted 'Miss Violet's Kitchen' in gold on a wooden sign. They hired three shop assistants from the area, who all looked a little like Miss Violet themselves. It proved so popular that in three months, Celia was looking for a property in London to do the same, found one in Oxford Street. A few companies, including one called Flower Foods, were trying to break into their market but were having no success. Their customers were loyal – and there were more of them all the time.

Celia kept the key for the office and shop in her pocket, always, her treasure. On one day, she felt daring and enquired with an agency about taking a light advertisement in Piccadilly Circus, but they told her that there was a long queue and it tended to go to the more established brands – Coca-Cola, Rowntree, Cadbury. Mr Mars had made a new chocolate bar at his factory in Slough and he had taken the space for nearly six months.

Rudolf said he was proud of Miss Violet's Kitchen – but she knew he was disappointed. She knew he thought that if she'd put the same effort into Winter Meats, she would have made that succeed too. There was no point telling him that the world had changed – it had not changed for him. One day, they would have Miss Violet up in lights in Piccadilly Circus and she would take him to see her and he really would be proud.

Tom had written and she'd written back. He'd come to visit Michael regularly, once or twice a month, but hadn't told the boy or the family the truth. They pretended he was visiting her. 'Why won't you let me tell my son the truth?' he said.

'I need you to prove it,' she said. 'I don't want you going in and out of his life. He has suffered so much.' Her heart swelled with fear that once Tom married and had children of his own, he would forget about Michael and leave them all behind. She saw his visits with confusion in her mind. Michael deserved to know his father and it would be cruel to keep him away. She could not imagine how Jonathan would see it, feared he might view it as disloyalty, so did not tell him.

Every visit made her heart hurt. But Tom was kind and patient, talked to them all, bought Michael and Lily presents. She forced herself to think rationally – it wasn't Tom's fault that he didn't love her. She couldn't resent him for that. Tom had written occasionally to Heinrich, received no response. At least he didn't blame her for that.

'You were right, Celia,' he said one day. 'That night in Baden – I didn't think about it again – not in this way. I didn't think it might have – consequences.'

She remembered Violet's words: *Men do what they want*. Tom wasn't like that.

'I should have done,' he was saying. 'I was so angry about what happened with Heinrich – I didn't think about you.'

'Thank you.' She couldn't think of anything else to say. She'd wanted him to love her, then. Now – he only felt sorry for her, guilty for not having thought. At night, her heart snaked with

244

fear, Tom would marry, set up a rich home and he and his wife would take Michael for himself.

In May, he mentioned to her on a visit that he was engaged, and her face clenched with panic. She didn't ask about the fiancée or the wedding plans, dreaded him telling her.

The children were still working hard for Mr Brennan. Emmeline had been right – he had been an excellent choice for a tutor. Lily was flowering under his close attention, answering comprehension questions, memorising history and geography. Michael was fond of history too, but she was most surprised by his love for art. No one in the family had ever been able to draw – and here was Michael, sketching trees, flowers, the house, the whole family – and then figments of his imagination, fantasy worlds with elves and pixies and fairies. He could spend hours and hours carefully drawing the details of a flower in the garden. Celia admired it, was proudly surprised by it, for she knew nothing of such detail, couldn't train herself to such minute attention, and yet Michael found – showed – a whole world in the varying colours of a single petal of a flower. And it was all thanks to Brennan – Celia would never have noticed, expected it, fostered it.

'He really is very talented,' said Mr Brennan. 'He might want to study art when he is older.'

Rudolf was dubious about art. 'He should be planning for Oxford,' he said crossly. Celia disagreed. Her son had a talent and in the new world, artists could make money too – what about Lowry, his canvases of hundreds of people, so alive that they could walk out of the painting any minute. Michael carried a sketchbook everywhere now, was always drawing – and even when he wasn't, she saw him looking at something – the whorl of wood on the table, her own hand and its interwoven webs of lines, and knew he was thinking of drawing them. Sometimes, she would creep into his room when he wasn't there and look over his sketches. She knew she shouldn't, that although it wasn't looking at a diary, still it was private, but she couldn't help herself. Looking at his drawings, she felt that they gave a pathway to the hidden rooms of his heart. She looked at pictures of Stoneythorpe, the gardens, the flowers – and her soul flowed when she saw he had drawn her, caught unawares and looking the other way, sketched with love. And other pictures too – some of the skyline of New York, the view he must have had from his constricted windows. And then some sketches that she didn't recognise, pure imagination – leaping dragons, monsters, fairy maidens chained to rocks, a fish of flowing, vibrant green passing through transparent water. One particularly elaborate, entrancing picture of a girl fleeing a monster almost had Lily's face. She traced her fingers over the picture. He barely wrote in the book – the odd name of a flower, a place, 'Mama' under her picture. But he had written 'Brennan' a few times, once under the maiden.

'You chose an excellent tutor,' Rudolf often said. 'So good with the children. And so unobtrusive. You would hardly know he was here.' Mr Brennan had his own key, let himself in quietly, walked up the stairs to the classroom where the children were waiting for him. Celia had asked him to stay for dinner, invited his mother, asked if they might like to pay a visit at Christmas, but he was very strict, said no. She supposed he was right – if you got too close to the family, then it would be harder when you had to leave them. That was what they dreaded. The day when Mr Brennan told them that he had got a job in a school – and of course he should because he was such a talented teacher – and he would be leaving them. They gave him a rise, repainted the classroom and bought new desks, offered him extra holiday but he never took it. Celia wondered if he was in love with Emmeline, wanted to be close to her and perhaps that was why he was so complaisant. She watched him – and he did follow Emmeline with his eyes. She pondered saying it, did not. Emmeline might panic and send him away – and Michael was so happy with him. Sometimes, she picked up essays of the children's, left in the schoolroom. Lily had written six pages about the misery of being trapped by your possessions, the cruelty they imposed, how things kept you down and enslaved. She thought of speaking to her about it – but then did not. It was only the natural extremism of being a young person, when it was all or nothing, no half area in the middle.

Just for fun, she asked Michael to draw Miss Violet – and the girl he produced was much better than the one they already had. She was more vibrant, more engaging, less beautiful but that was *better* – more like any pretty girl on the street. The first Miss Violet had had the sort of face that would always be beautiful, get more so when she was forty, fifty, into greater years. Michael's Miss Violet was the girl who was most beautiful in her youth, bright and shiny with hope. You could see the sheen of newness on her, the fresh arrival into the world, knowing little, happy because that was so. And oddly, even though she was blonde and slightly caramel skinned, when Violet had been dark haired and very pale, and although Michael had never seen her, she had a look of the real Violet about her. Something in her eyes that could switch so quickly from merriment to sadness, something searching, looking, even though, perhaps, she wasn't sure what it was.

She gave the first artist a pay-off and Michael's Miss Violet became the girl. She put pictures up of her in the shops, a giant one on a wall in London, smaller ones for posters on the Tube. 'We will get her up in Piccadilly Circus.' She gave Michael and Lily a small payment, to split between them, because otherwise it wouldn't be fair – and Mr Brennan a bonus.

Lily and Michael glittered with the sheen of change, every moment a new spark of electricity passed across them, altering their bodies and their minds. But she and Emmeline had merely lived longer, passed more days, done nothing with them. She could see the fine lines on the face of her sister, the thinning of the skin around the mouth. Her sister's golden hair was greying now, her waist thicker. Still, thought Celia, Emmeline was beautiful, more so, to her.

She found herself wondering about Emmeline's old fiancé, Sir Hugh, horrid anti-German snob – but still, he'd loved her once. She asked after him, and the vicar told her he'd died just after the war, from the Spanish flu. Celia counted the months and realised she'd been in Germany at the time. He said that Emmeline had been to the funeral and Celia wondered at her sister, at how much she didn't know about her.

'Emmeline,' she said one day, while they were washing up the breakfast plates in the kitchen. 'When did you last hear from Samuel?'

Her sister shook her head. 'I'm not talking about this. I told you last time. I can't remember just now.'

'Look, Emmeline, have you had a single letter from him since the first few when he set off?'

'Don't, Celia.'

'He hasn't written to you at all, has he?'

'Twice. At the beginning.'

She held her sister's soapy hand, lowered her voice. 'Emmeline. What if he's not coming back?' She couldn't say the rest. She couldn't say, *What if he's dead?* That would be too cruel. But it was what she thought. Four years gone and so long since she'd had any word from him.

She tried again. 'Emmeline. I know you're loyal. You're a good wife. But he's been gone for four years. Maybe you should start – looking elsewhere.' She restrained herself from mentioning Mr Brennan. He was so much younger – although of course there was the point that he was already fond of Lily.

Emmeline looked up. She was holding a plate in her hand, one of Verena's special breakfast plates. 'Never! I'm waiting for him. He's not dead! He's alive, I know it. And as long as he's alive, I'm his wife!'

She held up the plate. Celia stepped back. *She's going to throw it at me*, she thought. *She's going to.* Emmeline threw it on the floor at her feet and dashed from the room. Celia picked up a broom and began sweeping the bits into a pan.

'There's something I wanted to speak to you about,' Emmeline said, two days later. Had she noticed that Mr Brennan was following her with his eyes? But it wasn't that.

'We need to try and separate Lily and Michael. They're too close.'

'What are you saying? I don't understand.' They were in Verena's bedroom, surrounded by all her tiny bottles and vases. Emmeline had summoned her there, chosen it so no one would hear.

'We have to do something about it,' said Emmeline. 'Don't you see?'

'No. I don't. They're just fond of each other. And it's just a phase,' said Celia. 'It will pass. They'll find other friends, people their own age.'

'It's not a phase. They're completely dependent on each other. It's not healthy.'

'But there's nothing wrong with it.' Celia was gazing at one of the vases, swirled pink and purple. When Celia had been a little girl, Verena had sometimes kept loose change in them so if Celia wanted to buy sweets, sometimes her mother would go over the vases, emptying each one to find the few pennies she needed. Her mother probably kept more there now, she was so busy saying she didn't trust the banks after the Crash. But Celia worried that notes might be getting old and fragile in there, that when they took them out, there would be nothing but tiny pieces of paper, like snowflakes.

'Lily's fourteen. Michael's eleven. They're too old to behave like children. If I could, I'd send her to school like her brother. But Papa couldn't afford her as well. You should send Michael, ask Tom for the money.'

'Never. I'll never send him away.'

'Don't you see how well Albert is doing?' Emmeline was right, Celia had to admit. When Albert came home for the holidays, he was taller, browner, talked about how much he enjoyed school, and so many boys that she couldn't keep track of them all.

'That's different.'

'We have to do something. I think we'll start by saying there's to be no more being together unless there's an adult there too. They can't be alone any more.'

'Come on, Emmeline. They're going to hate that.'

'Celia, you were young once, so was I. Feelings run high. And there's no way back for girls.'

'I don't like what you're implying. Michael loves Lily. She's his cousin. Anyway, he's a child.' She was sitting too close to Emmeline. She could see the red lines in her eyes, the wateriness of the tear ducts. She looked away.

'Don't be naive. They're getting older. You were in love with Tom at thirteen.'

'That's different.' Celia paused. 'Did you know?'

'It was obvious to me. Probably not the rest of them, they're so blind. But that's what I mean. And you carried on mooning after Tom long after you should have done – and now look at you.'

Celia stood up. She walked to the window, clenching her fists, trying to control her feelings. The room felt suffocatingly hot, Emmeline's scent, the plump fatness of Verena's pillows. 'Oh, stop being so self-righteous. They're young. If they want to be together, they should be. It's only friendship.'

'Lily needs other friends.'

She gazed down on the garden, the trees around the sides, the overgrown flower beds, the fountain in the middle, all inspired by Verena's love for Versailles. She couldn't see either of them. 'But they're children.'

'My rules stand.'

'But listen, Emmeline, how about we let them play together after lessons? It's harmless.'

Emmeline shook her head. 'I've made up my mind. She's my daughter. I have to protect her.'

Celia almost hated her then. 'But Michael's had so little in life. So little happiness. This is all he's got. Don't take it away from him.' *Lily didn't need protecting from her cousin!*

'Oh, don't be so melodramatic. I'm not taking anything away from him. They still have each other. It's just – they're coming up to a dangerous time.'

Celia pushed her back against Verena's thick curtain. She wanted to break one of the tiny vases, smash it to the floor. 'They're friends. Nothing more. He's so young. They need each other.'

'Well, you can take whatever view you like, Celia. Fact is, I'm in charge when it comes to Lily and these are my rules for her from now on. I don't care if you agree or not.'

'You're wrong. What if they come to resent us?'

'I don't care. We know we're right.'

Celia ignored her. 'Not me. You. They're your rules.' She grasped her sister's hands. 'Don't do it. Please.'

Emmeline shook her head. 'I have decided. You can't change my mind.'

'I'll stop!' said Celia. 'I'll stop doing all this for the business so we can all live.'

She shrugged. 'Then we'll be poor. I don't care. These are my rules and I don't care whether you agree or not.' She hurried from the room.

INTERLUDE

So often when he couldn't find her, he knew where she'd be: in the room they thought was Louisa's, looking at her dresses.

He wanted to do what they used to do – explore the whole house, find out secrets. But Lily was changing. She wanted to talk about grown-up things. She was fascinated by Louisa. She was convinced she had been killed, and thought that if she looked through her belongings, she would feel closer to her.

'Look,' she said, holding one up, a pale-blue gown embroidered with sequins. 'Isn't it beautiful?'

He nodded, stared at the pile of gowns around her, heaps of pale yellow, green, pink and cream, sparkling bags, high-heeled shoes.

'These are party dresses, for London parties. For a pretty girl.'

He sat down on the broken bed. It was another room that they said was locked, but it wasn't really. Nobody ever checked.

'You're pretty.'

'Not as pretty as Aunt Louisa.'

'Prettier,' he said.

But she wasn't listening, she was looking through the gowns, sorting them, humming to herself. 'Let's never have secrets,' she'd said in the first days. But now there were secrets, not just of the grown-ups, but theirs too. Hers.

Mr Brennan was always talking. After art, Michael liked maths the most, the clean lines of the numbers, how they fitted together and there was always a right answer. Lily preferred composition, would write pages and pages of stories about things he barely understood: people flying through the sky, fish at the bottom of the sea, love stories between handsome men and girls who lived in lonely cottages in the wood, alone and waiting to be rescued.

He didn't know how she imagined such beautiful things. He knew that Mr Brennan was similarly amazed, for he took Lily's book and read it and when they were both supposed to be working on composition or reading or maths, Michael would sometimes look up and there was Mr Brennan, holding Lily's exercise book and gazing at it.

He'd hated Mr Brennan at first because there was less time for playing with Lily. But now, as she was changing, harbouring secrets, he found himself looking forward to their classes. For in the sitting room that they used as their schoolroom in the mornings, Lily was knowable, happy, keen to answer, always smiling. He could predict her, understand her. But then, in the afternoons when they were free together, he felt as if she was slipping away. Even when they were alone in a room together, she wasn't with him. Her mind was in another world.

So he drew. He drew and he drew and he drew, creating lines, systems, shading, focusing on detail. Lines made sense of the world when words only confused it. He drew Miss Violet for Mama and she had been delighted. She said that his picture had reminded her of her old friend, something in the eyes. But he'd never seen the friend – when he'd drawn Miss Violet, he'd been drawing Lily's eyes: sadness, excitement, anticipation and something else, a jumping, always out of reach quality he neither recognised nor understood.

When he went to see Grandpapa and look through the photographs, Lily didn't seem to mind any more. Once, Grandpapa had let him go early because he had a headache. He ran out to look for Lily but he couldn't find her anywhere. Then, when it was just time for supper, she reappeared.

'I've been looking for you!' he said.

She smiled beatifically. 'I went for a walk. Down to the woods.'

One day, while exploring the rooms upstairs, alone because Lily had gone off somewhere and he couldn't find her, Michael looked behind a bed and found a padded box containing two old pistols. They looked like ones from the war. He held it up, touched the rusty trigger and the end. There were bullets in it. You could shoot someone with it. Perhaps the owner already had.

'I found two guns upstairs,' he said to Rudolf, one evening while they were looking at photographs. 'I think they're very old.'

Rudolf shrugged. 'So much old stuff in this house. I never imagine any of it works. And now antique guns. I suppose they belonged to one of the soldiers in the hospital.'

'I think it still works.' His hand on the trigger, curving around it.

'Oh no.' Rudolf smiled. 'Now to these photographs.'

But Michael couldn't forget about it. At night, the gun spun in his mind.

TWENTY-NINE

Stoneythorpe, August 1933

A letter came from America. Celia tore it open. She stared in horror. Mr Galss had been right to suspect that there might be more of Arthur's debts – and she had been wrong to imagine that he would not borrow against Rudolf's name. The solicitor wrote that the bank noted below expected this money paid and the family was liable because Arthur had signed them all under his name. He had used Rudolf as guarantor and they must pay the money. He owed thousands upon thousands. The bank noted that they were willing to waive the interest that had accrued since he took the loan to the date of sending the letter, as they understood that the family may have overlooked the matter. But now, they would request it be repaid as soon as possible.

Celia stared at the letter. She'd never be able to repay them, not even if she got Miss Violet up in Piccadilly Circus and their products in every shop in London.

They would have to put the house on the market. They had to sell. Everything she had been working for. She'd put her marriage on hold, told Jonathan to wait. She'd thrown herself into trying to save the house, for them, for Michael. But now it was lost. However hard she worked, she couldn't beat Arthur's debts. They had to sell. Miss Violet's Kitchen was as nothing, hopeless, empty snow falling on them. The future she had expected, wanted, was broken and she had failed.

Michael heard his mother and grandparents talking. Some money had been lost. Someone had made a mistake. He heard his mother weeping when she told his grandparents. His grandmother screamed.

Stoneythorpe would have to be sold. He didn't want it to be. He didn't want to move again. He had thought he would stay here forever and ever. He wanted to live here with Lily and run through the garden with her.

Aunt Emmeline was trying to hide her tears, he could see. She was practical. He felt sorry for her. And then she said something terrible, a few days later. 'Well, we'll move house and things will have to change,' she said. 'It's time you were separated. We had been thinking about it before this news of selling – but now we're sure. You will go to school, both of you, like Albert. No need for a tutor. School is much better. Celia and I enjoyed school, didn't we?'

Celia shook her head. Emmeline lit up Winterbourne, beautiful, popular, good at games. Whereas she had been shy, out of place, always reading, girls like Eloisa mocking her.

Emmeline started talking about the sitting room she would have in the new house, blue and rosewood. The subject of school was closed. It had been decided.

And so the children saw the future. Everything they had would be over.

'Why are they doing this to us?' he said to Lily.

She gazed past him. 'They must be stopped.'

'I think we should have a party,' Celia had said at the dinner table, one night soon after.

'A what?' Emmeline looked up from her plate.

Celia pushed her dried-out beef to the back of the plate. 'A party. To say goodbye to the house. If we're going to sell it and never come back.' She was growing used to the idea. They could find a new home, put the past behind them. Michael had been taken from her here, Louisa had run away with Arthur. They could go to a new house, a different life.

'We haven't sold it yet,' said Rudolf, 'remember.'

'Well, we will. Only a matter of time. And surely summer would be best for a party. And this way we can celebrate it before we have to move too many things around.' The agent they'd already arranged to come and see their home had expressed concern that the house was too 'cluttered'. Things would have to go into storage. The modern buyer wanted a 'clean' look, apparently. Stoneythorpe was 'too Victorian' – in every way.

'And who on earth would come? We know no one.'

'Celia, what has got into you? You never have parties.'

'I just think we should say goodbye, that's all!' She didn't know what had got into her. The words had sprung into her head. In her heart, though, what she said was true, she wanted to wish goodbye to the house.

'We once had so many parties. When I was a little girl, you were always throwing them.' If they didn't have one final party now, then that would mean that the last party they'd ever thrown had been that disastrous one, just before the war, when no one but Tom and his sister had come, the whole village ignoring them because they were Germans and the enemy.

Celia stopped for breath and then she wasn't in the sitting room at all, but in the garden, just before the war, and they were waiting for the children to come to the party. The table was heavy with cakes, carrot, sponge, one thick with lemon icing. Mr Thompson and Mr Smithson had laid out all the tables and decorated them with bunting and paper stars. And there were games: pin the donkey, blind man's bluff and a box of lucky dip almost as tall as Celia. Jennie and Verena had spent hours wrapping up the presents for it. Celia had been in love with a big wax doll, with blonde hair and blue eyes, a beautiful thing, terribly expensive. Of course, at fifteen, she was too old for dolls, but something in her yearned for it, to be a child of seven and playing with such a beautiful toy. She'd helped, wrapped it carefully, covering its limbs with tissue paper and folding its velvet gown around its legs so that the material wouldn't crease. 'Good girl,' said Rudolf, watching her wrap it. He had bought it in London, carried it all the way home.

For two weeks, the house had been bustling, Rudolf planning, Mrs Bell conjuring pies and jellies, Verena organising the games.

And then they were waiting in the garden, the icing sliding off the cakes in the heat, buns glistening, and Jennie came around the corner.

'There aren't many children, Sir.'

'Oh, I am sure they are on their way! How many do you have now? Ten, twelve?'

Jennie dropped her head. 'Two, Sir.'

It was Tom and his sister, Maggie, only just seven. So Maggie had to be every child, pinning the tail on the donkey, playing blind man's bluff with Smithson. The tables stood to attention, full of food that no one would eat. The heavy icing on the lemon cake began to heat up and collapse in on itself. Maggie, exhausted, her eyes brimming tears for being watched by so many adults, was finally allowed to go home by Rudolf – but before she did, she was sent to dig deep into the lucky dip. Each time she took a present, Jennie shook her head. 'No!' she said. 'That's not the one!' And she did it over and over until the child pulled out a big parcel, wrapped in blue with purple ribbon. Maggie clasped it to her chest.

'Open it,' said Rudolf from the table.

Maggie stared at him.

'The poor thing's a little tired,' ventured Tom.

Rudolf gazed back. And then his voice cracked. 'Please,' he said, desperately. 'Open it, just for me.'

And Maggie, eyes of everybody upon her, carefully tore open the paper and then the tissue and pulled the doll out. She looked at it.

'It's beautiful,' Tom said. 'Say thank you, little one.'

Celia knew she was afraid of it, too grand, too expensive.

'It doesn't matter,' Rudolf said. 'As long as she had it.'

They watched Jennie take Tom and Maggie away. The sky reached down and touched them with its fingers of blue. *Didn't you realise?* it said. *The English don't want you here!*

Jonathan had seen all that, their great humiliation. And yet his increasingly infrequent letters said he still loved her, wanted her to come back, and that he couldn't leave America, his father's business. She was beginning to worry that the outlines of his face were growing fainter to her, something about it indistinct, as if she was looking at him through a window covered in mist, no matter how many times she looked at the photograph of them.

'It's an idea,' said Rudolf, slowly, looking up, breaking into Celia's thoughts. 'What do you think, children? A party?'

Michael and Lily were eating with them, which they didn't always do. They sat silently. It was five months since Emmeline's new decision that they could never be alone and Celia had to admit it was going better than she could have expected. They seemed to have accepted it – and they had begun to lead their lives separately. In the morning, they worked with Mr Brennan, then after lunch, walked separately around the garden. For the rest of the day, they'd read with the adults or rest before dinner. In January, Michael would be going to school with Albert at Harrow. And when they moved, they were going to try to find a school for Lily, just a day school so she could live at home.

'See, I was right.' Emmeline had whispered. 'They're young. They don't care.'

Celia sighed. Perhaps Emmeline had been right. Michael seemed accustomed to it, Lily too. Something within her sank at how he would go to school, make friends, move on to adult life, and forget about her. And it was right. He was almost a man. Children only wanted to be with you all the time when they were very young. It was too late now. She couldn't get those days back. The Whetstones had had them – and hadn't wanted them.

'Children?' prompted Rudolf.

Michael looked up, said. 'We could help.'

'I wish we could have a party!' said Lily. 'It would be wonderful. Imagine. We could make this place look like fairyland. We could put lights in the trees, cover the rooms with flowers. And people could dance in the gardens.'

She was looking upwards. Everybody was staring at her, surprised by her fervour. Celia looked across quickly – and saw Michael gazing at her too, not surprised, but mesmerized. She looked away, just in case Emmeline might see and follow her eyes. Lily was still talking about her plans.

'I just think it would be magical,' Lily said. 'Don't you think?'

'Well, we could certainly try,' said Rudolf, beaming at his grand-daughter.

'It would be nice to say a proper goodbye to the house,' said Verena, slowly.

'There we go, then,' said Celia, before Emmeline could start throwing cold water around. 'We have to have a party. Lily is in charge of the decorations. The rest of us can do the guest list and the food. When shall we do it?'

'September,' said Verena. 'After that it will be too cold.'

'That's a month away,' said Emmeline. 'We can't do a party in a month.'

'Of course we can,' said Rudolf. 'We don't have anything else to do.'

And so they did. The next month was a whirl, of letters and planning and moving furniture and discussing who might come, might not. They planned to have food laid out in the parlour, then outside, under the lights that Lily was talking of for the trees, people would walk and maybe even dance. Mr Brennan was superbly helpful – making lists of food, planning decorations, taking the children into town to buy what was needed. Celia asked him if he'd like to invite his mother, but he declined, said she grew shy at parties. He found them a string quartet, who'd come all the way from Winchester to play.

'This seems like a ridiculous expense,' said Verena. But Emmeline reminded her, when they'd sold the house, they'd have plenty of money – and they had to say goodbye somehow. Emmeline was being practical about the sale and Celia knew she hoped to take up their old flat in London, wait for Mr Janus there. Verena ordered caviar from London, venison, fancy puddings that would have to come down on the train packed up in ice. She shot off invitations to everyone she could think of. Lady Redroad, the old doyenne of the area before the war, was long dead, but Verena invited her son and his wife, who sent a reply saying they would most probably come. Their old servants, Jennie and Mr Smithson, married now and living in Winchester, where Mr Smithson ran a pub, said they'd come – with all five of their children. Rudolf offered to pay Mr Thompson's fare from Scotland, where he lived now – but he said he wasn't strong enough to come. Most of the other servants who'd been with them during the war were dead now.

The school even allowed Albert special dispensation to come – although none of his friends were allowed to accompany him.

'Why don't you invite friends, Celia,' Emmeline said.

'From Winterbourne? I'm not sure I even know where they are.' Nearly twenty years later. She tried to remember them, could conjure up only shadowy forms, shapes against the large windows at the back of the assembly hall. Popular Eloisa who had snubbed her – where would she be now? She tried to run through other friends. The only names she remembered were those of the ambulance girls: Waterton, Fitzhugh. The girls she hadn't really paid much attention to because her heart had been so caught by Shep. She supposed that Waterton, ex-Head Girl, always telling people what to do, constantly ordering, talking about Doing Your Bit, was busy organising church fêtes somewhere, the pillar of the community. She'd once seen mention of Geraldine Fitzhugh's marriage to an Earl, while idly flicking through the pages of *The Times*. Both of them would be far too busy to come.

'I don't think I have any friends,' she said, decidedly. 'I've invited Jonathan. That's enough.'

He had been at the last party, the one that had failed. Now it would be different. And they could go to America, once they had sold the house. They could try again with the American Girl, selling her breads and cakes and pastries and stews to the modern girl in Los Angeles, New York, Detroit.

'Unless you would rather invite Tom?'

'Stop it, Emmeline.'

'Because you can't have both, can you?'

'Emmeline, I said, stop it. I've invited Jonathan. And the rest is none of your business.'

'Of course not. We'll just stand by as you make a mess of things.'

At that, Celia felt her blood rise. 'Me make a mess of things? What about you? You run away, marry Mr Janus – and then we all have to tiptoe around you, let you say whatever you want? Of course, he's off fighting for freedom – saving the world. But he never bothers to write to you and so here you are in the same position as me – still living off your parents – and you're thirty-six! At least I do important work, manage the company.'

She threw out the last words, ran off, up the stairs. There, at her desk, she wrote a telegram to Jonathan, in case he hadn't received the letter in time. *We're leaving the house and we're having a party here. Please come.*

The pencil in her hand twitched, wanted to write to Tom, too. *Come.* She threw it to the floor. She sent the telegram to Jonathan. It might be impossible, difficult to travel at such short notice.

She wrote a letter to Tom after all. He wrote back that he didn't wish to say goodbye to the old house – the place where he'd been a servant. Anyway, he said, he was busy with the wedding. She had to force herself not to think of his fiancée, how pretty and engaging she must be.

Verena had invited people she hadn't seen in years – and even more surprisingly, most said they were coming! Everybody was helping. Even Lily and Michael were busying themselves with carrying things back and forth. For the past few weeks, the men and women from the village had been helping them clean the house, repair a few of the more obvious bits of damage, and now they were decorating the house with flowers. Rudolf had said they must spare no expense, should spend whatever they wanted. It was their party to celebrate the house that had been theirs for so long. They must go out with a bang.

THIRTY

Now the party was almost on them, Michael and Lily were laughing and busy, putting up decorations with Mr Brennan directing them, always helpful. Celia's heart pierced at their happiness, the finality of it, before separation, school and more of Emmeline's rules. They had told Mr Brennan that they aimed to send the children to school soon and he had been very polite about it, said it was better for the children to be at school and it had been a privilege to teach them. Celia saw him staring after Emmeline, felt pained for him.

Jonathan's car arrived from London two days before the party. She was amazed he had come all the way to see her. Her heart filled with joy. Life with him had been so simple. She went up to her room beforehand, put on the ring, felt dishonest and as if the ring would expose her, too clean, out of place.

'The place looks transformed,' he said.

'I thought you wouldn't come.'

'Almost like the old days.'

She nodded. 'They've been working at it.' A fear of going to America had filled her heart. What if, now the economy was improving, the Whetstones demanded Michael back? They'd have no rights in Britain, surely. But America? That was different. And even though the house was being sold, something was holding her close to it, as if there were roots going deep, love and history and fear of the future so long and tangled together that she didn't know where one started and another began.

'Michael's been so looking forward to seeing you,' she said. 'He's off somewhere with Lily. I'll go and find him.' Something in her wanted to hurry away, stop him from looking at her. And then Michael and Lily came hurtling through, saw Jonathan and wanted to show him the trees, the decorations, everything they'd done.

Celia kept talking, desperate not to let the silence in. She told him about Miss Violet's Kitchen and its success. He talked about his family and the business in New York. He mentioned that since Violet had taken the job he'd found for her in an office as a bookkeeper, she was earning enough to rent a better flat for her mother and herself.

Celia didn't ask after Hope. She still didn't know if Violet had told Jonathan. It was Violet's secret, not hers to tell. If Jonathan had not mentioned a child, then Violet surely had not got her back, perhaps not even seen her.

Violet was a safe subject, like the house, the business. Anything but the question – when will you come? She wondered, even, if he still wanted her to. Perhaps he had grown weary of waiting, fallen out of love.

Albert came home on the train, excited by time away from school, full of stories about rugby matches and the maths master who told jokes. They all bought new gowns, Rudolf said again how he could justify any expense as it was their last chance. The final party. Celia bought a long red gown in Winchester, covered in sequins, terribly expensive. Emmeline wore a primrose-yellow dress, embroidered in seed pearls over the bust, pearls tumbling down the skirt, like flecks of ice. Mr Brennan would admire her in it! She and Emmeline put up each other's hair. She thought of Arthur saying, *You never had a coming-out ball*. Well, this was it. The end of the house. A few people said they couldn't attend at the last minute – some cousins of Verena's, and Mr Brennan telephoned to say his mother's cold had worsened and needed his attention.

They woke up in the morning to the sun, pasted up the last of the flowers, opened up the door to the delivery of food. And then they were downstairs and the house was full and there was music playing in the sitting room and people dancing and Stoneythorpe was beautiful again, as it should have been for Emmeline's wedding to Sir Hugh, all the parties they would have had if the war had never happened.

People were laughing and talking and moving over to the table. Celia didn't recognise many of them, perhaps she had known them years ago but their faces were blurred now. There were colourful dresses, hair piled high with jewels and ribbons, men in black ties. Smithson asked her to dance and they whirled under the lights, surrounded by the other couples, pink-faced and happy. So happy! Why was everyone so happy? Smithson was explaining about his children. She nodded, smiled. The music came to an end, she breathed, bowed out. She stood on the edges, watching the dancers dive in. Albert was listening to the music, watching the men playing with rapt attention. Michael was talking with Lily in the corner. They both looked so smart, so grown up, it touched her heart. Lily's first grown-up dance, Michael's too. *They are friends, only children. Can't you see?* She thought of the speakeasy she'd been to with Jonathan and then it struck her – he was not there.

Celia walked away, under the lit-up trees to where it was darker. She leant against a tree, enveloped in the blackness. She didn't want to smile, think any more. Here it was quiet, the party noise just background laughter, like something turned down on the wireless. She could hear the night noises of the garden, insects settling, the rustle of mice and voles.

'I suppose you're trying to be alone.' Jonathan's voice.

'No.' He walked towards her. Closer. He held her hand.

'You haven't seemed to want to talk much.' They'd been in the garden together, just before the war, nearly twenty years ago. Little German Fräulein, he'd said, swooped down to her, kissed her. His cigarette lit in the dark. She'd been stunned by it – then the war had begun and other things had crowded it out of her mind.

'Celia. You know it's been four years. We've been engaged for four years. And we've been apart. There's something ridiculous in it.'

'I'm sorry.' The ring was huge, ungainly on her finger, felt wrong and out of place.

'We have a house, a life waiting for us. And your family. They can all come. Now you're selling Stoneythorpe, what's to stop you?'

She couldn't answer. Then she looked up. 'What's that?' She could just make out two figures hurrying down the garden. They were giggling. 'There's someone there!'

Jonathan didn't turn around. 'It's probably just someone playing a game. Someone in love. Like we're supposed to be.'

'But who is it?' The voices, whispered voices, she recognised them. She heard the woman laugh.

'It doesn't matter. Stop trying to change the subject.'

'Don't you think we should go and warn them? It's not really safe around here in the dark, where it's not lit. They might fall.'

'Celia, if they fall we'll hear them. Now, tell me. When I got your letter to come here, I thought, well, this is it. I'm being invited because we're telling everyone. Stoneythorpe is selling and Celia and the rest of them are going to come to America. And I get here and everything's the same. Nothing's changed. So, I've decided. We have to tell them tomorrow. We are going to marry. Move to America. They can come if they like, or not. But we are going.'

The noise had stopped. The couple had clearly run past, right down to the hedge. Or maybe they'd gone back up to the party again. Celia wanted to chase after the couple, say *How do you know you're happy? How do you know you wouldn't rather be running down the garden with someone else? Why him? Why her? How can you be sure?*

'Jonathan. I'm sorry. I just don't know.'

'Don't know what?'

'Whether I can move to America or not.'

She saw his eyes widen in the darkness. 'Oh.'

'It was so right in America. But – well, I'm not sure any more.'

'Why can't we be in America again, then?'

'My life is here. Michael's life is here. I think he wants to stay.'

'You had lives in America.' His eyes were bright, the whites hurt her against the darkness. He lit a cigarette and his face flamed briefly in the darkness.

'I know. But it doesn't seem it now.'

'Are you telling me that you don't want to marry me?'

She tried to look past him. 'No! I do. But – where do we live?' The lights up at the house were glittering. She could hear people laughing, talking.

'You live in America with me. You said you would before.'

'I told you, Jonathan. I just don't know. I can't tell. I wish I did know. I wish I was sure.'

'It sounds to me as if this is it. You don't want to be with me. Do you love me?'

'Yes! Of course I do.' Everything was so confused. 'I do love you. It's not about that. I just don't think I can live in America.'

'You want me to live here, is that it?'

'Yes. But you can't, I know that. But I feel like I belong here. With them. I do love you. But – I love them too.'

'It's not the same sort of love. I want to be your husband.'

'I'm sorry, Jonathan. It's just the way I feel.' The tears were fighting at the back of her eyes.

'We should go away. We haven't. That's what people in love do. Italy or somewhere warm with a beach. Or back to Los Angeles.'

She and Jonathan together in a hotel in Italy, looking out at the sea, admiring the view. Their problems forgotten, drinking wine on the balcony, talking about the future, a long road that gleamed. She could say yes, he'd take her and then she'd be free, happy. Or she could stay here in the tangle of her family's emotions, Tom who didn't want her.

She felt the tears on her face, couldn't say anything.

'Celia, this place drags you down. Your family does. You're not their servant.'

'I have to help them.'

'So you love me but you don't want to be married to me?'

'No! I just don't see – I feel I must stay here. At least to see them into another house.'

'What about me? I wait for your parents to die?'

The blood rushed in her head. 'It's not all my fault! Why can't you come here? Why can't you live here with us?'

'My life is in America.'

'Like mine is here! So why are you blaming me?'

He shook his head. 'You promised me you could live in America.' He turned away.

'No. Don't go. Please.'

He lit another cigarette, his hands bright in the flame. 'I'm going to go back now. I'm not going to stay. I'm going to leave and go back to America. If you don't write to me in a month, I'll consider the engagement off.'

The words seized her breath. She saw the lit end of the cigarette in the dark, heard the sound as he turned and began walking back up the garden. She leant against the tree, wept in the dark, cried for the past, for Arthur, Michael, Louisa and for her own heart that couldn't leave it all behind to be married to Jonathan. She was already regretting it. But then the tangle of family love clutched her, pulled her to the earth and her heart was shattering, breaking into a thousand pieces.

She could have chased after Jonathan then, begged him to come back, and said she didn't know what had come over her. She told herself – if he comes back, I will go with him. If he comes back, helps me to cut these roots away, I will go with him.

He didn't turn around. She watched his shadow walk up to the house. Then she wept again.

After what felt like an hour or so, she couldn't cry any more. Her face felt swollen. She wanted to wash it, lie down. The party sounds had receded. Perhaps she could hurry past them and straight up to her room, without too much questioning. She started to walk back.

Up at the house, the party had quietened. The string quartet had gone and the women from the village were helping Emmeline tidy up the food on the tables. There were people sitting in the parlour, talking. Smithson and Jennie were deep in conversation with Verena. Rudolf wasn't there.

'Oh, there you are,' said Emmeline, straightening up. 'I wondered where you'd got to. Jonathan came through in a hurry, said he had to get back to his hotel. I take it he saw you?'

Celia nodded. 'I think I have a cold. I'm going to bed.'

'Is Lily coming up behind you?'

Celia shook her head. 'I haven't seen her.'

'You haven't seen her? We thought they were with you.'

'Who?'

'Michael and Lily.'

'No. I've been alone. I didn't see anybody.'

'Emmeline, dear, they'll be in the house, somewhere,' said Verena, placatingly. 'They've probably hidden themselves away with some cake.'

'But, Mama, they're not allowed to. They're not allowed to be alone.' Emmeline's colour was rising, her voice frustrated and angry. 'You *know* that.'

'They're probably upstairs asleep,' said Jennie. 'It is late, after all. Albert's in bed. They're probably fast asleep too. Why don't we go and check?'

She heaved herself to her feet. Celia hadn't realised that Jennie was pregnant again. That would be number six. She wanted to ask her *How did you know? Were you quite sure? Didn't you think you might love someone else?*

'No, no, you mustn't go up the stairs. You need to rest,' said Emmeline.

'The exercise is good for me after sitting down all evening. Anyway, no one knows the nooks and crannies in this house better than me. It hasn't changed that much, after all.' She smiled at her husband, squeezed his hand.

'I'll come with you,' said Celia. She walked up with Jennie, asked her questions about the baby, ignored the slow hand clutching around her heart. The sound of two people – young people – giggling in the dark, running to the bottom of the garden. How long ago had that been – two, three hours ago?

They walked to Lily's room. The bed was neatly made. Celia looked in the wardrobe, couldn't be sure if anything was gone. But she knew that things had been taken. Something in her knew that they had.

She turned and ran to Michael's room, burst in through the

door. The bed was made too, the place neater than she'd seen it for a while. She pulled up the bed and looked in the bedside table. Michael's sketch book wasn't there. Her heart froze. She looked at the shelf over his bed. He was gone, Harvey the bear that she'd bought him on the first day in New York. The horse was gone from under the pillow, but the farm was still in a box under the bed. The air was strangely still, as if it had been empty for days, even though she knew it couldn't have been, of course it couldn't. She gazed at the empty room.

'What is it?'

Celia turned to Jennie but couldn't speak. She clutched her throat, tried, still nothing came out. All the times in New York she had been with Michael, turned around and panicked, and he'd been the other side of her all along. The fear that seized her heart in public places, in case they got separated, the relief when they had returned home together. All useless, all pointless. She grasped Jennie's hand.

'Celia, what is it?'

She felt dizzy, dark-headed. Her body was losing itself. She could hear Jennie shouting her name, then Emmeline and another voice she didn't recognise. But it was lost, lost under whispering voices running down the garden, laughter. She clutched for Emmeline's hand but it was too late. She was lost to the darkness.

INTERLUDE

Where had the idea come from? Neither of them could say. Perhaps it had always been there. They'd wanted to run, be free of the adult world of money, cruelty, compromise. One mother endlessly cutting out pictures of sofas and sitting rooms while the other could spend all day putting a bow on a jar. They had to make their lives different. And they had to hurry it up, when the adults started talking about London and schools and separation. They watched the plans for the party in the house. The others were absorbed, discussing guests, food, timings, music, their obsession with the tiny things that showed they'd forgotten about what was really important in the world, if they'd ever known it at all. Their mothers were talking about dresses and table layouts and they despised them for their pettiness. They knew about the important things: love, truth. *Only you understand me.* They'd told each other this, late at night, crept to each other's rooms. *I can't live without you.*

Lily said her family had always been like this, never keeping anything that mattered, forgetting, forcing everybody into their world of keeping to appearances, no matter what cruelty lay underneath. Michael wasn't sure, thought of his own mother and her fight to find him. But now – here she was, trying to separate them too. A big school near London full of boys where he would never see Lily again. Once the house was sold, Lily and he knew, it would be the end of everything. They were in the air and the adults were trying to pull them down to the ground. They had to jump.

At the end of the garden, in the dell, they hid clothes, warm things, a knife they'd taken from the upstairs rooms, money they'd taken from the adults, bits and pieces here and there. Books, his wooden horse, Harvey (Lily said it took up too much space but he insisted), his sketchbook and pencils (again she said they wouldn't be needed and he said he had to take them), things they couldn't leave behind. 'We have to travel light,' they'd agreed. They were going to be free, after all. But he knew that she was packing up the purple cat her father gave her and so many of the pretty things in her room – the stack of bracelets as slippery as ice, the purple cat that he wanted so.

The string quartet were playing loudly, the parlour was flooded with people laughing and talking. They slipped in between the people, no one noticing them. They stepped out into the garden, under the trees covered in lights. Then they smiled at each other and began to run.

THIRTY-ONE

Stoneythorpe, September 1933

'They can't have gone far.' Celia came round on the floor and thought she'd only been gone for a moment or two. Emmeline was standing over her, sorting through Michael's shelves. 'They must have left a note. There's nothing in Lily's room. It must be here.' Verena was talking, Jennie too.

Celia propped herself up, dizzily.

'Oh, you're awake,' said Verena. 'Mr Smithson has gone out with the men to look for them. They must be somewhere near.'

'Yes.' She'd run away once with Tom, barely got as far as the village. But something struck hard in her heart and made her fear that this was more.

'One of your father's friends saw them go out into the garden. That's why we thought they were with you.'

'I think I might have heard them run past. I heard two people, laughing, running. Whispering. It must have been them.'

Emmeline stopped moving things, turned around. 'You heard them?'

'I think so.'

'You *heard* them and you didn't stop them?'

'I didn't realise it was them.'

'What do you mean, you didn't realise it was them?'

'Stop it, Emmeline. You can't blame me. I didn't recognise them. It could have been anybody. Why would I have stopped them?' *They sounded so happy*, she didn't say. *They seemed in love.* 'I might blame you. You told them they were going to be split up even more in London.'

'Oh, that's got nothing to do with it. They've taken my money.

I kept it under my bed. Twenty pounds. I was saving that for the new house. Whose idea would that have been?'

Her sister was always dwelling on those magazines, looking over the ideas for decoration, clipping out the pictures, piles and piles of pictures of sofas and cupboards.

Celia struggled to her feet. 'I'm going to help the others find them. Emmeline, I'd like you to leave Michael's things alone. Go and wreck Lily's room if you must.' She stood up and folded her arms until they left. Then she ran downstairs and out into the garden. The trees were still lit by the fairy lights. She dashed to the bottom, her feet catching on the wet grass, shouted, 'Michael! Lily!' The words came back to her, weaving around the branches, skittering up to the clouds. If only she'd said something to Jonathan, followed the noise; if only they'd both walked out and seen Michael and Lily. She could hear the shouts of the searchers outside the garden, see the flash of torches. She walked back up the garden, through the doors of the parlour and pushed her way out of the front door. There were men from the village, assembling on the drive.

'Lily!' she shouted. 'Michael! Come back! I'm sorry.' She walked down into the group of men, asked for a torch. She was going to walk with them. She was going to keep on until she found them.

Celia opened her compact, checked her face for about the twentieth time since she'd sat down at the café table. She snapped it shut. Tom was now twenty-five minutes late. Perhaps he wasn't coming at all. The waiter was hovering, but there was no point ordering more tea if Tom wasn't going to come. She sighed, gazed out of the window again. She'd written to tell Tom, two days after it happened, after the search parties had been around and around the village and all the villages about, come back, found nothing. No one had seen them. He'd written back saying he'd help if there was 'anything he could do'. She hadn't replied, hoping he wouldn't be needed, that they would come back and it would all be over. Now, a week and a half later, no sign of them, she had written to beg him for help. The police had been all over the house, questioned them all dozens of times, taken clothes and toys as 'evidence', written endless reports.

'We will find them,' said the detective, but his voice trembled when he spoke and Celia knew he was lying. 'They have very little money. Lily's mother's won't last them long. So they'll be back soon.'

The newspapers gave it front pages for the first three days or so. 'Romeo and Juliet', the journalists called them. 'Love Triumphs over all'. There were a few articles about danger and children disobeying their parents – but one columnist said it was the triumph of romance in a cynical world. And if Lily and Michael were in love or Romeo and Juliet – what did that make her and Emmeline? The cruel parents, the wicked elders in the fairy story, forcing their children to do as they wished, not caring for their hearts.

It wasn't that, she wanted to say, looking at the papers. *We thought they were too young. Emmeline did.* So far she had fought herself down, not said to Emmeline, *Why did you do it?* Her sister was suffering, she didn't need Celia telling her what she already knew, that she had been wrong to try to separate them, for it had only pushed them further together. They'd sent Albert back to school, as quickly as possible, hoping he wouldn't read the newspapers. 'Don't worry,' she'd said to him, holding him on Winchester station platform. 'They'll be back in a moment of time!' They'd stuffed his box with biscuits and chocolates. She'd sent a telegram to Jonathan – just in case he'd seen anything at the time. He wrote kindly offering to come back – but said he'd seen nothing of value. She told him to remain, knowing she should send the ring back. The police sent him a list of questions which he returned swiftly – nothing there.

They'd had two viewings of the house, people who were clearly just coming to snoop about the crime. Celia told the agent to wait for a month, until all the gossip had died down.

'Don't you think we ought to bring Albert back from school?' Celia had asked. 'Just for a little while.'

Emmeline shook her head. 'It's better for him to continue. Take his mind off it.'

Celia supposed Emmeline was right. Home was a mess, Verena weeping, Rudolf hiding away in his study. He had taken it badly, worse than she could have expected. Celia heard him crying when she walked past his study door. She knocked, but he wouldn't answer.

Mr Brennan had come to express his sympathies, accompanied by his mother, a small, respectable-looking woman in a brown hat she was too shy to take off. Verena gave him two months' pay.

'Such a tragedy,' he said. 'I only wish I had some clue about what they were thinking, so I could tell the police. But I've racked my brains in our interviews and can't think of a thing.'

He looked so devastated by it, poor man. 'You weren't to know,' Celia said. 'It wasn't your fault. None of us realised.' He looked so very distressed. He'd loved them too, of course, felt just as betrayed that he had not realised they were running away. He was gazing at Emmeline again and Celia's heart dropped for him – no chance of that now. 'School is a factory,' he'd said at his interview, talked with such colour and attention that they knew he was the right one. Emmeline, heartbroken. She'd torn up her magazine pictures of sofas and sitting rooms, thrown them into the bin, confetti with no wedding.

Mr Brennan said the police had asked him about their state of mind. 'I really couldn't think of anything,' he said. 'They seemed perfectly normal. Excited about the party. We were all completely in the dark.' His mother was close to tears, he held her hand tightly. 'If only I'd been there at the party,' he said. 'I might have spotted something going on.'

Mr Brennan was right. They had all been in the dark – Celia most of all. She had been blind, hadn't seen a thing. The children had run past her and she had been too caught up in herself to even recognise the whisper of her own child.

'Hello, Celia.' She looked up into Tom's face. 'I'm sorry I'm late. I was kept at the office.'

'Thank you for coming.' He sat down and she cursed herself

for the electricity that ran through her body. And her vanity, that she'd fussed over her outfit, fretted at her hair, checked her mirror dozens of times.

'Is there any news?' He waved the waiter over. 'Tea please.'

She shook her head. 'They've vanished. It's like they have, at least. We can't find anyone who saw them after they left the garden.'

'No one?'

'We've searched, asked. The police have tried. Nothing.' They'd even all been up to speak to Albert at school – and the police came too. He said that he hadn't heard back from a letter he'd sent Lily. Emmeline was convinced he was telling the truth.

Celia looked back at Tom. 'We've tried everything. No one has any ideas.' She wasn't going to ask about his wedding, the beautiful fiancée, their plans for the future. She was probably sitting with her doting mother at this moment, working out her table plans.

'They must be hiding out in a city. Maybe they're even here.'

'I don't know how we'd ever find them here.'

'No. Maybe not. You don't have any idea why they did it?'

Celia told him about Emmeline's rules, separation, school. She trailed off, thinking of the sketchbooks, the dragon trying to capture the maiden with a face like Lily's. Had they been the dragon, she and Emmeline, trying to take Lily off to school?

'Don't blame yourself. Children have to go to school eventually. I'm sure they'll see the error of their ways and come back. Don't you recall when we ran away?'

His words jolted her. She'd never have imagined he'd remember. When she was seven, he nine, Rudolf had told them that they weren't allowed to go into the village – and so they'd made plans to escape. They'd stolen bread, cheese and knives from the kitchen and packed them up in a basket. She'd taken her journal and they'd both written letters to their families. Celia told Verena and Rudolf that she was going into the world to make her fortune and would come back, richer than King Midas. Tom wrote a letter to his mother but didn't show it to Celia. They took clothes and books and made plans to go to France. They crept down to the woods together in the early morning – and planned to spend the day there. But by late afternoon, they were bored and hungry for tea. Celia had been worrying about Rudolf and Verena being alone and when Tom said he was beginning to think twice, she almost hugged him. When they went back, Verena had just started searching for them.

Celia was about to reach across for Tom's hand. Then she remembered. 'You were whipped.' Tom had been punished for leaving his duties, beaten and locked in the stables overnight.

'That wasn't your father's idea.'

'But he could have stopped it.'

'Yes. He could have.'

Her heart filled. 'That was what you meant when you said the friendship wasn't equal, wasn't it?' They should have kept running. They should have never gone back.

'Listen, let's not talk about that now. Anyway, Celia, they'll find the world outside isn't so easy. Look, there must be some clues. Who was the last person to see them?'

'Me.'

'You?'

'I heard them. I was out in the garden, at night. I heard giggling and someone running past me. Two people. I didn't think anything of it.' *What were you doing there?* He would surely ask it.

'You always did like wandering around in the garden,' he said. 'Look, they clearly wanted to go. You can't force them back.'

'So we just have to wait for them.'

A tear was welling up in her eye, drying her throat. She'd thought that Tom might have a solution, be able to swoop in with his new money and his success and make everything right again.

'There's nothing you can think of? Not to find your son?' She was beginning to beg now.

He looked up at the word, jolted. It was the first time she'd used it. 'Well, I suppose we might try a private detective. You never know. He'd ask you for leads, though. Their thoughts in the run-up to it all.'

'I don't really know.' She felt shame once more. 'We were

planning the party. We were so caught up in it. We didn't really notice them.'

He raised an eyebrow. 'Oh yes, the party.'

'Jonathan came from America. He was asking me questions.' She had to send the ring back to him, even though he hadn't asked. She couldn't go back now. But the ring was so final.

'Oh, him. That was why you were outside. Talking to him. That was why you didn't think twice about people running past. He's always around, isn't he?'

'Look, Tom—'

'Is he going to find the children for you? I suppose you argued? It's always the way. Needed when you need me, otherwise nothing to you. What did you think I was going to be able to do, anyway? Find someone when the police can't?'

'I don't know. I just thought you might have an idea.'

'Well, there's nothing I can think of but a private detective. I suppose you want me to pay for it.'

'No! That wasn't what I meant. Of course not.'

He stood up. 'I'll give you the money. Find a detective and get them back. And when you do – you can tell him who his father is. I've played your game for far too long.'

'I'm sorry.' She tried to catch his hand, even though they were making a scene in the café. People were turning to look.

'I'm going to go now. You can write to me. If I can help. With money or whatever it is you want. I'll send you a cheque. But that's it!'

He hurried out of the café. She paid the bill quickly and followed him – but he had gone.

She walked towards the Underground, to head back to Victoria. She supposed she'd look up a private detective in the newspapers. It was hardly as if there was a street where they all had their offices, like Harley Street for doctors. She ducked down into the dirty staircase for Covent Garden. Something in her dreaded the idea of a private detective, searching over their belongings and asking questions, just like the policemen had. Verena would hate it. And she'd have to explain that she had been outside talking to Jonathan, considering breaking off their future forever.

Still, they had to try. Celia wrote to a Mr Pilsdown who advertised in the back of *The Times*. He had assured her by phone that 'missing persons' was one of his specialities. She promised him one hundred pounds as a retainer and invited him to look at the house. He arrived with a quiet young man whom he sent off to draw a plan of the grounds. She followed Mr Pilsdown as he sorted through Lily's things, Michael's books. He ran his hand over Michael's papers, admired a few sketches that had been left behind. She tried not to let his kind words pierce her heart. He took notes, looked at the windows, and checked the doors. Then they walked out into the garden. She showed him where they had been standing, took them both to the dell where she thought they'd probably planned it – and then to the gap in the hedge at the back where you could cut through to the forest.

'The police searched the forest,' she said. 'They're not there.' She held tight to the photograph of her son, taken by Rudolf at the studio in Mareton. The police had asked for it but she was never letting it go.

'We'll find those two, don't worry,' he said. 'They don't have much money. They can't have gone far.'

And yet. After Mr Pilsdown and his man had left, sent in a cab to the station, she ran upstairs, headed to Verena's bedroom. She burst in, to the chintz and the velvet and vases, dozens and dozens of vases. She started pulling at them, opening them, holding them upside down, tipping out keys and dust and dead flies. She pulled the Wedgwood boxes out, tugged off the lids, cast them aside. She opened the mystery novels, found nothing, flung them aside.

'What are you doing?' Emmeline and Verena stood in the door. Her sister stepped forward. 'Are you trying to wreck the place?'

'Did you have money in here?' Celia asked. Verena stood back. 'You did, didn't you? You had money in here.'

Verena gazed back, her eyes milky.

'Where is it? I know you had money in here. You always said you didn't trust the banks. Did you have money?'

Verena nodded.

'They took it,' said Celia, sitting back on the bed. 'They took the money. How much was it, Mama?'

She wrapped her arms around herself, made herself small. 'I don't know. Six hundred, a thousand. Maybe more.'

'Well, now they'll never come back,' Emmeline said. Her whole body sank. 'They took twenty from me, but they wouldn't have got far. But they stole yours. They could go anywhere.'

'They didn't steal it,' said Verena in the doorway.

'What?'

'I gave it to them.'

Emmeline was staring. 'What do you mean?'

Verena was breathing heavily.

'What do you mean, you gave it to them?' asked Emmeline.

Celia stood up. 'Come on, Mama.' She pushed past Emmeline, put her arm around Verena, and took her to sit on the bed. Her mother's shoulders were shaking.

'I didn't know,' she said. 'They just asked me for money. They said they needed it for something. I didn't know what. I didn't ask. I thought they were going to get something for the party.'

'With so much?' Emmeline kicked the doorway. 'How could you?'

'I wanted to give it to them,' she said. 'I sent Michael away. How could he ever forgive me? Then when he asked me for money – they both asked me for money – I thought, this is something I can do. I can give them the money. What do I need with it?'

Celia tried to make her voice gentle. 'Mama, if you were saving money, wasn't it to be used for their future? For school.'

Verena was weeping now, head in hands. 'They asked for it. I wanted to give it to them. I shouldn't have sent him away.' She was hiccupping as she spoke.

'No, that's true. But, Mama, don't you see? Now you've given them this money, they could be anywhere. They could go to France. Anywhere. We'll never find them now.'

'When were you going to tell us?' said Emmeline. 'When were you going to tell the police?'

'I was afraid you'd blame me.'

'Well, you were right. You were completely right.' Emmeline stormed from the room and they heard her footsteps hurtling down the stairs. Verena burst into another storm of weeping. Celia put out her arms, brought her mother to her, rocked her gently, as if she were the child.

Celia wrote to Jonathan to tell him what had happened. She couldn't go to America now. She could never go. She had to wait here until Michael came back. She took off her ring, wrapped it carefully in paper and put it in the parcel. Her heart broke in two. Rudolf was angry, said he couldn't understand how she couldn't have persuaded Jonathan to live in the house with them, but she hated hearing him talk about Jonathan's money and what that could have done. It had been about love.

This was her life now and she could never leave.

'We'll never find them now.' Emmeline was sitting in Lily's room, holding her pillow.

'I don't know,' said Celia.

'The only hope that the police gave us was that they didn't have much money. Now look.'

'Well, now they'll come back because they love us. Not because they have run out of money.'

'Maybe. But what if they don't think they can come back? What if they're afraid? We need to find them and tell them we want them back. This place is going to be sold, eventually. We won't be here. We shouldn't have ever let them be together at all. You should have sent him off to school first thing.'

'No! You can't blame him. They went together.'

Emmeline snorted. 'It was his idea, I bet. So you find them.'

But Celia didn't know what any of them could do this time. The children had disappeared – two birds flown up into the sky.

INTERLUDE

There was someone there. A person behind them. Michael swung around, looked for Lily. Nothing. The branches lay bare, the ground tangled with moss.

His heart clenched. Someone had got her. She was going to die. He ran forward, his heart smashing in his chest. It was his fault. He shouldn't have turned away. Well, he'd save her. He'd run to her and rescue her. He'd fight off whoever had her. Even if whoever it was had a gun, he'd fight him off.

'Lily!' he shouted. The words echoed back to him, mocking. 'Lily! Where are you?'

A bird fluttered up. The air around him was silent. Someone had her. He was stopping her from crying out.

'Don't be afraid!' he called out, as loud as he could. 'I'm coming to save you.'

And he was. He was a knight, there to save her, strong and true, better and braver than any of the knights in the stories. He didn't need a sword or even a horse. He rushed forward, broke through the branches. 'Don't worry!' he shouted. 'I'm coming!'

But there was nothing. No sign. He ploughed on. He didn't know where he was going. He felt hopeless, exhausted. Lily had the map. He looked around, could see nothing. It was so dark. The cool dread grasped his heart. There could be a murderer in the woods. But Lily was strong! She wouldn't give in. She'd fight back. And she had the weapon in her bag – a knife they'd found in one of the top rooms. He'd wanted to take the old gun, but she'd told him to leave it.

'Lily!' he cried. 'I'm coming.' But it was cold and damp and tiring and the branches snapped back in his face. He needed to sit down. *No!* But the tiredness was threading its way up his body, weighing down on his face and eyes. He sat down on the floor, leaning against a trunk. It was just for a minute, just briefly. He closed his eyes, willing himself not to feel fear, so that when he opened them, the world would be right again.

'We've been looking for you.'

His eyes snapped open. The moonlight darted through the trees above his head, too bright.

'It's you!' he said.

It *was* him. He was standing there. He was standing next to Lily. He had his arm around her. *What was he doing here? Had he followed them?*

'Hello, Michael.' Lily was smiling. 'We've been waiting for you. Now we can begin.'

THIRTY-TWO

Stoneythorpe, February 1934

'People can't just disappear,' said Mr Pilsdown. 'But these two – somehow – they have escaped us.' It was as if they had vanished into thin air. Over the last five months, he had interviewed everybody possible. Mr Brennan was the only one he hadn't spoken to; his mother said that he had gone to look for work in France. She'd given him a forwarding address in Rouen and he'd sent a letter.

'Apart from him, I've spoken to everyone. And I have – I am afraid to admit it – very few leads. It is as if they had help and assistance on the other side. But we know they didn't. So all I can say is that they must have got lucky. And they had that money, of course, which changes things. It's the perfect disappearance.'

Now the publicity about the disappearances had died down, they had begun offering people viewings of the house again – but there hadn't been much interest. The agent was not optimistic. It didn't suit modern tastes, too big, too ramshackle. 'We only need one person to love it,' Celia told herself. She wished they could keep it, so that Michael would come back to it, the only real home he knew. But she knew they couldn't. Arthur's debts were too large. She applied herself to the business. She put up Michael's picture of Miss Violet over department store displays, sent it off to be printed as a poster for the Underground and thought her heart would break. She worked on contracts, machine outputs, and accounts. She tried not to think about anything else. She locked the office at the end of the day, went home, talked to her parents and Emmeline, went to bed. She was working to make them a new life.

To save money, they lived in even fewer rooms. She walked in one day after a day of meetings to find Tom there. Emmeline and Verena were already with him. He was sitting upright, smartly dressed, his silver-topped cane beside him.

'Have you found out anything?'

'I wish I had news,' he said. 'But I came for something else. I had another idea.' He paused.

'Yes?' said Verena.

'You said the children love it here.'

'They do. As we did,' answered Celia.

'They didn't want to move to London.'

None of them answered. Celia waited. He surely hadn't come to them to repeat what they already knew.

'So I thought to myself, perhaps, after all—' he broke off.

Verena sighed, so quiet you'd nearly miss it.

'What is it, Tom?' Celia asked. 'What's your idea?'

He smiled, nervously. 'I thought I could buy Stoneythorpe. I cannot see it sold before we find them. Not if they were running away because you were selling it.'

'What?'

'If the children love it, I could buy it. Then they won't have lost it. They'll know they can come back.'

'Come back?' Celia stared at him. 'You'd buy Stoneythorpe so they could come back? You can't afford it.' Some other woman, Tom's wife, living in Stoneythorpe. Filling it with her children, smiling happily up from the bed as the doctor showed Tom his latest baby. Children dashing around the garden, climbing the trees.

'I can borrow. I've looked into it. It can be done. That is – if you want it to be. It's up to you.'

Celia could feel both her mother and sister looking at her. She tried to avoid their gaze. Emmeline was speaking: 'But how would it work? You buy it, you live here? And what if you're not here when they come back?'

He shook his head. 'I buy it. You live here.'

'We live here?' Not true, thought Celia. He was engaged. His *wife* would want it.

286

He nodded. 'You can pay me a rent if you like. I don't mind. It's not just this. I grew up here. I don't want to see it fall apart. Of course, I would love to come here sometimes. I should be in London, but there are other times. But it will be yours to live in.'

Verena breathed. 'Tom – Mr Cotton. That is such a very generous offer. Let me please discuss it with my husband. I'm sure he'll be delighted.' She spoke slowly, graciously, the tone Celia recognised was for talking with the serious, the dignified, those requiring respect.

'Of course,' he said. 'It would take me a month or so to get the money, anyway. You don't have anyone else who wants to buy it?'

'No! You can't have it, Tom.'

'Celia!' said Verena, as if she had been ten, not over thirty. 'Stop that!'

'But he can't, Mama. He can't come here as if he could buy us. You can't, Tom. It's not fair.'

He stared back at her. 'I'm not trying to buy you, Celia. I only mean the house. I want to keep it in the family. Our—'

'We're all wrong! We think that if we just keep the house, they'll come back? They've gone! We drove them away and it was all our fault. They're not coming back.'

'You don't know that, Celia,' said Emmeline. 'Please calm down. Tom's only trying to help.'

But the white heat had caught Celia and it was firing her. 'I don't need your money!' she said. 'I don't need your money to get Michael back. After all the times you've said you hated this house and you hated your life here, that every moment you spent with me was work you didn't want to do. All the rest of it. And now you want to buy the house. You say you won't live in it with us? It's not true. You'll visit for a little while. Then after you're married, your wife will want us out so you two can live happily ever after here.' What if she were very rich? And it was her money Tom was using to buy their home?

Tom was looking at her. She could see the pain behind his eyes. She kept going. She couldn't stop. She was talking, spewing out the hurt, all of it, the times she had tried to speak before and did not. Emmeline was telling her to stop and Verena, too, but she couldn't, kept forging on.

Tom stood up. 'You don't need to continue, Celia. I understand. You don't want me here, or my help. I was wrong to offer it.' He turned to Verena. 'Thank you for the tea. I'll go now. My car is outside.'

He looked back at Celia. She could say it then, speak, apologise, say she never meant it. The words wouldn't come.

He walked away. She watched him go. Then she ran to the hall, heard his car start. She leant against the wall, put her face against the cool marble.

The time afterwards was terrible. Verena and Emmeline had been angry with her, Rudolf so furious that he could barely speak. 'Our only chance to get it back,' Verena was weeping.

'We can't be dependent on him,' Celia said. 'Don't you see? He's engaged. He'd only buy it and move in here with his wife.'

'Of course we could be,' said Emmeline. 'He offered it. It's our only hope. But you threw it away. And now what – poverty?'

'Well, you go and get it back from him,' Celia said.

'Oh, don't be ridiculous!' Emmeline shouted. 'It was for you. Not for me. He was giving it to you! It's you he wanted.' She stood there, silent, stared at her. 'Well, if you won't take his money, then you need to get it. Make more money from the business. Or find a buyer.'

'And what about you?'

'Someone needs to look after our parents. Anyway, you got us into this mess. You can get us out.'

INTERLUDE

Michael opened his eyes. The light burnt his face, swords of it coming from the sky. He had been asleep.

'We've been looking for you,' said Mr Brennan again. He was smiling. He had his arms around Lily.

'Now we can begin,' Lily said, caught Michael's hand to help him up.

And so that's how it started, their story. Mr Brennan – call me Don, he said – had planned it all along, with Lily. Michael hadn't realised it, but of course that's what they'd been doing when he found them talking or when she went off to the woods alone. They were planning. And so Mr Brennan met them there, and took them to a house of another friend who was on holiday in France. They waited there while he went back home and checked for a few days to see that the coast was clear (he said the police wanted to ask him questions but he'd never say anything, ever).

Lily didn't want to talk to Michael, tried to brush him off.

'But I only ran away because I thought I was going to be with you! Just the two of us,' he said. He wondered about all the words they'd said together, that they wanted to be free, different to the adults. Mr Brennan was an adult!

'We are together,' she said, smiling. 'This is the best way. Always together.' She smiled and, like a flower, turned her face to the light.

Mr Brennan said he had somewhere for them all to live, forever. They were going to live in Year Zero. The children of the future.

PART FOUR

THIRTY-THREE

Stoneythorpe, January 1936

Celia was examining the accounts of Miss Violet's Kitchen in the sitting room. The world outside was changing but here at Stoneythorpe, they were not. She had written to Tom but he hadn't replied. Maybe he was married now. She hadn't heard from Jonathan. No one wanted to buy the house. And there had been no clue about Michael and Lily. The police said the file was still open but that they currently had no leads. Mr Pilsdown said that he was stumped. They had disappeared.

She gazed at a new letter. From Mr Crennet, who had taken over from Mr Pemberton, who had just retired to a small house near Devon. She tore it open and read that the agent had found a buyer. A girl's school. The agent said that was what was happening to all the big houses these days. Two thirds of the asking price.

They had had just three viewings over the last year. All three families had declared the house needed too much work.

Celia looked out onto the lawn and imagined the dell razed down to make a hockey pitch, girls playing lacrosse where Verena's fountains had been.

She had to let it happen. She turned to find her father.

'You're making us leave our home,' said Rudolf. Verena had shut herself in her room, weeping. Celia couldn't bear it either and felt cruel. She hated the thought of leaving the graves behind. They had to. Mr Galss wrote often that the banks were asking for the money.

Now, when she looked out onto the lawn, she saw Michael and Lily coming back. Not builders, tearing out the pipes, rewiring, plumbing in modern sinks for dozens of girls, and knocking down the walls to make dormitories. I can't leave you, she whispered to the garden. It had swallowed up Michael and Lily into thin air. One day it would give them back.

INTERLUDE

The New Children. That's what they were called. They'd create a new world, better than the last. They'd take everybody back to the beginning, Don said. This was the vision. Lily believed it, every word. Michael saw her writing it down, to better remember it, surreptitiously. They weren't supposed to write anything down. Because they were going to Year Zero – when they couldn't write. The written word had polluted mankind and the purity of his thought.

They went to a part of London but he didn't know where it was. They travelled across in the car of a man that he'd never met. He didn't introduce himself, they never did, but bundled them both in the back under the blanket and they drove. Michael wanted to leap out somewhere, take Lily with him. But then, Lily would never leave Mr Brennan, so he had to stay with her and make sure she survived. He'd promised that he would look after her.

The home was a tall house in London – a place he didn't know. There were already too many people living there, so many that all he wanted to do was hide. They didn't introduce themselves either, so who knew who they were, they were always different. The adults took the bedrooms and the children slept together in what would have been the sitting room.

Most of the beginning of the new world was going on in Russia, Don explained. They had learnt to live without possessions, all those things that cluttered you up, stopped you seeing what was really important. They were free. No names, no money, no jobs. Nothing that tied down ordinary humans, none of those emotions that activated their petty lives: jealousy, competition, avarice. Don talked about how people were so deluded in everyday life that all they wanted was to earn more, get more than their neighbours. It didn't matter how much it was, it just had to be more.

So Michael understood. All those words that Lily had said to him about being free of possessions. They had been Mr Brennan's first.

Don and the rest said they were free. The problem was that people were so far behind in their country. So you had to be careful, for everywhere were people who wanted to betray them. They were conventional, tied up in their lives of getting and spending, slaves to the men of business and the systems of money, comforted by the baubles that the system gave them. So they had to be always alert to anyone who seemed to be giving up on the group, thinking of leaving. Of course, if you wanted to leave, you could, they were free, freer than anyone else, but if you did, you had to go quickly without infecting others. No one had, as long as Michael had been there. Why would you want to? They had made life perfect.

Don reported to them from the corrupt world: a mother of six collapsing and dying while bathing her baby twins because she was starving; men who hadn't worked in twenty years, no jobs and the government kept men low by giving them relief that wouldn't feed a family. The country was starving and the government kept cutting relief, sitting in their fine dining clubs and expensive country houses. The government did this to keep the people down, because if the working classes were hungry, they wouldn't have the spirit to attack the government. Even when they did march to London, the government sent them away, told the women they should work in domestic service. They wanted the people to be starving, so when they did find a job, they were so desperate that they'd allow themselves to be treated as badly as the employer desired. They were all together, politicians and big business, making money out of misery, determined to keep people low and poor, because if you had working men with nothing to do but make dolls out of wood in the hope of selling them for a few pennies, you could do whatever you liked. And they did.

They needed to pull themselves out of the world of money because some would always have more.

Michael supposed that these were the sort of words Mr Janus had said, before he'd disappeared off to Spain. He knew Lily was thinking about her father because he saw her sit up when there was ever any mention of Spain, listen closely. But she never talked about it with him now.

They were just going to break everything apart and rise from it, the phoenix from the ashes. How they were going to smash everything, though, he didn't know. And people seemed to him to like buying things and watching cinema screens. Mr Brennan stood at the front and talked vaguely about how everybody would join their vision and then the world as they knew it would end, people would no longer be chained to the old ways of money, getting and spending, their false seductions.

Michael, Mr Brennan and Lily took a small room at the back but they weren't supposed to be there much. The whole idea of Year Zero was that they all lived together – Mr Brennan said that they'd pull down the walls if they could because walls were bourgeois and repressive – but they'd started trying to do it and they had realised that the house might fall – they needed all the walls to support the roof. So the idea was that they would *pretend* not to have walls. Thus, the less time they spent in their room the better. They should always be in the communal room, where everybody ate, cared for the babies and children, played, talked, read. Michael dreaded the days. They always seemed to have to explain the rules to him. He'd use a teacup and someone would tell him that he couldn't, he'd used that teacup before and he was wrong. You weren't allowed to use the same thing twice. Then you were almost owning it. And ownership was evil and pulled the whole world down with it. He'd sit and he'd sat in the same place yesterday and had to be moved. His favourite chair was in the far corner, a squashy, old brown one. Sometimes, when everybody was asleep – even though people slept in the communal room – he'd sneak down and sit in the chair. Just to feel as if he owned it. He wasn't going to give up his wooden horse and his bear. Lily still had her purple cat. He'd seen it under her pillow. If they took away his horse, he'd tell on her purple cat. But something told him that she'd be allowed to keep it, no matter what.

Michael said to Lily, 'I don't like this.' He missed Mama, all of the family and particularly Grandpapa, who'd showed him books in his study. He wondered if they could go home. 'Please,' he said to Lily.

'I'm staying.'

'But why do you like it here?'

That was clear enough. Everyone loved Lily. They looked up and smiled when she came into the room. Women patted the seats beside them and asked her to come and speak. The men nodded when she spoke. Mr Brennan was respected too. Michael was wary of him now, wanted to question everything he said. Why was what he said so important? What was the Secondary World? If he wasn't talking to Lily, he was talking to the group, droning on and on about the New World and the future.

There was so much work, too. He and the five other children, three boys, two girls, had to clean the communal room every day, then the kitchen after all the food had been prepared. The women were doing the washing then. They took the two toddlers with them as they cleaned and tidied. Mr Brennan and the other men were out giving speeches, persuading people to join. Lily usually went with him. When they came back, the meals had to be prepared (great vats of stew, always vats of stew), so the afternoon was chopping vegetables, stirring, under the instruction of the women. He sometimes tried to give the younger children lessons in whatever he could remember, even though he'd been told not to. School, too, was an oppressive system. But he could remember less and less, and it wasn't very easy to teach anything without books. After a few months, he'd given up, just let them play their jokes and games. He grew rather fond of Bear, a six-year-old boy who loved pretending to be planes, and Rainbow, a girl of maybe ten who made them all laugh by playing silly tricks, falling over and pretending she was stuck. The adults said laughter was the corrupt world's way of getting them drunk, forcing them to ignore their position of being exploited. But they usually let them laugh for a while, smile too, themselves.

Lily barely spoke to him. She was always too tired when they got back from speaking. At night, she wouldn't go up to sleep until Mr Brennan did, so Michael went early, listened to the shouts from downstairs, waiting for when Lily curled up next to him and he could pretend they were twins. She never did. He held tight to Harvey, his bear, too old for it he knew, not supposed to have it because possessions were a trap, there to distract you from your oppression, form a warm cocoon around you so you didn't realise you were trapped. He felt for the other children, not allowed toys, saw some of them taking carrots or potatoes to bed with them, wanting some type of doll or bear. He carved faces on their potatoes, great smiles, big eyes, thought of names for them. He gave them his tiny horse to play with, made them promise not to say. Then he lent Rainbow his bear. She wanted it desperately, but he couldn't give it to her. 'You know we're not supposed to have things. I'd get in trouble.' He thought of taking Lily's purple cat for them but he looked for it in her things and couldn't find it.

'Why can't I go lecturing too?' he asked.

They told him he was too young.

'Why do we get to keep our room?' Michael wanted to ask, didn't dare because he thought he'd never manage to get to sleep in the communal room. Other people had to move between rooms. But they were always allowed to keep theirs. He supposed that Mr Brennan must be very favoured.

THIRTY-FOUR

Berlin, 1936

The only way to stop the pain was by keeping moving. Celia busied herself with the business, so she didn't have to think about Michael, Lily, Tom, Jonathan. The bankers said she should try Europe. The sale to the girls' school was proceeding and Rudolf and Verena blamed her. She told herself that she was going to Europe for the business so they would have enough to buy a home. But really, she couldn't bear to be there to see it, her parents' misery as they packed their boxes.

She wrote to Tom. 'I am leaving for Germany. I don't know how long I will be. I can't stay any more. The empty house is too much. I can't bear that I have lost Michael again.' She didn't leave an address for him. She didn't want a reply. No one could help her in the dark hole, her pain that Michael might never come back.

She travelled to Paris and Madrid – and now Berlin, researching bringing Miss Violet to Europe. She had talked to department stores on the Champs-Élysées, showed pictures of Miss Violet to groups of young French girls, to see what they thought of her, visited possible factories outside Paris and in Lille and Lyons, as well as visiting some big French farmers. She had stayed in a grand hotel in Paris, looking out at the Place de Concorde, gazed out at the lights of houses where she knew nobody. Men tried to speak to her in the hotel restaurant, waiting in the lobby, on trains. She carried Michael's sketch of Miss Violet, the photographs of the products and the displays in Harrods, her shops in Oxford Street and Winchester. She came from Paris with orders, plans of hiring a salesgirl who spoke French.

When people found she was English, they wanted to talk about the King. The old King George was dead, died late at night in Sandringham and the new King was on the throne, young and glamorous, the Prince of Wales who had been so popular was now Edward VIII. Who would he marry, they all wanted to know. She had to tell them she knew as little about the royals as they did. Most of all, the French talked about war, much more than they did back at home. They feared Germany and invasion. 'Oh no,' she said. 'It won't happen.'

In Berlin she took a room in the hotel there. The city was all building, the new stadium going up, hundreds, thousands of men carrying bricks, climbing ladders, hammering steel. They were making a new road from the stadium to the palace, widening it so great processions could walk down it. They were chopping down the trees along the route, lime trees said to be the heart of Berlin, even though there was protest in the newspapers. The Olympics was coming and that was most important. So much talk in the newspapers about the Chancellor making Germany great again – it was as if no one knew that people in Europe were afraid of him.

She walked into the centre of the city and surveyed the great Wertheim department store, glass roof vaulting high into the sky. She imagined a big display of Miss Violet's Kitchen in the front window.

But the women looked so much more cast down than they had in England or France. They wore grey coats, shapeless hats, heads down as they hurried onto the trams. She wasn't sure if they would even like carefree Miss Violet at all. The men too were sombre – but the women looked so sad. She went to the Haus Vaterland, which housed the biggest café in the world, crammed with tourists and people after a long day's work. Surely they would be happy there. She wandered the Hungarian village inn, the Turkish café (so busy), wished Michael could be there to see the cowboys in the Wild West bar. There was a Rhineland café, surrounded by an artificial river, an hourly storm that showered the people wandering around the pretend countryside with rain. The Rhineland that they had occupied, without permission – it was what they said they wanted. But, despite that, all the fun of Haus Vaterland, still the Germans looked fearful, and refused to speak to her, a foreigner.

One of the bankers she met told her that Hitler had plans for a great new city, Germania, a dome that rose a thousand feet into the sky. The whole place would be rubble, allowing the new Germany to arrive.

There wasn't much interest in Miss Violet's Kitchen. Everyone was being told to buy German. The stores were polite but said that women in Germany wanted to cook for their husbands – that the Chancellor stressed the importance of being a good housewife and tins would not be popular.

'Well, Papa, I tried,' she said to the sky.

She travelled to see Johann, Hilde, Lotte and Heinrich in the Black Forest. Heinrich and Lotte were poorer than before. Hilde was still living at home although assisting with teaching at the local school. Johann was still making windmills out of matchsticks. Her heart tipped. If there was a war, how would they survive? 'You could come to England,' she said, but of course they would not and so they barely heard her when she said it.

'Tom is doing well now,' she wanted to say. 'He's rich.' If only Heinrich had acknowledged him, he could help them. But Lotte would never allow it and not even Hilde asked after him, her half-brother. She ate soup with them in their dark house, heard the news about the Olympics fourth- or fifth-hand from neighbours passing it along. They all shared the new gossip that the lesser newspapers were printing, that the English King was in love with an American – and in early December, it was proved to be true. Edward abdicated. Emmeline's beloved Princesses moved into Buckingham Palace, the little Elizabeth possibly the future Queen. Celia followed the news as avidly as anyone. But underneath it all she worried – that while the newspapers were watching Mrs Simpson, her tiny waist, strings of pearls, the German Chancellor was dreaming of expansion, of making the whole world like the restaurant, each country a captive playground for his imagination.

She wrote to her parents, saying that if they needed her to help with packing up the house, she'd come back. They didn't reply. Emmeline wrote short letters, no detail. She presumed they were busy and she felt guilty for not being there to help with all the movement of the things, years and years of belongings piled up in the rooms.

She followed news about the war in Spain, too, always hoping for sign of Mr Janus. She never said so to Emmeline, but guessed that her sister too was doing the same thing, buying newspapers, looking for hints.

She stayed with her aunt and uncle for far longer than she had expected. Hilde said she was grateful for her company and Lotte thought she brightened Johann. She told Heinrich that her son was Tom's but he refused to listen. Still she took comfort from being with Michael's grandfather, even if he would never admit it. They had celebrated Christmas together and spring drifted into summer. She had been in Germany for almost a year. She hated being away for so long, but Lotte and her cousins needed her. She felt useful, loved even, and even if Michael and Lily were gone, at least she was still helping her family somehow. Back home, the business was doing fine without her.

Eventually, one of the banks called her back to Berlin for a second meeting. They said they had an idea, a property they wished her to review. She arrived back in the city and found it entirely changed in such a short time. There were always military processions now, going back and forth, lines of the Hitler Youth or the League of German Girls or just groups of soldiers, sometimes followed by great black cars containing Nazi Party members and you had to salute. There were loudspeakers along the roads blaring out the words of Hitler and Goebbels about the return of the Empire and the greatness of Germany. She watched the Hitler Youth, marching. If she had been living here, Michael would have been forced to join.

The bank had hoped, it turned out, that she'd buy factories left over from a takeover. When she refused, they tried to sell her other buildings. They said there was no money left in Germany, they needed English money. She smiled, declined, said she would leave. But she stayed for the visit of the now abdicated Edward VIII and Mrs Simpson, gleefully touring a school that would create perfect Aryan boys. She waited in the crowds for their car, saw a tiny blond-haired man in a heavy coat step out with his wife, thin as a bird, held tight to his side as if by a sheen of mesh, and it was, for how could she or he escape, they had to be in love forever and after.

'Where he leads, other English will follow. They will see our greatness,' said the woman next to her. Celia watched the party members curtseying to Wallis, bowing to the Duke. She read the newspapers back at the hotel, Edward saluting outside a mine, visiting Hitler's mountain retreat. Berlin had gone Britain mad – there was a new British café in Haus Vaterland, serving up Yorkshire pudding and Cornish pasties. The radio praised England and the excellent foresight of the Duke. She clutched the photograph of Michael in her pocket and felt filled with fear.

The bank's idea for a property turned out not to be a good one. She would have to bear all the risk. It was time to return home.

In December, she woke up one morning to a knock at her hotel door. The woman said there was an urgent telephone call for her. She scrambled into some clothes, hurried downstairs. She picked up the telephone to hear Emmeline's voice, tinny, distant, the line sounding as if it had a million other breaths on it.

'Celia, you need to come back. They've closed the file. They say Michael and Lily are dead.'

INTERLUDE

Everything was supposed to be shared. Even people. That made Michael sick because it *wasn't true*. They said it, over and over. But over the past few months it had changed. He'd been told to move into the communal room. He lay at the end with the other children, couldn't sleep for all their snuffling and turning. And Mr Brennan and Lily remained in their old room.

Of course, he'd always known that Mr Brennan – Don – preferred Lily to him, right from the start. Perhaps he should have been better at hiding how much he had grown to dislike their old tutor, then maybe they would have invited him out with them. She was seventeen now, more beautiful than ever, her dark hair and bright eyes. It hurt his eyes to look at her.

He'd always known that Mr Brennan liked her.

But he hadn't thought she liked him best *back*.

And they were the children of men. They should like each other equally.

'This isn't how it's supposed to be, Lily,' he said. 'Everything's supposed to be shared.'

She smiled, that perfect beatific smile that she'd turned on him before, at Stoneythorpe, when he'd asked her where she had been. 'We *are* sharing,' she said.

'No, you're not.'

She smiled again. 'Some things are special.'

That night, alone in their room, he took out a pencil he had swiped from the downstairs room. Even that was breaking the rules, because no one was supposed to own anything, no one was supposed to keep anything for themselves. He took it out and he began to draw. He drew a line along the bottom of the wall, where he sat. No one could possibly notice that. They would surely think

305

it just a crack if they even looked at all! The walls in Stoneythorpe had been criss-crossed with cracks, so many that if a giant put his fingers in and pulled, the whole place might come falling down. He carried on tracing the line. Then, when he reached the edge where the line and the pillar met, he began to draw.

THIRTY-FIVE

Stoneythorpe, December 1937

Celia sat in the back seat of the car on her journey from Dover, leaning her head against the window. The glass was hot against her forehead. She kept moving, to capture another piece of cool clear glass, but there was no chance of comfort. Each time, it heated up quickly and everything was on fire again. The flames danced in her thoughts, black and dreadful, seizing her into their furious heart. 'Make it stop,' she said in her mind – and then she realised she had said the words aloud.

How could the police do it? They had made so little effort, it seemed, and then to close the file! To say they had probably died on the road or in the woods, at some point. She couldn't see it – and then she tried to and that was the horror. She knew in her heart that they weren't dead. Michael was still alive. She would know if he was dead. She was sure.

You didn't before, the voice came to her. *Your family said he was dead and you believed them.*

That was different. She knew him now. He was alive.

She took the old route to Stoneythorpe, the one she thought she'd never take again. She'd thought she'd be coming back to another house, a crammed little one in Winchester, maybe. But the message had been clear. Come to Stoneythorpe. She couldn't understand why, how, they were still there. But then, she'd said she'd come back to help and they had never asked her. She'd thought they were perhaps busy, that Emmeline hadn't wanted her to come back.

Emmeline opened the door and paled immediately. Then she flung herself into Celia's arms.

Celia held her close, stroked her back, painfully aware of her slept-in clothes, unwashed hair and body. Emmeline was weeping, incoherent words here and there. 'So awful... All alone... glad you're back.'

'I'm here now,' said Celia, patting her back. Although she wasn't sure how much comfort that could be to her sister. 'Don't worry. Don't cry.' She manoeuvred Emmeline back inside and managed to close the door. Celia stroked her hair. 'I know. I'm here to help you now. I'll do everything.'

Celia didn't ask why they still hadn't moved out – after over two years! – would do it later. She hugged her sister.

'The police are wrong,' she said. 'I know they're alive. Emmeline, it doesn't matter if they close the file. We are still looking, Mr Pilsdown is still looking. We know they're not dead!'

Emmeline was still crying. Celia tried to listen but a wave of tiredness from the journey was sparking, slowly, across her face. She tried to resist it, looked at her sister. The books all said that the Roman statues were probably garish, in their first instance, bright red lips, flaming blue eyes, a child's painting of a face, no light and shade, no subtlety. And then time wore it down and they were more handsome with no colour at all. Emmeline's face was still beautiful, the features regular, small chin, perfect nose. Time had taken all the colour away. And so maybe it wasn't true, that the statues had been less beautiful then, it was just something said to imagine that modern people weren't missing out on anything. She wanted to reach out, trace her sister's face. *Let's go back*, she felt her heart saying. *Let's go back ten, twenty years, when we were still children and we were all together.*

'I'm so sorry you've had to deal with it all,' she said. 'How are our parents?'

'Afraid of war. That's all they talk about. Papa said it was better for Michael to die this way because he'd only die in war.'

'No. I won't hear it!'

Emmeline sat down in one of the alcoves in the hall, the one that had once held a marble statue of Venus. It was gone, broken maybe, shattered into pieces. She leant back against the wall.

'I can hardly talk to them now,' she said. 'They're preoccupied by the news. It started just because you were in Germany and they were interested in the news from there. But then they started to talk about it the whole time, scouring the papers. They bought extra ones for detail.'

Emmeline started talking about Berlin, the Army, the Führer.

'I saw it first-hand,' said Celia. 'It's like a hysteria for him. Well it was. The people seem less willing to salute now but they have no choice. They're afraid of war too.'

'So if they're afraid and we're afraid, then why do it?'

'It won't happen,' Celia said, stoutly. 'We had a war to end all wars. It won't happen again.' But then. Those Hitler Youth wanted to fight. The grandeur of Empire. How could it be gained, they must think, other than through fighting?

Emmeline held out her other hand. It was cold from the marble too. 'Help me,' she said. 'Please help me.'

Emmeline had recovered and they were walking out, towards the garden.

'You will cheer them up,' she said. 'Tell them what it's really like in Germany. You can tell them that there's not going to be a war.'

Celia shook her head. 'I don't know if I really can,' she said. The loudspeakers screaming out the words. The party rallies on the radio. 'I'll try. Why haven't you moved – I thought the school needed to start work on adapting the house?'

'They have had a money problem. Mr Crennet has offered them a discount but still they're not sure. He thinks we might have to drop again.' She turned to Celia. 'How could this all be worth so little?'

Michael and Lily, walking up to the house, looking for them and finding teams of girls playing netball, stern teachers, a secretary saying they had no idea.

*

That night, Rudolf showered her with questions at dinner. He asked her about Germany, the people, Hitler, the economy. 'He hasn't been this animated since you left,' whispered Emmeline, squeezing her hand. 'You're a tonic for him.'

Rudolf grinned expansively. 'I knew my Celia would tell me the truth! You and Tom.'

Celia dropped her fork. She turned to Emmeline. 'Tom?' she whispered.

Emmeline shrugged.

'He came to visit. I wrote to him when the police first mentioned the notion of closing the case. He passed on a few things that the detective had said, nothing useful in any of them. We asked him to stay, two months ago. He comes and goes, he has his own work of course. But he's been a great comfort to Papa.'

Celia felt her blood rising, fury in her throat. 'The fiancée, wife even. Was she staying too?'

'Oh don't start. We asked. He came. We're lonely. I don't care what you think.'

'But—'

'You left us alone!'

'I was going there to help you!'

'He's been so kind!' She grasped Celia's hand. 'You're so lucky.'

'What?'

She lowered her voice, whispered. Rudolf was talking to Verena about the Führer, not hearing.

'You're so lucky that he loves you. I wish he loved me. I've been wrong about him all this time, I'd almost think of offering myself in your place, if I knew for sure that Samuel wasn't coming back, but I doubt he'd take me. It's you he wants.'

Celia looked at her sister's hand. She had to focus on the hand. She stared at it, four fingers, thumb, skin thin over the knuckles. Her heart was beating hard. It was too much. She wanted to tell her to stop.

'He's married. He has a wife. If he's coming, it's just to be kind to us.'

'He's not married. He said it was off.'

'Off?'

'I expect he'll come tomorrow,' said Emmeline. 'He'll be pleased you're back. Now I'm tired. I'm going upstairs.' She stood up and brushed past her, skirts catching. Not a statue, but human, someone real, blood rushing around her, feelings catapulting through her. *I wish he loved me.*

Why shouldn't he? Celia had said she could never love him, grown angry with him, sent him away. So why shouldn't he love Emmeline? He and her, they had none of the history of hurts and divisions, love and hate that Tom and Celia had. Their love could be pure, clean, not tainted by years of cruelties, lack of emotion, resentment. They could start again.

'You have him,' Celia whispered to her sister's back. *Emmeline, you take him.* If she said it out loud, everything would change. And then Michael's father would be always near, Tom could look after all of them. Because Emmeline was surely wrong to say that Tom could never love her. She was beautiful, graceful, *you wanted to protect her.* More fun than Celia, too, witty. Men often loved women and their sisters, didn't they? Celia had read gossip articles about Virginia and Vanessa Bell, exchanging men. In the Bible, weren't men supposed to marry a sister, if their wife was barren? Or something. It had been such a long time since she'd read it.

You have him. Simple words. All she had to say. Tom wanted to marry – and Emmeline was better for him than Celia. Gentler, less angry. If she loved her sister – and she did – she should be able to give him up. Emmeline had lost her husband, lost so much. Surely she deserved this.

Next morning, they were washing up in the kitchen together, after breakfast, when Emmeline heard the front door jangling.

'That must be Tom.'

'He has his own keys?'

Emmeline dried her hands, walked up the stairs, and towards the hall. Celia followed her. They walked through to the parlour and towards the French windows. There was Tom, his back to her. He was standing, smoking. Something in her wanted to run. She wanted to dash back into the house. But Emmeline had hold of her hand now and they were walking forward.

You have him. She couldn't say it.

'Tom,' said Emmeline, her voice too bright. 'Celia is here.' Her sister's voice wasn't normal. It struck hard at Celia's heart. Her sister was in love with Tom. She was in front of her now, saying something to her.

Why hadn't she thought? How long had it been? Was this the reason why she'd never found someone new, rather than Mr Janus, even after his long absence? Surely not, surely that couldn't be so. Emmeline never kept secrets – she would have said something long ago. And yet still, Celia watched her sister, face upturned to gaze at Tom, nodding at what he said. She should say it, give him to her sister. *I don't love him. I never will again. He's yours.* The words wouldn't come. A bird passed low over the trees at the side. It was one Celia didn't recognise – a kite, maybe. It swooped up. The prey it had seen wasn't there.

Tom turned. 'Hello, Celia. I'm so sorry we still haven't found them.' Her heart smashed, hit the floor. A thousand pieces of it flew into the air.

He caught her in his arms. *Like a brother-in-law*, she thought, was that it? A *brother*.

'I'm sure they'll come home eventually,' he said. 'Whatever the police say, I don't believe they're dead.'

'Thank you,' she said, strangled, pressed into his chest. 'Thanks for calling me home.'

He loosened her and she turned her head slightly. Emmeline was standing, just behind them, staring, and the look on her face made Celia's heart break again.

'Emmy—' she began to say. But her sister was walking away and Tom still had his arms around her and she felt as if he was telling the truth, that they would come back and be happy once more. He knew. He must know.

'Emmeline said about your – marriage. I'm sorry.'

He shrugged. 'She found someone else. A richer man. I expect they're married now.'

'Is that you, Tom?' Rudolf called from the dining room. 'Come and talk to us. Celia has brought news from Germany.' And they went in, talked of the cars, the factories, people's desires. She told him that Berlin was always being built, that the people saluted because they had to, talked of the power of the government. Rudolf's eyes were flaming, so bright he might have been feverish. 'The moderate Germans will win out,' she said. 'I feel sure.'

Tom shook his head. 'I don't think so. Something tells me we are on a course for war. Only war can stop it.'

She listened to them talk war, back and forth, her mind flooded with the boys marching.

'How's Albert?'

Emmeline played with her fork. 'Better than he was. Tom and I went to see him last week. He wants to stay at school. It's probably best.' They were eating from Miss Violet's jars, but Rudolf and Verena refused them, wanted a proper meal so Emmeline had cooked up some chicken and cabbage.

Albert had lost his father, sister, cousin, in such a short time. Easier not to think about it. 'I'm sure he's getting a good education,' she said.

'Oh yes,' Tom said. 'I spoke to some of the masters while we were up. They're very pleased with how he's buckling down.'

Celia cleared her throat. 'So what is the news on this money problem of the school? I don't think we should let them be so casual like this. Either they buy or no more.' In her heart, she longed for them not to, to have the place back so Michael could find them once more.

Emmeline looked at Tom. She didn't reply.

'What is it? Did something happen?' Her heart lurched. 'Has the school changed its mind?'

Emmeline was looking at her plate.

'What's happened?'

'It was me,' said Tom. 'I gave the girls' school money to wait.'

'You?'

'I know you didn't want me to buy it. So I won't. But they

were happy to stay the moving in, with a bit of money. Emmeline asked me to come and help with the business while you were on the continent. I thought I might as well do it from here.' He was talking fast. 'Miss Violet's Kitchen is doing well. You could release some of the capital and in a few years even keep the house, I'd say. As long as the country keeps getting richer. Your sister and father knew nothing, though. You took a risk leaving it in their hands.'

She'd wanted to keep the house, for Michael. But not like this. She stared at Emmeline. 'How could you do this? How could you let him?'

Emmeline sighed. 'Celia.'

Tom stood up. 'I was trying to help! And you throw it back in my face.' He flung his napkin down and took himself from the room.

'Look what you've done,' said Emmeline, turning to her.

'How could you let him? You should just have left. You know it. You were wrong to keep hanging around here.'

Emmeline stood up. 'You know nothing! Absolutely nothing!' She rushed from the room as well. Celia sat there, stared at her parents, then got up to go to bed too.

That night she lay in her empty room, unable to sleep. She heard banging doors, the creaks of the corridor outside. One was going to the other's room. They were both lying up there together, talking about her. Probably laughing at her. She shivered, anger and jealousy coursing through her mind.

INTERLUDE

Why did they always have to be together? Micheal didn't understand. What did the two of them have to talk about for all that time? They were always close together, sitting in the communal room, deep in conversation. And – even worse – they went up to the room that had been theirs together, even in the daytime. Yes, Lily was an adult now, she was eighteen. But why couldn't she talk to him? No one seemed to stop them. What did they find to talk about? Why *him*?

At night, he sent his heart up to Stoneythorpe. He sent it flying to his mother, imagined her receiving it, holding his love tight, not forgetting him.

He felt so lonely. He missed home, his mother, his grandparents, all of them. But most of all, he missed Lily. Surely if he just waited for long enough, she would invite him back again, be his friend once more.

He had begun to sense that the other people in the house were talking about Lily and Mr Brennan. He saw them look strangely at them when they left the room. The women in particular stared at Lily. When he watched them stare, a hot feeling crept up inside him, something like fear. He tried to push it down but it came flooding upwards and filled his mind and the words that it made weren't clear. He tried to grasp them, but he knew that it was trying to tell him: *stop. Make it stop.*

It heated his mind, twirled around his eyes, burned his face. *Something bad is happening. And you have to stop it.*

But he didn't know how to.

THIRTY-SIX

Stoneythorpe, December 1937

Next morning, they didn't speak about it. None of them mentioned Celia's outburst. They skipped and stepped around it as if it was a giant snowman in the middle of the place. They were polite. Emmeline received a letter from Albert and read it all to them. They had won again at rugby and Mr Stretton was particularly pleased with his latest English composition. The masters suggested he might try for Cambridge.

The newspapers were full of the latest fighter aircraft to be bought by the RAF and the excellent prognoses for Mr Joseph Kennedy, the man who some said might be the next US ambassador to Britain. Something about Mr Kennedy's photograph reminded Celia of Jonathan: handsome, confident that the world and everything it had was open to him. There wasn't much in the newspapers about Germany. They were more concerned with the former King, now living in France, than Germany and the little man she'd seen, lost in his coat in Berlin. Perhaps, she crossed her fingers, perhaps they were right. But she thought of the young men in uniform, lining up and marching through the streets and her mind tipped.

They were going to have a small Christmas, for Albert. They promised each other that they'd eat a proper meal of turkey. But nothing else, no decorations, no tree. Presents only for Albert. She decorated the Miss Violet's Kitchen shops in Winchester and London beautifully, though – a tree covered in little foil-wrapped biscuits and sweets, greenery decked around the walls, beautiful stacks of Christmas puddings and cakes in glowing red and green paper. She wondered about Tom – did he wish he was spending Christmas with the girl he was meant to have married, now buying presents for another, richer man? She sometimes saw clouds pass over his face, supposed it must be pain, was too shy to ask.

Rudolf wouldn't stop talking about the likelihood of war. He was always asking about it. 'The King should be practising shooting,' he said. 'For when the invasion comes.'

'There won't be an invasion,' Celia said.

She had got used to Tom being around on the nights he stayed, maybe three a week, the rest being spent in his home in London. At night, if he was in the house, she found it hard to sleep. One night, when Emmeline had gone to bed and she'd drunk wine at dinner, she found herself telling him about New York and finding Michael, pouring out the whole story about finding his address, and Violet, and conning her way into the Whetstones'.

'Do you think worse of me?' she asked.

He shook his head. 'Of course not. You did what you had to.' He smiled.

'It's astonishing to think they just gave him up to you, after all that time.'

'Yes.'

'For a lot of money. Celia, how could you afford it? Ten thousand dollars. Arthur had to find it for you?'

She blushed. She hadn't told him about Jonathan. She had barely mentioned him at all.

She shook her head.

'Look, Celia, I know you don't want my money, but at least let me give you that. Or half of it. Please.'

Her face flamed. It was like that day with the great new toy car. Tom could buy Michael with his money. It was all so easy for him. Her voice wanted to burst out but she pushed it down. She had taken money from Jonathan, after all.

'No,' she said, trying to be polite. 'There's no need.'

'Please.'

And then the truth was pushing at her heart, welling up like water inside her and she couldn't stop it. 'I didn't pay it. We didn't have it. Jonathan gave me the money.'

'Jonathan?'

'Michael's old university friend. He lives in New York.'

He stared at her. 'Oh, yes, I remember. Big, blond fellow. Always talking.'

'He helped us.'

'You let him buy your son for you?'

She looked away from him. 'I had no choice.' *You were just offering to do the same*, she wanted to say.

'Why would he do it for you? Was he in love with you?'

She blushed. Jonathan with her, running through the streets, his arms around her, asking her to marry him.

'He was, wasn't he? He was in love with you! And so he paid for your child.'

'It wasn't like that.' The scar just under his eye was a brighter red than it had been before.

'Did you tell him he was mine? Or did you try that soldier story on him too.'

She nodded, miserably.

'You lied to both of us. Well—' She saw him clench his fist. He stood up and in three fast steps had slammed out of the room.

She hurried out, passed Rudolf on the stairs. 'Did you see where Tom went?'

He shook his head, grasped her by the arm. 'Tell me again. Why do you think Adolf Hitler is so successful with the German people?'

She answered hurriedly, impatient with his constant questions about Germany, anxious to find Tom.

'But would a war be like the last one?' He looked like a child, then. Waiting for her to reassure him.

'Papa, Germany lost last time. They won't try it again. It's just this madman leading them.' She broke off. 'I'm sorry, Papa. I really must find Tom.'

She dashed into the garden but she couldn't see him. Perhaps she shouldn't chase him at all, he was so angry with her. Well, she reminded herself, what choice had she had? She had to get Michael back. Jonathan had offered. He'd loved her. She'd loved him. And she'd got Michael back. Who was Tom to tell her what to do, how she should have behaved?

'I think we really need to move,' she said to Mr Crennet at their next meeting. The interest was mounting. And Tom had paid the school for six months – but there was only two months of it left to go. He couldn't pay again, she wouldn't ask him. And she feared that that the school would change their minds entirely, find somewhere else for the lacrosse pitches and classrooms.

But the school agreed that the family could remain in it while they prepared for the maintenance work and made it habitable for three hundred girls. They had to pay a tiny rent, which infuriated Rudolf so much he wanted to ring the school and complain, until Celia had convinced him they were lucky. The governors said that they wanted someone living there for security.

There would be six months of work. Then they would have to move out and find somewhere else to live. Stoneythorpe would never be a home again.

They could delay no longer. They would have to find a new place to live. Celia went through the accounts. Once Arthur's debts had been paid, they would barely have enough for a small house in Winchester. Emmeline and Celia walked around Winchester looking at houses to rent. Celia said they were cosy, but Emmeline was angry, said they were tiny, few-bedroom places, poky front rooms, scrubby gardens.

'It's all your fault,' she said. 'Tom could have held them off again.'

'They'd have changed their minds. Anyway, the debts need to be paid. The interest is huge.'

After four days of it, they found a house that was bearable enough, not far from town, a Victorian house on the corner of a road, four bedrooms, and a small garden. The kitchen was in a bad way, but this way they got more space than the others, so they would have to bear it. And they'd still have the money for Albert to go to university, which Rudolf said was vital.

'Although what kind of home poor Albert comes back to, I don't know,' said Verena, sighing.

'Celia needs to help us,' said Emmeline. 'She needs to find a rich husband who can help us. Like Tom or Jonathan.'

'And what I do for the business means nothing?'

'You could never get as much money as a man could give you.'

What followed next was boxes. Boxes and boxes to be packed. Everything else from the house had to be collected together and put aside to be given away or thrown into the rubbish or wrapped up and piled to be stored. Mr Crennet had found a farmer who would give them part of his barn to store their belongings.

'Although why we're storing anything, I don't know,' Emmeline said. 'As if we will ever have a house that can contain them again. All thanks to you. Tom would have let us stay but you wouldn't let him.' Celia ignored her comment, carried on piling things up. They were in the sitting room, wrapping up the ornaments and putting them into boxes. They'd done the same in the war, when they were turning the place into a hospital, so she could pretend that it was only a temporary measure again. Mr Grey and his wife, who'd come from the village to help, took the ornaments from them when they'd wrapped them in newspaper, placed them in a giant cardboard box. After they'd finished with the ornaments, he started rolling up the rugs. Then he stood on a ladder to take down the portraits from the walls: Rudolf, Verena, Michael, Arthur, Emmeline, Celia. Then she thought her heart would break.

After the sitting room was nothing but an empty shell, stains on the walls where portraits had been, furniture covered over and waiting to be taken away, they cleared out the hall, wrapping up the marble statues in the alcoves. Rudolf was packing up the books in his study, Mrs Grey and some others were in the kitchen, wrapping up the cutlery and dinner services. Verena was giving them the saucepans – you hardly needed very many in the new place they would be living. Celia was grateful for Mr Grey, for his calm presence meant that Emmeline couldn't remark too much more about how everything was Celia's fault. The sisters didn't talk, just picked up ornaments and wrapped them up in angry silence.

After that there were the other rooms on the ground floor that had never been used for very much, those that hadn't already been converted into dormitories or classrooms, one full of broken furniture ever since the war, other sitting rooms that had always just been locked, unused. So wasteful, she thought now. Then they went up to the bedrooms.

'I'm not throwing away Michael's things,' said Celia. 'Or Lily's. We need to keep them for when they come back. We need to take them with us to the next house.' They were standing in Michael's room. Celia gazed at his things; the books, the space where the bear that she'd bought him in New York had sat.

'Where are we starting, ladies?' Mr Grey arrived at the door.

'A different room,' said Celia. 'One of the spare ones.' And so up they went to the top floor. They were easy enough, most of them packed high with junk, old beds from the hospital time that were still there. They should have thrown it all out long ago. But perhaps, Celia thought, they had never believed that they would ever leave.

'What are we going to do with it all?' said Emmeline.

Celia imagined it, a giant hole in the ground, full of things no one wanted, things they'd bought, desired once, and then not, snapped tables, old chairs, dolls with no legs. Her mind flitted back to New York, Arthur.

After a while, they climbed up to the loft and started looking through the boxes piled up there. Celia hadn't even been there since she was a child. She opened boxes of her old dolls and Michael's toy planes.

'We can't throw these away,' she said. 'They're our history.'

'Well, where do we put them?' asked Emmeline. 'What's the use of them now? You never missed your old doll before.'

She was right. Celia held up her doll, Magdalena, bought for her when she was seven.

Rudolf had taken her to a department store in London, they'd gone up into the toy section and he'd said she could choose a toy, any one she liked. She'd picked out Magdalena, blue eyes, long brown hair in ringlets, a neat red and green suit, with a matching hat. The pretty saleslady had said she'd made an excellent choice, then started showing them all the other things you could buy for her: a set of gowns, a nightgown, outside coats, rainwear. And a wardrobe made of oak to put them in, a grey dappled horse made of china for Magdalena to ride with a leather saddle and a harness. Rudolf had been filled with bonhomie, charmed by the woman behind the counter, and he said Celia could have the whole lot: clothes, wardrobe, horse. She'd walked out into the street, holding his hand and clutching the box with Magdalena in it, thinking she'd never feel sad again.

The saddle had snapped after a while and the horse had broken when Arthur had thrown it over a chair, pretending it was making a jump. Emmeline had wrecked two of the gowns with scissors and ink, when they'd been playing dressmakers. But Celia had kept Magdalena herself safe, hiding her under her covers in the daytime so the others wouldn't find her, brushing her hair at night, washing her porcelain face with a flannel once a week. And yet, then she'd forgotten about her and someone had packed her up into a box – and Celia had never even missed her apart from when she'd thought briefly about her again after Lily had been born, but then Michael came and she forgot everything.

She held her close. 'She's still a beautiful doll. There must be a child who'd like her.' She could have given her away years ago, to Lily or a child in the village. Instead, she'd kept her stuffed in the bottom of a box in the attic, no use to anyone.

'I shall give her to a child,' said Celia.

'Are you expecting to have another? You've left it a long time.'

Celia ignored her, pulled out the gowns from the box. The moths had got at the velvet dress, it was covered in holes and the lace collar was in tatters. But the raincoat was still wearable, and the nightgown was only a little yellowed. The red and green suit was worn and fraying at the edges.

'That's the sort of thing that needs to go in the bin,' said Emmeline. 'We can't take everything. You can't. The more space we use up of this barn, the more we have to pay.'

But in every box they opened, there were things they wanted. Their old schoolbooks and what even looked like old schoolbooks of Verena's. Emmeline found pairs of knitted baby shoes – which child's, she didn't know – children's outfits, a rocking horse. Some of it could even once have been Rudolf's. Things flowed everywhere.

'You know, I think we should just not open these,' said Emmeline, kneeling back, her hands covered in dust. 'If we never wanted them before, then we don't need them now. This is just taking up time.'

Celia wanted to argue. But still. Each box made her feel so sad – for time passed, people gone, days she could never get back. Perhaps there was something to be said for being free of it, all the memories, weighing you down, giving you pain because you could never return.

'We must check each one, surely?' she said. 'We should keep the old toys. Just a few of them.'

Celia gazed at the boxes. Rudolf and Verena had probably started with very little – but now, here it was, boxes and boxes of things, clothes, toys, books, so many of them that you couldn't tell who they'd once belonged to. Some of them were her brother's. The books he said she was too small to read, more of the toy planes that he'd hung from his bedroom ceiling. They were only things, she reminded herself. They didn't signify. It was the person who mattered. It was Michael who was special. But she had to look at a photograph to remind herself of what he looked like. He was gone, not real any more, held forever in 1916. And it didn't matter that thousands of boys had had planes like them. Michael had touched these, loved them. They still carried tiny pieces of his skin.

'Let's keep them all,' she said to Emmeline. 'We have to.'

They carried on through the house. So many doors that she'd thought had been locked simply came open in her hands. She pushed open a door back down on the third floor – and realised that the room had been Louisa's. There were two trunks in the corner. She walked over. Full of gowns, beautiful pale blue, delicate green, primrose.

'I didn't know these were still here,' she said to Emmeline. 'I'd forgotten.' The hotel must have sent them back after Louisa had died and someone put them up here. Carelessly. The gowns were thrown in any which way, tangled and crumpled as if they'd been stored in a hurry. Celia sat down against them, pressed a silk skirt to her cheek. 'How pretty she was.'

Emmeline stalked to the corner. There was a dirty pile of newspapers. Emmeline shook out one. 'It's from the trial. Who kept these?'

Celia moved closer, looked over her shoulder. Those words. She remembered every one. 'Throw them away. I can't bear to see them.'

'Poor Arthur,' said Emmeline.

Celia nodded, didn't trust herself to speak. The air around her broke and she was in New York again, held too tight by Arthur over the balcony. Why did it have to be her? Why was she the one who had to keep all the secrets?

They ate dinner with Rudolf and Verena, hands still covered in dust, no matter how much they cleaned them. Rudolf read the newspapers and listened to the wireless all day, and in the evening, he talked of the war, the soldiers mobilising, the building work in Berlin.

After, Celia and Emmeline bent over the washing up together. 'How long is Tom going to stay?' she asked Emmeline.

'I like having him here.' Emmeline passed her a dishcloth. 'You can dry.'

She dried the dishes, thinking rather than talking. Emmeline passed her another cup. And then there was a great bang, echoing around the house. And another. Emmeline dropped her plate, but they barely noticed it crash on the tiles. Celia rushed out, upstairs, following the sound. It had come from the parlour. Something must have fallen, a painting from the wall smashing onto the floor. But twice? She ran.

THIRTY-SEVEN

Stoneythorpe, December 1937

Tom was barring the parlour door. 'You can't come in,' he said. 'I forbid it.'

'What do you mean?' Celia threw himself at him, felt the warmth of his chest.

'You can't come in. Neither of you. You have to go and phone the doctor.'

'What's happened?'

'Quickly! Tell him to come quickly.'

She stared at him. The door was slightly ajar. She peered past and saw great things she didn't understand come crashing into her mind. Blood. Two bodies. She turned and ran to the telephone.

She was dialling the number for the doctor when she heard someone begin to scream. She tried to talk into the receiver and then she realised it was her.

The hours that followed were dreadful. The ambulance came, a black one because what was the use of colour now? Celia was walking asleep, not thinking because thinking was too terrible. Tom took care of everything – the arrangements, the doctors, the discussions about funerals.

'Where did they get the guns?' she asked. She was begging, asking. 'Where did the guns come from?' She couldn't see because the police were in the room.

'They were old,' Tom said. 'Maybe from the war. I suppose they were here for years. They'd probably forgotten about them.'

Until they tried to find them. Until they went looking.

Outside, in the garden, Celia tried to walk but crouched on the grass, crushed into a ball. She looked up and the sky was falling. A bird was fluttering above, just escaping, but it wouldn't, how could it, the sky would crush it too.

'There you are.' Tom came down to sit beside her and she held him, feeling as if she was drowning.

'He wanted to talk about the war. I told him I had to look for you. If I'd just spent longer talking to him.'

He drew her to him again. 'Don't blame yourself. They were afraid of a war. They were always talking of it.'

When had they decided? When had they thought: there is no turning back?

'What did you see?'

'Sorry?'

'What did you see? You walked into the parlour. You saw them. What did you see? What had they done?'

'I didn't see much, Celia. I just – walked in and I realised what had happened, so I – then I closed the door again. I came out.'

'You didn't go to look at them? How could you be sure they were dead?'

He looked away. 'I was sure.'

She looked up and the bird was still above them, swooping, circling. And then it dipped and flew high into the sky, almost to the clouds. 'Come back,' she shouted. The words echoed back.

'Who?'

'That bird. I wish it would come back.'

She couldn't make him understand. 'Oh, go to Emmeline! She needs you more!' She set off running down the garden, to the dell that was the only place she had left. She ran in under the weeping willow, threw herself onto the rock. 'Please,' she said. 'Please make time stop.'

When she eventually walked back to the house, the sky was beginning to darken. She stood at the door of the sitting room. There were men in there. She couldn't look in, walked to the dining room where the policemen were talking to Emmeline and Tom.

Which chair did they die in? Where did you find them? What she had seen through the door – the splashes of blood, the bodies. The shadow of what she had thought she had seen. The head.

'This is my sister, Celia de Witt,' said Emmeline.

The taller, fatter man with pale blond hair nodded. 'I am Detective Bilkson. This is Sergeant Dill. We are just asking a few questions. What light can you shed on your parents' state of mind, Miss?'

'They were afraid of the war. They didn't want another one.'

'And otherwise?'

'Otherwise. Well. They didn't want to leave here, but I thought they'd become accustomed to it. Ma – I mean Mother – seemed to be quite interested in the idea of living in town.'

'You've been away for some time, I believe.'

She nodded, sat down on a stool.

'And during this period? Did you think they'd changed?'

'I couldn't say. They thought that if I went to Germany, I'd tell them the truth. But I did think that war might come and I told them so. So I made it worse.'

Emmeline broke in. 'Not at all, Detective. It wasn't her fault.'

'I am simply trying to understand Mr and Mrs de Witt's state of mind. I am baffled, I might say. Two people, who seem reasonably content, then choose to die? I'm also baffled at the choice of the weapons. Those guns were antiques. That both fired on time, wielded by such elderly people. All I can say is that they must have been determined, don't you think?'

Emmeline sat upright, her face still. The heat was rising in Celia. She fought it down.

'And as I have told Mrs Janus, it is rare that these double pacts tend to work out. One almost always changes his mind, sometimes both. In the end, I believe humans are like cats. We prefer to drag ourselves off to die alone. And so I ask myself, what happened here?'

The heat was high in her now. She just couldn't stop it. It flooded into her mind and she was the bird over the garden and she just couldn't stop. 'Mr Bilkson. Detective. They were so afraid. War is real for them. They were terrified!'

Emmeline looked up at Celia, eyes wide – with what, Celia couldn't tell: fear, dread? But Celia wasn't stopping. 'Detective Bilkson – you don't understand! It's fine for you and all you English people who were born here to English parents. No one is going to tell you to *go home*! Or call you a traitor! Do you know what happened to us in the last war? That's what happened. We lost all our friends. Emmeline lost her fiancé. Someone wrote 'Go Home!' on our garden. And then it got worse. We were supposed to register with the police, not travel. And they took Papa away to a camp. You know, he didn't even get his own mattress there? They weren't even allowed to keep their own mattress, had to hand that in every morning. They didn't want them to have a single possession, because possessions make you human, feel secure – and they wanted my father and the other men to be always anxious. Do you know how many times we've lied, said we're English, changed our name? People would have killed us if they'd known the truth. And then, when all this might be happening again, you say you *can't understand*?'

'Miss – I do understand.' But she wasn't going to let him speak. Her heart wouldn't stop – although it held back other thoughts: *I've been with real Germans. They're not cruel or evil. They are afraid of war too!* And yet, some welcomed it, or at least those young ones who didn't know what it was. The Hitler Youth marching up and down in Berlin, defying their parents who said: Don't fight. Don't let us have another war.

'It was dreadful for us! Everybody thought we were the enemy. And even after the war, it wasn't much better. I made sure nobody knew I had a German father. I lied. But I saw what happened to those who didn't. Stones thrown at them in the street. Turned away from jobs. You're older than me, Detective Bilkson, I presume. You must have seen them. Desperate German men begging on the streets of London because they were forbidden to leave – they only had two weeks to get out, if you remember, and if they didn't manage then they had nowhere to go – and no one would employ them. They were begging for money. But they didn't always get it. Instead people threw things at them. Old vegetables, eggs, dog mess. And do you know what? I never saw them fight back. They just sat there, took it. That's how we were treated. And we will be again. While people like you are *fine*. I mean, I'm sure you've looked hard at our files. When Louisa died, all the newspapers could write about was how we were evil Germans. Killers! And that was years after the war. But that's how Germans were treated when we were at war, no matter how much we'd given the country. *Our* country. And you think my father could face that again? Or my mother? So you have no idea! You stand here and ask questions and say you are *baffled*? How dare you!'

The air in the room stood still. Celia looked at the detective's face, his stony eyes. She might have gone too far. They might all be arrested.

'It's true,' said Tom. 'Miss Witt is right.'

The sergeant coughed. 'This is a civilised country.'

Celia tried to agree. But she couldn't. The fire was still going, flowing up into her mouth. 'That's what everyone says! Great Britain is a civilised country! But it's not. You're polite and generous in your words and then under it all you are angry and furious and ready to knife anyone. You expect us Germans to sit there and take it. *You are lucky to be safe.* That's what they said to my father in the camp. Safe for what? To be tormented, deprived of everything, treated like an animal in the zoo? And you wonder he dreaded it all happening again?'

'Please calm yourself, Miss de Witt. You're clearly hysterical. I didn't mean to cause such upset. I was simply asking the questions that have to be asked.'

'For what? Other people in the police came to investigate when the children vanished. And they didn't find a thing. Nothing. Then they closed the file. They barely even tried.'

Detective Bilkson stood up. 'Perhaps the Sergeant and I might come back another day. When you have all calmed down.'

The word 'calm' infuriated Celia, but the fire had gone now. It was down, back in her heart, angry, flaming at herself, no one else. Her back ached from sitting on the stool.

'Yes, Detective Bilkson,' said Tom. 'I think that would be an excellent idea.' He stood up to show them out.

Celia jumped up, went to the window, hunted for the bird. It wasn't there.

'Thank you,' said Emmeline behind her. 'You told them the truth.' Celia clutched the old table, held tight to it, the only solid thing she could find.

'There's something you're not telling me,' Celia said, that afternoon in the kitchen, making tea. She looked at Tom. 'What is it?'

He busied himself with the teapot.

'You're not telling me something. You won't meet my eye. I know you.'

'There's nothing. I'm going to take this out.'

And yet there was, she knew there was. He was avoiding her. It was something about her parents. Or perhaps Emmeline. The death had shown him that he really loved her.

'Just tell me!' she said. 'I have to know!'

'There's nothing.' He walked out of the kitchen. She heard him balance the tray as he stepped through the door.

She went upstairs, tried to write to Jonathan. The words came out stiff and slow. How long ago it was that they were going to be married. She could have married him, encouraged Rudolf and Verena to live in America and then they would never have died.

Emmeline came and found her weeping. 'You wanted to sell, though,' she said, standing over her. 'Tom would have helped them for longer.'

'And then what? Arthur's debts get so big that they'd swamp us all. It had to be done.' She looked up at her. 'I knew they were unhappy. I didn't pay enough attention.' It must have been terrible, wandering around the house, everything packed away, sparse, like they were living without permission in an abandoned house. Every day closer to when they'd have to finally go.

Emmeline shook her head, sat down. 'Mama said to me that she'd welcome a smaller house, easier to look after. She was lying!'

The thought of Verena saying that, being brave, looking on the bright side, was almost more than Celia could bear. 'What about the thought of war?' she said. 'It was too much for them. They were too old. Too afraid.'

Emmeline shrugged. 'As that policeman said. How rare it was. He said *They must both really have wanted to do it.*'

'Oh God.' She had no more words.

Rudolf and Verena had been taken to the funeral parlour in Winchester. Celia went to see them. She wanted to touch their faces, hold their hands. But when she went into the dingy Chapel of Rest, she found that she couldn't see their faces. They were both wearing porcelain masks, like soldiers in the war had done. Their hair was wigs, Verena's piled high on her head in a way she would never have arranged it when she was alive.

'Can I touch their hands?' she asked the undertaker.

Rudolf was in his suit, Verena in her blue velvet day dress, both outfits looking old now.

He shook his head. 'We've had to embalm them. You'd find them awfully cold.'

'Please.'

'We find it upsets people more than it comforts.'

'I would be so grateful. I wouldn't tell anyone.'

He relented. 'Just this once. Just between us.'

He pushed a chair in between them and he took one hand of each out of the coffin, laid them in hers. He was right, the hands were cold, almost rubbery. She held them tight, as if she could almost force more blood into them.

She tried to talk to them, think of things to say. But all she could think of to talk about was Germany and what she'd seen there. 'You were right,' she whispered to them. 'The boys of the Hitler Youth marching up and down Berlin, growing older, ready to fight for the Party and the future – and Germany becoming great once more.'

On the way back home, the town gaudy with Christmas decorations, she stopped at a newsstand. Tom had told her not to look at the newspapers, but she had to know. Everyone else would have seen it.

'Do you have any old papers?' she asked the bearded, bored-looking man running the stall. 'From yesterday, the day before.'

He shrugged. 'Shouldn't think so, Miss. I can have a look for you, though. I should send them back, mind. So they will cost you.'

'That's fine.'

'I suppose I'm not busy. You give me a shout if any customers arrive.' He walked off to the back of the shop, came back five or so minutes later with a big bundle of papers. 'Two pounds to you, Miss.'

'One.' They were no use to anybody.

'One and six.'

'Done.'

She spotted the words: German, double suicide. 'Yes, these will do.' She handed over the money and bundled them up in her arm, went to catch a cab home.

Sitting in the back, chugging to Stoneythope, she read the front pages. *The Times* talked about the sadness of the 'senior generation', how they'd seen the world make mistakes and couldn't bear to see it again. Other newspapers talked about 'Germans', the inner heart of cowardice, how Germans had tried so hard to ruin the country once upon a time, might do so again. How they let spies in, tried to poison the wells.

'Here, Miss?' shouted the driver, over his shoulder.

'Just here, thank you.' As she sat up, she gazed uncomprehendingly at the sentences on the page, all the old German hatred, every word transported, it seemed to her, from 1914. Nothing had changed. The English had just been pretending all this time. When she'd been speaking to Detective Bilkson, she'd been seized by fury. But every word had been true. It was happening again.

THIRTY-EIGHT

Stoneythorpe, December 1937

When Celia got back, there was a letter on the hall table. From America. She tore it open. She scanned the words.

You know I waited. I hoped you'd change your mind. Even after you returned your ring. But I have found another to marry. I am going to ask her and I feel she will say yes.

Jonathan. A thousand miles away. Marrying someone else. A girl who loved America and would never leave. Her mind swooped with the first time they'd kissed, in the garden she could see from her room. Then in New York, when he came for her, after the dreadful ball, running into the hotel and there he was. Walking back to her room and then there together, holding tight to him as he took her to the bottom of the sea. Thinking about how if she had his baby, it would be a sibling for Michael. Going to the speakeasy, walking through the streets, the drink pounding in her head. Him with Michael, her family. The photo of her, clutching her bunch of flowers.

And now it was nothing. To be forgotten.

The other girl. She wondered about her, hoped she was kind and generous, couldn't help but jealously wonder how pretty she was. Their wedding, perhaps even in one of the hotels they had looked at, flowers, her white dress, smiling faces.

She walked to the window. The garden was empty, overgrown. Full of ghosts. Her parents, Arthur, Michael. Michael and Lily. Now Jonathan.

Wait for me! little girl Celia cried. *Wait!* Hurrying after the older children, trying to join in. And now they'd gone ahead of her again. She was left behind.

She walked out of the room, letter clutched in her hand. Down the stairs, through the hall. Tom was standing at the door, smoking.

'I didn't realise you were back from the Chapel of Rest,' he said. 'How was it?'

'They looked peaceful. Maybe content. They'd arranged Mama's hair.'

He shuffled his feet, looked down. 'So sad.'

'And then I had a letter. From Jonathan.'

'The man who gave you the money?'

She nodded. 'He asked me to marry him. I said I would. I was grateful to him. I thought we could make a life in America. And then I came back here – and I couldn't leave Papa and Mama. And Emmeline.'

'Ah, yes. The family.' He pulled the cigarette to his lips, drew hard.

'I probably shouldn't have said yes.' She was talking too much.

'So you didn't go back.' He pulled at the cigarette again.

His face was furious. She shouldn't be telling him. She told herself to stop talking. She couldn't. Tom kept smoking as she talked on, telling him about Michael and how Jonathan offered them both a new life.

He might not even be listening to her. He might be horrified by her. Talking about loving another man, then agreeing to be engaged without giving it any proper thought. She kept talking.

'And when did you tell him it was over?'

'He came to the party. The one—'

'So you invited him and told him you weren't going to stay with him. Poor chap.'

'I was telling him that when I heard the voices. Michael and Lily, rushing down.

'Ah. You said he was asking you questions.'

She watched the light of his cigarette, faint against the sun. He'd caught her to him in Baden and there had been people smoking in the background. Something within her longed for him to do it now. She shook herself. She had just been writing to Jonathan! And here she was, wishing for Tom to grasp her and hold her.

Her heart struck cold. Was it just because she wanted to take him from Emmeline? Shameful. She should be ashamed.

She looked down. 'It was a terrible thing to do. I was cruel to him.'

Tom dropped his cigarette, crushed it under his heel.

'You're too hard on yourself, Celia. I say he knew what he was getting into. Anyone knows how devoted you are to your family. You would never have stayed in New York.'

She had thought she would, once. She had offered herself to Jonathan in the first place. She got caught up in the idea of living with him in America, happily ever after. But she couldn't go back there, leave her family, and had feared that Michael might be taken from her again. And if he wouldn't come to England – then there was no answer. Love couldn't conquer all.

Tom looked away. His eyes clouded, an odd wry look on his face.

'So I've told you everything now,' she said. 'What about you? Have you told me everything?'

'Well, you're right. Emmeline got a letter. They're not going to sell you the house in Winchester any more. Too much scandal. We have to find another one.'

German. Too German. 'Never mind,' she said. 'I didn't like it much. But there's something else you're not telling me. What is it?'

His face hardened. 'Everything I need to. What do you want to know?'

'The thing you're still hiding from me. I know there's something.'

I am in love with your sister, she waited for him to say. *I love her and I want to marry her.*

'Go on,' she said. 'I wish you'd tell me.'

'There's nothing. Really. Nothing.'

'I know there's something.'

He leant back against the wall. 'How, Celia? How do you *know*?

Do you read minds? Or is it just because you keep so much secret that you think everyone else does too?'

She watched him go. Maybe he didn't even see it himself, that he was in love with Emmeline. It was unconscious. The minute someone told him, it would flower into truth. She imagined herself, the spinster sister, third wheel to Emmeline and Tom on a walking holiday, trotting along with Albert. Then it struck her with a rush of cold water. Emmeline was still young enough to have another child. Or two, three. She, Celia, would be the spinster-aunt nanny for their children, holding their hands on the holiday while Emmeline and Tom strode off happily in front. People around them would think how kind Emmeline and Tom were for taking their unmarriageable sister out.

In the days following, they tried not to talk, prepared for the funeral – which the church had said would have to be delayed until after Christmas. Not that it would be large. Rudolf and Verena hadn't had many friends in the past years and there weren't many relations left.

'I wrote to Heinrich and Lotte when it happened,' Emmeline said. Celia stole a glance at Tom. 'I haven't heard back.'

'I think we should go ahead without them,' said Celia. 'I don't think they could afford to come. And travel is difficult now.'

So there was no one from Germany to come and Verena's family were pretty much all gone, with Louisa, Matthew and Lady Deerhurst all dead.

Celia knelt down in the sitting room, by the bundle of papers. They had gone through everybody.

'So it might be just us, then?' she asked.

'My family will come,' said Tom.

'There will be others,' said Emmeline. 'The church, then back here for sandwiches.'

Celia thought of it, the sparse bare room where Rudolf and Verena had died, filled with people eating sandwiches.

Her heart filled. 'And after that we need to leave this house,' she said. 'I can't bear it so empty. The school can move in, we can leave and they can get the works done without us. We'll find something else.' The idea of the funeral, the empty obeisance, the fact that they were gone and nothing could bring them back. It filled her heart, sparked her body with pain.

Emmeline drew herself up. 'Like what?'

'A house, like the one we looked at before in Winchester. It will be perfectly fine. We need to be out of here, pay all the dues.'

'How can you say that, Celia,' said Tom. 'This was their home.'

'How can *I* say that? It's all right for you! You can go off and get married. But we can't live here any more. I can't! Am I going to spend the rest of my life sitting here, watching you two moon over each other? You can creep around, amuse yourselves with thinking I won't notice. Well, I'm not your spectator. So after the funeral, we all move out. The school gets the house and we make a new life.'

Emmeline and Tom were staring at her. Her sister was flushed, tears glistening in her eyes. Tom's expression she couldn't read.

Celia sat, made breathless by her own anger. One of them could speak.

Finally, Tom shook his head. 'What are you talking about, Celia?'

And that provoked more fury. 'What do you mean, what am I talking about? You go into her room at night! I know you do. I hear you!'

'Celia,' said Emmeline, urgently. 'Please.'

'You two are in love with each other! I've seen the way you look at each other. Her staring after you. I'm the biggest gooseberry in the world around you two lovers!'

'Lovers?' Tom was staring at her. 'Me and Emmeline? But – Celia.' He looked at Emmeline, tears running down her face. 'Celia, this is not—' He stopped.

'Hello,' said a cheerful voice behind them. 'The door was open, so I walked straight in. I thought I might find you here.'

Emmeline turned around. Celia did too, saw a skinny, sunburnt man with shaggy dark hair and a huge beard in a dark, scruffy coat, dirty trousers, boots that had split. And then in what Celia – and all of them – would later say was an almost unbelievable moment, not real, Emmeline tried to stand up, and instead she fainted and crashed to the floor.

INTERLUDE

Often, Michael wondered about the world around him. He wondered about the Prime Minister and the new King and Queen. The Children of the Future said that you should never think of such things, that these people were just put in as circus monkeys, distractions from what was really going on, which was great movements of power and capital, and the only way to escape from it was to ignore them all, altogether.

Most of all, he wondered about war. When he had briefly accompanied a group who were knocking on doors, he'd seen a placard saying news about Germany. Invasion! And in Spain, they were fighting still, but losing now. Uncle Janus might be suffering.

Don said it was all lies, that war was cooked up between the rich, just like they cooked up financial crashes, to keep the poor repressed. If people were always afraid of a crash, they never protested their job. And if they were always afraid of war, then they would never resist the government and always fall behind its efforts to make them all the same, all servants of power, wearing the poppy and talking about the sacrifice of ordinary men, claiming that type of memory had purity and anyone who didn't believe in it was wrong. You wear your poppy and you obey and you say you are *patriotic*.

'But will there be a war?' he'd asked.

Don shrugged. 'They always have wars. That's the only way they can control us. Nothing more effective. Those politicians cook up false fights over land and send us off to fight, telling us it's all about bravery and sacrifice.' Don was right, he understood now that the world worked thus. But, still, how could they stop it?

'But now, will they have one now?'

'Why not? It's fun for them.'

'But my family!' He'd heard so much from them about how cruelly the Germans here had been treated in the last war. Rudolf had been in prison.

'There is no such thing as family, remember,' Don said. 'We are your family.'

'Of course.'

Don raised his eyebrows. 'Don't forget it.'

And yet still, when he lay in the common room, listening to the snuffles and sighs of the others, not able to sleep, he thought of boys his age in Germany. He could guess what they were doing. They were marching with guns, practising, learning how to go to war. Something in him yearned to go too.

THIRTY-NINE

Stoneythorpe, December 1937

'Well, that's a welcome and a half,' the scruffy man said, advancing. 'A modern day *Odyssey*. Get back to my wife, and she faints flat on the floor.'

Celia had rushed to Emmeline, but now she was frozen next to her.

'Samuel?' It was his voice she recognised. And, thinking about it, he was the right height. But nothing else was the same! He was rake-thin and dirty, his beard so huge it obscured half of his face, the rest of it hidden by his straggly hair. And his eyebrows seemed to have expanded too – all of his hair had, while everything else had shrunk. His face – the bits she could see – was scorched red and brown. But staring at him, she picked out the old features, the long nose, sharp eyes, left ear that was prone to pointing out of his hair.

'What are you doing here?' she said. 'We – I – thought you were—'

'I said I'd come back, didn't I? Now, what's this with my wife?' He bent down to pick her up and carried her to the sofa.

'I'll get some water,' Tom said, hurrying out of the room.

Mr Janus patted Emmeline's forehead. 'I suppose it was a bit of a shock to her!'

'I should think so,' said Celia, gathering her feelings. 'She didn't tell me she'd heard from you.'

'She hasn't. No point writing. Post never gets through. And dangerous to know too much anyway.'

'But – Samuel – she thought you were dead.'

He was stroking her forehead. 'Still as beautiful as ever. You haven't changed a bit!'

Tom walked back in with some water. Mr Janus sat Emmeline up and tried to make her drink. 'Still out cold,' he said. 'But the pulse is beating hard. We'll wake her up.'

Celia tried again. 'Samuel. It's been eight years. Couldn't you have told us how you were? We all thought you were dead.'

He stroked Emmeline's forehead some more. 'I bet she knew I wasn't. She had faith.'

Celia felt as if she was hitting, over and over, at a wall that wouldn't move. 'But it's been so long! What if she'd remarried?'

'But she hasn't.' He stopped stroking her forehead as she stirred. 'Has she?'

'No – of course not.' Celia stole a look at Tom, now standing watching from the door. 'But she might have done.'

'Might, might. She knew I'd come back. And here I am. Not that I've been stunned by the welcome here. And what's happened to all the furniture?'

'Celia,' said Tom. 'Let's leave them. Emmeline will be fine.'

He was right. Emmeline would be fine. But she couldn't leave. 'Why are you back? And are you planning to stay?'

'I expect you've seen the news from Spain. War there. We couldn't stop it. Anyway, our movement is more needed here than there. You're facing a great war here, I'm sure, Germany against the world. And we're going to stop it.'

'And how, exactly?' said Tom

'You'll see. Peace always wins. Anyway, little sister Celia, perhaps you might find this weary traveller something to eat or drink. I'll take care of my wife. And what about my two? I take it they're at school?'

Celia froze. 'Albert is away at school. But Lily—'

'She's gone,' said Tom. 'She and Michael – Celia's son – ran away four years ago. We've tried – well, we've tried everything to find them.'

Mr Janus's face dropped. Celia couldn't read it. 'But—'

Her heart broke for him then. 'I'm sorry, Samuel. So sorry.'

'I don't believe it—'

'We still can't.'

His eyes dimmed, the colour somwhow changed. 'I told them—'

'What?' Emmeline, now fully alert, reached out, seized his hand. 'What do you mean? You know something!'

His face was flushed. Celia felt resentment flash across her heart.

He turned away. 'They wrote to me.'

'They wrote to you?'

'Celia,' said Tom. 'Come on. This can wait.'

'No. I want to hear it,' said Emmeline. 'Go on, Samuel. So they wrote to you?'

'They did. Same address all of you had, even though your letters must have been getting lost, theirs got there in the end. They wanted to come out and help with the struggle. They said they'd been learning the history of class struggle with their tutor, which I was pleased you'd ensured. I told them they were far too young, and anyway, it was wrong to run away. I told them not to.'

'Why didn't you tell us?'

'I told them not to. I didn't think they meant it.'

She imagined the tortuous toing and froing of letters, Stoneythorpe to Spain and back. How they must have made sure that the family would never find out, hiding letters. They must have had the help of one of the servants. How could she not have noticed? And how could she not have thought it was where they might go? They had thought they'd known their children, but really they had just lived in the same house, domestic intimacy meant nothing, the closeness of sharing possessions, breathing the same air wasn't really intimacy at all. They'd known nothing. They hadn't seen a thing.

Mr Janus's face was drained and shocked. 'I thought they had a pie in the sky idea. I didn't think they'd actually go. Where do you think they are?'

'We have no idea. We had – have – a private detective who said it was the perfect disappearance. And – the police have closed the file. They said they must be dead.'

'Dead! No! I won't have it!' He rose up, was shouting now. 'I will find them. Lily isn't dead! She can't be. Not my girl!'

Emmeline was holding her hands up to him, telling him it was fine, putting her arms around him.

'Come on, Celia,' said Tom again. 'Let's leave them.'

She turned back, watched Mr Janus stroking Emmeline's hair, like she was Sleeping Beauty, woken after a hundred years. And she thought, to him, she had been that, slumbering through a decade, everything that had happened just a dream, that she could be awoken and they could be happy once more. He would have been right – but Michael and Lily were gone.

FORTY

Celia and Tom barely saw Emmeline and Mr Janus again on the day he arrived back. They'd been closeted together. Then Mr Janus had borrowed some clothes from Tom, Emmeline had called for a cab, and they'd gone out together to Winchester.

Celia found herself feeling hope. Samuel had heard from the children. He might be able to think of something – a new lead.

'Don't you mind?' Celia had said to Emmeline, when they had met in the kitchen that night. 'Don't you mind that he was away for so long and never wrote? He wrote to the children.'

Emmeline shrugged. 'He's my husband.'

'We thought he was dead!'

'He's not. He's back. And I agreed *for better, for worse*. I was right to wait.'

'I know. But what if he goes again?'

'He won't. He's needed here. You'll see, Celia. He can stop the war.'

Celia picked up her tea cup. 'You never know.'

And then she almost dropped it when Emmeline turned, grasped her shoulders. 'Don't tell him,' she said, her voice urgent. 'Don't tell him about Tom.'

Celia shook her head. 'I would never.' She lowered her voice. 'And there's nothing to tell. Nothing happened. You were just friends. And I misread things because I was jealous.'

Emmeline nodded, her face bowed. 'Thank you.'

'Really. There's nothing to tell. It was nothing. You were just lonely. Glad to have a friend. And I misread the signs because of my own feelings.'

Emmeline smiled. She drew Celia to her. 'We are lucky,' she said. 'Don't you see? Samuel came back when we really needed him. He came back for us.'

Celia shrugged. But over the following days, her sister was proved right. Mr Janus shaved off his beard and cut his hair, bought new clothes – and then said he was going to *take charge of it*. He picked up the funeral arrangements, wrote letters, spoke to the undertaker. He talked to the police and Mr Pilsdown and wrote notes. He contacted the school to meet Albert and went to Winchester to look for houses, trying to be discreet so that the sellers wouldn't know it was the double-suicide family and not sell to them.

'Who's going to live there?' Celia asked, when he was showing them the plans of a Victorian house, just on the outskirts of the city.

'All of us,' he said. 'Anyone who wants to.'

Celia stole a look at Tom over the table. She couldn't read his face. She hadn't been able to, over the last few days. Whenever he thought no one was looking, she could see his thoughts crossing his face, like it was a kaleidoscope, shapes and emotions changing, restarting, joining together. She couldn't guess at what he was thinking.

She'd told Emmeline half of the truth in the kitchen. She had told her that her suspicions were borne of jealousy. But not of being in love with him. It was true, every word. If she had a kaleidoscope inside her, it had turned so all the colours were merged and her heart was swelling and she was thinking, *Why didn't I see this before?* She was in love with him. She loved him. But she couldn't tell him. She was floating in the sea, far from shore, waving at him. He couldn't see her.

Despite the funeral to come, their Christmas, with turkey and pudding, was pleasant, even a little cheerful at times, thanks to the return of Mr Janus and then Albert back for the holidays. But eventually the day of the funeral was upon them. It was sad and slow, quiet as they had expected in the icy graveyard. People from the village, some of the men from the old Winter Meats office, even the deputy headmistress from the local school, Mr Crennet and the shop assistants from Miss Violet's Kitchen in Winchester. They buried them out in the graveyard next to Michael and Arthur and Louisa. Celia felt guilty for not coming to see the graves of her brothers and cousin more. *I haven't forgotten you*, she said. But she had, in a way. She didn't come out to sit by them, talk to them. It made her feel too sad. She'd stayed in the world of the living.

'There won't be a war,' she had told them. 'I promise.' She had lied and thought that would be enough.

She and Tom did the washing up after the reception, still wearing their black clothes, not troubling themselves to change. She wanted to ask him a dozen things, but didn't know where to start.

Albert had come back from school taller and more handsome than ever. He looked like a man, Celia thought, a grown man she hardly knew. He embraced Mr Janus with restraint.

'I know I've been gone a long time,' he said. 'I'm sorry.'

'I told that to the chaps at school. They'd have teased me if I'd said I hadn't got a father. So I said you were in South America, making our fortune. You're not going to make me leave school, are you?'

Mr Janus shook his head. 'Of course not. Of course I wouldn't. Well, at least—'

Emmeline shook her head at him and he broke off.

'I'm nearly finished. Then I'll go to university.' Albert sat down on the sofa. 'I wish my sister was here. She doesn't even know that Grandpapa is dead. Why can't you just find her?'

'We've tried, dear,' said Emmeline. 'We keep trying.'

He glowered across at Celia. 'She used to like me best. Then Michael came along. She stopped writing to me at school. When she did bother, I knew Mamma had made her. I wasn't as much fun as him, I suppose.'

Emmeline put her arm around him. 'She'll always love her brother.'

He shook his head. 'At first, you all said she'd just wanted to run away for fun, and she'd come back. But it's been four years now. And she's not here. She wouldn't have done that if she were happy, would she? You must have made her unhappy.'

'Albert, please.' Emmeline was weeping. Celia looked at her nephew. How could they not have thought? All those cheerful letters about rugby and school dinners and masters. Under it all, he was furious.

'Albert, you're upsetting your mother,' said Mr Janus.

'Well, you'd know about that! Wandering off to God knows where for years on end and expecting us all to welcome you back? I bet you don't know either. What did she do to send them away?' He turned to Celia. 'Or was it you?'

She shook her head.

'So it was my mother, then. Give me an explanation!'

They couldn't. They couldn't think of anything to say.

INTERLUDE

Lily was screaming. Micheal couldn't bear it. He fought to get into the room, desperate to try to help her, but they wouldn't let him. The women barred it against him. He fought them, hearing her desperate cries.

'She's dying in there,' he said. They wouldn't let him go in. He heard Mr Brennan's voice, the voice of the other men and he begged them. 'Please!' They told the other men to take him downstairs and put him in the communal room.

He was fighting hard against them, when he heard another say, 'Let him stay. He might need to be here.'

'Poor boy,' a woman was saying.

'Poor girl, more like,' said another.

'She knew what she was doing.'

'She never had a chance,' said one of the men.

'So much for being free of the outside world,' said a woman.

They shushed her. A man inside the room was talking.

Lily's screams sounded as if something was tearing her in two. He threw himself at the door, and one of the men pulled him back. He was her cousin. He'd known her for the longest of all. Mr Brennan barely knew her.

'Don't let her die!' he shouted. 'Don't let her die!' His heart pulled up to the sky. *Somebody save us.*

FORTY-ONE

Stoneythorpe, January 1938

Albert blamed all of them – and perhaps he was right to. He wouldn't speak to Tom. And now he was refusing to go back to school until Lily and Michael had been found. Celia found herself staring at his handsome, smooth face. She remembered him begin born, after they'd fought their way out of the Victory celebrations, back to the Savoy, the midwives not realising at first that there was a second child behind him.

'You can't stay here forever,' said Emmeline. 'As you said, your schooling is important.'

'This is more so. I'm going to wait here until we find them!' Celia's heart banged hard in her chest. If there was a war, he would go. Tom, Mr Janus, even Jonathan would all be too old. Albert would go, into the trenches, fight, and shoot to kill.

'Don't go, Albert,' she said.

'What?' he said.

She shook her head. 'Ignore me.'

'I can't,' Tom had said. 'Really, I can't. This isn't the answer.'

But Rudolf and Verena wouldn't listen. They wouldn't be told. 'We need your help.'

He'd tried to avoid them, escaping when he saw one of them coming, hiding behind doors. But they waited for him, pressing, patient.

'We need to be ready,' Rudolf said. 'If they come here, I will go down fighting. Just help us do it. It's insurance for us. Peace of mind.' He held out his fingers, curved with arthritis, bright red and swollen. 'A simple task.'

'I can't,' Tom said again, looking at the old gun. He couldn't touch it. And then because nothing else would dissuade them, he told Rudolf about that day, June 1916, when he had been standing in a half circle with the other soldiers, waiting for the traitor. The officers had brought the traitor out, a black hood over his head. They positioned him in the middle. And then the officer tore the hood off and Tom saw it was Michael.

'Stop, sir,' he'd begged the officer. 'We can't. He's not a traitor.'

'Hold your gun, Cotton.'

'But, sir.'

'He is to be shot. He is a traitor.'

'Please.'

'Hold your gun.'

And he hoped that because he was to the side, Michael wouldn't see him, but of course his fuss meant that Michael turned his head – and saw who it was.

'Raise your guns.'

Michael looked at him and said something. And Tom held up his gun. He could shoot fast and first so that the others didn't get him. He would make sure he didn't suffer.

'Fire!'

He did. He held up his rifle and he fired. But the gun flew out of his control, to the side, and his shots hit Michael's feet. The other men killed him, the bullets raking him, jerking him, burrowing into his soul.

'That was then,' Tom said to Rudolf. 'I tried. I failed. I've not been near a gun since.'

'How long have you kept that confession, Tom?' asked Rudolf. 'Since the war? Nearly twenty years?'

'I told Celia. Jonathan Corrigan told her that Michael was shot. Someone forced him to tell her. And I told her the truth. Then she hated me. But he wasn't a traitor or a coward, but ill. After what he saw, he was ill!'

Tom knew about the raid that Michael had led on the German trenches. They had thought it was just corpses lying there. But they had been playing dead and they shot the regiment. Michael's friend, Wheeler, dying, drowning in his own blood.

Rudolf nodded. 'I knew that the regiment was lying. I thought they'd shot him for being German. And now here we are again. A war coming.'

'Don't you hate me?'

'No, not you. I hate the officers. I always knew they were lying. Verena doesn't know. And poor Celia, carrying it around by herself.'

'She's never forgiven me.'

'I forgive you. So she can too. You can tell her when she gets back.'

'Thank you.' The burden he had carried so long, weighing down his soul. He'd thought it would be a relief when it was taken from him. But something in him felt too light, as if not having it hurt even more. Then he knew. If it didn't hurt any more, then Michael was truly gone.

He had envisaged this confession so many times. It had never occurred to him that Rudolf already knew that the cause of Michael's death had been a lie.

'But you have to help us,' said Rudolf. 'When they invade, I will shoot back. I won't die like a coward.'

Tom looked dubiously at the gun. It was so old, too old surely to work. It was unreliable, could blast back any moment. 'That thing's not safe. At least buy a new one.' It belonged in an antique shop, a relic from the Crimean War.

Rudolf shook his head stubbornly. 'This has always been my gun. All I'm asking you to do is to help load it for me, this and its twin. It's just for insurance. We will fight them!'

'You shouldn't have loaded guns in the house. And they aren't going to invade. No one's going to invade. We're not even going to war.'

'Yes we are. And we're going to be ready this time.'

Tom stared at the wall of Rudolf's study, shadows on it where the family portraits had been. Someone had to save him.

'Please, Tom. You owe us this much. We have the gun. It was in the attic. We just need you to load it. And check it. Then you can forget about it.' *You owe it to us. You shot Michael. You made Celia pregnant.* He thought they didn't know about Celia, but he always felt guilty in front of them. He had done so much to ruin their happiness. And now all they wanted was for him to load the guns.

'Rudolf. I had to kill men in the war. I had to shoot Germans, crawling below me. I saw their faces come towards me and I shot them with my gun. Don't make me do it again.'

Rudolf reached out a gnarly, wrinkled hand. 'But this isn't the same. We are defending ourselves. We are defending us all.'

Tom felt his heart fold in on itself, like paper, and all his resistance was gone, and he said, 'Yes. Yes. I'll do it. Yes.'

And he had loaded it for them and readied the gun and Rudolf had taken it in his hand, very grateful, passed him the other. He'd believed them, how it would be a back-up plan, just in case there was invasion and how they were protecting the family. And then they had turned the guns on themselves. He could not tell Celia. He would never tell her. She and Emmeline worried over how Rudolf had managed to load them with his arthritic hands, concluded he must have forced himself through the pain. When they questioned it, he stayed silent, fearing they could see the truth written on his face.

FORTY-TWO

Celia didn't take a car from the station, preferring to walk. She was thinking about jars and Mrs Craigmire's idea about having two different puddings in one jar, when Mr Janus came up behind her.

'You made me jump!'

'Sorry,' he said. 'I wanted to talk to you.'

'Oh?'

'You're always so cool with me because I went away, aren't you?'

A car zipped by, heading towards Mareton. More and more of them, every day. Perhaps they'd buy a car, when the children came home – when, not if. She could drive it. They were still in Stoneythorpe. The girls' school had backed out permanently now, talking about financial concerns, the possibility of an approaching war. But Celia saw it in the bursar's eyes when he had met her with Mr Crennet – it was the double suicide, all the cruel words in the newspapers about Germans.

The wind was still chill. She pulled her coat around her. 'We didn't know where you were. We had no idea. You might have been dead. And the children – they wanted to go.'

'I told them not to.'

'But still they went.'

'Yes. Listen, anyway, I wanted to ask you. About that tutor...'

'Mr Brennan?'

'Did they question him?'

'Of course. But nothing.'

'Where is he now?'

'Last time they asked, he'd gone abroad.'

'I bet he had.'

'What do you mean?'

'Tell me, what did he look like?

'Tall, thin, hook-nosed, respectable, quite ordinary really.' She described him in as much detail as she could. 'And he had an odd thing, a blackish speck, just by the pupil of one eye.'

'A blackish speck in one eye?'

'That's right.' He asked her for more details, how large, which pupil, the rest of his appearance.

'Someone with the same name used to come around a little to our meetings. I didn't think anything of it – but he had the same eye. It sounds like the same man.'

'You mean a man used to come to your meetings and then he became our tutor?'

'It sounds like it. We never thought much of him, to be honest. He brought knives to the meetings. In the end, I asked him to leave. Maybe he wanted revenge.'

'Oh no. A tutor.' The answer was touching her heart. Patterns repeating themselves. 'You don't think?'

'I do. Someone had to have helped them. Who else could it have been?'

Celia felt sick. Her mind spooled back. 'Lily?'

'I suspect so.' She stared at him. He was right. It took a man to know it – a man who had been a tutor before. Who had done the same thing. They had been so blind. And all of it due to Mr Janus. Revenge on him for some petty division about who led what, how to conduct the revolution that would never happen. 'If it wasn't for you! This was all about you?'

'I doubt it. Maybe he fell in love with Lily. She's a pretty girl. You should have—'

'Hired a woman? How dare you say that! You left us alone. It was hard enough to find anyone.'

'Sorry, Celia. You're right.'

She held her hand to her head. She couldn't start arguing with him now. They had to think. 'But Mr Pilsdown, the private investigator, interviewed his mother and said it was all fine!'

'Perhaps he made a mistake. I'm sure she lied for him.'

'You're right. If you'd been here—' She stopped. He might have realised then. But *she* should have done. 'We would never have hired him if you'd been here,' she said, realising. 'We have to go and speak to his mother. Maybe she'll tell us.'

'I agree. I wonder if the only reason he started coming to us so keenly was because he wanted to see Lily.'

'I'm going to get the address. I'll ask Mr Pilsdown. As soon as we have it, we'll go.'

Pilsdown had missed it, they all had, it had taken Mr Janus to show them what had been staring them in the face.

Two days later, Celia and Mr Janus were on a train to Reading to visit Mrs Brennan. They had agreed that if she wasn't in, then they'd wait. They took a taxi from the station, drew up to the neat house, white painted windows, tidy garden, in a row of houses that all looked similar. Celia looked at Mr Janus and realised.

'You can't come,' she said. 'You have to wait.'

'What?'

'Two of us would be too much for her. We don't want to frighten her off. Anyway, if I fail, then you can try. It gives us two chances.'

He nodded. 'I see your point.' He leant forward. 'Drive up to the next road, please. I'll wait for you there.'

'Thank you.'

She stepped out and walked to the house, rang the doorbell. How many places she'd pretended to enter, told lies, the Whetstones', trying to find Michael. And here she was, doing it again. The door opened, chain on, and a woman in a fussy blue dress peered out. Her hair was a dark brown puff around her head. Everything about her, the neat dress, the hair, the garden with pink and blue flowers grown from Dutch bulbs in soldier-like rows, was pushing back the wildness, maintaining order.

'Mrs Brennan?'

'Yes.'

'I'm Celia Witt. I wonder if I could come in.' The woman was closing the door against her. 'You see, I've realised we owe Mr Brennan some money.'

'Money?'

'Yes. Quite a bit.' What terrible lies she was telling now. Although, when she thought of it, Brennan had been owed some salary, two weeks or so. They had forgotten – and he had not chased it. Perhaps that should have made them think.

Mrs Brennan opened the door and Celia continued talking, how sorry she was, how she realised that when she'd looked through the accounts, they owed him three months' salary and no one had given it to him. Mrs Brennan smiled, showed her into the sitting room, and offered her a cup of tea. Celia looked around the spotless sitting room while Mrs Brennan was in the kitchen, china ornaments arranged in perfect rows, sorted by animal type, a carpet that looked like it never bore dust. On her return, Celia talked of how sorry she was, said they must send a cheque immediately.

'Where shall we send it?'

'Oh you can send it here.' Too clever for her.

'You're sure he wouldn't like it for himself.'

Mrs Brennan patted her pristine hair. 'No, no.'

'Of course.' What were they going to do? Bring the cheque down and then have Mr Pilsdown follow her to the post office? Possibly that was the only answer. Celia looked round at a row of rabbits on a shelf, the pink notebook by a letter rack. They circled around each other, cheques, addresses. Celia complimented the house, told her how happy they had been with Mr Brennan's work.

Finally, there seemed no point in more. She stood up. 'Thank you for your hospitality, Mrs Brennan. I shall post over the money.'

Then the woman darted across, seized her hand. 'You haven't come about money, have you?'

'No.' Celia met her eyes and saw tears swelling in them.

'You want your child back.'

'I do. I miss him every day. My sister feels the same.'

'I know. You must do. He was my only one too.' She loosened Celia's hands, sat back down on the sofa. 'You're getting closer to them, aren't you? Promise me something,' she said.

'Anything.' Celia held herself still. Something was coming.

'If I give you the address, swear that you won't go after him, just the children. You'll let him go.'

She shouldn't promise. Every bone in her body was saying that she shouldn't promise. He had committed a crime. But what choice did she have?

'I promise.'

Mrs Brennan turned away, scribbled on a paper from the notebook. 'There!' she said, holding it out. 'You promised.'

'You have my word.'

Celia grasped the paper in her hand, stuffed it into her purse, shook Mrs Brennan's hand, let her show her out. When the front door had closed and she was out with the immaculate hydrangeas, she began to run.

Celia handed Mr Janus the paper, blindly. 'Here it is.' He had been right. How betrayed they had been, how blind. She and Emmeline congratulating themselves on appointing such a marvellous teacher. How they were always praising him. How sad they had been when they had told him he had to leave. He had been so calm, so accepting. Under it all, he had been making plans. Such lies. All the while, he'd been keeping them somewhere, while saying to the police and to the family that he didn't know a thing, blamed himself for not seeing anything earlier.

Mr Janus opened the paper and looked it over. 'East London. They're in east London.'

FORTY-THREE

London, April 1938

They got out of the taxi at Liverpool Street station. Emmeline clutched Mr Janus's arm, Albert next to them.

'Jack the Ripper Tour?' offered a man with a beard, holding a placard proclaiming MURDER!

Tom shook his head.

'They go on tours?' asked Emmeline.

'The grisly nature of the human mind,' said Mr Janus.

'Come on,' said Celia. They looked, she thought, no less out of place than the lost-looking tourists gathering around the Jack the Ripper placard. Women in headscarves hurried past them, looking mockingly, Celia thought. She wished Emmeline hadn't worn her best blue velvet coat. It was a little moth-eaten and threadbare, true, but it still cost more than the money some of these women saw all year. 'I want to look smart to see my daughter,' she'd said.

Celia turned to Mr Janus, who was looking out at the people, sizing them up, no doubt, for membership of his movement. 'Could you lead the way?'

He nodded. 'It's not far.' He stepped forward – and so they set off, not on a Jack the Ripper tour, but a walk to see Michael and Lily, five years on. Celia held Tom's arm through the streets, trying not to look like the fish out of water that she felt. They hadn't sent a letter to Michael and Lily saying that they were coming, fearing that if they did, and they were still where Mr Brennan's mother had said, they might flee.

'Shouldn't we tell them?' Celia had said. 'Rather than bursting in on them.'

Something about it didn't seem quite fair. But in her heart, she knew that she'd do anything to have even a brief meeting, even if the way they'd seized it was wrong. They walked around a corner, to a large pub, busy with other groups of out-of-place-looking tourists, gathered around more Ripper placards: 'INNOCENT WOMEN', 'HORROR'.

'The elites slay thousands of us every year, in the course of their power games,' said Mr Janus, loudly, as they walked around one group. 'And yet we're fascinated by the deaths of just a few.'

'Ssh.' Emmeline patted his arm.

It was astonishing to Celia how quickly Emmeline had settled into being Mr Janus's wife once more. Patting each other's arms, laughing, smiling across at him. *He could go again tomorrow*, Celia wanted to scream.

'This way,' said Mr Janus, briskly. 'I expect a war will kill our fascination with domestic murder,' he shouted over his shoulder.

They hurried after him, down narrow streets, hung over with washing lines, a stream of dirty water running down the middle of the road. They turned again, and again, into a side road. 'This is it, I think,' he said. They were in front of a tall house, eighteenth-century like all the others.

'I doubt they're here any more,' said Emmeline, under her breath.

Mr Janus stepped up smartly and knocked on the door.

The door cracked open and a woman's face appeared.

'Go away.'

'We've come for Michael and Lily,' said Mr Janus, moving forward. 'We know they're here.'

There were voices behind her. A baby crying.

The woman pushed the door closed – but Mr Janus was pushing back. 'We know they're here,' he said. 'Let us in.'

'Never!' A man appeared next to the woman and they pushed the door shut.

The group stood there, on the doorstep, looking up at the windows.

'Now what are we going to do?' said Albert.

'Wait them out?' said Celia.

'What, camp on the doorstep? Don't be ridiculous, Celia,' said Emmeline. 'We will have to come back with the police.'

'I won't let you,' said Albert. 'The police will arrest Lily and Michael too.'

'I don't think standing here on the doorstep is going to do much good,' said Mr Janus, dryly. 'And I agree with my son, I don't think we want to get the police involved either. Why don't I see if I have any friends who might be able to help us?'

'What, *them*?' snorted Emmeline. 'They'd make it worse.'

'I don't think we have any choice,' said Tom. 'We have to get in somehow. They won't let us in. And if we don't want to break in or ask the police – then we'll have to use someone else.'

'Give me a few hours. I'll come and find you,' Mr Janus said.

Celia cast a last glance at the windows. They might be up there. They could be looking down on them. She was a few feet away from Michael, possibly. And yet she still couldn't touch him.

'What about if they run?' said Celia. 'Shouldn't one of us wait?'

'I'll wait,' Tom said.

'And when I've got the men, I'll come back,' said Mr Janus. 'You lot – get a taxi back to Liverpool Street. Meet me at the station in four hours. We'll do it at night, so no one sees.'

'What if you don't find anyone?'

'Well, then, we will take men off the street.'

They sat in the station café, looking at scones, barely speaking. Celia worried. They were going to break into someone's home. If they were caught, then what? She and Emmeline arrested for breaking into a house? No one would care if they said they were trying to retrieve their children, they'd still be criminals.

'You can't go,' she said to Emmeline. 'It might be dangerous. What if they fight? We'll get dragged into it. You need to stay.'

'I'm going. It's my daughter. I'm going. You stay if you want to.'

'It could be dangerous, Mama,' said Albert. 'Aunt Celia's right.'

'Well, I will have to face it. I'm not leaving now. Why do you want to go, then?'

'I want to be there, too.' Her mind catapulted with scenes of terror and violence. The people, whoever was in there, fighting against Mr Janus's men. Shooting and knives, perhaps. Mr Janus had said Brennan had been interested in violent insurrection. She imagined him saying he would die for the cause. They could die. The children could die. It could be her last moment with Michael.

'They won't want us there,' said Albert. 'Well, maybe me. The rest of you. You know that. They might do anything to get away from you.'

'Look, stop this,' said Celia, breaking in. 'If we're all going, we have to stand together. We need to be there for them.'

They sat in silence. Pictures, terrible pictures fell across Celia's mind. To stop them, she tried to think of how Michael and Lily would have changed. Five years was so long, almost an unimaginable stretch of time for children. After she had missed so much of his life. More of his life had been away from her than with her. Everything had changed. But all she could see was the old Michael – and his lines were still not quite defined. She couldn't even see him.

At eight o clock, Mr Janus met them at Liverpool Street. 'I have the men,' he said. It was dark, the streets that had before looked bustling, cheerful, were gloomy, made her feel fearful. All the Jack the Ripper tourists had gone, tucked up in their hotel beds, she supposed.

'No one's come out,' said Tom, who'd come to meet them. 'From the front way at least. And it's so built up at the back, I can't see where they'd go.'

'Do you really think this is a good idea?' Celia said to Mr Janus. 'What if it goes wrong?'

'No option.'

'What if they're not there?'

'Well, then you dig deep into that company of yours and pay over some money to keep whoever is living there happy and cover any damage we make when we force the door. And then we start searching all over again.'

She clutched Tom's hand. 'I'm afraid.'

He squeezed her fingers. 'Don't be.'

She held his hand harder. It struck her – they were like any father and mother. Two parents, walking to find their son. She vowed that if she found Michael, she would tell him the truth about his father. There would be no more secrets.

As they were following Mr Janus, a large group of men slid in front of them. They were carrying big pieces of wood, like policemen's truncheons.

They curved around the corner, came to the house. There were lights on upstairs.

'Stand over there.' Mr Janus directed them to a house on the other side of the road. They obeyed, walked over.

The men called out to the windows. 'Let us in.'

'Now, please,' added Mr Janus. 'We know you're in there. We're being nice. Let us in.'

There was no reply.

He turned back to the others. His eyes were glittering. *He's enjoying this*, Celia thought. He was enjoying playing the role.

'So, gentlemen,' he said. And three of them flung themselves against the door and it burst inwards. They rushed in. Celia dashed forward. Tom caught her hand but she shook it off. She ran into a dank, dirty hallway and stumbled over broken wood. The men ahead of her were flinging open doors, shouting out 'Stay clear!' But the rooms were deserted, strewn with things, bits of old clothes, food packets, scraps of paper. 'They've left,' she heard Tom say behind her. 'They've just left. They must have just done it as I came to find you. Only five minutes. I was watching. They must have been watching me too. We're too late.'

Celia couldn't believe it. She hurtled to the top of the stairs, ran through the rooms, threw open the doors. Nothing. No one was there. She threw herself against a wall, sat down, closed her eyes. When she opened them again, the room was still quiet. She looked to the side. There was writing there, something scribbled on the wall, a picture. She looked closely. And then she felt sure. It was Michael's hand. She put out her finger, traced his writing. 'Lily,' he had written. Then her heart flew. 'Mama,' in the same hand. She followed the line he had drawn, across the bottom of the wall, and there was a sketch of a house, some trees, a pool. Her heart dropped. He had drawn the gardens. He had drawn the frontage of Stoneythorpe and the gardens. In secret, in pencil, at the bottom of the wall, where no one could see it, he had drawn the gardens. He had drawn their home.

He missed them. She clutched the photograph she always kept in her pocket. He must still be near. *She would find him.*

PART FIVE

FORTY-FOUR

Winchester, October 1938

It was six months since they had found the house in London – but it was, again, as if the children had vanished. They had given Mr Pilsdown all the information and he had been to London, questioned the neighbours and the shopkeepers and spent days there, simply asking people walking past what they knew of the house. They all said they knew nothing, that the people in the house kept themselves to themselves, that they saw adults, children and younger people but they couldn't distinguish which ones, had always felt it was better not to look too closely. When he asked them why, they had clammed up again.

'They were afraid of something,' he said to Celia. 'I hear this man in charge – Don, I believe – had a lot of power. No one wanted to get on the wrong side of him.'

It filled Celia with pain, that if these people had looked closely, they might have seen Michael and Lily, might have been able to rescue them! But, of course she was wrong, the 'disappearing children' story was years old now and no one remembered it but them. They had taken their information to the police, who had been unhelpful, said the children were over sixteen now and could do as they pleased. Albert had begun at Cambridge, along with his best friend from Harrow. At the school prizegiving, he'd won the prize for maths, but on the way home he'd wept and tried to throw it out of the window. 'Where's Lily?' he said. 'I wanted her to be there.'

Finally, after a lot of asking around, Mr Pilsdown had found that a woman working as a cook in one of the pubs that he had visited had been part of the group, chosen to escape. One of the waiters had let it slip to him by mistake.

'Finally,' said Mr Janus, when Celia was reading the letter. 'That man earns his money!'

The woman hadn't wanted to speak, she'd been shy and un-forthcoming and was particularly determined to be silent about Michael and Lily, said she knew nothing. But after Pilsdown pushed her hard, even threatened her with the police, she admitted that the people in the house had split because there had been a disagreement some time before – on what, she would not say – and Michael and Lily had gone. The people who had not let them in and then escaped when Tom came to meet them were the ones who had stayed. She would not say if the children had left with anyone else and next day when he had gone back to interview her again, she had fled.

'Well,' said Mr Janus. 'It is a start. He must continue. Keep making enquiries. And then perhaps we will get somewhere.'

That was all they could hope for, that he found someone else who had been with the group and who could tell them where Michael and Lily had gone. Celia clung to that – and the drawing of the garden, sketched out faintly on the peeling wall.

For now, however, she sat in her office in Winchester, waiting for Mr Crennet. The shops were busy in Winchester and London, and they'd bought a new one in Manchester. It was as if they couldn't stop expanding. She had ordered some catalogues to look into advertising. It was all very well thinking about the modern woman. You had to reach her as well. She looked at her newspaper as she waited.

Chamberlain had been to Germany, back and forth, first time on a plane. Then, when they were readying for the sirens and the evacuation and the blackout – he came back, talked of 'peace for our time'. The wireless blared it out. Germany wanted the Sudetenland from the Czechs. If the Führer got that, then they wouldn't want anything else. The war was over. It would always be over. Albert and Michael were safe and Rudolf and Verena had died for nothing. For the country was going wild for Chamberlain and what he said outside Downing Street was 'peace with honour'. He was on the Buckingham Palace balcony, waving out to the crowds, the hero. No need for the mobilisation of the army after all. Celia tried to believe it, forget the loudspeakers screaming out, the Nuremburg rallies replayed on the radio. The youth marching up and down, in Berlin, determined on the greatness of the Fatherland.

'He's like an innocent abroad. He thinks they're all British gentlemen,' she said.

'Those Czechs,' said Mr Janus. 'Sacrificed.' He was planning a rally to support them. 'The Czechoslovakian problem, indeed!'

'I've read that people want pieces of his umbrella,' said Albert. 'Like holy relics.'

But there was quiet from Germany. Perhaps Chamberlain had been right. Instead, they had other stories of human misery, thousands of refugees from Spain fleeing over the Pyrenees to France. The paper showed queues of them, hollow-eyed, sick-looking, about to die. If Mr Janus had stayed abroad, he would have been caught up in it, desperate too.

'I have good news,' said Mr Crennet, knocking and entering. 'Well, perhaps good and bad would be the best way to see it.' He was holding a letter.

He closed the door behind him.

'The bad news is that the government seem convinced we will go to war,' he said, sitting down.

She shook her head. 'The newspapers say no. How do you know?'

He held out the letter. 'Well, let us say, the Ministry of Food believes there will be a war. They are researching how to feed the nation in the event of war. I have had a request that we draw up our plans and bid for the contracts. They are predicting that many women will be drawn into the workforce and thus they will need our foods and suggest they are sold at subsidised rates in the factories where they will be making munitions and in the workers' restaurants across the country. They are working on the idea that there may be rationing, so we must be creative in what we make. It will necessitate new recipes.'

Celia took the letter from him and read it. She read through requests for confidentiality, details of what they expected, numbers of cafés, factories, workers' restaurants, instructions about the importance of nutritional value and a high energy yield due to the nature of war jobs.

'I don't believe it. We can't be having a war. Tell me it's not true.'

He shook his head. 'There is nothing we can do to stop it. What we can do is help the country prepare. Feeding the nation is paramount, as we are an island.'

She stared at the letter.

'Miss Witt. It seems clear to me that we are in the best position for this. We have the expertise and are far ahead of any of our rivals. It appears to me that we must do this.'

She gazed past him, to the display of bottles and cans behind. The advertising on the wall. They had wanted to make food for the office girl, the shopgirl. Not the woman making weapons. Not war. But he was right. They could feed everyone quickly and efficiently.

'What will be rationed, do you suppose? Lard, butter, sugar, eggs?'

'I expect so. Meat. We can try to get around it, non-rationed foods, although I doubt they yet know what exactly will be rationed or not. They want us to go in next week to discuss the contract. We will have to make some plans.'

She scribbled on her pad. 'And hope they are not needed because we'll have no war.'

'I believe that it will be inevitable,' he said, glancing at her newspaper. 'Hitler will stop at nothing.'

And he was right. Boys marching in Berlin, saluting. Believing, wanting.

Over the next week, Celia worked every moment she could, scribbling out recipes, used flour and vegetables with only a little cheese and meat to add flavour, make it seem more than it was.

The packaging had to be simple, plain, no bows and ribbons and pictures. They would need more factories and more workers.

On Thursday, at two in the afternoon, she and Mr Crennet travelled to the Ministry of Food. She wore her smarter grey suit, tried to arrange her hair. They sat at the end of a long polished table as dozens of men came in and out, asked them questions, gave numbers, pondered recipes. When Celia and Mr Crennet asked questions – how many women do you think? What about the housewives? What about the male workers? Will you concentrate the workers in parts of the country? – none of them could quite give an answer. They shook their heads and said gently that it was all only speculative.

But how can we give you numbers if you can't give anything to us? Celia wanted to shout, but did not. Instead, she and Mr Crennet smiled and nodded and he said, 'Oh yes, if war is announced, we could be ready to go immediately. We don't need any notice.'

Under the table, he kicked Celia gently. It was impossible! Entirely impossible! She had no idea how they'd do it.

'We'll need to rent properties for the factories and warehouses,' she said to the group of men at the end of the table. 'And we'll need to stock up on supplies. The minute war is announced, everyone will rush to the shops to pile up food.'

'That is a good idea,' allowed the man at the end.

'So we'll need an advance against the contract.'

He drew back. 'I'm afraid that is impossible, Miss Witt. You see, there is no contract unless there is war.'

'Of course! But to do this properly, we need money! And what you're saying is that you can't give it to us until war begins.'

'*If* war begins.'

'So we must recruit staff, rent and set up factories, warehouses, buy in the packaging and stockpile the food. And if there is no war, all that will go to waste.'

'I'm sure you can use them in other ways.'

'Well, I don't know we can.' Mr Crennet was nudging her under the table again. He would say that she was ruling them out by being like this, the Ministry would go to one of their rivals. She didn't care. They needed her.

'Because we don't even know when a war would start, if there was one,' she said. 'We might have to keep the factories and staff on for months. Keep buying stock. It can't be done.'

'I feel sure that someone can do it,' said the man, with dignity. 'Perhaps Flower Foods.'

Celia shook her head. 'I doubt they can either! And are the aircraft manufacturers expected to make planes for free, just in case?' she said.

'I cannot say. Not our area.'

'Oh of course they're not. Well, why should we? You should pay for what you're asking for. If you want things done properly. Otherwise, well, Mr Crennet and I and all the existing girls will do our best – but we can't start moving towards a war effort until you tell us and then it will be too late. There will be chaos.'

Mr Crennet nodded. 'Hunger.'

'An army marches on its stomach.' She leant forward. 'Please,' she had forgotten his name. 'Sir. You plan. We need to plan. We can't do it otherwise.'

One bald man was whispering to the one next to him and the one sitting at the end was writing on a pad. Celia smiled at them. The other side were conferring. She looked at Mr Crennet and they both sat quietly, looked out, waited.

The man at the end spoke: 'Let us consider, please, Miss Witt, Mr Crennet. We shall give this some thought.'

They wished them goodbye and walked out through the heavy door into the sun. 'I think you might have won them,' said Mr Crennet.

He was right. Three days later, they received a letter. Five thousand pounds to do advance planning and hire staff and rent factories. The Ministry would expect reports and they would visit at weekly intervals and expect to see the factories. Spot surprise visits would also be carried out. Any hint that there was a lack of proper budgeting and the project would be terminated. And it all must remain secret. No one must know it was war preparations.

'Etcetera!' said Mr Crennet closing the letter. 'We have success.'

'We have a lot to do,' she said. 'We need to start now. How long do you think it will be?' That was the way she thought now – not if, but when. The earth had shifted under her when they came out of the Ministry and she'd known, without even looking at a newspaper, that the world was turning, the boys were marching in Berlin, that Hitler was planning and the planes would thicken across the sky, trails of men walking across Europe, and France would again look like it had when she'd been there, no grass, all soil, pure war.

'How are we going to tell the workers this isn't about war?' she said. 'They'll guess.'

Mr Crennet shrugged. 'We say it's for an overseas market. And if they ask more, we tell them not to. They'll be grateful to have a job.'

She got back to find a letter from Jonathan. He wrote that he had not told her everything in the last letter. He was married now – and his bride was Violet. They both sent their best wishes.

Celia stared. Violet. 'He's married to *Violet*,' Celia said. She had imagined him marrying some society woman, like one of the girls at the ball. He'd told her he'd visited her, promised to check that she was well. And somehow the visits had turned into love. Violet wearing the too-large engagement ring that she had once worn. Yes, Violet was delicate, beautiful, needed his help. Perhaps he would help her find Hope. She was perfect for him – gentle, kind and she never wanted to be anywhere but America. And although Celia knew it was irrational, she couldn't help feel jealous, of him for loving Violet, of her for rebuffing all attempts at friendship, blaming her for being rich when he was the same, and envious of both of them, for finding a love that seemed, to her, looking in, purer and more simple than anything she could ever have, a gift.

INTERLUDE

Don came up to them after another night of shouting. 'There's no choice,' he said. 'We have to leave. This place is empty, false and corrupt and we should never have come.' Mirabel was crying at night and the others didn't like it. She was just a baby. The whole movement was supposed to be about children. And yet they didn't want one when they had one.

'And they don't want us here,' said Michael, under his breath. No one wanted them. They hated them here. He reached out his finger for the wall. He traced the line he had drawn, but didn't dare follow it round to the picture. If he saw it, he thought, he might begin to cry.

'But what about Mirabel?' said Lily. 'They can't keep her!'

'Of course not,' he said, snappily, waving his hand around. 'She comes too. But we have to leave. This place is a disgrace. We need to travel, find purer, find better. And that's not here. Year Zero can never be in Britain. This place is dry, cruel, materialistic. We deserve better! We must go abroad.'

'But where?' Michael asked. 'Where are we going to go?' His heart tugged at the thought of the other children, Bear and Betty and funny Rainbow, the ones who'd almost become his friends. He didn't want to leave them.

'And what about war?' he said. 'I thought there was supposed to be a war coming.'

'I have an idea,' Don said. He reached down, patted Lily, closely. 'It's what you've always wanted. We will go and find him.'

'Who?' asked Michael. But his heart knew, the words in his heart were growing and he saw from Lily's face that she knew the answer too. 'It's too dangerous,' he said. 'We can't!'

'It won't be dangerous with me,' said Don. 'I will look after you.'

'Don't go,' said Bear and Rainbow, still not understanding the rules – no attachments, no affection, love all a myth to keep them suppressed. He wanted to tell them he'd come back for them but knew he never could. He drew them all in his mind because he wasn't allowed to do it for real, sketched out their lines in his head so he wouldn't forget their eyes, mouth, small bodies. He left his toy horse with Bear and his bear with Rainbow. He begged them to hide them, keep them safe, even knowing as he did so that the adults would find them and take them away.

FORTY-FIVE

London, April 1939

Celia worked around the clock – for now they had to keep their own orders fulfilled and prepare for the Ministry. Mr Crennet found five new factories and staffed them. The first, just outside Nottingham, would make soups. 'Once we get going, we will be making five thousand cans a day,' Celia told Mr Greenwood, the man sent from the Ministry. He nodded, approvingly. 'Good. As soon as possible, please. That's the sort of yield we like.'

She nodded. 'Of course.' She'd been right. The earth was moving under her and the planes were ready, coming, rising. Two, three, six months until they were heavy in the sky like crowds of birds at dusk. Not long.

They set up a pie factory in Leicester, a meat patty factory in Lincoln and the one in Birmingham canned dumplings, cheese, vegetables and meat. The Ministry had decreed that puddings were still important and so they would make chocolate sponge, raisin sponge and shortbread biscuits, all in cans.

And the recipes were easy to change, for when things became short in supply. Take out some mutton, add more potato. Take out some leeks, add more potato. Take out some chicken, add more potato. Chocolate sponge with hardly any chocolate in it, they were probably going to have to use gravy colouring to make it brown. She didn't want to think about what would happen when they had to ration sugar and flour.

And if there was no war? They would go back to how they were, give up the factories, lay off the workers. But she knew it was coming. Mr Greenwood talked so seriously about transport, stressed the importance of secrecy. And the workers knew too – they didn't ask. Celia sat in her office and went through the figures, wondered how many people all over the country were going through figures – trains, aeroplanes, hospitals, guns, medicines, bandages, deaths. She thought of the boys marching in Germany, faces looking up to the sun.

'If I could give some advice, Miss Witt,' said Mr Greenwood on one visit. 'I would suggest a stepped-up advertising campaign. In our target cities for workers, ideally. We want your name in the minds of the girls – women – so that they will know you so well that they won't need to think about food or housekeeping. All their mind will be on their work.'

'Yes, of course,' she said. No point debating with him.

'Oh good. We also wondered if you might show Miss Violet doing things.'

'Like making munitions?'

He raised an eyebrow. 'Not quite yet. But just general fixing things.'

She wanted to laugh, it seemed so prosaic. But why not? The modern girl shouldn't have to wait for a man.

'How about a wireless. She could fix her own wireless?'

'Excellent. Excellent idea, Miss Witt.'

'I have always wanted to put a girl up in Piccadilly Circus. I want to see Miss Violet up in the lights! But we have been told there is a long queue.'

'Oh yes?'

'Perhaps you might consider looking into it?'

'Of course, Miss Witt.'

Three weeks later, a letter came. The agency would have a spot for Miss Violet at Piccadilly Circus in a matter of weeks. The price was astronomical, but she didn't care. In May, she, Emmeline and the staff from the shops travelled up to London by train – and stood at Piccadilly Circus as Miss Violet extended up above them, ten foot tall, in her best blue suit, holding out a jar. 'Don't stop to cook! Turn to a can!' Her heart was so swollen with joy.

Perhaps Michael would see it one day, admire it, come back. His drawing displayed to all London.

At night, in Mareton, there were practice runs. Men came to dig trenches, their flashlights and lorry headlights shining into Stoneythorpe's windows as they passed. Across London – apparently, the whole country – they were digging trenches in every park, men pulling up the flowers and piling up the soil to make shelters for them, the thousands of souls in London. Mr Janus, Tom and Albert followed the advice in the leaflet and built a refuge in the back garden, walls of sandbags with corrugated iron they bought in the market.

'We are going to war,' said Celia. 'We shouldn't look for the children. If Michael is with us, they will make him go to war.'

'The authorities will find them eventually,' said Tom. 'Conscription is conscription.'

Mr Janus shook his fist. 'It's all lies. We're serving big business whatever we do. The money men make money from war. I refuse to let it happen.'

'I'll go with you tomorrow,' Celia said. 'I'll go to London and I'll join the march.' And yet maybe peace was impossible, polluted, and indeed not peace if it could only be achieved by sacrificing others. The Youth she'd seen would be eighteen now, old enough to fight, ready to sacrifice everything for the Fatherland. 'Why would Hitler give anything to us? Why would he stop?'

Albert looked at them. 'Adults. You ruin the world. Then you expect us to agree and do what you say.'

'Well, hopefully, you can make it better,' said Celia.

Tom put his arm around her, then Emmeline, pulled them together. 'But war doesn't last. Not forever. We can survive it. We did before.' He clasped them closer. 'We have each other.' Celia felt her heart flood with affection and emotion. They had each other. And one day, they would have the children again.

One day, not long after, Celia arrived back from London and there was a letter for her on the hall table. She didn't recognise the handwriting and, peering at the postmark, saw it was from France. They didn't know anyone in France! She sat down on the chair and pulled it open, dreading it, nothing was good news any more, but she'd have to read it. It was like tugging the plaster off, you had to do it quickly. Handwritten, thin paper. She scanned the words, turned it over. Alicia Waterton. Her heart struck. Her old ambulance girl, Waterton, big and brash and bossing them all around, always telling them that 'mother said we should do our bit', former Head Girl of her smart girls' school.

Dear Celia,

It is years since I saw you and we were together in France. But I saw your picture in the newspaper a few years back when you were launching Miss Violet's Kitchen and I felt very proud of you. I hope you remember me from those days. I will never forget them. I sometimes see word of Fitzhugh in the society pages and I hear from time to time from Grant. I think of how young we all were, and I often think of Shepherd and how we are all living our lives and she has been stopped from this and she will always be young, always convinced, as we were, that we could change the world. I hope you remember us all fondly.

Life did not work out the way I had thought it would for me. I never married and suppose I will not now. I trained as a nurse after the war and lived with Mother while I worked at the hospital in Southampton. After she died, I decided to travel and I am with the Red Cross in the south of France now. We are very busy with the refugees who are coming due to the end of the war in Spain. We have thousands coming through every day and we do our best to cope with them. Many are starving. I do not know where they will go from here. I thought I could never be more tired than I was after a day driving in France, and now I can barely drag myself to bed after a day here. But I am older, I suppose, and feel less hope than I did.

But I did not write to share my troubles. I write because I think that you should come here. I am not entirely sure but I think you should. There is something you should see. I am sorry I cannot be clearer, but please believe me that I am serious and would not write unless I was.

If you come here, there are hotels in town where you could stay. I only have a small room on the camp with no space, otherwise you could stay with me. Please advise me what you would like to do. I am sure you are very busy but I will wait to hear from you.

I am pleased that life has worked out so well for you. I have often thought of you over the years – and as I say, how young we were then.

Yours sincerely,
Alicia Waterton.

Celia sat down and stared at the letter. Waterton. She couldn't imagine her as an older woman, the same age as Celia. In her mind, she was the same age as she had been then, tall and confident, talking endlessly.

Celia had always imagined that she would end up being a rich matron in Surrey or somewhere, happily telling the other mothers what to do, organising the tea rota at church, nursing classes for the Sunday school, harping on about her war work as an ambulance driver. Not in the camps in the south of France, surrounded by all those refugees. The picture Celia had seen in the newspaper, hollow-eyed, desperate women carrying children, men, their faces covered in scars, people who'd lost everything. The Waterton she had imagined talked forever about her children and her garden, not, as she must be, desperately asking for supplies and help, trying to keep people alive. How wrong Celia had been.

She didn't seem to want money, although Celia would send her some anyway. She didn't want Celia to go out and help – and what use would Celia be now anyway?

I am sorry I cannot be clearer.

What could it mean? Celia wracked her brain. If Waterton was ill or dying and wanted to tell her something, surely she would have said? And what could she have to tell her anyway? A secret? Celia felt she had had enough secrets to last a lifetime – but even if Waterton had one, what could it be? Nothing about their lives then could have been changed. She hoped that it wasn't something to do with Shep. Surely the poor girl couldn't blame herself for Shep's death? Maybe she was supposed to take that driving shift and gave it to Shep and felt guilty? She shouldn't! They were on the front line and any of them could have died at any time. But Celia knew how you could grip all the blame to your own heart, hate yourself for still being alive when others were dead.

She had to go. If that was it and poor Waterton had been keeping it to herself all these years – she had to travel there. Now that the expansion of the business was ticking along, she could easily leave it for a week or two if she travelled down to the south of France.

But what if war broke out while she was there? Her heart clutched with fear. She had to go, even more so, if war would break out. Waterton needed to tell her now. She would go, hear the secret, tell Waterton it wasn't her fault and get back as quickly as possible. Poor Waterton faced death every day. The least she could do was to get on a train to France.

Over the next week, Celia met Mr Crennet, organised the business, told Emmeline and Mr Janus.

'I should come with you,' Mr Janus said. 'You don't know what it's like down there.'

'No!' Emmeline cried. Celia looked from her sister to her brother-in-law – and knew. Emmeline thought that if her husband went to France, he would never come back.

'I will be fine,' she said. 'Really. I'm not going for long.' She tried to sound more confident than she felt. 'The town will be full of Red Cross people anyway. It will be perfectly safe.'

'They're starving there,' said Mr Janus, flatly. 'They'll kill you for what you have. They'll murder you for your shoes.'

'No, they won't. Anyway, I have to go. She needs me.'

'I've read there's cholera,' said Emmeline. 'You haven't seen her for twenty years. Over twenty years. Why are you doing this?'

Part of her thought the same. Why did she always have to be the one to keep the secrets. Why her? But she had to go. She wrote to Waterton, saying she was on her way. It might be that the letter arrived after her. She had to move fast.

FORTY-SIX

Perpignan, France, May 1939

Celia travelled across the Channel on a choppy ferry that made her sick, caught the train to Paris, and then to Perpignan. As she grew closer, the train started to fill up with nurses, Red Cross people, government workers. When she got out into a station bustling with people, nurses, men shouting in Spanish, she had no idea where to go. She walked to the main square, glad that she had a small bag. The town would be a perfectly ordinary pretty enough small French town – bakery, butcher's shop, toy shop – if it wasn't for all the soldiers walking around, policemen on every corner. Both hotels she tried were full – and then they directed her to a woman who lived two streets back from the main square, who had a spare room.

Celia walked over, knocked on the door and the woman showed her up a narrow staircase to a small room furnished in dark wood, a tiny bed with a pink bedspread, narrow window, clean enough. The woman said no breakfast, no meals, no visitors, and Celia nodded and paid over the money, extortionate but so it had to be if the town was full. She took off her hat, washed her face with the jug of water the woman brought up and headed back out into the square. She would go to a restaurant for something to eat and then tomorrow she would get out to the camps. She was beginning to wonder if she shouldn't have waited at Stoneythorpe for Waterton's reply. But she told herself that she'd find her. The Red Cross headquarters, wherever they were, would be able to direct her.

Three hours later, she was back in her room, ready to sleep. She'd eaten roast chicken and vegetables and started talking to two lady charity workers from Paris. They told her that the volunteers in the camps were rushed off their feet, distributing food and blankets, milk for the children, trying to get the supplies to the children first, the male volunteers attempting to stop the fights that broke out when the food arrived. They said everybody was exhausted, but even worse, couldn't see an end to the situation.

'Where are these people going to go?' one said to her. 'They have nowhere. They're all going to die here. And the world doesn't care.'

She lay in bed reminding herself of those words.

Next morning, Celia found a man who'd drive her out to the Red Cross headquarters, near one of the main camps. She queued up there and found that Waterton was in the Fifth Division camp. Celia left a note with the woman at the desk, staring at the piles of paper to the woman's side, worrying it would never reach Waterton. She turned away, left the queue of nurses and volunteers and soldiers.

She walked back to the village, rather than take a car again, talked to a journalist in the café for a while, walked back to her room and tried to sketch out some ideas for Miss Violet's Kitchen, if there wasn't a war. But her heart wasn't in it and she went back out again, sat in the town square with her notebook in her lap, watching the soldiers passing back and forth, the old men playing boules.

She went back to her house and a large blonde woman in a nurse's coat was waiting by the front door. She knew it was Waterton, from the set of the head on the shoulders, confident, in charge. That hadn't changed, no matter what else had. Celia walked up to her and touched her shoulder and the woman turned and flung herself into her arms. 'You came!' Waterton said. 'I didn't think you would!'

'I had to,' said Celia, muffled into her shoulder, but the woman couldn't hear her. Her shoulders were shaking and she was crying silent tears.

Waterton said she had three hours off as she'd volunteered to take the night shift and they went back to the roast chicken café, Waterton exclaiming about how she thought Celia would never come and how she hadn't changed a bit. 'Mother would be so thrilled to see it!' she said. 'We always kept up with Miss Violet's Kitchen!' She said that her mother cut out every mention in the magazines, had even travelled up to the shop in London for a birthday treat.

Celia felt ashamed for barely giving a thought to Waterton over the years. She called her Celia throughout and Celia struggled to address her as Alicia, gave up and omitted to use her name.

Waterton talked of her work in the camp – the unimaginable squalor, the poverty, the hopelessness, families separated, how disease spread like wildfire and all the children were malnourished. There was cholera, of course, but she and the other nurses in her section were particularly exercised by a measles epidemic that was circulating around the children.

'If they were better fed, we'd have more of a chance,' she said.

Celia offered the money she'd brought, said there was more to come, and Waterton was grateful, said all money had to go via HQ and she would take it in tomorrow. But, still, Celia thought, she was no closer to understanding the letter. Waterton looked exhausted, purple rings under her eyes and grey shadows on her cheeks, but she didn't look like she was *dying* (although who could tell these days?), and although she was keen to talk to Celia about the camps, none of it seemed very specific. Celia could have been any friend from home, a fellow nurse or charity worker even.

But Waterton hadn't just asked her to come all the way because she needed a friend. There had to be something.

'I often think of us, like you said,' Celia ventured when Waterton paused. 'We were all so young, out in France. We had no idea what was really happening. Looking back, I'm almost surprised more of us didn't die than just Shep.'

'Poor Shepherd,' said Waterton, shaking her head. 'So tragic.'

'It was no one's fault, you know,' Celia said carefully. 'Any one of us could have died driving along those roads. She was just very unlucky.' She thought of herself, desperately holding Shep, screaming up to the moon to save her and could hardly credit that she was talking of Shep so casually, eating lunch in a café in France. But she had to say this. No one was to blame.

'Oh no, I agree,' said Waterton. 'Of course, I feel the guilt of the survivor. You must too. But you mustn't blame yourself!'

'No,' said Celia, baffled. What on earth, then, did Waterton want?

Celia gave up, turned her attention back to her chicken. But then Waterton began to speak.

'I can't remember how many sisters you had,' she said. 'Was it two?'

'I have one. Two brothers. One died while I was in France. Near the Somme. The other in America, not long after the Crash.'

'Oh yes,' she said. 'I remember the news. And do they have children?'

Celia talked about Lily and Albert, Euan who died. She said that Albert was at school.'

'And Lily?'

'She ran away. We don't know where she is.'

Waterton nodded. 'How terrible for you all. And she is how old now?'

'She is nearly twenty. An adult. We can't always be chasing her. But still. We thought she was happy with us.'

'Did she run away alone?'

Celia looked at the table. 'No. With my son.'

'You had a son?'

And then Celia was talking about Michael and she couldn't stop. She spoke about how he was born, how he'd been taken from her, how she'd found him, told Waterton everything, said the father had been a friend, because Waterton would never meet Tom, so what did it matter.

Waterton nodded solemnly. 'I am glad you had a child, Celia. I suppose now I never will. Do you have a picture of him?'

Celia took out the picture, at least five years old now, and talked about his good looks, how much she loved him. It was comforting to be able to talk about him, to someone who wasn't going to get upset, like Emmeline – and really she had no one else to talk to. She didn't have a friend.

They talked about Stoneythorpe and selling it and Rudolf and Verena's death, and Waterton shook her head over it all. Then they talked about Waterton's mother and her decline into forgetfulness, the work Waterton did at the hospital. She talked of two near engagements with doctors, neither quite worked out.

'Time goes so quickly,' she said.

Celia nodded. 'I don't think I realised.'

Waterton agreed. 'I should be getting back soon,' she said. 'I'd like you to come with me.'

FORTY-SEVEN

Perpignan, France, May 1939

Celia paid for the meal and then accompanied Waterton on the Red Cross bus taking nurses and soldiers from the town to the camps. They settled together on a back seat and Celia looked out of the window as they left the town behind, moved into farmland, ploughed fields, cows grazing and strings of washing near the farmhouses.

They turned a corner and she could see dozens of low buildings, all surrounded by a tall fence of barbed wire, soldiers patrolling the perimeters. There was a gathering of men and women, sitting on the ground, in worn clothes, calling out to the bus as they passed.

'Who are they?'

'They think their children are here. Or husbands, or wives or parents. But they aren't – the HQ has checked the names. We can't let them in because they'd take anyone they could find.'

'What, they'd take any child?'

'Yes. They want to believe it's theirs. Anything rather than thinking theirs is dead.'

But Celia understood. She remembered learning about sheep from one of their farmers – that they were such keen mothers that if a lamb was orphaned, you could douse it in the smell of another existing lamb and its mother would believe it was hers. She craned back to look, her heart breaking for them.

The bus drove through a checkpoint of soldiers and Waterton signed her in at a small office. She stopped at a wooden door, unlocked it with a key from her waist. 'I have a veil here. Put it over your hair, and under. That's right. There are so many germs around, we ask all visitors to wear them to try to stay healthy.'

Celia wrapped the dark-blue veil tightly around her face, not entirely sure how it worked against germs but supposing something must have to.

'I forgot, have you had measles?' Waterton asked.

'When I was a baby, I think.'

'Good. You can't get it again.'

There were low cement blocks with wooden roofs. Celia walked past one and it was full of women, sitting on beds, nursing babies, talking, sleeping, all of them dressed raggedly, hair unarranged. A lot of them looked sick, coughing, sweating. Cholera, she supposed.

Waterton put her head in. 'I thought they were here. They're usually here.'

'Who?' Celia asked, but Waterton was walking on, nodding to the other nurses as she passed them.

'They must be queueing up,' she was mumbling. Celia hurried to catch up with her, sweeping her skirt out of mud and the rats hurtling about. It was even more awful than she expected, worse than her time during the war. Women slumped against the walls, throwing up, rubbish piled everywhere, flies, cries and moans from inside the buildings. She scrambled to keep up with Waterton. Ahead of them was a long line of older children and teenagers, queueing up near a table serving out food. 'That's it!' said Waterton, and seized Celia's hand. 'Come!'

They passed along the line, up to the servery. Two ladies wrapped in blue veils were passing out bowls of soup to the children, who were queueing up politely. Some of them held the hands of toddlers, siblings, others were carrying babies. They were ragged and dirty and very thin.

'These poor children,' said Celia, walking past them.

'Yes,' said Waterton. 'God knows what they've seen. Some of them are probably even adults but we don't know and neither do they, so why question?'

They came to the front of the queue and the volunteers greeted Waterton, respectfully.

'This is my friend, Miss Witt,' Waterton said. 'She and I might assist you with the queue, if we may.'

'Of course,' said the taller lady volunteer, looking curiously at Celia. 'Perhaps you might like to pass me and Mrs Craig the bowls, Miss Witt.'

Celia nodded and stood behind the stack of wooden bowls, passing one to the tall woman and one to Mrs Craig. They filled them up with soup and passed them forward. Waterton stood at the other side of the table, surveying the line.

The first was a black-eyed girl holding the hand of a small boy. She took a bowl of soup for herself, then loosened his hand to take one for him, put his hand on her skirt, clenching his fingers around the material. She murmured a quiet '*Gracias*', poked the child to do the same. Celia kept on working, staring into the faces of the children, willing herself to tell them apart, remember them, so they weren't just numbers, yet another part of the crowd of human misery.

Waterton patted a boy with russet hair on the shoulder, as he came forward. 'You're bowl monitor, with Jane and Marco, yes?' He looked blank and Mrs Craig started speaking in fast Spanish. 'Make sure you bring them all back,' said Waterton. He nodded.

'They want to keep them,' said Waterton, turning to Celia. 'Not to sell them. They just want to have something they can say is theirs.' Celia thought of her father and what he'd said about not having a mattress at the internment camp in the war. Because having things made you human. Her heart flooded as she looked at the children, so desperate for a possession that they'd keep a dirty soup bowl.

'Come on, children!' said Waterton. '*Vamanos!*'

Celia handed another bowl to Mrs Craig, looked at the child waiting for it. And then her heart crumbled. Two steps behind him was a boy, seventeen or so. He was looking at her. She stared again, clutched Mrs Craig. 'Are you quite well, Miss Witt?' She heard the woman's voice, her sensible, English voice speaking to her but she couldn't understand. Nothing was sensible. Behind him there was a girl, holding a baby and when she saw the baby,

Celia threw her arms around Mrs Craig, trying to hold on. 'Please!' she said. The boy was gazing at her.

'Mama?' he said. 'Mama?'

And Mrs Craig wasn't enough, her pillowy waist couldn't hold Celia and she was falling to the ground.

Celia woke up, lying on a bed in what looked like the nurses' station. She opened her eyes and looked up at a nurse she didn't recognise. 'I'll get Sister,' the woman said, and Celia lay back, clutching the corners of the bed. She heard brisk steps coming towards the bed, the rustle of a uniform skirt and knew it was Waterton.

'I am so sorry!' Waterton was saying, moving forwards to sit on the bed. 'I really am so sorry! I gave you such a shock.'

Celia sat up. 'Michael!' He had looked so different, so thin. His hair was so long that you could barely see his face. Lily's had been almost waist length, so matted.

'Where are they? I must go to them!'

Waterton touched her shoulder. 'No, no. Do lie back. You've had a shock. They're not going anywhere. As you observed, Celia, they can't get out of here. I didn't know, you see. I thought, but I didn't know. And I didn't want to give you false hope. It is your son, isn't it?'

'It is.' Celia could hardly believe she was hearing the words. 'And it looked like Lily with him.' Her head was spinning, circling, lost. 'But how did you know?' And then, her mind turned. *Mother cuts out anything to do with Miss Violet's Kitchen.* All the questions that she had asked her at lunch about her family had just been— 'You suspected. You knew they had disappeared.'

'It was all over the papers. I remembered the photographs. And then I came here and there were two children of sixteen or so, although they wouldn't say how old they were, clearly weren't Spanish, the nurses thought, so they sent me over to speak to them. They wouldn't say much. But I felt he was your son.'

'How?'

She smiled. 'He looks like you. But I wasn't sure. And he

393

wouldn't talk much – and she wouldn't talk at all. So I asked you here. I thought I'd put you together and you'd both know if you were mother and son. If you did not, you did not.'

'But we might not have recognised each other! Time has changed us!'

'Not that much.'

And Celia knew, then, why Waterton hadn't told her the truth, wrote to say *I cannot be clearer*. The women outside the camps willing to take any child, believing a baby was theirs because they were so desperate to have them. If the boy had merely looked a little like Michael but not been him, perhaps she too would have lied to herself, to everybody, said he was hers.

'I can't believe you recognised them.'

'Well, as I said, he looks like you. So does she, a little. And I remembered you from when you were about the same age, so possibly I saw it more. And there was something—'

'Something?'

Waterton shook her head. 'Never mind. Just – I don't know. A feeling.'

Celia looked at her. 'A feeling?' Something not being said. But Waterton shook her head and she thought best not to pursue it. She had them back, after all, and that was all that mattered.

'Is Mr Brennan with them?'

'Who? No. They came alone.'

'Let me see them, please.'

'You must be ready. The children here have been through much pain and sorrow. Few of them will talk.'

'They were in England for a long time. We think we just missed them. Just!'

'Let us go.'

'Well, Lily must be reasonably well if she is helping other women look after their babies,' Celia said, swinging her legs over the side.

'Oh,' said Waterton. 'But that is not another woman's baby. We believe that the little girl is hers.'

Celia held her heart. She didn't understand. She couldn't

understand. Lily had a baby? It couldn't be the case. She was a child. She couldn't have a child herself! The whole world was upside down. She gripped the wall but Waterton took her arm. 'Come,' she said. It was too much – but she had to be like Waterton, practical, no emotion. The children needed her. And she followed her, into a room that she said was the recreation room. Celia saw them in the corner, Michael and Lily and the baby and her heart was filled with air and light and she was running, hurtling towards them and then finally, finally they were in front of her and she was falling on them, gathering them in her arms.

'We've missed you so much,' she said. 'I thought I'd never find you again. They told me you were dead.'

Michael was holding tight to her, Lily too. 'You came to save us!' he said. 'I knew you'd come.'

FORTY-EIGHT

Perpignan, June 1939

After that, it was a flurry of passports and discussions and visas and interviews and nothing was as easy as Celia had expected. 'He's my son!' she wanted to say. 'And she is my niece! They have to come with me!' But it wasn't so easy, of course, and she had to sit for hours in HQ and have discussions with different women and men from the Red Cross and men from the army. The baby was particularly difficult, because even though Lily had arrived with her and said she was hers, she had no papers, no birth certificate, no name other than Mirabel, and Lily said she did not know her exact date of birth and would only say she was born in the city. The days dragged on, to the camp and back. Celia begged the Red Cross people – what if they caught the measles? What if Mirabel caught cholera? But things had to be done properly, they said. The children had travelled on false papers and even those were long since lost. Celia railed at the bureaucracy of it all. There were hundreds of children waiting to go, everything had to be done in order. So she watched them get thinner and thinner – and Lily had terrible lice in her hair – and Mirabel cried and cried.

She was only allowed to see the children for an hour a day in a cold room near the nurse's station. She told them that Mr Janus was back and well and keen to see them. She tried to tell them how happy she was to see them again, how she thought she'd lost Michael all over again, how she would listen to anything, that they should say why they had left and she would make sure it never happened again. But she didn't want to push too hard, make them feel guilty for leaving. They had suffered so much.

'We hoped to help in Spain,' said Michael. 'That's why we came. But the war was nearly over.'

'It was very brave of you,' she said, hoping that if she did so, they might talk about why they had, where Brennan was, but they did not. 'It must have been hard travelling here with a baby.'

Michael nodded. 'She was always crying. We tried to hide her but then she cried more.'

'Did Lily have him in London?'

He stared away. 'We're not supposed to talk about London.'

'Who said that?'

He shook his head.

'It was Mr Brennan, wasn't it? He took you?'

He shook his head. 'Don't ask me, Mama. Please.'

She told them about Stoneythorpe and that Verena and Rudolf were dead (although not how they died, that was too much for now). She meant to tell them that they'd probably have to sell the house soon, if they could find another buyer. She wanted to hold them both and never let them go, told herself that she had the rest of her life with them now and she shouldn't hurry them. She held tight to baby Mirabel, when Lily would let her hold her.

Waterton said that they guessed the baby was about seven months old, but they couldn't be sure. It must be that – if they were right about that house in east London – she had been born there. Perhaps that had been what prompted them to go, some kind of division. Who was the father? Michael looked after the baby, held her, fed her with the bottle of milk and always watched over her, but the father? Surely it couldn't be her son.

Celia asked Lily about the baby's name, hoping it would give some sort of clue.

'She was named after a doll I saw in London. Near the flat. Mama took me. I wanted it then but it was too expensive.'

'I'm sorry,' she said, to both of them. 'Whatever we did that drove you both away, I'm sorry. I wish you'd stayed and talked to us. We could have found an answer.'

Michael looked at the floor. 'You wanted to part us. You were going to send us to school.'

'We'll never separate you again. I promise.' She said it with certainty, but still. What on earth Emmeline would say when she arrived home with them – and a baby? She would blame Michael, be angrier with him than ever.

'I can't talk to them,' she said to Waterton. 'Not really.'

'You will get there in the end,' said Waterton. She had been in trouble with HQ for setting up the scene at the soup line, but she'd shrugged it off. 'They've suffered a lot. They need to trust you again.'

'You're right.'

'I'm always right.' Waterton grinned and Celia saw a hint of the girl she remembered – bossy, always taking charge.

'I just don't know how to thank you. You guessed. You knew just by looking at him.'

Waterton took her hand. 'Not entirely. Come and see.' She held her hand and Celia followed her. They walked between the accommodation blocks and through to the one where the children slept. Celia hadn't been allowed to see it – volunteers weren't allowed, let alone ones that had caused chaos in the soup queue. There were children in bed, ones too ill to come out. Waterton led Celia to the back of the neat row of beds. 'This is your son's bed,' she said. 'I noticed something. I should have reported him. Although I have no idea where he found a pencil from!' She pointed down to the floor and Celia crouched down. She looked at the wall. There was the same pencil line she'd seen before. Then a house.

'It looked like Stoneythorpe to me,' said Waterton. 'I always remembered the pictures in the papers of it, thought it would be nice to live somewhere so big and old. Why do you think they left in the first place? Why run away from a house like yours?'

Celia traced the line with her finger, couldn't answer because the truth was that they had run away from them, not the house.

The problems with the paperwork dragged on. In the end, Waterton suggested she hire a notaire from the town – and she went to a Monsieur Grenouille, who bustled in with papers and discussions and hurried everything up, for the price of hundreds of francs.

She sent a telegram to Stoneythorpe, and Mr Janus wrote back saying he'd come, but she told him that by the time he arrived, they'd be leaving.

And finally, she had them, three children with nothing more than their camp-issue clothes – and she had to stop herself from trying to touch them and hold them all the time, so afraid was she of losing them again.

'Thank you,' she said to Waterton – Alicia. 'I don't know how to thank you.'

'It's my job,' said Waterton, briskly. 'If only I could do it for all these children.' But her voice was trembling and there was a tear in her eye.

'Will you come back to England soon?' said Celia. 'It's dangerous here. What if – if – there is a war?'

Wateron shrugged. 'There is always war. I haven't died yet.'

'Come back to England.'

'What is there for me there? You have your family. You have your child and your niece – and the baby. And the business. But there is nothing for me. I belong here.'

Celia nodded. 'Will you write to me? Tell me how you are?'

'And you. I want to hear how the children are settling in.' She clasped Celia's hand. 'Be patient with them. Take them at their own pace.' Celia hugged Waterton hard, not wanting to let her go.

They caught a taxi straight to the café where they fell on plates of steak and potatoes, followed by custard pudding. Waterton had told her not to let them eat too much initially, but she couldn't help it. They were starving. Her child, her niece and Mirabel had been starving!

Michael stared at his plate. 'It doesn't seem fair that we are free to eat this and all the others have to stay behind.'

'I'm sure that people who know them will come and get them,' said Celia, lamely, because she knew it wasn't true, they were depending on Waterton and people like her to help them because there was no-one else. 'I'm sure there are a lot of French families who would take them in.' This was surely true. But the politicians wanted them kept together, cooped up because they saw them as a threat.

After they had eaten, she swept them to the station. She didn't want to stay in a hotel, wanted to get them away as fast as she could, before the visa types popped up with another problem. On the way, they all fussed over Mirabel, whether she was too hot, too cold, wanted feeding. Lily was so quiet, held her baby and the soft purple cat she wouldn't let go of. Celia found herself longing that someone else was there, that Mr Janus had come, and he could talk to their children, where she could not.

They clambered onto the train, took a compartment and Mirabel cried then fell asleep. Michael leant his head against the window, watching the countryside flashing past. He'd told her that he thought they'd been in the camp for three months.

She couldn't help it. The question she was supposed to be suppressing burst out. 'Why didn't you tell them who you were? I would have come to get you.'

He shook his head. 'We – Lily – thought *he* would come and get us. We were waiting.'

'When did *he* leave you?'

Michael shook his head, leant against the window again.

FORTY-NINE

Stoneythorpe, July 1939

They travelled through the night, stayed one night in Paris, then journeyed on to Calais, took the ferry and then they would go on to Stoneythorpe. Michael talked off and on but Lily would only really talk about Mirabel, wanting to discuss her feeding, sleeping, how she responded to stories. Celia said she was putting on weight rapidly – which was true. She seemed the healthiest of all of them. One night, when Michael was asleep, she asked Lily about the birth.

'Did you have a doctor helping you?'

Lily shook her head. 'We don't need doctors. That's what he said. They try and poison us with their medicine so we'll always be slaves.'

'Oh. Who said this?'

Lily shook her head but Celia knew it was Brennan. She had to remember her promise to his mother. Not to do anything. Not to tell the police. Although she had no idea where he was and Lily wasn't going to say.

'Did Mr Brennan go with you to Spain?'

Lily's eyes flickered and Celia knew she was right.

'Did he die?'

Lily shook her head. And then she said they had all travelled abroad to help the fight. But Mirabel was always crying and nothing seemed to go right so he took them to the camp, said he would come back for them.

She waited, didn't want to ask. The train rushed on.

'I knew he wasn't coming back. He didn't love us anymore. I could tell.'

'I'm sure he still did love you,' she said, weakly, only wanting Lily not to hurt. They would never have come with Celia, if they thought he was coming for them.

'How could he leave us there?' Lily turned to her and she was weeping. Celia took her in her arms. They carried on, through the night.

Tom came to meet them at Dover. He said that he'd waited to receive every boat until he found them. Emmeline had said in a letter to the hotel he was still staying with them, dividing his time between Stoneythorpe and London. They all depended on him.

'I thought you might need some help,' he said.

'I do.' She felt a rush of gratitude to him. She hated how awkward she was with them, with Lily in particular.

'We'll drive back to Stoneythorpe,' he said. 'I imagine you've had enough trains.'

They all nodded. He held them all, lifted Mirabel into the sky.

'Whose is the baby?' he said, as they were driving back, the three in the back, asleep.

'Lily's. And I don't know. Emmeline – I know what she'll say.'

'Ignore her. I should have come with you to France.'

He was right. 'I wish you had. It's too awful there. The people are suffering so much.'

'Well, that's just the beginning if there's a war. Although if you ask me, they can't go to war again.'

'I don't know. Maybe.' She knew what she'd seen. The Führer wasn't going to stop, all his desires were bound up in wanting land. So either they let him take every country he wanted – or they took him to war. And Michael would be old enough to go.

'You think they were with Brennan?' he whispered. 'What if he and his types come for her?'

'He left them, lying that he'd come back. But Lily knows he won't and even if he did – how could they forgive him, deserting them.'

Celia saw Lily's eyes fluttering. She looked out of the dark window, then fell asleep again.

When they finally arrived, Tom carried Lily and the baby upstairs, then Michael. Emmeline stood there at the door, watching.

'Should we wake them up to let them eat?' said Celia. 'Just Mirabel, maybe.' She took the warm bundle from Lily's arms and down to the kitchen. Emmeline took her noiselessly, fed her with a cup because there was no bottle. 'I'll do it!' she said. 'How would you know?' She rocked her to sleep and took her back upstairs to Lily.

Celia sat by Mr Janus and Tom in the sitting room. She was too tired to think, even to speak. Emmeline stormed in.

'How could you?' she said. 'It's all your fault.'

'Emmeline?'

She was framed against the hearth, a fire goddess, furious, aflame.

'What's he done to her? What has your son done to her?'

'I—'

'I knew it. Do you know, I knew it all along? I knew he was a bad sort. You got him from nowhere. He came from nowhere. And what kind of behaviour did he learn? Now we see! She was good before he came. She was perfect. And he came and ruined her – and now look at her. She's a child. And he's ruined her.'

'Emmeline—' Tom held out his hand.

'Oh, don't you start. He gets his corruption from you! You did it to Celia, all those years ago, and now your son is carrying on the tradition of ruining innocent girls.'

'I wanted Tom to, Emmeline,' said Celia. 'I did.'

But that made her even more furious, stamping her foot.

'Emmeline,' said Mr Janus. They had almost forgotten he was there. 'You'll wake everyone up. They'll hear.'

Celia levelled her gaze. 'Emmeline, you ran away with your tutor. Now Lily has done the same.'

Emmeline leapt forward, Mr Janus holding her back. 'She's right, you know.'

'Look,' said Tom. 'We don't know what's happened. Let's leave them to tell us, shall we?'

'I know what's happened. Michael dragged her off so he could do what he wanted to her. He was bad news.'

'It was Brennan. You know that.'

Mr Janus stood up. 'Let's discuss this tomorrow. We'll leave it until the morning.'

Celia sat on the sofa, listening to them walk upstairs, then the sounds of them walking around, over her head in their room. She lay back on the sofa.

Tom soothed her. 'Don't listen to what she says. She's just upset, that's all.'

'But what if she's right?'

'That's Brennan's child. She just can't admit it.'

That night, Celia woke up, her heart pumping hard. Her mind was running wild, overheated. She wanted to reach out and touch him. She ran to Michael's room, then Lily's. They were all there. She knocked on Tom's door, walked in. The fear bulged in her heart, ran riot. She couldn't help it. She reached down, shook Tom awake. 'I can't sleep. You were right. Someone might come for them.'

He opened his eyes. 'How would anyone know they were here? It's much more likely, if you ask me, that the pair of them will try to run away again.'

'They wouldn't!'

'Celia, let's get some sleep. Nothing is going to happen tonight.'

But she couldn't. She heard creaks and bangs, saw shadows passing the windows, but when she looked up, there was nothing there.

Next day, she told Lily and Michael how Rudolf and Verena had died. 'They killed themselves.' They both wept. Then Lily began to talk, words and words spooling out of her, nothing about the present but memories of Rudolf and Verena. They asked Celia questions and she told them every detail she could – although she realised as she did so that some of them were beginning to slip away from her. She told them about the funeral home, how peaceful they were.

'It was because you were selling the house,' said Lily, flatly. She was still clutching the purple cat, wouldn't let it go, held it as tightly as she held Mirabel.

Celia shook her head. 'Yes, a little. But they were afraid of war, most of all.'

'I would have looked after them!' said Michael. 'Why didn't they wait for us?'

The guilt on his face pained her heart. 'It wasn't your fault. It was the war.'

They still needed to sell the house. As Tom said, it would be impossible to sell if there was a war. But Celia knew the children wanted to stay. It was the only security they had. They'd lost everything else. How could they take them to a place in Winchester they'd never seen before?

'We need the money,' she said, forcing herself. 'Let's ask Mr Crennet to try the girls' school again. Offer them even more money off.'

'I'll try,' said Tom. 'The market is changing.'

Celia looked at all the boxes, everything they had loved packed away, and her heart sank. Emmeline and Tom were right. They should take what they could get. The children were back with them and that was all that mattered.

Lily was often silent. They were all looking, she thought, for those small moments when Lily began to talk and they thought that she was coming back to them. She would give them a little. And then she would stop, close off, and they did not know how to reach her again.

They agreed not to ask them questions, decided to share between them what they heard, judged that they would hear eventually. Celia thought Lily and Michael had mellowed, become pleased to see them, but then sometimes they closed off again and you couldn't talk to them. Lily wandered round the parlour, crying over her grandparents. They all took turns to hold Mirabel. Lily and Michael said very little. But sometimes, Celia turned a corner and heard them speaking to each other, whispering words she couldn't catch.

Albert came down from university and Celia's heart broke to see how distant he felt from his sister. He was trying to talk to them, just as they did, and none of them could get through.

Mr Janus spent most days out, meeting up with his anti-war society friends. Albert had gone to some of the meetings with him. She was grateful for Tom, always there with them.

Sometimes, Lily woke in the middle of the night, screaming, and Celia ran to her but got there and the door was barred. Lily said to her – and Emmeline who was usually there too – that she didn't need help, she had just had a bad dream. Celia bought Michael a sketchpad and pencils but he didn't seem to want to draw. 'Why not draw Mirabel?' she said. 'So we don't forget how she looked.' He shook his head.

The days passed. Celia sometimes looked out of the window, thought she saw a shadow. But then she looked again and it was gone. Nothing there. She was scaring herself, seeing things behind the trees.

She and her sister skated around each other, angry, resentful.

'Don't,' said Tom. 'Don't tell Emmeline what you're thinking. Honesty is overrated. Don't. It won't do any good to say it. I promise. Don't.'

'I'll try.'

And she did, she really did. She tried not to say it. She talked of different subjects, the baby's feeds, how there surely wouldn't be a war. Hitler would see sense – who would want to wreck the peace that had brought them so much?

'Try harder,' said Tom.

And then, in a small disagreement about how warm to make the baby's bottle, it all came. The leaves cleared away from the spring and it bubbled up and wouldn't stop.

'How do you know it was his idea to run away?' Celia cried.

'How do you know it wasn't her? She wanted to be with Brennan, not us, and Michael was her cover!'

The harsh words flowed and Tom came into the kitchen and Emmeline had slapped Celia and she was standing there, hand on face, outraged.

'Stop that!' he said, pulling them apart. Celia held tight to his hand, breathless and ashamed. 'You have to accept what they are now.'

'We should never have found them,' said Celia, breathing hard. 'With the war. We need to go. If we went to America, they wouldn't have to fight.'

'I'm not going to America. Or letting you take my grandchild. You can go alone.' Emmeline spat out her words, stalked out of the room, her hair awry.

Lily was talking more and Tom said Michael had told him a few things – Celia tried hard not to be jealous. Tom said Michael had told him a little about the house, said it was called Year Zero and they'd had many ideas. 'Sounds harmless enough,' said Tom. 'In the ideas at least.'

Celia nodded. 'You're probably right. I suppose at least we must be glad that someone took them in. Until. Well.' She looked at the floor. 'I don't suppose he is talking about that?'

He nodded. 'Michael won't say much. He won't talk. I think he is protecting her. Keeping her secrets.'

Celia was tossing, turning, couldn't sleep. Images flashed through her mind. Nothing would settle. She turned onto her side, tried to sleep again. Still the house creaked and banged around her. And then she sat up. Footsteps, passing her room. She waited, crept to the door. There was nothing. She thought she'd heard footsteps before, Emmeline going to find Tom. She'd been imagining it. But this was *real*. Someone was out there. She pulled a cardigan around herself, pushed on slippers, padded quietly out of her door, trying not to creak as she stepped.

She walked along the corridor and could hear nothing. Perhaps she had imagined it. Then she heard a tiny, muffled cry. The baby! She hurried forwards, down the stairs.

She looked down. There in the hallway, two figures, shadowed, bent close together. One was holding a baby. A woman. It was Lily. It had to be.

Celia stood there, watching. Was she with Michael? It didn't look like him – too tall. And it surely wasn't Tom. What were they *doing*? The baby was wrapped tightly, so it didn't cry, she supposed. They were deep in conversation, heads bent together. The man put his arm on her waist.

'I don't know,' the girl was saying.

He took her hand. She walked forward. The baby was whimpering.

Celia took a step and it creaked out. Lily looked up – and the man with her turned and she saw it was Mr Brennan. She hurtled down towards them and Lily screamed and Celia stopped halfway down.

'You're coming!' Brenan shouted at Lily.

Celia stood still, watched. Lily looked up at her – then at him. Celia could see – she was wavering. 'Stay with us, Lily,' she said. Lily looked at her and the baby, took a step away from Brennan.

'Don't you dare,' he shouted at her. Then he called up towards Celia. 'I'm taking both of them. They're mine.' He pulled the baby out of Lily's arms. Lily screamed again, pitched herself towards him and he caught her.

Celia threw herself down the rest of the stairs. 'Stop!' she shouted. And then she was running towards them and Brennan was dashing towards the door and suddenly there were more of them, Tom, Mr Janus, Emmeline, and Emmeline had Lily and the baby was crying and Tom was running after Brennan. Lily was screaming, weeping.

'I'll get her back!' he was shouting. 'I'll come for her!'

The men ran out into the darkness.

Lily was clutching at Emmeline. 'Don't call the police! Don't! I'll never speak to you again if you do.'

Celia ran past them, out of their great front door onto the drive.

It was so dark, she could see nothing. Men were shouting but she couldn't make out where they were. Then she heard a cry. She bent down. A child's cry. A baby. Her eyes adjusted and she saw it in the gloom. Mirabel's blanket! She reached down and there was the child. She picked her up and cradled her in her arms. She felt the child's warmth, held her close as the men's running feet were further and further away.

'I lost him.' Tom came in to the parlour, breathless. 'I lost him. Samuel is still going but I think Brennan's gone. I think he was hiding somewhere.'

Lily was holding the baby. 'Please don't call the police.'

'Give us one reason why not?'

'We have to,' Celia said. 'He was trying to take you away. And your child.'

'But I wanted to go. He needs me.'

'No, he doesn't.' Celia's heart turned, sickly. Patterns repeating themselves. 'He was the one you went with, wasn't he? We always thought that you and Michael ran away together. But it wasn't about you and Michael, was it? It was about you and him. You ran away with him.' They had given him no thought at all, the pale, shy man who'd done the teaching, poor, schoolmasterly, shy. They had ignored him. What revenge he had taken!

'We wanted to run away!'

Emmeline looked at her. 'He's the father of your baby. He took you and you were just a child.'

'Stop it! It's not true. You're making it low, when it was—'

'What – love?'

'More than that! We were being free, making a new society, we were going to be different from all of you, stuck in your world of money and spending and bills and how you say – men do this and women do that. You are all so cruel and rigid! You make people sit in these horrible holes that have nothing to do with the truth of their souls, nothing! You torment people. We could be free, men and women, loving and living together. All of us.' She clutched Mirabel close.

'He wanted to be free of your parents, I'd say,' said Tom. 'Men will say anythi—' Celia glared at him, cut him off.

'Maybe he's right,' Celia said. 'But couldn't you have stayed and tried to change us?' Although when she said it, she knew how foolish it sounded.

'He said he'd come back for us,' said Lily. 'And he did.'

'But how did he find you here?'

'He was looking for us,' she said, proudly, heart swelling. 'He loved us. He really did. He looked for us in the camps. In ours, there were people we'd known and they told him we'd come back to England.'

Celia shook her head. 'When did he start persuading you to run away?' And then she knew. When she had come into the room and he was showing them a picture of the world. The Secondary World. She'd heard the word freedom and he had stopped talking. Why had she not realised? She had seen nothing in Brennan's pale eyes, his maps, his quiet voice. And all the time his mind had been full of plans.

'Why Michael? Why did he have to come too?' She was aware she sounded petulant, couldn't help it. Why couldn't they just have left him behind? Why if they needed each other, did they have to have him as well?

'Because he needed to be free too! We couldn't leave him to your world. Oppressive, Brennan said.'

Tom raised an eyebrow. 'Was bringing Michael Mr Brennan's idea?'

'Mine. But of course he wanted him! We were friends.'

'Of course.'

Lily held the baby to her. Mirabel was asleep now.

'What have you done?' Celia heard herself saying, knowing she shouldn't say it. 'Didn't you think we'd miss you? Didn't you think your mother would be weeping every night, your father desperate? Didn't you think of me? I searched everywhere for Michael – and then I lost him again.'

Lily looked up at her, clear-eyed. Of course she didn't. Why would she? She was young, confident that the world was there to serve her, she didn't need to hold on to things, grasp hard to people like adults did. Family were just pulling you down, when you could go out and be free.

'I presume he had sent you a letter or something. Thrown stones at your window. Got you to come down. Or were you in contact for longer?'

She nodded, her hair over her face.

'You've been meeting him.' The creaks on the floorboards. The shadows from the windows. This time she had actually been right.

She saw a tear on Lily's face.

'And tonight was your chance to go.'

The tear dropped onto the baby's cheek.

'But you didn't. Why didn't you?'

She looked up at Celia. 'It's – different. He loves me. I know he loves me.' Tom snorted and Emmeline shushed him. 'But I have her, now, Mirabel. And I can't let her go. In the house, she'd be owned by everyone. You don't have parents. You don't have children. You share. I don't want to share her. I want her for me.' Celia looked at the baby's sleeping face, the tiny cheeks and the pale eyelashes. They had to do better with her.

'You share?' said Tom. 'Did you share each other too?'

'People always ask that sort of thing. It wasn't the point.' Lily laid Mirabel down. 'You all treat me like a child! I'm not a child. Mr Brennan saw that! Why can't you! I'm just as grown as the rest of you!'

Tom walked towards them. 'Look, Lily—'

The door opened and Michael was there, standing in his pyjamas. 'What's happening?' He looked at Lily. 'What's going on?'

'Brennan came back for her,' said Emmeline. 'And Mirabel. Samuel is trying to find him but we think we've lost him.'

Michael took a step towards Lily. 'And you were going to go? Without me?' She didn't reply. He looked around.

Emmeline shrugged. 'Without all of us.'

'But he abandoned us. We had nothing! He just left us in the mountains. We might have starved.'

'We didn't.'

'Only because the Red Cross found us! Why is he coming back for you now? I can guess. He wants money. Just like all the money we took for him last time. Does he want money?'

She shook her head.

'That's why you asked me where the key to Mama's office was. He's made you take her money.'

Celia felt in her pocket for her office key. Missing. There had been two thousand pounds in there.

'Is this true?'

Lily looked away.

It couldn't be true! Celia put her hand out to her son. 'Don't get upset, Michael. We don't know what happened.' But Michael wasn't listening. He was rushing forward, coming towards Lily, trying to grasp her. Tom threw himself between them, held them apart.

'You've always hated him!' she cried. 'I thought we were going away together! We'd come for you later!'

'He's always lying to you! Stay with me,' Michael was saying. 'Please stay with me.' Celia, gazing at him, knew he'd love Lily more than he ever did her, his own mother, no matter what, and knew she had been the same to her own parents, wanting to leave. How had she ever thought they would be different? She watched the anguish cross his face as he looked at Lily and knew he was flying from her, sure as if he were up in the clouds. She watched him soar, couldn't wave goodbye.

Celia went to check and a thousand pounds had gone. She forced herself not to say anything to Lily, let her father do it. She had been controlled by Brennan and too young. Too loyal. Emmeline refused to speak to her.

'Aren't you going to apologise?' Celia said to Emmeline. 'For everything you said about Michael?' Her sister's realisation, on that night, that Michael was only the cover. It should be enough, she knew – but still.

'Lily was perfect before he came. Your bad blood.'

'Mine?' She almost flew at her sister. But they had lost too much. They couldn't lose each other as well. She ran from the room instead.

Celia rushed outside, sat on the grass with her face in her knees. A fine mesh of moonlight lay over the flowers, the spiral of the clematis, the dancing whorls of the roses. She felt a coolness pass over her.

'You must be cold out here.'

She looked up at Tom. 'You told me not to say it.'

'Well, you were always going to. Perhaps things will be better now you have. You're not wrong, though. Whatever happened, it's not as simple as Lily says.'

'He was clever. And Lily too. They were in love, or at least she was. Trying to do anything to be together.'

In love. As she had been once. How pure it was.

They sat. She watched the dew glimmer on the grass.

'Would you come to America with us?' The words just came out.

Tom coughed, surprised. 'If there's a war?'

'Yes. I can't bear to see Michael fight. And I want to tell him the truth about you. If you agree.'

'Of course. But why America? Anywhere would do, wouldn't it? Is it because you want to be with *him*?'

'Who?'

'Jonathan.'

She shook her head. 'No. He's married now, anyway.' He and Violet. Happily ever after. 'Just America – it's young. Different.'

She couldn't leave the business, though. The Ministry needed her. She could send Michael on his own. Apart from him again. Her heart was torn.

They fell silent.

He stood for a while, looking over her. It was almost as if he had forgotten she was there. 'I should tell him the truth,' she said. 'About you. He needs to know.'

Tom nodded. 'But maybe we should wait. I can wait. He's had so many shocks.'

'I will tell him.'

'There will be war. It's inevitable.'

'But if there is to be a war, we should seize moments, shouldn't we? It might be our last chance.'

He was staring past her. She couldn't see his eyes, couldn't guess at his meaning.

'It's true,' she said, carefully.

He nodded. 'The future. What do you think about the future?'

'I don't know. I might join Mr Janus's anti-war protest. And even Mr Brennan wasn't wrong with those words Michael said he said about war. It's so hopeless.'

'Just before Mr Janus arrived, you were talking. All those things you said about Emmeline. You thought that Emmeline and I were in love with each other.'

'I did. I'm ashamed of it now. You just seemed so close.'

'I can't see how you ever thought that.'

Jealous. I was jealous!

Tom said, 'I was trying to help your sister. And your family. That's all. There wasn't anything else to it. Because I was doing it for you.'

'What?'

'Everything I was doing for your family. Emmeline, your parents, the house. It was only for you.'

She looked up at him. 'For me?'

'All of it. For you. For when you came back. When you sent me that letter saying you were going to Germany, I realised. I hurried to Stoneythorpe but you'd already gone.'

She breathed, thought. 'What were you going to say?'

'I was going to tell you not to go. I was going to say – you can't. When you said you could be gone for a long time, that you didn't know how long. That's when I realised. I had to stop you. All this time, I thought you were here. And when you were about to go – I thought that anything could happen. You could meet someone else there, fall in love with him. And get married. You wouldn't return.'

'You thought that?'

'Your letter was very final.' And he was right, it had been final. She had written it saying to herself: *This must be the last time.* She was going to forget about him, put him out of her mind. That's what she'd told herself. And instead it had done the opposite. He had come to find her.

She felt laughter bubbling up in her throat. 'We're always out of sync,' she said. 'Never in time.'

'What do you mean?'

And then everything that had happened made her feel grand and bold and the words came pouring out. 'Because every time I am in love with you, you're not in love with me. And back and forth! You love me, I don't love you. Over and over.'

She saw his face crumble. 'So that's what you're saying. You don't love me. I thought – when you were so angry about Emmeline. That there was—'

'No! No! That wasn't what I meant. Not at all! You know what I mean. Always at the wrong time.'

He crouched down to face her. 'Well, what about now? Is this the right time?'

The emotion sweeping her was so strong that she could hardly think. She almost wanted to push him away, it was so heavy, bearing her over. *This will be how it is*, a voice whispered, the air around it rushing as if she was holding a shell to her ear. *This emotion. You'll have to carry it every day.* The tide was battering her in the sea, pulling her forwards. She could let it – or she could run away, opt for what she knew. Safety.

She looked up, turned towards it. 'Yes,' she said. 'Yes, it's the right time.' The wave pulled her in.

Jonathan sent a letter inviting her and anybody who was with her to come to America to safety. He said that New York was the same and wrote about how safe America was. He said Violet sent her love. He wrote that they would all be welcome. He would care for them. Her heart cracked at his generosity. They discussed it – but really, how could they go? It scared Lily to go to town, let alone go to America. She wrote back, thanking him, saying they couldn't go – it would be too much for Lily, they must take it slowly. She said that she had Tom now, and Lily had a child.

Tom put his arm around her in the daytime, they stayed downstairs after everyone had gone at night. He held her tight and she tried to forget the others who were always with her, Jonathan, Arthur, Michael, Louisa, Shep, her parents. They surged back into her mind, but sometimes it was free, a blank page just for him and so she had to hope and cling to that, tell herself that eventually that would become more clear space to be filled up with love, the loss wound underground, always there but not at the front. She loved him, he loved her. That was enough.

The gas masks were issued in July to all of them. They went to the church hall in the next village and stood in a queue to be fitted by two weary volunteers. Even Mirabel had a mask in a canvas covering that tied around her legs like a nappy, made her look a bit as if she was diving under the water. They read the leaflet and practised putting them on, pulling the masks over their heads and tightening the straps. It felt hot and suffocating, smelled of disinfectant. When you breathed in, the mask stuck to your face and made you sick. Lily thrust hers off, refused to wear it and pulled it off the baby.

'Don't force her,' said Tom.

The leaflet said to keep them with them at all times, but that seemed too much so they debated keeping them in the cellar – but thought that would be too far away if the real gas came. So they stacked them in a pile in the sitting room corner.

Celia took Michael to her. 'I have to tell you about your father,' she said.

'It's Tom, isn't it?'

'You knew?'

'I guessed. Anyway, I look like him. Why didn't you want me to know?'

'I thought there had been enough change,' she said, carefully. When had he guessed? She had been trying to protect him. Instead she had only added to the lies.

'I'm sorry.'

'It doesn't matter. Can I go and see him now?'

'Of course.' She heard him thundering downstairs and to the dining room, where Tom was looking over some figures. She heard laughter and shouts. He was happy.

That night, Michael and Lily stayed up late, and after supper – Tom said they needed a break from Miss Violet's jars and asked Mrs Code from the village to bring up some pudding and they ate sponge and custard after the chicken – Lily brought the baby down to sleep in the parlour and Tom put some records on the gramophone. Mr Janus was out at a meeting but they supposed he wouldn't mind missing it, if it were only a small celebration.

They listened to the music. Fly away with me. Celia smiled, looked across at Michael, but he was gazing at Lily.

'We should dance,' said Tom. And so they did – he put his arms around her and they began, whirling around the room. She felt his hand against her back, leant into him. Emmeline was smiling, dancing with Mr Janus in her mind, and Michael and Lily were dancing too. And their arms were around each other and they were smiling and even though there would be a war, surely even now, whatever Mr Chamberlain said, and they had lost so much, they still had each other and there was music and they could dance. She looked through the window and the stars glimmered through the cloud.

FIFTY

Stoneythorpe, August 1939

Celia was rushing from bedrooms, opening the doors, shouting. The air around was hot, the stones under her feet were burning and the sky was on fire too. The log was in front of the back room and it was burning.

She started to panic, ran back and straight into Tom. 'We can't get out,' she said. 'Emmeline?' She'd run back for her.

'She's out. I helped her,' he said. 'It's just us.'

The heat was all around her. 'We can't get out,' she said again. The panic was flaming her chest.

'We can,' he said. 'Lucky you have your clothes on.' She started to tell him she'd been walking outside but he wasn't listening. And then he was tearing at her gown so she could put it over her mouth and seized her hand and he was pulling her up the stairs. The flames were burning at her feet and she couldn't breathe. She had taken Lily out and rushed back for Emmeline – but Tom had come back for her. Everything was on fire.

He was pulling her up the staircase. 'You need to jump,' he said. 'Then maybe we can go back another way. I don't know. But you need to jump.'

He pulled her to the upstairs window, by the top of the staircase.

She stared out. The whole place was flaming. 'I can't.' The house was on fire. The flames were coming high towards her. She looked down and all of it was burning. The house, their home, the place they had given so much to.

'I can't,' she said. 'I can't leave it.' Jumping. She couldn't do it. Arthur had jumped. Louisa had fallen. She couldn't do it too.

He grasped her, hard. 'What are you talking about? Come on! There is no time to lose!'

'I can't.' Something in her was dragging her down. They'd have nothing. She'd have nothing. They would have to start all over again. She didn't know whether she could do it. The moment was so violent, so absolute.

'You have to, Celia,' he said. 'You have to.' And as he was saying it, she knew he was right. She had to make a new life. She had to do it for Michael and Lily and baby Mirabel – and maybe for Tom, too. She held his hand and clambered onto the window ledge. She heard people shouting '*Jump!*' below her. She thrust herself from the window and saw below her Michael, Lily, Mirabel, Emmeline and Mr Janus. She fell out towards them. She felt as if she was flying.

She landed with a smash on the ground, even though they'd tried to catch her. Her whole body felt broken. The hot air burned her skin. Michael was standing over her.

'Are you hurt?'

'No.' Everything hurt. 'How's Tom?'

'He's fine. Don't get up. Wait for the doctor.'

But she had to. She couldn't just lie there. 'Help me up.' Michael pulled her up and it didn't hurt to stand. Just ahead of her, Tom was standing too. She leant against them, Tom and Michael, watched the house in flames. Lily stood there with the baby, a little apart from them but nearly together. For a moment, Celia thought she saw a figure at the window. A man, Brennan. But then she blinked and the window was empty of all but flames.

The fire danced forward, ate it all. The flames that you couldn't stop, not if it was your house, not if it was the whole of Europe, consumed by a new flame of anger and war. She watched it fall. Michael held her hand. Tom's arm around her. She held tight to their hands. In the morning the sun would rise again.

EPILOGUE

Everybody had gone to bed. Celia sat in the parlour. The house was quiet. And yet it wasn't. There were a hundred, thousand voices, speaking all the time. She could hear them, always. Her mind could never be free because they were always talking. No one would buy Stoneythorpe due to the war and so the voices would never let go. She could spend the rest of her life trying to keep it up, please all those voices who made her keep their secrets. And then Michael and Lily would have to do the same. Their children again, always attempting to shore up the place – and for what? It was only a house. She had given so much to trying to keep it. She couldn't let her children live like that, chained to bricks and mortar. And with war, everything would be lost, and big houses would be blights, taking up space that could be better used for everyone. Her heart tore for her love of it, her childhood, her parents. They had to live free of the shadows.

She couldn't do it. It would be a crime. But then...

She was the only one who could do it. Set them all free.

She found one of Tom's cigarettes, lit it. It reminded her of Red, running across the rooves of New York, always free. She held it up to the sky. The idea flooded around her. How they could never let go of it, however hard they tried. The insurance.

It was an act of love. It would set her free, set them all free. She stood up, walked to the window. She held the cigarette to the thick gold curtain at the window. A bright flame came and began dancing, like a tiny genie jumping up the curtain.

'But what are you doing?' cried the house. 'I did so much for you!'

She turned away, looked towards the sky. When she turned back to the curtain, there were a thousand genies, all dancing, gambolling across the thick gold. They made the world new. They would set them free, forever, so they could stop looking back. The genies danced further, tore on through the room. She watched them for a while. Then she turned to run upstairs to the bedrooms. 'There's a fire!' she shouted. 'Fire! Everyone! Run!' Michael, Lily, Mirabel. Tom, Emmeline, Mr Janus, they would all come running out. She'd done it now. No turning back.

The fire was behind her, burning it all down, and they would rush into the light. The world circled around them, all of it thrown into the air now, but it was their own, what they had made of it, how they would go on. And they would go on, whatever came, even if it was war. They had a new way now. The voices of everybody from the past, talking all at once, all the people who had come to the house, been a part of their lives, over all of the years. They could hear them now. They were walking beside her. The stars burned the darkness into a thousand pieces.

AFTERWORD

I heard the Witts in my mind for years. Fragments of Celia and the others came to me at odd times, their voices, their thoughts, even though I did not then know what I was hearing. The fragments grew more numerous, joined together and I finally began writing about them in 2010, fascinated by the lives of the Anglo-Germans in Britain, numerous when the war broke out, but forgotten in the rush to declare good/bad. I always knew I would take them to the moment of when the unimaginable happened once more, the thing that everything had been directed towards stopping: total war returning once more. At school, I learned the Treaty of Versailles off by heart for A level, the names of those countries that were given self-determination, and that, along with the huge reparations, would protect the world against the resumption of the horror of war. Kept low and poor, territorially and financially reduced, Germany would never fight again.

The opposite was true, of course. The Great Depression raked the world with its cruelties, yet none so much as Germany, where bad governance and crippling payments thrust the country into economic despair – and the febrile climate of resentment and fear that created the ideal conditions for the rise of Adolf Hitler and the evils of the party.

The Second World War saw the great sacrifice of humanity from across the world, some of which has often been obscured in the familiar narratives of the Second World War – the Empire soldiers who fought so bravely and were promised so much, the soldiers of Russia who arguably drove the outcome of the war. The Home Front saw great suffering, as those left behind tried to continue living amongst the loss and uncertainty. The photographs of the time are incredibly moving: a girl comforting her doll in the ruins of her home, children attempting to play in rubble and broken furniture. The human sprit fighting through in the midst of despair and loss.

Celia and her family see their world and everything around them change. Europe and America are broken and remade, altered forever, new forms coming from what was torn apart. The Edwardian security, the belief when Victoria died that her fondness for marrying her children into European families would protect against war, was broken apart. The Empire as they knew it would crumble, as countries fought rightly for independence.

Life for Anglo-Germans grew harsh again in the war. Once more they were reviled, mistrusted, hated. Celia and her family have to find a way through once more – but that is another story!

I am grateful to the archivists at the Imperial War Museum, the British Library, the Metropolitan Archives and the archives across the country that I used for this book, to look at letters, diaries and other books and records that told me so much about the period. The words that I have read have coursed through my mind, woven through my dreams, been everything for me so at times I was not living now but then.

It has been an incredible privilege to work on the Witts for so much of my life, a period in which my life has changed in ways I could not imagine too! I had wanted to write on the period ever since I saw the trenches in Flanders, on a primary school trip, unable to imagine then and now how men managed to live and fight in such tiny spaces, for years. And the more I read and researched, the more I realised how the First World War shaped lives and feelings for years to come – there was no cut-off point. I have learnt so much from the letters and diaries that I have read in archives and record offices across the country. The Witts are fiction – but every word they say is based on the reality of people in the past, who kept fighting and hoping, even after the war was over.

When I was a child, I made a time machine out of the box that the washing machine had arrived in and decorated it with foil. I put my brother in there and pretended to him it was a time machine. Now I make time machines out of words – thank you for coming in it with me.

I am very grateful to my editors: Clare Hey, who has edited this book so brilliantly and given so much sensitive thought and heart to the family and their story, and to Gen Pegg for being such a superb guide and inspiration and making raw words much better – thanks for everything! My first editors, Jemima Forrester and Jon Wood, were a guiding inspiration and were so generous and gave so very much to the book, when it at times seemed an overwhelming mass of emotion and history.

Thank you to Orion for their wonderful support, to Katie Espiner and David Shelley, Harriet Bourton and my brilliant publicists Gaby Wood, Sam Eades and Virginia Wollstonecraft who were always helping the book and did so much. They were always there for me and the books – and I am so grateful. It is very kind of you! And thank you to Gillian and everyone at Gollancz for making life fun! Thank you to Simon Spanton, who has so many brilliant ideas. I am very grateful to my wonderful agents, Robert Kirby and Ariella Feiner in London and Zoe Pagnamenta in New York, who are always there for me, agents and friends. And to Sue, Sue, Helen and all at Knight Ayton, who are very supportive and friends full of kindness. Most of all to Marcus and Persephone who have to live with me in a different time...

And thanks most of all to my readers, who have given me their time, sent me their thoughts and messages, written and reviewed online, and come to my events – I am so grateful and lucky to have shared some of your lives and I truly could do none of it without you. Thank you.